THE CIVIL WAR SOLDIERS
OF BRANFORD, CONNECTICUT

THE
CIVIL WAR
SOLDIERS
OF
BRANFORD,
CONNECTICUT
NORTH BRANFORD & NORTHFORD

Jane Peterson Bouley

BRANFORD, CT

ABOUT THE AUTHOR

Jane Peterson Bouley is the Branford, Connecticut Town Historian and has focused her research on primary material and resources with an emphasis on the nineteenth and twentieth centuries. She is the author or coauthor of *Damascus Cemetery*, *Mill Plain Cemetery*, *Supply Pond*, and other works. She is a recipient of an Award of Merit from the Connecticut League of Historical Societies and was inducted into the Branford Education Hall of Fame in 1999.

CONTENTS

Appendices

Indexes

x

BRANFORD'S CIVIL WAR SOLDIERS

Ackerman, John
Adams, James
Adams, John
Albee, Calvin
Albinger, John J.
Albinos, John
Allen, Henry
Ames, Charles
Arlington, Willoughby
Ashman, Robert A.
Averill, Adelbert C.
Averill, Daniel 2nd
Averill, David
Averill, Roland G.
Babcock, Marcus O.
Backes, Michael
Bailey, Heman W.
Baisley, John W.
Baldwin, George C.
Baldwin, George W.
Baldwin, Jerome A.
Bamberg, Casper
Bamberg, Martin
Barker, Ammi B.
Barker, Joseph
Barnes, George H.
Barnes, William H.
Barry, Charles
Bartholomew, Isaac C.
Bartholomew, John L.
Bartholomew, John N.
Bartholomew, Rodolphus
Beach, George W.
Beach, Harvey W.
Beach, Samuel
Beach, William H.
Beaumont, Harvey
Behrens, Gustave
Bennett, Joseph
Bird, Edward J.
Bishop, Austin
Blake, Halsey H.
Blakeslee, Charles P.

Blakeslee, Kirtland
Bliss, George
Bliss, Howard
Boardman, Henry D.
Booth, John H.
Boylan, Luke
Bradley, Franklin
Bradley, George G.
Bradley, Leonard
Bradley, Timothy
Bradshaw, William
Brennan, Michael
Brockett, Benajah
Brockett, Edgar L.
Brockett, Edward
Brockett, William E.
Brockett, William T.
Brown, Charles
Brown, Henry C.
Brown, James A.
Brown, Lawrence
Brown, William
Bub, William
Buell, Burton T.
Buell, Edward J.
Buell, Edwin A.
Bunnell, William R.
Bush, Malachi C.
Bush, Timothy G.
Butler, Charles
Butler, Jesse
Butler, Rufus A.
Butler, Samuel C.
Byington, Edwin M.
Calkins, Wilbur F.
Callahan, Timothy
Callihan, Stephen
Camp, Henry A.
Camp, Joel
Carey, Thomas J.
Carter, Charles
Carter, Edwin H.
Chaipel, Benjamin F.

Chaipel. William H.
Clanning, William Henry
Clark, Francis L.
Clark, Joseph
Clark, Thomas
Clifton, Robert
Coan, Jerome
Coates, Lewis
Cobleigh, William C.
Colburn, Elisha H.
Colwell, George W.
Colwell, Thomas
Condon, John
Condon, Patrick
Connelly, James
Cook, Samuel S.
Cooke, Samuel G.
Crosby, Richard
Cross, Edmund B.
Curtiss, Joseph
Cusher, Joseph
Danby, William
Daniels, Joseph
Daniels, Josiah
Dargan, Pierce
Davis, James
Davis, John
Day, Thomas
Dayton, Ambrose L.
DeBacque, Alfred
DeCourcey, Charles
Demuth, Jacob
Dibble, Elizur B.
Dietrich, Joseph
Dolph, Charles C.
Dolph, Edward B.
Donahue, John
Donahue, William
Donnelly, Edward
Donovan, Jeremiah
Doolittle, Horace A.
Dory, George W.
Dougherty, Robert

Dowd, Benjamin R.
Downey, Timothy
Duffy, Thomas
Edge, Reuben D.
Egan, George M.
Elton, George W.
Ely, Calvin L.
Ennis, James
Evans, Leverett E.
Evans, Thomas H.
Fairchild, Douglas
Ferguson, Charles M.
Field, Daniel W.
Fisher, Albert
Flynn, John
Foote, Delizon B.
Foote, Frederick
Foote, Isaac
Foote, Lozelle
Foote, Philo B.
Forbes, Edgar L.
Forbes, Levi
Ford, George
Forrester, Julius F.
Foster, Andrew
Fowler, DeGrasse, Jr.
Fowler, Samuel O.
Fowler, Walter E.
Fowler, William N.
Francisco, Clifford A.
Frazier, John
Freeman, Wilbur
Frisbie, Alonzo P.
Frisbie, Charles H.
Frisbie, John R.
Frisbie, Russell L.
Frost, Alva
Fuchs, Charles
Fuchs, Henry
Galligan, William J.
Galloway, William S.
Galpin, Joseph A.
Garlick, Seymour
Gilbert, Frederick A.
Gilbert, Wells
Gilde, James

Goodrich, Horace W.
Goodyear, Robert B.
Graham, William F.
Gray, Samuel N.
Green, Charles H.
Green, John
Griffin, Alexander
Grimes, John R.
Gutersloh, Christian
Hall, Isaac K.
Hall, James
Hall, John G.
Hall, Roger
Halling, William
Hanson, Peter
Hargent, John
Harlow, Henry P.
Harlow, Stephen P.
Harris, Theodore
Harrison, Benjamin F.
Harrison, C. Albert
Harrison, Elizur H.
Harrison, Franklin M.
Harrison, H. Lynde
Harrison, Lorenzo E.
Harrison, Nathan A.
Harrison, Sylvanus
Harrison, William H.
Hart, Henry T.
Hartson, Isaac Y.
Henry, James H.
Hickman, John T.
Higgs, Israel
Hill, Bryon
Hilline, Edward
Hilliner, John
Hipwell, John H. R.
Hitchcock, Oliver A.
Hogan, Michael
Holcombe, Dr. H.V.C.
Holmes, William W.
Hopkins, Albert F.
Hosley, Loring D.
Hosley, William B.
Hotchkiss, John
Houghtling, William

Howd, George W.
Howd, William T.
Hoyt, George E.
Hubbard, Henry W.
Hubbell, Alonzo F.
Hull, Eli
Hull, James C.
Huntley, William H.
Hutchinson, John
Hyde, James R.
Ives, William B.
Jacobs, Egbert
Jennings, Barney
Jepson, Benjamin
Jergenson, Emanual
Johnson, Campbell
Johnson, Charles
Johnson, Davis S.
Johnson, Elizur C.
Johnson, George
Johnson, Henry
Johnson, Henry E.
Johnson, Homer R.
Johnson, Josiah
Jones, Elijah B.
Jones, Peter
Jones, William S.
Jost, Jacob
Kelsey, Gilbert I.
Kelsey, Richard T.
Kennedy, James
Kerr, John
Kinneen, James
Kinneen, Michael
Kneringer, Matthias
Knight, Winthrop
Lamb, John
Lamm, Adam
Lanfare, Aaron S.
Lay, James W.
Lee, Frederick W.
Lee, Joseph
Lester, Thomas
Linsley, Atwood
Linsley, Benjamin M.
Linsley, Charles E.

Linsley, Charles F.
Linsley, Frederick A.
Linsley, Jacob F.
Linsley, James H.
Linsley, Jared, Jr.
Linsley, John S., Jr.
Linsley, Joseph F.
Linsley, Marcus M.
Linsley, Samuel M.
Linsley, Solomon F.
Linsley, William H.
Logan, Michael
Lull, Oscar S.
Lynch, Daniel H.
Lynhan, James
Maher, John
Maltby, Charles D.
Martin, James
Martin, John
Mason, Charles
McDermott, James
McGinley, James
McGinnis, John
McGowan, James
McGuire, Thomas
McKeon, Francis
Merring, Levi
Mix, Stephen
Mooney, Michael
Moran, John
Morris, William H.
Morse, James
Morton, Henry
Munson, Medad D.
Munson, William W.
Murphy, John
Myer, William
Myers, George W.
Neale, Daniel
Nelson, William
Nettleton, Joseph F.
Nichols, Henry Z.
Norton, Elias O.
O'Brien, Edward
O'Brien, John
O'Brien, Thomas

O'Callahan, Philip
O'Neal, John
O'Neil, Michael
Packard, Charles H.
Paden, Charles
Page, Elizur E.
Page, Henry
Page, Henry B.
Page, James B.
Page, Joel C.
Paine, Richard J.
Palmer, Ammi B.
Palmer, John Henry
Palmer, Luzerne A.
Palmer, Nathan A.
Palmer, Theodore
Palmer, W. Bradley
Pardee, Henry N.
Parker, William H.
Parsons, Edwin W.
Phelan, Thomas
Plant, Albert E.
Platts, Albert U.
Powell, John
Pratt, Eugene H.
Prout, George M.
Rapp, William
Rath, Gottfried
Reif, Christian
Reif, Lorenz
Reynolds, Peter F.
Reynolds, Stephen
Rich, James S.
Riley, Thomas
Robertson, Alexander
Roberts, Amos, Jr.
Robinson, Henry P.
Robinson, John S.
Robinson, Lorenzo
Rogers, Albert T.
Rogers, George S.
Rogers, Mason
Rogers, Walter
Rowland, George H.
Russell, Alfred
Russell, Charles

Sanford, Daniel
Schaffer, Henry L.
Schenck, Paul
Scranton, Dayton H.
Scranton, Francis S.
Scranton, Henry W.
Scranton, James H.
Scranton, Thomas Marvin
Shanley, Patrick
Sheldon, Edward D.
Shepard, Charles B.
Shepard, Harvey G.
Shepard, John F.
Shepard, Samuel S.
Sherman, Daniel
Sliney, David
Slowman, James
Smith, A. Judson
Smith, David L.
Smith, Edward L.
Smith, Elbert J.
Smith, Elizur G.
Smith, Frederick
Smith, Henry C.
Smith, Ira B.
Smith, Jacob A.
Smith, Josiah A.
Smith, Stephen
Smith, Thomas
Snow, Luther H.
Squire, Lyman F.
Stannard, John S.
Sternberg, John
Stevens, Charles C.
Stevens, Ellis M.
Stevens, Emmerson R.
Stevens, George
Stewart, James
Stone, Elizur C.
Stone, Horatio the younger
Stone, Horatio the elder
Stone, Walter A.
Stone, Watson W.
Strickland, Asa
Sullivan, Charles
Sullivan, Matthew

Sullivan, Philip

Sundelous, Peter

Talmadge, George W.

Talmadge, William

Tarbox, Augustus G.

Taylor, Henry

Taylor, Michael

Taylor, William L.

Terhune, Nicholas R.

Thayer, Elwyn M.

Thomas, Elbridge

Thompson, Richard E.

Todd, Andrew B.

Todd, Beri M.

Todd, Henry D.

Todd, Kirtland

Towner, John Edwin

Townsend, Sidney

Tubbs, John E.

Tucker, Allen

Tucker, Lewis M.

Tyler, Obed L.

Tyler, William A.

Underwood, William J.

Valleley, Frank

VanBenthuysen, Isaac E.

Vibbert, Nelson J.

Wallace, William J.

Wallack, George

Walter, Frank

Weed, Oscar

Wheaton, Albert F.

Wheaton, Merwin

Wheeler, George H.

White, Albert D.

White, James

White, William H.

Whitney, Henry M.

Wilder, John K.

Wilford, Edwin L.

Wilford, George G.

Williams, Charles M.

Willis, Joseph T.

Willis, L. Mortimer

Wilson, John

Wilson, Thomas

Winship, Hoyt F.

Woernley, Paul

Woodruff, Rev. Curtiss T.

Woodworth, Albert P.

Wright, Ellis C.

Yale, Solomon

Young, Charles A.

Young, William E.

Zink, Walter H.

Union soldiers entrenched at Fredericksburg (by Andrew J. Russell, Library of
Congress Prints & Photographs Division, LC-ppmsca-34476)

PREFACE AND ABBREVIATIONS

The Civil War Soldiers of Branford was written primarily as a reference book focusing on the soldiers' service and biographical information. The book provides historical background to the Town of Branford and its public records just before and during the war. The book will interest students of Branford history, descendants of the individual soldiers, and those interested in the specific regiments or battles.

The beginning of the book is a narrative about Branford and the soldiers' experiences such as enlistments, bounties, prisons, and hospitals. Finding the soldiers' pension and other military records is explained. The pension provides detailed information about the soldiers' military service, personal experience, and genealogical data. The narrative uses The Chicago Manual of Style for its formatting.[1]

The largest section of the book focuses on the soldiers' military and biographical information. Separate chapters were made for soldiers where more extensive information was available such as letters or diaries. The remaining soldiers are listed alphabetically. Each listing provides detail about the soldiers' service, pension, family, and vital records. The formatting for this section is in Register Style, a genealogical writing style.[2]

---

1   The Chicago Manual of Style, Sixteenth Edition (The University of Chicago Press, 2010).
2   Henry B. Hoff, editor, Genealogical Writing in the 21st Century, A Guide to Register Style and More (New England Historic Genealogical Society, 2002).

Spelling has been retained for original letters and diaries, but capitalization and periods were added. Most soldiers did not capitalize the first word of a sentence or use punctuation marks. An occasional word in a bracket has been added to better explain the context of the original document.

Abbreviations were used by the soldiers during and after the war in their correspondence:

Capt - Captain

Cav - Cavalry

Co. - Company or County

Col. - Colonel

Comm. - Commissioner

Conn. or Ct - Connecticut

Conn Reg Vol - Connecticut Regimental Volunteers

Conn Vols - Connecticut Volunteers

Corp - Corporal, sometimes for Corps

CV - Connecticut Volunteers

Dr. or Doct - Doctor

D.V.S. - Disabled Veteran Soldier

F. or Fd'kburg - Fredericksburg

F. or Ft. - Fort

Gen. - General

HA - Heavy Artillery

Inf - Infantry

LA - Light Artillery

Lt. or Lieut. - Lieutenant

Md - Maryland

Mt - Mount

Reg or Reg't - Regiment

Sgt. or Sergt. - Sergeant

Va - Virginia

VRC or VC - Veterans Reserve Corps

Other abbreviations used in the text are:

c. - circa

CMSR - Compiled Military Service Record

CVI - Connecticut Volunteer Infantry

G.A.R. - Grand Army of the Republic

JP - Justice of the Peace

NARA - National Archives and Records Administration

RG - Record Group

All places are Connecticut except where otherwise noted. The James Blackstone Memorial Library in Branford will be referenced as Blackstone Library. The archives of the Branford Historical Society are housed in the Blackstone Library as a separate collection and are referred to as the Branford Historical Society archives. The original Branford vital and town records were used and can be found at the Branford Town Hall, Town Clerk's office, 1019 Main Street. Certificate books began in 1890 for births, marriages, and deaths and are not paginated.

The information included in the biographies is derived from the soldiers' pension files, Compiled Military Service Record (CMSR), and the *Record of Service of Connecticut Men*. Photographs of gravestones from local cemeteries were taken by the author.

The terms Connecticut Regimental Volunteers, Connecticut Vols., Connecticut Volunteer Regiment, CV, CVI, and Connecticut Volunteer Infantry are all used interchangeably to denote a regiment.

INTRODUCTION

Branford, Connecticut, on the northern shore of Long Island Sound, was settled in 1644 by colonists from New Haven and Wethersfield. By 1700 some of the families moved north to what is today the Town of North Branford, which includes Northford, originally known as the Second and Third Societies. North Branford did not form a separate government until 1832. An in-depth study of the men who fought in the Civil War from Branford has never been undertaken. This book focuses on identifying Branford and North Branford[3] soldiers - their military service, pension records, and biographical information.

Vital records, original letters and diaries, newspapers, regimental histories, and soldiers' pensions at the National Archives in Washington, D.C. were used to research the military service of individual soldiers. Included in the study are soldiers who were born or buried[4] in Branford or North Branford, members of Branford's Grand Army of the Republic post, all the men in Co. B 27th Connecticut Volunteer Regiment, and veterans who came to Branford after the war.

An attempt has not been made to examine the human and social impact on the town but war affected every facet of community life. Some Branford men died in battle or from disease, others returned home sick and suffered chronic disabilities the rest of their lives. The women provided supplies for the soldiers and maintained the farms.

Company B of the Twentieth-seventh Connecticut Volunteer Infantry was raised in New Haven with men primarily from Branford and Wallingford. Branford's dentist, Calvin L. Ely, was elected captain. Forty-three men from Branford served in the company which saw action at the Battles of Fredericksburg and Chancellorsville, Virginia. The field reports submitted by the 27th are not very detailed and most published regimental histories do not mention the service of individual companies. By examining the pension records of the soldiers of Co. B, a detailed chronology of their service is presented. A brief history of the Tenth and Fifteenth Connecticut Regiments is also included, both of which had a significant number of Branford soldiers. An alphabetical list of Branford and North Branford soldiers summarizes their service, biographical information, and pension data. In the Appendix is a timeline, a list of soldiers by company and regiment, followed by a bibliography.

The use of the archives of the Branford Historical Society and the James Blackstone Memorial Library is greatly appreciated. Special thanks to all the librarians and individuals who responded to my requests for photographs, information, and assistance.

Jane Peterson Bouley
Branford, Connecticut
2013

---

3   For North Branford and Northford soldiers see Marion Doody Bradley, *Our Soldiers* (North Branford: Totoket Historical Society, 1995). The use of her files is appreciated.

4   The Charles R. Hale Collection of Connecticut Cemetery Inscriptions (herein The Hale Collection) recorded vital record information from gravestones throughout the state in the early 1930s including military inscriptions and markers. The Connecticut State Library is the repository for the collection.

SECTION
ONE

BRANFORD 1860-1864 AND
THE SOLDIER EXPERIENCE

Town Hall, Branford, Conn.

The Branford Town Hall was built in 1857 on the Green. (Branford Historical Society photograph collection)

BRANFORD DURING THE CIVIL WAR

Branford, Connecticut in New Haven County was settled by English colonists in 1644 and just before the Civil War was a small farming village with a population of 2,137.[5] Like many New England villages at this time, Branford was in transition with changes in transportation, employment opportunities, and demographics. The population of Branford increased 44% in the previous decade and in 1860 12% of its residents were born in Europe, primarily Ireland. Many men in town were involved in maritime activities. Branford-made goods were shipped along the Eastern Seaboard and to the West Indies. The Malleable Iron Fittings Company was established in 1854 and the Branford Lock Works in 1862; the latter provided employment for a growing Irish population and men started working in the factories instead of on the farm. Both companies grew substantially during the war and their output was among the highest in New Haven County.[6] There is no local documentation or oral history to indicate that Branford products were used in the war effort.

The State of Connecticut was by no means unanimous in its support of the war and there were strong opinions regarding the war and slavery.[7] The Democratic Party in Connecticut favored peace, negotiation,

---

5   U.S. census 1860, Branford, New Haven County, population schedule T-1045, 873-926, www.heritagequest.com.

6   A northern income tax was instituted in 1862 to fund the war, NARA M758; the ledgers for Connecticut are on rolls 7-11.

7   For a discussion of the political climate in Connecticut before and during the war see John Niven, *Connecticut For The Union, the Role of the state in the Civil War* (New Haven: Yale University Press, 1965); Matthew Warshauer, *Connecticut in the American Civil War* (Middletown: Wesleyan University Press, 2011) and Brother J. Robert, *A Political History of Connecticut During the Civil War*, Dissertation (Washington, D.C.: The Catholic University of America Press, 1941).

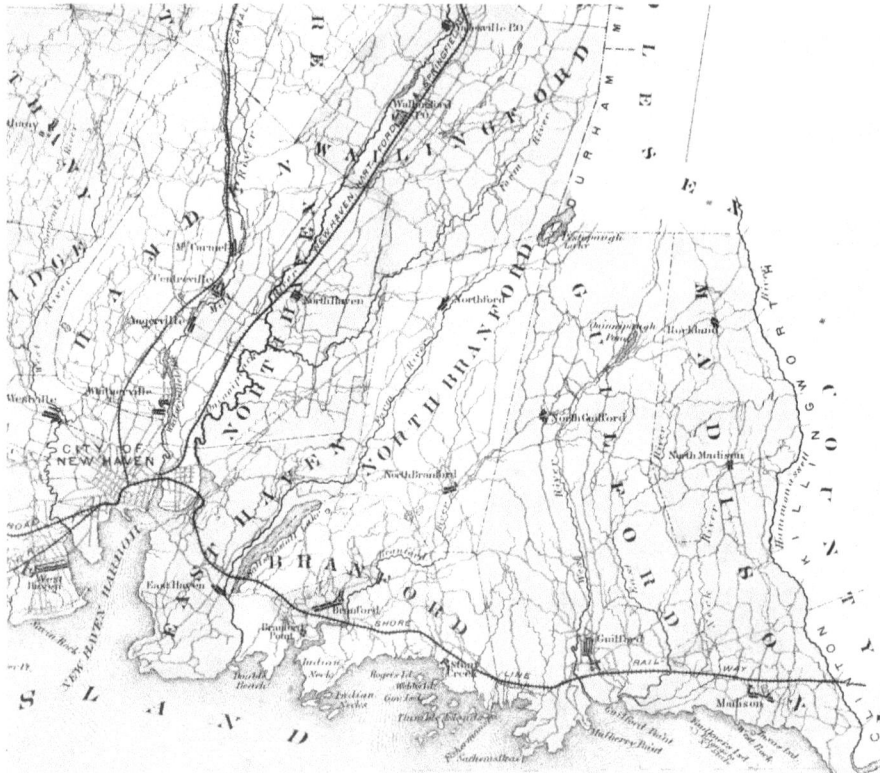

1868 map of eastern New Haven County showing Branford, New Haven, North Haven, East Haven, Guilford, Madison, and Wallingford. (Beers, Ellis & Soule, New York, 1868)

The Malleable Iron Fittings Company on the Branford River was established in 1854 and was the town's largest employer. The factory closed in 1970. (Branford Historical Society photograph collection)

and state's rights; the Republican Party was more pro-Union and anti-slavery. The majority of Branford men voted for the Democratic governor candidates Thomas Seymour, James C. Loomis, and Origen S. Seymour versus the Republican incumbent William A. Buckingham in every gubernatorial election during the war by an average margin of 250 to 146.[8] There was no Branford newspaper during this period and Branford men read and would have been influenced by the *New Haven Evening Register*, a pro-Democratic newspaper. Branford, however, favored the Republican Abraham Lincoln who received 157 votes versus 136 votes for Democrat Stephen A. Douglas in the 1860 presidential election.[9] The members of Branford's Board of Selectman changed every election during the course of the war and four different men represented Branford in the Connecticut General Assembly. Branford's representative Bradley Chidsey was placed on a "blacklist" for refusing to vote yes on legislation to pay for soldiers' bounties.[10]

Branford responded to Governor Buckingham's call for volunteer troops. At a special meeting held Saturday, May 18, 1861 at the Branford Town Hall the electors voted "To make an appropriation for fitting out a volunteer company from this Town and providing Support of the Families of Said Volunteers. Whereas there is now being formed in this Town a Rifle company to be composed of men enlisted from this and the adjoining Towns of East Haven, North Branford and Guilford...Voted that the Selectman of the Town of Branford be hereby authorized and directed to pay to the wife of the enlisted citizen of said Town the sum of one dollar and fifty cents for each week that he is in actual service for her support and to the mother or guardian of each child under the age of fourteen years the sum of fifty cents for each week the father shall be called out and to furnish at the expense of the Town one India Rubber Blanket and such other articles of clothing and conveniences for the comfort of the men in addition to what is furnished to him by the state, the amount of which shall not exceed four dollars each man so enlisted and voted that the sum of three hundred dollars be appropriated for the purpose aforesaid."[11] In 1862 the Branford Selectman certified that they had enrolled 214 men in the service.[12] North Branford certified that 125 men had enlisted; 28 others received exemptions from Surgeon Hubbard.

A special meeting was held October 13, 1862 "Whereas the President of the United states has recently called for 600,000 troops to assist in putting down the present rebellion, a Bounty of $150 shall be paid to encourage enlistment and furnish the quota of this town and shall be paid to each man from Branford who has enlisted or who may enlist under said calls in any company in the State provided he has not received a bounty from another town. The persons so entitled may elect to leave any part of the whole such bounty in the hands of said committee for the benefit of their families to be allotted as they see fit..."[13]

Branford had a grand list of $1,075,441 in 1864 and had expenditures for bounties and support of soldiers' families of $27,181, and an additional $14,300 was paid by individuals for bounties and substitutes. North Branford spent $15,403 and $4,800 respectively with a grand list of $533,867.[14]

There are a few other Branford town meetings regarding the Civil War:

At a Special Meeting held on January 7, 1865 a resolution was made to pay Henry Rogers, Ralph Blackstone and John B. Russell $150 each from the town treasury having furnished a substitute into the U.S. Army

---

8   Meeting of the Branford Electors, election for governor, Town Meeting Book A.
9   William J. Finan, *Branford in the Civil War*, typescript, 29 January 1962, 2; Blackstone Library Archives RG 3, box 7, folder 18.
10   *The Hartford Daily Courant*, 11 November 1863, www.genealogybank.com.
11   Branford Town Meeting Book A, 175.
12   Selectmens' returns of volunteers and men drafted 1862-1864, RG 13, box 111, for Branford, Connecticut State Library.
13   Branford Town Meeting Book A, 175, 192.
14   W. A. Crofut and John M. Morris, *The Military and Civil History of Connecticut During the Civil War of 1861-65* (New York: Ledyard Bill, 1868), 845.

just previous to November 17th 1864.[15] On August 25, 1865 a resolution was made "Whereas the General Assembly at its recent session validated and made obligatory upon this town the appropriation made in July 1863 to assist drafted men. Therefore for the purpose of paying such indebtedness, the selectman shall determine the amount due each man."[16] The town did not vote on the resolution concerning payment to substitutes or draftees and sought a legal opinion. At the October 2, 1865 meeting the town received a legal opinion that the act of the General Assembly about paying draftees did not make the Town of Branford indebted to those persons who furnished a substitute in consequence of the draft of July 1863. In order to avoid dispute or controversy, a resolution to pay the substitutes $300 carried by a vote of 54 to 52.[17]

The Connecticut General Assembly proposed an amendment to allow every male citizen the right to vote. A Special Meeting of the Electors of Branford was called on Monday, October 2, 1865 at 9 o'clock a. m. at the Town Hall "for the purpose of signifying their approbation or disapprobation of a proposed amendment of the constitution of this State viz: Every male citizen of the U.S. who shall have attained the age of twenty one years who shall have resided in the state for a term of one year…to be admitted to the privilege of being an Elector…and shall be able to read any article of the constitution or any section of the statutes of this state and shall sustain a good moral character; shall on taking such oath as may be presented by law become an elector." The proposal was defeated in Branford after the votes were counted: Nays 219, Yeas 90.[18] The amendment was defeated state-wide by over 6,000 votes.[19]

Two businessmen, both born in Branford, had an impact in the North and South during the war. Henry Bradley Plant was born at Branford in 1819 and was one of the developers of Florida, owning a vast network of transportation systems throughout the Gulf region and along the Eastern Seaboard. Before the war, he rose to head the New York operations of the Adams Express Company. When the conflict between the Northern and Southern states seemed evident, the Adams Express Company sold their southern interest to Henry B. Plant. His company carried all the packages of clothing for the Confederate soldiers free of charge during the war. Despite his northern roots, Plant transported Confederate money through his express business.[20] Henry Bradley Plant died at New York City on June 23, 1893 and was buried in Center Cemetery, Branford.

Henry Barker Norton was born at Branford in 1807 and moved to Norwich where he owned a steamship company, mill, and other businesses. He "rendered substantial service in chartering vessels, superintending the transportation of troops, and purchasing supplies at the beginning of the war. An upright, able, and influential business-man, he left his own affairs, and gave personal attention to the wants of the State in this emergency. He cheerfully spent months of time, refusing even the reimbursement of his expenses."[21] After the Battle of the Wilderness on July 24, 1864 Norton, "a patriotic and liberal citizen of Norwich, went to the Potomac at the request of Gov. Buckingham and was of great assistance" supplying the 18th Regiment.[22] Henry Barker Norton died at Norwich on 25 October 1891 and was buried there in Yantic Cemetery. There is also a gravestone for him at Mill Plain Cemetery, Branford.

---

15   Branford Town Meeting Book A, 255.
16   Branford Town Meeting Book A, 265, 269.
17   Branford Town Meeting Book A, 270, 274.
18   Branford Town Meeting Book A, 266-267.
19   Warshauer, *Connecticut in the American Civil War*, 186.
20   Edward A. Mueller, *Steamships of the Two Henrys, Being an Account of the Maritime Activities of Henry Morrison Flagler and Henry Bradley Plant* (Jacksonville, Florida, 1996).
21   Crofut & Morris, *Military History of Connecticut*, 71.
22   Crofut & Morris, *Military History of Connecticut*, 497.

William A. Buckingham of Norwich was governor of Connecticut during the Civil War. He was a supporter of Abraham Lincoln and a strong advocate for the Union. He worked tirelessly during the conflict and afterwards served as a U.S. Senator until his death in 1875. (Crofut & Morris, Military History of Connecticut, 58)

LOCK WORKS, BRANFORD, CONNECTICUT, U. S. A.

The Branford Lock Works was founded in 1862 providing employment for Irish emigrants and thrived during the Civil War. The company was purchased by Yale & Towne and moved to Stamford in 1902. (Branford Lock Works Catalogue 1893, Branford Historical Society archives)

Martha Russell[23] of North Branford was a poetess, author, and journalist. She was born at North Branford on January 17, 1817, daughter of Augustus Russell and Lydia Rose. During the Civil War she lived in Washington, D.C. working for the war department as a French translator. She was a friend of John Denison Baldwin and wrote for his newspaper the *Worcester Spy* (Massachusetts) from 1862 to 1865 under the pseudonym "Zeb." In her column she shared her observations of the war. Martha Russell died at Westfield, New Jersey on April 8, 1899 and was buried in Bare Plain Cemetery, North Branford.

Several men from Branford moved to southern states before the war for business opportunities and were shoe makers, farmers, or merchants. Charles E. Hoadley moved to Fredonia, Alabama and when the conflict began sent two of his daughters north to live with their uncle George Hoadley in Branford. Albert T. Rogers moved to Virginia in 1857 and was drafted into the 31st Virginia Artillery serving in the ambulance corps. Both men returned to Branford shortly after the war.

Branford's contribution to the war was sending its sons, husbands, and fathers to the battlefields. Most enlisted as privates and Dr. H.V.C. Holcombe, Branford's only physician, held the highest rank as surgeon of the 15th Connecticut Volunteer Infantry. About 30% of Branford's soldiers enlisted in 1861, the majority (64%) joined in the late summer and fall of 1862. The record of servicemen from Connecticut[24] lists 185 men from Branford in its catalogue. One hundred fourteen were actually residents and the remainder came from other towns to fill Branford's quota or were substitutes. Two Branford soldiers were killed in battle, eight died of disease, two died in prison, and one died of his wounds shortly after the war (11% of those serving).

North Branford had a population of 1,058 in 1860.[25] Sixty-eight men from North Branford and Northford served during the Civil War of which eighteen were probably not town residents. Four men were killed in action, seven died of disease, and one died in prison.

About 450 men associated with Branford and North Branford served in the Union Army or Navy during the Civil War. Of those soldiers, 312 received pensions after the war (69%).

---

23   For her biography see Everett G. Hill, *A Modern History of New Haven and Eastern New Haven County* (New York: S. J. Clark Publishing Co., 1918), II:681. Some of her papers can be found in the Totoket Historical Society (North Branford) and Branford Historical Society archives.

24   *Record of Service of Connecticut Men in the Army and Navy of the United States during the War of the Rebellion* (Hartford, Connecticut: Case, Lockwood & Brainard, 1889). Statistics in the sources vary. Blaikie Hines, *Civil War, Volunteer Sons of Connecticut* (Thomaston, Maine: American Patriot Press, 2002) provides an analysis of men and battles by regiment and town; sites 199 men from Branford.

25   U.S. census 1860, North Branford, New Haven County, population schedule M653-85, 789-*815*, www.heritagequest.com

MARCHING THROUGH NEW HAVEN.
(See page 60.)

The First Connecticut Light Battery leaving New Haven for the front (Beecher, First Light Battery, front piece)

ENLISTMENTS, BOUNTIES, DRAFT, PRISONS, DEATHS

ENLISTMENTS

When the call for volunteers was made by President Lincoln, public meetings, sermons, posters, and bounties all encouraged young men to enlist in the Union cause. Shortly after the first shots were fired at Fort Sumter a meeting was held in Branford. Colonel Levi S. Parsons presided and the people were addressed by Rev. Jacob G. Miller of the First Congregational Church, Dr. H.V.C. Holcombe, and others; recruiting began at the meeting.[26] In North Branford, "the people raised a hickory stick, the gift of an old Jackson man, Capt. Jonathan Rose; and unfurled a handsome flag on the identical spot, where, in 1776, after the Sabbath service, Parson Eells called the young men of his congregational together, and led them to war."[27] Patriotism was probably the foremost reason men from Branford enlisted; others joined for money, adventure, or to be with their friends. "The growth of each company was rapid or slow according to the popularity of the proposed officers, the influences of friends, the efforts made by advertising, by recruiting agents, by holding war meetings, and in some instances, by the offer

---

26 Crofut and Morris, *Military and Civil History of Connecticut*, 52.
27 Crofut and Morris, *Military and Civil History of Connecticut*, 54. Rev. Samuel Eells of the North Branford Congregational Church led a company to the defense of New York in 1776.

of money. Every recruit was taken to the appointed physician and carefully examined as to his physical ability. If he passed the test, he was sworn into the United States service, made to sign enlistment papers in triplicate, furnished a suit of blue clothes, and sent to drill with a musket."[28]

The men spent several weeks or months in camp drilling, marching, and learning military discipline. Diseases such as measles plagued the camps. The public frequently visited the camps and local women brought food, clothing, supplies, and often provided the flags for the regiment. There was great enthusiasm and support, especially at the beginning of the war when the troops left for the front.

The Regimental organization was vital to the war and to the soldiers. It provided a home away from home where the men often knew each other from civilian life. There was tremendous pride in the regiment; its officers, discipline, decorum, and performance during battle. After the war the soldiers formed local G.A.R. organizations, held annual reunions, marched in parades, attended state and national encampments, monument dedications, and funerals.

BOUNTIES

Bounties were offered by the federal, state, and local governments in various amounts for men who enlisted. Connecticut soldiers received a $100 bounty, twenty-five dollars when they enlisted and the remainder when their service expired. Towns provided extra support for the families and supplies and clothing for the soldier. Sometimes wealthy businessmen augmented the bounties. Each town was required to meet an enlistment quota which was filled quickly when the war began but became more difficult as the war dragged on. Sometimes men from other towns or states, through bounty brokers, enlisted from Branford to fill a quota or earn an extra bounty. Pay for the soldier was thirty dollars per year, paid in ten-dollar installments every four months. As the war progressed the soldiers' pay was often delayed for months, leaving their families destitute. The Connecticut legislature approved an act on June 27, 1861 providing the payment of a $300 annual bounty for the soldier and support of the family of each enlisted man. Ten dollars per month was provided for the wife and six dollars per month for each child, not exceeding two children under fourteen years of age. An additional ten dollars per month was provided to the family if the soldier was taken prisoner. The bounty was paid quarterly until the soldier was mustered out or if the soldier died continued until the expiration of his term of service.[29] Substitutes were not paid the bounty until later in the war when they also received the $300 state bounty. This created ill will between enlisted soldiers and the substitutes.

THE DRAFT AND DESERTIONS

The Militia Law of July 17, 1862 required all men between the ages of eighteen and forty-five to be enrolled for a possible draft and gave President Lincoln the authority to ask governors to draft men to fill their quotas. The draft for the Union, known as the Enrollment Act, was instituted on March 3, 1863. The draft was an encouragement to enlistment but only a small percentage of the eligible draftees ever served. The drafted men were known as "recruits" or "conscripts" and joined the regiment at camp or in the field. Some draftees did not desert and served honorably. The enlisted soldiers had a low opinion of the conscripts and the draft did not have the desired result of increasing the size of the army but instead lowered morale and increased desertions. The public felt the draft was an infringement of individual freedom and that

---

28   Homer S. Sprague, *History of the 13th Infantry Regiment During the Great Rebellion* (Hartford: Case, Lockwood & Co., 1867), 19.
29   Warshauer, *Connecticut in the American Civil War*, 63.

WAR POSTER.

ISSUED AT NEW HAVEN, CONN., JULY, 1862.

THE LYON REGIMENT

Will be raised by the authority of the Governor by the

TOWN of NEW HAVEN.

It can be Raised in

80 DAYS.

TERMS OF ENLISTMENT!!

State Bounty paid upon enlisting, if within 30 days,		$50.00
" " " during the first year, .	.	30.00
" Allowance for wife " "	.	72.00
" " " and two children,	.	48.00
United States Bounty paid upon enlisting,	.	27.00
" " " " at end of war,	.	75.00
" " Pay per month, . . .	.	13.00
Total pay in one year besides clothing and rations,		458.00

Good Men are Invited to meet the Committee at once.

LET THE LYON REGIMENT

Be first in the fieldand march to Washington
in 30 Days.

JOHN C. HOLLISTER,	HENRY D. PARDEE,
SAMUEL BISHOP,	B. L. BRYAN,
N. D. SPERRY,	CHARLES W. ELIOT,

FRANCIS WAYLAND,

Recruiting Committee, Cutler Building.

New Haven recruitment poster (Thorpe, History of the Fifteenth, 223)

unwilling soldiers made poor fighting men. Men with enough wealth hired substitutes for $300 or paid a commutation fee to avoid the draft. An industry developed of "bounty jumpers," men hired and paid as substitutes, sometimes using a fictitious name, then failing to report or deserting and repeating the process over again. There were charges of class discrimination and the new draft put a burden on immigrants since they did not have the means to hire a substitute.

Those already serving were encouraged to reenlist when their term expired and were given an additional bounty and a thirty-day furlough back home. Money from commutation fees were used for the reenlistment bounties. Often it seems a soldier survived two or three years of soldiering and battles only to be killed shortly after reenlisting.

Less than half of Branford's eligible men enlisted in the service. There were 253 eligible men on the 1862 draft enrollment list but only five from that list served and several found substitutes. The majority of Branford's soldiers had already enlisted. Only seven Branford residents enlisted after 1862, most serving in the Navy. For North Branford, eighty-two men were eligible for the draft but none served. Twelve North Branford residents found substitutes.[30]

The reasons for not serving were many including opposition to the war, fear of fighting, family concerns, the necessity of running their farms or businesses, and ill health.

PRISONS

Confederate prisons[31] were Libby and Belle Isle at Richmond, Virginia; Danville, Lynchburg, and Petersburg, Virginia; Salisbury, North Carolina; Charleston and Columbia, South Carolina; Millen, Macon, Atlanta, Savannah, and Andersonville, Georgia; plus others in Alabama and Texas. Both the North and the South used conditions at the prisons for their propaganda.

Libby Prison at Richmond, Virginia was infamous for its harsh conditions, particularly exposure to the elements and overcrowding. Before the war it was three warehouse buildings owned by the Libby family used for storing tobacco and other goods. It was converted for use as a prison in 1861 after the First Battle of Manassas. "Many thousands lived there month after month, wasting away, starving, dying of fever, of consumption, from insanity, despair."[32] In 1864 men still imprisoned at Libby were transferred to Macon or Andersonville, Georgia. After Union forces occupied Richmond, Libby was used for detaining Confederate officers. About 50,000 prisoners entered Libby Prison during the war. In 1888 the prison was sold, dismantled, transported, and was to be erected in Chicago; however, most of the building materials were sold. Another source says it operated in Chicago as the Libby Prison Museum from 1889 until 1895.[33] Belle Isle on the James River near Richmond was also used as a prison for enlisted Union soldiers. There were no deaths of Branford soldiers at Libby Prison since their captivity there was brief. Early in the war, prisoners from both sides were exchanged, but later in the war, exchanges were banned by President Lincoln.

Andersonville Prison in Georgia was the most dreaded place of captivity due to overcrowding, lack of food, filthy conditions, the heat, and mistreatment. Upon entering, "we looked in horror; before us were forms that had once been active and erect; stalwart men, now nothing but mere walking skeletons, covered

---

30   Further research might reveal more substitutes for Branford and North Branford men.

31   For the Connecticut experience in Confederate prisons see Robert H. Kellogg (of the 16th CVI), *Life and Death in Rebel Prisons: Andersonville, GA., and Florence, S. C.* (Hartford, 1865); and Homer B. Sprague (of the 13th CVI), *Lights and Shadows in Confederate Prison, A Personal Experience 1864-5* (New York: G. P. Putnam's Sons, The Knickerbocker Press, 1915).

32   *In Memory of the Men of Connecticut who Suffered in Southern Military Prisons 1861-1865, Dedication of the monument at Andersonville, Georgia* October 23 1907 (Hartford: State of Connecticut, 1908), 8.

33   The Encyclopedia of Virginia, www.enclopediavirginia.org.

Camp Tyler in Hanover, Connecticut (Beecher, First Light Battery, 30)

Libby Prison in Richmond, Virginia (Library of Congress Prints & Photographs Division, LC-cwp-02897)

with filth and vermin. Deaths were frequent, the old prisoners called it being exchanged."[34] Several Branford and North Branford men died at Andersonville. Confederate prisoners were held at various locations in the North, the treatment of the men varied depending on the facility.

Much of the 15th and 27th Connecticut Volunteer Regiments were held prisoners at Libby or Belle Isle in Richmond for less than two weeks before they were exchanged. Twenty-four other Branford or North Branford soldiers were confined at various prisons, seven of whom died.

DEATH AND DISEASE

Many books refer to the horrible death toll during the Civil War, the total of which surpasses all other American conflicts combined. Over 600,000 Northerners and Southerners lost their lives in the war but there were more deaths from disease than injury in the battlefield. Diarrhea and dysentery claimed 44,558 Union soldiers from spoiled food, poor nutrition, bad water, and exposure to the elements.[35] Many Branford soldiers suffered at some time during their service from these ailments and some were discharged for disability. The second leading cause of death was various fevers; referred to as camp fever, typhoid, remittent fever, malaria fever or malaria poisoning. Over 40,000 Union soldiers died from fever. About 20,000 men died of pulmonary disease, primarily pneumonia.

A group of prisoners at Andersonville waiting for their rations. (Photographic History of the Civil War, 7:130)

---

34   Kellogg, *Life and Death in Rebel Prisons*, 712.
35   For these statistics, see E. B. Long, *Civil War Day by Day, An Almanac 1861-1865* (New York: Da Capo Press, 1971), 712.

Fitch's Home For Soldiers, Noroton Heights, Conn.

Fitch's Home for Soldiers in Darien, Connecticut (Collection of the author)

KNIGHT HOSPITAL & FITCH'S SOLDIER HOME

KNIGHT HOSPITAL IN NEW HAVEN

Citizens' committees, particularly women's groups, raised money to assist soldiers' return to Connecticut for convalescing from wounds or disease. A soldier was more likely to recover and survive at the local hospital than at the field hospitals. The New Haven State Hospital became the primary care facility for Connecticut soldiers.

In the fall of 1862, the State Hospital in New Haven leased their building to the United States government for use as a military hospital. The one-hundred bed facility was expanded with wooden barracks and tents for up to 1,500 patients and became known as Knight U.S. Army General Hospital or Knight Hospital, named for New Haven physician Dr. Jonathan Knight. Knight was president of the General Hospital Society of Connecticut, one of the founders of the American Medical Association, and a professor at Yale College. The hospital was at the current Cedar and Howard Streets, and Davenport and Congress Avenues. The location is now part of the campus of Yale-New Haven Hospital.

Knight Hospital treated 25,340 patients during the Civil War and 204 men died there. A monument in Evergreen Cemetery was dedicated in 1870 to honor the soldiers who died at the hospital. [36]

---

36   Sharon B. Smith, *Connecticut's Civil War* (Milford, Connecticut: Featherfield Publishing, 2010); www.yale.edu/library; and www.ctmonuments.net.

FITCH'S HOME FOR SOLDIERS

A number of Branford Civil War veterans spent their last years as residents of Fitch's Home for Soldiers and Orphans in the Noroton section of Darien, Fairfield County.[37] It was also known as the Fitch's Soldier Home or Noroton Home. The complex was erected by Benjamin Fitch and dedicated on July 4, 1864 as a home for soldiers and soldiers' orphaned children. It was the first such home in the country and was personally financed and managed by Fitch until his death in 1883. The facility included a hospital, chapel, library, dormitories, parade grounds, art gallery, and administrative buildings. Residency was not restricted to Civil War veterans. In 1910 over 500 veterans were residing there and during the Depression up to 1,000. Admission was granted by a board of directors and disability had to be proven. At the home the soldiers received their food, some clothing, tobacco, newspapers, and other items. Most of the soldiers living there had very few possessions.

The State of Connecticut assumed control of the facility in 1887 and renamed it Fitch's Home for Soldiers. A new Veterans' Home and Hospital was dedicated by the state in Rocky Hill on August 28, 1940 that is still in use today.

The Connecticut State Library holds the discharge files of about 2,300 veterans who stayed at the Fitch's Soldier Home. The discharge papers are in fifteen boxes arranged by file number and the index can be found online on the state library's web site.[38] Over two thousand veterans are buried in Spring Grove Cemetery, Darien.

---

37 Thomas & Donna LaLancette, *A Guide to Civil War Monuments, Memorials and Markers of Connecticut*, 1997, volume one, Fairfield County, 47, includes soldiers buried in Spring Grove Cemetery; and Connecticut Department of Veterans' Affairs, www.ct.gov/ctva.
38 Connecticut State Library, www.cslib.org.

Henry C. Merwin of New Haven, Lieutenant-Colonel of the 27th Connecticut Infantry was killed at the Battle of Gettysburg July 2, 1863 leading the charge at the Wheatfield. (Sheldon, History of the Twenty-seventh, front piece)

THE TWENTY-SEVENTH CONNECTICUT VOLUNTEER INFANTRY

ORGANIZATION

Answering President Lincoln's call for volunteers, the 27th Connecticut Volunteer Infantry[39] was raised in the summer of 1862 with men from New Haven County. Some of the New Haven Grays who fought at the First Battle of Bull Run served as officers. Richard S. Bostwick of New Haven was elected Colonel; Henry C. Merwin of New Haven, Lieutenant-Colonel; and Theodore Byxbee of Meriden, Major. Each company had a captain, one or two first and second lieutenants, several sergeants, six or more corporals, a musician, and about seventy privates. Company B was organized in New Haven by Colonel Richard S. Bostwick and Calvin L. Ely of Branford was elected Captain. During August, September, and October 1862 eighty-six men enlisted in Co. B.; Branford and North Branford supplied forty-three soldiers in the company (51%), Wallingford thirty soldiers (35%) and other towns twelve men (14%). The

---

39 Using the *Regimental History of the Twenty-Seventh* by Sheldon and the essay by Frank D. Sloat "History of the Twenty-Seventh Regiment C. V. Infantry in *Record of Service of Connecticut Men During the War of the Rebellion*, with other sources, an attempt has been made to chronicle the military service of Co. B and more generally the 27th CVI. The Compiled Records of Events for the 27th only covers November 1862-March 1863. "It was difficult to get a report from April 1 to May 1, 1863, the Regiment was in the field and no report was made. Since that time Companies with their officers including the field officers were captured."

youngest soldier was eighteen years of age, the oldest forty-four and the average age was twenty-eight years. Enlisted men received a bounty of $100.

A member of the 27th Connecticut Volunteer Infantry re-enactors discovered that the companies had nicknames:[40]

Co. A - First company New Haven Grays   Co. F - Columbia Guards
Co. B - Hamilton Guards   Co. G - The Patriot Guard
Co. C - Monitors   Co. H - Marble Rifles
Co. D - Third company New Haven Grays   Co. I - Burnside Rifles
Co. E - Elm City Avengers   Co. K - Newall C. Hall Guard

The Twenty-seventh Regiment was mustered in at Camp Terry, New Haven on October 3, 1862 for a term of nine months. They trained at Camp Terry perfecting their discipline, military skills, organization, and equipment. "The New Haven Grays gave the 27th a full complement of knapsacks which were the best made, more serviceable and convenient than those furnished by the government, and consequently were highly prized."[41]

Camp Terry was a conscript camp at Grapevine Point, Fair Haven bound by Chapel, Lloyd, and James Streets, and the Quinnipiac River. Wooden barracks lined Chapel Street. It was named for General Alfred H. Terry one of New Haven's most distinguished soldiers and Colonel of the Second Regiment of the New Haven Grays. The 23rd, 27th, and 28th regiments trained there and the site later became the Bigelow Boiler Works.[42]

TO WASHINGTON, D.C.

In the evening of October 22, 1862 the Twenty-seventh left New Haven on the steamer *Quaker City*[43] for New York City. They boarded a train passing through Port Monmouth, Philadelphia and spent the night at Baltimore. They arrived in Washington, D.C. on the morning of October 25th and immediately after disembarking from the train marched across Long Bridge to General Robert E. Lee's peach orchard on Arlington Heights, Virginia, by then called Camp Seward.[44] The Regiment set up long rows of white tents. On October 26th the Twenty-seventh was assigned to Brigadier General John J. Abercombie's Division.[45]

Soon after arriving at Camp Seward it began to rain and the soil grew softer and softer into a sea of mud. "The storm continued at intervals during the twenty-sixth and as night approached a strong wind with pelting rain swept howling over the ridge, tearing many of the tents from their uncertain moorings."[46] "That first night was cold, very stormy with hard rain. We had no nourishment, or anything."[47] Some of the soldiers on picket duty that night got sick.

---

40 Broadside, 1995, New Haven Museum.
41 Lucke, Jerome B. *History of the New Haven Grays from Sept. 13, 1816 to Sept. 13, 1976* (New Haven, Connecticut, 1876), 287.
42 "New Haven Now and Then," *New Haven Evening Register*, undated, New Haven Museum, microfilm #122, column #42.
43 Hines, *Volunteer Sons of Connecticut*, 247.
44 Deposition, Charles Paden of Wallingford, 12 November 1889, in the pension file of John Condon.
45 General and Specific Orders, 27th Connecticut Volunteer Regiment, RG 13, item 240, 8; Connecticut State Library.
46 Sheldon, *Twenty-Seventh*, 12.
47 Deposition, Timothy Callahan of Wallingford, 12 November 1889, in the pension file of John Condon.

The steamer U.S. Quaker City transported the 27th Connecticut Regiment from New Haven to New York City on October 22, 1862.

A typical camp in North Virginia. (Library of Congress Prints & Photographs Division, LC-cwp-03892)

TO CAMP NEAR WASHINGTON, D.C.

At noon on October 27th, the order came to strike the tents for their move a few miles up the Potomac. They crossed over to Georgetown across the Aqua Duct Bridge, then followed the river and crossed the Chain Bridge back to the left bank where they camped. The day they left Washington, "it had rained hard and was very muddy; there was not anything of interest [that] occurred on the march."[48] The next day, October 28th, Camp Tuttle near Chain Bridge came into existence where the 27th settled into a month's routine to prepare for the campaign. The camp was situated on high ground with a view of the dome of the Capitol. "Some distance in front, and on the left, were thick woods, while the right was skirted by a road, across which were encamped the Twenty-fourth and Twenty-eighth New Jersey, and the One Hundred and Twenty-seventh Pennsylvania, which, with our own regiment, constituted a brigade of Abercrombie's division of the army for the defense of Washington."[49]

As soon as camp was established in its new location the Colonel issued a regimental order setting forth the program of daily duty, as follows: Reveille at six a.m.; guard mounting at eight; company drill from nine to eleven, and again from one to two; battalion drill from three to four, and dress parade at five p.m.; tattoo at nine and taps at half past nine. All this was varied by two days of picket duty every two weeks a few miles up the Leesburg turnpike.

The Chain Bridge over the Potomac River connected Washington, D.C. to Arlington and Fairfax, Virginia and was used by the soldiers as they marched south. (Library of Congress Prints & Photographs Division, LC-cwpb--04112)

---

48 *Compiled Records Showing Service of Military Units in Volunteer Union Organizations* (called the Records of Events), National Archives microfilm M594, roll 8. Reports for Connecticut infantry units are on rolls 5-8. The reports for the 27th have very little detail after 1862.
49 Sheldon, *History of the Twenty-Seventh*, 13.

With the approach of winter pine logs were cut and cabins built. On November 7, 1862 it snowed in northern Virginia and mid-November was cold and rainy. In November the Army of the Potomac listed 39,340 men on its sick rolls including 852 cases of typhoid; 14,002 cases of diarrhea and dysentery; 3,207 cases of rheumatism; 777 cases of bronchitis; and many other cases of respiratory illness and fever.[50]

TO CAMP NEAR FALMOUTH, VIRGINIA

On the last day of November 1862 marching orders came and rations were prepared. At nine o'clock the following morning the 27th with the other regiments in the brigade began the march to Washington, leaving their tents standing at Camp Tuttle. "Henceforth, shelter-tents, and for much of the time no tents at all, were to be our covering."[51] The first day they marched across Chain Bridge through Georgetown and Washington and down the Potomac fifteen miles. On December 2nd they marched twenty miles through pleasant countryside. On the third day they came within three miles of Port Tobacco and camped on the grounds of a plantation. December 5th was their last day marching on the Maryland side of the Potomac and they had to wait several hours in the rain for a ferry to cross at Acquia Landing. The rain changed into a driving snow. They camped at Acquia Creek on a hillside and rested for two days. The snowstorm still raged and the company was nearly out of rations. "First we scrape the snow away, put up out shelter tents, lay our rubber blankets down on the wet ground, then lay on them with our wet clothes on and cover ourselves with our woolen blankets. The cold comes up from underneath. I have not been able to sleep over four hours a night."[52]

On December 8th the Second Army Corps led the Grand Right Division for the final march to Falmouth, Virginia, arriving the next day.[53] "A few days before the Battle of Fredericksburg the company was on a forced march, the weather being very wet and Stormy."[54] They encamped "about one mile back of the town."[55] The Twenty-seventh was assigned by General Darius N. Couch of the Second Army Corps to the Third Brigade commanded by Colonel Samuel K. Zook. The Third Brigade was part of the First Division under the command of General Winfield S. Hancock. The First Division was part of the Right Grand Division led by Major General Edwin V. Sumner.

On December 9th they received orders to prepare four days of rations and clean their weapons. In the afternoon of December 10th, companies D and F of the 27th were assigned to picket duty along the Rappahannock River just above Falmouth.

"About 12 o'clock at night we were ordered to roll our blankets and tie them over our shoulders and to be ready to march at 4 o'clock. As soon as it was light we were in line and marched towards Fredericksburg."[56] The morning of December 11th they began the march toward Fredericksburg arriving near the Phillips House, headquarters of General Sumner. "We were just this side of the river and stayed overnight. Cannonading was heard day and night that probably has never been heard on this continent."[57]

---

50 Sutherland, Daniel E., *Fredericksburg & Chancellorsville, The Dare Mark Campaign* (Lincoln, Nebraska, University of Nebraska Press, 1998), 25.
51 Sheldon, *History of the Twenty-Seventh*, 17.
52 DeCusati, Andrew, "Connecticut Men Answer Lincoln's Call." essay, c. 1995, quoting a letter from William B. Crampton, Co. I 27th CVI, 9 December 1862.
53 O'Reilly, Francis Augustin. *The Fredericksburg Campaign, Winter on the Rappahannock* (Baton Rouge, Louisiana: Louisiana State University Press, 2006), 30.
54 Affidavit, Henry D. Boardman of Great Barrington, Mass., 26 December 1888, in the pension file of Edwin W. Parsons.
55 *Record of Events*, M594, roll 8.
56 Letter from Merwin Wheaton of Co. B 27th CVI, January 9, 1863 from Falmouth, Va. to his family in North Branford, copy from Marilyn Doody Bradley.
57 Letter, Merwin Wheaton.

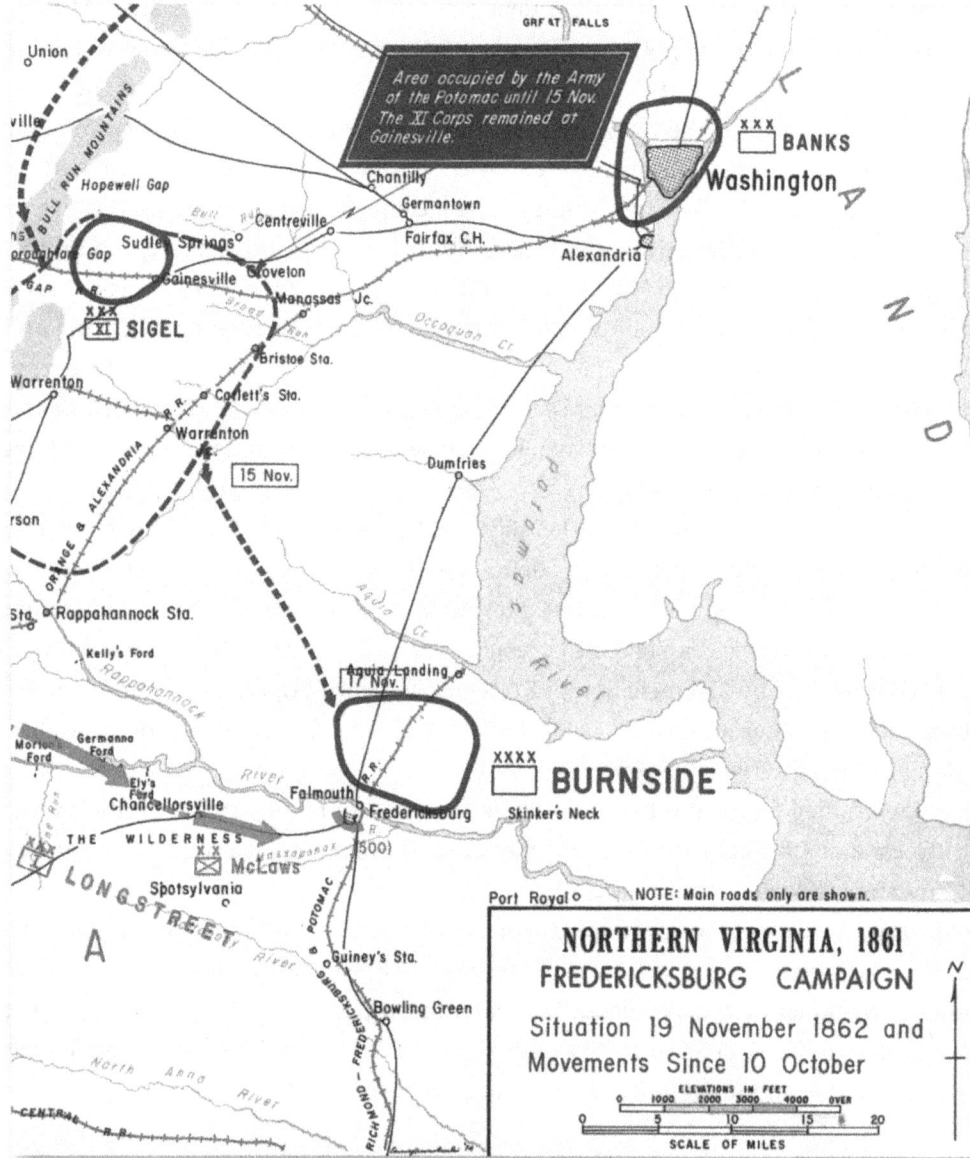

Map of North Virginia during the 1862 campaign showing key locations along the Rappahannock River. (Atlas for the American Civil War, map 24)

THE BATTLE OF FREDERICKSBURG, VIRGINIA[58]

Early in the morning of December 12, 1862, 375 men of the 27th Connecticut Volunteers moved from a point near Phillips House and crossed into Fredericksburg over pontoon bridges that had been built the previous day. "We were in the city. It was completely riddled with shot and shell, the houses were all blown to bits."[59]

The Twenty-seventh moved down Water Street and encamped by a pontoon bridge in the mud just below the town. "That night we lay right in the street without any fires and the mud [was] about a foot deep."[60] Co. B was detailed to lay pontoons across a stream uniting with the Rappahannock just below the town at Hazel Run. Mid-afternoon one of the rebel batteries began firing at the men and for a time there was a very brisk artillery duel. The Twenty-seventh was sheltered by the steep bank so rebels could not obtain accurate range and most of the shells shrieked harmlessly over their heads. "The Connecticut men hid beneath the steep bank of Hazel Run and refused to budge."[61]

On the morning of Saturday, December 13th "we got up at 5 in the morning & ate our breakfast of raw pork & hard bread."[62] The day was chilly and foggy until the sun broke through mid-morning. The Twenty-seventh with the other regiments of General Hancock's First Division formed on Sophia Street and marched to Caroline Street as artillery shells crashed in the city. About 12:30 p.m., the 27th with the 53rd Pennsylvania under the command of Colonel John R. Brooke advanced south of the railroad tracks at Frederick Street. "A murderous fire of grape, canister, shot & shell was opened upon us."[63] The Twenty-seventh lost some of its men when it passed the railroad depot.[64] Zook's Brigade advanced quickly 1,500 yards across an open field to try and take the Confederate fortifications at Marye's Heights.[65] They were met with terrific artillery and musket fire from the Confederate line hidden behind the stone wall at the base of the Heights. "At Fredericksburg, Virginia we faced the enemy fire acting under orders of Lieutenant George Elton of Co. B 27th Regiment Conn. vols. I remember that shot and shell was flying about us so thick that we got orders to lay low."[66] "I then began to realize the horrors of a battlefield, the groans of the wounded, the thunder of shells all mixed together, or perhaps 3 or 4 men blown all to pieces by a shell within a few feet from me. I did not get off that field until 10 o'clock in the evening for I was looking for Josiah and some of the rest of our boys."[67]

> *"It is a wonder to me that any of us came out alive but thanks be to God who doeth all things well."*[68]

---

58   For a detailed account of the experience of a 27th soldier at Fredericksburg, see the letters by Henry D. Boardman, George C. Baldwin, and Merwin Wheaton.
59   Letter, Merwin Wheaton .
60   Letter, Merwin Wheaton.
61   O'Reilly, *Winter on the Rappahannock*, 117.
62   Letter, Henry D. Boardman, 17 December 1862.
63   Letter, Henry D. Boardman, 17 December 1862.
64   O'Reilly, *Winter on the Rappahannock*, 303.
65   *Dedication of the Monument at Gettysburg, October 22nd, 1885. An Account of the Excursion From New Haven to Gettysburg and Return* (New Haven, Connecticut: Price, Lee & Co., 1885), 16.
66   Affidavit, Elizur B. Dibble of Branford, 25 July 1890, in the pension file of Henry A. Camp.
67   Letter, Merwin Wheaton. He married Carrie Johnson, sister of Josiah.
68   Letter, [George C. Baldwin] to home, 15 December 1862.

BATTLE OF FREDERICKSBURG.

During the Battle of Fredericksburg on December 13, 1862 seventeen men were killed and ninety wounded from the 27th Connecticut Volunteer Regiment. (Kurz & Allison lithograph, Library of Congress Prints & Photographs Division, LC-DIG-pga-01851)

The landing at Acquia Creek along the Potomac was a hub for transporting men and supplies to Falmouth, Fredericksburg, and Chancellorsville, Virginia. (Library of Congress Prints & Photographs Division, LC-cwp-01164)

Before the Battle of Fredericksburg, the 27th Connecticut was assigned to the Second Army Corps under General Darius N. Couch. (Library of Congress Prints & Photographs Division, LC-cwp-4a40418)

View of Fredericksburg, Virginia from the east bank of the Rappahannock. (by Timothy H. O'Sullivan, Library of Congress Prints & Photographs Division, LC-cwp-04325)

The 27th was detailed to lay the pontoon bridges across the Rappahannock and were the last regiment back over during the retreat after the Battle of Fredericksburg. (Photographic History of the Civil War, 2:91)

Wounded soldiers gathered at a field hospital after the Battle of Fredericksburg. (by James Gardner, Library of Congress Prints & Photographs Division, LC-cwph-03385)

Burying dead Union soldiers after the Battle of Fredericksburg. In 1865 a National Cemetery was established on Marye's Height and contains the graves of 15,000 soldiers who died at Fredericksburg. (Library of Congress Prints & Photographs Division, LC-cwp-1843)

The buildings of Fredericksburg, Virginia were riddled with gun and cannon shot during the battle. (Photographic History of the Civil War, 9:315)

The Twenty-seventh went the farthest up the heights that day within fifty yards of the Confederate wall.[69] The battle decimated the ranks of the 27th which became fragmented during battle. One-third of the 375 soldiers of the 27th were killed or wounded. Joseph Bennett, Patrick Condon, Josiah Johnson, and George Wilford of Co. B died shortly afterwards from their wounds.

> *"All drawn up in the line of battle, one Brigade*
> *after another, colors streaming, they marched*
> *boldly up like Tennyson's six hundred into*
> *the jaws of death. It was a grand sight. I*
> *lay where I could see it all plainly. They*
> *advanced no farther than the 27th. When they*
> *scattered and soon began to break and fall*
> *back a little, they were bullied by their*
> *officers and advanced a little farther amid*
> *the most terrific storm of bullets canister*
> *shot and shell…they soon broke and fell*
> *back…Our regiment behaved well – so far*
> *as we can see the whole operation was a*
> *prodigious blunder."[70]*

The temperature on December 13th reached 60 degrees but fell sharply that night below freezing. There was a truce to bury the dead on December 15th, many of whom were wounded and died of exposure. Many of the dead were left on the field. A small party returned on December 17th for further burials.

The army retreated from the city at night on December 15th. The Twenty-seventh was the last regiment left behind to bring up the rear and loosen the pontoon's moorings. During the retreat on December 16th there was a thunderstorm about 1 a.m. Later in the day about noon they arrived back at camp at Falmouth. The wounded were sent to hospitals in Alexandria and Washington, D.C.[71]

AT CAMP NEAR FALMOUTH, VIRGINIA

The Twenty-seventh spent that winter at camp near Falmouth. They build 130 log huts, seven-by-ten feet, each with a fireplace. The roofs were made with the canvas from the shelter tents. Furniture was made by the soldiers and cooking utensils fashioned from whatever scraps could be obtained. Provisions consisted of beef, pork, hard-tack, and fresh bread. The Twenty-seventh was initially furnished with Austrian rifles which were of an inferior quality but during the winter received new Whitneyville rifles manufactured in New Haven.

On January 20, 1863 there was a drop in temperature with wind and sheets of rain that lasted 36 hours. The brigade began to march for another attack on the enemy but the march was aborted due to the weather and they returned to camp on January 22nd in what became known as the "Mud March." The number of desertions increased but a pardon was granted if the soldier returned by April 1st.

---

69   Lucke, *New Haven Grays*, 295.
70   Letter, Corporal Samuel Beach of Co. B 27th CVI to home, 18 December 1862.
71   *Dedication of the Monument at Gettysburg*, 18.

The Twenty-seventh was engaged in picket duty along the Rappahannock during the winter and spring. The soldiers equipped with blankets and one day's rations formed in front of the Colonel's tent and after inspection marched a mile to General Hancock's headquarters to undergo another inspection. From there they marched two or three miles to the guard station along the river. Three-fourths of the time it was either rainy or snowing. On February 22nd they experienced the severest snow storm of the season and many of the men became ill in camp that winter from diarrhea and rheumatism.[72]

> *"I am well and harty. I am with my Company. We are in the same old Camp yet and I hope we shall stay here until our time is up. There is know excitement down hear just know but there may bea before long for the mud is a drying up fast & it will soon bea dry enuf to march. I think they will try to Cross the river when they move agane.*
>
> *I don't wish to Cross that River agin for it is a hard place to tackle you Can bet. I hope when we move that we shall move back toards Washington. We have only two months and a half longer to serv. Give my Respects to all and tell them I am tough as a nut."* your Uncle John S. Robinson, Falmouth, virginia[73]

THE BATTLE OF CHANCELLORSVILLE, VIRGINIA

The Twenty-seventh participated in the grand review of the Army of the Potomac by President Lincoln at camp in Falmouth on April 8, 1863, and was transferred to the Fourth Brigade under the command of Colonel John R. Brooke of the 53rd Pennsylvania. The Fourth Brigade was under the command of Major General Darius N. Couch of the Second Army Corps and Major General Winfield S. Hancock of the First Division. Major General Joseph Hooker was placed in command of the Army of the Potomac after the Battle of Fredericksburg. In mid-April orders were given to prepare to march and to dismantle the camp. It rained nearly every day of the march. On April 27th they marched to Kelly's Ford twenty-five miles above Fredericksburg. The roads were filled with marching Union regiments. The Twenty-seventh moved up river from Bank's Ford and crossed on pontoons at United States Ford. General Couch and Hancock's brigade reached Chancellorsville the night of Thursday, April 30th and camped near the town.

The Twenty-seventh was assigned to build entrenchments day and night and they got little sleep. On May 2nd at the break of dawn the Twenty-seventh marched onto the road and took its place in Hooker's line of battle. The building of entrenchments continued with the enemy firing about them. On May 3rd the Twenty-seventh held its position while other Union regiments were engaged in heavy fighting.

May 3rd was a Sabbath and the day Co. B and most of the 27th fought at the Battle of Chancellorsville, Virginia, sometimes called the Second Battle of Fredericksburg. Immediately after breakfast the Twenty-seventh with the exception of companies D and F who were engaged on picket duty were ordered down into the entrenchments. About 1 p.m. the regiment advanced to relieve the Second Division, Fifth Army Corps led by Major General George G. Sykes as they retreated. They marched at double-quick time down the hill into the ravine and were met by a heavy fire of musketry. Several men were wounded just as they

72   Sheldon, *History of the Twenty-Seventh*, 40.
73   Letter, John S. Robinson, Co. F 27th CVI, April 2, 1863 from Falmouth, Virginia to his family in North Branford. Robinson died June 18, 1863, age 27 from disease. The letter is quoted in Furgurson's book, page 57, the original is at the Fredericksburg and Spotsylvania National Military Park, vol. 117.

The 27th Regiment spent many hours on picket duty at camp near Falmouth, Virginia. Soldiers became ill from exposure to the rain and cold. (by Edwin Forbes, Library of Congress Prints & Photographs Division, LC-ppmsca-20741)

In January 1863 a second march to Fredericksburg began but was aborted due to the weather.
It became known as the "Mud March." (Harper's Weekly 14 February 1863, 104)

The Twenty-seventh was part of the 2nd Corps under Major General Darius Couch and arrived at Chancellorsville on April 30, 1863. (by Edwin Forbes, Library of Congress Prints & Photographs Division)

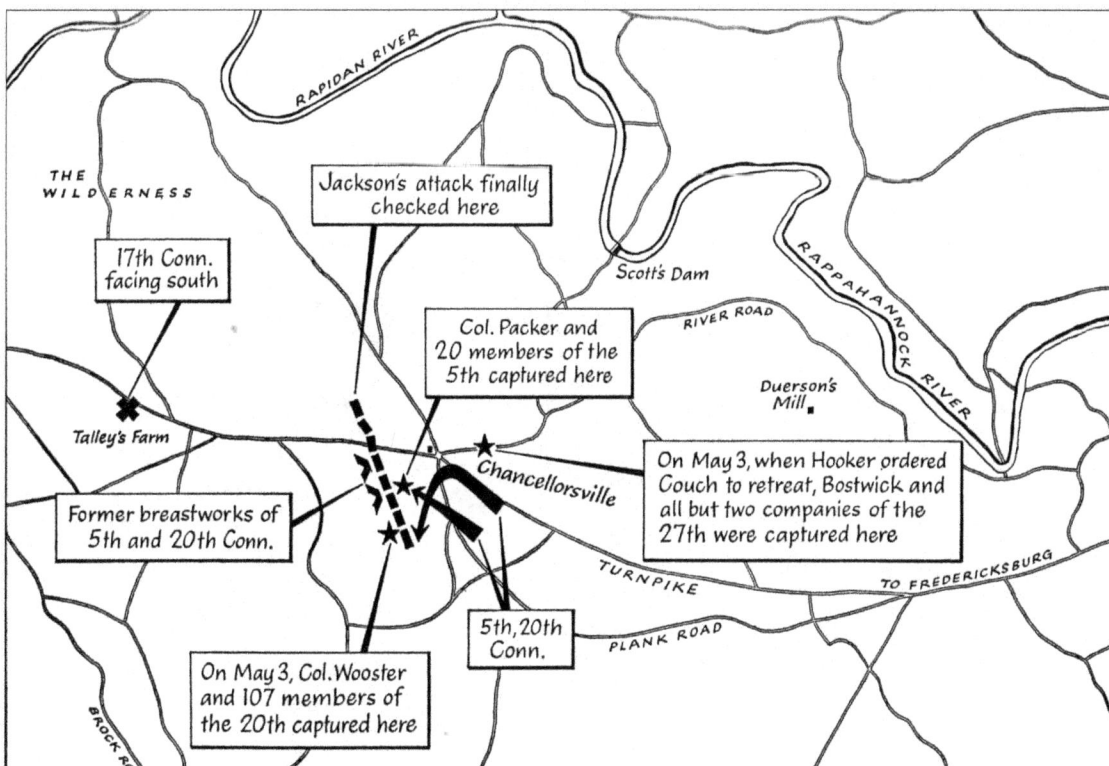

A map of the Battle of Chancellorsville, Virginia May 1-4, 1863 showing troop positions. (Niven, Connecticut for the Union, 231)

The Twenty-seventh Volunteer Infantry suffered its greatest losses at the Battle of Chancellorsville, Virginia on May 3, 1863 where 272 soldiers were taken prisoner. (Kurz & Allison lithograph, Library of Congress Prints & Photographs Division, LC-DIG-pga-01844)

The officers and some of the enlisted men were held at Libby Prison in Richmond, Virginia after their capture at the Battle of Chancellorsville. (Photographic History of the Civil War, 7:57)

entered the breastworks. "May 3rd 1863 acting under orders of Lieut. George Elton of Co. B Reg. Conn. vol. at Chancellorsville State of Virginia, we faced the Enemy's fire behind the entrenchments in the woods. I remember we had orders to get up and fire and then fall back again behind the entrenchments."[74]

The entrenchments were in a ravine surrounded by dense woods. These woods were locally called the Wilderness, thick with vegetation. Both sides became disorganized and it was hard to distinguish between friend and foe especially as night fell. While holding the line along the entrenchments the Twenty-seventh thought more troops were sent in as reinforcements but they were actually surrounded by the enemy. Soon the shelling stopped and a Confederate soldier appeared waving a flag of truce and slowly advanced. The officer identified himself as Lieutenant Bailey of a Georgia Regiment. After realizing they were surrounded by Confederate troops, officers Merwin and Bostwick surrendered and soon the enemy came pouring in on both flanks.[75] Word had never reached the 27th that the Union's line had been moved back. Eight companies of the 27th were captured that day at Chancellorsville totaling 272 men, including 38 members of Co. B.

PRISONERS OF WAR

Soon after their capture the men threw away their guns, many of them with the cartridges, into a rivulet near the entrenchments and some cut up their equipment. The captured troops were ordered to fall in and the 27th was marched up the road to General Lee's headquarters where they were relieved of their knapsacks, rubber blankets, shelter-tents, and canteens. The prized knapsacks given to the 27th by the New Haven Grays were consumed in a good bonfire to prevent them falling into Rebel hands.[76] Under strong guard, part of the group slept at the Spotsylvania[77] Court House yard and the others in the vicinity of the battlefield. The next day [May 4th] they marched and reached Guinea's Station, a small hamlet on the Richmond and Fredericksburg railroad. Fifteen hundred prisoners had already been assembled at this location before their march to Richmond.[78]

Near Guinea's Station was a house where Stonewall Jackson lay dying. Their stay at the station was prolonged until Thursday, May 7th with three days of misery in an open lot in intense heat. On Tuesday May 5th there was a terrific thunderstorm in the evening with heavy rain. "While in the hands of the enemy while en-route to Richmond, near Guinea Station there was a severe storm which lasted all night and into the next day. We had to lay on the ground with no shelter.[79] The only rations were three pints of flour per man, mixed with water and dried by the fire. The ground was flooded between ridges of earth by the heavy rain."[80]

The march to Richmond resumed Thursday morning, May 7th, escorted by the 12th South Carolina Regiment. The roads were almost impassable and muddy due to the recent heavy rains. On the route they passed through Bowling Green, a few miles east of the railroad, and by evening reached Milford Station. Just beyond the village they had to wade across the Mattapony River and halted for the night in a forest nearby. After a grueling march they bivouacked a short distance beyond Hanover Station. At this place each man received five medium-sized crackers and an ounce of bacon.

---

74   Affidavit, James B. Page of Cheshire, undated, in the pension file of Henry A. Camp.
75   Sloat, Frank D. "History of the Twenty-Seventh Regiment C. V. Infantry," *Record of Service of Connecticut Men During the War of the Rebellion*, 1889, 826.
76   Lucke, *New Haven Grays*, 287.
77   Also spelled Spottsylvania.
78   Lucke, *New Haven Grays*, 287.
79   Affidavit, James Kennedy of Wallingford. 19 September 1892, in his own pension file.
80   Statement, Richard B. Goodyear of North Haven, 27 January 1887, in the pension file of James Kennedy.

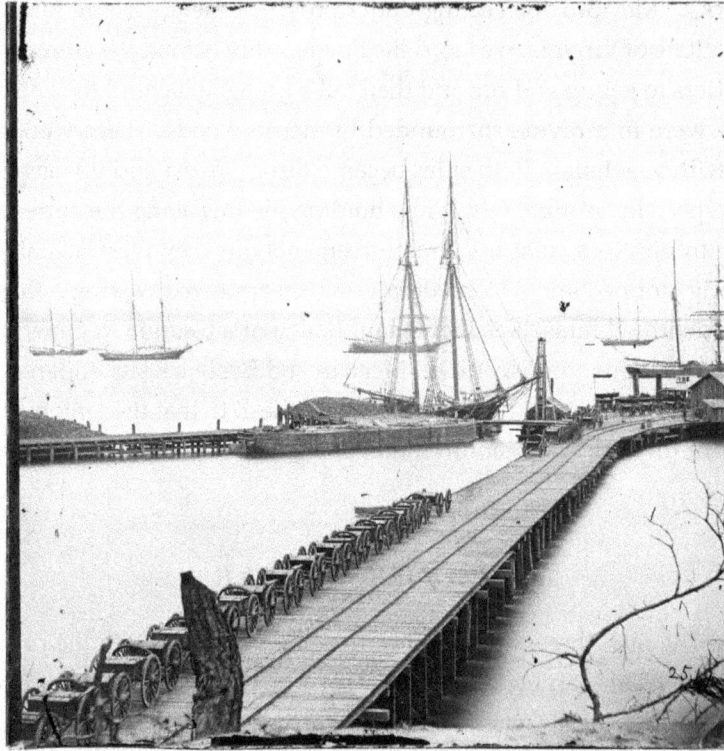

The soldiers of the 27th Connecticut Volunteers taken prisoner at the Battle of Chancellorsville were paroled at City Point, Virginia on May 14, 1863 and placed onboard a U.S. transport bound for Annapolis. (Library of Congress Prints & Photographs Division, LC-cwpb-01867)

A scene at Camp Convalescent in Alexandria, Virginia where soldiers of the 27th stayed after their release from prison. (Photographic History of the Civil War, 7:287)

May 9th was exceedingly hot and several soldiers were stricken with sun stroke. They marched through a succession of vile swamps skirting the Pamunkey and Chickahominy Rivers to within four or five miles of Richmond. The prisoners reached Richmond in the evening of May 9th and were ushered into a tobacco factory belonging to Crew and Pemberton situated on Carey Street opposite Libby Prison. Some privates were sent to Libby Prison where the commissioned officers had been sent arriving by rail from Guinea's Station. Due to overcrowding at the prisons some men were sent to Belle Island.[81]

Over one-thousand men were held at the tobacco factory, more than 300 men per floor. Most of the Twenty-seventh occupied the upper loft and almost every square foot of floor was covered with exhausted men. Many were so thoroughly exhausted they could not drag themselves upstairs without assistance from their comrades.

After several days they received word of their exchange and a U.S. transport was waiting for them at City Point. The commissioned officers were detained at Libby Prison several more days. They left prison at 3:30 p.m. on May 13th for the march to City Point, about thirty-five miles from Richmond. Crossing the James River into Manchester they took the turnpike road to Petersburg under the escort of the Southern cavalry. They were hurried forward for miles at double-quick pace. They rested Wednesday night in the woods due to a thunderstorm.

They reached City Point, Virginia Thursday, May 14th where they were paroled. From City Point they boarded a United States transport and traveled up the James River. They arrived at Annapolis, Maryland the morning of May 16th and were quartered in barracks in the rear of the town. Some of the paroled prisoners were sent to hospitals in Washington, D.C. on May 20th. After three days of rest at Annapolis the remaining soldiers arrived at Convalescent Camp, Alexandria, Virginia on May 21st. They remained at Camp Convalescent until they rejoined the rest of the Regiment at Baltimore, Maryland on July 20, 1863 for their trip back to New Haven.

The officers were released from Libby Prison on Saturday, May 23rd and arrived by train at City Point the same day. The officers and the other paroled prisoners were all re-united on May 29th at Annapolis. The officers returned to the front.

THE REST OF THE TWENTY-SEVENTH RETURNS TO CAMP

On May 5th about 2 p.m. the rest of the Union army retreated from Chancellorsville and recrossed the Rappahannock River the next morning. It rained all night and the river flooded its banks. They recrossed Kelly's Ford twenty-five miles above Falmouth and twelve hours later arrived at the old camp near Falmouth. After a few days, the regiment moved its camp two miles further back from the river. Dress parades took place as usual and duty at the old picket line on the Rappahannock was resumed. On May 13th several of the men wounded at Chancellorsville came back after nine days in a rebel hospital.

Only seventy-five soldiers remained of the 27th, mostly from companies D and F who were on picket duty along the river during the battle. Some soldiers of the Twenty-seventh were sick in the hospital and others wounded or killed at previous battles. The remaining soldiers were regrouped and placed under the command of Lt. Colonel Henry C. Merwin and Capt. Jedediah Chapman as part of the Second Army Corps.

---

81   Affidavit, William H. Barnes of Branford, 1 March1899, in his own pension file.

THE BATTLE OF GETTYSBURG, PENNSYLVANIA

On June 8, 1863, the Twenty-seventh received orders to be ready to march with three days' rations. Orders finally came on June 14th and at 3 p.m. the regiment moved up the river to Bank's Ford, retrieved their pickets, and moved toward Stafford Court House. This little hamlet was left behind in flames. For several days the Second Corps followed the roads near the Potomac, passing through Dumfries, Occoquan, Fairfax Station and arrived at Centreville on the nineteenth. They turned farther to the west crossing the old Bull Run battlefield. The troops moved silently over the field. After a march of twenty miles in the rain, the regiment arrived at ten in the evening of June 12th at Thoroughfare Gap in the Blue Ridge Mountains for four days of rest. Throughout the journey there was firing from the enemy.

The Second Corps advanced through Haymarket, toward the Potomac being followed by the rebel cavalry. The Corps pushed forward to Gum Springs and rested that night without pitching their tents. The regiment crossed the Potomac at Edward's Ferry at midnight on June 26th. The next three days they marched continuously up the valley of the Monocacy River, through many quiet Maryland villages, among them Poolesville, Frederick City, Liberty, Johnsville, and Uniontown. "We marched to Gettysburg from camp near Falmouth, Va. in the month of June 1863, the heat was oppressive."[82]

On July 1st, the Twenty-seventh Connecticut, with the Second Corps, moved up to Taneytown, just below the Pennsylvania State line. They were unaware that the first day of battle was already in progress. The Corps advanced rapidly to within three miles of Gettysburg and built entrenchments until midnight. At early dawn, July 2nd, they moved forward and took the place assigned them in the line about a mile and a half south of Cemetery Hill. They arrived at Cemetery Ridge at 8:00 a.m. as part of the Fourth Brigade and took position on the line from Cemetery Hill to Round Top.

That afternoon they moved forward to support the Third Corps. Between five and six p.m. the 27th entered the Wheatfield while the broken columns of the Third Corps were moving to the rear closely followed by the enemy. The Twenty-seventh and other regiments of the Fourth Brigade advanced and were exposed to a sweeping fire. Lieutenant-Colonel Merwin fell, mortally wounded, while leading his command of 75 officers and men of the 27th and Capt. Jedediah Chapman, Jr. was also killed in the charge. The Brigade moved forward, through the Wheatfield and beyond, forcing the enemy into the woods and across a ravine. The Union Brigade reached the ravine within pistol range of the enemy. After intense firing, the shattered line fell back. Afterwards, the Twenty-seventh marched to Brookes Avenue on Rose farm.

That night the Twenty-seventh was positioned in the line of battle midway on the ridge between Cemetery Hill and Round Top. On July 3rd, the 27th constructed entrenchments and remained in position but did not enter battle. On July 5th, the 27th moved from Cemetery Ridge and left Gettysburg by Taneytown Road, through Frederick City, and crossed the Blue Ridge by way of Crampton's Gap in pursuit of Lee's army. The march was slow due to rain and exhausted troops. Still in the vicinity of the enemy they were ordered to Falling Waters below Williamsport, participating in the capture of the enemy's rear guard. Leaving Falling Waters, the regiment moved with the Second Army Corps down the Potomac to Harper's Ferry and went into camp at Pleasant Valley.

Of the original eighty-six members of Co. B, few fought at the Battle of Gettysburg. Thirty-eight were captured at the Battle of Chancellorsville and were at Camp Convalescent, Alexandria, Virginia; seven had died of injury or disease; two officers previously resigned; twenty-five soldiers were sick or had been discharged due to disability. The pension records of Henry T. Hart and William Tyler state they fought

---

82   Statement, Lt. Frank H. Smith, Co. D 27th CVI, in the pension file of Calvin L. Ely.

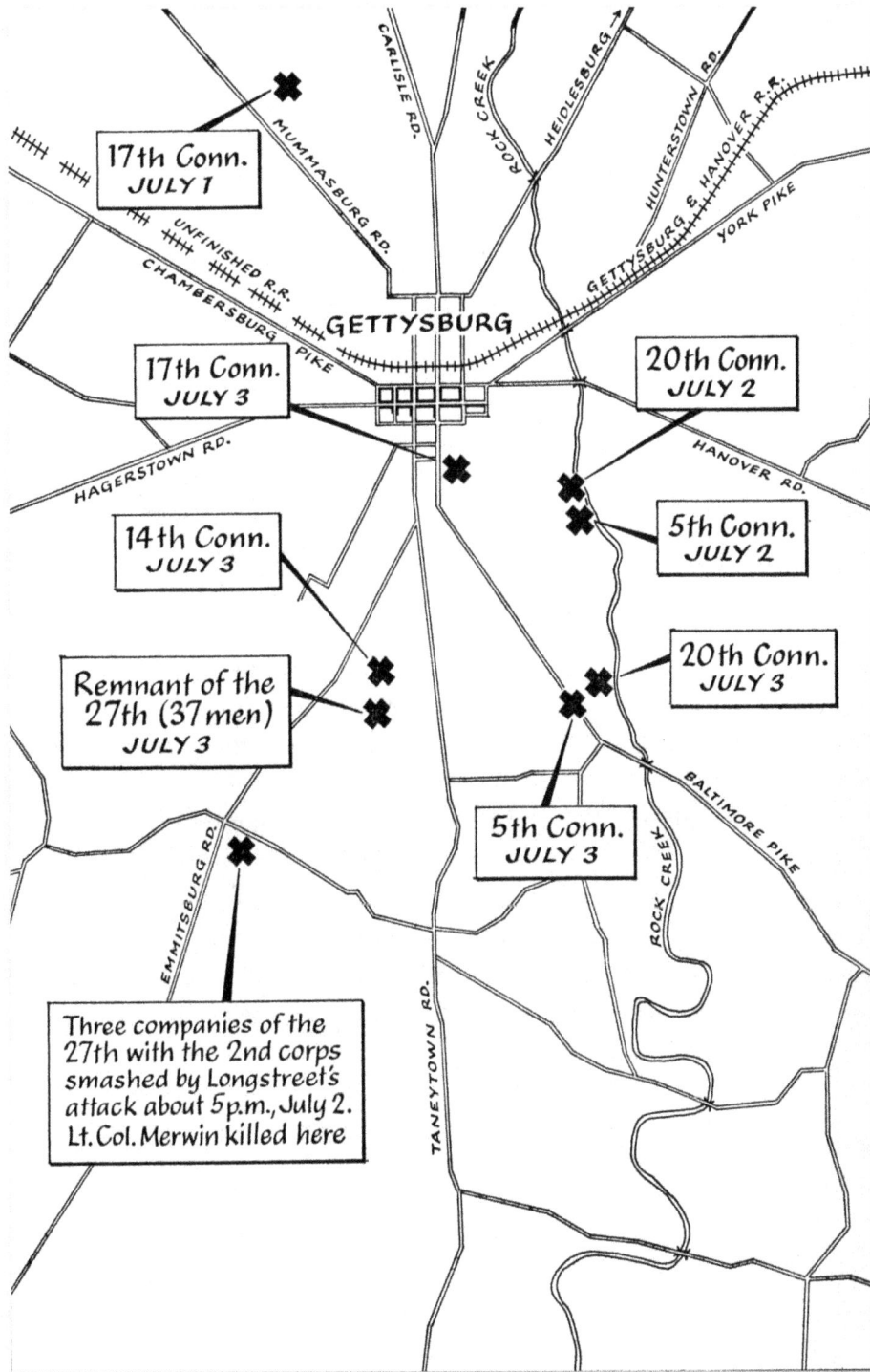

*Map of the Gettysburg battlefield July 1-3, 1863. The 27th fought at the Wheatfield under the
command of Lt. Colonel Henry C. Merwin. (Niven, Connecticut for the Union, 240)*

at Gettysburg and Joseph Cusher was wounded and captured at the battle. It is probable that Bryon Hill and Charles Paden were at Gettysburg as "they were with the regiment throughout the war." It is unclear whether Rodolphus Bartholomew, William R. Bunnell, Henry A. Camp, Calvin Ely, William Galligan, Roger Hall, Matthias Kneringer, Beri Todd, James Slowman, or Solomon Yale were with the regiment at Gettysburg or were sick or on other assignments.

Of the seventy-five officers and soldiers from the 27th Regiment that fought on July 3rd at Gettysburg, eleven were killed, twenty-three wounded, and four missing. The captured men were marched from Gettysburg to Staunton, Virginia, one hundred and eighty miles, then transported by railroad to Richmond. Joseph Cusher of Co. B was one of the captured men and was a prisoner on Belle Island for six weeks. He was paroled at City Point, Virginia on August 21st and discharged from Camp Parole on August 22nd about one month after the muster out of the rest of the regiment. He returned home so emaciated and worn down by hardship as to be almost beyond recognition even by members of his own company.

DISCHARGE

On the morning of July 18, 1863 the 27th Connecticut Volunteer Infantry was discharged from the Army of the Potomac. Early on July 19th, the remaining men from Gettysburg took the train to Baltimore. On the 20th, the detachment of paroled men from Annapolis and Camp Convalescent[83] arrived at Baltimore and the Regiment, now half its original number, was reunited. "When we were coming home in July 1863, seventy men of the Regiment joined us in Baltimore."[84] They took the train to Philadelphia and spent a night at the Battery in New York City. They left New York by rail and arrived at New Haven on July 22, 1863 exactly nine months from the date of their departure. They were escorted from the train station by several military companies and municipal authorities of New Haven to the north portico of the State House. Here they were received with an enthusiastic and hospitable welcome with throngs of people lining the streets waving flags.[85]

On July 27, 1863 at New Haven,[86] Co. B of the 27th Connecticut Volunteer Infantry was mustered out of service. Only William H. Beach and Nelson Vibbert reenlisted in other companies after their discharge.

Many of the men suffered from ailments due to exposure during the war from long marches, picket duty, poor nutrition, and days of constant rain in Virginia. The pension records of the soldiers of Co. B 27th Connecticut Volunteer Infantry reveal that the soldiers suffered from chronic rheumatism, intestinal problems, heart disease, and lung disease during their service. Seventy-one members of Co. B (84%) received survivor, invalid or old age pensions.

THE TWENTY-SEVENTH CONNECTICUT BATTLE FLAGS

Each regiment carried the Union or National flag and a regimental or state flag also called a standard or the colors. The flags were often given to the Regiments by local women. Both flags of the Twenty-seventh were six-six-and-one-half-feet, made of silk with gold fringe. Since January 1863, Sergeant John Sanford of Co. C carried the National flag and Sergeant James Brand of Co. I was the standard-bearer of the state flag since the 27th left New Haven.[87] The colors were carried at the Battle of Fredericksburg. At Chancellorsville, the

---

83   These were the men that were taken prisoner at the Battle of Chancellorsville and paroled.
84   Statement, James Kennedy of Wallingford, 16 July 1888, in the pension file of William J. Galligan.
85   For the welcome home see *The Connecticut War Record*, August 1863, I:22, citing The Journal and Courier, 23 July 1863.
86   Many of the men listed 25 July 1863 as their muster out date on their pension applications.
87   DeCusati, "Connecticut Men Answer Lincoln's Call."

THE BATTLE OF GETTYSBURG, P.ª JULY 3.ª 1863.

Only seventy-five officers and men of the Twenty-seventh fought at the Battle of Gettysburg on July 2, 1863. Lt. Colonel Henry C. Merwin and Capt. Jedediah Chapman were killed during the charge at the Wheatfield. (Currier & Ives lithograph, Library of Congress Prints & Photographs Division, LC-USZC4-2088)

The regimental and state flags used by the Connecticut troops during the Civil War were transferred to the new State Capitol on Battle Flag Day in 1879. (History of Battle Flag Day, 176)

regimental flags were left with Companies D and F who were on picket duty during the battle. No doubt, the flags would have been captured along with much of the 27th at the battle. The remaining members of the 27th carried the Regimental colors at the Battle of Gettysburg and upon reaching the ridge above the Wheatfield waved the colors defiantly at the enemy.[88]

As early as 1865, the battle flags were deposited at the State Arsenal in Hartford. Under a special act of the General Assembly the flags were to be permanently housed in cases at the State Capitol. On September 17, 1879 Battle Flag Day[89] was celebrated when eighty battle flags borne by Connecticut Civil War regiments were transferred to the new State Capitol. There was a grand patriotic celebration including a parade with 10,000 veterans attending. The National flag of the 27th was in good condition, the State flag in poor condition.

MONUMENTS TO THE TWENTY-SEVENTH INFANTRY AT GETTYSBURG

At the sixteenth reunion of the 27th Connecticut Volunteer Infantry at Pawson Park in Branford on September 4, 1884 a committee was appointed to raise funds to erect a monument at Gettysburg in honor of the Regiment. The Chairman was Capt. Frank D. Sloat and the committee included a representative from each company, Albert Harrison of North Branford represented Co. B. Funds were raised by the veterans, families, and friends of the regiment. The contract was awarded to St. Johnsbury Granite Co. of Brattleboro, Vermont at a cost of $950. Two-hundred participants left by special train on Tuesday, October 20, 1885 from New Haven to attend the dedication. They spent the night at Philadelphia, went by train to Gettysburg, and by carriage to the field. Hundreds of Gettysburg citizens attended the ceremony. The monument to the Twenty-seventh was dedicated on October 22, 1885.[90] Attending from Co. B were Sergeant Robert B. Goodyear of North Haven, Sergeant Samuel S. Cook of Branford, Corporal Albert Harrison, Corporal Isaac K. Hall of Wallingford, Musician Henry Z. Nichols of Branford, Privates Nathan Harrison of North Branford and Henry D. Todd of North Haven, and citizen Leverett T. Chidsey of North Branford. The monument was unveiled by Miss Ruby Merwin Osborn, niece of Henry C. Merwin. Also attending from the 27th Regiment were Frank D. Sloat, now a general but formerly captain of the regiment, and Rev. Winthrop D. Sheldon, author of the history of the regiment. A speech was given by Connecticut Governor Henry B. Harrison. The monument has a granite shaft, twenty-three feet high, with a bronze eagle at the top and stands in the Wheatfield, some distance from the road, where Col. Henry C. Merwin was killed. On the front of the monument is a highly polished shield with the Second Army Corps badge. It was the first regimental monument erected at the Wheatfield.

---

88   DeCusati, "Connecticut Men Answer Lincoln's Call."
89   History of Battle Flag Day, September 17, 1879 (Hartford, Connecticut: Lockwood & Merritt, 1879); and Ben C. Ray, The Old Battle Flags Veteran Soldiers' Souvenir, 1879.
90   *New Haven Register*, 17, 19, 22, 23, 24, 25 & 27 October 1885.

The monument to the 27th Regiment was the first monument dedicated at the Wheatfield. (Branford Historical Society photograph collection)

Veterans of the Twenty-seventh Connecticut Volunteer Infantry gather at the monument dedicated on October 22, 1885 in the Wheatfield at the Gettysburg Battlefield. (Branford Historical Society photograph collection)

27TH

CONN.

CVI

Erected-1885.

THE 27TH REG'T. CONN. VOLS.

COMMANDED BY

LIEUT. COLONEL HENRY C. MERWIN,

AND FORMING A PART OF THE

4TH BRIGADE, 1ST DIVISION, 2ND CORPS

CHARGED OVER THIS GROUND, THE AFTERNOON OF

JULY 2, 1863

THE 4TH BRIGADE FORCED THE ENEMY FROM THE

WHEATFIELD AND BEYOND THE WOODS IN FRONT

WHERE THE ADVANCED POSITION OF THE 27TH REGT.

IS INDICATED BY A TABLET ON THE CREST OF

THE LEDGE.

ON THIS SPOT LIEUT. COL. MERWIN WAS KILLED,

WHILE GALLANTLY LEADING HIS COMMAND OF

75 OFFICERS AND MEN, 38 OF WHOM WERE KILLED,

OR WOUNDED IN THE CHARGE. EIGHT COMPANIES OF THE

REGT. CAPTURED AT CHANCELLORSVILLE WERE STILL

PRISONERS OF WAR.

CAPT. JEDEDIAH CHAPMAN, JR. WAS ALSO KILLED IN THE

CHARGE WHILE COMMANDING A COMPANY, ORGANIZED FROM

DETACHED MEMBERS OF THE EIGHT COMPANIES TAKEN

PRISONERS AT CHANCELLORSVILLE.

THE 27TH REGT. CONN. VOLS.

WAS RECRUITED AND ORGANIZED

IN NEW HAVEN COUNTY, STATE

OF CONNECTICUT

JULY 2, 1863

QUI TRANSTULIT SUSTINET

The Twenty-seventh Regiment, though the smallest unit to fight at Gettysburg, has the most monuments: two large and three small. A second large monument to the 27th was paid for and sponsored by the State of Connecticut and stands on Brooke Avenue near the Rose Farm. The monument was dedicated on April 17, 1889 and cost $1,000 through an appropriation of the Connecticut General Assembly. The monument honors the seventy-five officers and enlisted men who served under Lt. Colonel Henry C. Merwin at Gettysburg.

27th Conn. Vols.　　　*Advanced Position*
4th Brigade　　　*Of This Regiment*
1st Division　　　*In The*
2nd Corps.　　　*Brigade Charge*
　　　July 2nd 1863.

27TH CONN. INFANTRY

Three smaller tablets for the Twenty-Seventh Regiment are at Gettysburg: the first, "In Memory of Lt. Col. Henry C. Merwin 27th C. V. who fell mortally wounded where the monument of his Regiment stands"; second, on the west side of Wheatfield: "Here fell Jed Chapman Capt. Co. H 27th Conn. Vols."; and third, at the edge of the Wheatfield: "This tablet indicates the advanced position of the 27th Regt. Conn. Vols. in its charge the afternoon of July 2, 1863."

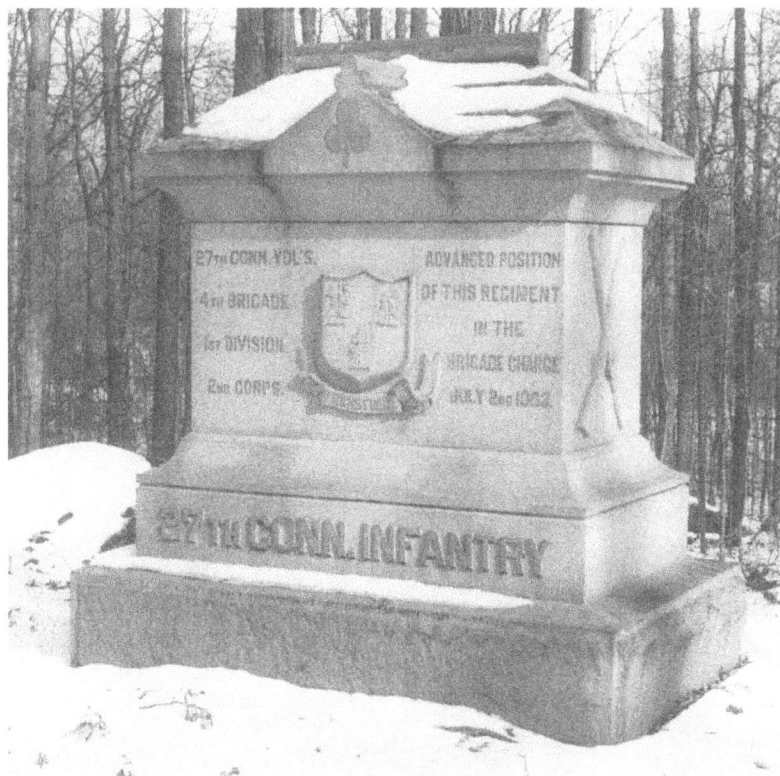

A second monument to the 27th Regiment was dedicated on April 17, 1889 on Brooke Avenue at Gettysburg and was financed by the State of Connecticut.

REUNIONS OF THE TWENTY-SEVENTH CONNECTICUT REGIMENT

The seventeenth reunion of the veterans of the 27th Connecticut Volunteer Regiment was held at Pawson Park in Branford on August 12, 1885. (Branford Historical Society archives)

The first reunion of the veterans of the 27th Connecticut Volunteer Regiment was held in 1868. Branford hosted the tenth reunion at the Town Hall on September 8, 1878.[91] After its formation in 1884, The Mason Rogers Post No. 7 of Branford hosted the sixteenth reunion on September 4, 1884 and the seventeenth reunion on August 12, 1885 both of which were held at Pawson Park.[92] Plans were made at the sixteenth reunion to erect a monument at Gettysburg in honor of the regiment.

The twenty-ninth reunion of the 27th Regiment was held at Lighthouse Point, New Haven on September 1, 1897.[93] Thirty-seven members of Co. B originally enlisted from Branford and twenty still survived. Attending from Branford were Capt. Calvin L. Ely, Edwin L. Wilford and Edward D. Sheldon.

---

91   *Shore Line Sentinel* (Guilford), 11 September 1878.
92   *New Haven Register,* 12 August 1885.
93   *The Branford Opinion,* 21 & 28 August 1897.

The 15th spent the first part of their tour of duty stationed at Camp Chase in Arlington, Virginia. (Thorpe, History of the Fifteenth, 20)

FIFTEENTH CONNECTICUT VOLUNTEER INFANTRY
ALSO KNOWN AS THE LYON REGIMENT

ORGANIZATION

On July 1, 1862 President Lincoln called for 300,000 volunteers to serve three years. Governor Buckingham issued a proclamation for the immediate formation of six or more Connecticut infantry regiments to be formed with 7,145 men. A meeting was held at the Music Hall in New Haven on Tuesday, July 8, 1862 which filled the hall and the Fifteenth Regiment[94] was organized with recruits from New Haven County. The regiment was named in honor of General Nathaniel Lyon, a Connecticut native and the first Union general killed in the war. Sixty men from Branford and North Branford were in the Fifteenth Volunteer Infantry, primarily in Companies B and K. Company B was comprised mostly from men of the New Haven Grays. The regiment was mustered into service at Camp Lyon, New Haven on August 26, 1862 for a term of three years.

---

94   For a history of the 15th CVI see Sheldon B. Thorpe, *The History of the Fifteenth Connecticut Volunteers in the War of the Defense of the Union 1861-1865* (New Haven: The Price, Lee & Adkins Co., 1893); the essay by George M. White in *Service of Connecticut Men*, 587-589; *Soldier's Record*, 16 October 1869, 2 & 4; *New Haven Daily Register*, 25 August 1862 for a list of men; *Branford Opinion*, 23 August 1912, 1.

TO WASHINGTON, D.C. AND VIRGINIA

The regiment left New Haven on August 28, 1862, under the command of Colonel Dexter R. Wright, arrived in Washington, D.C. on August 30th and proceeded to camp at Arlington Heights, Virginia. The next day they received their guns and tents and began guard duty at Long Bridge for six weeks. They remained at Camp Chase in Arlington as part of the defense of Washington, D.C. On November 1, 1862 the regiment was moved to Camp Casey at Fairfax Seminary, Virginia where they continued on guard duty through November. The weather was cold with snow and rain, malaria and typhoid fever significantly reduced the ranks at both camps. Benjamin R. Dowd died at Camp Chase and Samuel M. Linsley and Philo Foote died while at Camp Casey.

> *"We have had a verry pleasant trip from New Haven to this place for oft it rained like smoak when we marched through New York. Friday morning we got our breakfast in Philadelphia. From New York to Amboy we went by water, all of the rest of the way by rail. Took supper in Baltimore where we were complemented verry highly on the good looks of our regiment as we have been all the way through and had to sleep on the depot floor in Baltimore. But otherwise our treatment has been first rate all the way. We came through the country of New Jersey in the night so that I could not tell very mutch about its inhabitants. We arrived in Washington about ten o'clock Saturday and after we had our dinner we marched up on capital hill in the rear of the capital building. Last night I spent my first night in the open air with nothing but a blanket for covering. It comenced raining about midnight and as I pulled my rubber blanket over me I could not keep from laughing to hear the boys growl and swear as they waked up."[95]*

> *"November 1862 was a time of great sickness and many deaths in the Regiment at Camp near Fairfax Seminary, Va. Benjamin R. Dowd was violently attacked with Typhoid Fever and removed to Washington, D.C. Our Reg't Hospital was full of patients. I had the same complaint & unfortunately without Hospital comfort such as a bedstead & bedding. The patients were obliged to lie on straw cots on the floor thickly stowed in which condition many died averaging from 1 to 3 a day. Four from my company died at this station including my brother."[96]*

THE BATTLE OF FREDERICKSBURG, VIRGINIA

On December 1, 1862 the Fifteenth Regiment left Camp Casey for camp at Falmouth, Virginia on Acquia Creek opposite Fredericksburg. "About the first of December 1862 the Reg't started down through Maryland to Fredericksburg. Before reaching Aquia Creek we were overtaken by a Snow Storm. We were obliged to pitch our Shelter tents in the Snow which furnished but little protection."[97] The new camp was soon

---

95   Letter, John Edwin Towner to his sister Emily S. Holcomb of Branford, 31 August 1862. The letters of J. Edwin Towner to his sister are in the Branford Historical Society archives and will be referred to as Towner letters.

96   Letter, M. D. Munson, at New Berne, N.C.; captain Co. K 15th CVI, 21 March 1864, in the pension file of Benjamin R. Dowd.

97   Affidavit, Charles A. Hall of New Haven, 23 July 1890, in the pension file of Jerome Coan.

A view of Fredericksburg, Virginia in 1862. The 15th was part of the Connecticut Brigade at
the Battle of Fredericksburg in December 1862. (Thorpe, History of the Fifteenth, 32)

The 15th had picket duty at Portsmouth, Virginia from July 1863 until January 1864. (Thorpe, History of the Fifteenth, 223)

nicknamed "Camp Mud." The Fifteenth became part of the "Connecticut or Harland's Brigade" made up of the 8th, 11th, 15th, 16th and 21st Connecticut regiments under the command of Brigadier General Edward Harland. As part of Brigadier General Ambrose E. Burnside's Third Brigade, First Division, the Fifteenth crossed with its brigade and bivouacked in the town of Fredericksburg with the shells flying over their heads. On December 13th, the regiment was held in reserve along the Rappahannock River while other Connecticut regiments assaulted the rebel lines at Marye's Height. At six p. m. the entire Connecticut Brigade returned to the town. On Sunday, December 14th, the Connecticut Brigade stood ready for a full assault on Marye's Height but the Union command decided not to attack probably saving the Union forces from a complete slaughter. "The Reg't had been Marched to the Pontoon bridge I think on the morning of Dec 12th 1862 opposite Fredericksburg and halted the night resting on the Bridge until about 3 A.M. when the enemy Commenced Shelling us. We were ordered back out of range."[98] The regiment left at midnight and was one of the last regiments to leave Fredericksburg and returned to camp near Falmouth. The Fifteenth lost two men in the battle and eight were wounded.

ASSIGNMENTS IN VIRGINIA

After the Battle of Fredericksburg, the Fifteenth spent two months at camp near Falmouth, Virginia. On February 6, 1863 the regiment with the rest of the Connecticut Brigade moved to new quarters at Newport News, Virginia. They marched to Suffolk, Virginia on March 14th and saw action at the siege of that city. They proceeded to Portsmouth on June 20th as part of General John Adams Dix's Peninsula Campaign and by July 4th were within twelve miles of Richmond. They had marched a total of 120 miles for an assault which failed to materialize. The Fifteenth returned to camp at Portsmouth, Virginia on July 14th and had picket duty there until January 1864.

TO NEW BERN, NORTH CAROLINA AND YELLOW FEVER

On January 21, 1864 the regiment took the steamer *Spaulding* to Morehead City, North Carolina arriving there on January 23rd. The regiment spent several months in the New Bern, North Carolina area for defense and provost duty. Mason Rogers of Branford died on September 9, 1864 of yellow fever, the first afflicted with the disease. Dr. H.V.C. Holcombe of Branford, surgeon of the Fifteenth, predicted the disease would become epidemic and the other regiments were moved out of New Bern. In a short time more than half of the 15th was sick with fever putting extra strain on the remaining soldiers. It was not until the first frost in November that the disease subsided. More than seventy men died from yellow fever and a large number of recruits were added to the Regiment's ranks. In all, 3,000 soldiers and civilians were afflicted with yellow fever and 1,300 died. The officers and soldiers of the Fifteenth "rendered constant and invaluable service in nursing the sick and dying of their own regiment and among the citizens."[99]

> *"I supposed you could be anxious as the story has probably gone home that we were dieing with the Yellow Fever here, and it may be true though some of the Doctors deny it. True it is that some plague is here. People are dieing at the rate of ten a day, mostly citizens...There has been only two or three deaths in our Regt.*

---

98   Statement, George W. Talmadge of New Haven, 21 November 1888, in the pension file of Lorenzo E. Harrison.
99   Crofut & Morris, *Military & Civil History of Connecticut*, 712-713.

in two weeks. Perhaps this is oweing to haveing good Doctors. Doctor Holcomb is quite unwell but attends to his duties yet…

Well I should have tried to have written yesterday, but I was quite unwell. I have been out of the Hospital now four days. Have gained some strength but am quite weak yet. I left Wm. Linsley. and Ammi Palmer in there, both getting better. Linsley had a narrow escape. He was put in the dead room once. I never got as far as that, next door to it…The fever has abated some oweing probably to the weather being cooler. My Comp. has lost eight men and the Captain. Scarce aney of the Recruits have died. Doctor Holcomb has been very kind. His health is poor he kept going when he was not able to.

You speak of the deaths in our Regts. Sixty have died since the fever commenced. One name you mentioned stirred up memories, J. A. Sturges. He was one of our best boys. To me he was most dear as a brother. He was in the Hospital when I was and was getting better. He told me one day that he would be out before I was. One day he was taken down and died very sudden before morning. Death was very busy with us for a time, but the fever has gone now."[100]

THE BATTLE OF KINSTON, NORTH CAROLINA
(also known as Wise's Fork)

The Fifteenth Connecticut Regiment joined Colonel Charles L. Upham's Second Brigade for a surprise attack on Kinston, North Carolina on December 9, 1864. During the march there was a heavy rain, followed by snow, and the regiment could not cross the swollen river and was forced to return to camp. In early February, three hundred recruits from the western states joined the Fifteenth along with regiments from Massachusetts and New York.

There were skirmishes and heavier fighting on March 8, 1865 at Kinston. About one p.m., the Fifteenth along with the 27th Massachusetts were surrounded and captured by rebel forces. The Colonel of the 57th North Carolina stated that "During all my experience of army life, I have never seen such an exhibition of hard fighting as that given the 15th Conn. regiment at Kinston, N. C. We had to entirely surround them before they would surrender."[101] Company K, under Capt. Medad D. Munson of Wallingford, remained back in New Bern on provost duty on the 8th but participated in the fighting at Kinston on March 10th.

PRISONERS OF WAR

An account of the wounded and prisoners immediately after the battle was recorded by John E. Towner of Branford in his diary:[102]

"The wounded as fast as gathered at the mill were sent back a short distance to a field hospital in the rear of the rebel breastworks. Here those wounds requiring

100 Towner letters, 25 September, 22 October and 7 November 1864.
101 Thorpe, *History of the Fifteenth*, 94.
102 Thorpe, *History of the Fifteenth*, 101.

A hospital in New Bern, North Carolina. Many homes, schools, government, and commercial buildings were used as hospitals during the war. Tents, barns, and houses were used as hospitals in the field of battle. (Photographic History of the Civil War, 7:231)

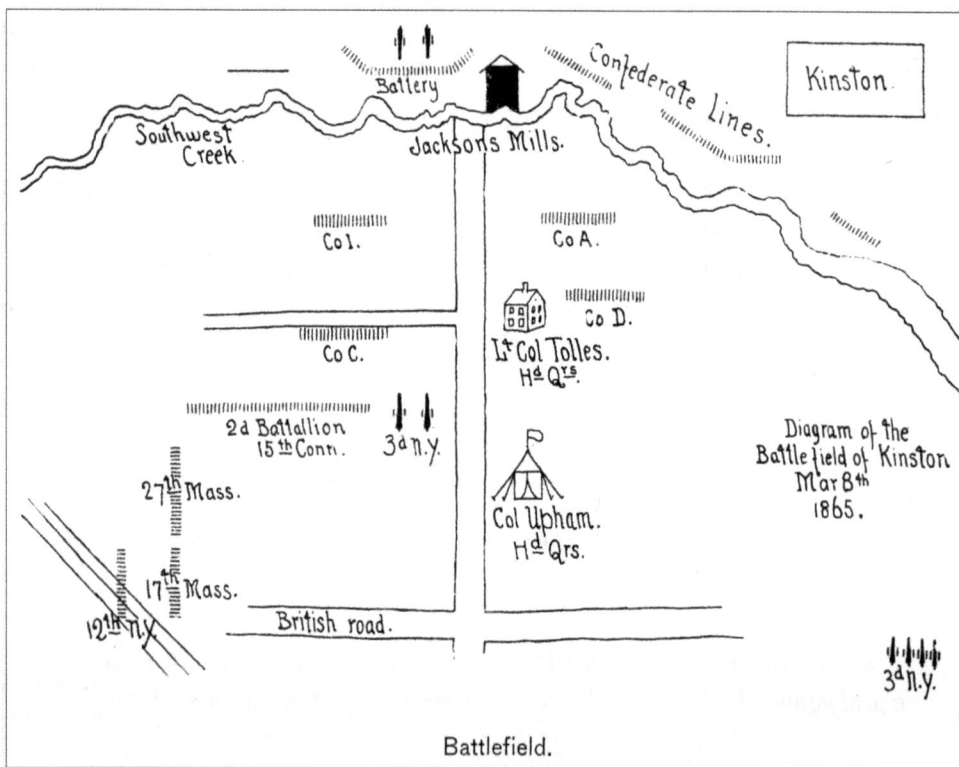

The position of the 15th Connecticut Volunteer Infantry during the Battle of Kinston, North Carolina on March 8, 1865. (Thorpe, History of the Fifteenth, 113)

immediate attention were dressed by the Confederate surgeons. It was at this place
that Palmer, of Co. B, had his arm amputated. Toward night we were taken across
the creek and up to Kinston. We were quartered in an old building standing on
the corner of the first square after crossing the river. Here all minor wounds were
attended to and the surgeons were busy until well along in the night. As fast as
cared for we were passed into an upper room to sleep on the bare floor and fortu-
nate were they who had saved their blankets."

The prisoners who were not wounded were marched to Kinston and sent by train to Goldsboro, North Carolina where they arrived about 9 p.m. Upon their arrival at Goldsboro, they were corralled in the Fair Grounds and slept on the cold ground, a portion of them were taken to the Court House for shelter. The wounded joined them from Kinston the next day. "They treated us very well, giving us the same rations they gave their own soldiers, one pound of corn meal, and one-third pound of bacon."[103] The women of Goldsboro offered the soldier many kindnesses, such as warm food, bandages, and coffee. During the night of March 10th, the prisoners were placed aboard the train for Weldon arriving at 4 a.m. where they were un-loaded and placed in an open lot and provided with tents. The officers were housed in an old church. The injured were left behind in Goldsboro and later sent to Salisbury Prison. On Sunday, March 12th the pris-oners were awakened and put on board the cars for Gaston, then marched about eight miles to a camp in the woods. Here Capt. White and Lieut. Solomon Linsley escaped. In the morning of March 13th they were marched about twelve miles to Clarksville Junction and slept near the village, the officers were quartered in a school house. From March 14th until the 23rd, the prisoners marched during the day and camped for the night. On Friday, March 17th, the officers were separated from the group and taken by train to Richmond and the enlisted men continued their march to Richmond. At 9 a.m. March 23rd, fifteen days from the time of their capture, the prisoners entered Libby Prison in Richmond, Virginia. The officers and enlisted men were in separate rooms but all on the second floor of the same building.

On Sunday, March 26th a parole for the prisoners was arranged and early that morning they were placed onboard the *William Allison* at Boulware's & Cox's wharf under a flag of truce. At Union headquarters at Aiken's Landing the steamers *New York* and *Manhattan* were waiting for them and transported them to Annapolis, Maryland where they arrived at Camp Parole on March 27, 1865. Most of the paroled prison-ers received a thirty day furlough back to Connecticut and reported to Camp Convalescent at Alexandria, Virginia about May 1st.

The wounded were sent by train to Danville, North Carolina. On March 24th they arrived at Salisbury Prison and were marched to the prison where they remained until the 27th. Since they were now paroled, they were sent to a hospital. On March 29th the injured soldiers went by train to Richmond and were housed in a building opposite Libby Prison and on March 30th they were transferred to a regular hospital. Sunday, April 2nd they were told to be ready to cross the lines the next day. No transport had been arranged and many walked through the night to reach the Union lines, carrying those unable to walk in blankets. They arrived at Annapolis on April 4th, eight days after the other paroled prisoners. Some of the wounded were sent to Paterson Park Hospital at Baltimore.

---

103 *The Connecticut War Record*, May 1865, 2:10:400.

MUSTER OUT

The members of the Fifteenth Regiment who were not captured remained at camp near Kinston, North Carolina and received the news of General Lee's surrender on April 12th. The officers who were captured at the Battle of Kinston returned on May 11th and the paroled men returned from Camp Convalescent on May 15th. The Regiment remained at Kinston on provost duty. The Regiment left Kinston on June 6, 1865 for New Bern, North Carolina and their anticipated release from service. On June 24th the newer recruits were transferred to the Seventh Connecticut Regiment.

The Fifteenth Connecticut Volunteer Infantry was mustered out at New Bern, North Carolina on June 27, 1865 after serving nearly three years. They were transported aboard the schooner *Recruit* to New York. On June 30th the men left by train for New Haven and were discharged on July 12, 1865.

Sixty men associated with Branford and North Branford served in the Fifteenth Regiment. Nine died of typhoid or yellow fever and eighteen men were taken prisoner at the Battle of Kinston, North Carolina on March 8, 1865.

Over seventy soldiers died at New Bern of yellow fever in 1864. (Photograph by Jim Dugan, 2008, with permission)

MONUMENT TO THE FIFTEENTH VOLUNTEER REGIMENT

A monument to the Fifteenth Connecticut Infantry was dedicated in 1908 at the National Cemetery in New Bern, North Carolina.

15th Conn. Vols.

To the men who died of

Yellow fever in 1864,

And those who fell in

Action before Kinston

March 8, 1865.

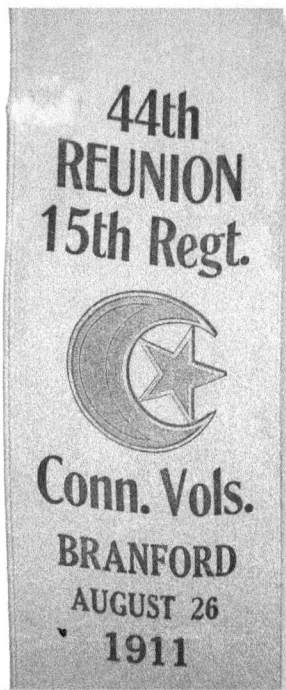

The forty-fourth reunion of the 15th Connecticut Volunteer Infantry was held at Branford on August 26, 1911. (Branford Historical Society archives)

REUNIONS OF THE FIFTEENTH CONNECTICUT REGIMENT

The first reunion of the veterans of the 15th Connecticut Volunteers was held on November 29, 1869[104] at Wallingford with 150 members present. The fourteenth reunion was held at Branford on August 25, 1882 by invitation of the Mason Rogers Post No. 7 G.A.R. The soldiers and their families met at the Town Hall where dinner was provided. Solomon F. Linsley was active on the reunion committee.

The twentieth reunion of the Fifteenth was again held at Branford on August 25, 1887.[105] After gathering at the train station, the veterans paraded down Main Street for their meeting at the Gaylord Opera House on South Main Street. A business meeting was held followed by announcements of those who had died; speeches by comrades, and dinner at the Town Hall. "Branford never does things in halves and the collation which awaited the hungry men was a sight to behold."

The thirtieth reunion was held at Branford on August 25, 1897.[106] After a parade and meeting at the Gaylord Opera House, two hundred veterans had dinner at the Town Hall, afterwards returning to the Opera House for further business. After the meeting, the guests were given a tour of the library. Only six surviving members of the 15th were still living in town: Ammi B. Barker, J. Edwin Towner, Samuel O. Fowler, Albert E. Plant, Charles H. Frisbie, and William H. Beach.

The forty-fourth reunion of the 15th Connecticut Volunteers was held at Branford on August 26, 1911. [107]

---

104 Thorpe, *History of the Fifteenth* states the first reunion was in 1869 but newspaper articles and ribbons of subsequent reunions suggest they began in 1867.
105 *The Branford Opinion*, 21 August & 28 August 1887.
106 *The Branford Opinion*, 28 August 1897 and 4 September 1897; *Shore Line Times*, 20 August 1897.
107 *The Branford Opinion*, 25 August 1911, page 1.

The 10th Regiment from Connecticut spent much of 1863 along the coast of South Carolina including the attack on Morris Island on February 13th. (Library of Congress Prints & Photographs Division, LC-cwp-04739)

TENTH CONNECTICUT VOLUNTEER INFANTRY

A significant number of Branford and North Branford soldiers served in the 10th Volunteer Infantry.[108] The regiment was organized in late summer 1861 for a term of three years and the men were mustered in at Hartford on October 26, 1861. They left for Annapolis, Maryland on October 31st for two months of drill and discipline. On January 2, 1862 they were transported and remained on a ship for five weeks before fighting on January 8th at the Battle of Roanoke Island, North Carolina, sustaining heavy losses including the death of Colonel Charles L. Russell of Derby. The Tenth spent the summer of 1862 in North Carolina on various assignments. On December 14, 1862 there was an engagement at Kinston, North Carolina and the Tenth attacked the enemy from the rear, captured 500 prisoners and artillery pieces but sustained significant losses.

On January 29, 1863 under Major General John G. Foster, the regiment was moved to South Carolina for the attack on Morris Island, landing on February 13th. The regiment had the reputation of being the "best drilled and best disciplined of any troop in service." On March 13, 1863 they fought at the Battle of New Bern and in April the Regiment took Seabrook Island from the enemy. By the end of summer 1863, sixty

---

108 For a history of the 10th CVI see Henry Clay Trumbull, *War Memories of an Army Chaplain* (New York: Charles Scribner & Sons, 1898); H. Clay Trumbull, *The Knightly Soldier: A Biography of Major Henry Ward Camp, Tenth Connecticut Volunteers* (Boston: Nichols and Noyes Publishers, 1865 & 1892); the *Diary of James H. Linsley 1862-1864*, University of Florida; and the essay by John L. Otis in *Service of Connecticut Men*, 394-396.

percent of the men were sick with typhoid fever. In late 1864 the Tenth Connecticut served briefly at St. Augustine, Florida, returning to Virginia on April 14, 1864.

On May 7, 1864 the Regiment was in action at Port Walthall Junction, Virginia and a new commander "expressed astonishment and admiration at its matchless steadiness in action." The Tenth Connecticut Regiment fought at the Battle of Drewry's Bluff on May 16th and lost thirty-six men. That summer the Regiment fought at Bermuda Hundred, Deep Bottom, Strawberry Plains, and Darbytown Road, Virginia.

The Tenth Connecticut Volunteers remained in Virginia during 1865 and spent the winter camped near New Market Road a few miles below Richmond.[109] The regiment received new recruits and substitutes, many of whom were "bounty jumpers." They saw action in 1865 at Hatcher's Run, Fort Gregg, and Petersburg, Virginia. Allen Tucker of East Haven, a member of Branford's G.A.R. post, received the Congressional Medal of Honor for gallantry as color bearer in the assault on Fort Gregg. The regiment was at Appomattox Court House during the surrender, leaving on April 15, 1865 for Richmond and left there on August 26th for Hartford. The Tenth Connecticut Volunteer Infantry was mustered out of service at Hartford on September 5, 1865 nearly four years after they were mustered in.

> *"The 10th Connecticut Volunteers was the first three-year local regiment to come home from the Civil War. They came to New Haven by boat and arrived at Union Depot at noon. Cheered by crowds, they were escorted by Colt's Band, Mayor Stillman, city officials, Light Guard, City Guard and citizens to American Hall where dinner was served. The 10th left with a full regiment; only 151 returned with nine officers. They fought in many battles and their battle flags were tattered, uniforms and boots in bad shape. The soldiers marched to camp on Park Street and stayed a week before their discharge. Merchants outfitted them with civilian clothes, underwear, boots, and hats. They were paid off and mustered out."[110]*

Thirty-three men from Branford and North Branford were associated with the 10th Connecticut Volunteer Regiment. Corporal George G. Bradley of Branford was killed at Darbytown Road, Virginia; Albert Wheaton of North Branford at Kinston, North Carolina; John Henry Palmer of North Branford at Petersburg, Virginia; David L. Smith died of disease; and John F. Shepard died in Andersonville Prison. A number of men were wounded, some more than once, and others were sick at New Bern, North Carolina with typhoid fever.

James H. Linsley of North Branford was captain of Co. C of the 10th Connecticut Volunteer Infantry and was wounded three times at Kinston, North Carolina; Strawberry Plain and Fort Gregg, Virginia. He was commended by the department commander for special service in the capture of the enemy's outposts near Dutch Gap, Virginia in July 1864.[111] Though he was eligible for discharge due to his injuries, he remained in active duty and was much admired by the soldiers.

The flag of the Tenth Regiment, badly worn and torn, is at the New Haven Colony Historical Society.[112]

---

109 Trumbull, *Memories of an Army Chaplain*, 35.
110 Unidentified newspaper article, 25 October 1945 in Ray Keyes Linsley, *Connecticut Linsleys The Six Johns* (Bristol, Connecticut, 1948), privately printed, 106.
111 Obituary of James H. Linsley, *Shore Lines Times*.
112 *Battle-Flag Day*, 190.

TROOPS IN POSITION AWAITING ATTACK AT BERMUDA FRONT, PREVIOUS TO THE ARRIVAL
OF GRANT'S ARMY, JUNE 3, 1864.

*The 10th Connecticut Volunteer Infantry fought at Bermuda Hundred in the Virginia campaign
during the summer of 1864. (History of the First Connecticut Artillery, II:503)*

The Tenth Volunteer Infantry is one of four Connecticut Regiments honored with a monument at Elm and Broadway Streets in New Haven dedicated on June 16, 1905.

10TH CONN. VOLUNTEERS

IN GRATEFUL MEMORY OF THE SERVICES

AND SACRIFICES OF OUR HEROIC DEAD,

WHO OFFERED THEIR LIVES ON THE ALTAR

OF CONSTITUTIONAL GOVERNMENT AND HUMAN

LIBERTY, THIS TABLET IS LOVINGLY

INSCRIBED BY THEIR SURVIVING COMRADES

OF THE TENTH CONNECTICUT VOLUNTEERS.

TOTAL NUMBER ENROLLED 1879

TOTAL CASUALTIES 1011

NUMBER OF ENGAGEMENTS 51

TERM OF SERVICE, SEPTEMBER 30, 1861, TO SEPTEMBER 2, 1865

SAFE AND HAPPY THE REPUBLIC WHOSE

SONS GLADLY DIE IN HER DEFENSE.

The 10th Connecticut Volunteer Regiment was at Appomattox Court House when General Robert E. Lee surrendered on April 9, 1865. (Photographic History of the Civil War, 9:127)

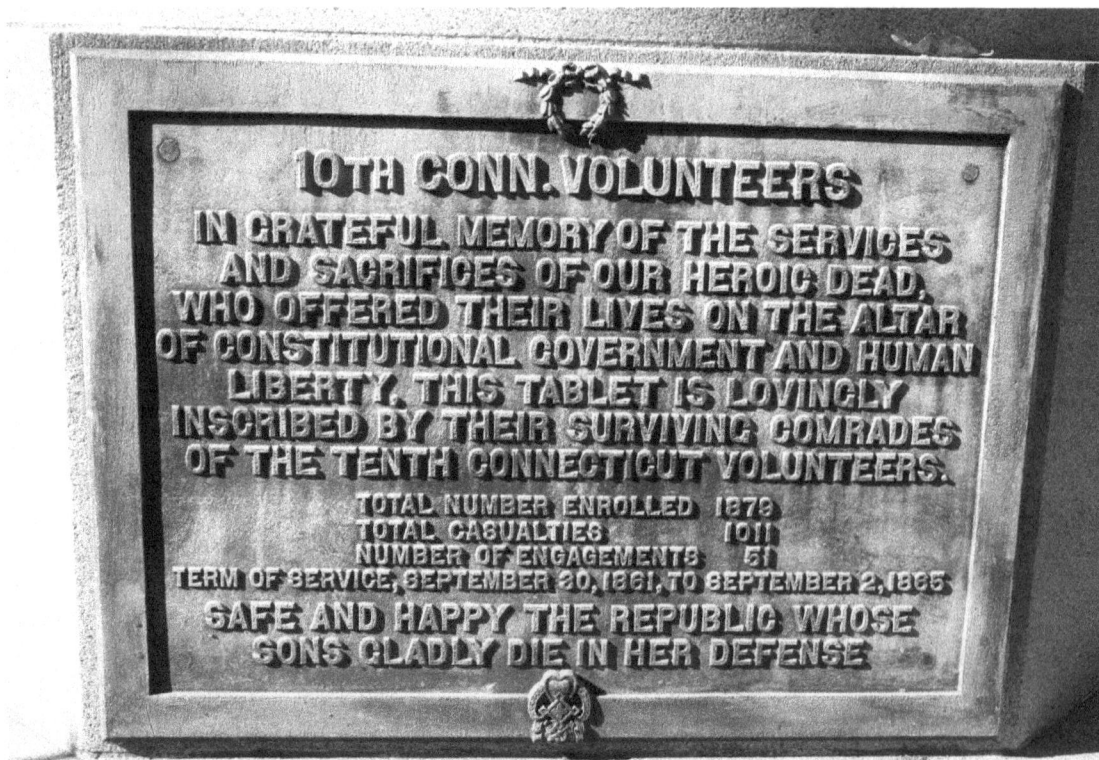

10TH CONN. VOLUNTEERS
IN GRATEFUL MEMORY OF THE SERVICES
AND SACRIFICES OF OUR HEROIC DEAD,
WHO OFFERED THEIR LIVES ON THE ALTAR
OF CONSTITUTIONAL GOVERNMENT AND HUMAN
LIBERTY. THIS TABLET IS LOVINGLY
INSCRIBED BY THEIR SURVIVING COMRADES
OF THE TENTH CONNECTICUT VOLUNTEERS.

TOTAL NUMBER ENROLLED 1878
TOTAL CASUALTIES   1011
NUMBER OF ENGAGEMENTS   51
TERM OF SERVICE, SEPTEMBER 20, 1861, TO SEPTEMBER 2, 1865

SAFE AND HAPPY THE REPUBLIC WHOSE
SONS GLADLY DIE IN HER DEFENSE

The 10th Connecticut Volunteers are one of four regiments honored with a monument in New Haven. (Photograph by Jane P. Bouley, 2011)

Guns and Crew at Fort Richardson, Arlington, Virginia, 1st Connecticut Heavy Artillery
(Library of Congress, Prints & Photographs Division LC-B811-2311B)

OTHER CONNECTICUT REGIMENTS

The following are regiments in which Branford and North Branford men
served in addition to the Tenth, Fifteenth, and Twenty-seventh.

FIRST REGIMENT CONNECTICUT HEAVY ARTILLERY
Originally the Fourth Connecticut Volunteer Infantry

The Fourth Connecticut Volunteer Infantry, later the 1st Connecticut Heavy Artillery,[113] was originally organized in May 1861 and mustered into service at Camp Mansfield, Hartford on May 23, 1861 for a term of three years. It was the first three year Connecticut regiment. Throughout the war part of the First Heavy Artillery was detached as part of the infantry while other companies remained in the regiment manning the artillery.

---

113 For a history of the 1st HA see *History of the First Connecticut Artillery and of the Siege Trains of the Armies Operating Against Richmond 1862-1865* (Hartford: Case, Lockwood & Brainard Co., 1893); Edward Ashley Walker, *Our First Year of Army Life, An Anniversary Address, Delivered to the First Regiment of Connecticut Volunteer Heavy Artillery at Their Camp Near Gaines' Mills, VA., June 1862 by the Chaplain of the Regiment* (New Haven: Thomas H. Pease, 1862); the essay by Henry L. Abbott in *Record of Service of Connecticut Men*, 116-119; and *Official Souvenir and Program of Monument First Connecticut Heavy Artillery Held on the State Capitol Grounds, Hartford, Conn. September 25, 1902* (Hartford: R. S. Peck & Co. Printers, 1902).

The regiment left Hartford on Monday, June 10, 1861 on the steamers *City of Hartford* and *Granite State* and camped in Maryland and near Washington, D.C. for nine months. Newly formed companies L and M joined them and the name of the regiment was changed to the 1st Connecticut Heavy Artillery, nicknamed the "First Heavies." They left camp on April 3, 1862 for the Virginia peninsula campaign and served at Yorktown, Chickahominy, Gaines Mills, and the Battle at Malvern Hill. Companies L and M were sent with their artillery to Fredericksburg on December 2, 1862 and companies B and M were at the Battles of Chancellorsville and Gettysburg. In 1863 and the spring of 1864, the regiment guarded forts at Alexandria, Virginia. The First Heavy Artillery participated in the Siege of Fredericksburg, Petersburg, and Richmond, Virginia through 1865. For the rest of their term they bombarded Confederate forts.

The First Connecticut Heavy Artillery was mustered out at Washington, D.C. on September 25, 1865 when their term expired and discharged at Hartford on October 1, 1865. Twenty-seven men associated with Branford and North Branford served in the regiment. Some of the Branford soldiers enlisted later in the war, others reenlisted and served four years. Malachi C. Bush died in prison after being captured at Cold Harbor, Virginia on July 27, 1862; James Davis, Walter Stone, and Sidney Townsend died of disease.

A monument to the First Connecticut Heavy Artillery was dedicated on the grounds of the Connecticut State Capitol on September 25, 1902.

THIS 13 INCH SEA COAST

MORTAR WAS IN ACTUAL USE

BY THE REGIMENT DURING THE

CAMPAIGN IN FRONT OF

PETERSBURG 1864 – 1865

AND WIDELY KNOWN AS THE

"PETERSBURG EXPRESS"

FIRST CONNECTICUT LIGHT BATTERY

The First Connecticut Light Battery or Light Artillery[114] was organized in September 1861 and mustered in at Meriden on October 26, 1861 for a term of three years. They were not organized into companies. They left for New York City on January 13, 1862 and spent most of 1862 and 1863 in South Carolina. They saw action in Virginia during 1864 and 1865. The regiment was mustered out at Richmond, Virginia on June 11, 1865 when their term expired. Seven men from Branford served in the 1st Connecticut Light Battery.

The First Light Battery is one of four Connecticut Regiments honored with a monument at Elm and Broadway Streets in New Haven.

---

114 For a history of the 1st LA see Herbert W. Beecher, *History of the First Light Battery Connecticut Volunteers, 1861-1865* (New York, A.T. De La Mere Publishing: 1901), 2 volumes; and the essay by Theron Upson in *Record of Service of Connecticut Men*, 98-99.

1st Heavy Artillery badge (Blackstone Library archives)

A monument in honor of the First Connecticut Heavy Artillery was dedicated on the grounds of the Connecticut State Capitol on September 25, 1902. (Photograph by Jane P. Bouley, 2011)

FIRST CONNECTICUT LIGHT BATTERY

KNOWN AS ROCKWELL'S BATTERY

MUSTERED IN OCTOBER 26TH, 1861

MUSTERED OUT JUNE 11TH, 1865

PARTICIPATED IN THE SIEGE OF CHARLESTON

AND OTHER BATTLES IN SOUTH CAROLINA

FT. FINNEGAN, FLA. JAN. 1862 TO MAY 1864

AND ENGAGEMENTS OF RICHMOND AND

PETERSBURG CAMPAIGNS

FROM MAY 1864 TO LEE'S SURRENDER IN 1865

THE TENTH AND TWENTY FIFTH ARMY CORPS

THE LEFT SECTION FIRST CONNECTICUT BATTERY, AT POCOTALIGO, S. C.

The 1st Connecticut Light Battery fought at Pocotaligo, South Carolina
on May 29, 1862. (Beecher, First Light Battery, I:123)

FIRST REGIMENT CONNECTICUT CAVALRY

The First Connecticut Cavalry[115] was organized at Meriden in October 1861, left Camp Tyler on February 20, 1862 for Wheeling, West Virginia and served in the Shenandoah Valley, including the Battle of Bull Run. They camped near Washington, D.C. in the fall of 1862 and were on picket duty at Stafford Court House and Baltimore. They spent the last part of the war in the Shenandoah Valley at Petersburg and Winchester, Virginia. The Regiment was detailed to escort General Grant to Appomattox when Lee surrendered on April 9, 1865. They performed provost duty in Washington, D.C. until August and a battalion was sent to Gettysburg for the laying of the cornerstone for the soldiers' monument on July 4, 1865. The Regiment was mustered out at Washington, D.C. on August 2, 1865 and discharged at New Haven on August 18, 1865. The First Connecticut Cavalry served their entire enlistment in Virginia and participated in 89 engagements including the Battles of Cedar Mountain, The Wilderness, Spotsylvania Court House, and Cedar Creek. Sixteen men from Branford served in the 1st Cavalry and several deserted. Aaron S. Lanfare received the Congressional Medal of Honor on May 3, 1865 for capturing the flag of the 11th Florida Infantry at Sailors Creek, Virginia on April 6, 1865.

SECOND REGIMENT VOLUNTEER INFANTRY

The Second Connecticut Volunteer Infantry[116] was organized in April 1861 for a term of three months. The regiment was divided into companies which also had state organizational names. For example, Co. H of the 2nd Connecticut Volunteer Infantry was known as Rifle Co. D. The regiment was mustered in at New Haven on May 5, 1861 and left on the steamer *Cahawba* on May 10th for Washington, D.C. for camp near the Capitol and then to camp in northern Virginia. The Regiment fought at the Battle of Bull Run on July 21, 1861, returned to Washington D.C. and was mustered out at New Haven on August 7, 1861 when their term expired. Five men from Branford served in the 2nd Connecticut Regiment and most reenlisted in other regiments.

SECOND REGIMENT HEAVY ARTILLERY
Originally the Nineteenth Connecticut Volunteer Infantry

The Second Regiment Connecticut Heavy Artillery[117] was organized in July 1862 as the 19th Connecticut Volunteer Infantry, also known as the Litchfield County Regiment. They were mustered in at Camp Dutton, Litchfield on September 11, 1862 and left for Washington, D.C. on September 19th for assignment near Alexandria, Virginia. The Regiment suffered severe losses at the Battle of Cold Harbor, Virginia on June 1, 1864 and served in Virginia for the rest of the war, seeing much action. The original members of the Regiment were mustered out on July 7, 1865 and others were mustered out at Fort Ethan Allen on August 16, 1865. Ten men associated with Branford served in the 2nd Heavy Artillery, Jacob Demuth was killed at Petersburg, Virginia and John Hipwell at Cedar Creek.

A monument to the Second Connecticut Heavy Artillery was dedicated on June 1, 2003 at Cold Harbor, Virginia.

---

115 For a history of the 1st Conn. Cavalry see the essay by Erastus Blakeslee in *Record of Service of Connecticut Men*, 56-60.
116 For a history of the 2nd CVI see the essay by James C. Coit in *Record of Service of Connecticut Men*, 18.
117 For a history of the 2nd HA see Theodore E. Vaill, *The County Regiment: A Sketch of the Second Regiment of Connecticut Volunteer Heavy Artillery, Originally the Nineteenth Volunteer Infantry, In the Civil War* (Winsted Printing Co., 1868 and 1908 edition); and the essay by James N. Coe in *Record of Service of Connecticut Men*, 173.

Members of Cavalry units rode and maintained stables of horses but some were foot soldiers. (Beecher, First Light Battery, I:404)

The 2nd and 3rd Connecticut Regiments joined in 1861 for a term of three months.
(Library of Congress Prints & Photographs Division. LC-USZC4-7989)

FIFTH REGIMENT VOLUNTEER INFANTRY

The Fifth Connecticut Volunteer Infantry[118] was organized in May 1861 for a term of four years and the men were mustered in at Hartford on July 22, 1861. They left for the front on July 29th for Maryland and Virginia. On August 9, 1863 they fought at the Battles of Cedar Mountain; Chancellorsville on May 1, 1864; and Gettysburg. In 1865 the Fifth Connecticut Volunteers were part of the Atlanta Campaign, the campaign of the Carolinas, and the march to Savannah. They were mustered out at Alexandria, Virginia on July 19, 1865. Fifteen men from Branford served.

A monument to the Fifth Connecticut Volunteer Infantry was dedicated in the Gettysburg Battlefield at the southern end of Culp's Hill in 1887.

SIXTH REGIMENT VOLUNTEER INFANTRY

The Sixth Connecticut Volunteer Infantry[119] was organized in August 1861 for three years and trained at Oyster Point in New Haven. Members of the Second Company Governor's Foot Guard joined Co. K. The Regiment was mustered into service on September 13, 1861 and left four days later on the steamer *Elm City* for Jersey City, then by rail to Washington, D.C. The Regiment was stationed in South Carolina in 1861 and 1862 in Georgia where they saw action at the Siege of Fort Pulaski and the Battle of Pocotaligo. During 1863 and 1864 they served along the coast as far south as Jacksonville, Florida and in the Virginia campaigns including Drewry's Bluff, Bermuda Hundred, Petersburg, and Darbytown Road. They were mustered out at Petersburg, Virginia on August 21, 1865 and transported on the steamer *United States* to New York City. They left New York for New Haven on the steamer *Nassau* where they were discharged on September 17, 1865. Eleven men from Branford served in the 6th Connecticut Regiment, Jesse Butler of North Branford died in action at Bermuda Hundred and Joseph Barker at Drewry's Bluff. Wells Gilbert, William T. Howd, and Richard Paine of Stony Creek were all in Co. K.

The Sixth Volunteer Infantry is one of four Connecticut Regiments honored with a monument at Elm and Broadway Streets in New Haven.

6TH CONN. VOLUNTEERS

ORGANIZED SEPT. 1861. MUSTERED OUT AUG. 21st, 1865

TOTAL NUMBER OF MEN WHO SERVED IN THE REGT. 1608

CASUALTIES 877

ENGAGEMENTS

PORT ROYAL, S.C., MORRIS ISLAND, S.C., SIEGE OF PETERSBURG

PORT PULASKI, GA., FORT WAGNER, S.C., DEEP BOTTOM, VA.

JAMES ISLAND, S.C., CHESTER STATION, VA., DEEP RUN, VA.

---

118 For a history of the 5th CVI see Edwin E. Marvin, *The Fifth Regiment Connecticut Volunteers, A History Compiled from Diaries and Official Reports* (Hartford, 1889); and the essay by E. E. Marvin in *Record of Service of Connecticut Men*, 220-223.

119 For a history of the 6th CVI see Charles K. Cadwell, *The Old Sixth Regiment, Its War Record, 1861-1865* (New Haven, Tuttle, Morehouse & Taylor:1875); and the essay by Charles K. Cadwell in *Record of Service of Connecticut Men*, 257-259; many from Co. K were later members of the Connecticut Second Company Foot Guard, see The Whitney Library, New Haven Museum.

The 5th Connecticut Volunteer Infantry fought at the Battle of Gettysburg. This is a view at cemetery ridge showing the gate house. (Abbott, The History of the Civil War in America, II:413)

The Sixth Volunteer Infantry is one of four Connecticut Regiments honored with a monument at Elm and Broadway Streets in New Haven.

POCOTALIGO, S.C., DREWRYS BLUFF, VA., CHAPINS FARMS, VA.

FORT FISHER, N.C. WILMINGTON, N.C.

AND MORE THAN TWENTY OTHER MINOR ENGAGEMENTS

AND AFFAIRS.

SERVICE

ARMY CORPS 19TH AND 24TH

DEPARTMENTS

DEPT. OF THE SOUTH. DEPT OF NORTH CAROLINA

ARMY OF THE JAMES ARMY OF THE POTOMAC

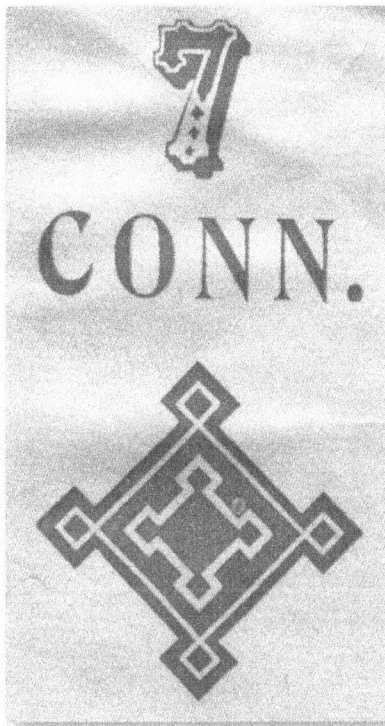

Veteran reunion ribbon of the 7th Connecticut Volunteer Regiment. (Blackstone Library archives)

SEVENTH REGIMENT VOLUNTEER INFANTRY

The Seventh Connecticut Volunteer Infantry[120] was a three-year regiment organized in August 1861 led by General Alfred H. Terry of New Haven. They camped at Camp English for drill and instruction. The soldiers were mustered in at New Haven on September 17, 1861 and left the next day for Washington, D.C. to be part of Sherman's North Carolina Corps. They camped and drilled for several weeks at Annapolis, Maryland and boarded steamers for Fort Monroe, Virginia experiencing several storms on the voyage. The Regiment arrived at Port Royal, South Carolina on November 4th. During the winter, the Seventh Connecticut camped at Tybee Island, Georgia and built fortifications. The Regiment manned the guns at the Battle of Pulaski in April and in the beginning of June moved to Charleston, South Carolina for the attack on James Island on June 16, 1862. That summer they served at the Battles of Pocotaligo and Fort Wagner and spent most of 1863 in South Carolina. In 1864, with other Connecticut regiments, they occupied Jacksonville, Florida and saw action at Drewry's Bluff, Deep Bottom, and Bermuda Hundred, Virginia. The Regiment was mustered out at Goldsboro, North Carolina on July 20, 1865 and discharged at New Haven on August 11th. Twenty-four men associated with Branford served in the 7th Connecticut Volunteer Regiment, William H. Harrison died of disease; John Davis died in prison; and a number of soldiers were wounded or captured. Henry Page, Timothy G. Bush, Jerome Baldwin, John H. Booth and William J. Underwood were all in Co. G.

---

120 For a history of the 7th CVI see Stephen Walkley, *History of the Seventh Connecticut Volunteer Infantry, Hawley's Brigade, Terry's Division, Tenth Army Corps 1861-1865* (Southington, 1905); Jerome Tourellotte, *A History of Company K of the Seventh Connecticut Volunteer Infantry in the Civil War*, 1910; and the essay by William H. Pierpont in *Record of Service of Connecticut Men*, 290-292.

Alfred H. Terry of New Haven was Colonel of the 2nd and 7th Connecticut Volunteer Regiments. He was promoted to Brigadier-General of the U.S. Volunteer troops and after the war continued his career retiring as a Major-General.

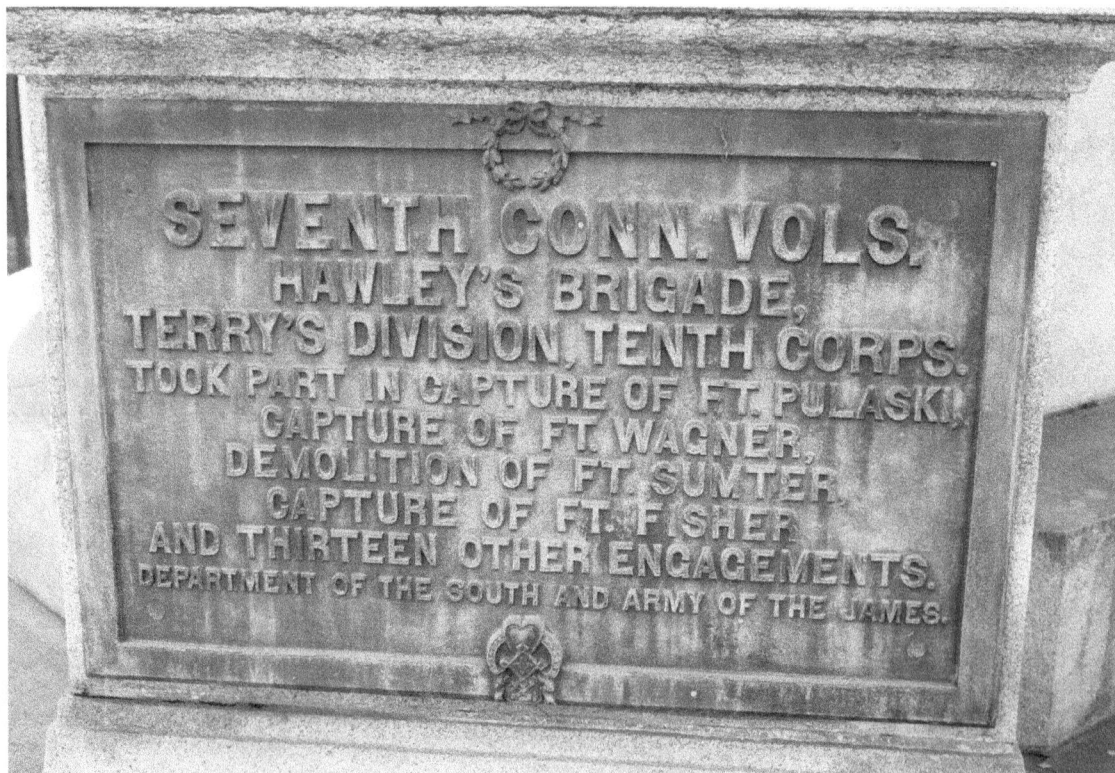

SEVENTH CONN. VOLS,
HAWLEY'S BRIGADE,
TERRY'S DIVISION, TENTH CORPS.
TOOK PART IN CAPTURE OF FT. PULASKI,
CAPTURE OF FT. WAGNER,
DEMOLITION OF FT. SUMTER,
CAPTURE OF FT. FISHER
AND THIRTEEN OTHER ENGAGEMENTS.
DEPARTMENT OF THE SOUTH AND ARMY OF THE JAMES.

The Seventh Volunteer Infantry is one of four Connecticut Regiments honored with a monument at Elm Street and Broadway Streets in New Haven.

A monument planned for Lafayette Park opposite the Connecticut State Capitol bearing a likeness of Generals Terry and Hawley was designed but the funds could not be raised. Instead, the Seventh Volunteer Infantry is one of four Connecticut Regiments honored with a monument at Elm and Broadway Streets in New Haven.

SEVENTH CONN. VOLS.

HAWLEY'S BRIGADE,

TERRY'S DIVISION, TENTH CORPS.

TOOK PART IN CAPTURE OF FT. PULASKI,

CAPTURE OF FT. WAGNER,

DEMOLITION OF FT. SUMTER,

CAPTURE OF FT. FISHER

AND THIRTEEN OTHER ENGAGEMENTS.

DEPARTMENT OF THE SOUTH AND ARMY OF THE JAMES.

EIGHTH REGIMENT VOLUNTEER INFANTRY

The Eighth Connecticut Volunteer Infantry[121] was organized at Hartford in September 1861 and served in the Virginia and North Carolina campaigns. They saw action at Antietam, Fredericksburg, Drewry's Bluff, Cold Harbor, and Petersburg, Virginia. After the war ended, the regiment had guard duty in Virginia. They were mustered out at Hartford along with the 11th Connecticut Volunteer Infantry on December 12, 1865. Only six soldiers associated with Branford were in the 8th Connecticut Volunteer Regiment.

A monument in honor of the Eighth Connecticut Regiment stands just outside the Antietam Battlefield.

8TH CONN. VOL. INFANTRY. 2D BRIGADE, 3D DIVISION, 9TH CORPS.

ADVANCED POSITION, 8TH CONN. V.I., SEPT 17, 1862.

ENGAGED 400. KILLED AND WOUNDED 194.

NINTH REGIMENT VOLUNTEER INFANTRY

The Ninth Connecticut Volunteer Infantry,[122] known as the "Irish Regiment," was organized at New Haven in October 1861 and most of the soldiers were of Irish birth. Joining regiments from Massachusetts, they headed to Mississippi and Louisiana and took part in the capture of New Orleans. The regiment suffered greatly from disease, lack of food, and poor sanitary conditions. Many men from the regiment died of fever and are buried in Vicksburg National Cemetery. During 1864, the regiment saw action at the Battles of Cedar Creek and Winchester, Virginia. They were mustered out at Savannah, Georgia on August 3, 1865

---

121 For a history of the 8th CVI see the essay by J. H. Vaill in *Record of Service of Connecticut Men*, 327-328.

122 For a history of the 9th CVI see Thomas Hamilton Murray, *History of the Ninth Regiment Connecticut Volunteer Infantry, "The Irish Regiment," in the War of the Rebellion, 1861-1865, The Record of a Gallant Command on the march, in battle and in bivouac* (New Haven, The Price, Lee & Adkins Co., 1903); and the essay by William H. Pierpont in *Record of Service of Connecticut Men*, 290-292.

and discharged at New Haven on August 8, 1865. Eight men associated with Branford served in the 9th Connecticut Volunteer Infantry.

A monument in honor of the 9th Connecticut Volunteers was dedicated on August 3, 1903 at Bay View Park in New Haven on the site where the regiment first encamped. The monument lists the names of all the soldiers. A monument to the Ninth Connecticut was dedicated on October 14, 2008 in Madison Parish, Louisiana opposite Vicksburg, Mississippi.

ELEVENTH REGIMENT VOLUNTEER INFANTRY

The Eleventh Connecticut Volunteer Infantry[123] was organized at Hartford on October 24, 1861 and mustered in on November 27, 1861 for a term of three years. The regiment left camp on December 16th for Annapolis and early the next year saw action at New Bern, North Carolina. On September 17, 1862 they fought at the Battle of Antietam, Maryland where they sustained heavy losses, 139 killed including every field officer. They fought at the Battle of Fredericksburg in December. The regiment camped at Newport News, Virginia until March 13, 1863. The Regiment participated in the Siege of Richmond and Petersburg, Virginia fighting at the Battles of Drewry's Bluff and Cold Harbor. The regiment lost half of its officers and nearly 400 men during the course of the war. The Eleventh was part of the advance into Richmond on April 3, 1864 and performed provost and police duty in Virginia until November. The Eleventh was mustered out at Hartford on December 21, 1865. Twenty-four men associated with Branford and North Branford were in the 11th Connecticut Volunteer Regiment, however, most were not town natives.

A monument to the Eleventh Connecticut Volunteer Infantry was dedicated on October 11, 1984 at Antietam near the Burnside Bridge in Sharpsburg, Maryland.

TWELFTH REGIMENT VOLUNTEER INFANTRY
ALSO KNOWN AS THE CHARTER OAK REGIMENT

The Twelfth Connecticut Volunteer Infantry[124] was organized at Hartford in September 1861 at Camp Lyon in West Hartford. The regiment left Hartford on February 24, 1862 by train to New York and boarded the ship *Fulton* arriving at Ship Island, Mississippi on March 8th. They were the first Union regiment to arrive in New Orleans on April 30, 1862. The Regiment occupied a Confederate fort, which they renamed Camp Parapet, where they remained for the summer on various expeditions. The Regiment served in the Mississippi River delta until July 1864 when it was sent to Fortress Monroe, Virginia and joined General Sheridan's Brigade. The Twelfth saw action at Winchester on September 19, 1864 and Cedar Creek on October 19th where many were captured. Those who did not reenlist were discharged at Hartford on December 2, 1864. The remaining soldiers spent the winter in Virginia and participated in the Grand Review at Washington, D.C. on May 23, 1865. They were mustered out at Savannah, Georgia on August 12, 1865 and discharged at Hartford on August 22nd. Twenty men associated with Branford and North Branford enlisted in the 12th Connecticut Volunteer Infantry. Levi Forbes of Branford died in 1866 from wounds and disease contracted while in the army; John Powell and James H. Scranton of North Branford died in prison; and

---

123 For a history of the 11th CVI see the essay by Charles Warren in *Service of Connecticut Men*, 431-432.
124 For a history of the 12th CVI see *Catalogue of the Twelfth and Thirteenth Connecticut Volunteer Infantry 1862* (Hartford:Case, Lockwood & Co., 1862); John William DeForest, *A Volunteer's Adventures, A Union Captain's Record of the Civil War* (Baton Rouge: Louisiana State University Press, 1974); and the essay by L. A. Dickerman in *Record of Service of Connecticut Men*, 471-473.

Assignments to Mississippi and Louisiana were dreaded due to the hot climate and disease. Sick soldiers were treated on hospital ships such as this one shown at Cairo, Mississippi. (Photographic History of the Civil War, I:243)

The 11th Connecticut Regiment suffered heavy losses at the Battle of Antietam, Maryland on September 17, 1862. (Photographic History of the Civil War, I:53)

James' brother Dayton H. Scranton died of wounds received at Port Hudson, Louisiana. James S. Rich came to Branford after the war and was the second to last surviving Civil War veteran in town.

A memorial to the Twelfth Connecticut Regiment stands in the Winchester, Virginia National Cemetery and was dedicated on October 19, 1896.

THIRTEENTH REGIMENT VOLUNTEER INFANTRY

47th

ANNUAL

RE-UNION

(14th)

C. V.

HARTFORD
SEPTEMBER 16
1911

The Thirteenth Connecticut Volunteer Infantry[125] was organized at New Haven in the fall of 1861 and mustered in on January 28, 1862. The Regiment left New Haven on March 17, 1862 on the ship *Granite State* and were transferred at New York Harbor onto the *City of New York*. They arrived at Ship Island, Mississippi on Sunday, April 13th and left on the same vessel, arriving at New Orleans on May 12th. During the summer they had provost and other duties around New Orleans. On September 29th some were chosen for a Reserve Brigade which fought at the Battle of Georgia Landing, Louisiana on October 27, 1862. Until mid-1864, the Regiment remained in Louisiana and saw action during the Siege of Port Hudson. In the fall of 1864 the regiment fought at the Battles of Winchester, Fisher's Hill, and Cedar Creek, Virginia. Those who had reenlisted were mustered out at Fort Pulaski, Georgia on 25 April 1866. The Thirteenth had the longest term of service of any state regiment. Thirteen men associated with Branford served in the 13th Connecticut Volunteer Infantry.

A monument to the Thirteenth Connecticut Regiment also stands in the Winchester National Cemetery.

FOURTEENTH REGIMENT VOLUNTEER INFANTRY

Veteran's reunion ribbon of the 14th Connecticut Volunteer Regiment. (Blackstone Library archives)

The Fourteenth Connecticut Volunteer Infantry[126] was organized on May 22, 1862 and rendezvoused at Camp Foote in Hartford. The regiment was mustered in on August 23, 1862 and left the same day for Arlington, Virginia. They fought at the Battle of Antietam, Maryland on September 17th and were among the Connecticut troops at Marye's Hill during the Battle of Fredericksburg. After camping in Virginia for the winter the men fought at the Battle of Chancellorsville, Virginia in May 1863. The regiment, now reduced in number, fought at Gettysburg on July 3, 1863. They spent the rest of their enlistment in the Virginia campaign seeing action at the Battles of Cold Harbor, Petersburg, Deep Bottom, Reams' Station, and Hatcher's Run. They participated in the Grand Review at Washington, D.C.

---

125 For a history of the 13th CVI see Sprague, Homer S., *History of the 13th Infantry Regiment During the Great Rebellion* (Hartford: Case, Lockwood & Co., 1867); and the essay by John C. Kinney in *Record of Service of Connecticut Men*, 510-511. The regimental history by Sprague provides detail about the life of the soldier, not just the military activities.

126 For a history of the 14th CVI see Page, Charles D., *History of the Fourteenth Regiment Connecticut Vol. Infantry* (Meriden: The Horton Printing Co., 1906); Stevens, Henry S., *Souvenir of Excursion to Battlefields by the Society of the Fourteenth Connecticut Regiment and Reunion at Antietam September 1891* (Washington, Gibson Brothers:1893); and the essay by Henry S. Stevens in *Record of Service of Connecticut Men*, 549-551. There are several other books published about the 14th Regiment.

on May 23, 1865 and were mustered out at Bailey Cross Roads, Virginia on May 31, 1865. The regiment fought in more battles and had more men killed in battle than any other state regiment.[127] Thirteen men associated with Branford served in the 14th Connecticut Volunteer Regiment, Henry B. Page, Francis S. Scranton, and Thomas M. Scranton died in the war; John L. Bartholomew and Michael Brennan died in prison.

A granite monument honoring the 14th Connecticut Regiment stands near Bloody Lane in the Antietam Battlefield. The Regiment fought here only three weeks after they were mustered in. Another monument to the Fourteenth Connecticut Volunteer Infantry stands in the Gettysburg Battlefield on Hancock Avenue and was dedicated in 1884. Two additional markers for the Regiment are at the Bliss house and barn in Gettysburg.

THE 14TH C.V. REACHED THE

VICINITY OF GETTYSBURG AT

EVENING JULY 1ST, 1863, AND HELD

THIS POSITION JULY 2ND, 3RD AND

4TH. THE REGT. TOOK PART IN THE

REPULSE OF LONGSTREET'S GRAND

CHARGE ON THE 3RD, CAPTURING

IN THEIR IMMEDIATE FRONT MORE

THAN 200 PRISONERS AND FIVE

BATTLE-FLAGS. THEY ALSO, ON THE

3RD, CAPTURED FROM THE ENEMY'S

SHARP-SHOOTERS THE BLISS BUILD-

INGS IN THEIR FAR FRONT, AND

HELD THEM UNTIL ORDERED TO

BURN THEM. MEN IN ACTION 160,

KILLED AND WOUNDED 62.

TWENTIETH REGIMENT VOLUNTEER INFANTRY

The Twentieth Connecticut Volunteer Infantry[128] was among eight Connecticut three-year regiments and the men were mustered in on September 8, 1862. They left for Washington, D.C. on September 11th and marched to Fairfax Station and Stafford Court House, Virginia, joining the Twelfth Corps. The regiment fought at the Battle of Chancellorsville on May 1, 1863 and lost eighty-five men. "It was a terrible battle. Our Regt is all cut to pieces."[129] They were among the first to arrive at Gettysburg and were in the front line at Culp's Hill. The Regiment was stationed in Georgia during 1864 and fought at the Battle of Peach Tree Creek on July 20, 1864. They were among the Union troops at the Siege of Atlanta and in 1865 saw action

---

127 *Battle-Flag Day*, 109.
128 For a history of the 20th CVI see John W. Storrs, *The Twentieth Connecticut: A Regimental History* (Ansonia, 1886); and the essay by Cecil A. Burleigh in *Record of Service of Connecticut Men*, 690-691.
129 Letter, Elizur G. Smith to his parents, 3 May 1863, in his own pension file.

Above, The 12th, 14th, and 20th Connecticut Volunteer Regiments participated in the Grand Review at Washington, D.C. on May 23, 1865. (Library of Congress Prints & Photographs Division, LC-USZ62-57018; Below, Photographic History of the Civil War, 9:258)

The Monument of the Fourteenth Regiment at Antietam, erected by the
State of Connecticut.

The Fourteenth Connecticut Volunteer Regiment fought at the Battle of Antietam three weeks after being mustered in. A monument to the Regiment stands near Bloody Lane. (History of the Fourteenth Regiment, 265)

The Regiment's Monument at Gettysburg.

A monument for the Fourteenth Connecticut Volunteer Infantry was dedicated in 1884 at the Gettysburg Battlefield on Hancock Avenue. (History of the Fourteenth Regiment, 249)

in North Carolina. They participated in the Grand Review at Washington, D.C. on May 23, 1865 and were mustered out on June 13, 1865. Twelve men associated with Branford served in the Twentieth.

A monument to the Twentieth Connecticut Volunteer Infantry, dedicated in 1885, was erected by the State of Connecticut in the Gettysburg Battlefield on Slocum Avenue.

TWENTY-NINTH REGIMENT VOLUNTEER INFANTRY

The Twenty-ninth Connecticut Volunteer Infantry[130] was formed in late 1863 and early 1864 after Governor William Buckingham signed a proclamation on November 23, 1863 allowing colored men to join the Union army. The proclamation was not without its opponents. William B. Wooster, former colonel of the Twentieth Connecticut took command. Twelve men enlisted from Branford; however, none appear to have been residents, but probably listed Branford to fill the town's quota when other cities' quotas had been filled. Several of the men were from New York, others from New Haven and the Complied Military Service Records list them all as "free men." Frederick Douglass addressed the men at camp near Fair Haven on January 29, 1864 and presented the colors, the regiment was mustered into service on March 8, 1864. They left New Haven on the *Warrior* and arrived at Annapolis, Maryland on March 22, 1864.

The Regiment participated in the Siege of Petersburg, Virginia fighting at the Battles of Bermuda Hundred and Fair Oaks. They were among the first troops to enter Richmond and acted as a bodyguard to President Lincoln. On June 10, 1865 they sailed from Richmond to Brownsville, Texas for provost duty. They were mustered out at Brownsville, Texas on October 14, 1865 and discharged at Hartford on November 25, 1865. Several of the "Branford" enlistees died of disease and a few had pensions.

A monument to the Twenty-Ninth Connecticut Volunteer Regiment was dedicated at Criscuolo Park, New Haven in 2008. The African-American Civil War Monument and Wall of Honor in Washington, D.C. was completed in 1997. The wall lists all the soldiers who served in state or federal colored regiments.

THE NEW HAVEN GRAYS

The New Haven Grays[131] were a local elite military company founded in 1816 as the New Haven Light Infantry Company and renamed the New Haven Grays. Members of the Grays enlisted in Co. A 2nd Connecticut Volunteer Infantry in April 1861 for a term of three months. The Regiment fought at the first Battle of Bull Run under the command of Colonel Alfred Terry on July 21, 1861. Many of the New Haven Grays reenlisted and served as officers in other regiments including the 27th. Mason Rogers of Branford was in the New Haven Grays before the Civil War. The New Haven Grays were integrated along with other home guards into the Connecticut National Guard serving at the Mexican border in 1916, in Europe during World War I, and in the Pacific theater during World War II.

---

130 For a history of the 29th CVI see Alexander H. Newton, *Out of the Briars: An Autobiography and Sketch of the Twenty-Ninth Regiment Connecticut Volunteers* (Philadelphia: Book Concern, 1910); Isaac J. Hill, *A Sketch of the 29th Regiment of Connecticut Colored Troops: Giving a Full Account of its Formation, of all the Battles through which it passes, and its final disbandment* (Baltimore: Maguire & Co., 1867); and the essay by Rev. Henry G. Marshall in *Record of Service of Connecticut Men*, 859-860.

131 For a history of the New Haven Grays see Jerome B. Lucke, *History of the New Haven Grays from Sept. 13, 1816; The New Haven Dailey Register*, 25 August 1862 (reprinted in *Shore Line Times*, 20 August 1897); and New Haven Grays archives, Whitney Library, New Haven Museum.

A monument for the Twentieth Connecticut Regiment stands on Slocum Avenue in the Gettysburg Battlefield. (Photograph by Jane P. Bouley, 2006)

The 29th Connecticut Volunteer Infantry at Beaufort, South Carolina. (Library of Congress Prints & Photographs Division, LC-cwpbh-03372)

The African-American Civil War Monument in Washington, D.C. (Photograph by Sharon D. Bouley, 2011)

The New Haven Grays fought in the first Battle of Bull Run on July 21, 1861 and most reenlisted as
officers in other regiments. (Library of Congress Prints & Photographs Division, LC-cwpb-01314)

THE U.S. NAVY

Seventeen men from Branford served in the Navy or Marine Corps during the Civil War. Most enlisted later in the war probably to avoid being drafted and they served one year or less. Several men were from seafaring families. Five Branford men - Adelbert Averill, Roland Averill, Marcus O. Babcock, Charles Linsley, and George S. Rogers all enlisted and served together. Most of the men enlisted and were discharged at the Brooklyn, New York Navy Yard and served on steamers in the blockade of South Carolina ports. The blockade of southern ports was known as the Anaconda Plan and was instituted by General Winfield Scott. There are no Compiled Military Service Records for the Navy and lists in other sources are often incomplete. Pensions for Navy veterans are on microfiche at the National Archives Records Administration in Washington, D.C. and some appear online. Some of the ships Branford men served on are listed below:[132]

> **USS *Clyde*** - She was the Confederate side wheel steamer *Neptune*; captured on June 1, 1863 and served the remainder of the war for the Union Navy.

> **USS *Florida*** - A 1,26-ton side wheel civilian vessel converted for use during the war in the blockades of Port Royal, South Carolina, Georgia, and Florida. In March 1865 she transported supplies and Confederate prisoners.

> **USS *Grand Gulf*** - A screw steamer that left New York on October 11, 1863 and joined the North Atlantic Blockading Squadron off Wilmington, North Carolina. She captured a number of Confederate blockade runners.

> **USS *Itasca*** - A Union wooden steamer assigned to the Gulf Blockading Squadron throughout the war, capturing a number of Confederate ships.

> **USS *Mercedita*** - A 840-ton civilian steamer built in 1861 at Brooklyn, New York and converted to a warship. In late 1862 the steamer joined the blockade of Charleston, South Carolina and was in the Gulf of Mexico toward the end of the war.

> **USS *North Carolina*** - A 74-gun ship built in 1820; was used as a receiving ship at the Brooklyn Navy Yard until the end of the war. After returning to New York, the sailors spent one or two days on board and were discharged from the *North Carolina*.

> **USS *Portsmouth*** - A wooden sloop-of-war built in 1843 in New Hampshire and served during the Mexican-American War. She served in the Gulf of Mexico Blockading Squadron in early 1862 and for the rest of the war as a station ship at New Orleans.

> **USS *Princeton*** - A 1,370-ton steamer built in 1851 with powerful guns and during the war was a receiving ship stationed at Philadelphia, Pennsylvania.

---

132 Data from www.history.navy.mil; *Dictionary of American Naval Fighting Ships* (Washington, D.C., Government Printing Office, 1964).

USS Mercedita

USS Florida

USS Portsmouth

USS *Quaker City* - A 1,428-ton side-wheel steamer with a powerful 20-pounder long rifle. She served in the Chesapeake Bay and Atlantic coast blockades and in 1865 in the Gulf of Mexico, capturing many Confederate ships.

USS *Rhode Island* - A 1,517-ton side-wheel steamer converted for war use in 1861 as a store ship. She participated in the assaults on Fort Fisher, North Carolina in 1864 and 1865.

USS *Savannah* - Built in 1842, the ship served off the Georgia coast until February 11, 1862 and for the rest of the war was used as an instructional vessel at the U.S. Naval Academy.

USS *Vermont* - An older ship commissioned in 1862 and served as a store, receiving, ordnance, and hospital ship at Port Royal, South Carolina. The *Vermont* left Port Royal on August 2, 1865 and was replaced at Port Royal by the *New Hampshire*.

USS *Wanderer* - Formerly a high-speed schooner used in the slave trade, she served throughout the war as a gunboat and hospital ship at Key West, Florida.

THE BRANFORD BATTERY

Branford Battery A[133] was organized in 1868 and grew out of the First Connecticut Light Battery. Among the forty charter members were Branford Civil War veterans Edgar Forbes, William T. Howd, Davis Johnson, and Elwyn Thayer. The Branford Battery, First Connecticut Artillery, served in the Spanish American War in 1898. Renamed Battery E, 103rd Regiment, 26th Division, Connecticut National Guard they served at the Mexican border under General Pershing to capture Francisco "Pancho" Villa in 1916 and a few weeks later were sent to Europe for the World War. They saw action in France at Chem des Dames, Chateau-Thierry, St. Mihiel, Meuse Verdun, Marne Torey, Belleau, Monthiers, Epieds, Turgny, and Forest de Fere. As Battery H, the men from the Branford Armory served in the Pacific during World War II. The Branford Battery was part of the 102nd Regiment Tank Company, 43rd Infantry Division in the Korean War.

The Branford Battery formed shortly after the Civil War and is still active today as part of the Connecticut National Guard. Field training took place at Pawson Park in the late 1800s. (Branford Historical Society photograph collection)

---

133 For a history of the Branford Battery see *The Branford Review* 10 January 1929, 23 January 1941, 28 March 1942, 20 April 1944, and 3 August 1950.

The Mason Rogers Post No. 7 G.A.R. poses in front of the First Congregational Church in 1893. For identification, see Appendix VIII. (Photograph by Harry O. Andrews, Branford Historical Society photo collection)

MASON ROGERS POST NO. 7
GRAND ARMY OF THE REPUBLIC

The Mason Rogers Post No. 7 of Branford, Grand Army of the Republic[134] was organized at the Academy on July 28, 1881 by Frank D. Sloat, Chief Mustering Officer of the Admiral Foot Post No. 17 of New Haven and Joel C. Page of the Parmelee Post No. 42 of Guilford.[135] The post was named for Mason Rogers of Branford who served in Co. B 15th Connecticut Volunteer Infantry and died of yellow fever at New Bern, North Carolina on September 9, 1864. The first officers were: Post Commander, Calvin L. Ely; Senior Vice-Commander, J. Atwood Linsley; J. V. Commander, Walter E. Fowler; Quartermaster, John Hutchinson; Chaplain, Henry W. Hubbard; Officer of the Day, Michael Kinneen; Guard, A. Judson Smith. Commander Ely made the following appointments: Adjutant, Joseph F. Nettleton; Sergeant-Major, Ammi B. Palmer; and Quartermaster Sergeant, Burton T. Buell. Several members were charter members of the Branford Battery A organized in 1868 which later became part of the Connecticut National Guard. Many veterans were also members of Widow's Son Lodge No. 66 F.A. & A.M.[136] of Branford before and after the war.

---

134 For a general history of the G.A.R. see Robert B. Beath, *History of the Grand Army of the Republic* (New York, Bryan, Taylor & Co. Publishers: 1889).

135 Blackstone Library Archives, RG 4, boxes 1 & 2, contain partial records of the Mason Rogers Post, particularly minutes from 28 July 1881 through 21 April 1904; see also *The Branford Review*, 26 May 1932, 1.

136 Ancient Free and Accepted Masons.

Grand Army of the Republic medal worn by the Branford
G.A.R. members. (Blackstone Library archives)

Grand Army of the Republic belt worn by Branford
veterans. (Branford Historical Society archives)

The Mason Rogers Post No. 7 hosted several Civil War veterans' reunions in Branford. This photograph was taken at
Pythian Hall on South Main Street, later the Community House. (Branford Historical Society photograph collection)

Post No. 7 met on the second and fourth Thursdays of the month at the Academy building on the Branford Green. The meetings consisted of the election of officers, guest speakers, an annual dinner, and discussion of upcoming events. The members participated in the Memorial Day parade, decorated veterans' graves, attended events in other towns such as the dedication of war memorials, attended funerals, and participated in the annual state or national encampments. They wore coats, hats, badges, and white gloves as their uniform. Officers were elected annually in November for the upcoming calendar year. About 1920, due to decreasing membership, the post no longer elected a commander or other officers but was led by an adjutant.

New members were mustered in at various times, some transferred from other posts. Some Civil War veterans never joined. The G.A.R. posts were run like a military unit with muster in dates, military officer rankings, and decorum with procedure and duty. Like any organization there were disputes and members were dropped, mostly for nonpayment of dues. There was one court martial for the stealing of post funds. Before 1900 the organization had 34-42 members in good standing.

After meeting at the Academy for nine years, the post rented a room above the Hutchinson Store at 272 Main Street[137] until 1897. Subsequently they met at the new Pythian Hall on South Main Street.[138]

In 1928 only two members of the post were living: Elwyn M. Thayer, a charter member and James S. Rich. The post is listed for the last time in the 1932 city directory.[139] Elwyn Thayer was the last surviving Civil War veteran and Post No. 7 member living at Branford.

The following is a list of members of the Mason Rogers Post No. 7:
denotes a charter member[140]

Ackerman, John (muster in 23 February 1882, transferred out 22 May 1884)
Averill, Adelbert C. (muster in 1 February 1882)
Averill, David (muster in 26 April 1883)
Averill, Roland G. (muster in 1 February 1882, dropped 25 September 1890)
Babcock, Marcus O. (muster in 23 October 1890)
Baisley, John W. (muster in 9 August 1883, dropped 25 September 1890)
*Baldwin, Jerome (muster in 28 July 1881)
*Barker, Ammi B. (muster in 28 July 1881)
Bartholomew, Rodolphus (muster in 1 March 1887)
Beach, George W. (muster in 28 March 1895)
Beach, Samuel (muster in 28 December 1882)
Bird, Edward J. (muster 9 November 1893)
*Bliss, George (muster in 28 July 1881, dropped 8 May 1884)
*Bradley, Franklin (muster in 28 July 1881, dropped 25 September 1890)
*Buell, Burton T. (muster in 28 July 1881, transferred 23 April 1885)
Buell, Edward J. (muster in 28 April 1882)

137 The address currently used for this building is 1094-1110 Main Street.
138 This building at 125 South Main Street later became the Community House and was torn down in 1963.
139 *The Branford Directory* (New Haven, Price & Lee Co., 1932), 142.
140 The Branford Historical Society archives has a framed certificate of the original members; also Mason Rogers Post meeting book, Blackstone Library Archives, RG 4, box 2, folder 1.

Most members of the Mason Rogers Post No. 7 are buried in Center Cemetery in Branford and have a G.A.R. gravestone marker.

Bush, Timothy G. (transfer in 13 February 1902)

Button?, E. (muster in 5 October 1916)

Cobleigh, William C. (muster in date not given)

*Cook, Samuel S. (muster in 28 July 1881, dropped 8 May 1884)

Cooke, Samuel G. (muster in 1 February 1882)

Crosby, Richard (muster in 28 April 1882, dropped 27 September 1884)

*Curtiss, Joseph (muster in 28 July 1881)

Daniels, Joseph E. (muster in 27June1889, suspended 22June1893)

*Donahue, William O. (muster in 28 July 1881)

Dory, George W. (transfer in 14 February 1891)

Downey, Timothy (muster in 23 March 1882, dropped 25 September 1890)

*Ely, Calvin L. (muster in 28 July 1881)

Forbes, Edgar L. (mustered in 30 September 1888, transferred 1890)

Fowler, Samuel O. (muster in 14 January 1893)

*Fowler, Walter E. (muster in 28 July 1881)

Frisbie, Charles H. (muster in 24 May 1883)

Garlick, Seymour (muster in 11 June 1891)

*Gilde,/Gildee/Gildea James (muster in 28 July 1881, dropped 25 September 1890)

Graham, William F. or Frank (muster in 11 May 1882)

Gray, Samuel N. (muster in 28 June 1892)

Hall, Roger[141]

Harrison, Nathan of North Branford (muster in 14 August 1884)

Hartson, Isaac Y. (transferred in)

---

141 According to his obituary, *The Branford Opinion*, 3 February 1905, 18; not found in the meeting books.

Hickman, John T. (muster in 23 June 1892)

*Hubbard, Henry W. (muster in 28 July 1881)

Huntley, William of New Haven (transfer in date not recorded)

*Hutchinson, John (muster in 28 July 1881)

*Johnson, Davis S. (muster in 28 July 1881)

*Johnson, Elizur C. (muster in 28 July 1881)

Johnson, Henry (muster in 22 April 1886)

Jost, Jacob (muster in 23 November 1882)

Kerr, John (muster in 23 February 1882)

*Kinneen, Michael (muster in 28 July 1881)

*Lay, James W. (muster in 28 July 1881)

Lee, Joseph (muster in 24 April 1890)

Lewis, Peter A. (muster in 26 September 1889, suspended 22 June 1894)

*Linsley, J. Atwood (muster in 28 July 1881)

Linsley, Charles E. (mustered in 21 July 1881)

Linsley, Charles F. (muster in date not given, dropped 25 September 1890)

May?, Wm. H.? (muster in 5 October 1916)

Neall, Daniel (transfer in 25 January 1883)

*Nettleton, Joseph F. (muster in 28 July 1881, dropped 28 June 1894)

*Nichols, Henry Z. (muster in 28 July 1881, dropped 25 September 1890)

Page, Elizur E. of North Branford (muster in 22 May 1884, discharged 25 January 1894)

*Page, Henry (muster in 28 July 1881)

Paine, Richard, Jr. (muster in 10 May 1883)

*Palmer, Ammi B. (muster in 28 July 1881)

Palmer, Bradley (muster in 23 February 1882)

Parsons, Edwin W. (muster in 29 October 1881)

Plant, Albert E. (muster in date not given)

Reynolds, Peter F. (muster in 9 August 1883)

Rich, James S. (muster in 28 June 1892)

Roberts, Amos, Jr. (muster in 21 September 1911)

Schenck, Paul (muster in 9 August 1886, dropped 25 September 1890)

*Sheldon, Edward D. (muster in 28 July 1881)

*Sliney, David (muster in 28 July 1881, dropped 25 September 1890)

*Smith, A. Judson (muster in 28 July 1881, dropped 22 June 1893)

Stevens, Emmerson R. (transfer in date not given)

Stevens, George (muster in 14 November 1895)

Stone, Watson W. (muster in 8 November 1883, dropped 22 June 1893)

Sullivan, Matthew (muster in 23 October 1890)

*Terhune, Nicholas R. (muster in 28 July 1881)

*Thayer, Elwyn M. (muster in 28 July 1881)

Todd, Andrew B. (muster in 21 September 1911)

*Towner, J. Edwin (muster in 28 July 1881)[142]

142 Also listed in the Mason Rogers Post record as J. Edward Turner.

Tubbs, John Edward (transfer in 28 April 1882, transfer out 19 October 1885)

Tucker, Allen Co. F 10th (muster in 15 February 1889)

*Tyler, Obed (muster in 28 July 1881, dropped 21 December 1883)

Tyler, William A. (muster in 22 February 1883)

*VanBenthusan, Isaac E. (muster in 28 July 1881, transfer out 29 March 1892)

Weed, Oscar (muster in 12 July 1883)

White, William H. (muster in 1 November 1906)

Whitney, Henry M. (muster in date not given)

*Wilford, Edwin L. (muster in 28 July 1881)

Woodworth, Albert P. (muster in 19 December 1907)

Young, William E. (muster in 27 February 1902, post drummer)

Zink, Walter H. (muster in 10 August 1881)

Post Commanders[143]

1881 - Calvin L. Ely

1882 - Walter E. Fowler

1883 & 1884 - Henry Z. Nichols

1885 - J. Edwin Towner

1886 - Nicholas R. Terhune

1887 - Elizur C. Johnson

1888 - Ammi B. Barker

1889 - J. Atwood Linsley

1890 - Henry W. Hubbard

1891 - Michael Kinneen

1892 & 1893 - Samuel G. Cooke

1894 - Samuel N. Gray

1895 - Elizur C. Johnson

1896 - Edward J. Bird

1897-1900 - Charles H. Frisbie

1901 & 1902 - Edward D. Sheldon

1903-1905 - Timothy G. Bush

1906-1908 - Charles H. Frisbie

1909 & 1910 - Oscar Weed

1911 & 1912 - Samuel G. Cooke

1913 - Elwyn M. Thayer

1914 - James W. Lay

1915 - Isaac P. Hartson

1916-1926 - Amos Roberts

1927 - no commander, adjutant Ammi B. Barker

---

143 List of commanders from the Mason Rogers Post No. 7 minute books, Branford city directories, and Connecticut GAR annual encampment booklets. There was no Branford newspaper from 1913 to 1928.

THE WOMEN'S RELIEF CORPS NO. 46 OF BRANFORD

The Grand Army of the Republic Women's Mason Rogers Relief Corps No. 46 of Branford was organized on February 6, 1893 with twenty-three charter members. The men called them the "Ladies of the W.R.C." Unlike the men's G.A.R., a woman did not have to be a veteran's wife to join. The women's group provided support for the men's group and hosted their own meetings and events. They provided charity by donating clothing, fuel, food and other relief to the needy. In 1943 there were still twenty-three members, six of whom were charter members. The Branford Woman's Relief Corps disbanded on December 31, 1960.[144] The records of the Branford W.R.C. can be found in the Blackstone Library archives.[145]

A photograph of the Grand Army of the Republic Women's Relief Corps No. 46 of Branford standing in front of the First Congregational Church after their first organizational meeting in 1893. (by Harry O. Andrews, Branford Historical Society photograph collection)

---

144 *Journal of the 18th Annual Convention, Hartford, April 5 & 6, 1963*, Department of Connecticut, Woman's Relief Corps, 13.
145 Blackstone Library Archives, RG 4, box 2, folders 10-12; included in the collection are meeting minutes and treasurer reports.

Women's Relief Corps medal worn by the Branford Corps No. 46. (Blackstone Library archives)

The Women's Relief Corps No. 46 members in front of the Civil War Monument on Memorial Day. (Branford Historical Society photograph collection)

The Branford Soldiers' or Civil War Monument was dedicated in 1885 on the Branford Green.
(Branford Historical Society photograph collection)

BRANFORD'S CIVIL WAR MONUMENTS

THE SOLDIERS' MONUMENT IN BRANFORD

Branford's Civil War monument[146] stands on a slight rise between the Town Hall and the First Congregational Church on the Branford Town Green. Soon after the local Grand Army of the Republic post was formed, the town and the G.A.R. formed a committee to raise funds to erect a monument on the Green. The members of the committee were: John Hutchinson, Samuel Beach, James W. Lay, Thorvald F. Hammer, John P. Callahan, Joseph Curtis, Edward F. Jones, and Joseph Lee.

The Mason Rogers Post No. 7 gave $1,000 toward the project, the Town of Branford $1,000, and the remainder was donated by citizens. The total cost for the monument was $3,000. The thirty-foot high monument was built by the Smith Granite Company of Westerly, Rhode Island. The granite monument consists of a large base, and two semi-bases. The upper one is inscribed G.A.R. 1885. Atop the shaft is a figure of a soldier or standard bearer, more than seven feet high, whose arms encircle a flag. The inscription on the north face reads:

---

146 *Unveiling And Dedication of the Soldiers' Monument at Branford, October 28th 1885,* Branford Historical Society archives, Family Papers RG 1, box 7A, folder 16; *Shore Line Times,* 30 October 1885; *The Branford Review,* 24 May 1928, 1; *New Haven Register,* 22 October 1885.

Compliments of J. HUTCHINSON, Branford, Conn.
THE SOLDIERS' MONUMENT OF BRANFORD.

Branford

To Her Brave Sons

Who Fought In The War

Of The Rebellion

1861—1865

Our Country One Flag

On the shaft are cut shields and engraved on them are the principal battles in which Branford's soldiers were engaged:

Antietam

Fredericksburg

Shiloh

Gettysburg

Vicksburg

Port Hudson

New Bern

Chancellorsville

The monument was dedicated on Wednesday, October 28, 1885. Work was suspended at the factories and the children were given a school holiday. Attending were Captain James Blackstone of Branford, Governor Henry B. Harrison, General Frank D. Sloat, and other distinguished citizens. A parade started at the train depot and ended at the Town Hall where dinner was served to the guests. Marshal Charles H. Frisbie rode a twenty-nine-year-old horse which served in the army and was wounded three times at the Battle of Gettysburg.[147] Georgie Barker, daughter of veteran Ammi B. Barker, tastefully dressed as a goddess of liberty, unveiled the monument.

---

147 Purchased by Samuel Plant of Branford from Col. Sanford H. Perkins of the 14th CVI.

A monument was dedicated in 1866 to North Branford soldiers who lost their lives in the service of their country and stands on a small Green next to the North Branford Congregational Church. (Photograph by Jane P. Bouley, 2011)

THE SOLDIERS' MONUMENT IN NORTH BRANFORD

The Soldiers' Monument on the North Branford Village Green[148] was erected to the memory of the defenders of the Union in the War of the Rebellion. A committee consisting of Russell Clark and Jonathan Foote of North Branford, and Henry Rogers of Branford was formed in 1865. About $2,000 was raised and the monument was made from granite from Stony Creek, Branford.[149] The monument was designed by Burdick & Company of Westerly, Rhode Island with lettering by Greene & Turner of Stony Creek. It stands twenty-feet high, consists of a large base, semi-base, and the shaft. The monument was dedicated April 12,1866 with an oration by General Edward M. Lee of Guilford. The inscription on the shaft lists the soldiers from North Branford who died during the war:

1865

OUR SOLDIERS

JAMES H. SCRANTON

CO. F 12. C. V. DIED IN SALISBURY PRISON, N. C.

---

148 Rockey, J. L., *History of New Haven County, Connecticut* (New York: W. W. Preston & Co., 1892), II:95; and *The Branford Review*, 26 April 1928, 7. Rockey states it was the first Civil War monument in the United States but just in Connecticut two monuments preceded it.
149 Rockey attributes the granite to the Stony Creek Quarry but the color favors granite obtained by Burdick & Co.

FEB. 1865 AE. 22.

J. HENRY PALMER

CO. K 10. C.V. DIED APRIL 11, 1865 OF WOUNDS

RECEIVED BEFORE PETERSBURG, V. A. AE. 26.

WALTER A. STONE

CO. F 1. CONN. ART. DIED AT HOME

OCT. 31, 1862 AE. 20.

ALBERT F. WHEATON

CO. A 10. C.V. KILLED AT BATTLE OF KINSTON

N. C. DEC. 15, 1862. AE. 27.

JOSIAH JOHNSON

CO. B 27. C. V. DIED JAN. 5, 1863 OF WOUNDS

RECEIVED AT BATTLE OF FREDERICKSBURG

V. A. AE. 23.

JOHN S. ROBINSON

CO. F 27. C. V. DIED AT BALTIMORE, M. D.

JUNE 18, 1863 AE. 27.

DAYTON R. SCRANTON

CO. F 12. C. V. DIED IN L. A. DEC. 18, 1863. AE. 23.

A veterans' monument for the Revolution, Civil War, and World War was erected on the Northford Green in 1920 and lists thirty-two men serving in the Civil War. Another veterans' memorial was erected at Stony Creek, Branford in 1954.

The T289 pension card for Nathan Harrison of North Branford provides several details. The "late rank" is left blank inferring he was a private. He served in Co. B 27th Connecticut Infantry. He applied for an invalid pension on June 26, 1880 and received an application and certificate number. His death date is given at the bottom of the card and his widow applied for a pension on December 5, 1911 receiving a new application and certificate number. It is his widow's certificate number 736,091 under which the pension is filed. It can be found at the National Archives and never received an "C" or "XC" number. (T289 Civil War pension index, www.fold3.com)

CIVIL WAR PENSION RECORDS

Pension records for Civil War Union soldiers are filed using a numbering system. The soldier initially received an application number and a different certificate number when the application was approved. The widow of a soldier may have applied for continued pension benefits after the soldier's death or as a new pension application. In both cases she received a pension and certificate number. About 1900, some but not all active pensions received new numbers beginning with a "C" or "XC." The former is a pension for the soldier and the latter a pension for a widow or minor. Some of the "C" or "XC" pensions can be found at the National Archives. Others, especially those that were still active in the 1930s or later, were retained by the Department of Veterans Affairs. Copies of these pensions can be requested through the Veteran's Services Administration.

It is the final number issued, usually the certificate number but occasionally the application number, under which the pension is filed at the National Archives. In general, the later the soldier or widow applied the larger the certificate number. Navy and Confederate pensions are not included and are a separate category.

Pensions could be applied for by the soldier, his widow, a parent, or on behalf of minor children. There were many Civil War pension legislative acts, each successive one providing benefits for a larger pool of applicants with less stringent requirements. A summary of a few of the pension acts are as follows:

Act of July 14, 1862 - Pension benefits provided to soldiers who were partially or permanently disabled as a direct consequence of military duty, or for their widows, minor children under the age of sixteen, or dependent parents or siblings. The amount of the benefit was determined by rank and level of disability.

1873 - An extra benefit was provided to widows for each dependent child under the age of sixteen.

Act of June 27, 1890 - Benefits were provided to every veteran with some disability as a result of service or for disability developed afterwards. Soldiers received a pension when they reached the age of seventy. Widows of soldiers serving in the Union Army could apply for a pension by proving the following:

- that the soldier served the Union for at least ninety days during the Civil War;
- that he was honorably discharged;
- that the widow provide proof of the soldier's death, but it need not have been the result of his army service;
- provide proof of her marriage to the soldier and that she remained a widow;
- that the widow is without other means of support other than her daily labor;
- that she married the soldier prior to June 27, 1890, the date of the act.

Act of May 1, 1920 - A widow could receive benefits if she was married to a soldier before June 27, 1905 providing that he served for ninety days or more and was honorably discharged; or if the soldier was discharged because of disability or died, regardless of financial condition. The pension rate was $30 per month with $6 additional for each child under the age of sixteen.

Act of June 9, 1930 - Rate increased to $40 per month.

Before 1890, the soldier had to prove a disability and inability to work that was a direct result of military service. The pension files often have numerous affidavits from neighbors, fellow soldiers, and physicians. A widow had to prove she was the wife of the soldier, sometimes a vital record or marriage certificate could not be found. These files also have numerous affidavits which reveal important historical and genealogical information. Some applications were approved without difficulty, while others, especially those of widows, were delayed for several years with the applicant having to provide many documents. Often attorneys were hired to process the claims. The government hired physicians and examiners to evaluate the soldier's or his widow's claim.

The statistics in the field during the war were sometimes not recorded, lost, or misrepresented the true facts. A soldier may be listed as a deserter when in fact he was a patient in a hospital. This record of desertion stayed in the soldiers' record and had to be disproven through testimony when they filed their claim. Sometimes the commanding officers or regimental physicians were deceased. The pension boards were divided into regions and men living in Connecticut were under the jurisdiction of the Boston board. The pension boards were accused of fraud, incompetence, and class prejudice. In turn, soldiers often misrepresented their illnesses, military service, and other information in order to receive a pension.

FINDING A CIVIL WAR PENSION RECORD

There are a number of finding aids to locate pension records for Civil War Union soldiers. The soldier's name, state of service, and unit is first determined. The name of the soldier can be ascertained from a number of documents. These include family records, obituaries, county or town histories, genealogies, G.A.R. records, soldiers' homes, or cemetery records. Most states have published Civil War military histories with soldier rosters. There are published regimental histories and more specific published works on military units or soldier diaries. Many books, research aids, and pension indexes are online.

Pensions are filed by the state of service and regiment, not under the place of residence at the time of the application. By using one of several indexes, the pension application or certificate number can be determined. The original Union pension records are at the National Archives in Washington, D.C. and can be viewed only on-site but copies can be ordered online or by mail.

The pension number has to be exactly right to locate the pension at the National Archives. The majority of pension numbers are easy to read. The most common problem is determining the application or certificate number due to poor or faded hand writing in the indexes or the number was changed with a "C" or "XC" identifier. Fortunately, there are several alternate indexes and using all of them may be needed for the most difficult cases. The following National Archives records are helpful:

RG 94, M535 - Compiled Military Service Records (called the CMSR)
The CMSR was developed in the 1890s for the pension boards to document the military service records of Civil War soldiers applying for pensions. Muster rolls, hospital records, payments, prisoner of war, and death records were included. On cards and placed in individual envelopes for each soldier, the envelopes are organized by state, regiment, soldier's name, and company. Officers, volunteers, and enlisted men have CMSR files. Some soldiers may have multiple envelopes if they served in more than one unit. The CMSR cards for some states are microfilmed, those for Connecticut are not and can be viewed only on-site at the National Archives. There are also CMSR envelopes for other wars but none for Navy personnel.

T288 - General Index to Pension Files, 1861-1934[150]
On microfilm, this is the most up-to-date index of Civil War pensions and includes the "C" and "XC" certificate numbers and additional widows' pensions. The index cards are arranged alphabetically by the soldier's surname, state, and unit.

T289 - Organizational Index to Pension Files of Veterans, 1861-1900[151]
This microfilm does not include the "C" or "XC" numbers or as many widows' pensions. The certificate number on the T289 is usually accurate for soldiers who died before 1900. The cards are arranged by state, branch of service, regiment, company, and surname. The T288 and T289 sometimes have slightly different information such as a death date and place. This index should be checked if the certificate number is hard to read on the T288.

150 The T-288 is available at www.ancestry.com
151 The T-289 is available at www.fold3.com

A1158 - Numerical Index to Pensions

This microfilm is arranged numerically by the certificate number but may not include the "C" or "XC" numbers. It is useful if the number on the T288 or T289 is faint or hard to read. It also provides the soldier's name, state, and unit.

Pension records often provide information not found in other sources. The files may include birth, baptism, marriage, and death records; names, births, deaths, and residence of children; divorce information; names of neighbors, family members, co-workers and fellow soldiers; medical data, places of residence, occupation, physical description, original letters, and details about the soldier's military service. By examining the pension records of the soldiers of a company or regiment, a timeline of events and service can be developed.

The National Archives and Records Administration (NARA) in Washington, D.C.
is the repository for Federal records including Civil War pensions.
(Library of Congress Prints & Photographs Division, LC-highsm-15633)

SECTION
TWO

BRANFORD AND
NORTH BRANFORD SOLDIERS

BRANFORD AND NORTH BRANFORD SOLDIERS

Section two focuses on the soldiers' military and biographical information. Each alphabetical listing provides detail about the soldiers' service, pension, family, and vital records. The formatting for this section is in *Register Style*, a genealogical writing style.[152] Data not found in the soldiers' pension records, Compiled Military Service Record (CMSR), or the *Record of Service of Connecticut Men* is footnoted. Photographs of gravestones from local cemeteries were taken by the author.

---

152 Henry B. Hoff, editor, *Genealogical Writing in the 21st Century, A Guide to Register Style and More* (New England Historic Genealogical Society, 2002).

GEORGE C· BALDWIN

Co. B 27th CVI, private, enlisted 21 August 1862, died 25 January 1863, no pension

George C. Baldwin, age 19, of Branford enlisted on 21 August 1862 and was mustered in on 3 October 1862 as a private in Co. B 27th CVI for a term of nine months. "Capt. Gilbert & Mr. Ely called to have George[153] and I enlist. I enlist my name with 7 others into the Hamilton Guard, 68 men enlist in our company. Our Co. of 83 men were sworn into the U.S. Service at half past 2 o'clock."[154] At the time of his enlistment he was described as five feet ten inches tall, light complexion, hazel eyes, brown hair.

He fought at the Battle of Fredericksburg on 13 December 1862 with the rest of his company. "Today is the 23d of Dec. (Tuesday). I have felt pretty limpsy since the battle. I have got a cold and some diarrhea." Among family papers on a U.S. Sanitary Commission card are his last words "I am dying I believe in Jesus there is no other [not legible]."[155] He died at Regimental Hospital near Falmouth, Virginia of Typhoid

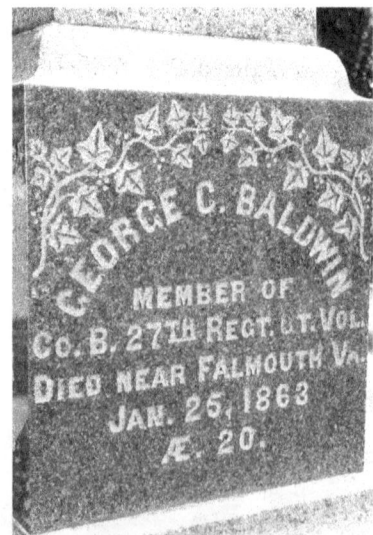

---

153 Probably George W. Baldwin.
154 Diary of George C. Baldwin, 1862, August & September; courtesy of Winston Visbeck.
155 Courtesy of Winston Visbeck.

Fever on 25 January 1863 at 5 o'clock. His body, corpse #156, was shipped to Branford the next day[156] and he was buried in Center Cemetery, Branford. His company, regiment and place of death are engraved on his stone and there was a G.A.R. marker on his gravesite in 1934.

George Crosby Baldwin was born in New York, son of John Rogers Baldwin and Harriet Rodgers of Branford. His father did not receive the rest of his bounty until 1901.

Thursday, Dec. 15th 1862 Camp near Falmouth[157]

To all at home,

I am safe well and sound.
I have been in one battle but through a kind providence
I came out without a scar. When I sealed my last letter
last Thursday morn about half past 6 o'clock, the firing
commenced an hour after we are in the ranks, we
march a couple of miles and halt near Gen. Sumner's
headquarters or where it used to be. we stay there all day
and encamp near there for the night. Bradley Palmer
was sick that day he went back to camp and conse-
quently was not in the fight of Saturday. It was a
sight to see our batteries of artillery hurrying to the
front, cannonading continues nearly all day.
I left my knapsack with 2 pair of stockings 2 shirts
my portfolio handkerchief & c. in camp, the same
as the rest of the regiment. I carried my rubber and
woolen blanket haversack and canteen. We cross
the Rappahannock Friday morning on a pontoon
bridge, stay in the street till noon, the boys all got
tobacco, some buy it in the street, others get backloads
of it in boxes out of the river, it is said the rebels
threw $80,000.00 worth of tobacco into the river. At noon
half of your company are detailed to load two pontoon
boats, and the other half of the Co., I among it, to
build a pontoon bridge across a creek for artillery
to pass over, while we are building it the rebels shell
us, shell strike on every side of us. we crawled
under the bank a while and then finished the bridge,
went up back to the wharf. Sam Beach and I lay
down in the road which does not lack of mud
but we slept some for all that, next morning the

---

156 Adams Express Company receipt, courtesy of Winston Visbeck.
157 Copy of partial letter courtesy of Mabel Baisley Kerrigan, original belonged to David Baldwin of Branford, now de-
      ceased. The letter is not signed but can be attributed to George C. Baldwin, mentions his sister Helen.

boys make cakes of flour and water and grease, the
brigade fall in and go up to the street above us "Carolina
Street," stack arms and stay in the street till noon
when brigadier Gen. Brooks sings out, "fall in third
brigade', we take arms and march for the rebels, go
by the depot, and not a great way farther on I threw
away my blankets. we were ordered to fall down
behind a little knoll, be there 2 or 3 minutes the
shells just clearing our backs, when we are ordered to
charge, we roust up and go double quick, when
shot and shell scatter the regiment. I tried to keep
with them, but did not. I looked in vain for some
thing to fire at besides our own men but I am con
fident that I did not shoot any of our men.
I finally for to the front beyond our own men
and fired away my gun when I was lying
down in the gutter, the shells struck around me and
threw a shower of dirt on me, the musketry
sounded like popcorn. I lay there till about an hour
after sun down, when I crawled off having fired during
the afternoon 49 times. I went down the street and came
across Dan Averill and Bill Tyler, we found a few more
of our regiment and went down to the river. we went into an
old house and staid there till morning. I did not have
any blanket but slept pretty well. next morning we
crawled out looking pretty scabby for we were covered with
sand and dirt. the orders were to report in the street,
about 75 men was all that could be mustered of
the regiment. Sam Beach and I go up to the hospital
where we see George Wilford, he is wounded with two
balls in his back, one in his leg and one in his hand.
Ed Wilford was wounded in the leg but not so but that
he walks on it. Sam and I go from the hospital near
[part of letter missing]
pair of buckskin gloves. I did not buy any but picked
up a noble pair on the battlefield. In the afternoon
of Sunday our company about a dozen of us go and
stand guard to the hospital. the hospital is or was a
nice building in the street of the city. there is Sam
Beach, Harvey Beaumont, Dan Averill, Henry Boardman,
Henry Hubbard, Joe Cusher, Merwin Wheaton and myself
stand at the doors to keep folks from going into the
building and getting in the way of the Doctors. we
took turns all night. Harvey Beach was in the house,

*he was detailed to carry the wounded off the field.
in the morning I see George S. Rogers and Henry Beach
they were both in the fight, but not wounded. by
the way Josiah Johnson was brought in last night. he
is wounded in the leg below the knee by a ball. Joseph
Bennet was also brought in sometime I don't know
when, he was upstairs and I did not see him till
Monday noon, was wounded by a ball in the arm
pretty bad. The rebels threatened shelling the town
at one o'clock this Monday afternoon but they did
not fire but a few. We boys made litters of boards, doors
blinds & c. and carried Josiah Johnson across the river,
without his leg being dressed. I helped carry Joe Bennet
across. George Wilford was carried on a stretcher. I
gave Bennet my woolen blanket so I have been
without any of my own ever since. To day is the 23d
of Dec. (Tuesday). I have been writing this above for 4 or 5 days.
this is secesh paper and I guess you will think I have
not a secesh pencil. I would have written before, but
I have felt pretty limpsy since the battle. I have
got a cold and some diarrhea and when I feel like
doing anything I help my tent mates get wood and
water. we are encamped near Falmouth. I have not
written to you or anyone else since Sunday Dec. 7th, except
one I mailed the 11th which I learn you have got by
the letter I got last night, which Father, you said, you
wrote in the Post office. I also received Helens letter dated
Dec. 10th and one from John R. Rossiter, an answer to one I
wrote him in Camp Tuttle. he says he is keeping school
in Madison. I got those three letters last night, which I
am very thankful for. Bradley has not got quite well
but is on the gain, he sends his respects. George Sam I believe
has got a diarrhea, but does duty the same as myself. Wil ( )
is well, but the whole regiment feel about alike having
been on a march, on picket duty, and through the battle.
It was lucky that about 250 of our men were out on picket
during the fight. Our Chaplain was wounded through the
right lung. Capt. Ely and Lieut. Elton went into the battle
with us, Capt. has been about sick ever since. he was not
wounded, Elton got knocked off or fell off from a stonewall.
he has had the rheumatism ever since. Lieut. Fields was
not in the fight, I believe he has got the dyspepsia. There
was not any of Co. B killed. Thomas Barrett orderly of Co.
H was killed, Capt. Sweizer of the dutch company was killed.*

newspaper Fowlers son was wounded and has since died. he
was orderly of Co. A. I saw the Colonel and Major Byxbee
on the field. I think Lieut. Col. Merwin did not go out with us.
It is a wonder to me that any of us came out alive but
thanks be to God who doeth all things well. On Monday
night, Sam Beach, John Hotchkiss, Merwin Wheaton, Henry Beach
and a few others of Co. B including myself went into the stoops
of an old house that had been pretty well shelled and lay
down there. we stay there till between 10 and 12 o'clock, in
the meantime, Sam gets up with another fellow go up to
the upper pontoon bridge where the troops were crossing a
regular stream. Sam came back, our regiment had gone, and
we were soon paddling for the bridge. we mixed up with the
troops and crossed over. there were two bridges, artillery crossed over
one of them, we went a mile or two. Sam, John Hotchkiss, Merwin
Wheaton and myself keep together.
[rest missing]

Crossing over the pontoon bridge below Fredericksburg (Library of Congress
Prints & Photographs Division, LC-ppmsca-33279)

Samuel Beach was a corporal in Co. B 27th Connecticut Volunteer Infantry. (Hart, Representative Citizens, 322)

SAMUEL BEACH

Co. B 27th CVI, corporal, enlisted 25 August 1862, mustered out 27 July 1863
pension application #661780 for the soldier and later received by his widow Harriet

Samuel Beach[158] of Branford, age 35, enlisted on 25 August 1862 and was mustered in on 3 October 1862 as a corporal in Co. B 27th CVI for a term of nine months. He fought at the Battle of Fredericksburg on 13 December 1862 with the rest of the company. He did not fight at the Battles of Chancellorsville or Gettysburg. He was sent to General Hospital, First Division, Second Army Corps near Brooks Station, Acquia Creek, Virginia on 1 May 1863 for illness and served as a hospital attendant.[159] "I left the Regiment and went to the Hospital at Aquia Creek some time after the battle of Fredericksburg and was not with the Regiment until we came home."[160] He was transferred to Finley Hospital, Washington, D.C. on 13 June 1863 when the General Hospital was dismantled and a few days later sent to Camp Convalescent in Alexandria. "He never fully regained his health."[161] Beach joined the rest of the Regiment at Baltimore and was mustered out at New Haven on 27 July 1863. He was the brother-in-law of Samuel G. Cooke.

---

158 For his biography see Samuel Hart, *Representatives Citizens of Connecticut, Biographical Memorial* (New York: The American Historical Society, 1916), 32.
159 Letter, Samuel Beach to his wife, 12 May 1863.
160 Deposition, Samuel Beach of Branford, 14 March 1885, in the pension file of Nathan A. Harrison
161 Hart, *Representative Citizens of Connecticut*, 33.

*Harriet Cooke, wife of Samuel Beach. Samuel was married with
three children when he enlisted. Many of his letters speak of the
farm, when crops were planted and harvested and who to hire.
He made suggestions but often said the decision was hers and
seemed to have the utmost confidence in her ability to run the farm.
(Branford Historical Society photograph collection)*

Samuel Beach gravestone, Center Cemetery

He applied for an invalid pension on 22 December 1891 under the act of 27 June 1890 but died before receiving a pension. There are very few documents in his pension file. He was married at Branford by Rev. Timothy P. Gillette of the First Congregational Church on 30 March 1851 to Harriet Atwater Cooke of Mendon, Illinois. Neither were previously married or divorced. After the war, he returned to Branford and was a farmer and proprietor of the summer resort known as Pawson Park. He was a member of the Mason Rogers Post No. 7 G.A.R. of Branford and was on the committee for the Branford Soldiers' Monument.

Samuel Beach died at Branford on 18 February 1892 and was buried there in Center Cemetery. He was born at Branford on 27 July 1827, son of Samuel Beach, Jr. and Mary Barker.[162]

Harriet A. Beach applied for a widow's pension on 12 May 1908 under the act of 19 April 1908. Harriet Atwater Cooke Beach died at Branford on 10 May 1916 and was buried there in Center Cemetery. She was born at Branford on 6 February 1832, daughter of Increase Cooke and Harriet Griffing.[163]

The following are excerpts of his letters to home, primarily to his wife Harriet.[164]

Camp Eathan Allen
Tues Oct 28th 1862

Dear Wife

........Revilie beats at
6 in the morning when the roll is called.
Guard mounting at 8 company drill from 9 to 11
dinner, company drill from 1 to 2, Battallion drill
from 3 to 4 - Dress parade at 5. We have had short
allowance some of the time since we have been here
but we are getting into better shape now. I enjoy
myself as well as expected. havent got sick of it yet
I am afraid I shall not be able to carry my knapsack
and endure any long marching. It is a week to day since
we left Camp Terry. I feel first rate.....

Your devoted
Husband S Beach

---

162 Branford Vital Records, 1786-1840, 355.
163 Branford Vital Records, deaths, 1916.
164 Samuel Beach, fifty letters to home, courtesy of John H. Beach, 2011.

Camp Eathan Allen
Sunday morn Nov 16 1862

Dear Harriett

*……….. We bought a peck of sweet Potatoes
for 25 cts & a peck of Apples for the
same, last Friday. my part of the bill
was only 8 cts. and 10 of us have bought
Victor Hugo's novel Les Miserables for
$2.50 or 25 cts a piece - 5 volumes at 50 cts each
So that we expect to have some reading
now. Wilder[165] is reading Fantine now…….*

*Sending much love to all
Your aff Husband S Beach*

Maryland Tuesday noon
Dec 2nd 1862

My Dear Wife

*We are on the move. We started
from Fort Eathan Allen Monday morn
about 9 or 10 in the forenoon cross
Chain Bridge, down through Georgetown
into Washington and the Capitol
down by the Navy yard & cross the
Eastern Branch Bridge into Maryland
down to F Carroll[166] nearly opposite
Alexandria. The 15th is just behind us. there
are great quantities of troops moving
now we suppose to join Burnside*

Co. B 27th Vols

**Woods opposite
Fredericksburg Va Dec 10th 1862**

Dear Sister[167]

*I have been down on the banks of the
Rhappahannock this forenoon with Doll[168]
& Hen Nichols[169]. Saw Fredericksburg across
the river & the rebel pickets. Falmouth is
this side. the view from the Bank this
side was very beautiful more so than
anything I have Seen Since I came to
Virginia. The air was very smoky so
that we could not see very distantly.
could see the steeples of the churches &
Court House The rebel pickets could be
seen very plainly.
Our camp is back from the river a while in
the woods but could be very easily shelled
by the rebels if they were disposed. There
is not much danger. We think We could
knock Fredericksburg into a cocked hat in
a very short time. We have had quite a
severe march from Chain Bridge here*

*Samuel Beach lived at 93 East Main Street, Branford
and the house is still owned by a descendant (Branford
Historical Society photograph collection)*

---

165 John Wilder of Co. B 27th CVI
166 He uses F for Fort.

167 His only sibling Anna who married Austin Babcock
     in 1863.
168 Rodolphus Bartholomew of Co. B 27th CVI
169 Henry Z. Nichols of Co. B 27th CVI

Camp near Falmouth Va
Wednesday Dec 17th 1862

Dear Wife

You have no doubt heard
all about our Great Battle at FkBurg
We think it was a big battle and a few
of us have no such desire to be in
another like it. You probably have ex-
tended and ful reports in the papers much
more so than I can give. A man in
the engagement as a private knows
but very little of the scope or obstinacy
of the conflict except right in his im-
mediate vicinity.....
The enemy were all entrenched and out of sight
while we were exposed to their full fire and across
from the batteries our loss was very great, much greater
than theirs I think. I wonder we were not all killed
we lay close to the ground a perfect rain of bullets
roaring of cannon screaming & bursting of shell....
The night of the Battle
all the next day - night & next day were spent
in caring and dressing the wounded and taking
[them] across the river, the third night
we were all removed across the river and the
Bridges swung around in the morning.....
And now may Heaven bless you
all and receive our thanks that he has spared & brought us
through great perils Is the prayer for you aff Husband

                    S Beach

Camp near Falmouth Va
Friday morning March 27th 1863

My Dear Wife

...............we will have to move from
here no doubt. We don't know where we are going
but indications lead to the opinion that we
shall soon have another encounter with the
Rebels. God deliver us from another defeat
I was out picketing last Tuesday again - had
a pretty hard time again, it rained all night.
The Rebs sent a small boat across to us with some
tobacco & a note. the seargent took it. We are
forbidden to touch them or have any com
munication with them.

General Hospital 1st Div
2nd Corps Tuesday May 12th

My Dear Wife

I came here about the 1st of May.
........I think Old Joe[170] will make another
strike before long. They are trying to
merge the two companies of our Reg't
probably be another examination by
the Surgeons tomorrow when some
more will be sent away to their Reg't
My chance of going is about as
good as any in our Reg't perhaps
I will write you soon after the decis-
ion. let it be what it may.

---

170 Major General Joseph Hooker

Henry D. Boardman of North Branford was a private in Co. B 27th Connecticut Volunteer Infantry and was discharged for disability. The pipe was given to him by the poet Walt Whitman while he was a patient in the hospital.

HENRY D. BOARDMAN

Co. F 4th CVI, private, enlisted 23 May 1861, discharged disability 11 October 1861
Co. B 27th CVI, private, enlisted 29 August 1862, discharged disability 23 March 1863
pension #XC-2677051 for the soldier and later for his widow Mary

Henry D. Boardman of North Branford originally enlisted at New Haven on 23 May 1861 as a private in Co. F 4th CVI which subsequently became the 1st Connecticut Heavy Artillery. He was sick in the hospital from 5 August until 31 August 1861. He was discharged for disability at Camp Engalls, North Arlington, Virginia on 11 October 1861 after being unfit for duty for forty-six days. In 1890 Edwin C. Dow of New Haven, commander of Co. F for three years, attested that Henry Boardman was a member of said company and was honorably discharged.

Boardman, age 19, reenlisted on 29 August 1862 and was mustered in on 3 October 1862 as a corporal in Co. B 27th CVI for a term of nine months. He fought at the Battle of Fredericksburg, Virginia on 13 December 1862 with the rest of the regiment. He was admitted to Campbell Hospital in Washington, D.C. on 29 December 1862 with diphtheria. He remained hospitalized and was discharged on 23 March 1863 from Campbell Hospital due to disability.

At the time of his second enlistment he was described as five feet seven inches tall, light complexion, brown hair, blue eyes, occupation seaman. He was discharged due to diphtheria and scrofula, the latter of which he had before his enlistment. Henry D. Boardman, age 24, was married at Branford by Rev. Elijah C. Baldwin of the First Congregational Church on 21 January 1869 to Mary Emma Wardell, age 17. Neither were previously married or divorced. They had seven children living (in 1898): Victor H., born

1869; Lottie E., born 1871; Frank W., born 1874; Grace A., born on 3 December 1884; Sidney H., born on 1 March 1887; Mary E. [E. Irene], born on 17 January 1889; and Coe Austin, born on 7 May 1893 at Springfield, Massachusetts.

He applied for an invalid pension[171] on 12 August 1890 under the act of 27 June 1890. He was living at Great Barrington, a fish and meat dealer. His son Coe's birth record states that Henry was born at West Henrietta, New York[172] and Mary E. Wardell was born at Baltimore, Maryland. Henry D. Boardman was chaplain of the D. G. Anderson Post No. 196 G.A.R. of Great Barrington, Massachusetts.[173]

Henry Decatur Boardman died at the home of his daughter Grace Porter in New Haven on 11 May 1906. He was born at West Henrietta, New York on 15 May 1843, son of Sidney Boardman and Martha Kelsey, both born at Northford. He was buried in Mahaiwe Cemetery, Great Barrington. His company and regiment are engraved on his stone and there was a Civil War marker on his gravesite in 2011.

Mary E. Boardman of 6 River Street, Northampton, Hampshire Co., Massachusetts applied for a widow's pension after his death. She and the soldier had not lived together for eight years but were never divorced. She received an extra benefit for her son Coe A. Boardman born in 1893. In 1940 she had been living with her daughter Dr. E. Irene Boardman of Prospect for about twenty years. Her son Sidney H. Boardman lived at 91 Walnut Road, West Barrington, Rhode Island in 1944; daughter Grace Porter lived at 28 Chapel Street in Woodmont; and her sister Mrs. Arthur Smith at 100 Wintergreen Avenue, Hamden. It appears she visited and stayed with various family members for extended periods of time.

A letter was sent to the pension board from her daughter Dr. E. Irene Boardman[174] of Prospect notifying them that Mary E. Boardman died on 31 April 1946. She was buried in Mahaiwe Cemetery, Great Barrington.

The American poet Walt Whitman spent many hours in the hospitals around the Washington, D.C. area and at the front comforting soldiers and observing the effects of war. He published his observations in several books. Henry Boardman is referred to as H.D.B. in "A Connecticut Case."[175]

The author and poet Walt Whitman. (Photographic History of the Civil War, 9:21)

"This young man in bed 25 is H. D. B., of the 27th Connecticut, company B. His folks live at Northford, near New Haven. Though not more than twenty-one, or thereabouts, he has knock'd much around the world, on sea and land, and has seen some fighting on both. When I first saw him he was very sick, with no appetite. He declined offers of money — said he did not need anything. As I was quite anxious to do something, he confess'd that he had a hankering for a good home-made rice pudding — thought he could relish it better than anything. At this time his stomach was very weak. (The doctor, whom I consulted, said nourishment would do him more good than anything; but things in the hospital, though better than usual, revolted him.) I soon procured B. his rice-pudding. A Washington

---

171 His pension is at the Veterans Administration.
172 His death certificate at New Haven states he was born at Northford, informant Mrs. C. H. Porter.
173 Information from his grandson Rev. Boardman W. Kathan of Prospect, March 2010.
174 Dr. E. Irene Boardman (1889-1980) was one of the first female physicians in New Haven County and a pioneer in public health in Connecticut. See www.greatwomen.org National Women's Hall of Fame.
175 Whitman, Walter. *Specimen Days & collect* (Philadelphia, Pennsylvania: David McKay, 1882), 32; many thanks to Marion Doody Bradley of North Branford for referring this essay to me.

The interior of a hospital in Washington, D.C.
(Library of Congress Prints & Photographs Division LC-DIG-cwpb-0424604246u)

After the war, Boardman lived in Great Barrington, Massachusetts and was buried there
in Mahaiwe Cemetery. (courtesy of Rev. Boardman W. Kathan)

lady, (Mrs. O'C), hearing his wish, made the pudding herself, and I took it up to him the next day. He subsequently told me he lived upon it for three or four days. This B. is a good sample of the American eastern young man—the typical Yankee. I took a fancy to him, and gave him a nice pipe, for a keepsake. He receiv'd afterwards a box of things from home, and nothing would do but I must take dinner with him, which I did, and a very good one it was."

A copy of a letter written by Henry D. Boardman to his sister Amelia Boardman Stowe shortly after the Battle of Fredericksburg is in the possession of the family.[176]

Dec 17th 1862 Camp before Fredericksburg Va

Dear Sister, The last letter: which I wrote on the 10th inst. I mailed yesterday. On the morning of the 11th we commenced the bombardment of F. [Fredericksburg] the Artillery fireing with occasionly a volley of musketry fireing was kept up all day. The pontoon bridges meanwhile were built. Some fireing during the night. The shells landed about ½ a mile from us.

We crossed the river at 7½ o'clock a.m. the 12th inst. & took possession of the town. but little resistance made. a few killed & some wounded. Every house, nearly, in the city was riddled by shot & shell. some of the rebel dead were left in the town, unburied. A great deal of Artillery fireing during the day. the shot & shell from our Artillery as well as the shell batteries passing over our heads. some men wounded, by our own Artillery on the other side of the river. Found $70,000 dollars worth of tobacco in the river, it wasn't damaged much, had all the tobacco I wanted or shall want for a long time. In the afternoon 15 of us were at work below the town building pontoon bridges. When the rebel batteries opened upon us & drove us away from our work & caused us to seek shelter under a high bank beside the river. the shell dropped in the river & all around us, but fortunately none us were hurt. One of the shells passed over our head & struck a long way off on the other side of the river & wounded three of the 15th CV. Our Artillery silenced the rebel batteries after a while & we finished our work.

On the 13th that was last Saturday (the day of the battle) we got up at 5 in the morning & ate our breakfast of raw pork & hard bread. got our brigade in line of battle in Caroline St. at 10 o'clock. the rebels commenced shelling the town, a good many of the men & horses of different Regts were killed & wounded. at 12½ o'clock a man in Co K was struck by a shell. he was standing about as far from me as from the house to the pig pen. we started at once. A murderous fire of grape, canister, shot & shell, besides heavy vollies of rifles & musketry was opened upon us at once. We were about ¾ of a mile from the rebel batteries when we started. went up Caroline St. & turned down the railroad in about 4 minutes - Cap. Schwitzer of Co. K & one of his seargents were killed by a shell about thirty feet from where I was. we were going on a run, didn't stop but went continually

---

176 Copy in the possession of Rev. Boardman W. Kathan. The original letter was sent to the National Park Service at Fredericksburg, Virginia in the 1950s.

*The 27th Connecticut Volunteer Regiment went the farthest up Marye's Height on December 27, 1862
during the Battle of Fredericksburg, Virginia. (Harper's Weekly, 27 December 1862 cover)*

passing over the dead dying & wounded. threw away our blankets & haversacks. After getting half way to the rebs the most murderous crossfire was opened on us it took us from the right & left as well as from the front. we rec'd orders to lay down to avoid the shot & shell. lay on our bellies in the mud half an hour nearly all the shots passing over us. soon the order came, "forward 27th" jumped up & charged up the hill. All around me the men were falling thick & fast. Up, up we went but no troops could stand the fire.

The battle continued until 7 at night it was terrific, describe it I cannot. no one who hasn't been there can imagine, can realize anything about it. Geo Wilford when we went into the fight was my right hand man. he had Six balls hit him, one went through his hand, one through the leg, two in his back & two just grazed him. Josiah Johnson was behind me in the ranks, he got a ball through his leg, will probably have to have it amputated. I was knocked about 10 feet by a shell before it exploded & slightly stunned. Left the field at 9½ o'clock in the evening, could hardly se anywhere on that bloody field without putting our feet on the dead & wounded. That large field sent up one continual groan. The wounded would pray, "For God's sake give me water" and some would say, "O God let me die." This has been one of the bloodiest battles ever known. Old soldiers who have fought at Fair Oaks, Antetum & have been the heroes of numerous battles say that it was by far the hottest fire they ever knew. Sunday morning, out of the 320 men of our

Gravestone of Henry D. Boardman in Maihawe Cemetery, Great Barrington, Massachusetts. (Photograph by Nancy Lee Kathan, with permission)

The 27th CVI was assigned to the 3rd Brigade under General Samuel K. Zook just before the Battle of Fredericksburg. Zook was killed at Gettysburg on July 3, 1863 (Library of Congress Prints & Photographs Division, LC-cwpb-05071)

regt who went into the fight on 75 reported, all but 320 were over to Falmouth doing picket duty. Monday morning 120 had been found & a great many of them was wounded. I helped bury three of ours. The rebels gave us from morning until 1 P.M. to evacuate the city with our wounded. When I left the city I had two rifles & blankets slung on my back & Lieut Elton leaning on my shoulder. The rebels were shelling the city. their shells were whistling over our heads & bursting in the air. Crossed the pontoon bridge & got to a place of comparative safety. had been up two nights & in one of the hottest battles ever known. The excitement carried me through & our officers say I did my duty well. out of 60 cartridges which I carried onto the field I had 17 left. We led the brigade, 5 regts. of old troops who have been in all the battles of the last two years were behind us. Gen. Zooks when he gave the order "forward 3rd brigade" saw us charge up the hill on the run, turned to the old troops & said "see them dam greenhorns go. follow on there you God dam sons of - ----." The men got up but the fire which the green 27th had passed through was too hot for them & they broke & ran away. Gen Zooks put spurs to his horse & dashing up to us said "nobly done 27th, nobly done." His horse was quickly shot from under him & he was stunned & lay on the field 4 hours. I never want to see another battle. I saw 8 men killed by one shell as they lay on the ground. the color bearer had stuck the staffs of the colors into the ground. they were about 3 rods from me. a shell came down in the midst of them & exploded, killing every one of them, but the colors still continued to wave over the dead - 8 killed by one single shell. This is scratch paper & came from F. (?). I must close. My love to Mother & all the others. If you or Mother want any money go to the bank & get it. Aunt M has the book.

H. D. Boardman

George G. Bradley of Branford enlisted on 14 September 1861 in Co. C 10th CVI and was killed on 13 October 1864 near Darbytown Road, Virginia. (Branford Historical Society photograph collection)

GEORGE G. BRADLEY

Co. C 10th CVI, 1st sergeant, enlisted 14 September 1861, reenlisted 17 February 1864,
killed 13 October 1864 near Darbytown Road, Virginia
pension #46937 for his widow Lois

George Granniss Bradley, age 28, of Branford enlisted on 14 September 1861 as a private in Co. C 10th CVI. At the time of his enlistment he was described as five feet six inches tall, light complexion, grey eyes, light hair, occupation machinist. He was promoted to corporal on 2 January 1862 and to sergeant on 23 October 1862. With his regiment he fought at the Battle of Roanoke, North Carolina on 8 February 1862. He was sick in the hospital at New Bern, North Carolina April through June 1862 and was promoted to 1st sergeant on 7 January 1863. From March 1863 until 16 February 1864, he was on detached service at Hartford and Fair Haven by order of Brigadier General Alfred H. Terry. He served under Capt. James H. Linsley. He was the father-in-law of Samuel N. Gray of the 1st Connecticut Cavalry.

He reenlisted at Hartford in the Veteran's Volunteer Corps 17 February 1864. He was on detached duty in Connecticut working at the U.S. draft rendezvous station at New Haven from March until June 1864. He was back at the front with the regiment in July and August 1864. He was reported absent without leave in September 1864 during the march from Petersburg to the inner defenses of Richmond, north side of the James River. He died at the field hospital on 13 October 1864 from wounds received the same day at Darbytown Road, near Richmond, Virginia. There is a government furnished gravestone for him at Center Cemetery, Branford and there is a marker at the gravesite. He was born at Branford on 3 May 1833, son of

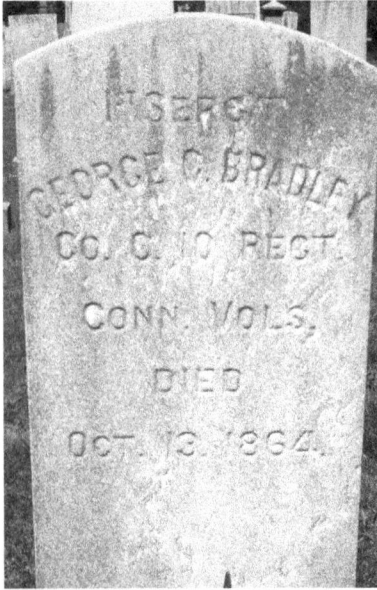

Major Bradley and Rosella Baker.[177] At the time of his death he was 31 years of age and left a widow, five children and a sixth child born three months after his death. He was the brother of Leonard Bradley.

Lois E. Bradley applied for a widow's pension on 18 November 1864. She was married to the soldier under the name of Lois Elizabeth Rowland at Branford by Rev. Lucius Atwater of the First Baptist Church on 25 May 1851. Their oldest child Lois R. was born at Branford on 12 February 1852.[178] The second child, Florence I. was born at New Haven on 22 December 1853.[179] The births of the last four children were registered in Branford: Luroff Orlando on 16 August 1856, Alida Genevieve on 7 December 1858, Castilla Zerilda on 2 January 1861, and Georgia on 13 December 1864. Lois E. Bradley never remarried. After the war she lived at Branford, New Haven, and Newark, New Jersey with her daughter Alida Bangs.

A letter in the file dated 24 June 1916 notifies the pension board of the death of Lois E. Bradley of 335 Roseville Avenue, Newark, New Jersey on 9 June 1916.[180] She was buried in Center Cemetery, Branford. She was born at New York City, daughter of John Rogers Rowland and Mary Ann Lanphier of Branford.

The following are excerpts from the diary of George G. Bradley kept for nine months in 1863:[181]

Daily Pocket Diary For The Year 1863, published in New York

front page
George G. Bradley, 1st Sergt Co. C 10th Reg CV, belonging to Branford,
Conn
Steal not, keep not
this book for fear of Shame
For in it you see the owners name
If this book is lost let the
finder return it to me.
For it will be of no
benefit to thee.
name of my wife Lois E. Bradley, Branford, Conn

---

177 Branford Vital Records, Town Meeting Book A, 228.
178 Statement, Ann M. Lay of Branford, 3 November 1864, whose husband Dr. Willoughby Lay was present at the birth. The birth was not recorded in the Branford Vital Records.
179 Statement, Mary Bottomly of New Haven, 10 August 1866, was a neighbor present at the birth.
180 Letter from grandson C. Clifford Bangs of Newark, New Jersey; son of Paul H. Bangs and Alida Bradley.
181 Branford Historical Society archives, RG1, box 32, folder 11.

1863
January

Thursday, 1Jan1863 - The beginning of the new year 1863, cold and windy, cloudy. No Duty today, as for myself fed [the] Sick, had requested oysters and cider at ten last. Saw the old year out the new-year in cribbing. Sitting in barracks at new borne, NC. Lt Coffin taken to the beat with an escort.

Friday, 2Jan - Regiment on Brigade review in the forenoon, Battalion Drill in afternoon, the bodies of hill. Wells Perkins arrived last night. Went with A flag of truce and yet I am not too weel today, wrote to Calvin Ives last night

Wednesday, 7Jan - Clear and cold, on the Sick list, went to the doctors, Brigade Drill this afternoon, Skirmish Drill this afternoon. I was this Day promoted to be orderly Sergeant of company C 10th CV.

Thursday, 8Jan - Attended guard mounting and Drill without commencing to act in my new capacity.

Friday, 23Jan - Skirmish Drill this morning, orders to cook three days rations and keep them ahead, Drawed clothing for part of the company.

Saturday, 24Jan - No Drill today, cleaned barracks for inspection in evening, minstrel performance in Co. quarters, got provisions for the march.

Monday, 26Jan - At one oclock orders to be ready to march at seven at nine, got on the cars for Morehead City passing the little villages of Crouton, Newport barracks, Carolina City and arrived at Marchead? at one and went on the vidette (sentry box).

Thursday, 29Jan - All hands on deck to clean Ship, all good natured, everything pleasant, got another mast mare, marines arrived, got underway at three oclock and went to Sea, wind blowing, fresh boys got sick.

Friday, 20Jan - Sea running heavy all night, almost all men Sick, run back fog six hours at five about Ship, prospect of a change in the weather, ran on course all night.

February
Sunday, 1Feb - Arrived at Port Royal.

Tuesday, 3Feb - Weather very stormy, wind blowing heavy. Wrote a note to Brother Leonard at Beaufort in the 6th reg CV.

Saturday, 7Feb - Got leave to go to Beaufort, Capt arranging off passes, went on board the Steamer Wyoming at two o'clock. Started at Six, arrived a Camp at 8 o'clock, found Leonard, stayed all night.

Monday, 9Feb - Packed early in the morning, landed at 12 o'clock, marched about half the night then camped for the night. Made coffe, carried Three days rations ashore with us, had shelter tents.

Wednesday, 18Feb - Preparing for review, won't have any for it rains. Out of 38 men there is Sick one Sergt., two Corp, two colonels. Can't stand this climate, feel bad myself, kidney affliction.

Wednesday, 25Feb - Drill as usual and other camp duties. More orders returning us to liberty. Going to give us more fresh vegetables, very lame myself in knee. Got bounty checks.

March

Sunday, 1March - Had company inspection, attended divine services, Luke 11th, verse very pleasant.

Wednesday, 4March - Cold and windy but clear. Drills as usual, hear of the capture of Savannah.

April

Wednesday, 1April - Called to arms this morning, some excitement but it died out, the rebels [are] alive and so are we. We will fight them yet and give them fits.

Sunday, 5April - Taken off from the reserve and placed on pickett on the outposts in the north of Tealbrook island. Very pleasant. Lieut Lindsley and myself, one or the other, on the outposts constantly. Saw the enemy twice.

Monday, 6April - Co. C still on the outpost. See the enemy calvary every few hours. The bombardment of Charleston commenced, lasted for three hours then Stopped for the night.

Friday, 10April - Got new tents, pitched them. Got news of the attacks on Beaufort, Port Royal.

Tuesday, 21April - Windy but warm. Rumor of there being 50 thousand troops on the way here. Got our pay for four months. My pay 73.40

Thursday, 30April - Were relived from pickett by the 24th Mass. Returned to camp, caught an alligator seven feet long. Were mustered for pay, drawed clothing.

May

Thursday, 14May - News of the capture of Fredericksburg but very conflicted. No mail. All the furloughed men assigned to leave tonight.

Friday, 15May - No boat yet, the boys depressed about the furlough failure. Some hard language used.

Saturday, 16May - News of Hooker being in front of Richmond and had been repulsed three times.

Sunday, 24May - Very pleasant. All packed and ready to leave, got on board at twelve o'clock for Hilton head on the Delaware barge. Got A fever headache.

Friday, 29May - Clear and pleasant. Every thing quiet, no news of the furlough. There is some dissatisfaction among the men. Got up at eleven to work on the fort three miles from camp.

June

Thursday, 4June - News of the capture of Vicksburg.

July

Sunday, 5July - Had inspection, very warm. Was very Sick this afternoon, insensibly for four hours from the pain, oh for home then.

Saturday, 11July - Very warm but pleasant. Arrival of a boat from Folly island, the seige (siege) very successful. The Sixth Conn. lost 60 men killed or wounded, missing. Heavy firing still.

Sunday, 12July - Very heavy up toward Charleston. Arrival of another boat, the Seige progressing and favorably. The news of the capture of Vicksburg July 4th.

Tuesday, 21July - Left Stono at Seven o'clock for Morris island, arrived at noon. Found the regt all right and joined it. No firing, all quiet. Was told by capt. appointed men to go home after the drafted men.

Wednesday, 22July - Very warm. The Seige progressing. Saw Leonard last night again today. I am expecting to leave every day or hour for home

Friday, 24July - After a good nights rest and early the next morning discovered a vessel throwing cotton overboard. We sent chase and captured her at about eleven o'clock, took all hands on board of the Arago and her in tow.

Saturday, 25July - Very pleasant. Expect to arrive in new york tomorrow at four o'clock. We have the prize in tow.

Thursday, 30July - Showery, got a leave of absence until Monday. Arrived at home at half past eleven, all the folks in the neighborhood calling to see me. Met with a good reception, had a Shake.

Friday, 31July - Very cool and pleasant. Enjoying myself very well, all the neighbors flocking into see me.

August

Saturday, 1August - Very cool and pleasant. Made a visit to the shop and Saw all the boys, all glad to see me [The Branford Lock Shop].

Sunday, 2August - The house full all day. Took a ride at eve, the house full all evening. Leave tomorrow morning.

Monday, 3August - Very warm. Arrived at camp at half past one and found that Col. Otis had been there.

Thursday, 6August - Put in command of the different details, Found everything very loose, no regularity. My wife came to see me, got a pass, stayed overnight.

Saturday, 8August - Arrived at camp at five in the morning, called the roll at Seven. Had a visit from my wife and sister. Rainy at sundown.

Wednesday, 12August - Made preparations to leave, left at twelve for long wharf. Went on board of the Detroit.

Sunday, 16August - Entered the potomac at daylight, at Sunrise were boarded by the Blockade. Arrived at Alexandria at five, went ashore to get some beef.

Monday, 17August - Very pleasant. Making preparations to leave at eleven for Warrnetown Junction, got one days rations in ( )sacks. Arrived at the headquarters of the 2nd Army Corp. at Seven o'clock.

Tuesday, 18August - Gave the conscripts in charge of the provost marshal and started for Bealton station distance seven miles. Left there at one for Alexandria, arrived at five and left for Washington for the Soldiers Retreat.

Thursday, 20August - Left Washington for New york at eight o'clock, arrived in New York at Seven. Were carried to the New England rooms and had supper and got rid of some of the dust by washing.

Friday, 21August - Left NY in the three o'clock boat for New Haven, proceeded to the camp.

Saturday, 22August - The drafted Negroes were sent away to Rhode Island to join the RI Negro Brigade.

Tuesday, 25August - Stayed at home and went blackberrying in the afternoon.

Saturday, 29August - Sent away 254 conscripts to the 20th. I was sent to the city to arrest one of the privy guards by the order of Gen. Hunt. Took and brought him before the Lieut.

Sunday, 30August - Father came to see me. Got a pass to visit my sister.

September
Saturday, 5Sept. - The men leave today. Cooked 1221 lbs. of beef at night.

Sunday, 6Sept. - Sent away 325 guard and conscripts. Went home a foot and stayed all night.

Sunday, 20Sept. - The conscripts leave today. 270 for the army of Virginia. Went over to sister Julias and found my wife there. Stayed over night.

Wednesday, 30Sept. - Send home my clothes to get them washed and send this Book, to old for use longer, please preserve it.

[Signed underneath Lois E. Bradley but all of above is in George's handwriting]

THOMAS J. CAREY

Co. E 15th CVI, private, enlisted 14 August 1862, mustered out 27 June 1865
pension #551835 application for the soldier and later received by his widow Libbie

Thomas J. Carey, age 24, of North Branford enlisted at New Haven on 14 August 1862 and was mustered in on 25 August 1862 as a private in Co. E 15th CVI for a term of three years. He saw action at Fredericksburg, Virginia on 13 December 1862, during the Siege of Suffolk, Virginia in the spring of 1863, and in the Peninsula Campaign of July 1863. He was not taken prisoner at Kinston, North Carolina. Carey was mustered out with the rest of his regiment at New Bern, North Carolina on 27 June 1865 and discharged at New Haven on 12 July 1865.

He applied for an invalid pension on 16 May 1891 under the act of 27 June 1890 for age related illness. The pension was denied due to failure to prove disability and he never received one during his lifetime. At the time of his enlistment he was described as five feet five inches tall, florid complexion, blue eyes, brown hair, occupation farmer. Bradley in *Our Soldiers* states he ran the 15th regiment laundry. He also, with others from the 15th, ran a school for children of loyal North Carolina soldiers and freed slaves. Since his discharge he lived at Cheshire where he died on 8 August 1902.[182]

Libbie Carey of Cheshire applied for a widow's pension on 4 September 1902. She was married to the soldier under the name of Libbie Nichols [Elizabeth] at Plymouth, Connecticut by Rev. B. Eastwood of St.

---

182 No gravestone is listed in the Hale Collection.

Peters Church on 13 September 1865. He was age 26, born at Wakeford, Ireland, living at North Branford; she was age 23, born and living at Cheshire. Neither were previously married or divorced. No children are mentioned in the pension file but children are listed in census records. She was living at Cheshire in 1910 and died on 17 or 18 November 1916. She was born at Cheshire on 15 August 1842, probably the daughter of Jesse L. Nichols and Elizabeth Hall.

The following are excerpts from his 1865 diary:[183]

March 1st 1865

Help me father to keep the pages of this book Free from the record of sin.

March Saturday 4th

Abraham Lincoln takes his seat for another four years.

March Wednesday 8th

The rebels were upon us in overwhelming Nos & captured nearly all the Regt. I made my escape with others as soon as I saw resistance was of no avail. Reached our rear lines in safety completely tired out. The Rebels attacked our new position & shelled us with great energy. A man of the 48th Indiana, Henry Layman, was killed by my side. The Lord knows the fate of those left and captured.

March Friday 10th

The rebs charged our lines still further & were handsomely repulsed. Their loss must have been immense, 900 reported taken. I went out to see the effects of the days work. The rebel dead are a fearful sight. Lord deliver me from such a death. I fired towards the enemy for the first time.

March Saturday 11th

Adjutant sent a squad of us out to bury the dead.

April Friday 14th

A dispatch from the front states Lee has surrendered to Grant. Such news as this awakens the liveliest emotions in camp. We talk of home with bright anticipations tonight. Thank God for our successes. Let Peace be proclaimed and God glorified.

April Monday 17th

Wrote and sent letter to E. The crushing intelligence of Pres Lincolns death reaches us. Fearful news.

May Wednesday 3rd

Very involved with school and church. School for 200 is short of supplies and teachers.

---

183 Thomas J. Carey Diary, #5116-z, Southern Historical Collection, Louis Round Wilson Special Collections Library, University of North Carolina at Chapel Hill, www.lib.unc.edu/wilson.

June Tuesday 27th

Were mustered out.

July Saturday 1st

We are on the ocean sailing.

July Monday 4th

Reached New York in morning. Took train at 3 PM & reached New Haven at 5 PM. Marched through several streets & then to the State house. Then we were dismissed & I came out home. Home again.

September Wednesday 13th

The day of my marriage. At seven oclock this morning Libbie & I [were] joined in holy matrimony. The Rev. Mr. Eastwood officiated at 8.

Samuel G. Cooke was a lieutenant in the Illinois Infantry and commander of the 44th U.S. Colored Troops.
He returned to Branford after the war. (Beers, Biographical Record of New Haven County, 1052)

SAMUEL G. COOKE

**Co. A 50th Illinois Infantry, 1st lieutenant, enlisted 14 October 1861, wounded
commander of Co. J 44th U.S. Colored Troop, prisoner, discharged 25 May 1865
pension #801964 for the soldier and later for his widow Cornelia**

Samuel G. Cooke[184] enlisted at Quincy, Illinois on 14 October 1861 as a corporal in Co. A 50th Illinois
Volunteer Infantry. He was promoted to sergeant in February 1862. On Oct. 4, 1862 he and another
sergeant took nine prisoners of the 1st Arkansas Infantry.[185] From November 1862 until 28 February 1863 he was on detached service in the Enquirer Department. He was sick in the First Field Hospital at
Cornith, Mississippi in March until 20 May 1863 when he returned to the company. In May and June 1864
he was detailed as a recruiting officer. He was discharged at Rome, Georgia on 7 June 1864 by reason of
promotion. "He participated in the battles of Fort Henry, Fort Donelson where he was slightly wounded,
Shiloh, Corinth; sieges of Corinth and Vicksburg, and was in the Atlanta campaign under Gen. Sherman in
1864. He was on detached duty for three months."

On 4 July 1864 he was 2nd lieutenant of the 106th U.S. Colored Infantry and was promoted on 6 August
1864 to 1st lieutenant and given command of Co. I 44th U.S. Colored Infantry. He was on special duty as
commander of Co. I from 31 October 1864 until 30 April 1865. He was captured at Dalton, Georgia on 13

---

184 For his biography see *Commemorative Biographical Record of New Haven County, Connecticut*. (Chicago: J.H. Beers & Co.,
     1902), 1052.
185 Beers, *Biographical Record of New Haven County*, 1052.

October 1864 and paroled at Villanow, Georgia on 15 October 1864. He was in the Battle of Nashville in December 1864.[186] He was discharged for disability at Chattanooga, Tennessee on 25 May 1865. His name appears on the Wall of Honor at Washington, D.C.; plaque No. C-57 44th Regiment U.S. Colored Infantry.

He applied for an invalid pension on 7 March 1884. At the time of his enlistment he was described as six feet tall, dark complexion, dark hair, dark eyes. "That about the middle of November 1864 at Chattanooga, Tennessee I had an attack of severe piles and about the 1st of December 1864 went with the regiment to Nashville. En route at Block House, [the] No. 2 train was fired into by two batteries of artillery under General Forest and stopped on Stone river bridge. I was in the third car on the span and in getting off had to jump some 12-15 feet which strained me severely. We had a 16 hour fight when came up a heavy shower and it was very cold. We escaped & got into Nashville where we suffered severely from exposure as we lost all our blankets when we left the train. In a few days I was obliged to go to the hospital." He was wounded at the battle of Fort Donelson, fought at the battle of Shiloh, and was at the Siege of Vicksburg.[187]

He was married at Branford by Rev. Elijah C. Baldwin of the First Congregational Church on 20 October 1868 to Cornelia Augusta Palmer. Neither were previously married or divorced. They had the following children, all living in 1915: Charles W., born on 14 September 1869; Lizzie L., born on 3 January 1872; Susie B., born on 13 April 1874; Harry G., born on 20 March 1878; and Addison T., born on 15 June 1884. Since his discharge he lived at Branford. He was a charter member and commander of the Mason Rogers Post No. 7 G.A.R. of Branford. He was the brother-in-law of Samuel Beach and W. Bradley Palmer.

Samuel Griffing Cooke died at Branford on 21 October 1915 and was buried there in Center Cemetery. He was born at Mendon, Adams Co., Illinois on 31 August 1835, son of Increase W. Cooke and Harriet Delia Griffing, born at Guilford and Branford.

Cornelia A. Cooke of Branford applied for a widow's pension on 12 November 1915. She died at Branford on 1 October 1925 and was buried there in Center Cemetery. She was born at Branford on 31 October 1844, daughter of Wilman Palmer and Susan Cornelia Bradley. [188]

Among Samuel Beach's letters are two from his brother-in-law Samuel G. Cooke:

---

186 Beers, *Biographical Record of New Haven County*, 1052.
187 *The Branford Review*, Civil War Veteran's Legacy, 18 June 2005, 1.
188 Branford Vital Records, deaths, 1925.

Cornith Miss Oct 19th/62

Dear Brother

Having heard that you
are in the army & thinking a few lines from
an old soldier might be acceptable. I have
Seated myself to communicate with you.
…..Well, Sam how do you like soldiering?
something is'nt it..
I was very much surprised when I heard you
had enlisted. I hardly see how you could
leave home yet I think it the duty of every loyal
man to shoulder his musket and help crush
out this wicked rebellion.
We are now encamped in Cornith & doing guard
duty in town some of our boys have gone to
Collumbus to day to guard prisoners……
you have probably heard of the battle of C---[189].
we had a hard time of it but came off victorious
after two days fighting. A long & tedious march
then followed. but we couldn't catch
the old rat and returned to C---. we have
been left to garrison the place as our regt
is small. we are reduced to 425 men about half
our original number. time and war have
truly thinned our ranks. I don't know how
long we shall remain here perhaps all
winter. it is very strongly fortified and
presents a very diferent appearance
from what it did a month ago. I was
out with a foraging party the other day
after corn. we took contrabands along to do
the work while we stood guard.
the country is laid waste
for many miles around here and is
almost entirely deserted by the natives.
we are about 30 miles from Pitsburg Landing.
while we were out on the march we lived off
the surrounding country. sweet potatoes were
quite plenty and we were not at all bashfull
about helping ourselves & woe to the chicks

that showed themselves. we got some kids too
they are very nice eating in fact we appro-
priated whatever we came across not even sparing
the old gray goose……
Remember me to Cousin Adison Taylor
I guess he will remember me.
I used to go to school with Lewis tucker[190]
in Pave street what kind of man was he.
What kind of army have you got? we have the
enfield[191] *now at first we had old muskets then*
Belgium rifles. A few more words and I must close.
you will probably have strange feelings when you go
into battle but put your trust in God and all
will be well. write soon yours truly

> *Saml G. Cooke*
> *Co A 50th Illinois*

Hospital of the 50th Reg Illinois

Dear Brother. Cornith Miss. April 18th /63

Your last was rec'd
yesterday and I was truly glad to
hear from you again. As I told
Hatt I wrote You a long letter & never
rec'd an answer. I see you didn't
get it. Since I last wrote I have
traveled considerably. I went to Vicks-
burgh with a lot of Snow balls (as you
Call them) to work on the canal.
I stayed there 3 weeks when the contraban
ds were turned over to Gen Shermans
division & we were relieved & ordered
back to our respective regts. When at
Vicksburgh we worke[d] in water over knee
deep this was not very good for our health &
in about a week after I got back to the
company I had to come to the Hospital.
I am much better now but am quite

---

189 Battle of Cornith, Mississippi October 3-4, 1862.

190 Lewis Tucker of Co. B 27th CVI died from disease
      while at camp in New Haven.
191 Enfield rifle.

weak. I have been here nearly 3 weeks.
I was sorry to hear of the death of Geo. Baldwin
I recollect him well. Yet what a comfort to hear that
he was prepared. I am glad you have
such good living. we live very well at
present but have seen some very
few potatoes. I should like some of
those of fashioned yellow turnips. they
dont raise many of them our west.
Speaking of the country I don't like it
around here at all I like it very
well up at Clarksvill in Tenn it is quite
pleasant there, but I cannot say that I like
it any better than Ill, or Conn. I have quite a
love for old Conn yet…..
I join with you in hoping
that this rebilion may soon be put
down & I feel confident that the
time is not far distant. I fear
that owing to the many reverses
the eastern army has met with.

They have lost confidence in them-
selves & their leaders & feel almost
discouraged, is not this the case? I think
you will soon hear of important
movements in the west perhaps
before this reaches you. They have stoped
the papers so we dont know what is
going on but feel shure that something
is up. that we might crush them
out in the west & then come & give
you a helping hand. I hardly think
they could stand before the heroes of Donels-
on Pittsburgh Landing & cornith combined
with your splendid army. But it is
all in the hands of him who doeth all
things well. let us trust him beleiving that
in due time he will deliver us from our present
trouble with regards to all friends I remain your

Bro
write often Sam

Calvin L. Ely, Branford's only dentist, was elected captain of Co. B 27th CVI and served throughout the war. (J. G. Steiger Gallery, New Haven; courtesy of Joan Paine Johnson)

CALVIN L. ELY

Co. B 27th CVI, captain, enlisted 19 August 1862, mustered out 27 July 1863
pension #616274 for the soldier and later for his widow Sarah

Calvin L. Ely[192] of Branford enlisted at New Haven on 19 August 1862 and was commissioned on 18 September 1862 as captain of Co. B 27th CVI for a term of nine months. He served throughout the war as captain of the company. He fought at the Battle of Fredericksburg on 13 December 1862 with the rest of the company. "Capt. Ely went into battle with us."[193] "Capt Ely has done no duty since the fight - diarrhea I believe."[194] He did not fight at the Battle of Chancellorsville and it is unclear if he was at the Battle of Gettysburg.[195] Ely was mustered out with the rest of his regiment at New Haven on 27 July 1863.

On 24 February 1863 Ely was arrested by Col. Richard S. Bostwick of the 27th being charged by Major Edward Venuti of the 52nd New York Regiment with neglect of duty and disobedience of orders. Supposedly, while on guard duty, he allowed a Union soldier to swim across the river to converse with the enemy. "Capt Ely is under arrest for some small irregularity."[196] Ely was tried on 4 March 1863 at the Headquarters

---

192 For his biography see Beers, *Biographical Record of New Haven County*, 448.
193 Letter, [George C. Baldwin] to home, 15 December 1862.
194 Letter, Samuel Beach to home, 1 January 1863.
195 Credited with fighting in the Battle of Gettysburg in his biography.
196 Letter, Samuel Beach to home, 4 March 1863.

of Hancock's Division, found not guilty and released. A similar charge was also levied against another soldier by the same Major. Further research could be done in the record for the details of the trial.

Ely states "I served as Capt. of Co. B 27 Ct Vol Inf. from Oct. 3/62 to July 28/63. I was with the company the whole time but not all the time on duty or in command because of sickness. I was sick in camp for a long time with pneumonia and jaundice."[197] Richard S. Bostwick stated "While on picket duty opposite the City of Fredericksburg, Va. he contracted a severe cold which resulted in Pneumonia in the month of March [1863]. In April when the regiment was about to move to take part in the Battle of Chancellorsville, the said Ely was unable to endure the march and was sent to a Hospital in the field at or near Brook's Station."[198] Another soldier stated that Ely contracted a severe cold "during a severe snow storm and for a time was dangerously sick and not sufficiently recovered to move to Chancellorsville, and was sent with other sick men to Brook's Station where he remained until about June 1st. I would also say that Captain Ely was an officer who always performed every duty to which he was assigned, and was willing and anxious to accept his share of duty even when sick."[199]

Frank Smith of Co. D 27th CVI stated "During the march to Gettysburg during the month of June 1863, Capt. Ely was prostrated by sun stroke and removed to an ambulance in the line of march. He had previously been sick with pneumonia and jaundice caused by a severe cold contracted while on picket duty opposite Fredericksburg in February of the same year and was still weak."[200]

Calvin L. Ely applied for and received an invalid pension on 5 May 1890. At the time of his application he was described as sixty years of age, five feet four inches tall, light complexion, brown hair, blue eyes, living at 123 West Main Street, Branford. He moved to Branford in 1849. In 1878 he was living at Omaha, Nebraska.[201] The sun stroke resulted in damage to his right eye, and eventual loss of sight, making it impossible for him to still perform his occupation as a dentist.

197 Deposition, Calvin L. Ely of Branford, 6 July 1895, in the pension file of George W. Elton.
198 Statement, Richard S. Bostwick of Brooklyn, NY; 20 February 1890, in the pension file of Calvin L. Ely.
199 Statement, George F. Peterson of New Haven, 23 April 1890, in the pension file of Calvin L. Ely.
200 Statement, Lt. Frank H. Smith, Co. D 27th CVI, in the pension file of Calvin L. Ely.
201 Deposition, Calvin L. Ely, 8 July 1878, in the pension file of L. Mortimer Willis.

Dr. Ely was the first commander of the Mason Rogers Post No. 7 G.A.R. of Branford. (from Beers, Biographical Record of New Haven County, 448; in frame - Blackstone Library archives)

Ely was one of the founders and first commander of Branford's Mason Rogers Post No. 7 G.A.R. He was also a cornet player and founder of the Branford Brass Band. He made many statements concerning the service of men under his charge for their pension applications.

Captain Calvin Luther Ely died at New Haven on 12 March 1905 and was buried in Center Cemetery, Branford. His rank, company, and regiment are engraved on his stone and there was a Civil War marker was on his gravesite in 1934. "Captain Ely was a faithful and efficient officer, and is highly esteemed by a large circle of friends."[202] He was born at Cheshire on 7 November 1828, son of Calvin Ely and Nancy E. Alford.

Sarah B. Ely applied for a widow's pension on 11 April 1905. She was married to the soldier under the name of Sarah Louise Beers at Branford by Rev. Calvin H. Topliff of the First Baptist Church on 5 June 1850. Their children are not named in the pension file.

Sarah Beers Ely died at Branford on 5 October 1921 and was buried there in Center Cemetery. She was born at Branford on 2 June 1832, daughter of Lester Beers and Mary Stedman.[203]

Dr. Calvin Ely was a founding member and cornet player in the Branford Military Band
(by Harry O. Andrews, Branford Historical Society photograph collection)

202 *The Ely Ancestry, Lineage of Richard of Plymouth, England* (New York: The Calmut Press, 1902), 399.
203 Branford Vital Records 1786-1840, 359.

Dr. Hubert V. C. Holcombe was the highest ranking Branford soldier during the Civil War as surgeon of the 15th CVI. He never fully recovered from illness contracted during his service and died in 1874. (Thorpe, History of the Fifteenth, 50)

DR· H·V·C· HOLCOMBE

Co. F 8th CVI and Co. C 15th CVI, surgeon, enlisted 25 April 1862, wounded 24 April 1863 mustered out 27 June 1865; pension #372992 for his widow Mary H. Holcombe later Bartholomew

Dr. H.V.C. Holcombe[204] of Branford enlisted on 25 April 1862 and was mustered in on 2 May 1862 as first assistant surgeon of the 8th CVI and was a member of Co. F. At the time of his enlistment he was described as six feet tall, dark complexion, black eyes and black hair.[205] Before leaving camp at New Haven, the men of Branford presented Surgeon Holcomb with a fine horse.[206] He was promoted to surgeon of the 15th CVI and mustered in at Newport News, Virginia on 14 August 1862; part of the Second Brigade, Third Division, Ninth Army. At the Battle of Fredericksburg on 11 December 1862 he was wounded in the head, "not seriously."[207] After the battle he performed many amputations in the field hospital.[208] He was wounded at Edenton Road, Virginia on 24 April 1863 and was appointed acting brigade surgeon at Portsmouth, Virginia on May 6, 1863. He was sick several months in 1863 and on leave for sixty days until 20 October 1863 for chronic diarrhea and vomiting as a consequence of remittent fever contracted in June 1862 at New Bern, North Carolina. He requested and was granted a leave of twenty days

---

204 For his biography see Stanley B. Weld, *Connecticut Physicians in the Civil War* (Connecticut Civil War Commission, 1961-65), 36-38.
205 His discharge papers and obituary can be found in the Branford Historical Society archives, RG 1, box 18, folder 13.
206 Thorpe, *History of the Fifteenth*, 15.
207 Thorpe, *History of the Fifteenth*, 39.
208 Obituary for Dr. H.V.C. Holcombe, undated, Branford Historical Society archives, RG 1, box 18, folder 13.

dated January 6, 1864 "My wife has just died in camp making it necessary for me to remove her remains to Connecticut, in addition her Father died but a short time previous leaving me the sole executor of his Estate. I am also but lately made the executor of my own Fathers estate, all of which business requires my immediate attention."[209]

He was the physician in charge at New Bern, North Carolina when nearly half of the 15th Connecticut Volunteer Infantry contracted yellow fever in the fall of 1864. Afterwards he was granted a leave of absence for thirty days for inflammation and abscess of the liver. He was captured in 1864 and confined at Libby Prison, Richmond, Virginia and paroled the following March. He was placed as surgeon-in-chief of the camp near Kinston, North Carolina the beginning of 1865. Dr. Holcombe was mustered out with the rest of his regiment at New Bern, North Carolina on 27 June 1865 and discharged at New Haven on 12 July 1865.

"Under the care of Surgeon H.V.C. Holcomb, the sick are skillfully attended to, and rapidly restored to health, and there can be no doubt that the regiment [the 15th C.V.] was never in better condition than at present. Holcomb is classed among the ablest operators of the army, as is fully evinced from the number of successful operations performed by him at the battle of Fredericksburg, while in the division Hospital, and fortunately for the sufferers not terminating fatally in one single instance. Very few in the volunteer service have had the experience in gunshot wounds, gained in the wars of Florida and Mexico, which he possesses. Dr. H. is a general favorite with those who know him well…"[210]

"When the disease had attacked our regiment, so that our regimental hospital was becoming more and more occupied; I desire to bear testimony to the admirable manner in which the affairs of our regiment hospital were administered by Surgeon Holcombe and his corps of assistants…As I now remember, Surgeon Holcombe had three wards, where those suffering with the fever were received."[211]

J. Edwin Towner makes several comments about Dr. Holcombe in his letters:[212]

> *6 October 1862 Camp Chase - I believe that Doctor Holcomb is the best old school doctor in the army.*

> *16 June 1864 New Berne - Doct Holcomb is well and is liked by the men for he stands up for them and is a good friend.*

> *25 September 1864 New Berne - Doctor Holcomb is quite unwell but attends to his duties yet.*

> *12 October 1864 New Berne Regimental Hospital - Doct Holcomb has not been well of late though he has attended to his duties until yesterday when he gave up.*

> *22 October 1864 New Berne - Doctor Holcomb has been very kind.*

> *14 November 1864 Camp of 15th C. V. - Doct Holcomb ought to be remembered by every <u>Christian</u>.*

> *27 November 1864 - Doctor Holcomb went home today. We miss him.*

> *8 December 1864 Sunday - Doct Holcomb [is] back from furlough.*

---

209 Letters, H.V.C. Holcombe to Chas. P. Brown, Adjutant 5th Reg't Conn. Vols, in Holcombe's CMSR.
210 Undated article, Branford Historical Society archives, RG 1, box 18, folder 13.
211 Thorpe, *History of the Fifteenth*, 233, report by Capt. M. A. Butricks, Co. I.
212 Towner letters and diary, Branford Historical Society archives.

Surgeons treated soldiers in their quarters or after a battle in makeshift field hospitals such as the U.S. Ford Field Hospital north of Chancellorsville. (by Edwin Forbes, Library of Congress Prints & Photographs Division)

The desk used by Dr. H.V.C. Holcombe during the Civil War where he kept his records. (The Connecticut Historical Society, Hartford, Connecticut)

Dr. H.V.C. Holcombe's gravestone.

Dr. Holcombe was born at West Granville, Massachusetts on 5 January 1828, son of Dr. Vincent Holcombe and Susanna Mills. He graduated from Castleton, Vermont Medical School; traveled in Mexico for two years with a trading company, practiced with his father at Granville, Massachusetts and came to Branford in 1854. "Even before his enlistment, he was active in making patriotic speeches in town."[213]

He was married first on 16 August 1852 to Annice Eunice Squire of Branford. "While visiting her husband in camp near Portsmouth, Va., [she] was attacked with Typhoid Fever; that she was treated during her illness by Dr. H.V.C. Holcombe & himself; that he was present at the time of her death, which occurred in the camp about Jan. 6, 1864; that her age was thirty-four years; that her body was embalmed in camp and taken by her husband to Branford, Conn. where it was buried."[214] She was born at Branford on 4 September 1829, daughter of Orin Dates Squire and Annice Frisbie.[215] She was buried in Center Cemetery.

Dr. Hubert Vincent Clairborn Holcombe returned to Branford after the war. His health never fully recovered from wounds and illness during his service. "Dr. Holcombe became an invalid in 1872 and was unable to practice."[216] He died at Branford on 4 August 1874 and was buried there in Center Cemetery. There was a G.A.R. marker on his gravesite in 1934. His desk used during the war with his papers is at the Connecticut Historical Society.[217] He never applied for a pension.

At the sixth annual reunion of the 15th CVI held at North Haven on August 25, 1874, the following resolution was passed:

"Whereas, we have been called to mourn the loss by death of an estimable member of our association, Surgeon H.V.C. Holcomb, of Branford, Conn., and whereas, in his relations with the regiment as its surgeon, as well as in his intercourse with us personally, he entitled himself by his professional services to our warmest gratitude, and by his unfaltering courage to our respect and admiration therefore:

Resolved, That we will ever hold in grateful remembrance the faithful and fearless service our surgeon rendered us in times of peculiar Trial, and the warm heart which made his friendship as endearing as his services were indispensable."[218]

His widow Mary H. Holcombe of Branford received a pension after his death until the time of her remarriage. She was married to the soldier as his second wife under the name of Mary Jane Hill at Branford by Rev. Frederick D. Lewin of Trinity Episcopal Church on 6 September 1865. She was not previously married or divorced. Dr. Holcombe had no children.

She reapplied for a pension on 9 June 1892 under the act of 27 June 1890 after the death of her second husband. She was married second at Branford by Rev. Zenas Smith on 25 December 1877 to David Daggett Bartholomew of Branford. He died at Branford on 2 November 1884 and was buried there in Center Cemetery.[219]

Mary Hill Holcombe Bartholomew died at Branford on 21 November 1897 and was buried there in Center Cemetery. She was born at North Guilford on 19 July 1839, daughter of Eliab Hill and Mary Ann Scranton.[220]

---

213 Weld, *Connecticut Physicians*, 36.

214 Statement, Dr. Edward O. Cowles of New York City, late assistant surgeon 15th CVI, in the pension file of Dr. H.V.C. Holcombe.

215 Branford Vital Records, 1786-1840, 410.

216 Affidavit, Emma C. Palmer, 17 July 1877, in the pension file of Luzerne A. Palmer.

217 Originally it was in the possession of the Blackstone Library, contained his register and prescription book. See *The Branford Review*, 6 July 1994, 3 and Connecticut Historical Society, MS 92085. The Holcombe papers are especially useful for someone researching medical practices during the Civil War.

218 Thorpe, *History of the Fifteenth*, 159.

219 Branford Vital Records, 1863-1895, 231; The Hale Collection, Branford, 85.

220 Branford Vital Records, deaths, 1897.

Before the Civil War, Aaron S. Lanfare served in the Mexican War and was a sea captain for the Trowbridge Fleet of New Haven. (Branford Historical Society photograph collection)

AARON S. LANFARE

Co. B & Co. K 1st Cavalry, 1st lieutenant, enlisted 16 November 1861, reenlisted 1 January 1864, mustered out 2 August 1865, pension #491552 for his widow Eliza

Aaron Stevens Lanfare[221] is the only Branford soldier to receive the Congressional Medal of Honor. He was born at Branford on 27 September 1824, son of Oliver Lanfare and Lois Willard.[222] Before the Civil War he served in the Mexican War (1846-1848) for three years on the frigate U.S. *Savannah*.[223] Afterwards, he was a sea captain for the Trowbridge fleet of New Haven trading to the West Indies. He was master of the ship *Reindeer* of New Haven and was honored by Queen Victoria for service rendered to the brig *Dominica* of Exeter, England on 2 April 1860[224]. He was given an engraved telescope by the Queen.

Aaron S. Lanfare of Branford, age 37, enlisted on 16 November 1861 as a corporal in Co. B 1st Connecticut Cavalry for a term of three years. He was promoted to commander sergeant on 1 November 1862. He saw action with his regiment at Cedar Creek, Winchester, Saylor's Creek, [225] and Appomattox, Virginia. He reenlisted on 1 January 1864 in Co. B and was promoted to 2nd lieutenant on 3 July 1864. The same day he

---

221 Various spellings - Lanfare, Lanfair, Lanfaer, Lanphier, Lamphere. For information see Manzella, Nancy, Profiles of Connecticut Civil War Soldiers, *Connecticut Genealogy News*, Fall 2010, Vol. 3 No. 3, 11.
222 Branford Vital Records, 1786-1840, 338.
223 Affidavit, Eliza J. Lanfare of New Haven, 27 December 1893, in the pension file of Aaron S. Lanfare.
224 Branford Historical Society collection.
225 Also spelled Sailor's Creek.

was transferred to Co. K 1st Connecticut Cavalry and promoted to 1st lieutenant on 29 October 1864. On 6 April 1865 at the Battle of Saylor's Creek, Virginia Lanfare captured the flag of the 11th Florida Infantry. For his bravery, he was awarded the Congressional Medal of Honor on 3 May 1865. Lanfare was mustered out at Washington, D.C. on 2 August 1865 and discharged with the rest of his regiment at New Haven on 18 August 1865.

After the war, Lanfare returned to New Haven and was a spice merchant and sea captain. He was master of Henry Trowbridge's bark *Mayflower* of New Haven which sailed from New York to Barbados, West Indies on 19 August 1875. The vessel never arrived nor was heard from again and was presumed lost at sea.

A government furnished gravestone was placed in Center Cemetery, Branford in 1986 next to the gravestone of his grandfather Oliver Lanfare. The flagpole at the Branford Post Office was dedicated to Aaron Lanfare in 1961 and rededicated in 1984 when a new post office was built on Park Place. In 2011 a new plaque was made and placed on the Branford Green.[226] The plaque reads:

In Memory Of
1st Lt. Aaron S. Lanfare
Co. B 1st Connecticut Cavalry
Awarded
The Congressional Medal Of Honor
On May 3rd 1865
For His Heroic Action At
The Battle Of Saylor's Creek, VA.

---

226 *The Branford Review*, 7 June 1984, 1; the original plaque was replaced by the Town of Branford in 2011.

Aaron S. Lanfare is the only Branford native to receive the Congressional Medal of Honor.

Eliza J. Lanfare of New Haven applied for a widow's pension on 3 October 1890 under the act of 27 June 1890. She was married first at Baltimore, Maryland to Edward G. Page on 15 March 1848. He was born in Maine. About one year after their marriage, he sailed from their home at Baltimore as a ship mate bound for New Orleans. He apparently died at New Orleans of yellow fever and she received word about his death about one year later. No record of his death or witnesses could be found. She did not have children with Edward Page. Her name on the marriage record to Aaron Lanfare was given as Purse, raising suspicion about her first marriage. The pension board wanted absolute proof that her first husband and Aaron Lanfare had died which, of course, could not be provided, despite an affidavit from the Trowbridge family and others. Her pension was rejected and she reapplied on 27 December 1893. The case was sent for special examination and was again rejected. There are many affidavits in the file from family members and neighbors.

She was married second as Eliza Jane Purse at Baltimore, Maryland by Rev. Allen on 4 March 1851 to Aaron Lanfare. He was not previously married or divorced. After their marriage they lived at Baltimore from 1851 to 1854, New Haven from 1854 to 1859, and Branford in 1860. They had four children: Agnes Stevens, born at New Haven on 15 January 1854; Mary Emily, born at New Haven on 10 May 1857; Adelle Matilda, born at New Haven on 9 December 1858; and Jessie Freemont, born at Branford on 20 February 1862.

After the death of Aaron Lanfare she lived at New Haven with her oldest daughter Agnes Woodward except for two years in Macon, Georgia. W. H. Huntley, special examiner at New Haven for the pension board, asked that the case be reopened on 3 October 1898 as "a matter of justice." "The claimant is about 73 years old & is in broken down health. She is the widow of the very bravest of men during the rebellion and cannot get a little help for the few years she has to live."[227] Papers in the file dated 3 March 1900 indicate she still had not received a pension but at the time of her death her "last payment was on 4 December 1902."

Eliza J. Lanfare died at New Haven on 21 February 1903. She was born at Baltimore, Maryland on 26 June 1826, daughter of Gilbert Purse and Susanna Dickinson.

---

227 Affidavit, W. H. Huntley of New Haven, special examiner, 2 February 1894, in the pension file of Aaron S. Lanfare.

A gravestone at Center Cemetery, Branford for Aaron Lanfare was placed by his descendants in 1986.

Depiction of a Union soldier capturing a Confederate flag during a battle. (Harper's Weekly, 17 September 1864 cover)

Connecticut State Library, Picture Group 540, Connecticut General Assembly Portraits.

JAMES H. LINSLEY

Co. C 10th CVI, captain, enlisted 25 September 1861, wounded, mustered out 24 August 1865
pension #607303 for the soldier and later for his widow Kate

James H. Linsley[228] of North Branford enlisted at New Haven on 25 September 1861 as a private but was mustered in on 22 October 1861 as a sergeant in Co. C 10th CVI for a term of three years. He was promoted to 1st sergeant on 25 May 1862 and 2nd lieutenant on 23 October 1862. With the regiment he fought at the Battle of Roanoke Island, North Carolina on 8 February 1862. He was wounded in the head at Kinston, North Carolina while in charge of the Provost Guard on 14 December 1862. He was again wounded in the head at Strawberry Plain, Virginia at the battle near Malvern Hill on 26 July 1864. He was in Hampton Hospital near Fortress Monroe about one month then in Officer's Hospital at Annapolis, Maryland until 10 October 1864. He was promoted to 1st lieutenant on 11 October 1864 and to captain on 19 November 1864. He was in the hospital at Point of Rock, Virginia from 3 April 1865 until 12 May 1865. He was wounded a third time in the right thigh in the charge at Fort Gregg, Virginia on 2 August 1865. Capt. Linsley was mustered out with the rest of his regiment at Richmond, Virginia on 25 August 1865 and discharged at Hartford on 5 September 1865. He was the brother of Benjamin M. and John S. Linsley. After the war he served in the Connecticut legislature.

---

228 For his biography see Rockey, *History of New Haven County*, II:102.

He applied for an invalid pension on 12 January 1880. At the time of his first enlistment he was described as five feet six inches tall, light complexion, hazel eyes, brown hair, occupation farmer. During the Roanoke Expedition he contracted malaria and was also wounded three times in the head and right thigh. "He was wounded three times - at Kingston, N. C. in December 1862; at Strawberry Plains, Virginia in July 1864; and at Fort Gregg, Virginia in April 1865. He was commended by the department commander for special service in the capture of the enemy's outposts near Dutch Gap, Virginia in July 1864."[229]

He was married at Thetford, Vermont by Rev. William S. Palmer on 19 September 1865 to Catherine Dean Conant. Neither were previously married or divorced. They had two children living (in 1898): Eleanor Bonney Linsley, born on 20 March 1870, and Arthur Maltby Linsley, born on 9 August 1873.

Captain James Halsey Linsley died at Northford on 2 December 1903 and was buried in Northford Cemetery. His rank, company, and regiment are engraved on his stone and his name appears on the Northford Veterans' Monument. He was born at North Branford on 5 September 1835, son of John Stephen Linsley and Eliza Ann Halsey. He left his widow, a son Arthur M.,[230] and a daughter Eleanor B. Johnson of Pomfret.

Kate D. Linsley of Northford applied for a widow's pension on 8 January 1904. She stated that her name was Catherine, but she has never used it, preferring Kate. Kate Conant Linsley died at Northford on 22 June 1915 and was buried in Northford Cemetery. She was born in New Hampshire, probably at Charlestown on 1 May 1832, daughter of Dean Conant and Almira Bonney.

A diary kept by James H. Linsley for 1862-1864 and several letters can be found online, some excerpts:[231]

January 1-2, 1862

In camp at Annapolis where we have been since Nov. 5th. In the yard is a large tupil tree under which Gen. Washington once had his headquarters.

January 3

An abundance of liquor finds its way into camp. Many of the guards are susceptible of corruption.

January 14

This morning finds us anchored at Cape Hatteras. Many of the boys lost their rations and the swearing ceased when the boat was pitching among the waves.

January 31

The most gratifying event is the reception of a mail, once more connecting us with the loved ones left behind. Newspapers few and far between also furnish a world of gratification to all.

---

229 Obituary, *Shore Lines* Times, as quoted in *Connecticut Linsleys*, 105.
230 According to his obituary, his son was incompetent and a patient at the Hospital at Middletown.
231 James H. Linsley Diary, University of Florida, George A. Smathers Libraries, www.ufdc.ufl.edu.

March 21

Col. Drake [A. W. Drake of 10th] will leave us tomorrow on account of his health, we shall probably never see him again. The regiment will be extremely sorry to lose him, a good soldier and good commander.

April 27

Voluntary turnout of the regiment to go to church. Going to church with guns is somewhat repugnant to the feelings of most of our men.

June 17

Went on duty after the longest fit of sickness I ever had.

December 14

Battle commenced by Wessell's brigade. Return over bridge, Kinston abandoned, bridge burnt. Highly complimented by our Generals.

December 17

Battle at Goldsboro, mostly artillery. Terrible destruction of the rebels, only one [of our] artillery men loss in six hour fight.

September 13, 1863

In command of 150 men at work on Battery Gregg. Got a daguerreotype at Cooleys to send home.

Captain James Halsey Linsley of the 10th Connecticut Volunteers was wounded a third time during the charge of Fort Gregg, Virginia on August 2, 1865. (by Haas & Peale. Library of Congress, Prints & Photographs Division, LC-cwpb-04739)

October 12

Officer of Day. Find myself very lame from strain and injuries by the sand bags yesterday. Gave out the state bounties.

January 1, 1864

Anniversary of President's proclamation of Freedom celebrated by Freedmen of Florida.

July 26, 1864

I was sent with sharpshooters to assist 11th Me in retaking the line and a few minutes after I received a severe wound in head and was carried to camp.

July 27

Removed to hospital at Point of rocks, rough riding over corduroy and stumps.

July 29

Arrive at Chesapeake Hospital Fort Monroe where my wound begins to receive proper care. Roughest experiences at front preferable to Hospital.

October 8

Leave Hospital for the front.

October 11

Rejoin regiment and receive commission of 1st Lieutenant. A pleasant greeting from the men, brigade commander, and officers. Homelike to sit again by the campfires and listen to what had been done in my absence.

November 25

Our turkeys arrive and the soldiers have a reminiscence of home which is substantial.

Officers Hospital[232]

Annapolis, Md
Oct 7th 1864

Dear Mother

*I applied yesterday for orders to
go to the regiment which I received
today and start tomorrow morning.
I look [at] the scab of my wound yester
day and considered it healed. I do not
wish to remain in Hospital a day
after I am fit for duty.
There are too many officers
willing to shirk duty and sacrifice
honor by lying around the Hospital
Dear Mother I trust you will not
worry too much about me and feel
reconciled to my remaining in the
army while the war lasts. The
same Benevolent Providence watches
over me here as at home
I feel that the last three years
have not been spent entirely in vain
by me I feel that my character has
been growing I trust in some respect
better. I love my friends
better and my country more than when
the war commenced.
I could scarcely leave the service now
with honor. I felt my determination (?)
the other day when seeing the poor
fellows who came down from Richmond
and as long as the son of any other mother
remained unreleased from that cruel bondage.
Ever your affectionate son*

Halsey

Camp 10th Conn Vols

In the Field Va.
Dec. 6th 1864

My Dear Kate

*Yours of Oct. 23rd
was duly received and I trust
you will forgive me if I have
been over punctilious in writing
your reply to my last before I
write again. Yours was received
this morning and I feel that
Heaven has been kinder to me
than I deserved in blessing me
with your confidence and
affection.
   The people of Connecticut
have it less worked up to the
necessity of recruiting the wasted
ranks of the Tenth They have
seen its bullet riddled and
battles stained banner carried through their streets in
political processions
Accordingly they have sent
us two Invoices of Substitutes
gathered now nearly every nation,
and Kindred and tongue under
Heaven. some of which are Mexicans
Greeks, Swedes, Irish, Spanish,
Canadians, Italian, Scotch,
English, Swiss, Brunswickers,
Germans, French etc. etc. We have
been busy all day arming and
equiping them.
I fear I am already
late for the mail so good
night and believe me ever*

Affectionately yours
James H. Linsley
Capt. 10th Conn Vols.

232 Linsley letters, Southern Historical Collection at
the Louis Round Wilson Special Collection Library,
University of North Carolina at Chapel Hill, www.lib.
unc.edu/wilson.

JOHN S. LINSLEY, JR.

**10th CVI, hospital steward, enlisted 14 August 1862, to Co. A 1st Battalion 14th Regiment
discharged 15 October 1865; pension #829692 for the soldier and later for his widow Mary**

John S. Linsley, Jr. of New Haven, age 24, enlisted at Fort Trumbull, New London on 14 August 1862 as a private in the 10th CVI, unassigned and was discharged on 14 October 1862. He reenlisted in Co. A 1st Battalion 14th U.S. Regiment on 15 October 1862. Upon reaching camp in Virginia, he was appointed hospital steward and treated many soldiers during the outbreak of typhoid fever and contracted the disease. After the Battle of Fredericksburg, he returned to Fort Trumbull, New London and continued as hospital steward. In May 1864 he went before the Army Medical Board at New York and received his appointment as Hospital Steward for the U.S. Army and was sent for duty at Bedloe's Island, New York, a hospital for officers. Later he was transferred to Battery Barracks and Transit Hospital and matriculated from Bellevue Medical College.[233] He was discharged at Transit Hospital, New York City on 15 October 1865. He was the brother of Benjamin M. and James H. Linsley. He was graduated in 1866 from the New York Homeopathic College.

He applied for an invalid pension on 28 July 1899 due to age related illnesses. At the time of his enlistment he was described as five feet six inches tall, fair complexion, light hair, blue eyes and was a medical student. He was married at Bridgeport by Rev. Alexander M. Hopper on 10 October 1866 to Mary Walker

---

233 Letter from his daughter Mary Linsley Horton, in *Connecticut Linsleys*, 108.

Lyon. He was age 28, born at Northford, living at New York City; she was age 26, born and living at Bridgeport. Neither were previously married or divorced. They had four children: Mary, born on 14 October 1867; Lillian, born on 8 October 1870; Edyth, born on 23 March 1873; and Gertie [Gertrude], born on 22 January 1875 who died before 1897. The first three daughters were living in 1915. Cornelius J. Horton married Mary Linsley in 1889.

After his discharge he lived at New York City from 1865 to 1902 and was a practicing physician; to Redding, Connecticut from 1902 to 1905; and 1905 to Baldwin Place, New York. They summered in Northford.

Dr. John Stephen Linsley, Jr. died at Baldwin Place, Somers, Westchester Co., New York on 18 March 1917 and was buried in Northford Cemetery. His name appears on the Northford Veterans' Monument. He was born at Northford on 19 January 1838, son of John Stephen Linsley and Eliza Ann Halsey.

Mary W. Linsley of Baldwin Place, New York applied for a widow's pension on 23 April 1917. She moved to the home of her daughter Edyth Linsley at Plainville immediately after the death of Dr. Linsley. Mary W. Linsley died at Plainville on 18 May 1932 and was buried in Northford Cemetery. She was born at Bridgeport on 12 April 1840, daughter of Horace Lyon and Mary Eleanor Beach.

John S. Linsley was near death from typhoid fever at camp near Falmouth, Virginia in March 1863. His brother Maltby was allowed to nurse him and their father John S. Linsley, Sr. made the trip to see his sons after Maltby Linsley also got sick. Benjamin Maltby Linsley was presumed killed after the Battle of the Wilderness in 1864. Excerpts of several letters from the family follow:[234]

March 8th, 1863.
Camp Near Falmouth, Va.

Dear Father; God's goodness still spares
him [John] in the land
of the living. Last Sabbath John was
very low this Sabbath Morn he is in
agony. Oh! how I wish I could relieve him
but I must trust in the Mercy of my Savior
his will be done.
John's moaning is pitiful, for two
nights he was delirious — yesterday he
called the names of each of the family first
"good bye father" – next he called "Harvey"

in the Afternoon called "Mrs. Linsley" several times
very loudly when I asked him what he wanted and
tried to console he said he wanted mother.
He wanted milk too – wanted me to
get him some fresh milk – from our cows.
He is not able to speak now and I can not
understand, it seems that a very short time
must decide his case for life or death.

Maltby

234 Linsley letters, Southern Historical Collection, University of North Carolina, www.lib.unc.edu/wilson .

[March 1863]
Hospital Tent   Near Falmouth, Va

My Dear Wife

*   When I maild my last*
I designed to have written you sooner than this
I left Washington 8 oclock Thursday morning on
board a steamer most densly crowded with men
mostly soldiers who had been home on furlough
now returning I could obtain no seat or rest for
my foot. We arrived at Aqia Creek about 11 oclock
distance 55 miles. After a good deal of inquiry
found the Hospital tent of the Regiment.
And am happy & thankful to the good Lord
that I found my dear boys comfortably well.
Maltby met me at the door with sallow eyes
having been troubled with jaundice. Johns eyes
were bright which filled me with thankfulness.
At this moment a dead soldier is laid at the tent
side who died last night at another Hospital.
I have just reminded John of his obligation to God,
for his goodness, in sparing him while others fall –
O! my God fill his soul with thy goodness.
My dear Wife still pray for me and yours
here do not worry about me

*   As ever your loving Husband*
*   J S Linsley*

Camp Bear Falmouth Va.
Sunday March 15th. 1863.

My Dear Mother; Brother John is
very much better and I am still
permitted to take some care of
him. I hope I may be able by this
letter to relieve you of much un-
necessary anxiety. We need be very thank-
ful that God has been so merciful to
us. How much prayer can accomplish!
How much I owe you and Hannah who
have always done so much for me
I hope the time will come when I can
make some demonstration of reciprocal
affection by deeds.

*   Much love to all.*
*   Your loving Son Maltby.*

Elias O. Norton of Guilford enlisted on 14 November 1861 in the First Light Battery. Transcriptions
of his letters are at the Guilford Free Library. (Beecher, First Light Battery, I:415)

ELIAS O. NORTON

1st LA, private, enlisted 3 November 1861, discharged 13 November 1864
pension #832543 for the soldier and his widow Anna

Elias O. Norton, age 18, of Guilford enlisted at Meriden on 3 November 1861 and was mustered in on 14 November 1861 as a private in the 1st LA for a term of three years. With his regiment he saw action in South Carolina and at the Battles of Drewry's Bluff, Bermuda Hundred, Deep Bottom, and Petersburg, Virginia. He was discharged with the rest of his regiment at Fortress Monroe, Virginia on 13 November 1864 when his term expired. His brother William B. Norton of Guilford was in the same regiment.

Comrade Elias O. Norton later recalled the action at the Battle of Proctor's Creek: [235]

> *We had gone into Battery under the brow of*
> *the bluff, so that our horses might be protected,*
> *and moved our pieces by hand to the front, and*
> *commenced firing. I was lead driver on the left*
> *piece of the left section, I had just dismounted*

---

235 Beecher, *History First Light Battery*, I: 415-416.

and stood by the head of my near horse, holding
a line from both of them, when a spherical-case
shell came from the enemy's line and killed
Comrade Henry L. Wilmot, who was Number 2,
instantly, hit my near horse in the forehead, both
of the swing horses and one of the wheel horses.
At the same time the swing driver had one of
his arms taken off above the elbow, and Lieut.
Metcalf, who was hitching his horse to the limber,
was mortally wounded. Lieut. Metcalf and
myself, with the swing driver, all stood in line
and I have often wondered how I escaped getting hit.
When I looked round to see what had happened I did not see the swing
or wheel driver, and did not know until after the fight that the swing driver
Comrade Charles Bissell had lost his arm. I found myself alone with six
horses, four of them badly wounded and all of them pretty well mixed up.
I went to work and succeeded in getting everything off the wounded horses.
except the surcingle and piled them into the limber. It took me some
time to accomplish it, as I had to duck quite often on account of
the shells from the enemy. I then took the two horses that were
uninjured and with the limber started for the
rear to get some more horses which were in
reserve. When I got about half through the
woods I saw Comrade Hart Landon sitting at
the foot of a tree fanning himself with his cap.

ON PICKET.

An etching of members of the 1st Connecticut Light Battery while on picket duty. (Beecher, First Light Battery, I:177)

Stopping my team I asked him what was the
matter with him and he replied that he was
wounded and not able to walk. I lifted him on
top of my load of harness and he rode there
until he crossed the railroad, when it hurt him
so much that he wanted to get down. I stopped
and took him off and hoisted him on my back,
holding him with one arm and leading the
two horses with the other. I had carried
him quite a distance in that way when I looked
ahead and saw the wheel driver coming toward
us. I stopped and put the comrade on the ground until the driver came to
us. I asked him if he would look after the horses while I attended to my
comrade. I soon found two soldiers with a
stretcher, and placing Comrade Landon on it,
sent him to the hospital. I did not see Comrade
Landon again until I was discharged and reached
home.

He applied for an invalid pension on 14 July 1890 under the act of 27 June 1890. After his discharge he lived at Bristol, Guilford, and New Haven. He was a member of the Merriam Post No. 8 G.A.R. of Meriden and a charter member of the Guilford Light Battery, Platoon A. At the time of his enlistment he was described as five feet eight inches tall, light complexion, brown hair, gray eyes, occupation farmer. He was admitted to the Fitch's Soldier Home[236] at Noroton Heights on 15 November 1907 and was dishonorably discharged on 18 March 1908 for drunkenness and creating a disturbance in the ward. Albert A. May of the Merriam Post was appointed his conservator by the Guilford Probate Court on 18 May 1908.[237] Norton was admitted to New Haven Hospital on 18 October 1908 and readmitted to the Soldiers' Home on 25 October 1908. He was a resident of the National Home in Hampton, Virginia in late 1913. He was admitted to Noroton Heights several more times, discharged on numerous occasions for "drunkenness, absence without leave, and disregard for the rules of the home." He was last admitted on 27 January 1914. His sister Elizabeth N. Bates of Guilford is mentioned in his file. "He resided in Guilford until about ten years ago [1907] and went to New Haven where he resided about five years after which he went to the Soldiers home in Noroton where he lived until his death."[238]

Elias Ogden Norton died at the Fitch's Soldier Home on 16 February 1917 and was buried in Stony Creek Cemetery, Branford. He was born at Guilford on 25 July 1844, son of Joseph O. Norton and Susan Morgan.[239]

Anna Eliza Smith was married to the soldier at Bristol by Rev. N. J. Seeley on 15 November 1866, they were both of Guilford. Neither were previously married or divorced. They had one son Edwin Elias, born

---

236 Fitch's Home for Soldiers, Deceased Veterans Discharge Files 1882-1932, box 11, file 2717.
237 May later resigned as conservator "I want nothing to do with him and I am mighty glad of it I can assure you. He is a bad egg." The toll on Civil War soldiers and mental health issues is a relatively new area of study, see Michael Sturgess, "Soldier's Heart," *Connecticut Explored,* Spring 2011, Volume 9, No. 2, 44.
238 Obituary, *Shore Line Times,* 22 February 1917, 4.
239 Alvan Talcott, *Families of Early Guilford, Connecticut* (Baltimore, Maryland: Genealogical Publishing Co., 1984), 917.

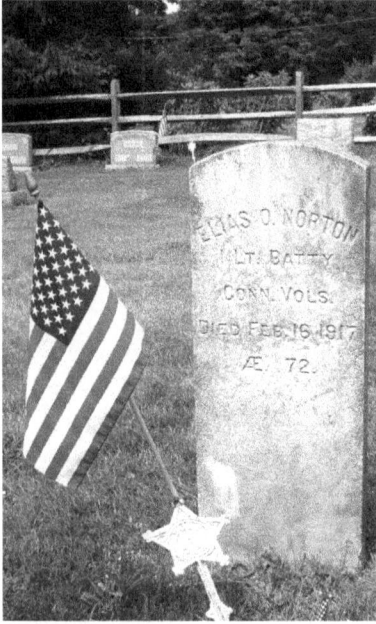

on 15 November 1867, living at New Haven in 1920. She applied for a pension on Elias' record in 1908. Elias Norton deserted her on 15 September 1907 and she moved to New Haven to live with her son. They were never divorced. After much difficulty and many affidavits including letters by commissioners and the soldier's conservator who stated "she was a person of good moral character," she received half of his pension on 28 September 1910 under the act of 3 March 1899 because he failed to provide support.[240]

After the soldier's death; Anna Norton, age 71, of New Haven applied for a full widow's pension on 6 March 1917. She died at New Haven on 22 September 1920 and was buried in Stony Creek Cemetery.[241] She was born at Bath, England on August 29, 1846; daughter of Thomas H. & Ann Smith.

The Guilford Free Library has the transcriptions of forty letters written by Elias O. Norton to his family in Guilford during the course of the war. The letters are quite detailed about the activity of his regiment, his health, the food they ate, and questions about home. Some of his letters are religious and testify to his love of God. Some excerpts:

Beaufort, S. C. April 18-19 /62

Your advice in requesting me to seek salvation shows that you have a great desire in my welfare, allow me to thank you, for your kind advice. The army is a very trying place for a young man, for there are all sorts of temptations and evil companions all around him. I have not had a drop of liquor since we came here and I don't expect to again.

Beaufort, S. C. June 12th / 62

We had the satisfaction of throwing some shell over their sand fort on the main land and they scattered some I can tell you. They are terribly afraid of artillery. Probably Richmond will be ours before you receive this.

Beaufort, S. C. June 26th /62

Bill is up to James island near Charleston [his brother William]. He says that they can see the rebel flag on Fort Sumpter. God Speed the time when he can see the stars and stripes floating on it instead of that ridiculous flag called the secesh.

July 6th 1862

I cannot believe that Gen mccellen noble army is cut to pieces. I gues that we are stuck for a year or more but that does not worry me.

---

240 Norton tried to prevent her from receiving part of his pension.
241 Branford Sexton Records 1884-1932, 96; no gravestone was found.

Beaufort, S. C. July 13th 1862

We expect we shall go to Virginia to join McClellan army. I wish I could send you some figs, they taste prety good. I have often thought how I should like to be home and taste of those apples.

Wednesday July 16th 1862

I suppose that you have seen the illustration of the fight in Frank Leslie[242] on James Island. It was a hard fight for a short time and it is a miracle that none of our boys got hurt or killed. The Evarts boys wasnt any where near the fight. They had the gun fever the morning before the fight and lay in their tent. We have plenty of green corn, cucumbers, tomatoes, squashes if we have the money to pay for them. We get first rate watermelons by paying 20 cts. We can get ink by paying 10ct and for those that chew can have the pleasure of paying 20cts.

July 28 1862 Beaufort, S. C.

I think that the war is not so near at an end as it was two or three months ago. I suppose that they will have to draft in G [Guilford] to raise the number of men required. There are some that I should like to see drafted.

Beaufort, August 4th 1862

We are both well and in firstrate spirits. Although there is hundreds of sick men on this island yet we have never been visited with sickness. But still our turn may come yet. We have had fresh-meat soup with onions and turnips in it for dinner and it was very nice. I had a rattle snake jump at me one night [while on picket duty] but I jumped out of his way and saved myself. There is all kinds of animals up ther such as alligators, rats and these large kinds of lizards. We have thunder showers most every night and some very hard ones to. You cant begin to think how extremely hot it is here. You don't know anything about hot weather in old Guilford. There is more danger dying by sickness than getting shot.

Camp Stevens near the ferry

Beaufort, S. C. Sept 7th /62

I have not seen a stone or rock of any kind since we left N. Y. What would Father think to go where he could not see a bit of stone wall or stone of any kind.

Beaufort, S. C. Jan 29th/63

We are both well and hope that this find you enjoying the same blessing. We have just got our stables covered so that it is much warmer for our horses. I have not spoke to a white woman in over a year what do you think of that. I would give all my old boots if I could be home to night and have a talk with you. I would like to have a skate on Blake's pond to night for about an hour and then go up to the house and get a piece of mince pie and set over a good fire and crack walnuts.

Beaufort, S. C. April 10th 1863

We left Beaufort last Saturday and have 12 pieces of artillery on this boat and are now in Stone

---

242 *Frank Leslie's Illustrated Newspaper* also called *Leslie's Weekly*. Was an important source of news about the war especially the engravings of battles and soldiers' daily life.

inlet six or seven miles from Charleston but we left and came back to Beaufort. I don't know why we came back without doing any fighting. We have a prayer meeting in the church to night and I can't find words to express the happiness and joy that I have experienced since I resolved to become a christian.

Beaufort, S. C. May 15th 1863

I guess I won't write any more for I am not very strong yet. I forgot to say I had the Typhoid fever and I think the doctor broke it up very quick.

Beaufort, S. C. May 25th 1863

We are both well. I am on duty again but not very strong. Lost about twelve pounds of flesh while I was sick.

Bermuda Hundred June 26th

There is heavy firing to day in the direction of Petersburg. President Lincoln passed along the lines the other day with Gen Butler and staff. That was the first time that I ever see him.

The 1st Connecticut Light Artillery spent much of 1862 and 1863 at Beaufort, South Carolina (by Timothy H. O'Sullivan, Library of Congress Prints & Photographs Division, LC-cwpb-00735)

THOMAS O'BRIEN

Co. B 27th CVI, private, enlisted 5 September 1862, prisoner, mustered out 27 July 1863
pension #680992 for the soldier and later for his widow Ellen

Thomas O'Brien, age 31, of North Haven enlisted at New Haven on 5 September 1862 and was mustered in on 3 October 1862 as a private in Co. B 27th CVI for a term of nine months. He fought at the Battle of Fredericksburg on 13 December 1862 with the rest of the company. He was captured at the Battle of Chancellorsville, Virginia on 3 May 1863, held prisoner at Richmond, and was paroled at City Point, Virginia on 14 May 1863. He reported to Camp Parole, Maryland on 16 May 1863, was sent to Washington, D.C. on 20 May 1863 and spent the remainder of his service at Camp Convalescent, Virginia. With the rest of the Chancellorsville paroled prisoners, he rejoined the Regiment at Baltimore on 20 July 1863. O'Brien was mustered out with the rest of his regiment at New Haven on 27 July 1863.

He applied for an invalid pension on 2 October 1890 under the act of 27 June 1890. He was living at 114 Canal Street, New Haven and was described as five feet nine inches tall, light complexion, blue eyes, brown hair, occupation farmer. "I misplaced my collar bone while building Breastworks in the night with Timber at Chancellorsville, Va. I fell down and a Timber fell on me striking me on the Left Shoulder. I contracted my Deafness while a Prisoner at Ginennius [sic Guinea] Station on our way to Richmond by being exposed in the Rain taking a severe Cold which settled in my Head. I first discovered my varicose veins right after the Battle of Fredericksburg Dec. 13 1862." He states he was born at County Cork, Ireland on 24 December 1833.

Thomas O'Brien died at New Haven on died 21 March 1908 and was buried in St. Bernard's Cemetery, New Haven.

Ellen O'Brien of New Haven applied for a widow's pension on 25 April 1908. She was married to the soldier under the name of Ellen Gibbons at New Haven by Rev. P. Mulholland on 7 June 1876. He was age 43, living at North Haven, she was age 35, living at New Haven, both were born in Ireland. The pension application was referred for special examination to determine the question of legal widowhood and a possible first marriage for the soldier. He stated in his application on 4 June 1898 that he was married first to Eliza Fitzgerald. No record could be found of a first marriage. After considering a number of depositions and the lack of evidence, the pension board determined Ellen was legally married to Thomas O'Brien. Abstracts of some of the depositions are included due to their genealogical significance.

Ellen O'Brien stated "I can't tell you my age. I was born in Ireland and came here when I was about 12 or 13 years old, before the war. I think Buchanan was president. I lived in New York City before coming to New Haven, sewing dresses in a factory. I was married to Thomas O'Brien in 1876 here in New Haven. My maiden name was Ellen Mary Teresa Gibbons. I came to New Haven three or four years before my marriage. I did not know him prior to coming to New Haven. I had no brothers and sisters. Both my mother and father had been married twice. I had three half brothers on Mother's side; William, Patrick and Willis Delly. On father's side was William and James Gibbons. James was in the Irish Brigade that went out of [New] York State. He was in the Soldiers Home in Milwaukie last I knew. He is a pensioner. Patrick Delly was in the Rebel Army. He had a home in Vicksburg, Mississippi. My mother died there about 1865 or 1866. William Gibbons was in Sacramento, Calif. some 20 years ago. My cousin Wm. Fay of New York City, I used to correspond with him. Wm. and Willis Delly were in the South when I came over to America and I never saw them. I came to the United States with Patrick and Wm. Fay. William was in Scotts Cavalry. He lived in New Haven when I came here. He was married and I came to visit him. I got work and stayed. He had no children. They left New Haven before I was married. Where he went I don't know, never heard from him since. There were four half sisters: Mary Ann Deely was in the South when I came over; Bridget Gibbons, Sabrina Gibbons, and myself. They were in New York when I came over. They were all married. Kate Sabrina married Martin Fay and she had ten children, including Wm and Patrick referred to above. Bridget married Pat. Deely. They had no children. They always lived in Oak St., NY. They are dead. They are all dead except possibly Wm. and Patrick Fay."

Did your husband have any brothers or sisters? "I heard him say he had one brother John and one sister Mary. I never saw them. I think they were older. My husband was born in Ireland. He said he was 17 or 18 years old when he came to this Country. He came right to New Haven. His mother and father were dead since he was six months old. He never saw them [his brother and sister] since he was a child. He first lived with Willys B. Hemingway at Quinnipiac Pt., Mrs. [Hemingway] is still alive. He worked as a deck hand on a steamboat from New Haven to New York. After our marriage he worked at Bell Dock for the Steam Boat Co. My husband had some cousins here, David Foley. He was in the army. David Foley died in New Haven a couple of years ago. He was never married."

Were you ever married before? "No sir, I was not." Was your husband ever married before? "I don't think so." Did he have children before he married you? "No, the children belong to me. I have three children by Thomas O'Brien. They are all dead."

"I was married June 6, 1876. The witnesses were sisters Helena Buchanan and Martha N., wife of Thos. McGuire. I boarded at their mother's house and worked as a domestic. I was married in the house. Our oldest child Augustin Thomas was born the second of Dec. 1876. The next was Ellen and Sabrina, no middle names, only about a year difference in age. They were born in this house. My husband died here."

Your husband in 1898 stated he had been married to Elizabeth Fitzgerald before he married you. "My husband or anyone else never told me anything about it. I never knew any relative of Elizabeth Fitzgerald."[243]

Nora Foley, age 43, of New Haven, widow of William Foley, stated "I have known claimant Ellen O'Brien some 30 years. My husband was a distant cousin of Thomas O'Brien. My husband's father brought Thomas up until he was old enough to be on his own. I never knew Thomas had a previous marriage."[244]

The first wife's niece, Catherine E. Mackey, was interviewed. "My mother told me that Thomas O'Brien was married to Eliza Fitzgerald in New Haven before the war. After they were married they lived with her parents Patrick and Elizabeth Fitzgerald in Woodbridge. They had a farm there. But, grand-father Fitzgerald died in Ireland. My father Garrett Fitzgerald was Eliza's brother. I was born in New Haven. When I was 11 years old we moved to Cheshire. My parents later came back here and I have lived here ever since. I remember when Thomas O'Brien came home from the army, his wife Eliza was not in New Haven and he couldn't find her. He came to our house at Cheshire for about a week and gave his canteen to me. I don't know whatever became of Eliza. I understand Thomas had a little girl he left with his wife when he went in the army who would be 47 years old if alive. Mother said she was the same age as my brother John who is dead. I don't remember if I ever saw her. Mother told me the little girl died but when or where I don't know. Thomas O'Brien never lived with Eliza after the war."

Ellen O'Brien, widow of Thomas O'Brien died on 23 August 1918.

---

243 Deposition, Ellen O'Brien of New Haven, 1 February 1909, in the pension file of Thomas O'Brien.
244 Deposition, Nora Foley of New Haven, 1 February 1909, in the pension file of Thomas O'Brien.

MICHAEL O'NEIL

Co. B 27th CVI, private, enlisted 1 September 1862, prisoner, mustered out 27 July 1863
pension #896986 for his widow Mary

Michael O'Neil, age 20, of Branford enlisted on 1 September 1862 and was mustered in on 3 October 1862 as a private in Co. B 27th Connecticut Volunteer Infantry for a term of nine months. He fought at the Battle of Fredericksburg on 13 December 1862 with the rest of the company. "Mike ONiel is doing first rate Seems to enjoy himself well."[245] He was captured at the Battle of Chancellorsville, Virginia on 3 May 1863, held prisoner at Richmond, and was paroled at City Point, Virginia on 14 May 1863. He reported to Camp Parole, Maryland on 16 May 1863, was sent to Washington, D.C. on 20 May 1863 and spent the remainder of his service at Camp Convalescent, Virginia. With the rest of the Chancellorsville paroled prisoners, he rejoined the Regiment at Baltimore on 20 July 1863. O'Neil was mustered out with the rest of his regiment at New Haven on 27 July 1863.

"Michael O'Neil was a loyal soldier with devotion to duty."[246] "After the war we returned to Branford. We worked together in the Branford Lock Shop. I never heard he reenlisted."[247]

---

245 Letter, Samuel Beach to home, 4 January 1863.
246 Affidavit, Dr. Robert B. Goodyear of North Haven, 12 November 1919, in the pension file of Michael O'Neil.
247 Deposition, Obed L. Tyler of Noroton, 23 May 1920, in the pension file of Michael O'Neil.

He never applied for a pension, and did not join the Branford G.A.R. One comrade said he did attend reunions. Michael O'Neil died at Branford on 1 March 1918 and was buried there in St. Agnes Cemetery. He was born in Ireland on 6 October 1842, son of John O'Neil and Mary Flarherty.

Mary O'Neil applied for a widow's pension on 27 March 1918. Her application was sent for special examination concerning Michael O'Neil's first marriage, and why he never applied for a pension though he was eligible. A question of desertion was often proposed in these cases. A sister of his first wife was found, "My name is Mary Josephine Johnston, widow of Thomas Johnston, age 83 years. My sister Catherine O'Connor was married to Michael O'Neil, we called him John O'Neil. I believe his father's name was Michael, a farmer, and John as we called him, or Michael, Jr. was a locksmith from Branford, Connecticut. I first met him in Hamilton, Ontario, Canada. I did not know him until after his marriage to my sister. They were married in Kingston. I do not know why he was in Canada. My sister Catherine went for a visit to Kingston and he was boarding next door. He was a nice fellow."

Did you know if Mr. O'Neil had run away from the Army? "Well, I heard him tell father and mother he and a lot of others had been in jail. My sister only knew him six months before they married. There is one child born to Catherine who is yet surviving, Minnie Whalen, of New Haven, Connecticut. Her name was really Mary but we called her Minnie. There were two other children born to Catherine who died in infancy. Catherine died in child birth at the birth of the third one. The second was born in Branford, Connecticut and the third one in Hamilton, same place where Minnie was born. I believe his marriage to my sister was his first. There must be a record of her death in Saint Mary's Cathedral in Hamilton. I am the only surviving sister. Ellen, widow of my brother Thomas was still living in Hamilton last year. No, I never did hear talk of Michael O'Neil deserting the U.S. Army. I did know he married again and had seven children. That information came from a letter from his daughter Minnie. Yes, I saw him after Catherine died when he came for the child, Mary or Minnie. He had left her with mother and we had her about six months until he came for her. That was the last time I ever saw him or my niece. He took the child to his parents who lived then about four miles from Branford as I understand it. Patrick O'Connor was my father and my mother was born Catherine Kelleher."[248]

A record was found at St. Mary's Cathedral at Hamilton, Ontario, Canada. Catherine O'Connor O'Neil died at Hamilton on March 22, 1868 age 23 in child birth.

The pension board was still not satisfied with some of the information about the case. Mary Whalen of New Haven was interviewed. "I was born July 13, 1865 in Hamilton, Ontario, Canada. My occupation is domestic for Mrs. Reed, 374 Orchard Street, New Haven. My parents were Michael O'Neil and Catherine O'Connor. My parents were married in Hamilton, Canada but I can't tell you the date. I was the only child born to them. You have shown me a picture and I can safely say it is my father Michael O'Neil who was a soldier in the Civil War in the 27th Connecticut. He had no other service that I know of. He was born in Ireland but reared in Branford. My father never told me why he went to Canada. My mother died in Hamilton in March when I was two. My father remarried a woman named Mary Ahern and there is no sociability between us. His parents John and Mary O'Neil brought me up. My mother had a brother Thomas O'Connor, he died in Hamilton two years ago. I am the widow of William Whalen."[249]

"I am 76 years of age and have lived in and around Branford all my life. I knew the O'Neil family very well. John O'Neil had two sons, Michael and John, and I think three daughters. One daughter Katherine Shay is still living, I believe, but is in the Sanatorium at Norwich, Connecticut, age 69 years of age. My

248 Deposition, Mary Josephine Johnston of Portland, Oregon, 12 September 1920, in the pension file of Michael O'Neil.
249 Deposition, Mary Whalen of New Haven, 17 August 1920, in the pension file of Michael O'Neil.

brother, George Baldwin, served in the same company as Michael O'Neil. My brother George died in the service. It runs in my mind that Michael left here and married a woman in Canada. I never heard that he reenlisted. No, I never heard he was a deserter, I don't think he was. By his first marriage he had a daughter Mary. I have met her many times. She worked for a number of years for the Beach family of East Main Street, my relatives."[250]

Michael O'Neil was married second at Branford by Rev. John Sheriden of St. Mary's Church on 6 January 1872 to Mary Ahern. In the file is a copy of the 1890 Federal census for Michael O'Neil and family at Branford, New Haven County, enumerated on 3 June 1890. The family consisted of: Michael age 47, Mary age 44, John N. age 16, Francis M. age 14, Florence E. age 13, Catherine A. age 10, Charles W. age 8, and James E. age 5. He had one sister Catherine Shay, living in 1920; and a daughter Mrs. Whalen living at 374 Orchard Street, New Haven. "His brother John O'Neil went west 40 years ago and I don't know what became of him."[251]

On her application, Mary O'Neil states that she was married to the soldier on 22 October 1862 at Branford and his first wife died on 7 July 1866. This conflicts with the Branford vital record marriage date of 6 January 1872. That record states Michael O'Neal age 29, born Ireland, of Branford, was married at Branford by Rev. Sheriden on 6 January 1872 to Mary Ahern, age 23, born Ireland, of Madison.[252] A deposition by Mary O'Neil in 1919 confirms the 1872 date.[253] She was not previously married. "He said he went to Canada right after discharge because it was dull here and he found work in Canada. He told me he had been married in Canada in Saint Catherine on July 7, 1866. Her name was Catherine O'Connor and that she died one year after their marriage. My home has been in Branford for over 50 years. I do not think Mr. O'Neil ever applied for a pension."[254]

Mary O'Neil died at Branford on January 18, 1935 and was buried there in St. Agnes Cemetery.[255] She was born at Waterford Co., Ireland on March 17, 1851, daughter of John Ahern and Mary Dusee. She was living at 53 Harrison Avenue, Branford with her daughters Florence E. O'Neil and Kathryn A. O'Neil.

---

250 Deposition, Helen Baldwin of Branford, 17 August 1920, in the pension file of Michael O'Neil.
251 Deposition, Mary O'Neil of Branford, 19 October 1920, in the pension file of Michael O'Neil.
252 Branford Vital Records, 1863-1895, 143.
253 Deposition, Mary O'Neil of Branford, 15 March 1919, in the pension file of Michael O'Neil.
254 Deposition, Mary O'Neil of Branford, 15 March 1919, in the pension file of Michael O'Neil.
255 Branford Sexton Records, 1933-1966, 3. A gravestone for Michael and Mary O'Neil does not appear in the Hale Collection and one could not be located.

Albert E. Plant of Branford enlisted on 7 August 1862 as a private in Co. B 15th CVI.
(by Stayner & Smith, Newbern, N. C.; Branford Historical Society photograph collection)

ALBERT E. PLANT

Co. B 15th CVI, private, enlisted 7 April 1862, prisoner, mustered out 27 June 1865
pension #476990 for the soldier

Albert E. Plant[256] of Branford enlisted at New Haven on 7 August 1862 and was mustered on 25 August 1862 as a private in Co. B 15th CVI for a term of three years. "His regiment was attached to General Getty's Division of the Ninth Army Corps." He saw action at Fredericksburg, Virginia on 13 December 1862, during the Siege of Suffolk, Virginia in the spring of 1863, and in the Peninsula Campaign of July 1863. He was captured with much of his regiment at the Battle of Kinston, North Carolina on 8 March 1865, confined at Libby Prison, Richmond on 23 March, and paroled at Boulware's & Cox's wharf on 26 March 1865. He reported to Camp Parole, Maryland on 30 March 1865, received a thirty day furlough and afterwards reported to Camp Convalescent, Virginia. Plant was mustered out with the rest of his regiment at New Bern, North Carolina on 27 June 1865 and discharged at New Haven on 12 July 1865. He was described as a "Good Soldier."

He applied for an invalid pension on 6 August 1889. At the time of his enlistment he was described as five feet four inches tall, dark complexion, brown hair, hazel eyes, occupation farmer. At Fredericksburg, Virginia in December 1862 he contracted rheumatism while on picket duty on the banks of the Rappahannock. He contracted deafness from the firing of artillery at Newport News, Virginia in the spring of 1863.

---

256 For his biography see Beers, *Commemorative Biographical Record of New Haven County*, 1228.

He was married at East Haven by Rev. D. William Havens on 20 September 1871 to Bessie W. Upson. She died at Branford on 4 September 1910 and was buried there in Center Cemetery.[257] They had three children (living in 1898): Albert B., born on 14 October 1872; Mary E., born on 5 June 1887; and Ray U., born on 26 February 1890. He was a charter member of the Mason Rogers Post No. 7 G.A.R. of Branford.

Albert Edward Plant died at Branford on 21 December 1914 and was buried there in Center Cemetery. There was a G.A.R. marker on his gravesite in 1934 and 2011. He was born at Branford on 6 November 1841, son of William Plant and Polly Beach.[258]

While he was in the service his father William Plant died at Branford on 28 March 1864.

Camp opposite Fredericksburg, Va
Saturday Dec 27th 62

My Dear Father

*I received
your very kind letter yesterday.
I also received one from Louisa
and was very much pleased
to hear from you both. It
seems by your writing that you
had not heard from me since
the battle and could not tell
whether I was in the land of
the living or no. But rest
assured that I am and enjoying
good health. I never was better
in my life. I weigh without
my overcoat - 124 lbs Which is
not very bad for the
fodder the US gives me.
You said in your letter that
you thought the battle of*

*Fredericksburg was the greatest
battle ever fought on this continent.*

*I think so too. On Saturday the
firing was incessant; fairly deafening
at times. I do not wish to see
anything like it again. You also
said that you thought a repetition
of the same would cause a Revolution
at the North. That is the mind
of every soldier as far as I can
learn. They differ from you in
on[e] thing They don't wish to wait
for a Repetition. They want the
thing settled now; and so do I.
I will draw you a map of our
position during the battle and
as near as I can the battle
ground. The places where we lay
at different times I have made a
cross so that you can see
the part our Regt took in
the fight. It is not very plain
but you can get some idea from it.
That is the way it looked to me
when I was there. You also*

---

257 Branford Vital Records, deaths, 1910.
258 Branford Vital Records, Town Meeting Book A, 233.

*gave me some good advice which
I thank you very much for it
and will try and profit by it.
I think that this war will do good
as well as evil. It will learn those
that have a home how to prize it.
Your hogs done well better than
I expected. I hope everything will do as well.
By the papers I see that Hay is
rising and Barley commands a good
price Good. Have you
sold anything yet. Well Father I
will close this letter now. Write me
as soon as you receive this. Your letters
do me so much good. My love
to Mother and all at home*

*With much love I
remain your Dear son A. E. Plant
I sent you a 10$ Check.*[259]

*After the war Albert E. Plant owned a large farm on
the Branford Hills. (Beers, Biographical Record of New
Haven County, 1228)*

---

259 A copy of this letter and his discharge paper are in the Branford Historical Society archives, RG 1, box 28, folder 2.

*A map drawn by Albert E. Plant for his father showing the positions of various forces
at the Battle of Fredericksburg. (Branford Historical Society archives)*

(Photographic History of the Civil War, 6:271)

GEORGE S. ROGERS

Co. B 27th CVI, corporal, enlisted 25 August 1862, prisoner, mustered out 27 July 1863
reenlisted U.S. Navy 1 September 1864, discharged 1 September 1865
pension #391838 for his army service and #34921 for the Navy

George S. Rogers, age 20, of Branford enlisted on 25 August 1862 and was mustered in on 3 October 1862 as a corporal in Co. B 27th Connecticut Volunteer Infantry for a term of nine months. He fought at the Battle of Fredericksburg on 13 December 1862 with the rest of the company. He was captured at the Battle of Chancellorsville, Virginia on 3 May 1863, held prisoner at Richmond, and was paroled at City Point, Virginia on 14 May 1863. He reported to Camp Parole, Maryland on May 16th, was sent to Washington, D.C. on 20 May 1863 and spent the remainder of his service at Camp Convalescent, Virginia. With the rest of the Chancellorsville paroled prisoners, he rejoined the Regiment at Baltimore on 20 July 1863. Rogers was mustered out with the rest of his regiment at New Haven on 27 July 1863.

He reenlisted in the U.S. Navy at the Brooklyn, New York Navy Yard on 1 September 1864. "We enlisted together in the Navy and were together until discharge."[260] He served as a Landsman on the U.S.S. *Vermont* until 18 September 1864; on the *Grand Gulf* until 2 August 1865 as a Landsman and Ordinary Seaman; on the *Portsmouth* until 13 August 1865; and on the *North Carolina* until 1 September 1865 when he was discharged from the Brooklyn Navy Yard.

---

260 Affidavit, Marcus O. Babcock of Branford, 2 October 1909, in the pension file of George S. Rogers.

He applied for an invalid pension on 26 June 1880 based on his service in the 27th Connecticut Volunteer Regiment. He applied for a Navy pension and received several rejections, failing to prove inability to work. The pension file is large with many depositions and he eventually received a pension. At the time of his enlistment in Co. B he was described as five feet ten inches tall, light complexion, blue eyes, brown hair, occupation wood turner. While on picket duty at Falmouth, Virginia about January 1, 1863 he contracted chronic diarrhea from exposure, camping on low marshy ground and drinking poor water. He was treated in January 1863 for diarrhea and in March 1863 for jaundice. Since the war he lived at Binghamton, New York.

He was married at Binghamton, New York by Rev. J. L. Adams on 18 March 1869 to Mary E. Allard. Neither were previously married or divorced. They had the following children: Dr. Walter Allard Rogers, born on 9 August 1870, 1915 of Portland, Oregon; Harry A., born on 7 September 1872, died June 1882; and Minnihaha (Minnie), born on 15 December 1873, 1915 living at home. His wife Mary died at Binghamton, New York on 12 January 1911.

George S. Rogers was living at Branford when he enlisted in the 27th CVI. He does not appear in the 1860 census at Branford and no connection to the Rogers family at Branford could be found. He was a tent mate with Walter E. Fowler while in the 27th and named his son after Fowler. He remained friends with several fellow Branford soldiers and sailors, visiting them through the years. The death of his wife Mary was noted in the *Branford Opinion.*[261]

George S. Rogers died while visiting St. Petersburg, Florida on 3 January 1920 and was buried at Spring Forest Cemetery, Binghamton, Broome Co., New York. He was born at Eaton, New York on 12 July 1842. His daughter Minnie Rogers submitted a request for payment for the expenses of his funeral and burial.

He provided excerpts to the pension board from his diary:

> *"I went into the Army weighing 145 lbs. Camp life at first seemed to agree with me. I gained in flesh until I weighed 160 lbs. When I got sick I ran down to 119 lbs About July 1st 1864. I started for the seashore at my Dr.'s suggestion as he could not help me. I had a bad cold with my other troubles.*
>
> *I went to the Brooklyn Navy Yard and tried to enlist as a Marine, was examined, did not pass the examining board said I not physically qualified for the service. I went to New Haven and shipped on a (?), it agreed with me. I improved in weight, strength and health. I gained 8 lbs. in a short time and looked quite like a sailor, sun burnt and weathered. A friend wrote me from home [that] I was subject to a draft and if I did not want to take my chances I had better try the navy and try it again. I did so. A friend, an officer on the Grand Gulf shipped me on that boat. He having needed seaman bad at that time and I wanted to go just as bad. I knew I could not stand it in the army again and I would not stand a draft. I shipped as landsman soon got my role as Ordinary seaman, was Capt. of a gun.*
>
> *I shipped as Landsman for 2nd Class Sloop of War U.S. Steamer Grand Gulf for one year at Brooklyn Navy Yard, N.Y. examined & sworn in Sept. 1st 1864. Went aboard the U.S. Receiving Ship Vermont Sept. 2nd, examined again, remained aboard Vermont until Sept. 19th*
> *Went to see [sic] Sept. 23 Convoying U.S. made Steamer Ocean Queen to Aspinwall, CA., arrived Oct. 3rd Sailed on return trip Oct. 6th. Arrived in N.Y. Oct. 16 saild for Aspinwall again Oct. 24th. Arrived at Aspinwall Nov. 3rd, saild for New York Nov. 5th where we arrived Nov. 16th. Ships Co [was] transferred to Vermont and reserved for Grand Gulf. Grand Gulf went on Dry Dock for*

---

repares [sic] preparing it for Ft. Fisher fight. Went home on liberty Dec. 23rd. Returned Jan. 4th 1865. Grand Gulf crew transferred back aboard Grand Gulf Feb. 22nd1865. March 7 went to sea towing Torpedo boat Casco. Anchored at Norfolk Navy Yard Mar. 12, went to sea Mar. 17th Key West Mar. 22nd, went to sea Mar. 23 Mobile Mar. 26anchor 5 A.M. 28th. Pensacola 2 P.M. 28th April 1st went to sea 4th came to Anchor with the West Gulf Blockading Squadron off Galveston, Texas. Left West Gulf Blockading Squadron June 23rd New Orleans June 25th West Gulf and Mississippi Squadron Consolidated. Grand Gulf relieved flag ship Portsmouth. Grand Gulf crew whose time expires on or before Sept. 1st transfered to Portsmouth

Aug. 4th to go to Brooklyn Navy Yard for discharge. Portsmouth sliped her cable and Aug. 6th Arrived in New York, Anchored at Battery Aug. 27th, transferred to the U.S. Receiving Ship North Carolina Aug. 31st. Sept. 1st Discharged from North Carolina at Brooklyn Navy Yard.

The above is correct in fact and substance, the names, places and vesels and dates are correct and taken from my diary kept by myself at the time. I was a good soldier and sailor and very proud of it. I believe myself worthy and entitled to a pension and I need it."

Very Respectfully
Geo. S. Rogers
38 Chestnut St.
Binghamton, N.Y.

Edward D. Sheldon of Branford was a member of Co. B 27th Connecticut Volunteer Infantry and was discharged for disability in 1863. (Beers, Biographical Record of New Haven County, 644)

EDWARD D· SHELDON

**Co. B 27th CVI, private, enlisted 20 August 1862, discharged disability
pension #810887 for the soldier**

Edward D. Sheldon[262] of Branford, age 20, enlisted at New Haven on 20 August 1862 and was mustered in on 3 October 1862 as a private in Co. B 27th CVI for a term of nine years. It is not clear if he fought at the Battle of Fredericksburg. He was sick in the hospital beginning December 1862 for cold and influenza. His CMSR does not have much detail. He was discharged on 28 July 1863 from Lovell General Hospital, Portsmouth, Rhode Island. It is not clear from the records in the file whether he was on duty at times during his enlistment or in the hospital the entire time. He was the brother-in-law of Charles A. Young of the same company.

He applied for an invalid pension on 24 October 1891 under the act of 27 June 1890. His application does not mention a disability received during his service. In 1907 he was described as five feet seven inches tall, light complexion, grey hair and grey eyes. He was married first at Norfolk, Litchfield Co. by Rev. Joseph Eldridge on 29 November 1870 to Eunice Emeline Geer. She died at New Haven on 10 February 1875 and was buried in Center Cemetery, Branford. He was married second at Norfolk by Rev. Dr. Lewis H. Reid of Salisbury on 17 October 1877 to Marion Josephine Geer, sister of his first wife. She died at Branford on 23 February 1911 and was buried there in Center Cemetery. He was married third at Milford by Attorney

---

262 For his biography see Beers, *Biographical Record of New Haven County*, 644.

Orma W. Platt on 22 April 1912 to Mary A. Harvey. She was living in 1915. None of his wives were previously married. He had one son by his first wife, Robert Truman Sheldon, born at Branford on 24 November 1871.[263] He was a charter member and commander of the Mason Rogers Post No. 7 G.A.R. of Branford. He represented Branford in the Connecticut General Assembly in 1895.

Edward D. Sheldon died at New Haven on 21 October 1915 and was buried in Center Cemetery, Branford. There was a G.A.R. marker on his gravesite in 1934. He was born at Branford on 18 April 1843, son of Truman Sheldon and Almira Appleby.

The following is a letter written by Edward D. Sheldon:[264]

Camp Ethan Allen
27 Reg't, Co. B U.S.A.
Oct 28th 1862

Dear Mother

*As I had nothing
to do for a short time it came
into my head that I would
write to you.
We have moved from the camp
seward to this camp which [is] much
pleasanter. we arrived at camp
seward Saturday at 2 PM. if we
had any other quartermaster than
Mr Harrison[265] I believe we should
have to lie out in the rain over
Sunday. Monday after it had
slacked raining Charlie[266], Henry
Beach, Major Hendrick and myself
went over to Fort Ward about
4 miles distant. we see Lewis and
Lorrin. you never see a person so
pleased to see anybody as they were*

*to see us. Lewis said he never expected
to get back from Harrisons Landing.
he has been very sick.
You need not ever be afraid of the
rebles [sic] taking Washington. where we
were first encamped or just above
us were rifle pits that extended to
the Potomac and across it and 5 or 6
miles below us then theres 3 forts
between Camp seward and fort
ward which is about 3 ½ miles and so
on for miles. then the woods are
all cut off as far as you can see
and there they lie to rot and nostt(?)
and do nobody any good.
I will finish my story about
going over to the fort. we got back
to the camp we found the tents
all struck and knapsacks packed
ready to march in 30 minutes.
I packed up and was ready as soon
as they were. all of the Reg't received
musket[s] all but about seventy of our
company. Charlie and I was one*

---

263 Branford Vital Records, 1863-1895, 25.
264 Branford Historical Society archives, RG 1 Family Papers, Sheldon family, box 8, folder 6. Also included is a diary fragment from 1863 of his trip from Virginia to Lovell Hospital in Portsmouth, Rhode Island and his discharge paper.
265 Quartermaster Lynde Harrison
266 Charles A. Young of Branford, Co. B 27th CVI, Edward D. Sheldon's brother-in-law.

of the number. we was not sorry
we did not receive them. we left
the encampment about 5 PM
and reached here at 9 PM.
the Colonel nor any of the field
officers except the Major
knew of a rout[e] but it happened to
be the longest on[e] he could have
taken it being 13 miles the shortest
rout[e] 5 miles. we averaged 3 ¼ miles an
hour, when we arrived here our tents
had not so we had to turn in on
the grass but it was cold. I was
glad to get up in a short time
and pull for a camp fire. it was the
coldest night that I have
seen since last winter.
They gave us Enfield rifles
yesterday afternoon and I expect
4.0 rounds of carterages [sic] tomorrow.
our regimental came last night
at dress parade. revile at 6 AM

morn report right away after roll
call
at 8 camping drill from 9 to 11
dinner at 12 if there is any. camping
drill from 1 to 2 battalion drill
from 3 to 4 dress parade 5 PM
supper 5 ½ revile at 9 PM taps
9 ½ PM put out your lights and go
to bed. the Col gave out orders tonight
Co
rations and be on hand at 5 ½ AM
tomorrow morn for picket duty. our
turn will be about a week from next
Monday. it is getting late and
I must close. Charlie sends his love
to all and I do the same.

from your affectionate Son
Ed
Direct to
Co B 27th Washington DC
care of C L Ely

Edward D. Sheldon sent a letter from Camp Ethan Allan to his mother shortly after the regiment left New Haven. (Branford Historical Society archives)

Elizur G. Smith was chief bugler for the 20th Connecticut Volunteer Regiment. (Beecher, First Light Battery, I:23)

ELIZUR G. SMITH

Co. A 20th CVI, musician, enlisted 12 August 1862, discharged 30 May 1865
pension #243153 for his minor child

Elizur G. Smith of Branford enlisted on 12 August 1862 and was mustered in on 8 September 1862 as a musician in Co. A 20th CVI. With his regiment he fought at the Battle of Chancellorsville, Virginia on 1 May 1863. "Have a slight hurt on the Calf of my leg caused by a piece of shell."[267] He was admitted to the General Hospital at Fairfax Seminary, Virginia on 14 June 1863 for epitasis and transferred to Chestnut Hill Hospital, Philadelphia on 17 June. He was admitted to Knight Hospital, New Haven on 24 March 1864 for rheumatism. After a furlough he was transferred to the Convalescent Ward, Bedloe's Island, New York on 20 April 1864 and was returned to duty at Louisville, Kentucky on 3 May 1864. He was admitted to Brown Hospital, Louisville on 7 June 1864 with debility and was on furlough from 28 October until 19 November 1864. He was discharged on 30 May 1865. After his discharge he lived at Branford.

He was married at Meriden by Rev. G. H. Deshan on 3 January 1872 to Ellen J. Slate. She died at Branford on 29 July 1874, age 29 and was buried there in Center Cemetery. He did not remarry.

Elizur Grant Smith died at New Haven Hospital on 27 July 1883 and was buried in Center Cemetery, Branford. There was a G.A.R. marker on his gravesite in 1934. He was born at Branford on 25 September

---

267 Letter, Elizur G. Smith to his parents, 3 May 1863, in his own pension file.

1843, son of Grant Smith and Rebecca Sperry.[268] He never applied for a pension.

His mother Rebecca Smith of Branford, as guardian, applied for a pension on 8 September 1886 on behalf of Harry Warren Smith, only child of the soldier. Harry was born at Branford on 7 January 1873 and received a pension until the age of sixteen. He probably lived with his grandmother until her death at Branford on 5 April 1890.[269]

The pension file of Elizur G. Smith contains a number of original letters sent by the soldier to his parents in Branford. Some of his letters were sent while he was a patient in the hospital. He was never well after the war according to various affidavits in the file. He indicates that he was the chief bugler for the entire brigade.

Loudon Valley Nov. 22nd 1862

Dear Parents,

I received your letter last night and one from Brownson. As for Harpers Ferry being taken I expect New Haven will be occupied by the whole Rebel army about the same time. do not be alarmed at any rumors you hear about us. The Rebels have got too much to attend to where they are and at Richmond to make any invasion. The Rebel Guerillas are apt to make a raid any time but they always go back to their holes again. I received the box last Saturday I think it was, I was very much pleased I can tell you to receive it although I could not eat much that was in it as I was not well and could not eat anything but it done me good so much good that I got well almost immediately. A week ago last Sunday I did not feel very well and lost my appetite on Monday evening the General sent for us

to go to his headquarters which were temporarily on top of the heights as they expected an attack from the Rebs I suppose but where they were to come from I cant see for there is not any force within 30 or 40 miles of here but up the mountain. I went going where I never was before (nor don't want to be again) it was about 11 oclock at night and raining & so dark that I could not see two feet from the road. to make the best of it is not as good as the cart paths at home in the woods well I got to the Generals tent after an hours hard walking and lay down in a sweat in his tent had not been there more than half an hour when a Corporal came scared half to death with the report that one of the Pickets was shot so the Gen. called me up [and] had me sound the alarm and then I had the privilege of following his August Majesty over the rocks & stones about an hours [piece missing] a tent a little way from his own but where the ground was about two feet higher. I suppose he thought he would know

268 Branford Vital Records, 1863-1895, 29.
269 Branford Vital Records, 1863-1895, 241.

what was going on better had his bed
brought up then which I had the privi-
lege of sleeping front of his tent out
doors in the rain. I was so tired that I
went right to sleep and when I woke up in
the morning was pretty stiff I have not
been well since have had the jaundice
in addition to Diarrhea and sickness
from exposure that night but I
feel quite like myself today and
shall be as good as ever in a day to two
a great many have got the jaundice
but all get well in a short time.
As regards the box you are going to send
you can send it by Adams Express they do
just as well as any others. I wish
you would put in my
scarf and get a new bow for the
fiddle or some new hair in the
old one till I get to see that it is in
good shape. The box will cost much
less by Adams Express than by
Heinsdale one of the drummers had
a box today that was only 4 days
on the way. you can address it to
Capt. Timothy Guilford Co. A
20th Reg C.V. Harpers Ferry Va.
and put this mark + on the cover
and then I can tell it without
opening it at my Captains tent or
can get it if he is not there.
there is nothing new down here as
I can think of. We, the drum corp
tent with them have a cook and
muse ourselves we have got a first
rate cook. Two or three of the pears
and four of the grapes in the box spoilt
but the rest of the things were in
excellent condition. the singing
book I was very glad to get we
had quite a concert on Sunday

evening it seemed like. the music-
able we had to have in church
Give my thanks and regards to
those who sent things in the box
and to all enquiring friends.

> *Aff your Son*
> *EG Smith*

Sunday
U.S. Ford May 3rd [1863]

My Dear Parents
*   We have been*
fighting more or less for
the last three days. today
and last night we had a
terrible hard battle. I am
all right. Have only a
slight hurt on the Calf of
my leg caused by a piece
of shell. it makes my leg
a little sore & stiff but it
will be so that I can go
as well as war(?) by tomorrow
or next day. Our Regt is
all cut to pieces. I am now
about 2 ½ miles from the
battle field have just come
up over there with one
of the Drs hospital. I was
ordered back up. I could
do nothing up there in front.
our success was very
doubtful when I left.
I don't [want] you to worry for I am
all right and probably
shall be. no more now
Your aff son
EG Smith

Camp of the 20th C.V. June 12 1863

My Dear Parents

*I received yours of the 7th
Inst last evening. <u>I left the Hospital</u>
day before yesterday as the Doct thought
I was well enough but he was mistaken
I have not any strength at all and last
night just after I got your letter
I had another spell of Bleeding &
bled a good deal and am very
<u>weak this morning</u>. I shall stay
at this place until I get stronger
I was intending to go back to Hed. Is.
yesterday we but(?) my nose bleeding
stopped me. I don't want to
go to the Hospital if I can get
out of this scrape any other
way but as I cannot unless
I wait a while and perhaps get a
discharge but that is uncertain,
therefore if you can get me into
the N.H. Hospital you had better
do it. You can state my case to
Dr Jewett and with the words
of one or two others to certify to
my complaint I think you will
have no trouble in getting me
transferred. <u>It has hurt me</u>
a good deal to blow the bugle for
three months past and now
I cannot blow at all. And Doct
Terry has told me to give it up.
So I am of no use now at all as
a musician and they cant make
anything else of me.
I cannot write more as the
mail is about to close.
Remember me to Aunt Laura &
all.*

    *Your aff Son
    EG Smith*

U.S.A. Hosp Chestnut Hill
Philadelphia Pa June 24th 1863

My Dear Parents
   *I have just received
yours of the 22nd Inst
with $200 enclosed. I do not
think I shall leave here very
soon although we cannot tell
but we may be sent away at
any time. The Hosp. is nearly
full now and I suppose that
as soon as they get them all
settled and find out where
the Patients belong that they
will do as they have done
before. that is send them to
their state Hospitals.
I got a pass yesterday and went
down to Philadelphia and spent
most of the day. I tell you it
was quite a relief to get out doors
once more. I am glad that you
have seen Col. Ross I hope you
like him I should like to see
him myself but guess I'll have
to wait awhile. I dont hardly
know what to think about staying
here but from all appearances
now I shall stay here for some
time unless you get an order
from the Surgeon General for
my transfer to N.H. Hospital
I am feeling about the same but it
is getting warm here again and
<u>I begin to</u> have the headache and
<u>the blood</u> begins to rush to my
<u>head</u> I should not be surprised
<u>if I had</u> another Bleeding spell
<u>soon but</u> I may not.
The Hospital is about full now
if not quite so. They do not give*

any Furloughs here unless in
cases when it is very necessary to
save life or something of that
kind. The Ward Master who
I am on the best of terms with told
me that he would tell me when
& how I could get a discharge
but it would cost me $45.00
what do you think about it
I would be willing to give twice
that to get out of the service
but will wait awhile and
see how things are going to
turn up. I must close now
Remember me to all

> *Your aff Son*
> *address as before   EG. Smith*

U.S.A. Hosp Chestnut Hill

Philadelphia Pa June 27 1863.
My Dear Parents

I have just received
yours of the 25th Inst and also
two letters which were written while
I was at Fairfax Seminary Hosp.
one written by Father and the other
one that Albert Page directed
and I also got A.L. Pages[270] letter
I am sorry that I could not
get those letters before as they
were opened by some one most
likely at the other Hosp. where
I was. I think that the
only way that I can be got
home is for you to get an order
from the Surgeon General at
Washington for my transfer to
New Haven. I think you can
easily get an order on a recomem-

dation from Col. Ross and no
doubt you can without.
The Doctor of this ward took a
specimen of my writing in to
the office this morning and
I am pretty sure if a clerkship
here. The Ward Master tells
me that he is sure that
I shall have a good berth
here and that if I get one
that I can stay about as
long as I like if I only
look out for myself and
take care to please them all
I can when I first begin.
I told him that was just
the way I should do if I got
a place here but I would
rather wait a week or so
and see if I could not get
home. I am feeling pretty well
except when it is warm. but
my constitution is not what it
was once and never will be
again and there are many
other Buglers as bad and worse
off than I am. there were
several that I saw while on
the way here and they all
were broken winded as you
might say. some were so bad
that they bled from the lungs
a great deal and I have no
doubt but that had I kept
on, or rather been able to bugle
much longer that I should
have bled as from the lungs
as well as from the nose.
I would like to get
a good berth here as a clerk
but yet I dont think that
the confinement would suit
me although I cannot stir
around much but yet I want

---

270 Albert L. Page of Branford

to be in the open air. I have
been out of doors only once
since I have been here. they
allow six passes a day and as
there are 60 in this Ward it
takes several days to get around
to all you see.
I suppose you have a good many
visitors now as you by this
time got settled.
As you have said, "I am
only a Patient now." but if
I get a clerkship I have to
be detailed and then that
gives me a place as long
as they want me or I am
unfit to do even that.
And I would not be reported
as being well and besides
Colonel Ross could
not order me back without
the Surgeon saw fit to let
me go. I think I have received
all your letters except those
that you sent to the Reg.
Give my regards to all

    Your aff Son
    EG Smith

U.S.A. Hospital Chestnut Hill
Philadelphia Pa June 30 1863

    I have just received
your letter the 27th Inst.
I am feeling about the same as
I have. no better nor worse.
I shall not do anything about
that matter at present as
I think that they may
discharge me here as the
Doctor told me yesterday
that I would not be able

to Bugh again and that I
<u>must give it up entirely.</u>
Now you see I can do nothing
else as I am mustered in
as a musician unless I
choose to and then according
to the U.S. Army Regulations
I cannot and I think that
before a great while the
Doctor will conclude upon
something. The money that
you sent I was very glad
of as I was in want of
a few things and had but
very little change.
We are going to be paid
off here in a few days but
not more than one or two
months pay. so you need
not send me any more
unless I send for it.
It is quite warm here today
but it has been quite cool
and we have had considerable
rain of late. Give my regards
to all. address as before.

    Your Aff
    EG. Smith

U.S.A. Hospital C. Hill
Monday Aug 24 1863

My Dear Parents

I received yours
of the 19th Inst yesterday.
I am feeling the same as usual
and am enjoying myself well
There is a Surgeon here from
Washington who is examining
all that are subjects for
the Invalid Corps or their

*Regiments. Many who have had
an easy time here for
the last 3 or 4 months have
got to go to their Regiments
but as I am declared by the
Surgeons here to be unfit for
either Invalid Corps or
Regt I have not been ex-
amined and probably shall
not be. The Surgeon in charge
will do all he can to keep me
here as long as I consent to
do duty that I am doing
now. they cannot compel me
to do anything else and therefore
I have the advantage of them.
If I was only a common Bugler
or musician it would be
different but I still rank
as chief musician of my
Brigade and consequently
cannot put me under any
one else. I hear that my
Corps the (12th A. C.) is going
to Charleston. I would
like to go then too were I well*

*& strong enough to stand
that climate.
I think the boys will have
a hard time of it down
there. I should like to
have been home to see Uncle
Sheldon. I suppose he is as
odd as ever.
I would like my collars
like the one you sent me
you can send them by mail
best the postage will not be
much.
I shall probably come home
if I can get a "leave of
absence" soon after pay day
next month. by that time
my Bugler Corps can get
along a little while without
me. I must close now
as it is dinner time and
the mail closes soon
Regards to all*

*Your son
E G Smith*

J. Edwin Towner of Branford served as 1st sergeant of Co. C 15th Connecticut
Volunteer Infantry (Branford Historical Society photograph collection)

JOHN EDWIN TOWNER

Co. C 15th CVI, 1st sergeant, enlisted 15 July 1862, wounded, prisoner, discharged 1 June 1865
pension #1084230 for the soldier

J Edwin Towner[271] of New Haven enlisted at New Haven on 15 July 1862 as a private but was promoted to 1st sergeant on 1 August 1862. He was mustered in on 25 August 1862 in Co. C 15th CVI for a term of three years. While stationed near Washington, D.C. "Sergt. Towner was in command of a three inch steel rifled gun and it made several effective shots."[272] His regiment was at Fredericksburg, Virginia on 13 December 1862, participated in the Siege of Suffolk, Virginia in the spring of 1863, and in the Peninsula Campaign of July 1863. His rank was reduced to private on 1 July 1864 upon his request.

He was wounded and captured at Kinston, North Carolina on 8 March 1865. With the wounded, he was left behind at Goldsboro and sent by train to Salisbury Prison. He was a prisoner at Salisbury Prison on 13 March and spent a few days in the jail at Danville, North Carolina on 27 March 1865.[273] He was sent to the hospital at Richmond on 30 March for a right sided wound. After his release he was a patient at Division No. 1 General Hospital, Annapolis, Maryland and transferred to Patterson Park General Hospital, Baltimore on 10 April 1865. He received a thirty day furlough to Connecticut. He reported to Depot Camp, Hartford after his furlough and was discharged from there on 1 June 1865.

---

271 For his biography see Beers, *Biographical Record of New Haven County*, 550.
272 Thorpe, *History of the Fifteenth*, 70.
273 Beers, *Biographical Record of New Haven County*, 550.

He applied for an invalid pension on 10 May 1904. At the time of his enlistment he was described as five feet seven inches tall, gray eyes, light hair, light complexion, occupation machinist. He lived at New Haven at the time his enlistment until 1870, then returned to Branford. The family states that his health was shattered by the war and he abandoned his hope of working for the railroad and returned to farming. He was married at Branford by Rev. Elijah C. Baldwin of the First Congregational Church on 16 November 1872 to Susan Driver Hoadley. Neither were previously married or divorced. She died at Branford on 22 March 1897 and was buried there in Mill Plain Cemetery. They had three children: Anna Pearl, born on 17 February 1874, died on 17 July 1899; Merle Eugene, born on 3 October 1875; and Laura Emily, born on 27 July 1877, died on 16 September 1910. He was a charter member and commander of the Mason Rogers Post No. 7 of Branford. He was commander when the Branford Civil War monument was dedicated and was an adjutant of the state G.A.R.

J. Edwin Towner died at Branford on 22 August 1916 and was buried there in Mill Plain Cemetery. He was born at Branford on 21 January 1840, son of John Towner and Martha Tyler.

His diary was quoted in the *History of the Fifteenth* by Thorpe especially after the Regiment's capture at the Battle of Kinston, North Carolina.[274]

"The wounded as fast as gathered at the mill were sent back a short distance to the field hospital in the rear of the rebel breastworks. Here those wounded requiring immediate attention were dressed by the Confederate surgeons. It was at this place that Palmer, of Co. B had his arm amputated. Toward night we were taken across the creek and up to Kinston. We were quartered in an old building standing on the corner of the first square after crossing the river. Here all minor wounds were attended to and the surgeons were busy until well along in the night. As fast as cared for we were passed into an upper room to sleep on the bare floor and fortunate were they who had saved their blankets."

---

274 Thorpe, *History of the Fifteenth*, 101 & 145-146.

Above, left: J. Edwin Towner after the war (Branford Historical Society photograph collection). Above right: Eli Walter Osborne of the New Haven Grays was captain of Co. C 2nd Volunteer Infantry and commissioned as major of the 15th Connecticut Volunteer Regiment. He was wounded and captured at Kinston, North Carolina and died at a Confederate Hospital in Danville, North Carolina on April 6, 1865. His papers are at the New Haven Museum Whitney Library. (Beers & Mansfield Gallery, New Haven; Branford Historical Society photograph collection)

Towner's letters to home are in the archives of the Branford Historical Society.

Speaking of his experience in Salisbury Prison, he says:

"The surgeon, a gruff old fellow came toward evening; I remember him for pouring some turpentine in my wound. Our rations consisted of rye coffee, a loaf of rye bread, about three by four inches (for two days), and rice soup; the soup was very thin. We had a promise of meat once in eight days; the bread was merely flour and water, mixed and baked; as to its solidity, you can judge. Our wounds became inflamed and offensive for want of care. On the 15th (March), the rations of the well prisoners were reduced one-half, but ours remained the same. I went in to see Lieut. Bishop who was in the next building, and found him lying on a stretcher propped up with blankets; he seemed cheerful and said he was trying to pull through. I have thought since that the brave fellow was keeping up appearances to encourage the others when he knew his own case was hopeless. Major Osborne lay beside him. A Catholic priest came to see us, and he was the only clergyman to my knowledge who visited the prison. Lieut. Bishop died at 8 o'clock, Friday evening, March 17th.

At Greensboro we were taken to a large open field and lay out all night; the wind blew strongly from the northwest, and as many of us had neither blankets nor overcoats, we suffered bitterly from the cold; I had an overcoat, and so gave my blanket to Major Osborne. After arriving at Danville, while we were marching down the street, a group of rebel officers on the balcony of a hotel, thought to guy us, supposing we were ' Sherman's bummers,' and said that 'Uncle Robert would use Sherman right smart when he got at him,' but our fellows advised them to 'take in Mar's Bob out of the wet when uncle Billy gets up this way'. Rations were not at all abundant here, but the thing we most needed was salt. On the morning of the 29th, we were called at daybreak to take the cars for Richmond. Some were too weak from lack of food and condition of their wounds to start, among them Corporal Frank Phillips and Major Osborne. We left them under fair treatment in a hospital and turned toward Richmond."

The Branford Historical Society is the repository of ninety-five original letters and their transcriptions written by Towner during the war to his sister Emily S. Holcomb of Branford. Included in the collection is his diary dated 1865. He signs the letters J. E. Towner, John E. Towner, Ed, J. Edwin Towner but most often Edwin. He tells his sister about daily and regimental activities. He is not afraid to give his opinion on a variety of subjects and has a negative view of commanding officers and how the army was run. The letters give a young soldier's view of the war, politics, and matters at home. His letters reveal the life of a soldier and the importance of news from home, some excerpts:

Camp Chase Sept. 8, 1862

Dear Sister,

If you know how good it seems to hear from you, you would keep that pen going the larger part of the time. A letter seems so good. My girl has not wrote yet. She ought to, dont you think so. If she don't, I shall give her fits when we are homeward bound again. I have enough to eat. Some of the time we have been a little short oweing to green officers, but Uncle Sam provides enough, and when we get regulated we shall get potatoes at least once a week. It is my duty to draw all of the rations from the Comesary and after they are cooked to deal them out to the men. My duties are rather heavey. I will try to give you one days work. First at revilie in the morning I have to get the men out and call the roll. Roll call over, next morning report has to be made out and handed to the Adjutant. Next, ration bill and rations drawn. Next, guard detail of my company - I make out and march the men out for guard mounting. That over, two or three hours drill. Dinner and first Sergeant call to receive our detail for next day's guard. Being over, then comes drill again, then roll call, and dress parade. After dress parrade with one of the commissioned officers (generally the Captain), I make the report to the Sergt Major of the number of men present, then supper. Next, retreat is sounded, and I call the roll and make another report. And taps, when the lights have to all be put out, finishes the day. Is not that enough?

Camp Casey Sept. 16th, '62

Dear Sister,

I am tired of guarding Long Bridge. We were there all day yesterday and last night till 9 oclock this morning when we were relieved. It is hard work standing at the gate examining passes. I was six hours on duty and six hours off, and I think in the twelve hours that I was on duty at least six thousand men and teams were passed across. I only got about two hours sleep last night for the moquietoes and rats were so troublesome that there was no chance for comfort.

Camp Chase Sept. 22nd 1862

Dear Sister,

We have had one review of our Division already which resulted in the choice of our Regiment as body guard of General Casey and in consequence we have been dubbed as Caseys Pets

Mail Wagon (Photographic History of the Civil War, 8:35)

by the other Conn. Reg'ts. I believe that I was not disapointed when I told the boys in New Haven that Captain Smith was the best Captain in the Regiment. Every day I think more and more of him. He's both a man and an officer.

Camp Chase Arlington Heights Va.
Sept. 28 [1862]

Dear Sister,

Generall Casey has sent for our flag and color bearer to stand in front of him, and has been heard to say that our Reg't was the finest looking body of men and the best marching of any volunteer Regt he has ever seen. Quite a compliment for us considering the short time we have in the field. But our Regt does march well and is very well drilled all things considered. We have not got rid of guarding Long Bridge yet. Our prospects of going into active service seems to be bright at times, but the brightness soon dims in this Va. Dust. You may think that you have dust up home, but I can assure you that sutch is not the fact. We can tell when bodies of troops or baggage trains are moveing through. They are severall miles and great bodies of dust will rise and fill the air looking verry mutch like a cloud. I should think it would suffocate the horses. They have to work hard for Uncle Samuel and get no thanks and verry little to eat for it.

Camp Chase Oct 6th 1862

Dear Sister,

Well I am sick in two different ways: sick of the leaders of our Armies and sick in body.
I have not been feeling verry well for some time. The consequence is that Captain went after Doctor Holcomb, and he concluded that I had fever enough for two men and gave me a powder. It has loosened every one of my front teeth. Our Second Sergeant was, upon application of Captain Smith, reduced to the ranks. He was Collar Sergt and being an Irishman, all of the Irish feel verry indignant, and say they wont fight. He was reduced for insubordination, refusing to obey orders and so Capt made an example of him.

October 29th/62

Sister Emily,

Yess, you may send me a box and I will tell you what to send in it: two pair of draws, two woolen shirts (I don't care what color) but something good, a pair of gloves for comfort, and if you go to New Haven get me a couple of pair of cheep white gloves for dress parade, large size, a box of black pepper and one of cayenne ground, a box of anguintun if handy to get (for the body guards are numerous here), and if there is any spare room send me a little box of butter and one of honey, that's all. Make the box as small as possible.

Nov. 7, 1862

Dear Sister

Tell Aunt Harriett that the south cannot take Washington while the Fifteenth is here. If we had Generalls, instead of Civil Engineers, our Army would have been in Richmond long ago.

Camp Near Fredericksburg
December 16th

Dear Sister,

You must excuse my long silence. After a long tedious march we arrived at this camp on last Wednesday, and after pitching our tents, or apologies for tents, we tried to compose ourselves for the night but were soon roused out to get ammunition and to prepare for a fight. In the morning we were drawn up in line and after stacking our arms were told to hold ourselves in readiness to march at minutes notice. How the canon roared. We were in good range of the enemy. In the morning we were marched down to the bank of the river and lay on the road side till late in the afternoon when the enemy threw some shell among us mortally wounding one man and severely two more. One of the shells passed but a few feet from me. It was my first experience, and I wished it might be my last. Just at night we crossed the river and entered the Cit. It presented a ruinous aspect. We lay by the road side all night - in the morning we marched down by the river's bank. Soon the batteries commenced to play and shot and shell flew over our heads. Some of the shell from our own batteries burst over our heads wounding six men, two from our own regt., one of them in my Co. I got to fill a canteen with water when one burst and a piece struck where I had been sitting. Thank God I escaped that time. We have escaped thus far. The 27th has lost many men.

Good bye
Pray for us
15th C V Washington Sumners Division

Camp near Fredericksburg Feb 1st/63

Dear Sister,

We had preaching this afternoon, the fist since we have been out here. Our drunken Chaplain is off on a furlough, and our quartermaster got the Chaplain of the Eighth, the only one in the Brigade, to officiate. He is a good one. He said he often heard the men say they would not fight any more for this government.
Butcher Hooker is going to Richmond. He will start with two hundred thousand men and have one hundred thousand left when he gets there.
Write often for I like to hear from Home

J Edwin Towner
1st Sergt. Co. C. 15th Regt. C.V.

Suffolk Va April 6th 1863

Dear Emily,

We shall probably stay here this summer or for some time yet. You know the war is to be at an end in three months. Dont you believe it I only wish it would be so, and then there would be some prospects of our going home. I have got entirely disgusted with this climate, quite pleasant one day blowing "great guns" the next and finally finishing off with an old fashion snow storm. Any one who would be willing to shed his blood in defense of such a climate ought to be put in a lunatic asylum for the rest of his days. What aint knee deep with mud is covered with sand which rises in clouds when the sun shines and wind blows, nearly putting ones eyes out. As for Suffolk, it is built like English Villages. One main street running through it where all the Respectables reside, and any quantity of by lanes and allies where the nigs and poor whites live. There are severall churches, some quite nice.

Camp behind the Breastworks
Suffolk, April 20th 1863

Dear Emily,

You have probably heard ere this that Rebs under Longstreet have laid seige to this place in right good earnest. They are working verry cautious and may accomplish their object, but I hardly think it probable for we have been greatly reinforced during the past week. On Sunday the Post Commissary issued rations for forty seven thousand men and more troops have since come. Two trains came this morning well loaded.

Emily S. Holcomb

Branford, Conn. Suffolk, Va May 7th 1863

Sister Em.

I am not a favorite now with the Capt. The reason I could easier tell than write, when an Officer tells me to knock a man down I shall do as I please about obeying the order, and that's just what I did do. Now as to being a favorite with the men, why I never have carried favor with anyone, and shall not for I do not care enough about my office to turn my hand over to retain it. A private's berth is an honorable one enough for me.

Camp near Battery Stevens

Suffolk, Va May 17th

Dear Sister,

You ought to see the flowers here. They are splendid. I saw three of the boys comeing in a short time since with splendid Bouquets. I wish that I could send you some. It is spring now in all its beauty. So glorious, and oh, how the mosquitoes and gnats bite. We have got splendid groves of pines all around us. The river winds snakelike in front and for the world looks like the river at home, just about as wide, lined with meadows on each side just the same.

Camp Conn

Suffolk June 17th/63

Sister Emily,

I send you as a curiosity a "Soldier's Daily Prayer."

NOT ORDERED BY THE WAR DEPARTMENT
SOLDIER'S DAILY PRAYER
OUR FATHER, which are in Washington, UNCLE ABRAHAM be thy name;
Thy victory won; Thy will be done, at the South as at the North; Give us this day our daily rations of Crackers and Pork; and forgive us our short-comings as we forgive our Quartermasters; Lead us not into temptation to steal Whisky, but deliver us from all Sutlers; For thine is the POWER, the SOLDIERS and NEGROES, for the space of TWO YEARS.

Amen
For use of Colonels, Captains, Sergeants, Corporals, Privates, "or any other man."

Conn. Camp of the 15th C.V.

Near Portsmouth July 23rd '63

Dear Sister,

Delay is dangerous as rumors are ripe that we are to leave this delightful locality for some raid into Seceshia toward Petersburg it is said. I hope we may go. I would rather face the enemy's bullets than another week of drunkenness like the last, and today seems to clap the climax of drunkenness. One Sergt. of our Co'. lays in his tent dead drunk and one Corporal has got drunk and been fighting. He is snoring like a thunderclap. We are liveing high at present, plenty of cucumbers and all other garden vegetables. The darkies come on the Camp in crowds with gingerbread pies, milk and every other nice thing that will sell. Green corn is in the market at Portsmouth, and new potatoes in any quantities. If that young lady who is boarding with you is good looking, just give her my best respects. By the way, you may whether she is or not.

Camp of the 15th Conn Vols.

Near Portsmouth Va ,

December 27th 1863

Dear Sister,

That coat has been in conflict all through the siege of Suffolk and in two engagements, once on the Edenton road, and once on the Providence Church road. Besides, it was a bed for me in camp mud, and kept me warm through the day, it has been at New Port News, Suffolk, Falmouth, Hampton, Yorktown, White house, Hanover Courthouse, Aylets, New Kent Court House, Portsmouth, and Norfolk, Southmills and Deep Creek. Can aney coat do better, a faithfull friend in need. Thanks for your Merry Christmas, and good wishes generally. Happy New year to you and those you love. Cant accept your invitation, cant possibly oweing to my haveing formed an engagement with Uncle Sam. and he cant spare my services for aney length of time.

Camp of the 15th Conn

Newbern, N.C. Feb. 11th/64

Sister Emily,

If you should happen to wake up some fine morning and find yourself here, you would think yourself in some Northern City, for New Berne is a northern city. There is not even the usuall accompany-ment to southern cities, Hogs in the streets. Such glorious Shade trees are only to be found in New Haven. It is nestled down here on the banks of the Neuse & Trent Rivers. Well, "a thing of beauty is a joy forever" and Newbern is beautiful.

Mrs. Emily S. Holcomb Out Post at Red House near
Branford, Connecticut Newbern N.C. March 29th 1864

Dear Sister.

….if our Officers were more mindful of the welfare of the men, they would have a better command. We will try and end this war soon. but I think the chimes of a new year will be rung ere Peace is declared. Now I am no Profet but mind what I say, 1865 will see this war ended. Dont deceive yourself in varrily hopeing that it will be before. Some of the Boys say "why dont you go and be examined for a commission in a collored Regt." and they predict for me a captaincy if I would. If the love of the collor was strong enough in me I might.

Camp of 15th Conn Vols
Sabbath Eve May 8th 1864

Sister Em,

A man in our Regt who has been away from home for the last year and a half has had an increase in his family lately. Perhaps he sent it home in a Letter
excuse me

Camp of 15th C.V.
June 1st [1864]

Gen. Grant is progressing very slow. In my opinion the end of the conflict will be the annialation of one and nearly of both Armies. Nothing short of this will stop the war. We may yet be drawn into the conflict. It has been our good luck to keep clear of it thus far, though we have endured maney hardships and have always been where we were ordered. We could do no more than this.

Camp of 15th Conn Vol.
New Berne Feb. 19th 1864 [1865]

Dear Sister,

Soldiering and married life are a great deal alike, plenty of Skirmishing, and some severe engagements. Will and I went down to the Cemetery today to see the graves of our comrades. It is a sorry sight. The yellow fever made sad havoc in our ranks. Many of the soldiers bodies have been dug up and sent north.

Corporal Albert F. Wheaton of North Branford was the flag bearer at the Battle of Kinston, North Carolina and died from his wounds. (Crofut & Morris, Military & Civil History of Connecticut, 754.)

ALBERT F· WHEATON

**Co. A 10th CVI, corporal, enlisted 12 September 1861, killed 15 December 1862
pension #103191 for his father Abram R. Wheaton**

Albert Francis Wheaton of North Branford enlisted at Hartford on 12 September 1861 and was mustered in on 2 October 1861 as a corporal in Co. A 10th CVI for a term of three years. With the rest of the regiment he fought at the Battle of Roanoke Island, North Carolina on 8 February 1862 and was the company's flag bearer. He was sick in the U.S. General Hospital at Portsmouth, North Carolina in July and August 1862. He was wounded at the Battle of Kinston, North Carolina on 14 December 1862 and died the next day in the field hospital. He was buried in the field of battle. His name appears on the North Branford Soldiers' Monument. He was the first cousin of Merwin Wheaton.

His father Abram R. Wheaton, age 55, of North Branford applied for a pension on 13 October 1866. Abram was married at North Branford on 16 September 1834 to Eliza A. Page who died at North Branford on 8 February 1861, age 46. The soldier left no widow or children and provided support for his father. Abram Ransom Wheaton died at North Branford on 20 January 1876, age 64 and was buried there in the Congregational Cemetery.[275] Abram R. Wheaton was born at North Branford, son of Daniel Whedon and Rachel Bishop.

---

275 The Hale Collection, North Branford, 21.

There is an account of Albert F. Wheaton's death by Rev. Henry C. Trumbull, chaplain of the 10th Regiment:[276]

> *In the first severe engagement of which I was a witness, one of the color-corporals was badly wounded, and was borne to the rear and laid on the ground at the field hospital. As I knelt by the corporal his first words were: "I did what I could to guard the colors, Chaplain. I'd stand by them to the last." "I know you would, Corporal," I replied, "you were always faithful." "Where's the regiment now?" he asked. "It's gone on, and finished its work," I said. "Glory!" he cried. As the surgeon told me that the corporal had but a few minutes to live, I asked him if he had any message to send to his parents. "Tell them," he answered, "that I gave my life for liberty, and I only wish I could give another."*

> *I visited the country home of one of my dear dead soldier boys, several years after, and I realized anew how the incidents of that conflict were an ever-fresh reality with those who had given their choicest treasures to make the conflict a success. This soldier boy was one of the color-guard who was shot in the first severe battle in which I had a part. He had sent by me his dying message to his parents, that he was glad to give one life for liberty, and I had buried him on the field where he fell. To his parents he was simply still away at war. As I sat before them in their quiet farmhouse home, they talked about Albert as their temporarily absent boy.[277]*

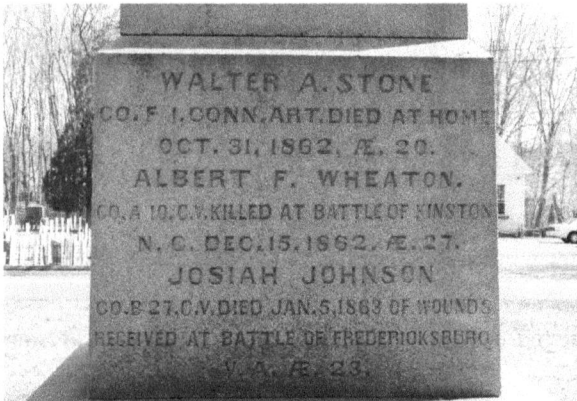

The eulogy for Albert F. Wheadon was delivered by Rev. William Bronson Curtiss at the North Branford Congregational Church on January 4, 1863:[278]

> *"He united with his church May 3rd 1857 & has lived among you for the most part until a little more than a year since. His early life you all know better than I. My first acquaintance with him was made three years last July when I first came to this place to preach. I spoke with him as he returned from the third sermon & shall not soon forget the cordial manner in which he welcomed me. I found him to be the same warm hearted cordial Friend in all our subsequent intercourse. When the 10th Regiment C. V. was forming he felt it his duty to enlist in the service of his country & went into camp in the city of Hartford. When his regiment broke camp they went to N. Y. & from there to Newbern, N. C. as part of Gen. Burnsides Division. His regiment has won unfading laurels in the*

---

276 Trumbull, *Memories of an Army Chaplain*, 159.
277 Trumbull, *Memories of an Army Chaplain*, 130; Trumbull speaks of his parents, his mother had already died but his father Abram had remarried.
278 Sermons of William B. Curtiss, Connecticut Historical Society, MS 93234, box 2, folder A.

various contests in which it has been engaged from that time to the present. Our Brother went forth to the field of strife not as a man of blood: not as a aspirant of fame; not with the hope of pecuniary seward but as an honest christian man <u>to</u> <u>do</u> his duty to God & his country…he yet heard his company's call & with him to hear was to obey. His letters to his friends state he felt he was in the path of duty. His heart was alive to the perils of the soldiers life he accepted the dangers as part of the trial he must endure but put his trust in God.

Whilst at Newbern he was taken sick & sent to the hospital & whilst there his papers were made out for an honorable discharge from the service & he might have returned to his friends. But health being restored he declined accepting the discharge & returned to his regiment. He fell wounded through the breast in the battle before Kinston, N. C. Dec. 14th & died on the 15th age 25 years & 5 months. He had been a professing christian a little more than 6 years & in that time his endeared himself to all. But he has fallen. His last words as they come to us from that far off field are tell my friends that if I had another life I would cheerfully give it to secure liberty of my country. His companions in arms bear honorable testimony to his courage & promptness in his discharge of duty… His remains rest in a soldiers grave with two others buried with him. He will hear no more the trumpet calling him to the deadly conflict; he will witness no more the field of carnage; he will never again join his companions in the gallant charge. He has stood guard for the last time upon the field of valor. We cannot doubt he has been promoted by the great Captain of our salvation…

Martha Russell of North Branford, an author and Civil War correspondent wrote the following poem in memory of Albert F. Wheaton:[279]

Our Color Bearer
*Albert F. Wheaton, Killed at Kinston, North Caroiina
December 14, 1863*

*"What of Albert?" do you ask me! Albert
        who our colors bore.
Through the quaking swamps to Beaufort-
        by the sluggish Neuse's shore
"Where the battle raged the fiercest-
        thickest fell the leaden storm
Bearing high the proud old banner,
        might be seen his stalwart form.
"Forward 10th" Clear rang the order,
        and compact as a rock
Our grim, restless column rushed,
        onward to the shock
One prayer for those we cherished,
        one deeply indrawn breath*

279 Totoket Historical Society, North Branford. The family used Whedon or Wheadon but his military papers spell his name Wheaton.

Ah, we reaped an ample harvest
    on that fatal field of death.
I was next but one to Albert,
    as we fiercely onward pressed.
I heard the cursed Minie ball
    that struck him in the breast.
Tom Davis caught the standard
    and we left him where he lay
But deeply we avenged him
    in that fierce and bloody fray.
Then my turn came - a saber cut
    on the right arm - just here
I could not grasp my musket-
    they sent me to the rear
Where I found my stricken comrade,
    all unconscious of the pain
The dreadful sights and fearful groans
    that pierce the heart and brain.
"No hope the surgeon muttered,
    but kindly bade me stay
To bathe his burning lips and brow
    and hear what he might say
What sacred word or token he night send
    to those who wait
Around the wide old hearthstone,
    the tidings of his fate.

A shell came shrieking past us
    his eyes flew open wide.
'How goes the day?" he murmured.
    "Tis ours", a voice replied.
"We have whipped the traitors soundly-
    full fast they broke and fled."
A flash of joy lit up his face
    "Thank God! Thank God." he said.

Then, his poor parched lips moved feebly,
    yet though I never stirred
But bent with listening eye and ear,
    I could not catch one word.

But knew by the soft radiance
    that overspread his face
He was thinking of the dear ones,
    in his far off native place.
Perhaps he saw his father's face-
    his sister's dear - who knows
Or heard the murmur of the stream
    that by their garden flows.
Or saw again his mother's grave
    where she sleeps amid his race
Good men and true, each one of them,
    in their own day and place.

Or heard once more the church bell smite
    throughout the morning air.
Calling each village household
    up to the place of prayer
And joined again the song of praise
    to God the wise and just.
In whose great love in life and death,
    I know he put his trust.

And so I trust he did not hear
    the dreary, gurgling sound
Of crimson lifeblood dripping
    from that fearful, ragged wound.
But my heart seemed nigh to bursting
    as the slow hours waned away
And I saw the death-camps gather
    the face grow parched and grey.

And I cried "O, friend and comrade
    for the sake of God above
Have you no word or token to send
    to those you love?
He looked up as if still seeing the old flag
    and faintly cried
"Tell them I redeemed my promise-
    I bore it till I died!"

OTHER SOLIDERS, ALPHABETICALLY

ACKERMAN, JOHN
Co. K 5th CVI, private, enlisted 21 June 1861, reenlisted, mustered out 19 July 1865, pension #506165 for the soldier and later for his widow Harriet

John Ackerman of New London enlisted at Hartford on 21 June 1861 as a private in Co. K 5th CVI for a term of three years. With his regiment he fought at the Battles of Gettysburg on 3 July 1863, Cedar Mountain on 9 August 1863, and Chancellorsville on 1 May 1864. In 1865 the Regiment was part of the Atlanta Campaign, the campaign of the Carolinas, and the march to Savannah. He was missing in action after the Battle of Silver Run, North Carolina on 2 March 1865.[280] Ackerman reenlisted as a veteran in Co. K on 21 December 1863 and was mustered out at Alexandria, Virginia on 19 July 1865.

He applied for an invalid pension on 12 June 1880. He was described as five feet five inches tall, light complexion, brown hair, blue eyes. While on duty at Milledgeville, Georgia about December 1864, he injured his left side by a fall while tearing up railroad tracks. He was treated at Savannah and contracted consumption. He lived at New London before and after the war and was living there during the 1880 federal

---

census.[281] He moved to Branford for a short period of time and was mustered in on 23 February 1882 as a member of the Mason Rogers Post No. 7 G.A.R. He was transferred back to the W. W. Perkins Post No. 47 G.A.R. of New London on 22 May 1884.

John B. Ackerman died at New London on 13 October 1900 age 69 and was buried in Duck River Cemetery, Old Lyme. His company and regiment were engraved on his stone and there was a G.A.R. marker on his gravesite in 1934.

Harriet M. Ackerman of New London applied for a widow's pension on 20 October 1890. She was married to the soldier under the name of Harriet M. Beckwith at New London by Rev. Jabez S. Swan on 28 March 1867. He was age 30, a machinist, born in Germany, living at New London. She was age 21, born at Old Lyme, living at New London. They had the following children (living in 1898): Cora DeWolf, born on 11 April 1868; and Lulu Hopper, born on 14 December 1869. Harriet Ackerman was born in 1846, died in 1928 and was buried in Duck River Cemetery, Old Lyme.[282]

ADAMS, JAMES[283]
Co. I 10th CVI, private, enlisted 23 November 1864, deserted 4 August 1865

James Adams of Branford enlisted on 23 November 1864 as a private in Co. I 10th CVI and deserted on 4 August 1865. He does not appear in the 1860 census at Branford.

ADAMS, JOHN
Co. F 27th CVI, private, enlisted 25 August 1862, mustered out 27 July 1863, pension application #911105 for the soldier

John Adams of North Branford enlisted at New Haven on 25 August 1862 and was mustered in on 3 October 1862 as a private in Co. F 27th CVI for a term of nine months. He fought at the Battles of Fredericksburg and Gettysburg with the rest of his company which was on picket duty during the Battle of Chancellorsville. John Adams was mustered out with the rest of his regiment at New Haven on 27 July 1863. He does not appear in the 1860 census at North Branford but is listed on the draft rolls as Class 3.

He applied for an invalid pension on 22 August 1890 under the act of 27 June 1890 claiming disability from a gunshot wound to the right knee at the Battle of Gettysburg and in another place said he was "bruised by a shell." He was living at Arden, Washington Co., Pennsylvania. Though a wound to his knee was verified by a physician's exam, he never received a pension. The cause for the rejection was not stated except the pension board noted "it was a curious case."

---

281 U.S. census 1880, Waterford, New London County, Connecticut, population schedule, T9-109, dwelling 89, family 90, page 742, www.heritagequest.com.

282 The Hale Collection, Old Lyme, 8.

283 There are a number of soldiers who enlisted or were drafted in 1864. Their residence was given as Branford when they enlisted, however, there is usually no record of their actual residence in town. It is possible that Branford was filling its quota and providing a bounty to men from other towns or the men were substitutes. Basic information about this group of soldiers is included but extensive research was not undertaken.

ALBEE, CALVIN
Co. I 15th CVI, private, enlisted 9 August 1862, killed 8 March 1865, pension #81193 for his widow Hannah

Calvin Albee, age 44, of Durham enlisted at New Haven on 9 August 1862 and was mustered in on 24 August 1862 as a private in Co. I 15th CVI for a term of three years. He saw action at Fredericksburg, Virginia on 13 December 1862, during the Siege of Suffolk, Virginia in the spring of 1863, and in the Peninsula Campaign of July 1863. He was killed at the Battle of Kinston, North Carolina, also known as the Battle of Wise's Fork, on 8 March 1865. His personal effects were captured by the enemy.

Calvin Albee of Durham was killed at the Battle of Kinston, North Carolina on 8 March 1865. His family came to Branford after the war. (Branford Historical Society photograph collection)

Calvin Albee was born at Lyme on 1 June 1815, son of Benjamin Albee and Lydia Otis. At the time of his enlistment he was described as five feet ten inches tall, fair complexion, blue eyes, brown hair, occupation shoemaker.

Hannah M. Albee of Durham, Middlesex Co. applied for a widow's pension on 28 August 1865. She was married to the soldier under the name of Hannah Maria Scranton at Durham by Rev. David Smith on 14 January 1836. He was living at Saybrook and she at Durham. At the time of her pension application, she had one minor child Ellen J. Albee, born on 18 December 1855. There were older children not named in the file and she did not remarry after the death of the soldier.

She removed to Branford where two of her daughters had settled. She became a member of the First Congregational Church at Branford on 1 July 1867, transferred from the Methodist Church of Durham.[284] She remained at Branford the rest of her life.

Hannah Maria Albee died at Branford on 28 September 1906 and was buried there in Center Cemetery.[285] She was born at Durham on 21 February 1817, daughter of Timothy Scranton and Hannah Hotchkiss.

A pocket bible was given to Calvin Albee by his wife when he went to war. After the Battle of Kinston, Joseph Atwood of the Second Connecticut Volunteers and a resident Woodbury found the bible with the name Calvin Albee, Durham, Conn. written on the fly leaf. He tried in vain to locate the Albee family but finally forty-four years later the bible was returned to Mrs. Charles Palmer of West Haven, daughter of Calvin Albee.[286]

ALBINGER, JOHN J.
Co. C 15th CVI, private, enlisted 11 August 1862, prisoner, mustered out 27 June 1865
pension #419762 for the soldier and later for his widow Bridget

John J. Albinger, age 32, of Branford enlisted at New Haven on 11 August 1862 and was mustered in on 25 August 1862 as a private in Co. C 15th CVI for a term of three years. He saw action at Fredericksburg, Vir-

---

284 First Congregational Church Records, Branford, 5:147.
285 Branford Vital Records, deaths, 1906.
286 Undated newspaper article, Branford Historical Society archives.

ginia on 13 December 1862, during the Siege of Suffolk, Virginia in the spring of 1863, and in the Peninsula Campaign of July 1863. He was captured with much of his regiment at the Battle of Kinston, North Carolina on 8 March 1865, confined at Libby Prison, Richmond on 23 March, and paroled at Boulware's & Cox's wharf on 26 March 1865. He reported to Camp Parole, Maryland on 30 March 1865, received a thirty day furlough and afterwards reported to Camp Convalescent, Virginia. Albinger was mustered out with the rest of his regiment at New Bern, North Carolina[287] on 27 June 1865 and discharged at New Haven on 12 July 1865.

He applied for an invalid pension on 24 September 1890 under the act of 27 June 1890. At the time of his enlistment he was described as five feet four inches tall, ruddy complexion, hazel eyes, brown hair, occupation farmer. "Joe Albinger has been sick but is doing duty now. Joseph Albinger is sick by turns, he has been well for the last two weeks, the chills bother him."[288] "Joe Albinger is hale and hearty and he does his duty well."[289] During the march from Kinston, North Carolina to prison in Richmond, Virginia he had to sleep on the ground with no shelter. He suffered from deafness in his ears, lumbago and rheumatism in his hips and left legs as a result of exposure.[290] "Nearly his whole regiment was captured on the 8th of March 1865 at Kingston, N. C. They were marched for 18 days to Richmond and on this march was obliged to sleep or camp during the nights on the cold and damp ground."[291]

John Joseph Albinger of Branford was a private in the 15th Connecticut Volunteer Infantry and captured with much of his Regiment at the Battle of Kinston, North Carolina on 8 March 1865. (Photograph by Ramsdell Studio, New Haven; courtesy of Carol Fogarty Young)

John Joseph Albinger died at Branford on 10 November 1894 and was buried there in St. Mary's Cemetery.[292] He was born in Germany, son of John and Anne Albinger.

Bridget Albinger, age 51, of Branford applied for a widow's pension on 24 November 1894. She was married to the soldier under the name of Bridget Curtin at New Haven by Rev. John Smith of St. John's Church on 22 August 1862, both were living at Branford. Neither were previously married or divorced and she did not remarry after his death. She had the following children under the age of sixteen (in 1894): Loretta, born on 31 May 1879, John Francis, born on 8 June 1881, and Josephine, born on 30 November 1884.

Bridget Curtin Albinger died at Branford on 29 August 1923 and was buried there in St. Mary's Cemetery.[293] She was born at County Cork, Ireland on 18 November 1845, daughter of Cornelius Curtin and Ellen Leahy.[294]

287 There are various spellings in the soldiers' files - Newbern, Newburn, Newberne, New Berne, New Bern.
288 Towner letters, 3 August and 19 September 1863.
289 Towner letter, 19 February 1865.
290 Affidavit, Dr. A. J. Tenny, 1 October 1890, in the pension file of John J. Albinger.
291 Affidavit, Dr. Arthur J. Tenney of Branford, no date, in the pension file of John J. Albinger.
292 Branford Sexton Records, 1884-1932, 16; no stone is recorded in the Hale Collection but a curbing with his name was found in 2012, partially buried.
293 Branford Sexton Records, 1884-1932, 107.
294 Branford Vital Records, deaths, 1923.

ALBINOS, JOHN
Co. H 11th CVI, private, enlisted 10 February 1864, mustered out 21 December 1865, no pension

John Albinos of Branford enlisted on 10 February 1864 as a private in Co. H 11th CVI and was mustered out at Hartford on 21 December 1865. He does not appear in the 1860 census at Branford.

ALLEN, HENRY
Co. F 17th CVI, lt. colonel, enlisted 11 August 1862, wounded, mustered out 19 July 1865, pension #220514 for the soldier and later for his widow Francis

Henry Allen of Norwalk enlisted on 11 August 1862 as a 1st lieutenant in Co. F 17th CVI for a term of three years. He was promoted to captain on 23 March 1863. He was slightly wounded from a gunshot to the fore finger of his left hand at the Battle of Gettysburg on 3 July 1863 and rejoined the regiment on 21 August 1863. He was promoted to major on 5 March 1864 and to lieutenant colonel on 20 May 1865. He was on a leave of absence for thirty days in October 1864. Allen was mustered out with the rest of his regiment at Hilton Head, South Carolina on 19 July 1865 and discharged at New Haven on 1 August 1865.

Lt. Colonel Henry Allen, above, commanded the 17th Connecticut Volunteer Infantry after the other officers were killed in battle. (Crofut & Morris, Military & Civil History of Connecticut, 568)

"My great uncle by marriage, Henry Allen, became commander of the 17th Connecticut Regiment when all the higher ranking officers were killed. He took part in many of the major battles and was at Gettysburg. A monument to this Regiment is on Barlow's Hill in the Memorial Park. My father, John Wilkinson Nichols, unveiled this monument at the time of its dedication when he was a small boy."[295]

Henry Allen of Norwalk, Fairfield Co. applied for an invalid pension on 26 March 1879. He was described as five feet ten inches tall, dark complexion, dark hair, black eyes, occupation clerk. Since his discharge he resided in Rhode Island, New York, and Washington, D.C. While in the line of duty he contracted "the disease of the lungs." He was sent to the Field Hospital and then to Baltimore, Maryland and was granted a leave of absence for thirty days. The bones of his finger were shattered by a gunshot wound at Gettysburg, and the "finger to this day remains of no use."[296] "He had disease of the lungs, an injury to his left side, and a sprained ankle. In my opinion he was incapacitated for any kind of manual labor at the time of his discharge. I have not seen him since until this week and found him still

---

295 Note from Rowena Nichols Mercer, undated, Branford Historical Society archives, RG 3, box 7, folder 12. The folder includes a pencil drawing of the monument.
296 Declaration, Henry Allen, 25 March 1879, in his own pension file.

suffering from the lung disease."[297] "While at or near Germania Ford, Va. as Capt. of Co. F on or about the 25th of April, 1863 he was drenched by the fording of said stream in the rain. The following morning he was attacked with a severe ailment in his lungs which lasted through his service. He was exposed afterwards in the service, particularly in a cold Northeasterly storm on Morris Island, S.C. in the latter part of Aug or Sept 1863. He had repeated lung and bronchial trouble with hemorrhages. Further, about Oct 1863 he was drenched at folly Island, SC in a storm while expecting an attack of the enemy."[298]

Henry Allen's pension file is large with many affidavits. The pension board accused him of falsifying his pension application but no reason is given. He did receive a pension.

Henry Allen died at Branford on 13 September 1885 and was buried there in Center Cemetery. His rank and regiment are engraved on his stone. He was born at Norwalk, son of William and Sophia Allen.

Frances Allen of Branford applied for a widow's pension after his death. She was married to the soldier under the name of Frances Almena Remington at Providence, Rhode Island by Elias H. Richardson of the Congregational Church on 14 September 1865.

Frances Allen died at Branford on 5 June 1911 and was buried there in Center Cemetery. She was born at North Providence, Rhode Island, daughter of Joseph and Alcy A. Remington.

AMES, CHARLES
Co. H 10th CVI, private, substitute, mustered in 12 November 1864, deserted

Charles Ames, age 20, served as a substitute for John B. Russell of Stony Creek, Branford. He was mustered in at New Haven on 12 November 1864 as a private in Co. H 10th CVI for a term of three years. He was described as five feet four inches tall, blue eyes, brown hair, dark complexion, unmarried, born in Canada, occupation tobacconist. He deserted before Richmond, Virginia on 26 November 1864. He does not appear in the 1860 census at Branford.

ARLINGTON, WILLOUGHBY
Willoughby Arlington served as a substitute for George M. Prout of Branford. He enlisted on 3 September 1864 at the Brooklyn Navy Yard.[299]

ASHMAN, ROBERT A.
Co. A 124th New York Infantry, private, enlisted 8 August 1862, wounded, mustered out 21 June 1865, pension #532520 for the soldier, application for his widow Alice and minor children

Robert A. Ashman, age 18, enlisted at Goshen, New York on 8 August 1862 and was mustered in on 5 September 1862 as a private in the 124th New York Volunteer Infantry for a term of three years. With his regiment he fought at the Battles of Chancellorsville, Wilderness, and Cold Harbor, Virginia. He was wounded at the Battle of Spotsylvania Court House, Virginia on 12 May 1864 and sent to Harwood Hospital, Washington, D.C. where he was mustered out on 21 June 1865. At the time of his enlistment he was described as five feet five and one half inches tall, brown eyes, brown hair, dark complexion, occupation farmer.

---

297 Affidavit, Dr. Sabin Stocking of Glastonbury, in the pension file of Henry Allen.
298 Affidavit, William H. Noble of Bridgeport, 24 November 1882, in the pension file of Henry Allen.
299 Statements of Navy substitutes, RG 13, box 96, 2nd Congregational District, Connecticut State Library.

He applied for an invalid pension on 3 October 1867. Robert Adolphus Ashman was born at Monroe, Orange Co., New York on 22 March 1844, son of Robert Adolphus Ashman and Charlotte McElroy. He was married first at Paterson, New Jersey on 9 June 1867 to Maria Rhutten.[300]

He was living at Monroe, New York in 1870 with his father and came to Branford by 1874.[301] He was married at Guilford by Rev. Henry Robinson on 27 October 1869 to Alice Mary Hotchkiss, daughter of John Hotchkiss a Branford Civil War soldier. Robert Ashman was living in 1884 and died before 6 July 1887 when his wife Alice applied for a widow's pension. He may have died at Carillo, Costa Rico on 28 November 1885[302] or 30 November.[303] "Robert Ashman was a veteran of the Civil War who died of yellow fever in South America and was buried there."[304]

Alice Hotchkiss Ashman applied for but did not receive a widow's pension since the soldier was never divorced from his first wife. As guardian, she applied for a pension for the soldier's minor children on 29 June 1889 but the pension was not granted. Mollie Ashman of Tennessee, also claiming to be the soldier's widow, contested the pension claim. The soldier may have married Mollie Caruth on 8 July 1884.[305]

Alice Ashman was married second at New Haven on 10 November 1887 to David Steel Ashman, younger brother of the soldier.[306] He was born at Monroe, Orange Co., New York on 27 June 1856, died at Stony Creek, Branford on 16 October 1904 and was buried in Stony Creek Cemetery. Alice Ashman died at Stony Creek on 13 August 1930 and was also buried in Stony Creek Cemetery. She was born at Branford on 8 October 1852, daughter of John Hotchkiss and Georgianna Tucker.[307]

AUGUR, REUBEN N.
see Daniel Lynch

AVERILL, ADELBERT C. or CHARLES A.
U.S. Navy, seaman, enlisted 1 September 1864, discharged 1 September 1865, pension #19263 for the sailor and later for his widow Estella

Adelbert C. Averill, age 21, of Branford enlisted at the Brooklyn, New York Navy Yard on 1 September 1864 and first served as a landsman on the U.S.S. *Vermont* until 18 September 1864; then as an ordinary seaman for the rest of the war on the U.S.S. *Grand Gulf* until 2 August 1865, the U.S.S. *Portsmouth* until 31 August 1865 and was discharged from the U.S.S. *North Carolina* at the Brooklyn Navy Yard on 1 September 1865. He was the first cousin of Roland Averill and nephew of David Averill.

He applied for an invalid pension on 29 April 1892 under the act of 27 June 1890 for age related illnesses. His claim was rejected because his diseases were not covered under the act. He reapplied several times and was rejected. He was again rejected on 1 February 1900 but it appears he finally received a pension in 1902.

---

300 GenForum posting, www.genealogy.com, 22 August 2000.
301 Birth of son Herbert. At the time of his marriage in 1869 he was living at Port Jarvis, New York.
302 GenForum posting, www.genealogy.com, 22 August 2000.
303 Branford Probate records, 39:59.
304 Obituary of son Frederick William Ashman, *New Haven Register*, 11 May 1943. Robert Ashman was a railroad engineer and it appears traveled for work.
305 GenForum posting, www.genealogy.com, 22 August 2000. Robert and Mollie had a son Winston Ashman born on 14 March 1885 at Riceville, McMinn Co., Tennessee. Robert and Alice Ashman had a child born at Branford on 2 November 1885. Mollie remained in Tennessee and never remarried.
306 New Haven Vital Records, marriages, 1887.
307 Branford Vital Records, deaths, 1930.

Adelbert C. Averill of Branford spent nearly one year aboard the U.S.S. Vermont as a landsman in the U.S. Navy. (Library of Congress Prints & Photographs Division)

At the time of his enlistment he was described as five feet nine inches tall, blue eyes, grayish brown hair, florid complexion, occupation seaman. He had a tattoo on his right arm with the initials A.C.A. His full name was Charles Adelbert Averill but he was known also as A.C. Averill and signed his name Adelbert C. Averill. He was a member of the Mason Rogers Post No. 7 G.A.R. of Branford.

Adelbert Charles Averill died at Branford on 6 August 1907 and was buried there in Center Cemetery.[308] He was born at Roxbury on 26 May 1843, son of Daniel Averill and Jane Bradley, born at Branford and New Lebanon, New York.

Estella N. Averill of Branford applied for a widow's pension on 11 September 1907. Her claim was sent for special examination to determine the value of her property and her means of support. The pension file is large with many depositions. She was married to the soldier under the name of Estella Nancy Shepard at Branford by Rev. Elijah C. Baldwin of the First Congregational Church on 29 January 1873, ages 29 and 26. Neither were previously married or divorced. They had only one child, Roy Victor born at Branford on 16 September 1879. She did receive a pension.

Estella N. Averill died at 98 Harbor Street, Branford on 4 December 1921 and was buried in Center Cemetery.[309] She was born on 22 August 1846, daughter of Baldwin Shepard and Nancy Smith. She was born, married, and died in the same house.

AVERILL, DANIEL 2ND
Co. B 27th CVI, 1st sergeant, enlisted 21 August 1862, prisoner, mustered out 27 July 1863, pension #768052 for the soldier and later for his widow Lucy

Daniel Averill, 2nd of Branford, age 23, enlisted on 21 August 1862 and was mustered in on 3 October 1862 as 1st sergeant of Co. B 27th CVI for a term of nine months. Captain Ely described him as the "orderly sergeant and a brave and faithful soldier."[310] He fought at the Battle of Fredericksburg on 13 December 1862

308 Branford Sexton Records, 1884-1932, 52; no stone was found and none is recorded in the Hale Collection.
309 Branford Sexton Records, 1884-1932, 101; no stone was found and none recorded in the Hale Collection.
310 Blackstone Library Archives, RG 3, box 2, folder 1, Daniel Averill orderly book, contains a list of men in Co. B & their height.

with the rest of the company. He was absent on furlough in Connecticut on 8 February 1863. He was captured at the Battle of Chancellorsville, Virginia on 3 May 1863, held prisoner at Richmond, and paroled at City Point, Virginia on 14 May 1863. He reported to Camp Parole, Maryland on 16 May 1863 and spent the remainder of his service at Camp Convalescent, Virginia. With the rest of the Chancellorsville paroled prisoners, he rejoined the Regiment at Baltimore on 20 July 1863. Daniel Averill was mustered out with the rest of his regiment at New Haven on 27 July 1863. He was the first cousin of David Averill and William A. Tyler and brother-in-law of Nicholas Terhune.

He applied for an invalid pension on 29 September 1890 under the act of 27 June 1890 citing disabilities. At the time of his enlistment he was described as five feet nine inches tall, dark complexion, black eyes, black hair, occupation farmer. The application was rejected on 26 April 1892. He again filed on 9 March 1897 and this application was rejected on 12 May 1898. The second rejection was upheld on appeal. Averill applied under the act of 11 May 1912, by then a resident of the Fitch's Soldier Home at Noroton Heights, age 72. This pension application was approved for $19.00 per month.

Since the war he lived at Branford until 1876, at Naugatuck from 1876 to 1888, and returned to Branford in 1888. He was admitted to the Fitch's Home for Soldiers[311] at Noroton Heights on 9 October 1911. At the time of his death his possessions included his discharge and service papers, and one overcoat.

Daniel Averill died at the Soldiers' Home on 11 November 1913 and was buried in Center Cemetery, Branford. His company and regiment are engraved on his stone and there was a G.A.R. marker on his gravesite in 1934 and 2011. He was born at Branford on 9 July 1839, son of James Averill and Amanda Bassett.

Lucy E. Averill filed for a widow's pension on 21 November 1913. She was married the soldier under the name of Lucy Elizabeth Pond at Branford by Rev. Elijah C. Baldwin of the First Congregational Church on 1 January 1866. Neither were previously married or divorced. She did not remarry after his death and the soldier left no children.

Daniel Averill of Branford was 1st sergeant of Co. B 27th Connecticut Infantry and is buried in Center Cemetery. (Branford Historical Society photograph collection)

Lucy Pond Averill died at New Haven on 29 July 1922 and was buried in Center Cemetery, Branford. She was born at Branford on 19 September 1844, daughter of Russell Pond and Lydia Tyler.[312]

---

311 Fitch's Home for Soldiers, Deceased Veterans Discharge Files 1882-1932, box 13, file 3195, Connecticut State Library.
312 Branford Vital Records, deaths, 1922.

AVERILL, DAVID

Co. B 1st Cavalry, private, enlisted 28 October 1861, discharged disability 16 May 1864, no pension

David Averill of Branford enlisted on 28 October 1861 and was mustered in at Meriden on 2 November 1861 as a private in the 1st Connecticut Cavalry for a term of three years. With his regiment he served in many engagements in Virginia including Battles at Cedar Mountain and the Second Bull Run. He was discharged for disability on 16 May 1864.

He never applied for a pension. After the war he lived at Branford and was a member of the Mason Rogers Post No. 7 G.A.R. of Branford. He was the uncle of Adelbert and Roland Averill and the first cousin of Daniel Averill, 2nd and William A. Tyler.

David Averill died at Branford on 27 April 1887 age 56 years and 6 months and was buried there in Center Cemetery.[313] His regiment is engraved on his stone and a G.A.R. marker was on his gravesite in 1934 and 2011. He was born at Branford, son of David Averill and Polly Morris. He was married at Branford by Rev. Henry Olmstead of Trinity Episcopal Church on 27 February 1854 to Elizabeth Charlotte Foote.[314] They had two children not listed in the pension file. She was born at Branford on 28 April 1836, daughter of David Austin Foote and Mary H. Curtiss.[315] She died at Branford on 27 September 1920 and was buried there in Center Cemetery.[316] She did not apply for a pension.

AVERILL, EDMUND M.
see John O'Neal

AVERILL, JARVIS
see John McGinnis

AVERILL, ROLAND G.

Marine Corps, private, enlisted 16 August 1864, discharged 23 November 1865, pension #11107 for his widow Fannie and minor children

Roland G. Averill, age 21, of Branford enlisted at the Marine Barracks, Brooklyn, New York on 16 August 1864 as a private in the U.S. Marine Corps. The Marine Corps was small during the Civil War and served with the Navy. He served on the U.S.S. *Grand Gulf* and returned to the Brooklyn Barracks on 11 November 1865 and was discharged there on 23 November 1865. He was the first cousin of Adelbert Averill and nephew of David Averill.

At the time of his enlistment he was described as five feet ten inches tall, hazel eyes, black hair, dark complexion, occupation tailor. He never applied for a pension. He was a member of the Mason Rogers Post No. 7 G.A.R. of Branford.

---

313 Branford Vital Records, 1863-1895, 235.
314 Branford Vital Records, 1852-1863, 3.
315 Branford Vital Records, Town Meeting book A, 235.
316 Branford Vital Records, deaths, 1920.

Roland Gelston Averill died at Branford on 17 October 1894 and was buried there in Center Cemetery.[317] A G.A.R. marker was on his gravesite in 1934 and 2011. He was born at Branford on 3 May 1843, son of John Averill and Almira Hemingway.[318]

Fannie M. Averill applied for a widow's pension on 27 December 1894. She had two children under the age of sixteen: Carrie M. [Carolyn], born on 23 July 1879; and Harry R., born on 13 May 1882. She was married to the soldier under the name of Fannie M. Palmer at Branford by Rev. Elijah C. Baldwin of the First Congregational Church on 27 November 1867. Neither were previously married or divorced.

Fannie M. Averill died at Branford on 20 September 1919 and was buried there in Center Cemetery. She was born at Branford on 7 March 1847, daughter of Joel B. Palmer and Lucinda Clanning.

BABCOCK, MARCUS O.
U.S. Navy, landsman, enlisted 1 September 1864, discharged 1 September 1865, pension #20125 for the sailor

Marcus O. Babcock of Branford enlisted on 1 September 1864 at the Brooklyn Navy Yard, New York. He served as a landsman on the U.S.S. *Vermont* until 18 September 1864; as a landsman and coxswain on the U.S.S. *Grand Gulf* until 2 August 1865; on the *Portsmouth* until 31 August 1865; and was discharged from the U.S.S. *North Carolina* at the Brooklyn Navy Yard on 1 September 1865. He may have also served on the U.S.S. *Savannah*.

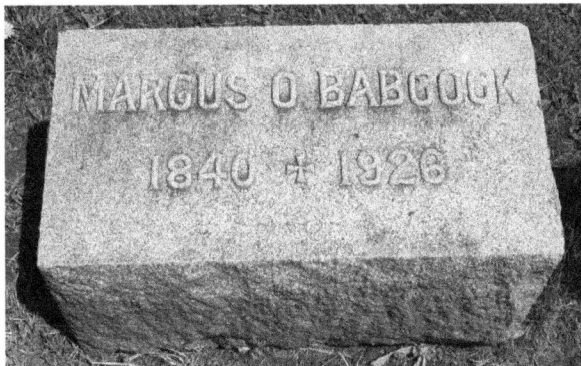

(Photographic History of the Civil War, 6:279)

---

317 Branford Vital Records, deaths, 1894.
318 Branford Vital Records, Town Meeting Book A, 237.

He applied for an invalid pension on 18 January 1892 under the act of 27 June 1890. At the time of his enlistment he was described as five feet six inches tall, hazel eyes, brown hair, occupation seaman. He was married at Branford by Rev. David Bishop of Trinity Episcopal Church on 31 December 1868 to Rebecca Hobart Robinson. Neither were previously married or divorced. They had the following children: William Robinson, born on 6 August 1870, died young; Lauretta Hobart, born on 20 August 1872; and Anson Tyler, born on 21 June 1875. His wife was born at Branford on 22 February 1843 and died there on 28 January 1923. Since his discharge he lived at Branford. He was a member of the Mason Rogers Post No. 7 G.A.R. of Branford.

Marcus O. Babcock died at Branford on 29 March 1926 and was buried there in Center Cemetery. A G.A.R. marker was on his gravesite in 1934. He was born at North Lyme on 23 August 1840, son of Russell William Babcock and Wealthy Ann Emmons. [319]

BACKES, MICHAEL
Co. B 27th CVI, private, enlisted 10 September 1862, prisoner, mustered out 27 July1863, pension #689760 for his widow Catherine

Michael Backes[320] of Wallingford, age 32, enlisted on 10 September 1862 and was mustered in on 3 October 1862 as a private in Co. B 27th CVI for a term of nine months. He fought at the Battle of Fredericksburg on 13 December 1862 with the rest of the company. He was captured at the Battle of Chancellorsville, Virginia on 3 May 1863, held prisoner at Richmond, and paroled at City Point, Virginia on 14 May 1863. He reported to Camp Parole, Maryland on 16 May 1863, was sent to Washington, D.C. on 20 May 1863, and spent the remainder of his service at Camp Convalescent, Virginia. With the rest of the Chancellorsville paroled prisoners, he rejoined the Regiment at Baltimore on 20 July 1863. Backes was mustered out with the rest of his regiment at New Haven on 27 July 1863.

He never applied for a pension. Michael Backes died at Wallingford on 19 October 1889 and was buried there In Memoriam Cemetery. He was born in Germany on 22 September 1829, son of John and Elizabeth Backes. He came to the United States in 1835 and to Wallingford in 1853.

Catherine Backes, age 72, of 168 South Main Street, Wallingford, applied for a widow's pension on 31 July 1908 under the act of 10 April 1908. She was married to the soldier under the name of Catherine Helmstaldter at Newark, New Jersey by Rev. F. A. Lehlbach on 15 May 1853. Neither were previously married or divorced and she did not remarry after his death.

Catherine Backes died at Wallingford on 2 December 1915 and was buried there In Memoriam Cemetery. She was born in Germany on 7 June 1836, daughter of Peter Helmsteadtor [sic] and Catherine Leice.

Seventy-one years after the death of Michael Backes, his three daughters Catherine Russell, Grace Sanders, and Rebecca Breckenridge, all living at 168 South Main Street, Wallingford, applied for a pension on the service of their father stating they were dependent on his support. All three were in their in their seventies or eighties and widowed. The claim was disallowed and was the only example found of a pension claim by children years after the death of the soldier. The file includes the daughter's birth records.

---

319 Branford Vital Records, deaths, 1926.
320 For his biography see Rockey, *History of New Haven County*, I:413.

BAILEY, HEMAN W. also HERMAN
Co. H 13th CVI & Co. E 13th Battalion, corporal, enlisted 27 January 1862, wounded, mustered out 25 April 1866, pension #154172 for the soldier

Heman W. Bailey, age 20, of Durham enlisted at New Haven on 27 January 1862 and was mustered in on 28 January 1862 as a private in Co. H 13th CVI for a term of three years. With his regiment he served in the New Orleans area including the Battle of Irish Bend on 14 April 1863 and the Siege of Port Hudson. He was discharged at Port Hudson and reenlisted as a veteran in Co. E on 2 February 1864. He was promoted to corporal on 1 July 1864. Through much of 1864 he suffered from diarrhea and fever. He received a severe gunshot wound to the left side of his face at the Third Battle of Winchester, Virginia on 19 September 1864 and was taken prisoner. He was brought from the field to a rebel hospital at Sheridan Depot on 24 September and was paroled at James River, Virginia on 22 February 1865. After his release he was treated at a hospital in Little York, Pennsylvania about six months. He was transferred to Co. E 13th Battalion on 24 December 1864 and his rank was reduced on 28 October 1865. Bailey was mustered out with the rest of the 13th Battalion at Fort Pulaski, Georgia on 25 April 1866.

He applied for an invalid pension on 9 May 1878. At the time of his enlistment he was described as five feet seven inches tall, light complexion, grey eyes, brown hair, occupation farmer. After his discharge he lived at Northford for 18 years, Middletown for 10 years, then Durham. He appears at Northford as a pensioner in 1883.

His pension claim was sent for special examination to determine if his deafness was caused by the gunshot wound he received at the Battle of Winchester. There are many documents in the file from physicians. He had total deafness in his left ear and partial deafness in his right ear associated with dizziness. He also had difficulty eating due to damage to his jaw and numbness of the left side of his face. He was granted a one fourth disability pension in 1878 but within a few years received an increase.

He was married first at Durham by Rev. J. W. Sessions on 6 June 1867 to Lydia S. Bassett. Lydia died at Northford on 25 April 1876. He was married second at New Haven by Rev. Edward Hawes on 12 January 1877 to Anna A. Scranton. Anna died at Rockfalls [Connecticut] on 23 March 1887. He was married third at Middletown by Rev. Frederic Gray on 4 May 1895 to Mrs. Helen Holt. Helen died at Durham on 17 May 1910. He married a fourth time at the Methodist Episcopal Church in Middletown by Rev. Flint on 16 October 1912 to Cora Josephine Burchard. She was living in 1915. He had one son, Elmer James Bailey, born at Northford on 16 March 1871[321] by his first wife, living at Middletown in 1915.

Heman Wesley Bailey died at Middletown on 27 June 1923 age 83 and was buried in New Cemetery, Durham. His company and regiment are engraved on his stone and a G.A.R. marker was on his gravesite in 1934. He was born at Durham on 6 October 1841, son of Eleazer and Damaris Bailey. He was baptized on 25 November 1853 at the Methodist Episcopal Church in Durham.

BAISLEY, JOHN W.
U.S. Navy, steward, enlisted 3 January 1864, discharged 3 August 1864, pension #31549 for the sailor

John W. Baisley of New York enlisted on 3 January 1864 as a Navy first class boy and later as a steward. He served on the U.S.S. *North Carolina* from 9 January 1864 to 16 April 1864 and on the U.S.S. *Clyde* from

---

321 On another pension application he states that Elmer was born in 1870. Elmer's birth is not in the North Branford Vital Records.

Above, John W. Baisley of New York served in the U.S. Navy and came to Branford after the war. (courtesy of Mabel Baisley Kerrigan)

30 June 1864 to 15 August 1865. The *Clyde* saw service running blockades in Florida. He was discharged at the Philadelphia Navy Yard on 5 August 1865.

He applied for an invalid pension on 11 June 1892 under the act of 27 June 1890. At the time of his enlistment he was described as five feet four inches tall, light complexion, hazel eyes, auburn hair. Since his discharge he lived at New York City and came to Branford about 1874. He was a member of the Mason Rogers Post No. 7 G.A.R. of Branford.

He states on his pension application "I, John W. Rabbeson was born July 1st 1844 at Greenpoint, Long Island. Rabbeson was my mother's name. At about nine weeks after my birth my mother left me in the care of A. E. Egbert of Greenpoint and I lived with him as my guardian until age 11 yrs. I never saw my mother again and never saw my father until 1870. After the war I returned to the use of my own name [Baisley] and was married to Sarah Ann Fisher by Rev. Dr. Maher at the Church of the Immaculate Conception, at East 14th St., New York City, on the 13th day of February 1870."[322] He was age 24, she was age 18, both were born at and living at New York City. Neither were previously married or divorced. They had the following children: J. W., Jr., born at New York City on 29 November 1870; G. H. [George], born at New York City on 12 March 1873; Emogene F., born at Branford on 15 December 1875, died September 1883; Silas S., born at Branford on 30 October 1877; Thomas A., born at Branford on 15 December 1879; James A., born at Fair Haven on 22 October 1871, died on 4 March 1906; Estelle L., born at Branford on 12 October 1883; Lauretta L., born at Branford on 7 February 1886; Joseph V., born at Branford on 19 Jan 1890; Sadie, born at Branford on 30 July 1888; Violet, born at Branford on 27 September 1892; and Raymond A., born at Branford on 22 February 1894.

Sarah Fisher Baisley died at Branford on 18 February 1903 and was buried there in Center Cemetery.[323] She was born at New York City on 22 June 1852, daughter of George W. Fisher and Elizabeth Reilly.

John William Baisley died at New Haven on 21 April 1917 and was buried in Center Cemetery, Branford.

BALDWIN, GEORGE W.
Co. B 27th CVI, private, enlisted 21 August 1862, prisoner, mustered out 27 July1863, no pension

George W. Baldwin, age 28, of Branford enlisted on 21 August 1862 and was mustered in on 3 October 1862 as a private in Co. B 27th CVI for a term of nine months. He fought at the Battle of Fredericksburg on 13 De-

---

322 Statement to Attorney Frank J. Kinney of Branford, 22 June 1907, in the pension file of John W. Baisley.
323 Branford Vital Records, deaths, 1903; a gravestone was placed by the family in 2006. Thanks to Mabel Baisley Kerrigan of Branford for information about her great-grandfather.

cember 1862 with the rest of the company and "had a ball [go] through his cap."[324] He was captured at the Battle of Chancellorsville, Virginia on 3 May 1863, held prisoner at Richmond, and paroled at City Point, Virginia on 14 May 1863. He reported to Camp Parole, Maryland on 16 May 1863, was sent to Washington, D.C. on 20 May 1863 and spent the remainder of his service at Camp Convalescent, Virginia. With the rest of the Chancellorsville paroled prisoners, he rejoined the Regiment at Baltimore on 20 July 1863. George W. Baldwin was mustered out with the rest of his regiment at New Haven on 27 July 1863. He was in Co. B 27th CVI Pioneer Corps.[325] He never applied for a pension.

He was married at Branford by Rev. Elijah C. Baldwin of the First Congregational Church on 1 October 1874 to Betsey Franklin.[326]

George W. Baldwin died at Branford on 29 September 1878 age 47[327] and was buried there in Center Cemetery. A G.A.R. marker was on his gravesite in 1934. He was born at Mount Carmel, New York, son of Arva Baldwin and Harriet Carpenter.

BALDWIN, JEROME A.
Co. G 7th CVI, private, enlisted 27 August 1861, wounded, prisoner, discharged 12 September 1864, pension #629733 for the soldier and later for his widow Lydia

Jerome A. Baldwin of Branford enlisted at New Haven on 27 August 1861 and was mustered in on 7 September 1861 as a private in Co. G 7th CVI for a term of three years. He was shot in the right leg and taken prisoner at the Battle of Drewry's Bluff, Virginia[328] on 16 May 1864. He was originally reported as missing in action. He was confined at Richmond, Virginia on 18 May 1864 and sent to a hospital in Richmond on 21 May 1864. Afterwards, he was sent to prison at Andersonville, Georgia. He was paroled on 13 August 1864 and reported to Aikens Lodge, Virginia on 22 August 1864. He was sent to Division Hospital, Maryland on 24 August and discharged on 12 September 1864.

Jerome Baldwin of Branford served in the 7th CVI. He was wounded and captured at the Battle of Drewry's Bluff, Virginia in 1864. (by F. D. Bradley Studio, New Haven; Branford Historical Society photograph collection)

He applied for an invalid pension on 3 March 1865 under the act of 14 July 1862. At the time of his enlistment he was described as five feet six inches tall, dark complexion. He received a penetrating flesh wound in the upper leg but no bones were broken. He initially received a one fourth disability due to the leg wound at $2.00 per month. He was a charter member of the Mason Rogers Post No. 7 G.A.R. of Branford.

---

324 Towner letter, 16 December 1862.
325 Sheldon, *History of the Twenty-Seventh*, 122.
326 Branford Vital Records, 1863-1895, 149.
327 Branford Vital Records, 1863-1895, 221.
328 Often spelled Drury in the records.

Jerome A. Baldwin died at Branford on 21 March 1907 and was buried there in Center Cemetery. A G.A.R. marker was on his gravesite in 1934. He was born at North Branford on 19 March 1835 although at the time of his enlistment his birth was given as 19 March 1836. He was the son of Giles Baldwin and Elizabeth Bush.

Lydia Baldwin, age 69, of Branford applied for a widow's pension on 5 April 1907. She was married to the soldier under the name of Lydia Sherwood at Peekskill, Westchester Co., New York by Thomas A. Whitney, JP on 28 February 1867. He was living at New Haven and she at Cortlandtown, Westchester Co., New York. Neither were previously married or divorced, and she did not remarry after his death. She lived at Branford since her marriage. They had no children.

Lydia Baldwin died at Branford on 19 December 1916 and was buried there in Center Cemetery. She was born at Scruff Oaks, New York on 1 August 1837, daughter of Joshua Sherwood and Lydia Canfield.[329]

BAMBERG, CASPER
Co. C 11th CVI, private, enlisted 25 September 1861, discharged for disability 25 February 1863, pension #257453 for his widow Mary

Casper Bamberg[330] of North Branford enlisted at New Haven on 11 September 1861 and was mustered in at Hartford on 27 November 1861 as a private in Co. C 11th CVI for a term of three years. He was discharged for disability from Camp Convalescent, Virginia on 27 February 1863. He was the father of Martin Bamberg and related to Michael Bamberg both of the same company.

At the time of his discharge was described as 54 years of age, five feet two inches tall, fair complexion, blue eyes, grey hair, occupation farmer, born in Germany. The cause of his discharge was old age and rheumatism contracted while in the service. "On the march to South Mountain, Md on the 14th day of September 1862, said Casper Bamberg fell over a stump & was injured by the fall, over the hip on one side. He was obliged to fall back & was sent to some hospital I think at Middletown. I never saw him after we left there."[331] After his discharge he lived at New Haven and Yalesville. About two months before his death he moved to Bridgeport. He never applied for a pension.

Casper Bamberg died Monday, 19 September 1881 on the steamer *Herder* while on passage from New York to Hamburg for a visit to Germany. A copy of his death certificate filed at Hamburg is in the file. His name appears on the Northford Veterans' Monument.

Mary Bamberg of Bridgeport applied for a widow's pension on 1 August 1885. She was married to the soldier under the name of Mary Bamberg at Dagmar, Saxony by Rev. Angel on June 1841. A copy of the original marriage certificate in German and translated in English is in the file. "Bamberg, Casper only son of the farmer Jacob Bamberg of Tachbach was married with Maria Margaretha, oldest daughter of the farm

---

329 Branford Vital Records, deaths, 1916.
330 Correspondence concerning his pension can be found in the Noble Pension Records, RG 13, box 4, case 58, Connecticut State Library.
331 Affidavit, Michael Bamberg. of New Haven, 26 June 1888, in the pension file of Casper Bamberg. Michael Bamberg was a brother or brother-in-law and was also in Co. C 11th CVI.

laborer Michael Bamberg of Tachbach on the 16th of May 1841; Bridegroom's age 30, bride's age 20; Certified June 16th 1886 from the Dueal Parish office, Schubart." They were cousins. After "much trouble" she succeeded in getting a copy of the ship's record which stated the cause of death was weakness. The ship's physician could not be found.

Mary Bamberg died at Bridgeport on 26 June 1913 and was buried in Lakeview Cemetery, Bridgeport. Her son Christian F. Bamberg, age 54, of 487 Ogden Street, Bridgeport applied for reimbursement for her burial on 21 July 1913.

BAMBERG, MARTIN
Co. C 11th CVI, private, enlisted 25 September 1861, discharged 24 October 1864, pension #718926 for the soldier and later for his widow Emma

Martin Bamberg of North Branford enlisted at New Haven on 25 September 1861 and was mustered in at Hartford on 27 November 1861 as a private in Co. C 11th CVI for a term of three years. With his regiment he saw action at New Bern, North Carolina and the Battle of Fredericksburg. After Fredericksburg he was sick in the hospital. Martin Bamberg was discharged when his term expired at Hartford on 24 October 1864. He was the son of Casper Bamberg of the same company.

He applied for an invalid pension on 27 February 1886. While in the line of duty at Fredericksburg, Va. about November 1862 he contracted diarrhea and rheumatism resulting in disease of the liver and heart. "While at Fredericksburg, Va. Feb. 1863 he had a severe attack of diarrhea and was taken to Regimental Hospital and after being there for some time was not fit to return to duty and was sent to General Hospital at Washington, D.C."[332] "Before the war he was a Healthy boy. When he returned he was a wreck, thin of flesh, emaciated, his former vigor gone and always said Army life ruined his health. I know he came near Death when we were in Newbern, NC with Typhoid Fever as I was a member in the same Company."[333] There is another affidavit in 1889 from his uncle Andrew Bamberg, age 65, of New Haven. After his discharge he lived at New Haven and moved to Yalesville in 1870.

Martin Bamberg died at Yalesville, Wallingford on 13 February 1911 and was buried there In Memoriam Cemetery. His company and regiment are engraved on his stone and a G.A.R. marker was on his gravesite in 1934. He was born in Germany on 14 September 1844, son of Casper Bamberg and Mary Bamberg. His name appears on the Northford Veterans' Monument.

Emma Bamberg of Yalesville applied for a widow's pension on 18 February 1911. She was married to the soldier under the name of Emma Cramer at New Haven by Rev. John G. Lutz on 28 November 1872. He was age 28, living at Wallingford; she was age 22, living at New Haven; both were born in Germany. Neither were previously married or divorced and she did not remarry after his death. They had the following children living (in 1898): Frederick W., born on 5 November 1878, Edwin C., born on 29 December 1883, and Lizzie C., born on 23 December 1891.

---

332 Affidavit, John Rooney of Fairfield, 15 November 1889, in the pension file of Martin Bamberg.
333 Affidavit, Michael Bamberg of New Haven, 14 November 1889, in the pension file of Martin Bamberg.

BARKER, AMMI B.
Co. C 5th CVI, private, enlisted 21 June 1861, discharged 26 July 1861, Co. B 15th CVI, private, enlisted 6 August 1862, prisoner, mustered out 27 June 1865, pension #A10-26-27 for the soldier and later for his widow Julia

Ammi B. Barker of Branford first enlisted at Hartford on 21 June 1861 as a private in Co. C 5th CVI. It was discovered he was still a minor and he was honorably discharged on 26 July 1861. "My father came with a writ of habeas corpus and took me home."[334] He enlisted second at New Haven on 6 August 1862 and was mustered in on 25 August 1862 as a private in Co. B 15th CVI for a term of three years. He saw action at Fredericksburg, Virginia on 13 December 1862, during the Siege of Suffolk, Virginia in the spring of 1863, and in the Peninsula Campaign of July 1863. He was captured with much of his regiment at the Battle of Kinston, North Carolina on 8 March 1865, confined at Libby Prison, Richmond on 23 March, and paroled at Boulware's & Cox's wharf on 26 March 1865. He reported to Camp Parole, Maryland on 30 March 1865, received a thirty day furlough and afterwards reported to Camp Convalescent, Virginia. Ammi Barker was mustered out with the rest of his regiment at New Bern, North Carolina on 27 June 1865 and discharged at New Haven on 12 July 1865. He was the brother-in-law of George W. Beach.

He applied for an invalid pension on 30 December 1891 under the act of 27 June 1890. At the time of his enlistment he was described as five feet nine inches tall, dark complexion, grey eyes, brown hair, occupation mechanic and lock maker. He was married first at Branford by Rev. David D. Bishop of Trinity Episcopal Church on 25 November 1868 to Anna L. Hull. She died at Branford on 2 July 1887 and was buried there in Mill Plain Cemetery. They had five children: Harold E., born on 14 November 1869; Georgia L., born on 16 April 1872; Etta, born on 3 August 1874; Ernest M., born on 11 April 1876; and Robert R., born on 7 April 1877. Georgia and Robert were living in 1898. He was a charter member, commander and quartermaster of the Mason Rogers Post No. 7 G.A.R. of Branford. His daughter Georgia unveiled the Branford Soldiers' Monument at the dedication in 1885.

Ammi B. Barker died at Branford on 19 August 1927 and was buried there in Mill Plain Cemetery. He was born at Branford on 8 March 1844, son of Eliphalet Barker and Martha W. McCoy.

Julia E. Barker applied for a widow's pension on 30 August 1927. She was married first to Civil War soldier William F. Graham (see Graham, page 313). She was married second to Ammi B. Barker at Branford by Rev. Palmer G. Wightman of the First Baptist Church on 5 December 1893.

Julia E. Rogers Graham Barker died at New Haven on 17 July 1929 and was buried in Center Cemetery, Branford.[335] She was born at Norwich on 7 September 1849, daughter of Asa Lee Rogers and Lorinda C. Curtiss.

---

334 Pension declaration, Ammi B. Barker of Branford, 17 May 1912, in his own pension file.
335 Branford Vital Records, deaths, 1929.

BARKER, JOSEPH
Co. K 6th CVI, private, enlisted 9 September 1861, killed 16 May 1864 at Drewry's Bluff, Virginia; no pension

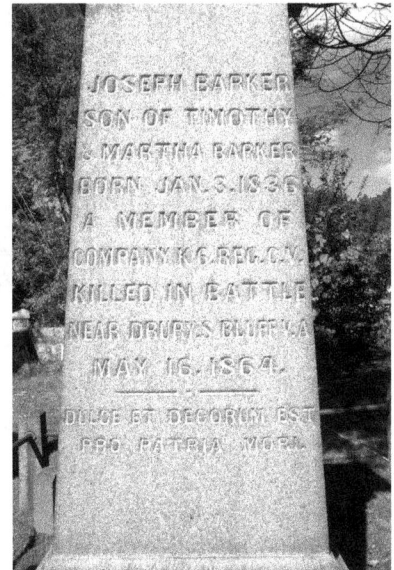

Joseph Barker of Branford enlisted at New Haven on 9 September 1861 and was mustered in on 12 September 1861 as a private in Co. K 6th CVI. With his regiment he served in Georgia, South Carolina, Florida and in the Virginia campaigns. He was killed at the Battle of Drewry's Bluff, Virginia on 16 May 1864.

He was born at Branford on 3 January 1836, son of Timothy Barker and Martha Leonard. [336] His name, regiment and place of death are engraved on the family monument in Damascus Cemetery, Branford.

BARNES, GEORGE H.
Co. K 15th CVI, private, enlisted 11 August 1862, mustered out 27 June 1865, pension #391659 for the soldier

George H. Barnes, age 24, of North Branford enlisted at New Haven on 11 August 1862 and was mustered in on 25 August 1862 as a private in Co. K 15th CVI for a term of three years. On 31 December 1862 he was present but sick in quarters. He entered Regimental Hospital on 1 November 1863 and returned to his company on 10 December 1863.[337] During the first half of 1864 he was the assistant company cook and in July he was sick in Knight Hospital, New Haven. He returned to his regiment as assistant company cook for the rest of 1864 and was not taken prisoner at Kinston, North Carolina since he was on light duty. George Barnes was mustered out with the rest of his regiment at New Bern, North Carolina on 27 June 1865 and discharged at New Haven on 12 July 1865. He served under Capt. Medad D. Munson of Wallingford.

He applied for an invalid pension on 18 February 1887. In the Fall of 1862 while near Long Bridge, Potomac Flats, he contracted malaria and at Fredericksburg had a severe attack of rheumatism. "I was sick and in the Camp all the time for two to three months I did little or no duty until we reached Newport News." "He was detailed as a caterer for officers as he was unfit for duty."[338] At the time of his enlistment he was described as five feet seven inches tall, light complexion, blue eyes, brown hair, occupation farmer. Since his discharge he lived at Durham for two years and since 1 April 1867 at Northford. He was married at Durham by Rev. M. Hurd to Carrie Louise Bailey. She died in 1917 and was buried in Northford Cemetery.[339] They had no children.

336 Branford Vital Records, 1786-1840, 378.
337 Statement, Charles F. Beckley, 30 April 1887, in the pension file of George H. Barnes.
338 Statement, Capt. M. D. Munson of Wallingford, 23 March 1887, in the pension file of George H. Barnes.
339 The Hale Collection, North Branford, 64.

George H. Barnes died at Northford on 21 February 1917 and was buried there in Northford Cemetery. A G.A.R. marker was on his gravesite in 1934. He was born at Northford on 15 March 1837, son of Seneca Barnes and Martha Hart. His name appears on the Northford Veterans' Monument.

BARNES, WILLIAM H.
Co. A 27th CVI, private, enlisted 2 September 1862, prisoner, mustered out 27 July 1863, pension #174483 for the soldier and later for his widow Mary

William H. Barnes of New Haven enlisted on 2 September 1862 and was mustered in on 3 October 1862 as a private in Co. A 27th CVI for a term of nine months. He fought at the Battle of Fredericksburg on 13 December 1862 with the rest of the regiment. He was captured at the Battle of Chancellorsville, Virginia on 3 May 1863, held prisoner at Richmond, and paroled at City Point, Virginia on 14 May 1863. He reported to Camp Parole, Maryland on 16 May 1863 and spent the remainder of his service at Camp Convalescent, Virginia. With the rest of the Chancellorsville paroled prisoners, he rejoined the Regiment at Baltimore on 20 July 1863. William Barnes was mustered out with the rest of his regiment at New Haven on 27 July 1863.

He applied for an invalid pension on 8 July 1891 under the act of 27 June 1890. He claimed partial disability from chronic diarrhea and sun stroke during the Battle of Fredericksburg and while in Libby Prison. "During the Battle of Chancellorsville, Va I was several days skirmishing and on picket duty and was completely used up. The next day we held the old line of Battle until noon Sunday May 3d 1863 until surrounded by the enemy and were marched off to Richmond which took a week. We arrived in Richmond on Sunday May 10. I had been helped along by companions having suffered sun stroke on the way. Was sick all the time while in Libbie Prison and also on Belle Island where they [the enemy] put us Libbie being so crowded."[340] His initial application was rejected as no pensionable degree of disability was found. He later received a pension based on age.

At the time of his enlistment he was described as five feet six inches tall, light complexion, blue eyes, brown hair, occupation clerk. After his discharge he lived at New Haven and summers at Stony Creek, Branford where he ran the Pot Island House. He was a member of the Admiral Foote Post No. 17 G.A.R. of New Haven.

William Harrison Barnes died at New Haven on 3 December 1908 and was buried in Fair Haven Union Cemetery. He was born at Chautaque, New York on 6 July 1840, son of Henry Barnes and Jeanette Potter, born at Southington and Hamden.

Mary Elizabeth Barnes of New Haven filed a widow's pension on 16 December 1908. She was married to the soldier under the name of Mary E. Farley at Ansonia by Rev. Mead on 19 March 1872. He gives their marriage place as Portchester, New York by Rev. William H. Borden.[341] Neither were previously married or divorced and she did not remarry after his death. A public record of their marriage could not be found and the marriage certificate was misplaced. The soldier's sister-in-law Etta J. Barnes, age 72, of New Haven attested to the marriage. His sister Louise C. Goodrich also lived at New Haven, age 65, in 1909. William and Mary Barnes had one son William Henry, born at Branford on 12 September 1875 who was alive in 1909.[342]

Mary E. Barnes died in 1929 and was buried in Fair Haven Union Cemetery.[343] She was born in New York.

---

340 Affidavit, William H. Barnes of Stony Creek, 1 March 1899, in his own pension file.
341 Pension application, William H. Barnes, 28 January 1899, in his own pension file.
342 Branford Vital Records, 1863-1895, 40, copy in the pension file. The birth year was given as 1876 on the pensioner's application in 1899.
343 The Hale Collection, New Haven, 1099.

BARRY, CHARLES
Co. E 7th CVI, private, substitute, mustered in 1 December 1864, deserted, no pension

Charles Barry served as a substitute for Edwin A. Ennis of Branford. He was mustered in at New Haven on 1 December 1864 and deserted on 20 February 1865. His name does not appear in the 1860 census for Branford or North Branford.

BARTHOLOMEW, ISAAC C.
Co. K 8th CVI, private, enlisted 18 September 1861, discharged disability 12 December 1862, pension #443222 for the soldier and later for his wife Clarissa

Isaac C. Bartholomew of Wallingford enlisted at Hartford on 18 September 1861 and was mustered in on 23 September 1861 as a private in Co. K 8th CVI for a term of three years. He was sick in the hospital at New Bern, North Carolina from March until June 1862. He returned briefly to duty on 29 June 1862 and was sent back to the hospital. He was treated at New Bern, Fortress Monroe General Hospital and Knight Hospital in New Haven where he was discharged for disability on 12 December 1862. He was on the 1863 draft list for Branford, Class 3, age 33, discharged from the 8th CVI, married, occupation boatman.

He applied for an invalid pension on 7 May 1863. In 1886 he was described as five feet seven inches tall, light complexion, light hair, blue eyes, occupation joiner. At or near New Bern, North Carolina on 12 March 1862 he contracted general debility from exposure and over work while going to said town and at the battle. After his service he lived at Branford, East Haven, and New Haven (Fair Haven).

Isaac Chauncey Bartholomew died at New Haven on 28 September 1896. He was born at Wallingford on 22 October 1830, son of Chauncey Bartholomew and Sophronia Parmelee.[344]

Clarissa A. Bartholomew applied for a widow's pension on 23 October 1896. She was married to the soldier under the name of Clarissa Ann Addis at Wethersfield by Rev. Mr. Kirby on 3 November 1851. She was not previously married and did not remarry after his death. She was born at Middletown on 16 December 1833, daughter of Austin Addis and Lucy Ann Phillips.[345] She was living at New Haven in 1900 but probably died by 1910.

BARTHOLOMEW, JOHN L.
Co. F 14th CVI, private, enlisted 6 August 1862, died 13 October 1864 in prison, pension # 142098 for his widow Henrietta A. Bartholomew later Plumley

John L. Bartholomew of New Britain enlisted at Hartford on 6 August 1862 and was mustered in on 23 August 1862 as a private in Co. F 14th CVI for a term of three years. He was wounded at the Battle of Antietam, Maryland on 17 September 1862. With his regiment he fought in battles during the Virginia campaign at the Wilderness, Spotsylvania, Cold Harbor, and Deep Bottom. He was wounded and captured at the Battle of Ream's Station, Virginia on 25 August 1864 and died in Salisbury Prison, South Carolina on 13 October 1864. There is a gravestone for him in Northford Cemetery, North Branford which reads "Company F. 14 Regt. Connecticut Volunteer. Died at Salisbury Prison South Carolina Oct. 13, 1864." A G.A.R. marker was on his gravesite in 1934 and his name appears on the Northford Veterans' Monument.

---

344 George Wells Bartholomew, *Record of the Bartholomew Family* (Austin, Texas: Salem Press, 1885), 323 and 407.
345 Barbour Collection, Middletown, 3:335.

John Luther Bartholomew was born at North Branford on 24 April 1835, son of Gerard Bartholomew and Henrietta Johnson.[346]

Henrietta A. Bartholomew of New Britain applied for a widow's pension on 19 June 1865. She was married to the soldier under the name of Henrietta Amelia Johnson at North Branford by Rev. Asa C. Pierce of the Second Congregational Church[347] on 11 December 1859. He was age 24, she age 23, both born and living at North Branford. They had one son born at New Britain on 31 July 1861 as Samuel Gerard Bartholomew but his name was changed to John after the death of his father. Originally the first name was left blank in the New Britain vital records and was later filled in with the name John. On 28 January 1870 John Bartholomew, age eight, was residing at North Haven with his mother Henrietta A. Plumley. There is no further record in the file for the son John Bartholomew. He was alive in 1880, age 18, living with the Plumleys at Guilford.[348]

She was married second at Montowese, North Haven by Rev. Alpha H. Simonds on 24 September 1869 to Henry Plumley of North Haven. Plumley died at Northford on 25 March 1899 age 80 and was buried in New Northford Cemetery. He was born at Potsdam, New York, son of Benjamin and Lucy Plumley. He never served in the military. Her pension was terminated upon her marriage to Plumley but was reinstated after he second husband's death. She had three children by Plumley.

Henrietta Bartholomew Plumley died on 4 August 1925 and was buried in New Northford Cemetery. She was born at North Branford on 28 June 1836, daughter of John Benjamin Johnson and Maria Moulthrop.[349] Her daughter-in-law Mrs. Addie L. Plumley was living at Clintonville in 1925 and helped care for Henrietta during her last illness.

BARTHOLOMEW, JOHN N.
Co. G 13th CVI, 1st sergeant, enlisted 14 December 1862, discharged disability 8 November 1862, pension #715529 for the soldier and later for his widow Ellen

John N. Bartholomew of Branford enlisted at New Haven on 14 December 1861 and was mustered in on 8 January 1862 as 1st sergeant in Co. G 13th CVI. He was in the Regimental Hospital [at Ship Island, Mississippi] on 22 April 1862 and discharged back to duty on 24 April. He entered St. James Hospital, New Orleans on 23 July 1862 and returned to duty on 13 August. He was in Regimental Hospital at Camp Henry, New Orleans on 16 October 1862 and was discharged for disability at New Orleans, Louisiana on 8 November 1862.

He applied for an invalid pension on 13 November 1879. At the time of his discharge he was described as five feet eight inches tall, light complexion, blue eyes, brown hair, occupation mechanic. While on duty at Ship Island, Mississippi on 23 April 1862 he was disabled by diarrhea caused by exposure while rafting

---

346 St. Andrews Episcopal Church Records, North Branford, I:67.
347 Another name for the Northford Congregational Church.
348 U.S. census 1880, Guilford, New Haven County, Connecticut, population schedule, T9-107, dwelling 117, family 145, page 565, Henry Plumley & family, www.heritagequest.com.
349 North Branford Vital Records, I:43.

wood to the island. When he was discharged he had no use of his arms and limbs. His application was denied and he did not receive a pension until the age of seventy for age related illnesses.

He was married at New Haven by Rev. John W. Leek of the Methodist Episcopal Church on 6 February 1862 to Ellen Brown Hull. He was age 23, living at Branford; she was age 19, living at Clinton. Neither were previously married or divorced. They had one son William N., born at New Haven on 15 August 1867. Since his discharge he lived at New Haven [Fair Haven] until 1882, Branford until 1884, New Haven until 1888, two years in California 1888-1890; and New Haven 1890-1907. From 1908-1910 they were living at Wareham, Plymouth Co., Massachusetts.

John Newton Bartholomew died at Concord, Merrimack, New Hampshire on 20 December 1910 where he had resided eight months at the home of his son William N. Bartholomew. He was buried in Center Cemetery, Branford.[350] He was born at Branford on 26 November 1838, son of John Bartholomew and Charlotte Squire.[351]

Ellen B. Bartholomew of Concord, New Hampshire applied for a widow's pension on 9 January 1911. She died at Concord, New Hampshire on 24 May 1916 and was buried in Center Cemetery, Branford.[352]

BARTHOLOMEW, RODOLPHUS
Co. B 27th CVI, wagoner, enlisted 22 August 1862, mustered out 27 July 1863, pension #469960 for the soldier

Rodolphus Bartholomew, age 43, of Branford enlisted on 22 August 1862 and was mustered in on 3 October 1862 as a wagoner in Co. B 27th CVI for a term of nine months. Upon arrival at camp in Washington, D.C. he was detailed throughout the war as an ambulance driver at the front. He fought at the Battle of Fredericksburg on 13 December 1862 with the rest of the company. While performing his duty at Falmouth, Virginia in February 1863 he contracted chronic diarrhea and rheumatism brought on by exposure and drinking bad water. He was treated at the Regimental Hospital in Falmouth and at Acquia Creek, Virginia General Hospital for two or three weeks. In March and April 1863 he was on the muster rolls for the ambulance corps. In May and June 1863 he was treated at the Finley General Hospital in Washington, D.C. for five or six weeks. It is unclear whether he was at Gettysburg after his release from Finley Hospital. Rodolphus Bartholomew was mustered out with the rest of his regiment at New Haven on 27 July 1863.

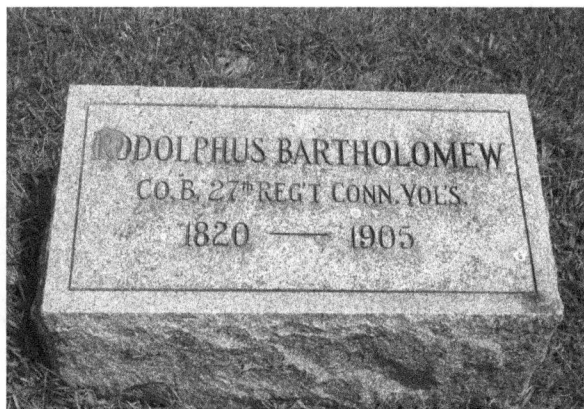

William Linsley of Branford, in an affidavit dated 24 August 1894, stated that the claimant "was a healthy man before the war. He came home broken down physically from lying on the ground and exposure. I have often met him since the war, walking with a cane." James R. Way of Branford stated that Bartholomew "was a strong, robust man" but since the war "has been a great sufferer."

---

350 Branford Sexton Records, 1884-1932, 62; no stone was found.
351 One of his applications gives his birth as 1839. He later claims the person filling out his application made the error. His birth is not in the Branford Vital Records. Henry C. Woodstock of Branford in a letter dated 30 January 1909 states he had seen the family bible originally belonging to the soldier's father. It states that Newton Bartholomew was born on 26 November 1838.
352 Branford Sexton Records, 1884-1932, 80.

Rodolphus Bartholomew of Branford served in the ambulance corps during his enlistment.
(Photographic History of the Civil War, 7:313)

Bible found by Bartholomew on the Chancellorsville battlefield. (Branford Historical Society archives)

He began receiving a pension on 22 August 1889 for disability. He reapplied on 15 June 1904 for an increase, then 83 years old. At the time of his enlistment he was described as five feet ten inches tall, light complexion, brown hair, blue eyes, occupation farmer. He was a member of the Mason Rogers Post No. 7 G.A.R. of Branford.

Since the war he resided at Branford. He was married at Branford by Rev. Timothy P. Gillette of the First Congregational Church on 15 June 1848 to Elizabeth Griffing who died at Branford on 4 November 1877. He did not remarry after her death. He had four children living (in 1898): Clifford G., born on 1 April 1849; Robert D., born on 24 March 1851; Elizabeth Brainard, born on 8 July 1854; and Ernest S., born on 11 October 1858.

Rodolphus Bartholomew died at Branford on 20 August 1905 and was buried there in Center Cemetery.[353] His company and regiment are engraved on his stone and G.A.R. marker was on his gravesite in 1934. He was born at Durham on 30 June 1820, son of Leman Bartholomew and Laura Foote both of Branford.

BEACH, GEORGE W.
Co. M 1st HA, corporal, enlisted 10 December 1861, discharged 24 February 1865, pension #870219 for the soldier and later for his widow Alice

George W. Beach, age 24, of Branford enlisted at New Haven on 10 December 1861 and was mustered in on 24 February 1862 as a private in Co. M 4th CVI which became the 1st HA. "George Beach came into camp today, he is Colonel Tylers orderly."[354] He fought with his regiment at Chickahominy and Malvern Hill, Virginia in 1862 and at the Battle of Fredericksburg on 2 December 1862. In 1863 and 1864 his regiment guarded forts in Alexandria, Virginia. He was promoted to corporal on 10 May 1864 and discharged at Petersburg, Virginia on 24 February 1865 when his term expired. He was the brother of Harvey W. and William H. Beach, and the brother-in-law of Ammi Barker.

He applied for an invalid pension on 29 June 1891 under the act of 27 June 1890. At the time of his enlistment he was described as five feet eight inches tall, dark complexion, brown hair, hazel eyes, occupation stage driver. He was a member of the Mason Rogers Post No. 7 G.A.R. of Branford.

He was married first at Branford on 25 December 1865 to Harriet Eliza Barker who died at Branford on 27 May 1881 age 34. He had seven children (living in 1898): Andrew E., born on 19 July 1867; Lucelia G., born on 21 September 1869; Minnie, born on 17 December 1872; Harry U., born on 15 January 1875; Mabel E., born on 3 January 1878; Annie D., born on 19 July 1885; and Esther J., born on 12 October 1890. They were all living in 1916 listed as: Andrew E., Lucelia Genevieve Beach Porter, Minnie Beach Ferris, Harry U., Mabel Beach Stannard, Annie D. Beach Morton, and Esther Josephine.

George Washington Beach died at Branford on 24 March 1919 and was buried there in Center Cemetery. He was born at Branford on 17 December 1840, son of Timothy Beach and Esther Cooke.

Alice A. Beach of Branford applied for a widow's pension on 23 April 1919. She was married to the soldier as his second wife under the name of Alice Gibson Appleby at Madison by Rev. James A. Gallup of the Madison Congregational Church on 17 April 1883. He was age 35, living at Branford; she was age 22, living at Madison. She was not previously married or divorced and did not remarry after his death.

---

353 Branford Vital Records, deaths, 1905.
354 Towner letter, 22 September 1862.

George Washington Beach of Branford, a corporal in the 1st Connecticut Heavy Artillery fought at the Battle of Malvern Hill, Virginia on 1 July 1862. (by G. White; Abbott, The History of the Civil War in America, II:109)

Alice Beach died at Branford on 22 October 1931 and was buried there in Center Cemetery.[355] She was born at Madison on 31 May 1861, daughter of Charles Appleby and Jane Gibson.

BEACH, HARVEY W.
Co. B 27th CVI, private, enlisted 25 August 1862, prisoner, mustered out 27 July1863, pension #520671 for his widow Cornelia

Harvey W. Beach,[356] age 27, of Branford enlisted on 25 August 1862 and was mustered in on 3 October 1862 as a private in Co. B 27th CVI for a term of nine months. He fought at the Battle of Fredericksburg on 13 December 1862 with the rest of the company. During the battle "he was detailed to carry the wounded off the field."[357] He was captured at the Battle of Chancellorsville, Virginia on 3 May 1863, held at Libby Prison, Richmond, and paroled at City Point, Virginia on 14 May 1863. He reported to Camp Parole, Maryland on 16 May 1863 and spent the remainder of his service at Camp Convalescent, Virginia. With the rest of the Chancellorsville paroled prisoners, he rejoined the Regiment at Baltimore on 20 July 1863. Harvey Beach was mustered out with the rest of his regiment on 27 July 1863 at New Haven. After the war, he was a captain in the state militia for five years.[358] He was the brother of George W. and William H. Beach and the brother-in-law of Henry W. Hubbard of the same company and regiment.

---

355 Branford Vital Records, deaths, 1931; neither have a gravestone.
356 For his biography see Beers, *Biographical Record of New Haven County*, 984.
357 Letter, [George C. Baldwin] to home, 15 December 1862.
358 Beers, *Biographical Record of New Haven County*, 984; his obituary *New Haven Register* 4 May 1881 states he was a captain in the old militia.

Harvey W. Beach of Branford was a member of Co. B 27th Connecticut Volunteer
Infantry. (Beers, Biographical Record of New Haven County, 984)

Harvey Willis Beach died at Branford on 3 May 1881 and was buried there in Center Cemetery. He was born at Branford on 1 May 1834, son of Timothy Beach and Esther Cook. [359] He never applied for a pension.

Cornelia H. Beach applied for a widow's pension on 24 July 1891. She was married to the soldier under the name of Cornelia Hannah Hubbard at Branford by Rev. Ralph H. Bolles of the First Baptist Church on 16 November 1856. Neither were previously married or divorced. They had one daughter Ada Venilia, born on 8 November 1877, still a minor in 1891, deaf and dumb. Their older children are not named in the pension.

Cornelia Hubbard Beach died at Branford on 27 January 1911 was buried there in Center Cemetery. She was born at Durham on 27 December 1835, daughter of Richard Hubbard and Rhoda Andrews.[360]

BEACH, WILLIAM H.

Co. B 27th CVI, private enlisted 21 August 1862, prisoner, mustered out 27 July 1863, Co. H 15th & Co. K 7th CVI, enlisted 28 December 1864, discharged 11 August 1865, pension #614570 for the soldier

William H. Beach of Branford enlisted on 21 August 1862 and was mustered in on 3 October 1862 as a private in Co. B 27th CVI for a term of nine months. He fought at the Battle of Fredericksburg on 13 December 1862 with the rest of the company. He was captured at the Battle of Chancellorsville, Virginia on 3 May

---

359 Branford Vital Records, 1786-1840, 377.
360 Branford Vital Records, deaths, 1911.

1863, held prisoner at Richmond, and paroled at City Point, Virginia on 14 May 1863. He reported to Camp Green Barracks, Maryland on 16 May 1863; was sent to Washington, D.C. on 20 May 1863 and spent the remainder of his service at Camp Convalescent, Virginia. With the rest of the Chancellorsville paroled prisoners, he rejoined the Regiment at Baltimore on 20 July 1863. William Beach was mustered out with the rest of his regiment at New Haven on 27 July 1863. He was the brother of George W. and Harvey W. Beach.

William H. Beach reenlisted at New Haven on 28 December 1864 as a private in Co. H 15th CVI for a term of three years. He was transferred to Co. K 7th CVI on 24 June 1865 when the rest of the 15th CVI was mustered out. Beach was mustered out with Co. K at Goldsboro, North Carolina on 20 July 1865 and discharged at New Haven on 11 August 1865.

He applied for an invalid pension on 20 September 1890 under the act of 27 July 1890. On the march to Fredericksburg on 10 December 1862 he contracted rheumatism from exposure lying on the wet ground which has now resulted in total blindness of his left eye. His condition improved and he reenlisted, but again fell ill, was treated at the hospital near Acquia Creek and was sick when he returned home. At the time of his enlistment he was described as five feet eight inches tall, dark complexion, dark eyes, black hair, occupation farmer. He was married to Margaret Terhune who died at Branford on 4 April 1885.[361] He never remarried. Since his discharge he lived at Branford and was admitted to Fitch's Soldier Home in 1900 but returned home. His son George L. Beach of Branford was appointed his conservator on 29 October 1910.

William Henry Beach died at Branford on 28 April 1911 and was buried there in Center Cemetery. A G.A.R. marker was on his gravesite in 1934. He was born at Branford on 18 August 1826, son of Timothy Beach and Esther Cook.[362]

BEAUMONT, HARVEY
Co. B 27th CVI, private, enlisted 9 September 1862, prisoner, mustered out 27 July 1863, pension #1,084,857 for the soldier

Harvey Beaumont[363] of Wallingford, age 25, enlisted on 9 September 1862 and was mustered in on 3 October 1862 as a private in Co. B 27th CVI for a term of nine months. He fought at the Battle of Fredericksburg on 13 December 1862 with the rest of the company. He was captured at the Battle of Chancellorsville, Virginia on 3 May 1863, held prisoner at Richmond, and paroled at City Point, Virginia on 14 May 1863. He reported to Camp Parole, Maryland on 16 May 1863, was sent to Washington, D.C. on 20 May 1863 and spent the remainder of his service at Camp Convalescent, Virginia. With the rest of the Chancellorsville paroled prisoners, he rejoined the Regiment at Baltimore on 20 July 1863. Beaumont was mustered out with the rest of his regiment at New Haven on 27 July 1863.

---

361 Branford Vital Records, 1863-1895, 232.
362 Branford Vital Records, 1786-1840, 377; his pension gives his birth as 18 August 1825.
363 For his biography see Rockey, *History of New Haven County*, I:416; and Beers, *Biographical Record of New Haven County*, 1091.

He applied for an invalid pension on 17 May 1904. He was described as five feet eleven inches tall, hazel eyes, brown hair, light complexion, occupation farmer, and had a scar from a broken right leg. He resided at Wallingford since the war. He was married first at Durham on 7 April 1881 to Melissa Lizzie Foster. She died at Wallingford on 10 December 1882 and was buried there in Center Street Cemetery. He was married second at Durham by Rev. Chesbrough on 25 October 1884 to Julia Ann Mix, daughter of Elihu Mix and Polly Hull. Julia was married first at Durham on 26 March 1882 to Henry Bailey. Bailey died at New Haven Hospital on 4 January 1883. Julia Ann Beaumont died in 1922 and was buried in Center Street Cemetery, Wallingford.[364] Harvey Beaumont had one child living (in 1904): Edmund Mix Beaumont, born on 18 June 1890.

Harvey Beaumont died at Wallingford on 15 September 1927 and was buried there in Center Street Cemetery.[365] He was born at Wallingford on 7 May 1836[366] or 5 May 1840,[367] son of John Beaumont and Ann Tyler.

BEHRENS, GUSTAVE
1st LA, private, enlisted 15 September 1864, mustered 11 June 1865, no pension

Gustave Behrens of Branford enlisted and was mustered in on 15 September 1864 as a private in the 1st LA. With his regiment he saw action during the Siege of Richmond. He was mustered out with the rest of his regiment at Manchester, near Richmond, Virginia on 11 June 1865. He does not appear in the 1860 census at Branford.

BENNETT, JOSEPH
Co. B 27th CVI, private, enlisted 25 August 1862, died 25 December 1862 from wounds received at Fredericksburg, pension #114929 for his father Gilman Bennett

Joseph Bennett, age 23, of Branford enlisted 25 August 1862 and was mustered in on 3 October 1862 as a private in Co. B 27th CVI for a term of nine months. He was wounded at the Battle of Fredericksburg on 13 December 1862, and sent to the hospital at Georgetown, Washington, D.C. "Joe Bennett was wounded by a ball in the arm pretty bad. I helped carry Joe Bennett across [the river] and gave him my woolen blanket."[368] He died in the hospital from his wounds on 25 December 1862, a left arm amputation with infection and other serious injuries.

His father Gilman Bennett of Northfield, Merrimack Co., New Hampshire was a farmer and stone cutter. He applied for a pension on 26 September 1867 which was approved on 18 June 1868 since he relied on his son for financial support. In 1875 a special investigation was ordered and there are many affidavits in the file attesting to Gilman Bennett's ability to perform manual labor. It was concluded that the father was not dependent on his son's income and could still perform manual labor. Subsequently, a bill was introduced in the House of Representatives to grant his pension. The bill was referred to the Committee on Invalid Pensions who examined the evidence and reported adversely. Bennett submitted additional testimony from himself, his son-in-law and daughter, and others.

---

364 The Hale Collection, Wallingford, 52. She is buried in the Mix family plot.
365 The Hale Collection, Wallingford, 115. He is buried with his first wife.
366 Birth on pension application, 13 May 1904. This date is confirmed by Wallingford Vital Records V-1:190.
367 Beers, *Biographical Record of New Haven County*, 1091.
368 Letter, [George C. Baldwin] to home, 15 December 1862.

The soldier, Joseph Bennett, resided at home in New Hampshire until 1859, came home two or three times for work, and finally left April 1862 and enlisted that same year. At the time of his enlistment he had worked at a lock factory in Branford for two months. He forwarded his bounty of $100 to his sister Sarah which was given to his father.

Gilman Bennett testifies that he was the father of the soldier Joseph Bennett born in 1840. Gilman was married at Sandwich, New Hampshire on 27 November 1829 to Betsey Williamson and they lived together until her death on 5 September 1849. He had four children: Joseph who died at age 14 months before the birth of the soldier, Frances, born about 1837; Joseph, born 1840; and Sarah, born about 1846. The two daughters were still living. Sarah was married in November 1871 to Joseph J. Mowe and lived in Tilton, New Hampshire. Frances Bennett, age 38 in 1874, a cripple since birth, lived with her father.

There is no evidence in the file that the pension was ever reinstated. The family could not prove the father was supported by the son Joseph. Testimony that Gilman Bennett could still walk five miles to his daughter's house at the age of 68 years and the tone of the investigator's report supports this premise. Gilman Bennett died at Northfield, New Hampshire January 1879.[369]

BIRD, EDWARD J.
Co. D 5th New York Vols, private, enlisted 9 May1861, wounded, discharged 14 May 1863, Co. A First U.S. Regiment, private, enlisted 17 December 1864, discharged 2 September 1865, pension #1061819 for the soldier

Edward J. Bird enlisted at New York City on 9 May 1861 as a private in Co. D 5th New York Volunteers. He was wounded at Bull Run, Virginia on 30 August 1862. "I was wounded in the neck and taken from the field in an ambulance." He was admitted to General Hospital, Patterson Park, Baltimore, Maryland on 3 September 1862 and transferred on 19 September to General Hospital, West Building, Baltimore. He was discharged shortly after his release from the hospital at New York City on 14 May 1863. He reenlisted at Washington, D.C. on 17 December 1864 in Co. A 1st Regiment U.S. Veteran Volunteer Infantry. He was discharged from Co. A at Washington, D.C. on 2 September 1865.

At the time of his enlistment he was described as five feet five inches tall, light complexion, blue eyes, light brown hair, occupation brass finisher. Since his discharge he lived at New York City and since 1867 at Branford. He was a member and commander of the Mason Rogers Post No. 7 G.A.R. of Branford.

He was married at New York City by Rev. Everett of the Church of the Nativity on 19 January 1864 to Elizabeth McGlinchy. She died on 9 April 1882 probably at Branford. He had the following children: Rosa A., born on 12 May 1868, died on 12 July 1868; Elizabeth, born on 25 June 1865, died on 20 November 1907; Henry, born on 16 September 1869; Alice, born on 17 November 1871; Joseph, born on 10 February 1874; Edward, Jr., born on 1 March 1876; Margaret, born on 22 May 1879; and Philip, born on 23 September 1881. The last six were living in 1915.

---

369 *International Genealogical Index* [IGI], www.familysearch.org.

Edward J. Bird died at Branford on 28 June 1923 and was buried there in St. Agnes Cemetery.[370] He was born at New York City on 24 November 1937, son of Edward Bird and Bridget McNulty. He was baptized the same day at St. Mary's Catholic Church, New York City.

BISHOP, AUSTIN
Co. I 15th CVI, private, enlisted 14 August 1862, died 13 February 1863, pension #9851 for his widow Eliza

Austin Bishop, age 44, of Branford enlisted at New Haven on 14 August 1862 and was mustered in on 25 August 1862 as a private in Co. I 15th CVI for a term of three years. In December he was sick in his quarters. He was admitted to Harwood Hospital, Washington, D.C. on 8 February 1863 and died there on 13 February 1863 from chronic diarrhea. At the time of his enlistment he was described as five feet five inches tall, dark complexion, hazel eyes, brown hair, occupation carpenter, born at North Haven.[371] He was living at Stony Creek, Branford during the 1850 and 1860 census. The wife of Austin Bishop died on 22 July 1854 age 27.[372]

Eliza E. Bishop of Stony Creek applied for a widow's pension on 29 June 1863 under the act of 14 July 1862. She was married to the soldier probably as his second wife under the name of Elizabeth Judd at Meriden by Rev. Harvey Miller on 24 September 1854; he was of Branford, she of New Haven. They had no children.

BISHOP, MARTIN C.
see Philip O'Callahan

BLACKSTONE, RALPH
see Julius F. Forrester

BLAKE, HALSEY H.
Co. G & I 24th CVI, musician, enlisted 1 September 1862, mustered out 30 September 1863, pension #XC2636372 for the soldier and later for his widow Virginia

Halsey H. Blake of Middletown enlisted as a musician on 1 September 1862 in Co. G 24th CVI and was mustered in on 18 November 1862 for a term of ten months. His rank was reduced to private by consolidation of the regiment and he was transferred to Co. I on 1 March 1863. Blake was mustered out on 30 September 1863.

He applied for a pension on 4 January 1892 under the act of 27 June 1890. Before the war he lived at Middletown and after his discharge lived at New Haven and moved to Short Beach, Branford about 1920. His pension is at the Veterans Administration.

Halsey Horatio Blake died at New Haven on 25 October 1930 and was buried in East Lawn Cemetery, East Haven.[373] He was born at Middletown on 6 September 1842, son of Edwin Blake and Lucretia Andrews.

---

370 Branford Vital Records, deaths, 1923.
371 John Guy Bishop, *Record of the Descendants of John Bishop one of the founders of Guilford in 1639*, 1951, 103 states that the Austin Bishop who died on 13 February 1863 in Harwood Hospital was from New Milford, Pennsylvania and was married to Sarah Griffing.
372 Branford Vital Records, 1852-1863, 3.
373 Branford Vital Records, deaths, 1930.

Virginia R. Blake of Branford applied for a widow's pension on 5 November 1930. Virginia Ruth Miller Blake died at the home of her granddaughter Mrs. Edward C. Spahr, Jr. in Milford on 30 October 1939 age 91 and was buried in East Lawn Cemetery. She was born at Middletown, daughter of Watrous Ives Miller and Ruth Lucretia Prout of Meriden.[374]

BLAKESLEE, CHARLES P.

Co. E 15th CVI, private, enlisted 8 August 1862, discharged disability 4 February 1863, pension #502121 for his widow Delia

Charles P. Blakeslee, age 23, of North Branford enlisted at New Haven on 8 August 1862 and was mustered in on 25 August 1862 as a private in Co. E 15th CVI for a term of three years. By December he was sick in U.S. General Hospital, Broad Street, Philadelphia. He was discharged from General Hospital, Chestnut Hill, Philadelphia, Pennsylvania on 4 February 1863 after being unfit for duty for sixty days. "He was sick since the 25th September 1862 and has done 3 weeks of duty since entering the service. He received an injury on his left side from lifting when in the army." At the time of his enlistment he was described as five feet eleven inches tall, light complexion, hazel eyes, brown hair, occupation mechanic. After his discharge he returned to his home at Northford. He never applied for a pension.

Charles P. Blakeslee died at New Haven on 19 April 1900 and was buried in Montowese Cemetery, North Haven. He was born at Northford on 12 August 1839, son of Edward Blakeslee and Lucretia Holt.[375] His name appears on the Northford and North Haven Veterans' Monument.

Delia A. Blakeslee of New Haven filed for a widow's pension on 28 April 1900. She was married to the soldier under the name of Delia A. Brockett at Montowese, North Haven by Rev. General Jackson Ganun of the Baptist Church on 25 March 1864. Neither were previously married or divorced. The public record for the marriage at North Haven was destroyed by fire. In 1900 Rev. Ganun was living at New Haven and wrote a letter to the pension board confirming the marriage.

Delia A. Blakeslee died on 12 March 1918 and was buried in Montowese Cemetery, North Haven.[376] She was born at North Haven on 12 June 1842, daughter of Gustavus Brockett and Adeline Barnes.[377]

BLAKESLEE, KIRTLAND

Co. F 7th CVI, private, enlisted 1 February 1864, mustered out 20 July 1865, pension #C257544 for the soldier

Kirtland Blakeslee of North Branford enlisted on 1 February 1864 as a private in Co. F 7th CVI for a term of three years. In September and October 1864 he was sick in the hospital. In November and December 1864 he was sick at Knight Hospital in New Haven. It appears he rejoined the regiment but may have been absent in May and June 1865. Kirtland Blakeslee was mustered out with the rest of his regiment at Goldsboro, North Carolina on 20 July 1865 and discharged at New Haven on 11 August 1865.

He applied for an invalid pension on 26 January 1889. At the time of his enlistment he was described as five feet four inches tall, dark complexion, black eyes, black hair, occupation mechanic. "I enlisted to meet

---

374 *The Branford Review*, 2 November 1939, 3.

375 North Branford Vital Records, I:44B.

376 The Hale Collection, North Haven, 63.

377 Edward J. Brockett, *The Descendants of John Brockett, One of the Original Founders of New Haven Colony* (Orange Chronicle Co., Orange, New Jersey: 1905), 101.

North Branford's quota. I was born at North Haven on 26 June 1846. I was an only child and my mother died when I was less than one year old and I only lived with my father for a short time after my mother's death. I was cared for by my mother's sister Sarah Jane Robinson who was living at Durham, Middlesex Co. I lived with my father after his remarriage when I was about six or seven years old but stayed only a short time. I was then taken to live with my grandmother on my father's side and lived with her for a short time. I then stayed a short time with George Peck at Cheshire and was hired out to work for Wm. M. Fowler at Northford in the summer of 1860. During this time I chose for my guardian the husband of my mother's sister A. J. Robinson. My father parted from his second wife and married a third wife and I never received any support from him after 1860."[378]

Since his discharge he lived in different places in Connecticut: Wallingford, Meriden in 1866; North Haven in 1868; New Haven in 1870; and since May 1871 in Huron Co., Ohio. He was married at Norwalk, Ohio by C. A. Bray, JP on 9 March 1872 to Anna Maria Lockwood. Neither were previously married or divorced. They had no children. She was living in 1920 and died by 1935. In later life they lived with her niece Anna Moss at New London, Ohio.

Kirtland Blakeslee died at New London, Huron Co., Ohio on 8 December 1935 and was buried there in Hartland Cemetery. His name appears on the Northford Veterans' Monument.

BLISS, GEORGE
Co. B 2nd Massachusetts Vols, private, enlisted 23 December 1863, discharged 14 July 1865, pension #XC2871369 for the soldier and later for his widow Mary

George Bliss of Medfield, Massachusetts enlisted on 23 December 1863 as a private in Co. B 2nd Massachusetts Regiment Veteran Infantry Volunteers, 3rd Brigade, 1st Division, 20th Army Corps for a term of three years. He was discharged on 14 July 1865.[379] He was the brother of Howard Bliss.

He applied for an invalid pension on 30 August 1898 under the act of 27 June 1890. Since his discharge he lived at Branford. He was married at Branford by Rev. Elijah C. Baldwin of the First Congregational Church on 23 October 1872 to Mary Emma Smith.[380] He was a charter member of the Mason Rogers Post No. 7 G.A.R. of Branford. His pension is at the Veterans Administration.

George Bliss died at New Haven on 4 June 1919. He was born at Seymour on 8 August 1844, son of Lemuel Bliss and Emeline French.[381]

Mary E. Smith, living in New Jersey, applied for a widow's pension on 28 October 1919. She was born at Shandaken, New York on 13 November 1855.[382]

BLISS, HOWARD
Co. H 20th CVI, sergeant, enlisted 20 August 1862, mustered out 13 June 1865, died 6 August 1865, pension #158744 for his widow Fannie and minor son Frank

Howard Bliss, age 26, of Seymour enlisted on 20 August 1862 and was mustered in as a private in Co. H 20th CVI for a term of three years. He was promoted to corporal on 20 July 1863 and to sergeant on 31 October

---

378 Statement, Kirtland Blakeslee, 11 November 1881, to Lester L. Leach, Huron County, Ohio.
379 J. Homer Bliss, *Genealogy of the Bliss Family in America* (Boston, 1881), 184.
380 Branford Vital Records, 1863-1895, 145.
381 *Genealogy of Bliss Family*, 184.
382 *Genealogy of Bliss Family*, 184.

Fannie Barker was the wife of soldier Howard Bliss and in 1875 married James B. Pelton.

1863. He was sick in January 1865 but returned to duty. Bliss was mustered out on 13 June 1865 and died at Branford on 6 August 1865 as a result of his service[383] At the time of his enlistment he was described as five feet ten inches tall, light complexion, blue eyes, born hair, occupation polisher. He was born at Seymour on 17 July 1836, son of Lemuel Bliss and Emeline French.[384] He was the brother of George Bliss.

Frances E. Bliss applied for a widow's pension on 12 February 1866. She was married to the soldier under the name of Fannie Eliza Barker at Branford by Rev. Jacob G. Miller of the First Congregational Church on 24 November 1859. He was born at Seymour, living at Branford.[385] As Frances E. Larkins, guardian, she applied for a pension for her minor son Frank H. Bliss on 19 June 1871. Frank Howard Bliss was born at New Haven on 18 April 1863.

Frances Barker Bliss was married second at New Haven on 23 January 1871 to George Larkins and was divorced from him at New Haven on 17 September 1875. Her pension terminated upon her marriage to Larkins. Frances was married third at North Haven on 6 August 1875 to James B. Pelton as his second wife. Pelton died at New Haven on 6 August 1906 and was buried in Center Cemetery, Branford. He was born at Madison on 22 August 1822.

Frances "Fannie" Pelton reapplied for a pension after the decease of her third husband James B. Pelton. She lived at Branford and New Haven.

Frances E. Pelton died at New Haven on 24 January 1923 and was buried in Center Cemetery, Branford. She was born at Branford on 12 October 1839,[386] daughter of Eliphalet Barker and Martha W. McCoy. Her son Frank Howard Bliss died at Branford on 4 July 1938 and was buried there in Center Cemetery.[387]

BOOTH, JOHN H.
Co. G 7th CVI, private, enlisted 28 August 1861, prisoner, discharged 19 July 1865, pension #XC2689286 for the soldier and later for his widow Arabelle

John H. Booth of Branford enlisted at New Haven on 28 August 1861 and was mustered in on 7 September 1861 as a private in Co. G 7th CVI for a term of three years. He reenlisted as a veteran in Co. G on 11 January 1864. He was captured at Richmond, Virginia on 1 October 1864 and paroled in February 1865. Booth was discharged with the rest of the regiment on 19 July 1865. He was not in the 1860 census for Branford or North Branford.

383 Branford Vital Records, 1863-1895, 205.
384 *Genealogy of Bliss Family*, 535; at the time of his enlistment he says he was born at Derby.
385 Branford Vital Records, 1852-1863, 14.
386 Birth date from her gravestone; her birth is not in the Branford Vital Records.
387 *The Branford Review*, 7 July 1938, 1.

He applied for an invalid pension on 30 December 1891 under the act of 27 June 1890. His pension is at the Veterans Administration. He was living at New Haven in 1900 and 1910.

John Henry Booth died at New Haven on 19 December 1914 and was buried in West Cemetery, Meriden. He was born at Meriden on 22 February 1844, son of John H. Booth and Louisa Hill.[388]

Arabelle H. Booth applied for a widow's pension on 16 March 1915. She was living at New Haven in 1920 age 60.

BOYLAN, LUKE
Co. I 15th CVI, enlisted 5 August 1862, died 13 October 1864, pension #56441 for his widow Ellen and minor child

Luke Boylan[389] of Branford enlisted at New Haven on 5 August 1862 and was mustered in on 25 August 1862 as a private in Co. I 15th CVI for a term of three years. He died in Regimental Hospital at New Bern, North Carolina of yellow fever on 13 October 1864 and was buried there in Union Cemetery.[390] At the time of his enlistment he was described as age 26, five feet four inches tall, dark complexion, gray eyes, brown hair, occupation laborer, born at Cavan, Ireland. He does not appear in the 1860 census at Branford but is on the draft list.

Ellen Boylan of New Haven applied for a widow's pension on 17 December 1864 under the act of 14 July 1862. She was married to the soldier under the name of Ellen McCormick at St. Patrick's Church, New Haven by Rev. Matthew Hart on 28 September 1858. They were ages 21 and 22, both born in Ireland and living at New Haven. They had one child Ellen, born at New Haven on 20 July 1859 who was eligible for a pension until 19 July 1875. The file mentions Bernard Boylan of New Haven.

BRADLEY, FRANKLIN
Co. A 27th CVI, private, enlisted 30 August 1862, mustered out 27 July 1863, pension #482654 for the soldier and later for his widow Martha

Franklin Bradley of New Haven enlisted on 30 August 1862 and was mustered in on 3 October 1862 as a private in Co. A 27th CVI for a term of nine months. He was sick most of his enlistment and was mustered out with the rest of his regiment at New Haven on 27 July 1863.

He applied for an invalid pension on 25 June 1880 and received a one half disability. At the time of his enlistment he was described as six feet tall, dark complexion, brown hair, grey eyes. On 6 December 1862 on the march from Camp Tuttle near Chain Bridge, Virginia to Falmouth, Virginia he was sick with diarrhea due to exposure at Acquia Creek in a snow storm lasting over two days, also from fatigue from the long march. He was unfit for duty on 21

CIVIL WAR
FRANKLIN L. BRADLEY
27TH REG. CO. A CONN. VOLS.
DIED JUNE 6, 1898
AGE 63 YRS. 11 MOS.

---

388 New Haven Vital Records, deaths, 1914.
389 Listed in the T288 index as Lulis Boylan and on his pension as Louis Boylan.
390 *The Connecticut War Record*, December 1864, 2:5:336.

December 1862 and sent to Campbell Hospital in Washington, D.C. from 29 December 1862 to 8 January 1863. He was a patient in McKinn's Mansion Hospital, Baltimore, Maryland from 9 January 1863 to 15 January 1863. He was reported as deserted. "When I left McKinn's Hospital I came to my home in West Haven, town of Orange with the exception of about a week in February when I staid with my Mother and Sister in Southington and was confined to my bed."[391] He was in Knights' Hospital, New Haven from 12 April 1863 until about 18 June 1863.

Previous to his enlistment he was a farmer at Cheshire for three years and a merchant at West Haven for two years where he enlisted. He came to Stony Creek, Branford in April 1864. Since his discharge he has done only light work due to his condition, keeping a few boarders and sailing a boat. "He was in poor health when he came to Stony Creek."[392] He was a charter member of the Mason Rogers Post No. 7 G.A.R. of Branford.

He was married at Meriden by Rev. George C. Creevey on 11 June 1856 to Martha E. Perkins. He was age 21, born and living at Cheshire; she was age 17, born and living at Meriden. Neither were previously married or divorced. Their daughter Emma Burgess, age 34, wife of Seavy L. Burgess, was living at Meriden in 1898. His other children are not mentioned in the file.

Franklin Lyman Bradley died at Stony Creek, Branford on 6 June 1898 and was buried in Stony Creek Cemetery. His company and regiment are engraved on his stone and his name appears on the Stony Creek Veterans' Monument.

Martha E. Bradley of Stony Creek applied for a widow's pension on 21 October 1898. She died at Stony Creek on 20 October 1910 and was buried in Stony Creek Cemetery. She was born at Meriden on 4 August 1839, daughter of Sherlock Perkins and Amanda Griswold.[393]

BRADLEY, LEONARD
Co. G 6th CVI, sergeant, enlisted 26 August 1861, reenlisted 7 March 1864, mustered out 21 August 1865, pension #846584 for the soldier

Leonard Bradley of Farmington enlisted on 26 August 1861 and was mustered in on 4 September 1861 as a private in Co. G 6th CVI for a term of three years. He reenlisted as a veteran in Co. G on 7 March 1864. With his regiment he served in South Carolina, Georgia, and in the Virginia campaigns of 1865. He was promoted to corporal on 30 March 1864 and to sergeant on 10 June 1865. Leonard Bradley was mustered out with the rest of his regiment at Petersburg, Virginia on 21 August 1865 and discharged at New Haven on 17 September 1865. He is identified as the brother of George G. Bradley of Branford by the latter's 1863 diary:

> *Feb 3 - Wrote a note to Brother Leonard at Beaufort in the 6th reg CV.*
> *Feb 5 - Capt going to try to go to Beaufort and take me with him. There I shall see Leonard.*
> *Feb 7 - Got leave to go to Beaufort, Capt arranging off passes, went on board the Steamer Wyoming at two o'clock. Started at Six, arrived a Camp at 8 o'clock, found Leonard, stayed all night.*

391 Declaration, Franklin Bradley, 19 June 1883, in his own pension file.
392 Affidavit, Dennis S. Page of Stony Creek, 18 January 1883, in the pension file of Franklin Bradley.
393 Branford Vital Records, deaths, 1910.

Feb 16 - Got a letter from Leonard and half pound tobacco. Wrote to Leonard yesterday, Sent it to him by Sergt. Hovy, Leonard is well.

April 22 - Went on board a transport and saw Leonard.

July 23 - Very warm. The Seige progressing. Saw Leonard last night again today.

Leonard Bradley applied for an invalid pension on 15 December 1891 under the act of 27 June 1890. After his discharge he lived at Meriden. He was married about 1860 to Martha M. Talmadge who died in 1911 and was buried in East Cemetery, Meriden.

Leonard H. Bradley died at Meriden on 30 June 1915 and was buried there in East Cemetery. A Civil War marker was on his gravesite in 1934. He was born at Branford on 7 February 1840, son of Major Bradley and Rosella Baker.[394]

BRADLEY, TIMOTHY
Co. C 10th CVI, corporal, enlisted 25 October 1862, discharged 7 October 1864, pension #470822 for the soldier

Timothy Bradley, age 19, of Branford enlisted at Hartford on 7 October 1861 and was mustered in on 22 October 1861 as a private in Co. C 10th CVI for a term of three years. He was soon promoted to corporal. In March and April 1862 he was sick in the hospital at New Bern, North Carolina. With the rest of his regiment he fought at the Battle of Roanoke Island, North Carolina. He was sick in his barracks in January and February 1863 and left behind at New Bern, North Carolina. In March 1863 he was on furlough in Connecticut. He was with the regiment in May and June 1863. In 1864, he was sick in Chesapeake Hospital, Fortress Monroe, Virginia during May and June; and in July and August was on detached service at that hospital. In August and September 1864 he was sick in Grant General Hospital, Willet's Point, New York Harbor. Timothy Bradley was mustered out at Hartford on 7 October 1864 when his term expired. He served under Capt. James H. Linsley of North Branford. He was the first cousin of George G. Bradley of the same company.

He applied for an invalid pension on 22 July 1889. At the time of his enlistment he was described as five feet seven inches tall, light complexion, grey eyes, sandy hair, occupation farmer. He had typhoid fever at New Bern, North Carolina and was sick for four months in Regimental Hospital. He contracted fever and rheumatism at the Siege of Charlestown in the summer of 1863 and was put in the hospital at St. Augustine, Florida and was there about three months. When the regiment got to Gloucester Point, Virginia he was put in the hospital at Hampton, Virginia and stayed there about three months and afterwards was transferred to Willett's Point Hospital, Long Island for about two months. He returned to the regiment at the front at Petersburg, Virginia in the summer of 1864 and was on light duty until his discharge. "Army life ruined his health."[395] Since his discharge he suffered from rheumatism and had to use a cane. Since the war he lived at New Haven. He was a member of the Admiral Foote Post No. 17 G.A.R. of New Haven.

He was married at New Haven by Rev. Hutchins on 17 May 1875 to Leone M. Loomis. Neither were previously married or divorced. She died in 1907 and was buried in Mapledale Cemetery, New Haven.[396] They had one son: Fred L. Bradley, born on 10 February 1876 who was living at New Haven in 1924.

Timothy Segemond Bradley died at New Haven on 23 July 1924 and was buried there in Mapledale Cemetery. There was a G.A.R. marker at his gravesite in 1934. He was born at Branford on 17 October 1842, son of Timothy Bradley and Grace Barker.

---

394 Branford Vital Records, Town Meeting Book A, 228.
395 Affidavit, Warren M. Shepard of New Haven, 16 July 1889, in the pension file of Timothy S. Bradley.
396 The Hale Collection, New Haven, 935.

Michael Brennan of Branford, a private in the 14th Connecticut Volunteer Infantry died while in prison and was buried in Andersonville National Cemetery. (Connecticut Men in Southern Prisons, 46)

BRADSHAW, WILLIAM
Co. B 27th CVI, private, enlisted 1 September 1862, mustered out 27 July 1863, no pension

William Bradshaw, age 44, of Wallingford enlisted on 1 September 1862 and was mustered in on 3 October 1862 as a private in Co. B 27th CVI for a term of nine months. He was sick November and December 1862 at the Patent Office General Hospital at Washington, D.C. On 8 December 1862 he was transferred to a hospital in Baltimore per order of the medical director and was sick there in January 1863. May and June 1863 he was sick at Emory General Hospital at Washington, D.C. and July and August 1863 at Lovell General Hospital, Portsmouth, Rhode Island. It does not appear he fought in any battles due to illness. Bradshaw was mustered out with the rest of his regiment on 27 July 1863 but was not present. After his discharge he lived at Wallingford. He did not apply for a pension.

He is probably the William Bradshaw born on 18 July 1817, died on 10 March 1890, buried in Walnut Grove Cemetery, Meriden. [397] His wife Maria died on 11 May 1900.

BRENNAN, MICHAEL
Co. I 14th CVI, drafted 25 July 1863, died 3 July 1864, no pension

Michael Brennan of Branford served as a substitute or was drafted on 25 July 1863 as a private in Co. I 14th CVI for a term of three years. He was a prisoner at Andersonville, Georgia and died while in prison on 3 July 1864. He was buried in the National Cemetery at Andersonville.[398] He does not appear in the 1860 census at Branford.

---

397 The Hale Collection, Meriden, 37.
398 *Connecticut Men in Southern Prisons*, 53.

BROCKETT, BENAJAH
Co. F 7th CVI, private, enlisted 8 September 1861, discharged 20 July 1865, pension #A5-19-26 for the soldier and later for his widow Elizabeth

Benajah Brockett, age 18, of North Branford enlisted at New Haven on 8 September 1861 and was mustered in the next day as a private in Co. F 7th CVI for a term of three years. He reenlisted as a veteran in Co. F on 22 December 1863. He was honorably discharged at Goldsboro, North Carolina on 20 July 1865.

He applied for an invalid pension on 11 October 1890 under the act of 27 June 1890. At the time of his enlistment he was described as five feet four inches tall, light complexion, blue eyes, light hair, occupation farmer. His military service was claimed by East Haven on the draft enrollment of 1863. His service of two years, five months, and fourteen days was reduced to one year, four months, and twenty-eight days due to desertion. He was reported as deserted on 22 February 1864 after failing to return from furlough. He was arrested on 9 March 1864 and sent back to his regiment on 13 March 1864. He arrived at Fort Monroe, Virginia on 16 March and was admitted to Foster General Hospital at New Bern, North Carolina on 23 March 1865. There is a discrepancy in the record whether the desertion was in 1864 or 1865; there is no record of a court martial. The reduction of time toward his pension was cancelled on 27 April 1915. Since his discharge he lived at Holyoke, Massachusetts 1872; Barkhamsted 1882; Amsterdam, New York 1887; Meriden 1890; New Haven 1891; Westfield, Massachusetts 1892; since then at Hagaman, New York.

He was born at North Haven on 5 January 1845, son of Justus Brockett and Mary Anne Robinson. He was married first at Springfield, Massachusetts to Eliza Cook who died in 1880.

Benajah Brockett died at Hagaman, New York on 18 June 1925 where he was buried. He is sometimes listed as Charles B. Brockett (see discussion below).

Elizabeth Brockett applied for a widow's pension on 7 July 1925. She was born at New York City on 9 September 1861. She was married to the soldier under the name of Elizabeth Kissinger at Amsterdam, New York by Rev. William Norman Irish of St. Ann's Church on 18 June 1883. He was called Charles E. or Charles B. Brockett and as long as she knew him he was known as Charles. She knew his name was Benajah but he preferred Charles because it was easier to pronounce. She was not previously married or divorced. She stated that the soldier was never previously married and claimed she never knew he was.[399] There are a number of documents in the file about this matter, Elizabeth did receive a pension. They had two children: Isabelle, born on 23 June 1884; and Edward R., born on 1 October 1899. Elizabeth and her two children were all living at Hagaman, New York in 1926.

---

399 Statement, Elizabeth Brockett, Hagaman, N.Y., 12 January 1926, in the file of Benajah Brockett.

BROCKETT, EDGAR L.

Co. F 7th CVI, private, enlisted 29 August 1861, discharged 20 July 1865, pension #960423 for the soldier and later for his widow Catherine

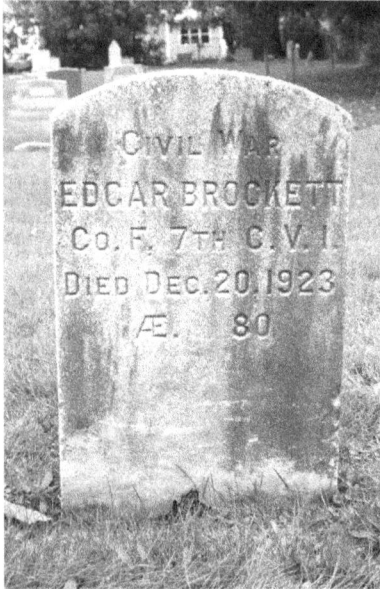

Edgar Brockett of North Branford enlisted at New Haven on 29 August 1861 and mustered in on 9 September 1861 as a private in Co. F 7th CVI for a term of three years. He was discharged at St. Helena Island, South Carolina on 22 December 1863. He reenlisted the same day as a veteran in Co. F. and was mustered out with the rest of his regiment at Goldsboro, North Carolina on 20 July 1865 and discharged at New Haven on 11 August 1865. He was the twin brother of Edward Brockett of the same company.

He applied for an invalid pension on 11 February 1880. At the time of his enlistment he was described as five feet six inches tall, light complexion, light hair, blue eyes, occupation farmer. While on duty aboard the steamship *Illinois* in the city of Port Royal on or about 16 November 1861, he was taken sick and remained so for twenty-two days and was weak until July 1862. He was taken with diarrhea at James Island and has never fully recovered. He also contracted malaria at Cockspun Island about 22 April 1862. He was reported as deserted at New Haven on 19 February 1864 and was arrested on 9 March 1865. His term of service was reduced for his pension.

He was married at Lebanon Springs, New York by William F. Kendal, JP on 17 September 1866 to Catherine "Katie" Louise Beach. She states in her application they were married at Pittsfield, Massachusetts by G. W. Twinging. No record of their marriage could be furnished. They were remarried on their 25th anniversary at Bridgeport by Rev. Charles Palmer on 8 April 1892. They had the following children (living in 1898): Ida Maria, born on 6 December 1867; Grace Emma, born on 5 November 1869; Charles Edgar, born on 27 February 1871; Edna Katie, born on 29 September 1874; Oscar Lenord, born on 27 October 1876; and Louis Jerome, born on 4 March 1878. A record of the children's baptisms is also in the file. The following children of Edgar and Catherine L. Brockett were baptized by Rev. William E. Vibbert of St. James Parish, East Grand Avenue, New Haven: Ida Maria, Grace Emma, and Charles Edgar on 5 August 1877. Son Louis Jerome was born on 6 March 1879 and baptized at St. Paul's Church, Chapel and Olive Streets, New Haven on 16 April 1892.

Edgar L. Brockett died at East Haven on 20 December 1923 and was buried there in Green Lawn Cemetery. He was born at East Haven on 10 February 1843, son of Justus T. Brockett and Mary Ann Robinson, born at North Haven and North Branford.

Catherine L. Brockett of East Haven applied for a widow's pension on 16 February 1924. She was living at East Haven in 1930 with her daughter Ida Oppel.

Outlying Picket in the Woods by Winslow Homer. (Harper's Weekly, June 7, 1862)

BROCKETT, EDWARD
Co. F 7th CVI, private, enlisted 29 August 1861, discharged 20 July 1865, pension #548634 for the soldier and an application by his widow Eleanor

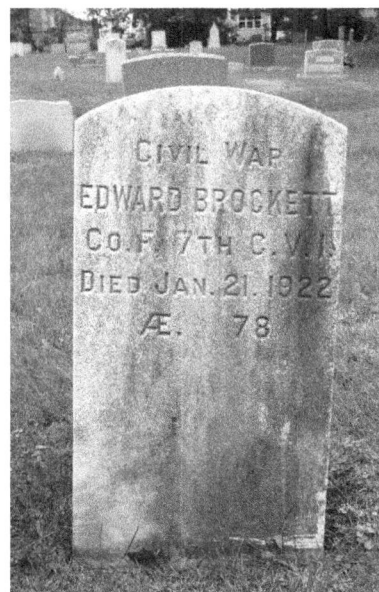

Edward Brockett of North Branford enlisted at New Haven on 29 August 1861 and was mustered in on 9 September 1861 as a private in Co. F 7th CVI for a term of three years. In November and December 1861 he was in the hospital at Hilton Head, South Carolina. He was mustered out on 22 December 1863 and reenlisted the same day as a veteran in Co. F. He was reported as deserted at New Haven on 22 February 1864. He was arrested on 21 February 1865, sent to the draft rendezvous station at New Haven and returned to his regiment. Edward Brockett was mustered out with the rest of his regiment at Goldsboro, North Carolina on 20 July 1865 and honorably discharged at New Haven on 11 August 1865. He was the twin brother of Edgar Brockett of the same company.

He applied for an invalid pension on 22 May 1889. At the time of his enlistment he was described as five feet six inches tall, light complexion, blue eyes, light hair, occupation farmer. "In August 1862 while on picket duty at Seabrook Ferry, we marched eight miles in the burning hot sun. While returning I became over heated and a heavy shower came up and drenched me. I contracted a severe case of typhoid fever which lasted about three months and has affected me ever since." Since his discharge he resided at North

Branford, New Haven, and East Haven. His time of service was reduced due to desertion.

He was married first at East Haven by Rev. D. William Havens of the Congregational Church on 4 July 1867 to Mary Ames Lincoln. She died on 5 October 1913. They had the following children living (in 1915): George C., born on 3 September 1868; Albert L., born on 28 September 1870; Esther May, born on 1 April 1876; and Elizur Edward, born on 29 December 1880.

Edward Brockett died at East Haven on 21 January 1922 and was buried there in Green Lawn Cemetery. He was born at East Haven on 10 February 1843, son of Justus T. Brockett and Mary Ann Robinson. There was no public record of his birth.

Eleanor V. Brockett of East Haven applied for a widow's pension on 18 March 1922. She was married to the soldier under the name of Eleanor V. Needham at East Haven by Rev. Clark on 19 March 1914. She was married first on 29 November 1889 to J. G. Needham. Needham died at New York in November 1893. It is not clear from the file whether Eleanor Brockett received a pension.

BROCKETT, WILLIAM E.
Co. K 15th CVI, private, enlisted 9 August 1862, mustered out 27 June 1865, pension #963471 for the soldier and later for his widow Hattie

William E. Brockett, age 18, of North Haven enlisted at New Haven on 9 August 1862 and was mustered in on 25 August 1862 as a private in Co. K 15th CVI for a term of three years. He saw action at Fredericksburg, Virginia on 13 December 1862, during the Siege of Suffolk, Virginia in the spring of 1863, and in the Peninsula Campaign of July 1863. He was on picket duty during the Battle of Kinston, North Carolina. William E. Brockett was mustered out with the rest of his regiment at New Bern, North Carolina on 27 June 1865 and discharged at New Haven on 12 July 1865. He served under Capt. Medad D. Munson of Wallingford.

He applied for a pension on 19 April 1901. At the time of his enlistment he was described as five feet nine inches tall, dark complexion, dark eyes, black hair, occupation farmer. He was married first at Northford by Rev. Sheldon Davis of St. Andrews Church on 30 March 1869 to Grace Caroline Clark. They had seven children: Walter Dudley, born on 18 December 1869; Frank Shelton, born on 25 September 1871; Ethel Maria, born on 14 March 1880, died on 24 July 1880; Lawrence Beach, twin, born on 4 May1881; Clarence Lewis, twin, born on 4 May 1881; Orrin Newcomb, born on 12 September 1882, died 25 October 1892; and Benjamin Alexander, born on 6 May1891. Grace Clark Brockett died at New Haven on 26 November 1902 age 51 years and 12 days. She was born at Haddam, daughter of Lewis and Grace Clark.

He was married second at Glastonbury by Rev. Francis P. Batcheler on 7 December 1904 to Hattie E. Friar of Glastonbury. After his discharge he lived at North Haven, New Haven and summered at Brockett's Point, Branford. He was a member of the Admiral Foote Post No. 17 of New Haven and active in the state's G.A.R. activities.[400] His name appears on the North Haven Civil War Honor Roll.

William Elfred Brockett died at New Haven on 29 November 1924 and was buried in Center Cemetery, North Haven. He was born at North Haven on 1 April 1845, son of William Atwater Brockett and Louise Eaton.[401]

Hattie E. Brockett applied for a widow's pension on 9 February 1925. She was born at Glastonbury on 2 December 1854. She was married first under the name of Hattie Elvira House at Hazardville, Enfield by Rev. George W. Miller on 26 October 1878 to Rufus R. Friar. He was age 33, living at Rockville, born at Fitchburg, Massachusetts; she was age 23, born and living at Glastonbury. They had one daughter Emma Jane

---

400 Obituary, *New Haven Register*, 1 December 1924.
401 *The Descendants of John Brockett*, 174-75.

Friar, born on 6 November 1869, living in 1897. Rufus Rawson Friar was married first to Mary A. Stone who died at Rockville on 7 August 1877 age 34 years & 2 months. Rufus R. Friar enlisted on 16 August 1862 at Concord, New Hampshire as a private in Co. G 13th New Hampshire Volunteers and was discharged on 21 June 1865. He was a pensioner #972087. Friar died at Glastonbury on 2 August 1901 and was buried there in Green Cemetery. He was the son of Robert L. Friar and Betsey C. Gibbs, born at Poughkeepsie, New York and Coventry.

Hattie E. Brockett was living at New Haven in 1930.[402]

BROCKETT, WILLIAM T.
Co. B 15th CVI, private, enlisted 5 August 1862, mustered out 27 June 1865, pension #591914 for the soldier

William T. Brockett, age 21, of East Haven enlisted at New Haven on 5 August 1862 and was mustered in on 25 August 1862 as a private in Co. B 15th CVI for a term of three years. He was fined $5.00 by a Regimental Court Martial on 9 October 1862 which was deducted from his pay, the reason was not stated. From 31 October 1862 until April 1864 he was detailed as a teamster on an ammunition train. William T. Brockett was mustered out with the rest of his regiment at New Bern, North Carolina on 27 June 1865 and discharged at New Haven on 12 July 1865. He was the brother of Edgar and Edward Brockett.

He applied for an invalid pension on 16 July 1890 under the act of 27 June 1890 due to age related illnesses. At the time of his enlistment he was described as five foot six inches tall, dark complexion, hazel eyes, brown hair, occupation shoemaker.

He was married at East Haven by Rev. D. William Havens of the Congregational Church in 1866 to Nancy Smith. She died by 1897 and was the daughter of Stephen Smith and Ann Depatra of Northford. He had one child living (in 1897): Ada B. Kumm, born on 27 September 1871. After the war he lived at Northford; 1897 at New Britain; 1898 at New Haven; and in 1903 at Newark, Essex Co., New Jersey. Ada Kumm was living at Meriden in 1907.

William T. Brockett died on 9 January 1907 and was buried at New Northford Cemetery, North Branford. His company and regiment are engraved on his stone. He was born at East Haven, son of Justus T. Brockett and Mary Ann Robinson.[403]

BROWN, CHARLES
Co. C 29th CVI, corporal, enlisted 13 November 1864, mustered out 24 October 1865, pension #343754 for his mother

Charles Brown of Branford enlisted at New Haven on 13 November 1864 as a private in Co. C 29th CVI for a term of three years and joined the regiment on 16 January 1865. His service was credited to Branford. He

402 U.S. census 1930, New Haven, New Haven County, Connecticut, population schedule, T626-277, dwelling 347, family 452, page 256, www.heritagequest.com.
403 *The Descendants of John Brockett*, 181.

was promoted to corporal on 1 October 1865 and discharged at Brownsville, Texas on 24 October 1865. He does not appear in the 1860 census for Branford. His name appears on the Wall of Honor at Washington, D.C.

BROWN, HENRY C.
Co. E 1st HA, private, enlisted 18 December 1863, mustered out 25 September 1865, pension #942587 for the soldier and later for his widow Margaret

Henry C. Brown of North Branford enlisted on 18 December 1863 as a private in Co. E 1st HA for a term of three years. With his regiment he fought in the Virginia campaign including Chickahominy and Malvern Hill. Henry C. Brown was mustered out with the rest of his regiment at Washington, D.C. on 25 September 1865 and discharged at Hartford on 1 October 1865. He does not appear in the 1860 census at Branford or North Branford.

He applied for an invalid pension on 8 August 1890 under the act of 27 June 1890. Henry C. Brown died at Poundridge, New York on 15 August 1923. Margaret E. Brown applied for a widow's pension on 30 August 1923.

BROWN, JAMES A. or BROOM
Co. M 2nd HA, enlisted or drafted 13 February 1864, deserted, no pension

James A. Brown of Branford enlisted or was drafted on 13 February 1864 and deserted on 28 July 1864. There was no additional military record. He does not appear in the 1860 census at Branford. A request for information about him was submitted to the *Solders' Record*:

Duncannon Oct. 1 1868

Rev. C. H. Seibke, Sir,

During the late war a young soldier by the name of James A. Brown wandered from the Shenandoah Valley and died here of congestive chills, August 23d 1864. He was buried in the Lutheran cemetery.

    We never knew his history, or where he enlisted until this summer. We raised money to get him a tomb-stone and thought we would try and find his friends. We first wrote to the Adjutant General of your State, and learned that he enlisted in Co. N [sic M] 2nd Heavy Artillery, Feb. 13th 1864, and gave his residence as Branford, New Haven Co. Conn. We have written twice to the P. M. at Branford but have received no reply, which we do not understand. Not seeing any Lutheran minister's address at that place, I thought perhaps you would feel interested on behalf of our honored dead, and try to find out all the information in your power. Please let us know as soon as you can, we would like to have the tomb-stone set up before the winter sets in. Please answer as soon as convenient.

    Address,
    Miss Susan McLaughlin
    Duncannon,
    Perry Co., Penn.

P. S. He came to our place about 3 o. c. in the afternoon, told where he came from, but did not give his name.

The letters J.A.B. were on his arms. The next morning when the family got up he was dying in a chill. We called two doctors who said he was dying and there was no help for him. He could not talk to tell us anything. He was about 17 years old and very beautiful.

It seems strange that such mystery hangs over him for four years. Please try and find out his parents or friends. Why has not the P. M. announced our letter?

Inquiries or information concerning the above matter may be addressed to Rev. C. H. Siebke, 102 Olive Street, New Haven, Conn. or this office."[404]

BROWN, LAWRENCE
Co. D 11th CVI, private, substitute, mustered in 1 December 1864, deserted

Lawrence Brown served as a substitute for Virgil H. Rose of North Branford. He was mustered in at New Haven on 1 December 1864 as a private in Co. D 11th CVI and deserted on 7 June 1865. There was no further military record. He does not appear in the 1860 census at Branford.

BROWN, WILLIAM alias WILLIAM MCMINN
Co. I 14th CVI, drafted 25 July 1863, wounded, discharged disability 31 May 1864, pension #XC2807721 for the soldier and later for his widow

William Brown, alias William McMinn, of Branford served as a substitute or was drafted on 25 July 1863 as a private in Co. I 14th CVI for a term of three years. He was wounded at Morton's Ford, Virginia on 6 February 1864 and discharged for disability on 31 May 1864. He does not appear in the 1860 census at Branford. He applied for an invalid pension on 1 June 1864 and died on 7 September 1898. His wife applied for a widow's pension on 20 December 1917 and was living in New York. His pension is at the Veterans Administration.

BRYAN, WILLIAM, JR.
see William Bub

BUB, WILLIAM or BUBB
Co. I 1st HA, private, substitute, enlisted 8 December 1863, to Co. I 1st HA, deserted, no pension

William Bub, age 19, served as a substitute for William Bryan, Jr. of Branford. He was mustered in at New Haven on 3 December 1864 as a private in Co. I 1st HA for a term of three years. He was described as five feet four inches tall, black eyes, light brown hair, dark complexion, unmarried, born in Germany, occupation teamster. He deserted on 4 April 1865 and was "a deserter therefrom." He was dishonorably discharged by general court martial on 29 November 1865.

---

404 Letter from Miss Susan McLaughlin of Duncannon, Penn. to Rev. C. H. Siebke of New Haven; *The Soldiers' Record*, 24 October 1868, vol. 1 no. 16, 121; Connecticut State Library digital collections. No reply was submitted to the newspaper.

BUELL, BURTON T.

Co. H 25th CVI, wagoner, enlisted 27 August 1862, discharged 27 August 1863, pension #781662 for the soldier and later for his widow Juliet

Burton T. Buell of Glastonbury enlisted at Hartford on 27 August 1862 and was mustered in on 11 November 1862 as a wagoner in Co. H 25th CVI for a term of nine months. With his regiment he served in Louisiana at the Battles of Irish Bend and Port Hudson. Burton Buell was mustered out with the rest of his regiment at Hartford on 26 August 1863.

He applied for an invalid pension on 28 December 1891 under the act of 27 June 1890. After the war he lived at Southington and appears at Branford in the 1880 census. He was a charter member of the Mason Rogers Post No. 7 G.A.R. and was transferred out on 23 April 1885 when he moved back to Southington.

Burton Tracy Buell died at Plainville on 17 February 1914 and was buried in Oak Hill Cemetery, Southington. He was born at Chatham, probably the son of Titus and Electa Buell.

Juliet J. Munson Buell applied for a pension on 11 March 1914. She died in 1917 and was buried in Oak Hill Cemetery, Southington.

BUELL, EDWARD J.

Co. B & D 75th Ohio, private, enlisted 16 December 1863, prisoner, discharged 13 January 1865 pension #462861 for the soldier

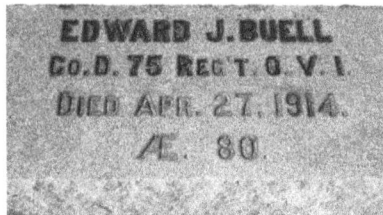

Edward J. Buell[405] enlisted on 16 December 1863 at Athens, Ohio as a private in Co. D 75th Ohio Volunteer Infantry and on 30 December 1864 was transferred to Co. B 75th Ohio. He was missing in action at Gainesville, Florida on 17 April 1864, brought from Salisbury Prison, North Carolina; confined at Andersonville Prison on 22 February 1865 and was paroled at Aikens Landing, Virginia on 24 February 1865. He was admitted to Hospital Division I at Annapolis and given a thirty day furlough on 16 March 1865. He reported back to duty at Camp Chase, Ohio on 3 May 1865 and was discharged from there on 13 June 1865. He was the brother-in-law of Watson W. Stone.

He applied for an invalid pension on 1 June 1880 for apoplexy and epilepsy contracted from exposure to the hot sun at St. Augustine, Florida. At the time of his enlistment he was described as five feet eight inches tall, medium complexion, blue eyes, dark hair, occupation laborer. After the war he lived at Ohio; Elsie, Clinton Co., Michigan about twenty year; returned to Connecticut in 1875 living at Clinton, North Branford, East Haven, and Branford. He was married first to Lovina J. Manley who died at Winthrop, Connecticut on 20 March 1875. They had three children: Minnie A., not mentioned in 1898; Clifford Agustin, born on 5 April 1870, living in 1898; and Elbert Earl, born on 18 January 1874, living in 1898.

---

405 For his biography see Rockey, *History of New Haven County*, II:98.

He was married second at Clinton by Harry E. Burns on 6 June 1876 to Dorlisha Amelia Stone, daughter of Heman Stone and Mabel Field of Clinton. She was the widow of Charles Griswold of Guilford.[406] She was born at Cayuga Lake, New York,[407] died on 18 April 1906 age 74 and was buried in Bare Plain Cemetery, North Branford. They appear at Branford in the 1880 census, North Branford in 1900 and he was living with his son Clifford at East Haven in 1910. He joined the Mason Rogers Post No. 7 G.A.R. of Branford on 28 April 1882.

Edward J. Buell died at Short Beach, Branford on 27 April 1914 and was buried in Bare Plain Cemetery, North Branford. There was a G.A.R. marker at his gravesite in 1934 and 2011. He was born at Clinton on 6 June 1835,[408] son of William A. Buell and Rosetta Stevens. His name appears on the Northford Veterans' Monument.

BUELL, EDWIN A.
Co. K 15th CVI, private, enlisted 11 August 1862, mustered out 27 June 1865, pension #C2534544 for the soldier and later for his widow Mary

Edwin A. Buell[409] of North Branford enlisted at New Haven on 11 August 1862 and was mustered in on 25 August 1862 as a private in Co. K 15th CVI for a term of three years. He saw action at Fredericksburg, Virginia on 13 December 1862, during the Siege of Suffolk, Virginia in the spring of 1863, and in the Peninsula Campaign of July 1863. He was on picket duty during the Battle of Kinston, North Carolina and during April 1865 on detached duty. Edwin Buell was mustered out with the rest of his regiment at New Bern, North Carolina on 27 June 1865 and discharged at New Haven on 12 July 1865. He served under Capt. Medad D. Munson of Wallingford.

He applied for an invalid pension on 17 June 1892 under the act of 27 June 1890. At the time of his enlistment he was described as age 28, five feet five inches tall, fair complexion, brown eyes, brown hair, occupation tin smith and farmer. He came to Northford in 1858 and lived there after the war except for two years in Clinton from April 1872 to August 1874. He was married at Guilford by Rev. A. C. Hurd on 28 January 1869 to Mary Amelia Barnes. They had no children. She was born at North Branford in 1839, daughter of Seneca Barnes and Mary Hart of Northford and died in 1911. She was buried in New Northford Cemetery,.

Edwin A. Buell died on 4 March 1911 and was buried in New Northford Cemetery. His company and regiment are engraved on his stone. He was born at Clinton on 8 December 1831, son of Horace Buell and Polly Kelsey.

406 Talcott, *Families of Guilford*, 1163.
407 North Branford Vital Records, deaths 1906.
408 His birthplace is given as both Clinton and Medina Co., Ohio in the pension file.
409 For his biography see Rockey, *History of New Haven County*, II:98.

William R. Bunnell of Northford was the drummer boy for Co. B 27th CVI. Depicted is
a sketch of a drummer along the Rappahannock by Edwin Forbes.

BUNNELL, WILLIAM R.

Co. B 27th CVI, private, drummer boy, enlisted 25 August 1862, mustered out 27 July 1863, pension #658401 for the soldier and later for his widow Isabella

William R. Bunnell, age 18, of Branford enlisted at New Haven on 25 August 1862 and was mustered in on 3 October 1862 as a drummer boy in Co. B 27th CVI for a term of nine months. He received an injury by falling off a log in December 1862 while building winter quarters at Falmouth, Virginia.[410] He was laid up for several weeks. It is unclear whether he fought in the Battles of Fredericksburg or Gettysburg. He did fight at the Battle of Chancellorsville on 3 May 1863. Bunnell was mustered out with the rest of his regiment at New Haven on 27 July 1863.

He applied for a pension on 13 October 1890 under the act of 27 June 1890. At the time of his enlistment he was described as five feet eight inches tall, medium complexion, hazel eyes, grey hair, occupation farmer. Bunnell claims he had an ongoing disability caused by sun stroke suffered in June 1863 a short time before the Battle of Gettysburg. Since his discharge he lived at New Haven until 1864 and since that time at Northford. He was married at the Davenport Church, New Haven by Rev. J. N. Patridge on 4 June 1873 to Isabella C. Chittenden, ages 28 and 24, both of New Haven. She was born at Durham. They had two children living (in 1898): Robert K., born on 1 December 1874; and William Leroy, born on 19 October 1882.

William R. Bunnell died at North Branford on 2 March 1908 and was buried in New Northford Cemetery. His company and regiment are engraved on his stone. He was born at Derby on 13 April 1845, son of Russell R. Bunnell and Alexa King, born at Northford and Scotland.

Isabella C. Bunnell of Northford received benefits after his death under the act of 19 April 1908. She was living in 1920.[411] She was the daughter of William Wolcott Chittenden and Rebecca Amelia Augur.

BUSH, MALACHI C.

Co. E 1st HA, private, enlisted 31 January 1862, prisoner, died 15 July 1862, pension #267489 for his father Gilbert Bush

Malachi Cook Bush of Branford enlisted at New Haven on 16 December 1861 and was mustered in on 1 February 1862 as a private in Co. E 1st HA. He was sick in May and June 1862 in Regimental Hospital, Gaines Mills, Virginia. He was taken prisoner at Cold Harbor, Virginia on 27 June 1862 during action at Golden Hill and reported as absent and deserted. He "supposedly" died in prison at Richmond, Virginia about 15 July 1862 from typhoid fever. There is a gravestone for him at Damascus Cemetery, Branford which reads "Died in Civil War" and his name is on the New Haven Soldiers and Sailors Monument on East Rock. He was the brother of Timothy G. Bush.

His father Gilbert Bush of Branford applied for a pension on 29 May 1888. Gilbert Bush was married at Wallingford by Rev. Matthew Noyes of the Northford Congregational Church on 2 May 1837 to Hermoine

---

410 Affidavit, Dr. R. B. Goodyear of North Haven, 8 May 1893, in the pension file of William R. Bunnell.
411 U.S. census 1920, North Branford, New Haven County, Connecticut, population schedule, T625-190, dwelling 93, family 98, living with her son Robert K. Bunnell & family, page 92B, www.heritagequest.com.

Calista Cook. They had four children (living in 1862): Timothy G., age 21; Malachi C., age 18; Ann A., age 16; and Emily C., age 12, born on 19 December 1850. His wife Hermoine Bush was an invalid in 1862. She died at Branford on 20 July 1887 age 74 and was buried there in Damascus Cemetery. The soldier, Malachi C. Bush, was born at Branford on 21 April 1844[412] and worked on his father's farm at the time of his enlistment.

Gilbert Bush died at North Branford on 6 October 1900 age 86 years, 3 months & 16 days and was buried in Damascus Cemetery, Branford.[413] He was born at Stony Creek, Branford, son of Gilbert Bush and Thankful Cook.

BUSH, TIMOTHY G.
Co. G 7th CVI, 2nd lieutenant, enlisted 27 August 1861, mustered out 20 July 1865, pension ##XC2688587 for the soldier and later for his widow Mary

Timothy G. Bush of Branford enlisted at New Haven on 27 August 1861 and was mustered in on 7 September 1861 as a private in Co. G 7th CVI for a term of three years. With his regiment he served in Georgia, at the Battles of Pocotaligo and Fort Wagner, South Carolina and served in the 1865 Virginia campaign. He was discharged at St. Helena Island, South Carolina on 21 September 1863 and reenlisted as a veteran in Co. G on 22 December 1863. He was promoted to 2nd lieutenant on 10 March 1865. Timothy Bush was mustered out at Goldsboro, North Carolina with the rest of the regiment on 20 July 1865 and discharged at New Haven on 11 August 1865. He was the brother of Malachi C. Bush.

He applied for an invalid pension on 15 August 1895 under the act of 27 June 1890. He was mustered in on 13 February 1902 as a member of the Mason Rogers Post No. 7 G.A.R. of Branford and was later commander. He was previously a charter member of the Admiral Foote Post, New Haven and also a member of the J. C. McCoy Post at Columbus, Ohio.[414] After his discharge he lived at New Haven; Columbus, Ohio; Nashville, Tennessee; Kentucky; and returned to Branford about 1895. His pension is at the Veterans Administration.

He was married first at New Haven on 31 January 1864 to Phebe Ann Seward. She was born at New Haven on 20 June 1844, daughter of Harvey Seward and Harriet E. Ramsdell. She died at Nashville, Tennessee on 9 September 1887 and was buried there in Mt. Olivet Cemetery.[415]

---

412 Family bible belonging to Gilbert Bush in the pension file of Malachi C. Bush, witnessed by Henry H. Stedman of Branford, 29 July 1889. The bible is now in the possession of Dorothy Bush Makula.
413 North Branford Vital Records, deaths, 1900.
414 Records Mason Rogers Post No. 7 G.A.R, Blackstone Library Archives, RG 4.
415 Bush family bible.

Bible carried by Timothy G. Bush during the war. (Courtesy of Dorothy Bush Makula)

Timothy Gilbert Bush died at Branford on 22 October 1914 and was buried there in Center Cemetery. A G.A.R. marker was on his gravesite in 1934 and his name appears on the Stony Creek Veterans' Monument. He was born at Branford on 2 September 1841, son of Gilbert Bush and Hermoine Calista Cook.[416]

Mary A. Bush applied for widow's pension on 2 December 1914. She was married to the soldier at Nashville, Tennessee by Dr. William Green on 21 May 1887.[417] Mary Anice Spain Bush died at Branford on 5 June 1948 age 99 and was buried there in Center Cemetery. She was born at Nashville, Tennessee on 6 October 1848.[418]

BUTLER, CHARLES alias CHARLES F. T. PETERS
Co. D 15th CVI, enlisted 17 September 1864, prisoner, to Co. D 7th CVI, mustered out 20 July 1865, pension #860084 for the soldier and later for his widow

Charles Butler of Branford enlisted or was drafted on 17 September 1864 as a private in Co. D 15th CVI. He was captured with much of his regiment at the Battle of Kinston, North Carolina on 8 March 1865, confined at Libby Prison, Richmond on 23 March, and paroled at Boulware's & Cox's wharf on 26 March 1865. He reported to Camp Parole, Maryland on 30 March 1865, received a thirty day furlough and afterwards reported to Camp Convalescent, Virginia. He was transferred to Co. D 7th CVI on 23 June 1865 and mustered out with the rest of the regiment at Goldsboro, North Carolina on 20 July 1865.

He applied for an invalid pension on 24 September 1891 under the act of 27 June 1890. He is probably the Charles F. T. Peters living at Warwick, Lancaster Co., Pennsylvania in 1900 and Reading, Berks Co., Pennsylvania in 1910 with his wife Katie.[419] He died at Reading, Pennsylvania on 16 September 1916. His widow applied for a pension on 21 September 1916.

---

416 Bush family bible.
417 Bush family bible.
418 Branford Vital Records, deaths, 1948; her parents are recorded as unknown. The 1900 census indicates she had a first marriage.
419 U.S. census 1900, Warwick, Lancaster Co., Pennsylvania, population schedule, T623-1426, dwelling 355, family 400, page 19A, Charles F. T. Peters age 59, born Germany; Kate B. age 47, born Wurtenberg; married 25 years. U.S. census 1910, Reading, Berks Co., Pennsylvania, population schedule, T624-1315, dwelling 349, family 351, page 17B, Mary McQuad, Charles F. Peters age 69, born Germany; Kate E. age 58, born Germany, married 25 years, www.ancestry.com.

BUTLER, JESSE

Co. F 6th CVI, private, enlisted 26 August 1861, killed 17 June 1864, no pension

Jesse Butler of New Haven enlisted on 26 August 1861 and was mustered in at New Haven on 7 September 1861 as a private in Co. F 6th CVI for a term of three years. He reenlisted as a veteran in Co. F on 24 December 1863. He was killed at Bermuda Hundred, Virginia on 17 June 1864. There is a gravestone for him in Northford Cemetery, North Branford which reads "Company F 6 Regt. Connecticut Volunteer, Killed Bermuda Hundred, June 17, 1864." His name is on the New Haven Soldiers and Sailors Monument on East Rock and on the Northford Veterans' Monument. He was living at North Branford in 1860.[420]

BUTLER, RUFUS A.

Co. G 7th Ohio Volunteer Infantry, private, died 10 October 1861 of disease, pension #135764 for his mother Mary

Rufus Alfred Butler enlisted at Camp Dennison, Edinburgh, Portage Co., Ohio on 20 June 1861 as a private in Co. G 7th Ohio Volunteer Infantry. He died at Charleston, Virginia on 10 October 1861 of camp fever.

His mother Mary applied for a pension on 7 October 1869 under the act of 14 July 1862. She was the widow of Rufus Butler and was dependent on her son for support who operated an engine at a saw mill. Another son Edward died on 6 October 1864 in the war. Mary Russell was married at Branford by Rev. Timothy P. Gillett of the First Congregational Church on 25 July 1824 to Rufus Butler.[421] She was born at North Branford on 2 April 1802, daughter of Jonathan Russell and Eunice Dudley.[422] The family moved to Ohio about 1830. Rufus Butler died at Atwater, Portage Co., Ohio on 16 June 1862 and had been unable to work for several years. She had one half interest during her lifetime of ten acres of land and a log house. Mary Russell Butler died at Atwater, Ohio on 31 July 1885.

BUTLER, SAMUEL C.

Co. G 29th CVI, private, enlisted 29 December 1863, mustered out 24 October 1865, no pension

Samuel C. Butler of Branford enlisted at New Haven on 29 December 1863 and was mustered in on 8 March 1864 as a private in Co. G 29th CVI for a term of three years. His service was credited to Branford. He was left behind sick at Bermuda Hundred, Virginia on 13 August 1864. He was sick at Post Hospital, Brownsville, Texas beginning 12 August 1865 through September. Samuel Butler was mustered out at Brownsville, Texas on 24 October 1865. His name appears on the Wall of Honor at Washington, D.C.

---

420 U.S. census 1860, North Branford, New Haven County, Connecticut, population schedule, M653-85, dwelling 179, family 190, page 873, Jesse Butler, age 22, born Conn., farm laborer living with Jonathan Fowler, www.heritagequest.com.
421 Branford Vital Records, 1786-1840, 334.
422 Talcott, *Families of Guilford*, 1031.

BYINGTON, EDWIN M.

Co. I 15th CVI, private, enlisted 4 August 1862, prisoner, mustered out 27 June 1865, pension #C2-550-274 for the soldier

Edwin M. Byington, age 18, of North Branford enlisted at New Haven on 4 August 1862 and was mustered in on 25 August 1862 as a private in Co. I 15th CVI for a term of three years. From May 1863 through June 1864 he was assigned to the Pioneer Corps. He was captured with much of his regiment at the Battle of Kinston, North Carolina on 8 March 1865, confined at Libby Prison, Richmond on 23 March, and paroled at Boulware's & Cox's wharf on 26 March 1865. He reported to Camp Parole, Maryland on 30 March 1865, received a thirty day furlough and afterwards reported to Camp Convalescent, Virginia. Byington was mustered out with the rest of his regiment at New Bern, North Carolina on 27 June 1865 and discharged at New Haven on 12 July 1865.

He applied for an invalid pension on 8 September 1890 under the act of 27 June 1890 due to age related illness. At the time of his enlistment he was described as five feet eight inches tall, fair complexion, hazel eyes, brown hair, occupation carpenter. He was living at Killingworth in 1880 and New Haven from 1900 to 1907.

He was married at New Haven by George Lansing Taylor on 15 February 1875 to Hattie Lucretia Dudley. Neither were previously married or divorced. She was born on 14 August 1849 and died on 18 January 1900, daughter of Wyllis Dudley and Mary Lucretia Wilcox of Killingworth.[423] They had three children living (in 1900): Frederick R., born on 6 August 1877; Mary I., born on 3 December 1879; and Lawrence E., born on 28 October 1882.

Edwin Minor Byington died at New Haven on 27 March 1907. He was born at North Branford on 24 May 1845, son of Darling Byington and Martha Benton. His name appears on the Northford Veterans' Monument.

CALKINS, WILBUR F.

Co. K 27th CVI, drummer, enlisted 9 September 1862, prisoner, discharged disability 27 July 1863;, reenlisted Marine Corps 16 August 1864, discharged disability 10 May 1865, pension #150471 for the soldier and later for his widow Rowena

Wilbur F. Calkins of New Haven enlisted at New Haven on 10 September 1862 and was mustered in on 18 October 1862 as a drummer boy in Co. K 27th CVI for a term of nine months. He was at the Battle of Fredericksburg on 13 December 1862 with the rest of the company. He was reported missing after the Battle of Chancellorsville, Virginia on 3 May 1863, held prisoner at Richmond, and paroled at City Point, Virginia on 14 May 1863. He reported to Camp Parole, Maryland on 16 May 1863, was sent to Washington, D.C. on 20 May 1863. According to his pension application he was at the Battle of Gettysburg on 2 July 1863. Calkins was mustered out with the rest of his regiment at New Haven on 27 July 1863. His father Henry D. and brother Arthur B. Calkins were also in the 27th CVI.

He reenlisted, now living at Branford, at the Marine Corps Barracks, Brooklyn, New York on 14 August 1864 as a drummer boy. He was discharged from the Marine Corps for disability on 5 May 1865.

He applied for an invalid pension under the acts of 14 July 1862 and March 3, 1873. At the time of his first enlistment he was described as age 20, five feet three inches tall, fair complexion, blue eyes, brown hair. He developed a right hernia at Fredericksburg, Virginia on 15 January 1863 lifting logs into a cart for the

---

423 Talcott, *Families of Guilford*, 324.

Wilbur F. Calkins was a drummer in Co. K 27th Connecticut Volunteer Infantry and fought at the Battles of Fredericksburg, Chancellorsville, and Gettysburg. (Beecher, First Light Battery, I:250)

building of winter quarters. He was treated at the field hospital near Fredericksburg. He was discharged from the Marine Corps for disability due to the hernia. He later applied for an increase in his pension due to deafness caused by the loud shelling at Gettysburg on 2 July 1863. The application for deafness was sent for special examination since he was a drummer boy and supposedly not in action. Calkins explained that the musicians were detailed to care for the sick and wounded during the battle and were close to the lines. After his discharge from the Marine Corps he returned to New Haven to the home of his parents and lived in New Haven, Fair Haven and West Haven until 1885. He removed to Campville, Litchfield Co. and was living there in 1895. His brother Arthur B. Calkins lived at Cleveland, Ohio since the war and was living in 1895 and his mother "is living still and lives with me." He was a member of the L. W. Steele Post No. 34 G.A.R. of Torrington.

Wilbur Fisk Calkins died on 2 July 1897 age 52 and was buried in Northfield Cemetery, Litchfield. His company and regiment are engraved on his stone. He was born at Terryville, son of Henry D. and Harriet Calkins.

Rowena M. Calkins of Torrington applied for a widow's pension on 24 August 1897. She was married to the soldier under the name of Rowena M. Ball by Rev. John Pegg, Jr. at New Haven on 9 August 1868. He was age 23, living at Terryville; she was age 17 born and living at Newark, New Jersey. Neither were previously married or divorced. Her application was rejected on 29 July 1898 because the soldier's death was not caused by his service. He died after an emergency operation for his hernia contracted during the war but died from complications. She requested the case be reopened and she did receive a pension. The pension file is very large with depositions from the soldier, his wife, physicians, and neighbors attesting to his physical disability and their marriage. She was living at Newark, Essex Co., New Jersey in December 1900 but returned to Torrington by December 1902. She was living at Torrington in 1913 and Verona, New Jersey in 1917. Several letters from her are in the file requesting an increase pension due to her destitute circumstances and the local G.A.R. was providing her with fuel and food. She received an increase to $20 per month by an act of Congress dated 3 March 1917.

Rowena Ball Calkins died on 24 October 1932 probably at Waterbury.[424]

CALLAHAN, TIMOTHY also CALLAGHAN/O'CALLAHAN/O'CALLAGHAN

Co. B 27th CVI, private, enlisted 10 September 1862, wounded, mustered out 27 July 1863, pension #543379 for the soldier and later for his widow Sarah

Timothy Callahan, age 30, of Wallingford enlisted on 10 September 1862 and was mustered in on 3 October 1862 as a private in Co. B 27th CVI for a term of nine months. He was "slightly" wounded at the Battle of Fredericksburg, Virginia on 13 December 1862 and sent to Division General Hospital, St. Paul's Church Branch, Alexandria, Virginia. In January through April 1863 he was at Knight Hospital, New Haven. By 20 July 1863 he was transferred to the invalid corps, unfit for duty but able to work at the Knight General Hospital in New Haven. He was described as 30 years of age, grey eyes, brown hair, height five feet nine inches, light complexion. He was born in Cork, Ireland; had been in the hospital for four months and sixteen days from his wound, had loss of his right finger, and was of good character. Timothy Callahan was mustered out with the rest of his regiment at New Haven on 27 July 1863.

He applied for an invalid pension on 29 May 1865. At the time of his enlistment he had been living in Wallingford for four or more years and was a laborer working in the spoon factory. He signed his depositions with his mark.[425]

Two of his children; James L. Callahan age 24, and Bridget H. Callahan, age 26 submitted an affidavit dated 17 February 1900. Since their births they stated they lived with their father in Wallingford. For about ten years their father has been in poor health, unable to work. The soldier had seven children living (in 1898): Mary Ann Roach, born on 16 September 1857; John, born on 4 July 1859; Ellen Lynch, born on 7 June 1863; Timothy, born on 9 July 1854; Edward, born on 15 September 1870; Bridget, born on 12 December 1873; and James, born on 15 December 1875.

Timothy O'Callahan died at Wallingford on 13 April 1902 and was buried in Holy Trinity Cemetery, Wallingford. He was born at Fermoy, Cork, Ireland on 25 December 1830, son of John O'Callaghan and Bridget O'Dwyer, both born at Fermoy.

Sarah Callahan applied for a widow's pension on 12 June 1902. She testified she was married to the soldier under the name of Sarah Leahy at Meriden by Father Wallace of St. Roses Church on 17 August 1855. The witnesses were all dead, neither the present rector nor the town clerk could furnish a record of evidence. The file had a number of depositions.

In 1902, James Barry of Wallingford, age 75 years, states "I have known Timothy Callahan since he was a small boy, before he left Ireland, and knew him to the date of his death. He was married only to Sarah Leahy, his wife, and I was godfather to their first child, born in 1856. They lived together at Colony Street, Wallingford." Also in 1902, Michael O'Callaghan, age 63 years, of 114 North Colony Street, Wallingford, states that he was the younger brother of Timothy Callahan. He stated that Timothy and Sarah were married in 1855 and neither had been married before, nor did Sarah remarry after the death of the soldier. Sarah and the soldier had eleven children. Francis J. Curtis, age 77, of Wallingford, states that Sarah Leahy lived with his family until 1855 when she married Timothy Callahan.

---

424 In 1930 she was living at Waterbury in a convalescent hospital.
425 Deposition, Timothy Callahan of Wallingford, 12 November 1889, in the pension file of John Condon.

CALLIHAN, STEPHEN

Co. C 1st Cavalry, private, enlisted 17 December 1864, prisoner, furloughed, failed to return

Stephen Callihan of Branford enlisted on 17 December 1864 as a private in Co. C. 1st Connecticut Cavalry. He was captured at New Market, Virginia on 9 March 1865 and released on 26 March 1865. He was given a thirty day furlough on 31 March 1865 but failed to return. There is no further military record. He does not appear in the 1860 census at Branford.

CAMP, HENRY A.

Co. B 27th CVI, private, enlisted 2 September 1862, wounded, mustered out 27 July 1863, pension #546318 for the soldier

Henry A. Camp, age 18, of Wallingford enlisted on 2 September 1862 and was mustered in on 3 October 1862 as a private in Co. B 27th CVI for a term of nine months. He testified in 1876 that "while at the Battle of Fredericksburg, Virginia, I was struck with a piece of shell striking the collar bone, dislocating the same and the effects of which I still suffer. Also on 3 May 1863 at the Battle of Chancellorsville, Virginia, while on the way to the Hospital being sick with lung trouble at the time, was struck with a shell on my head above the left eye which causes him at times to be confined to his bed. He was treated at Fredericksburg in a dwelling home from 13 December 1862 to January 1863 and at Chancellorsville from May to June 1863." There is no record of injury or any hospital records in his CMRS. On file with his pension papers from the war department is a document that states he was excused from guard duty on 25 December 1862 due to lung trouble and was admitted to the Regimental Hospital on 13 February 1863 with acute bronchitis and returned to duty on 21 February 1863. It is unclear if he fought at the Battle of Gettysburg. Henry Camp was mustered out with the rest of his regiment at New Haven on 27 July 1863.

Comrade Elizur B. Dibble states that at Fredericksburg during heavy firing by the enemy, "I saw Henry A. Camp fall down very suddenly and after laying on the ground a minute or so I crawled up to him being at the time only a few feet from him. I spoke to him and he said his right shoulder was hurt and he seemed to be in pain. I could see right away that his right shoulder was hurt and saw the place where the shell hit and his coat was torn and there was a hole in his cap. I saw him after the battle and could see his shoulder was dislocated. I remember that night after the battle of hearing one of the sergeants of the Co. saying that Henry A. Camp and his Father Joel Camp were both wounded and missing. I do not remember seeing him until about the 16th [December 1862] after our Division had fallen back across the Rappahannock. I saw him then, his arm was in a sling and his shoulder bandaged. I saw the wound a few days after. His shoulder was very much swollen and discolored, a black and blue spot about 2 ½ by 3 inches in size as near as I can remember. I do not know whether bones were broken. He was not sent to the hospital but was off duty for a month or more. I know he had trouble carrying his knapsack. I remember this because I shared the same quarters with him for several weeks after the battle."[426]

Solomon H. Woods stated that "about the 20th of June 1863 I was in command of Co. L 27th C. V. and that Henry A. Camp was a member of my company at that time at a place called Ginn Springs, Va. He reported to me that he was unable to carry his knapsack due to an injury and accordingly I ordered his knapsack transferred to the baggage wagon."[427]

---

426 Affidavit, Elizur B. Dibble of Branford, 25 July 1890, in the pension file of Henry A. Camp.
427 Affidavit, Solomon H. Woods of Berlin, 17 May 1890, in the pension file of Henry A. Camp.

Comrade James B. Page of Wallingford stated that while at the Battle of Chancellorsville "while we were about to fall back I heard Henry A. Camp say he was hurt or wounded. I turned partly around and saw blood on his face. I then crawled up to him being at that time only a few feet from him. I looked and [could] see a wound very near his left eye. I know he was then ordered to the rear. I am certain it was the work of a shell or fragment of a shell. I remember his shoulder being hurt at Fredericksburg and him not being able to carry a knapsack."[428]

Comrade George E. Rogers of Milford stated that "while facing the enemy fire in [the] line of duty under orders of Lieut. George Elton of co. B 27 Reg. Conn. vol. May 3rd 1863 at Chancellorsville State of Virginia I was with Henry A. Camp behind the entrenchments in the woods."

Comrade Almond E. Clark of Milford stated that "we faced the enemy at the battle of Chancellorsville under the orders of Lieut. George Elton of Co. B Reg. Conn. vol. I saw Henry A. Camp after the battle and was tent mate with him. I saw the wound over his left eye brow and he said it affected his sight. I also remember him telling me about being wounded at Fredericksburg. His right shoulder still troubled him very much while on march. I must say that Henry A. Camp was a good and plucky soldier and faced the Enemy's fire when he was entitled to be in the hospital."[429]

George E. Rogers added that "I was just about ten or twelve feet from him. In a few minutes he came up to me holding a handkerchief over his Eye Brow. He then took the handkerchief off his Eye brow and I [could] see then it was quite a bad wound."[430]

Henry A. Camp applied for a pension on 28 April 1876. He was admitted on 12 December 1912 to the Eastern Branch National Home for D.V.S. in Maine and discharged on 17 April 1914 to 280 Grand Avenue, New Haven. Previously he was living at Madison.

In 1926 Henry Camp states he was born at Wallingford on 25 January 1844, son of Joel and Mary Camp and lived with them until the war. At the time of his enlistment he was described as five feet six inches tall, light complexion, grey eyes, brown hair, occupation farmer, factory hand and mechanic. Since his discharge he resided at Yalesville, Wallingford, New Haven, Madison, and Noroton Heights. He was employed at the Simpson-Nickel Silver Company in Wallingford from 1858 until 1890.

Camp was admitted to the Fitch's Soldier Home[431] at Noroton Heights on 14 January 1908 and discharged on 22 September 1911. He was readmitted on 5 December 1922, a resident of New Haven. He was a metal buffer by trade and owned no property. Before his last admission, he had been at the National Home in Togus, Maine and had requested the transfer. At the time of his death his possessions included glasses, clothes, button and thread, a ring, writing chest, tools, razor, a fishing pole, and trunk. His daughter Mrs. William Bennett of Yalesville signed for his possessions.

He was married first to Ellen M. Davidson who died at Yalesville on 20 September 1893. He was married second at Clinton by Rev. R. H. Sherman on 22 February 1896 to Emma A. Cutler. His second wife died before 1922. He had three children living (in 1898): Frederick, born on 5 November 1868; Joseph, born on 20 July 1877; and Harriet, born on 4 January 1879.

Henry Alonzo Camp died at the Fitch's Soldier Home in Noroton Heights on 4 December 1927 and was buried there in Spring Grove Cemetery. He was born at Wallingford, son of Joel Camp and Mary Hawes.

---

428 Affidavit, James B. Page of Cheshire, undated, in the pension file of Henry A. Camp.
429 Affidavit, Almond E. Clark, 29 April 1895, in the pension file of Henry A. Camp.
430 Affidavit, George E. Rogers of Milford, 3 September 1895, in the pension file of Henry A. Camp.
431 Fitch's Home for Soldiers, Deceased Veterans Discharge Files 1882-1932, box 11, file 2745.

CAMP, JOEL
Co. B 27th CVI, private, enlisted 10 September 1862, prisoner, mustered out 27 July 1863, no pension

Joel Camp, age 40, of Wallingford enlisted on 10 September 1862 and was mustered in on 3 October 1862 as a private in Co. B 27th CVI. He served in the same company with his son Henry A. Camp. He fought at the Battle of Fredericksburg on 13 December 1862 with the rest of the company. He was reported missing after the Battle of Chancellorsville, Virginia on 3 May 1863, held prisoner at Richmond, and paroled at City Point, Virginia on 14 May 1863. He reported to Camp Parole, Maryland on 16 May 1863, was sent to Washington, D.C. on 20 May 1863 and spent the remainder of his service at Camp Convalescent, Virginia. With the rest of the Chancellorsville paroled prisoners, he rejoined the Regiment at Baltimore on 20 July 1863. Joel Camp was mustered out with the rest of his regiment at New Haven on 27 July 1863.

"My father was at my side when I was wounded at the battle of Fredericksburg, Virginia but is now deceased."[432] Joel Camp died on 6 August 1868 and was buried in Center Street Cemetery, Wallingford.[433] His company and regiment are engraved on his stone and a G.A.R. marker was on his gravesite in 1934 and 2006. He was the son of Enos Spencer Camp and Mary Parmelee of Durham. His widow Mary married second Lucius Royce.

CARTER, CHARLES
Co. G 20th CVI, private, enlisted 14 August 1862, mustered out 13 June 1865, pension #738965 for the soldier and later for his widow Julia

Charles E. Carter of North Branford enlisted on 14 August 1862 as a private in Co. G 20th CVI and was promoted to corporal on 15 October 1862. The regiment saw action at Chancellorsville, Gettysburg, the Atlanta campaign, and was present at the Grand Review. Charles Carter was mustered out with the rest of his regiment at Fort Lincoln, Washington, D.C. on 13 June 1865. He does not appear in the 1860 census at North Branford but was on the draft list. He applied for an invalid pension on 17 May 1890.

Charles Edgar Carter died at Clinton on 18 February 1912 and was buried there in Clinton Cemetery. He was born on 26 May 1839, son of Charles Carter and Jerusha Doane.

His widow Julia applied for a widow's pension on 28 February 1912. Julia Jerusha Carter died at Clinton on 24 March 1923 and was buried there in Clinton Cemetery. She was born at Clinton on 12 September 1842, daughter of Jacob Stannard and Sally Post.

CARTER, EDWIN H.
Co. K 11th Illinois Infantry, corporal, killed 15 February 1862 pension #109730 for his father Benjamin

Edwin H. Carter of LaSalle, Illinois was mustered in at LaSalle on 9 August 1861 as a private in Co. K 11th Illinois Infantry for a term of three years. He was promoted to corporal and was killed in action at Fort Donelson, Tennessee on 15 February 1862.

Edwin Hopkins Carter was born at Branford on 5 December 1843, son of Benjamin Linsley Carter and Phebe Beach.[434] He appears at LaSalle, Illinois in 1860, age 17, living with his brother Samuel Beach Carter.

---

432 Statement, Henry A. Camp of Wallingford, 19 May 1890, in his own pension file.
433 The Hale Collection, Wallingford, 18.
434 Branford Vital Records, Town Meeting Book A, 238.

THE STORMING OF FORT DONELSON, TENN., FEB. 15, 1862

Branford native Edwin H. Carter was killed during the storming of Fort Donelson,
Tennessee on February 15, 1862. (Currier and Ives)

A third brother, Henry Harrison Carter of LaSalle was captain of Co. K and was killed at Pittsburg Landing, also called the Battle of Shiloh, Tennessee on 6 April 1862.

His father Benjamin L. Carter, age 64, of Branford applied for a pension on 21 June 1867. He claims he was wholly dependent on the support of his son Edwin. Benjamin Carter was married at Branford by Rev. Timothy P. Gillett of the First Congregational Church on 24 March 1824 to Phebe Beach. She died at Branford on 14 September 1847 age 43.[435] Benjamin Linsley Carter died at Branford on 4 December 1887 and was buried there in Center Cemetery. He was born at Branford on 28 March 1803, son of Thomas Poledius Carter and Sally Linsley.[436]

Flora A. Carter of Branford, widow of Benjamin L. applied for accrued pension payments on 19 December 1887. She was married to the pensioner under the name of Flora A. Hart at the home of Elias Hart in Cornwall, Connecticut by Rev. Joshua Maynard on 2 July 1850. There is no indication in the file she received payments since she was not the mother of the soldier. Flora Hart Carter died at Branford on 10 December 1895 age 84 and was buried there in Center Cemetery.[437]

---

435 Branford Vital Records, Town Meeting Book A, 308.
436 Branford Vital Records, 1786-1840, 280.
437 Branford Vital Records, deaths, 1895.

CHAIPEL, BENJAMIN F.

Co. B 12th CVI, corporal, enlisted 1 November 1861, discharged disability 2 May 1863, pension #431049 for the soldier and later for his widow Nancy

Benjamin F. Chaipel, age 41, of Branford enlisted on 1 November 1861 as a corporal in Co. B 12th CVI for a term of three years. In September and October 1862 he was detailed as a nurse in the hospital at Camp Parapet, Carrollton, Louisiana. His rank was reduced to private in late 1862 and he was treated at U.S. Marine Hospital, New Orleans from January through March 1863. Benjamin Chaipel was discharged for disability from the U.S. Marine Hospital on 2 May 1863. He was the father of William H. Chaipel of the same company and father-in-law of Obed Tyler.

He applied for an invalid pension on 11 March 1889. At the time of his enlistment he was described as five feet six inches tall, light complexion, grey eyes, brown hair, occupation farmer. He was born at Waterford, Connecticut. He was sighting a cannon during a company drill and fell down, landing between the spokes of a wheel. He injured his right knee, foot, and hip. One record states he broke several ribs which he denied. He was treated at Regimental Hospital at Camp Parapet, Louisiana about three months and then taken to the hospital at Camp Kearney for about one month. While he was in the hospital he got rheumatism. He was then taken by ambulance to Marine Hospital in New Orleans where he was discharged. He waited for transportation home for about one month. Since the war he has been lame, walks with a cane, and suffers from disability. The origin of the injury was sent for special examination. Since Co. B was an infantry unit, there was a question why Chaipel was handling a cannon. There are many depositions in the file. Several state that part of Co. B of the 12th CVI was trained in heavy artillery at New Orleans. Since his discharge he resided at Branford.

Benjamin F. Chaipel died at Branford on 15 April 1896 and was buried there in Center Cemetery.[438] His rank, company, and regiment are engraved on his stone and a G.A.R. marker was on his gravesite in 1934.

Nancy L. Chaipel of Branford applied for a widow's pension on 1 July 1896. There are no papers in the file concerning her application. She died at New Haven on 13 June 1906 and was buried in Center Cemetery, Branford.[439]

438 Branford Vital Records, deaths, 1896; his parents are not recorded.
439 New Haven Vital Records, deaths, 1906; *Shore Line Times*, 21 June 1906.

CHAIPEL. WILLIAM H.
Co. B 12th CVI, private, enlisted 1 November 1861, deserted, no pension

William H. Chaipel of Branford enlisted on 1 November 1861 as a private in Co. B 12th CVI for a term of three years. He deserted and was sentenced to one year of hard labor on 6 November 1863 by general court martial. He was transferred back to his company on 20 November 1864 but failed to report. There is no further record. He was the son of Benjamin F. Chaipel.

He was married at Branford by Rev. Alpha H. Simons of the First Baptist Church on 26 December 1867 to Rosamond C. Mousey.

William H. Chaipel died at New York City 20 February 1897 age 57 and was buried in Center Cemetery, Branford.[440] A G.A.R. marker was on his gravesite in 1934.

CHIDSEY, LEVERETT
see Alexander Robertson

CLANNING, WILLIAM HENRY
U.S. Navy, seaman, 10th CVI, no pension

Among the Branford G.A.R. papers is a hand written list of "fallen heroes" buried at Center Cemetery. Henry Clanning is on that list but there is no gravestone. He was at Branford in 1860, age 24, a seaman, living with Seth Bradley. He is on the August 1862 Branford Selectman list of men who had enlisted from Branford to fill the town's quota. William Henry Clanning died at Branford on 15 July 1867 age 30, unmarried, born at Clinton, a boatman.[441] He was the son of Henry Clanning and Parmelia Willard.

Information concerning his service can be found in an article entitled "An Enigmatic Civil War Letter and The Affair of The Brig Joseph."[442]

U States Ship of war
Princeton Philadelphia
March 19th 1862

Dear Mother
I suppose you will think
it very strange to receive

---

440 *The Branford Opinion*, 27 February 1897; The Hale Collection, Branford, 49.
441 Branford Vital Records, 1863-1895, 207.
442 Heritage Quest May/June 1987, issue #10, 34; plus correspondence with the author of the article Pamelia S. Olson of Tacoma, Washington with Betty M. Linsley of Branford, 20 January 1987 through 8 August 1987; in the possession of this writer.

(Photographic History of the Civil War, I:97)

a letter from me and to
find me in the navy
my object in writing
these few lines to you
is to caution you not
to write to me again
untill you hear from
me again, as I have left
the army and joined the [navy]
and it will cause me trouble
I will write
to you again as soon
as I can so don't
worry. I have sent
you two likenesses.

Love William H Clanning"[443]

443 Letter from William H. Clanning to his mother Parmelia Stannard of Branford, March 19th 1862 (in Heritage Quest May/June 1987, issue #10, 34.)

According to the above referenced article, he first served on the brig *Joseph* which was captured by the Confederate privateer the *Savannah* on 3 June 1861.[444] The boat was sent to Georgetown, South Carolina, condemned and sold. The crew was imprisoned there for several months. Sometime between his release from prison and March 1862 his letter refers to being in the Army, yet implies that perhaps he deserted to join the Navy again. He is probably the Wm. H. Claming who rendezvoused at Boston on 31 August 1861 and served on the *Philadelphia, New York,* and *Itasca*.[445] He reenlisted in the Navy at Philadelphia on 11 March 1862 as a seaman, age 24. He served on the *Rhode Island* and was discharged on 7 June 1862 as an invalid.

He subsequently enlisted at New Haven on 29 September 1862 as a private in the 10th CVI for a term of three years. He was described as age 25, five feet seven inches tall, hazel eyes, dark hair, dark complexion, occupation sailor, born at Clinton. It appears he reenlisted or continued his service in the 10th CVI on 29 September 1863 and his name appears on a muster roll at Hartford on 17 March 1864. His name does not appear in the *Record of Servicemen of Connecticut* but does on the Soldiers and Sailors website.

CLARK, FRANCIS L.
Co. A 18th CVI, private, enlisted 4 August 1862, prisoner, mustered out 27 June 1865, pension #440452 for his widow Annie

Francis L. Clark of Lebanon enlisted at Norwalk on 4 August 1862 and was mustered in on 18 August 1862

as a private in Co. A 18th CVI for a term of three years. He was taken prisoner at the Battle of Winchester, Virginia on 15 June 1863, confined at Belle Isle and paroled on 2 July 1863. With the rest of the released prisoners he was sent to Camp Parole, Annapolis, Maryland and returned to his regiment in October 1863. The regiment fought at battles in Virginia during 1864 and 1865 including New Market, the second Winchester, and Cedar Creek. Francis Clark was mustered out with the rest of his regiment at Harper's Ferry, Virginia on 27 June 1865 and discharged from Hartford.

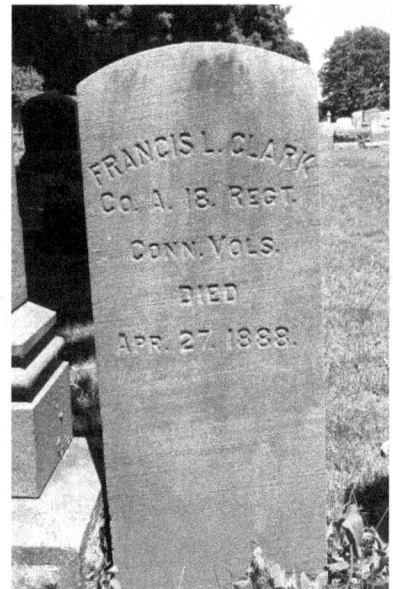

He was married first to Sarah Lovina Dean. She was born at Canaan and died at Branford on 26 October 1878 age 31 years, 9 months & 25 days in child birth;[446] daughter of Horace Dean and Caroline Marvin. He first appears at Branford in 1878 and was living at Branford in 1880 with his wife Annie and twin children, age 2. He never applied for a pension.

Francis Lincoln Clark died at Branford on 27 April 1888 age 42 years, 11 months & 18 days[447] and was buried there in Center Cemetery. His company and regiment are engraved on his stone and there was a G.A.R. marker on his gravesite in 1934. He was born at Lebanon, son of Erastus Clark and Bethiah Arnold.

Annie Clark of Branford applied for a widow's pension on 27 April 1888.

---

444 For more information concerning the capture of the *Joseph,* see The War of the Rebellion: A Compilation of the Official Records of the Union and Confederate Navies.
445 *Index to Rendezvous Reports,* NARA T-1099, page 208, par 2.
446 Branford Vital Records, 1863-1895, 222.
447 Branford Vital Records, 1863-1895, 237.

CLARK, JOSEPH
Co. C 15th CVI, private, enlisted 16 December 1864, failed to report, no pension

Joseph Clark of Branford enlisted on 16 December 1864 as a private in Co. C 15th CVI. He was transferred from New Haven to the company on 7 January 1865 but failed to report. There was no additional military record. He does not appear in the 1860 census at Branford.

CLARK, THOMAS
1st LA, private, substitute, mustered in 17 August 1864, mustered out 11 June 1865, pension application #226070 for his widow

Thomas Clark, age 42, served as a substitute for Lyman H. Foote of North Branford. He was mustered in at New Haven as a private in the 1st LA for a term of three years. He also served in Co. B Wisconsin Infantry and Co. B 4th U.S. Artillery. With his regiment he saw action during the Siege of Richmond and was mustered out with the rest of his regiment at Manchester, near Richmond, Virginia on 11 June 1865 when his term expired. He was described as five foot six inches tall, blue eyes, black hair, ruddy complexion, married, occupation joiner. He does not appear in the 1860 census at North Branford. His wife applied for a widow's pension on 12 May 1876.

CLIFTON, ROBERT
Co. I 14th CVI, private, drafted 25 July 1863, deserted, no pension

Robert Clifton of Branford served as a substitute or was drafted on 25 July 1863 as a private in Co. I 14th CVI and deserted on 7 November 1863. He does not appear in the 1860 census at Branford.

COAN, JEROME
Co. E 15th CVI, corporal, enlisted 9 August 1862, to 41st Co. 2nd VRC, discharged 8 August 1865, pension #528918 for the soldier

Jerome Coan[448] of Branford enlisted at New Haven on 9 August 1862 and was mustered in on 25 August 1862 as a corporal in Co. E 15th CVI for a term of three years. "I performed my regular duty in the Regt until about the last of Oct 1862 when my Brother Joseph Coan was prostrated with Typhoid fever while on duty as Cook of Co. E. I was detailed to take care of him and was with him until he died Nov 7th 1862. It was about this time I was taken with chills and intermittent fever. My Brothers remains was sent home for Burial and I was granted a seven days furlough to attend the funeral. During the funeral service I was attacked with a severe chill and taken home. I returned to my Regt at Fairfax Seminary, V.A. after being absent ten days and was excused for overstaying my furlough. The Regt marched to Falmouth through snow and mud and I was placed in the Regimental Hospital tent at Falmouth. I was sent to Division Hospital at Windmill Point, VA from there to Lincoln Hospital, Washington DC; from there to Portsmouth Grove Hospital, Rhode Island and came near to dying about the 20th of April 1863. I was transferred to Knight Hospital, New Haven. During my convalescence I was assigned to duty as a clerk in Major P. A. Jewets

---

448 For his biography see Rockey, *History of New Haven County*, II:170; and Beers, *Biographical Record of New Haven County*, 802.

Office, Surgeon in charge of [the] Hospital. In Feb 1864 I was detached as a clerk in the Provost Marshalls Office in New Haven where I served ten months. I was then transferred to the 41st Co. 2nd Battalion VRC and served as clerk until my term expired."[449] His rank was reduced to private on 31 August 1863 due to sickness. Coan was mustered out at Hartford on 15 August 1865.

He applied for an invalid pension on 3 February 1889. At the time of his enlistment he was working at Branford and after his discharge he returned to North Guilford. His service was listed by the Guilford selectman but credited to Branford. He was described as five feet six inches tall, dark complexion, hazel eyes, black hair, occupation clerk. He was married first on 23 March 1856 to Frances Dorcas Griswold who died at North Guilford on 1 February 1859. He was a member of the Parmelee Post No. 42 G.A.R. of Guilford.

Jerome Coan died at North Guilford on 4 November 1899 and was buried in North Guilford Cemetery. He was born at North Guilford on 19 June 1834, son of John Coan and Betsey Hart.[450]

Mary F. Coan of Guilford applied for a widow's pension on 29 December 1899. She was married to the soldier as his second wife under the name of Mary Francis Judd at North Guilford by Rev. Oliver Hopson of St. John's Church on 14 September 1869. She was not previously married and did not remarry after his death. They had the following children: Joseph Franklin, born on 19 August 1870; and Frances Louise, born on 16 November 1873.

Mary F. Judd Coan died at North Guilford on 28 March 1908 and was buried in North Guilford Cemetery.[451] She was born on 18 August 1846 in Bethlehem, daughter of Henry Green Judd and Sarah Rebecca Raymond of Bloomfield later of North Guilford.

A letter from Jerome to his sister Phebe appears in the Coan Genealogy:[452]

Lincoln General Hospital
Washington, D.C.
Feb 23ᵈ 1863

Dear Sister
*   Yours of the 19th inst*
I have just received and
have just finished a letter to
Ornin and I hasten to pen
a few words to you in answer
to your kind and welcome letter

a few days ago I shall write to
Mother in a few days I want you
Keep an eye on Mother and if she
is in need of any money let me
Know and I will send an order

---

449 Affidavit, Jerome Coan of Guilford, 27 May 1886, in his own pension file. His brother to which he refers was his twin Joseph and they enlisted and served in the same company.
450 Ruth Coan Fulton, *Coan Genealogy 1697-1982* (Peter E. Randall Published: 1982), 179 gives his mother as Phebe Ann (Fowler) Coan but she died in 1821 or 1827 and his father married second Betsey Hart.
451 The Hale Collection, Guilford, 131.
452 Fulton, *Coan Genealogy*, 180.

on the Savings Bank for some
for her give my love to all and
write soon

From Your loving Brother
Jerome

COATES, LEWIS

Lewis Coates was listed on the Branford G.A.R. Post's hand written list of "fallen heroes" buried in Center Cemetery. His gravestone reads "Louis F. Coates, died August 20, 1880 age 40." There is a Masonic symbol on his gravestone and a G.A.R. marker was on his gravesite in 1934. He joined the Branford Widow's Son Lodge No. 66 F.A. & A.M. on 28 February 1863. The Branford Vital Records gives his age at death as 48 years, 1 months & 10 days, unmarried, a seaman, born in New York. [453] The *Shore Line Times* calls him Captain Coates, aged 48. He is probably the Lewis Coats, age 17, living at Branford with Levi Forbes in the 1850 census; in 1870, age 36, a seaman, living with W. Lynde Shepard; and in 1880, age 45, an oysterman, living with George Averill. The 1850 and 1870 census lists his birthplace as Connecticut, the 1880 census lists New York as the birthplace of he and his parents. No pension was found.

COBLEIGH, WILLIAM C.
Co. G 6th CVI, private, enlisted 26 August 1861, wounded, mustered out 21 August 1865, pension #618898 for the soldier

William C. Cobleigh of New Britain enlisted at New Haven on 26 August 1861 and was mustered in on 4 September 1861 as a private in Co. G 6th CVI for a term of three years. He reenlisted as a veteran in Co. G on 7 March 1864. He saw action at Drewry's Bluff, Virginia on 16 May 1864 and was wounded at Bermuda Hundred, Virginia on 20 May 1864. Cobleigh was mustered out at Petersburg, Virginia on 21 August 1865 and discharged at New Haven on 17 September 1865.

He applied for an invalid pension on 31 January 1883. At the time of his enlistment he was described as five feet eight inches tall, fair complexion, dark hair, blue eyes, occupation laborer. He was "severely wounded in the left groin by a mini ball and has been disabled since." He was treated in his tent and later at Hospital Steward at New Haven. An examining surgeon in 1883 stated that "we think that the disability is a fraud."[454] Since his discharge he lived at Guilford, Branford, and Noroton Heights. He was a member of the Mason Rogers Post G.A.R. No. 7 of Branford.

---

453 Branford Vital Records 1863-1895, 225. Died as a result of a fall, there is no other information in the record. There are a number of soldiers in the Union Army with the name of Lewis Coates and it is possible he served in the Navy. He was not a member of the Mason Rogers Post No. 7. His probate record (Branford Probate 7:339-440) lists assets of personal property of $237.94. After expenses a legacy of $72.79 was left to the Masons of Branford, no heirs are named.
454 Surgeon's certificate, L. L. Paddock, 6 June 1883, in the pension file of William C. Cobleigh.

He was admitted to the Fitch's Soldier Home[455] at Noroton Heights on 16 August 1907. He was married at New Haven on 24 March 1864 to Jane C. Burdick. Neither were previously married or divorced. His brother was a witness to the marriage and was living at San Francisco, California in 1898. Jane B. Cobleigh died at Branford on 19 May 1907 and was buried in West Cemetery, Guilford. They had one son (living in 1898): Frederick W., born at Guilford on 19 May 1871.

William C. Cobleigh died at the Fitch's Solders Home on 17 June 1910 and was buried in West Cemetery, Guilford.[456] He was born at New Britain or Southington on 1 March 1838, son of Amasa Cobleigh and Sarah Carrington.

COLBURN, ELISHA H. alias WILLIAM H. LOWRY
Co. A 3rd Inf. Delaware Volunteers, pension #XC2680449 for the soldier and later for his widow Iminild

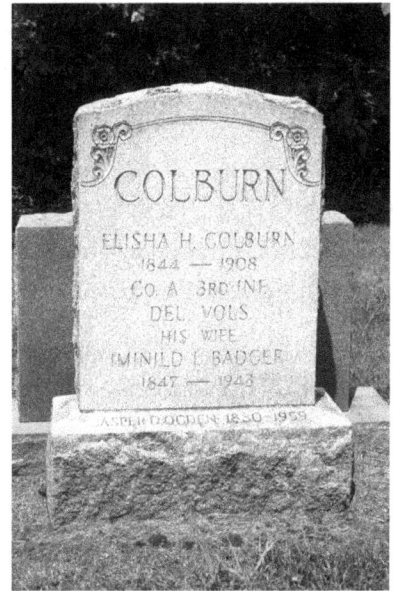

Elisha H. Colburn, alias William H. Lowry, enlisted as a private in Co. A 3rd Delaware Volunteer Infantry. He is probably the Elisha Colburn at Pomfret, Windham Co. in 1860, age 16, in the household of Rozal S. and Lydia Colburn. He appears in the 1870 and 1880 census at Windham County with his wife Iminild and children.

He applied for an invalid pension on 9 September 1887, the pension is at the Veterans Administration. He was married on 5 December 1866 to Iminild T. Badger.[457]

Elisha H. Colburn died on 15 March 1908 age 64, and was buried in New Northford Cemetery, North Branford.[458] His company and regiment are engraved on his stone.

Iminild Colburn applied for a widow's pension on 27 March 1908. She was living at Philadelphia in 1910 and at Hatfield, Montgomery Co., Pennsylvania in 1920.

COLWELL, GEORGE W.
Co. A 1st Cavalry, private, enlisted 9 December 1864, discharged 10 June 1865, no pension

George W. Colwell of Branford enlisted on 19 December 1864 as a private in Co. A 1st Connecticut Cavalry and was discharged on 10 June 1865. He does not appear in the 1860 census at Branford.

---

455 Fitch's Home for Soldiers, Deceased Veterans Discharge Files 1882-1932, box 11, file 2686.
456 *The Branford Opinion*, 23 December 1910; no stone is listed in the Hale Collection.
457 Connecticut marriages 1829-1867, www.familysearch.org.
458 The Hale Collection, North Branford, 80.

COLWELL, THOMAS
**Co. B 9th CVI, private, enlisted 8 September 1861, discharged for disability 27 November 1862,
Co. C 5th CVI, private, enlisted 27 August 1863, to Co. F 20th CVI, mustered out 19 July 1865,
pension #326894 for the soldier**

Thomas Colwell of New Haven enlisted on 8 September 1861 as a private in Co. B 9th CVI. He was discharged for disability on 27 November 1862. He reenlisted, then called of Branford, on 27 August 1863 as a private in Co. C 5th CVI for a term of three years. He was transferred to Co. F 20th CVI on 13 June 1865 and mustered out at Alexandria, Virginia on 19 July 1865.

He applied for an invalid pension on 30 June 1880. After his discharge he lived at New Haven. His wife Ellen was born in 1818, died in 1878 and was buried in St. Bernard's Cemetery, New Haven.[459]

Thomas Colwell died in 1891 and was buried in St. Bernard's Cemetery, New Haven. There was a Civil War maker on his gravesite in 1934. He was born in Ireland.

CONDON, JOHN
**Co. B 27th CVI, private, enlisted 10 September 1862, discharged 9 March 1863 for disability,
pension #472880 for the soldier**

John Condon, age 30, of Wallingford enlisted on 10 September 1862 and was mustered in on 3 October 1862 as a private in Co. B 27th CVI for a term of nine months. In November and December 1862 he was sick at Stuart's Mansion General Hospital at Baltimore. He was sick in a hospital at Washington, D.C. January and February 1863 and had been hospitalized since 1 December 1862. John Condon was discharged for disability on 9 March 1863 per order of Lt. Col. McKeloy, commander of Camp Convalescent.

He applied for an invalid pension on 23 May 1885. At the time of his discharge he was described as five feet seven inches tall, light complexion, blue eyes, brown hair, occupation silversmith, born in Ireland. He was unfit for duty for fifty-nine days at Camp Convalescent, Virginia and was discharged due to incipient phthisis which "existed prior to enlistment." There is a lengthy deposition from Condon in his pension file concerning the supposed "disability existing prior to enlistment." He states "I got sick my first night at Arlington Heights. I was on guard duty and it had rained, the water was up to our knees and I took a cold and had a cough and was sick in my tent. I was in the hospital in Washington, D.C. with pneumonia at the time of the battle of Fredericksburg and then sent to the hospital in Baltimore. I was sent back to Washington to the Convalescent Camp and then I got my discharge. I came right back to Wallingford after discharge and have had that cough ever since. After discharge I have lived in Wallingford and New Haven and my occupation is as a laborer. Before enlistment I was a mechanic in a factory and made good wages. Since my discharge I have been unable to work in the factory because I have not been able to do a full day's work, working odd jobs as I am able."[460]

Dr. C. L. Baldwin, age 66, of Wallingford testified "that he knew the soldier before the war and he was never treated for lung trouble, [Condon] came to Wallingford in 1853. When he returned from the war, he had a bad cough and was quite feeble, it seemed to me a case of incipient consumption. I have been his physician since his return and he has never recovered from his pulmonary troubles."[461]

---

459 The Hale Collection, New Haven, 1353.
460 Deposition, John Condon of Wallingford, 12 November 1889, in his own pension file.
461 Deposition, C. L. Baldwin of Wallingford, 12 November 1889, in the pension file of John Condon.

Othneil J. Martin stated that he has been the judge of probate for the town of Wallingford for 18 years. He has known the soldier since he came to Wallingford thirty-five years ago. That [Condon] has "frequently worked for me both before and some after the war. He was a laborer and also sometimes worked in the factory. I have always considered him a straight forward, honest and industrious man. He was as tough a man before he enlisted as any man I ever knew. I went to New Haven to see the 27th off. I saw him as soon as he came home, he looked bad and I hardly knew him."[462]

Charles Paden stated that he worked with him at the spoon factory before enlisting and "that he was a hard working, laboring man, and I never heard anything otherwise. John Condon was on guard duty the first night at Arlington Heights. I was under shelter. It was a bad, stormy night, cold, rained very hard. I did not see him but heard he had a cold, and afterwards was sent to the hospital. I did not see him until we were mustered out. He was very weak and feeble and has never had his health since that night in the Peach Orchard."[463] The same day Timothy Callahan stated "that we had no nourishment, or anything, that first day at Arlington Heights. I never saw John Condon on duty again, he was sick in his tent, coughing. He was sent to the hospital."[464] There are other depositions in the file. It appears that he was finally granted a pension under the act of 27 June 1890.

John Condon was married at New Haven to Nellie Sullivan who died before 1889. He states that his marriage certificate was "lost in the Tornado in Wallingford." He had four children living (in 1898): Michael age 43, Bridget age 39, Mary Russia age 36, and Kate age 34. He states that he cannot read or write.

John Condon died on 7 November 1901 age 70 and was buried in Holy Trinity Cemetery, Wallingford.[465] His wife, listed as Mary, died on 24 December 1887 age 50 and was buried in the same cemetery.

CONDON, PATRICK
Co. B 27th CVI, private, enlisted 10 September 1862, died 28 December 1862 from wounds received at Fredericksburg, no pension

Patrick Condon, age 18, of Wallingford enlisted on 10 September 1862 and was mustered in on 3 October 1862 as a private in Co. B 27th CVI for a term of nine months. He was wounded at the Battle of Fredericksburg on 13 December 1862 and sent to the hospital. "Pat Condon the Irishman who had his leg amputated we hear this afternoon is dead."[466] He died at General Hospital, Annapolis, Maryland on 28 December 1862 from an amputation after being wounded and was buried the same day. His death record names a sister Mary Bryan of Patucket, Rhode Island [Pawtucket].

CONNELLY, JAMES
Co. C 1st Cavalry, private, enlisted 19 November 1864, deserted, no pension

James Connelly of Branford enlisted on 19 November 1864 as a private in Co. C 1st Connecticut Cavalry. He deserted on 10 March 1865. He does not appear in the 1860 census at Branford.

---

462 Deposition, Othneil J. Martin of Wallingford, 12 November 1889, in the pension file of John Condon.
463 Deposition, Charles Paden of Wallingford, 12 November 1889, in the pension file of John Condon.
464 Deposition, Timothy Callahan of Wallingford, 12 November 1889, in the pension file of John Condon.
465 The Hale Collection, Wallingford, 143.
466 Letter, Samuel Beach to home, 1 January 1863.

COOK, SAMUEL S.
Co. B 27th CVI, sergeant, enlisted 19 August 1862, prisoner, mustered out 27 July 1863, pension #889097 for the soldier

Samuel S. Cook[467] of Branford, age 36, enlisted on 19 August 1862 and was mustered in on 3 October 1862 as a sergeant in Co. B 27th CVI for a term of nine months. He fought at the Battle of Fredericksburg on 13 December 1862 with the rest of the company, was bruised by a shell and treated for several days. "There were times during the winter of 1862 & 1863 that I took the company out for dress parade when Lt. Elton was sick."[468] He was captured at the Battle of Chancellorsville, Virginia on 3 May 1863 and held prisoner at Richmond. On 13 May 1863 he was admitted to the hospital at Richmond for dysentery and paroled at City Point, Virginia on 15 May 1863, one day after the rest of the prisoners. He reported to Camp Parole, Maryland on 16 May 1863. He was admitted to Hope Division Hospital at Annapolis, Maryland for a contusion on 17 May 1863 and remained there until 13 June 1863 when he was sent to Camp Parole, Maryland. He was sent to Camp Convalescent, Virginia on 17 July 1863. He was not at the Battle of Gettysburg. "I was with the company until my capture at Chancellorsville and did not join them again until we were mustered out."[469] With the rest of the Chancellorsville paroled prisoners, he rejoined the Regiment at Baltimore on 20 July 1863. Samuel S. Cook was mustered out with the rest of his regiment at New Haven on 27 July 1863.

He applied for an invalid pension on 12 September 1892 under the act of 27 June 1890. On 17 February 1893 he stated that "on or about Feb. 15th 1865 I received an injury on my left side going to the spring for water and slipped on the ice. I fell, striking my side and back." He reapplied under the act of 11 May 1912, age 86 years, a shoemaker. He was described as five feet ten inches tall, dark complexion, grey eyes, dark hair. He was married at Branford by Rev. Timothy P. Gillett of the First Congregational Church on 10 October 1849 to Caroline Celinda Page. He had two children living (in 1898): Alice E. Cook Nichols, born on 18 January 1851 and Anderson Scott Cook, born on 9 October 1860.

Above, Samuel Cook age 80.
(Branford Historical Society
photograph collection)

His wife Caroline Cook died at Branford on 16 September 1910 and was buried there in Center Cemetery.[470] He was a member of the Mason Rogers Post No. 7 G.A.R. of Branford.

Samuel S. Cook died at Branford on 19 February 1914[471] and was buried there in Center Cemetery. A G.A.R. marker was on the gravesite in 1934. He was born at Branford on 17 November 1825, son of Samuel Cook and Peggy Hobart.[472]

---

467 For his biography see Rockey, *History of New Haven County*, II:64.
468 Deposition, Samuel S. Cook of Branford, 6 July 1895, in the pension file of George W. Elton.
469 Deposition, Samuel S. Cook of Branford, 6 July 1895, in the pension file of George W. Elton.
470 Branford Vital Records, deaths, 1910.
471 Branford Vital Records, deaths, 1914.
472 Branford Vital Records 1786-1840, 362.

CROSBY, RICHARD

Co. A 15th CVI, private, enlisted 18 July 1862, prisoner, mustered out 27 June 1865, pension #348451 for the soldier and later for his widow Bridget

Richard Crosby, age 37, of Meriden enlisted at New Haven on 18 July 1862 and was mustered in on 25 August 1862 as a private in Co. A 15th CVI for a term of three years. He was sick in quarters in January and February 1863 opposite Fredericksburg, Va. He was captured with much of his regiment at the Battle of Kinston, North Carolina on 8 March 1865, confined at Libby Prison, Richmond on 23 March, and paroled at Boulware's & Cox's wharf on 26 March 1865. He reported to Camp Parole, Maryland on 30 March 1865, received a thirty day furlough and afterwards reported to Camp Convalescent, Virginia. Crosby was mustered out with the rest of his regiment at New Bern, North Carolina on 27 June 1865 and discharged at New Haven on 12 July 1865.

He applied for an invalid pension on 14 December 1876. At the time of his enlistment he was described as five feet eight inches tall, dark complexion, dark hair, born in Ireland. "I had an attack of rheumatism while on picket duty on the Rappahannock near Falmouth, Va. after the Battle of Fredericksburg. I got wet crossing a brook and had to lie all night on the cold ground." "After the Battle of Fredericksburg, V.A. he was sick with rheumatism and as near as I can remember was sick until the next summer. He cooked for the company and did some duty in the ranks after that. March 8, 1865 we were made prisoners and on the march to Richmond, V.A. he had another attack and had to be helped along by his comrades. We were all discharged soon after that."[473] He was married at New Haven by Rev. Matthew Hart of St. Patrick's Church on 15 January 1854 to Bridget Carney. Neither were previously married or divorced. After his discharge he moved to Branford where "I worked in the shop as a molder but all the other molders were Copperheads and soldier haters." He was a member of the Mason Rogers Post No. 7 G.A.R. of Branford.

Richard Crosby died at Branford on 21 May 1892 age 69 and was buried there in St. Mary's Cemetery.

Bridget Crosby of Branford applied for a widow's pension on 28 July 1892. She died at Branford on 13 April 1901 and was buried in St. Mary's Cemetery.[474] She was born in Ireland, daughter of Patrick Carney and Mary Roach.

CROSS, EDMUND B.

Co. B 27th CVI, 2nd lieutenant, enlisted 19 September 1862, prisoner, mustered out 27 July 1863, no pension

Edmund B. Cross of New Haven enlisted on 19 September 1862 and was mustered in on 3 October 1862 as a corporal in Co. B 27th CVI for a term of nine months. He fought at the Battle of Fredericksburg on 13 December 1862 with the rest of the company. On 25 March 1863 he was promoted to Sergeant-Major and on 1 May 1863 to 2nd Lieutenant. He was captured at the Battle of Chancellorsville, Virginia 3 May 1863,

---

473 Letter, Ammi B. Barker of Branford, 20 June 1888, in the pension file of Richard Crosby.
474 Her name is not on the gravestone.

held prisoner at Libby Prison, Richmond, and paroled on 23 May 1863 with the other officers. Cross was mustered out with the rest of his regiment at New Haven on 27 July 1863.

Edmund B. Cross died at New Haven on 1 August 1863 from typhoid fever contracted while in the service and was buried in Grove Street Cemetery, New Haven. He was born at New Orleans, Louisiana.[475]

CURTISS, JOSEPH
Co. B 12th CVI, private, enlisted 27 September 1861, discharged 2 December 1864, pension #C2534555 for the soldier

Joseph Curtiss, age 37, of Newtown enlisted on 27 September 1861 as a private in Co. B 12th CVI for a term of three years. With his regiment he served at New Orleans and at the Battles of Winchester and Cedar Creek, Virginia. Curtiss was discharged with the rest of his regiment at Hartford on 2 December 1864.

He applied for an invalid pension on 18 January 1892 under the act of 27 June 1890. During the war he had the measles in the spring of 1862 at Ship Island, Mississippi that affected his eye sight and also contracted rheumatism while serving in the state of Louisiana.

He was living at Branford from 1870 until 1890. His wife Jane E. Tayler died at Branford on 20 January 1890 age 42 and was buried there in Center Cemetery.[476] He was living at New Haven in 1900. He states that his wife is dead and all his children are over twenty-one years of age. He was a charter member and quartermaster of the Mason Rogers Post No. 7 G.A.R. of Branford. He was on the committee for the Branford Soldiers' Monument.

Joseph Curtiss died at New Haven on 13 June 1910 and was buried in Center Cemetery, Branford.[477] A G.A.R. marker was on his gravesite in 1934 and 2011. He was born at Newtown on 5 April 1844, son of Cyrenus Curtiss and Christa Ann Beardsley.[478]

CUSHER, JOSEPH
Co. B 27th CVI, private, enlisted 10 September 1862, prisoner, mustered out 22 August 1863, Co. A 2nd HA, enlisted 23 August 1864, discharged 2 December 1864, no pension

Joseph Cusher, age 21, of Branford enlisted on 10 September 1862 and was mustered in on 3 October 1862 as a private in Co. B 27th CVI for a term of nine months. He fought at the Battle of Fredericksburg on 13 December 1862 with the rest of the company. He was on picket duty during the Battle of Chancellorsville. He fought at the Battle of Gettysburg, was captured on 2 July 1863 and reported missing in action the next day. He was confined at Richmond, Virginia on 21 July 1863 and paroled on 21 August 1863 at City Point, Virginia. On 22 August 1863 he reported to Camp Parole, Maryland upon his release from the rebel prison

---

475 The Hale Collection, New Haven, 16. Other than his birthplace, New Haven Vital Records provides no further information.
476 Branford Vital Records, 1863-1895, 241.
477 The Hale Collection, Branford, 96; New Haven Vital Records, deaths, 1910.
478 Their gravestones are next to his in Center Cemetery.

and was mustered out the same day. He was sent to the place of his enrollment [New Haven] on 28 August 1863.

He reenlisted on 23 August 1864 as a private in Co. A 2nd HA. He was mustered out at Fort Ethan Allen, Washington D.C. on 18 August 1865 and discharged at New Haven on 5 September 1865.

Before his enlistment, he was living at Branford in 1860, listed as Joseph Cushing, age 19, born in New York,[479] a farm laborer, working for Elias Gould. In 1864 his place of residence was listed as Branford.

DANBY, WILLIAM or DENBY/DEMBY
Co. I 29th CVI, private, enlisted 2 January 1864, discharged 2 June 1865, no pension

William Danby of Branford enlisted at New Haven on 2 January 1864 and was mustered in on 8 March 1864 as a private in Co. I 29th CVI for a term of three years. His service was credited to Branford. He was sent to Knight Hospital, New Haven from the conscript camp on 5 February 1864 and returned to duty on 10 March 1864. He was on detached duty beginning on 19 April 1864 until July 1864 as a teamster at Beaufort, South Carolina. In August and September 1864 he was on duty with the regiment. He was sick in the hospital at Fort Monroe, Virginia beginning 5 November 1864 through April 1865. He was discharged on 2 June 1865 and mustered out at Fort Monroe on 18 August 1865. His name appears on the Wall of Honor at Washington, D.C.

DANIELS, JOSEPH
Co. K 2nd Vermont Volunteer Infantry, sergeant, enlisted 4 May 1861, discharged 15 July 1865, pension #743056 for the soldier and later for his widow and minor child

Joseph Daniels of Panton, Vermont enlisted on 4 May 1861 as a private in Co. K 2nd Vermont Infantry for a term of three years. He reenlisted in Co. K on 21 December 1863 and was promoted to corporal on 4 August 1864. Joseph Daniels was promoted to sergeant on 1 January 1865 and was discharged on 15 July 1865.[480]

He applied for an invalid pension on 19 September 1884. He was mustered in as a member of the Mason Rogers Post No. 7 G.A.R. of Branford on 27 June 1889 and was suspended on 22 June 1893.[481] He does not appear in the 1880 census or 1895 city directory at Branford.

Joseph Daniels died on 5 October 1910.[482] His widow applied for a pension on 15 October 1910.

DANIELS, JOSIAH or JOSIAH H.
Co. C 31st U.S. Infantry, private, enlisted 2 January 1864, died 30 June 1864, no pension

Josiah Daniels of Branford enlisted on 2 January 1864 as a private in Co. C 31st U.S. Colored Infantry and died on 30 June 1864. His name appears on the Wall of Honor at Washington, D.C.

479 U.S. census 1860, Branford, New Haven County, Connecticut, population schedule, M653-85, dwelling 668, family 748, page 873, www.heritagequest.com.
480 *Revised Roster of Vermont Volunteers 1861-1866*, (Montpelier, 1892).
481 Mason Rogers Post G.A.R., Blackstone Library Archives, RG 4, box 2, folder 5.
482 Civil War pension card, T-288; place not given.

DARGAN, PIERCE alias DARGIN, DORGAN, DROGIN, DURGAN
11th CVI, unassigned, enlisted 19 February 1864, discharged 23 February 1864, Co. F 7th CVI, private, enlisted 1 February 1865. discharged 2 October 1865, pension #593128 for the soldier, later for his widow Mary G. Dorgan and minor child Ruth

Pierce Dargan enlisted at New London on 19 February 1864 in the 11th CVI. He was unassigned being under age and size and was discharged on 23 February 1864 from Fort Trumbull. He was described as age 17, born in Ireland, five feet three inches tall, light complexion, blue eyes, red hair, occupation tinner. He reenlisted, then of Branford, on 1 February 1865 as a private in Co. F 7th CVI and was discharged at New Haven on 2 October 1865.

He applied for an invalid pension on 16 May 1890. "While on detached duty on [the] steamship Ivory from Goldsboro, N.C. to Norfolk, Va. about May 1865, the hoisting tackle became disarranged crushing him. He was transferred to Hampton General Hospital and from there to New Haven General Hospital. He was discharged from the hospital in New Haven on 2 October 1865 after the regiment had already been mustered out. The examining doctor stated that no defects were found and the soldier suffers from intemperate use of alcohol. I believe him to be a malingerer in his application for a pension."[483] He did receive a pension.

After the war he went to California and was in the mining business working in many states and territories. From 1886 to 1890 he was living at Hailey, Idaho and from 1897 until 1902 at Challis, Custer Co., Idaho.

Pierce Dorgan [sic] died at John Hopkins Hospital in Baltimore, Maryland on 19 October 1902 where he had been a patient for ten months. He was buried at Loudon Park National Cemetery, Baltimore.

Mary G. Dorgan, age 33, of Challis, Idaho applied for a widow's pension on 9 December 1902. She was married to the soldier under the name of Mary Geraldine O'Brine or O'Brien at Hailey, Alturas Co., Idaho Territory by Rev. E. M. Nattini on 29 June 1886. Neither were previously married or divorced. Mary Dorgan of Derby, Connecticut, sister of the soldier, testified that her brother was only married to Mary G. O'Brien.[484] They had two children: Pierce, Jr., born on 2 July 1888 at Hailey, Idaho; and Ruth, born on 1 January 1893 at Clayton, Idaho. There was no public record of the children's births and they were not baptized.

Mary G. Dorgan was married second at Challis, Custer Co., Idaho by Rev. G. L. McDougall of the Congregational Church to Joseph Rodger Prassuer on 20 October 1904. Her pension ceased upon her remarriage.

On 11 January 1905 Mary E. Prasseur, guardian, applied for a pension for the minor child [Ruth], daughter of the soldier Pierce Dargan.

DAVIS, JAMES
Co. B 1st HA, private, enlisted 6 September 1864, died 27 November 1864.

James Davis of Branford enlisted on 6 September 1864 as a private in Co. B 1st HA. He died on 27 November 1864. He does not appear in the 1860 census at Branford.

---

483 malingerer= pretend to be ill to avoid work.
484 Affidavit, Mary Dorgan of Derby, 2 April 1903, in the pension file of Pierce Dargan.

DAVIS, JOHN
Co. D 7th CVI, private, enlisted 24 August 1861, prisoner, died 28 October 1864, pension #246651 for his widow Sarah and minor child

John Davis of Branford enlisted at New Haven on 24 August 1861 and was mustered on 5 September 1861 as a private in Co. D 7th CVI for a term of three years. He was sick in camp at Fort Pulaski, Georgia June 1862. He reenlisted as a veteran in Co. D at St. Helena, South Carolina on 22 December 1863. He was captured at Drewry's Bluff, Virginia on 16 May 1864, confined at Richmond and sent to Andersonville Prison on 23 May 1864. He died there on 28 October 1864 of starvation. He does not appear in the 1860 census at Branford.

His widow, now Sarah E. Beers, applied for a pension on 19 July 1865 for her minor child Arthur L. Davis. She was married to the soldier under the name of Sarah Ester Reynolds at Carmel, New York by Rev. John Warren on 9 June 1859. Before the war they lived at Brewster, Putnam Co., New York where their son Arthur L. Davis was born on 11 June 1860. In 1887 Arthur was living in Delaware Co., New York. She was married second at Brewster, New York by Rev. A. D. Vail on 28 October 1866 to Cyrus Beers of Walton. She lived at Brewster Station from 1863 until the Fall of 1866 and since then at Walton, Delaware Co., New York.

DAY, THOMAS
Co. E 27th CVI, enlisted 9 September 1862, prisoner, mustered out 27 June 1863, pension #352169 for his minor child Thomas

Thomas Day of Madison enlisted on 9 September 1862 and was mustered in on 3 October 1862 as a private in Co. E 27th CVI for a term of nine months. With his regiment he fought at the Battle of Fredericksburg on 13 December 1862. He was captured at the Battle of Chancellorsville, Virginia on 3 May 1863, held prisoner at Richmond, and paroled at City Point, Virginia on 14 May 1863. He reported to Camp Parole, Maryland on 16 May 1863, was sent to Washington, D.C. on 20 May 1863 and spent the remainder of his service at Camp Convalescent, Virginia. With the rest of the Chancellorsville paroled prisoners, he rejoined the Regiment at Baltimore on 20 July 1863. Day was mustered out with the rest of his regiment at New Haven on 27 July 1863.

He never applied for a pension. He was married at St. Patrick's Church, New Haven by Rev. Matthew Hart on 12 June 1858 to Winnifred Kane, both of Madison. She died at New Haven on 3 October 1887. She was born in Ireland, daughter of John and Ann Kane. She never applied for a pension.

Thomas Day died at Madison on 11 April 1884 age 60 and was buried in St. Mary's Cemetery, Branford.[485] There was a G.A.R. marker at his gravesite in 1934. He was born in Ireland.

---

485 The Hale Collection, Branford, 105. He does not appear in the 1880 census for Branford nor is his death in the Branford Vital Records.

Sarah A. Shay of New Haven,[486] guardian for his minor child applied for a pension on 20 Aug 1890 under the act of 27 June 1890. The child, Thomas Lorenzo Day was born at Madison on 1 April 1878.

DAYTON, AMBROSE L.
Co. K 15th, private, enlisted 11 August 1862, mustered out 27 June 1865, pension #407679 for the soldier

Ambrose L. Dayton, age 19, of Wallingford enlisted at New Haven on 11 August 1862 and was mustered in on 25 August 1862 as a private in Co. K 15th CVI for a term of three years. He was sick in the hospital at Windmill Point, Virginia near Acquia Creek in January and February 1863 and was admitted to Armory Square Hospital at Washington, D.C. on 8 February 1863. He was furloughed from 20 February until 10 April 1863. He was detached to the Invalid Corps on 19 May 1863 until his return to his company on 13 October 1863. Dayton was mustered out with the rest of his regiment at New Bern, North Carolina on 27 June 1865 and discharged at New Haven on 12 July 1865. He served under Capt. Medad D. Munson of Wallingford and was the brother-in-law of DeGrasse Fowler, Jr.

He applied for an invalid pension on 7 August 1884. At the time of his enlistment he was described as five feet nine inches tall, dark complexion, black hair, brown eyes, occupation mechanic. He contracted typhoid pneumonia from exposure during guard duty at Camp Mud near Fredericksburg, Virginia soon after the Battle of Fredericksburg. "He was very sick and I never expected to see him again alive, he was deranged all the time."[487] He was in three different hospitals for nearly a year including General Hospital at Camp Mud [Camp Falmouth], General Field Hospital at Wind Mill Point, and Armory Square Hospital, Washington, D.C. "His father came down and got permission to take him home."[488] He was on furlough back home for fifty days and bed ridden most of the time. After his furlough he returned directly to Armory Square Hospital. He was away from his regiment about eleven months. When he returned to the company, "his health was very much impaired and he was many times excused from duty."[489]

His pension based on continued problems with his lungs was denied. He writes to the pension board "The examination I had in Hartford was a farce and nothing more. Three of us waited two and one half hours when Dr. Jarvis examined three of us at once in as many minutes and did it without even have us remove our over Coats."[490] There are a number of affidavits in the file attesting to his sickness during the war and his inability to work since.

He always lived at Wallingford but spent two months in North Carolina and Florida for his health. There is no personal information about a marriage or children in the file. He was married first to Caroline

---

486   She is perhaps the daughter of Thomas Day born about 1865 and states she supported the child. Thomas and Winnifred Day had older children.
487   Affidavit, William Mix of Meriden, 26 September 1884, in the pension file of Ambrose L. Dayton.
488   Affidavit, Henry N. Pardee of North Branford, 26 February 1884, in the pension file of Ambrose L. Dayton.
489   Affidavit, John H. Russell of North Haven, 21 April 1888, in the pension file of Ambrose L. Dayton.
490   Letter, Ambrose L. Dayton of Northford, 25 May 1885, in his own pension file.

and appears with her at Middlefield, Middlesex Co. in the 1870 census, ages 27 and 25. Maltby Lewis Dayton, probably their child, died at Middlefield on 8 October 1869 age 3 months & 18 days and was buried in Northford Cemetery.[491] In 1880 he was living at Wallingford, age 36, a boarder in the household of Selden & Sarah Austin. He was married, probably second, to Mary Holmes who died on 17 July 1891 age 45 and was buried in Northford Cemetery.[492]

Ambrose Lorenzo Dayton died on 21 December 1891[493] and was buried in Northford Cemetery. He was the son of Jonathan Hezekiah Dayton and Polly Eliza Todd of Wallingford. His name appears on the Northford Veterans' Monument.

DEBACQUE, ALFRED
Co. G 7th CVI, private, substitute, mustered in 29 November 1864, wounded 14 January 1865,, deserted, no pension

Alfred DeBacque, age 22, served as a substitute for Augustus R. Rowley of Branford. He was mustered in at New Haven on 29 November 1864 as private in Co. G 7th CVI for a term of three years. He was described as five feet ten inches tall, hazel eyes, light brown hair, ruddy complexion, unmarried, born in France, occupation glass blower.[494] He was wounded at Fort Fisher, North Carolina on 14 January 1865 and deserted on 2 April 1865 never returning from a furlough.

DECOURCEY, CHARLES
Co. B 11th CVI, private, to U.S. Navy, discharged 10 February 1865, no pension

Charles DeCourcey of Branford enlisted on 11 March 1864 as a private in Co. B 11th CVI for a term of three years. He was transferred to the U.S. Navy on 22 April 1864 and served on the U.S.S. *Minnesota* and U.S.S. *Wyalusing*. He was discharged from the Navy on 10 February 1865. He does not appear in the 1860 census at Branford.

DEMUTH, JACOB
Co. D 2nd HA, private, enlisted 31 December 1863, wounded 22 June 1864, died 24 June 1864, no pension

Jacob Demuth of Branford enlisted on 31 December 1863 as a private in Co. D 2nd HA. He was wounded at Petersburg, Virginia on 22 June 1864 and died two days later. He does not appear in the 1860 census at Branford.

---

491 St. Andrews Episcopal Church Records, Northford, 3:118; gravestone at Northford Cemetery.
492 *A Dayton Record*, Charles Nathan Dayton, typescript at New Haven Museum, 204; The Hale Collection, North Branford, 71; she was living in Massachusetts at the time of her death per St. Andrews Church Records 3:124.
493 Thorpe, *History of the Fifteenth*, 326. His name is on the gravestone in Northford Cemetery but no date.
494 Muster & Descriptive Rolls of Substitutes, RG 13, box 97, 2nd Congressional District, Connecticut State Library.

DIBBLE, ELIZUR B.
Co. B 27th CVI, private, enlisted 9 September 1862, prisoner, mustered out 27 July 1863, pension #316008 for his widow Ann

Elizur B. Dibble, age 20, of Branford enlisted on 8 September 1862 and was mustered in on 3 October 1862 as a private in Co. B 27th CVI for a term of nine months. He fought at the Battle of Fredericksburg on 13 December 1862 with the rest of the company. He was captured at the Battle of Chancellorsville, Virginia on 3 May 1863, held prisoner at Richmond, and paroled at City Point, Virginia on 14 May 1863. He reported to Camp Parole, Maryland on 16 May 1863, was sent to Washington, D.C. on 20 May 1863 and spent the remainder of his service at Camp Convalescent, Virginia. With the rest of the Chancellorsville paroled prisoners, he rejoined the Regiment at Baltimore on 20 July 1863. Dibble was mustered out with the rest of his regiment at New Haven on 27 July 1863.

Elizur Brockway Dibble died at Branford on 12 February 1891 and was buried there in Damascus Cemetery. His company and regiment are engraved on his stone and there was a G.A.R. marker on his gravesite in 1934. His name appears on the Stony Creek Veterans' Monument. He was born at Branford on 13 June 1842, son of Richard Dibble and Betsey Brockway.[495] He never applied for a pension.

Ann G. Dibble, age 53, of Branford applied for a widow's pension on 11 March 1891. She was married to the soldier under the name of Ann Griswold Meigs at Guilford by Rev. William S. Smith on 8 March 1864. Neither were previously married or divorced and she did not remarry after his death. One son, Charles was under the age of 16 years in 1891, born at Branford on 19 June 1876. She had four children living (in 1891): Annie B. (Dibble) Vedder, George F. Dibble, William A. Dibble, and Charles Dibble.

There are several statements in the file to prove the soldier had a disability due to war service. "On or about March 12th 1863 in Camp near Falmouth, Va he was taken ill with Rheumatism, the result of exposure in a long rain storm and about April 28th 1863 was sick with diarrhea."[496] "He suffered from rheumatism during the war, aggravated while in prison. After his parole from prison, he was sent to the convalescent camp at Alexandria where he remained about six weeks. He joined the Reg't on his return home. He was very sick about a year after his return home and was never well again."[497] "My son Elizur B. Dibble returned from the war sick with Dysentery and was attended 7 or 8 months by Dr. I. P. Leete and soon after his return had Rheumatism so badly that he could scarcely move without assistance. For more than a year he was unable to do any labor from that time to his decease suffering from sharp pain in his spine."[498]

Ann Griswold Dibble died at Branford on 21 December 1908 and is buried there in Damascus Cemetery.[499] She was born at Haddam on 15 November 1837, daughter of Nathan Meigs and Lois Charlotte DeWolf.[500]

---

495 Branford Vital Records, Town Meeting Book A, 230.
496 Affidavit, Harvey Beaumont of Wallingford, 3 March 1894, in the pension file of Elizur B. Dibble.
497 Affidavit, Henry A. Camp, 24 February 1894, in the pension file of Elizur B. Dibble.
498 Affidavit, Richard Dibble of Branford, 31 March 1893, in the pension file of Elizur B. Dibble.
499 Branford Vital Records, deaths, 1908.
500 Branford Vital Records, deaths, 1908.

DIETRICH, JOSEPH

Joseph Dietrich, age 21, served as a substitute for John H. Harrison of North Branford. He was mustered in at New Haven on 25 August 1864 as a private in the 1st Connecticut Cavalry, unassigned, for a term of three years. He was described as five feet five inches tall, blue eyes, light hair, fair complexion, unmarried, occupation printer, born in Germany.[501]

DOLPH, CHARLES C.

Co. D 7th CVI, private, enlisted 3 September 1861, wounded, to Co. I 19th CVI, discharged 15 July 1865, pension #382113 for the soldier and later for his widow Hannah

Charles C. Dolph of Branford enlisted at New Haven on 3 September 1861 and was mustered in on 5 September 1861 as a private in Co. D 7th CVI for a term of three years. He was wounded at Pocotaligo, South Carolina on 22 October 1862. He reenlisted as a veteran in Co. D on 22 December 1863 at St. Helena, South Carolina and was on furlough March and April 1864. He was wounded at the Battle of Drewry's Bluff, Virginia on 14 May 1864. He was admitted to Knight Hospital, New Haven on 13 June 1864 and transferred to Co. I 19th CVI at Elmira, New York on 30 January 1865. Charles Dolph was discharged for disability at Elmira, New York on 15 July 1865.

He applied for and received an invalid pension in 1866. At the time of his enlistment he was described as five feet eight inches tall, light complexion, gray eyes, light hair, occupation farmer. At the Battle of James Island he was wounded by a bursting shell on the right arm which since has made it useless for lifting. The wound was dressed by a surgeon in the field not belonging to the regiment and he was sent to Regimental Hospital and stayed about six weeks. He was wounded a second time on the right side at the Battle of Drewry's Bluff on 14 May 1864, the bullet entering his right side and coming out near the back bone causing damage to his lungs and spine. He was taken to the rear and treated at Regimental Hospital at Point Lookout for nearly two months. He was transferred to the hospital at New Haven where he remained for nearly a year. He was transferred to the invalid corps for three or four months where he was discharged in July 1865.

He was born at North Branford and was living at Branford in 1860. He was married first to Mary C. Dolph who died at Branford in December 1861.[502] In 1870 he was living at Westport, Fairfield Co.[503] From 1873 to 1879 he was living at New Haven and later at Leetes Island, Guilford where he died.

Charles C. Dolph died at Guilford on 13 July 1889 age 64 and was buried in Evergreen Cemetery, New Haven.[504] He was the son of Charles Dolph and Harmony Chittenden, born at Guilford and Saybrook.

Hannah M. Dolph of Leetes Island, Guilford applied for a widow's pension on 26 July 1889. She was married to the soldier under the name of Hannah M. Parcell by Rev. C. T. Mallory at Portchester, New York on 1 February 1864. She was not previously married.

---

501 Muster & Descriptive Rolls of Substitutes, RG 13, box 97, 2nd Congressional District, Connecticut State Library; his service is not found in *Record of Service of Connecticut Men*.

502 Branford Vital Records, 1852-1863, 14.

503 U.S. census 1870, Westport, Fairfield Co.; population schedule M593, Roll 99, dwelling 453, family 531, page 278, www.heritagequest.com.

504 The Hale Collection, New Haven, 819.

Society of the Fourteenth Regiment at Cemetery Hill, Gettysburg, September 16, 1891.

The veterans of the 14th Connecticut Volunteer Regiment had a reunion at Gettysburg
on September 16, 1891. (Page, History Fourteenth Regiment, 253)

DOLPH, EDWARD B.
Co. B 27th CVI, private, enlisted 9 September 1862, died 20 March 1863 near Falmouth, Virginia from disease, no pension

Edward B. Dolph, age 22, of Wallingford enlisted on 9 September 1862 and was mustered in on 3 October 1862 as a private in Co. B 27th CVI for a term of nine months. He fought at the Battle of Fredericksburg on 13 December 1862 with the rest of the company and was on the company roster in January and February 1863. Edward Dolph died at Regimental Hospital near Falmouth, Virginia on 20 March 1863 of typhoid fever and was buried in Center Street Cemetery, Wallingford.[505] He was probably the son of Milo and Mary Dolph.[506]

DONAHUE, JOHN or DONOHUE
Co. A 9th CVI, private, enlisted 8 February 1864, died 3 August 1864, no pension

John Donohue of Branford enlisted or was drafted on 8 February 1864 and died on 3 August 1864.

505 The Hale Collection, Wallingford, 128.
506 1850 and 1860 U.S. census, Cheshire, New Haven County.

DONAHUE, WILLIAM or DONOHUE
Co. G 14th CVI, private, enlisted 5 August 1862, mustered out 31 May 1865, pension #546883 for the soldier

William Donohue of Madison enlisted at Hartford on 5 August 1862 and was mustered in on 23 August 1862 as a private in Co. G 14th CVI for a term of three years. With his regiment he saw action at Antietam, Maryland, Gettysburg and many battles during the Virginia campaign. He was detached to the Pioneer Corps on 30 April 1864 and was mustered out at Baileys Cross Roads, Virginia on 31 May 1865.

He applied for an invalid pension on 31 August 1882 which was rejected on 16 November 1885. He re-applied on 12 August 1890 under the act of 27 June 1890 and was again rejected, the pension board stating his disability did not prevent him from performing manual labor. He was treated from February to May 1863 at the field hospital, Stony Mountain near Culpepper, Virginia for fever and bronchitis. At the Battle of Gettysburg he contracted fever, rheumatism, and sunstroke and suffered from deafness from the noise of the cannons. His company was on Cemetery Hill immediately in front of the artillery. At Martins Ford, Virginia in January 1864 he cut his left foot with an axe while cutting timber for a bridge resulting in the loss of two toes. At the time of his enlistment he was described as five feet ten inches tall, dark complexion, blue eyes, light hair. He was married at New Haven by Father Lynch on 9 February 1876 (her name is not given). His wife Mary Jane Donohue died at Branford on 23 May 1899 age 56.[507] He had no children living in 1898. Before the war he lived at Chester for two years then Madison where he enlisted. After the war he returned to Madison for two years and since then lived at Branford. He was a charter member of the Mason Rogers Post No. 7 G.A.R. of Branford.

William O. Donohue died at Branford on 3 December 1906 and was buried in St. Bernard's Cemetery, New Haven. He was born at County Cork, Ireland March 1839, son of William Donahue and Margaret O'Connor.[508]

DONNELLY, EDWARD
Co. F 15th CVI, private, substitute, mustered in 24 August 1864, discharged disability 18 January 1865, no pension

Edward Donnelly, age 19, served as a substitute for Elias E. Potter of North Branford. He was mustered in at New Haven on 24 August 1864 as a private in Co. F 15th CVI for a term of three years. He was described as five feet six inches tall, fair complexion, blue eyes, dark hair, unmarried, born in "Canada West," occupation boatman. He was discharged at New Bern, North Carolina for chronic valve disease of the heart on 18 January 1865, contracted before he enlisted.[509] He does not appear in the 1860 census at Branford or North Branford.

DONOVAN, JEREMIAH
Co. C 5th CVI, private, enlisted 16 December 1864, failed to report, no pension

Jeremiah Donovan of Branford enlisted or was drafted on 16 December 1864 as a private in Co. C 15th CVI. He was transferred from New Haven to the company on 7 January 1865 but failed to report.

---

507 *The Branford Opinion*, 27 May 1899.
508 Branford Vital Records, deaths, 1906.
509 Report of Sick and Wounded, Blackstone Library Archives, Holcombe papers, RG 5, box 1, folder 4; and his CMSR.

DOOLITTLE, HORACE A.
1st LA, private, enlisted 18 October 1861, discharged 12 August 1865, pension #660249 for the soldier and later for his widow Julia

Horace A. Doolittle of Cheshire was one of four brothers who served in the Civil War. He came to Branford about 1900. (Beecher, First Light Battery, II:769)

Horace A. Doolittle, age 23, of Cheshire enlisted at Meriden on 18 October 1861 and was mustered in on 26 October 1861 as a private in the 1st LA for a term of three years. He reenlisted as a veteran in the same regiment on 26 December 1863. He was admitted to Knight General Hospital, New Haven on 12 February 1864 and returned to duty on 24 November 1864. He was with the regiment when it entered Richmond and saw the Union flag hoisted above the Confederate capital. He was admitted to Stuart General Hospital, Richmond, Virginia for dysentery and transferred on 27 April 1865 to Point of Rocks Hospital at James, Virginia. He was admitted to Satterlee General Hospital, West Philadelphia, Pennsylvania on 21 May 1865 and transferred to Knight Hospital, New Haven on 22 July 1865. Doolittle was mustered out at New Haven on 12 August 1865. Three of his brothers served in the 20th CVI.

He applied for an invalid pension on 10 February 1880. "For five years before my enlistment I lived at Cheshire and my occupation was as a farmer. I was in perfect health. In the spring of 1863 I was first troubled with diarrhea and was treated at various hospitals. After my discharge I was terribly emaciated and treated for one year, only able to walk several yards. After two years of careful diet, I was able to resume my occupation but continued with attacks."

He was living at Cheshire during the 1860, 1870, and 1880 census. He first appears at Branford in 1900.

Horace Augustus Doolittle died at Branford on 17 February 1903 age 65 and was buried in Hillside Cemetery, Cheshire.[510] He was born at Cheshire on 7 May 1839, son of Amasa Lewis Doolittle and Maria Merriman.

Julia Doolittle applied for a pension after his death. She was married to the soldier under the name of Julia L. Andrews at New Haven by S.W.S. Dutton on 20 October 1860. They were both age 23, born at Cheshire and Hamden. Neither were previously married or divorced. They had one son living (in 1908): Frederick H., born on 19 February 1878 at Cheshire.

Julia Doolittle died at Branford on 28 September 1921 and was buried in Hillside Cemetery, Cheshire. She was born at Hamden on 25 November 1837, daughter of Rebecca Andrews.[511]

---

510 Branford Vital Records, deaths, 1903.
511 Branford Vital Records, deaths, 1921.

DORY, GEORGE W.
Co. I 10th Mass. Infantry, private, enlisted 21 June 1861, discharged 10 November 1862, Co. G 2nd U.S. Artillery, enlisted 11 November 1862, to Co. L 1st U.S. Artillery, discharged 11 November 1865, pension #965988 for the soldier and later for his widow Anna

George W. Dory enlisted at West Springfield, Massachusetts as a private in Co. I 10th Massachusetts Volunteer Infantry on 21 June 1861. He was discharged at Stafford Court House, Virginia on 10 November 1862 and reenlisted on 11 November 1862 as a private in Co. G 2nd U.S. Artillery. He was transferred to Co. L 1st Regiment Artillery ninety days before his discharge and was discharged at Fort Schuyler, New York City on 11 November 1865.

He applied for an invalid pension on 30 June 1880 which was denied. At the time of his enlistment he was described as five feet seven inches tall, light complexion, blue eyes, light hair, occupation farmer. After his discharge he came immediately to New Haven until 1876, then Hartford until 1885, came back to New Haven until he moved to Branford. He was a member of the Mason Rogers Post No. 7 G.A.R., transferred from the Admiral Foot Post No. 17 of New Haven on 14 February 1891.

He reapplied for a pension on 7 December 1899 stating he was not a pensioner. He had an injury of his left leg and shell wound of the left foot but waived these for his pension. He claimed disability for diarrhea and injury of his face and right eye received at Arlington Heights, Virginia from the bursting of a musket at Fort Cass. He could not see out of that eye for three months and wore a patch. He lived in Massachusetts five years before his enlistment and for three years in West Springfield. Before that he lived at Holyoke and Indian Orchard, Massachusetts. He was in the tent hospital on Capitol Hill, Washington, D.C. six or seven days with measles the last of July 1861 and from the hospital he went back to the company at Kalaram Heights and the next day the company started for Brightwood, Maryland. While at Brightwood, and not fully recovered from the measles, he contracted severe diarrhea with fever and chills. He was treated in camp and later sent to Regimental Hospital by stretcher from his tent. He was removed to Columbia College Hospital and was sick about fourteen weeks. When he was back on duty he was excused for days because of continuing health problems.

He was baptized on 11 June 1843. His father was a civil engineer and was working in Wales. His father came to this country first then sent back for George, a brother and a sister. He came over with friends. He was not over three years of age but remembers the ship. During the summer and fall of 1850 he lived with his father James Thomas Dory at West Haven. In 1860 he lived in Ashley Mills, West Springfield, Massachusetts with Sylvester Ashley until his enlistment in 1861.[512]

George Dory served in the Massachusetts Infantry and U.S. Artillery. He died at Branford in 1925 and was buried in Center Cemetery. (Branford Historical Society photograph collection)

---

512 There are several long depositions from George W. Dory in the file.

George William Dory died at Branford on 6 July 1925 and was buried there in Center Cemetery. A G.A.R. marker was on his gravesite in 1934 and 2011. He was born at Kingsley Avon, England on 22 April 1842, son of James Dory and Mary Rose, both born in England.[513]

Anna M. Dory of Branford applied for a widow's pension on 12 August 1925. She was married to the soldier under the name of Anna Melintha Hosley at Branford by Rev. Henry Olmstead of the Trinity Episcopal Church on 26 June 1879. He was age 33, living at Hartford; she was age 25, living at Branford. Neither were previously married or divorced. She was born at East Haven on 22 May 1854, daughter of Benjamin Adolphus Hosley and Lois Whitney Ward. They had no children. She was buried on 17 September 1935 in Center Cemetery, Branford.[514]

DOUGHERTY, ROBERT or DOROTY, DOGERTY, DOGHERTY, DOHERTY
Co. A 9th CVI, private, enlisted 20 August 1861, discharged 5 June 1865, pension #748786 for the soldier

Robert Doherty of Branford enlisted at New Haven on 20 August 1861 and was mustered in on 27 August 1861 as a private in Co. A 9th CVI for a term of three years. He received a gunshot wound to his right hand in the fight at Christian Pass, Mississippi in April 1862. He was absent without leave on 31 August 1863, apprehended for desertion on 26 October 1863 and in confinement at New Orleans on 31 October 1863. He was still in confinement from 31 December 1863 through 30 June 1864 awaiting sentence at court martial. He was in confinement at Ship Island, Mississippi on 31 August 1864. He was admitted to Camp Rendezvous near Alexandria, Virginia from Ship Island on 14 February 1865 for pneumonia. He was transferred to Knight General Hospital, New Haven on 5 May 1865 where he was discharged on 5 June 1865. Other military records show him sick at various times in 1863 and 1864 but absent without leave and desertion in 1865. He apparently received an honorable discharge.

He applied for an invalid pension on 24 February 1891 under the act of 27 June 1890. He was described as five feet seven inches tall, red hair, sandy complexion. While on duty at New Orleans in the winter of 1863 he contracted rheumatism resulting in disease of the heart, also lung fever resulting in disease of the lungs. "He was a healthy man before the war and since his return he has not been healthy and very sick a number of times."[515] After the war he settled in Branford where he had a brother. There are very few papers in the file and no depositions from the soldier. He did receive a pension.

He was married at New Haven by Father Ganan in 1866 or 1867 to Ellen Kelly. Neither were previously married or divorced. They had the following children (living in 1898): Katie, Robert, Lizzie and Annie. He did not know the dates of their births but they were all over eighteen years of age. Ellen Dougherty died at Branford on 23 December 1907 and was buried there St. Mary's Cemetery.[516]

---

513   Several documents in the file give his birthplace as West Haven which was for a period of time was his place of residence.
514   Branford Sexton Records, 1933-1966, 9.
515   Affidavit, Lynde Rowland of Branford, no date, in the pension file of Robert Dougherty.
516   Branford Vital Records, deaths, 1907; no gravestone was found.

Robert Dougherty died at Branford on 2 September 1908 age 78 and was buried there in St. Mary's Cemetery.[517] His company and regiment are engraved on his stone and there was a G.A.R. marker on his gravesite in 1934 and 2011. He was born in Ireland, son of Robert Dougherty.

DOWD, BENJAMIN R.
Co. K 15th CVI, private, enlisted 11 August 1862, died 4 December 1862, pension #23865 for his widow Juliette S. Dowd later Juliette Foote

Benjamin R. Dowd, age 26, of North Branford enlisted at New Haven on 11 August 1862 and was mustered in on 25 August 1862 as a private in Co. K 15th CVI for a term of three years. He died in Washington, D.C. at a private residence on 4 December 1862 of typhoid fever. His wife was present at the time of his death and took his effects. There is a monument and a government issued gravestone for him in Northford Cemetery, his company and regiment are engraved on both stones. His monument reads "He Died at Washington, D.C.; Dec. 4, 1862: AE. 28 Yrs. We gave him to God and his Country." He was born at North Branford, son of Benjamin Dowd and Ruth Stevens.[518] His name appears on the Northford Veterans' Monument.

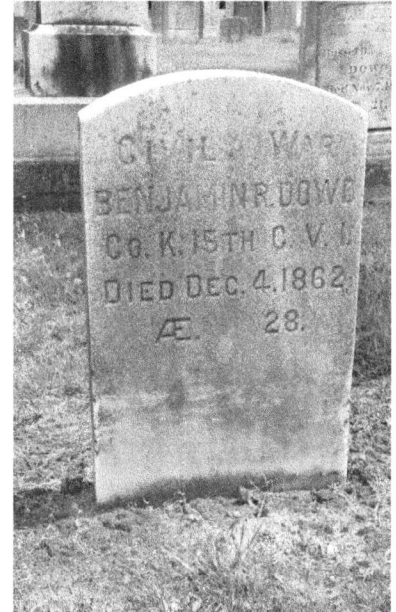

> "November 1862 was a time of great sickness and many deaths in the Regiment at Camp near Fairfax Seminary, Va. Benjamin R. Dowd was violently attacked with Typhoid Fever and removed to Washington, D.C. Our Reg't Hospital was full of patients. I had the same complaint & unfortunately without Hospital comfort such as a bedstead & bedding. The patients were obliged to lie on straw cots on the floor thickly stowed in which condition many died averaging from 1 to 3 a day. Four from my company died at this station including my brother. Dowd avoided entering our Reg't Hospital being taken by a friend—brother-in-law I think through permission of the Surgeon in charge to his own private residence in Washington."[519]

At the time of his enlistment he was described as five feet eleven inches tall, fair complexion, blue eyes, black hair, occupation farmer. His service was listed by the Guilford selectman but credited to North Branford. "In November 1862, Dowd, with the rest of the company was on picket duty about 4 miles South of Fairfax Seminary in Virginia & while on said picket he was exposed to a severe cold storm and was attacked with typhoid fever & was sick in Camp about ten days & while so sick he was removed by Mr. Downs[520] his Brother in law to a private boarding house where he died."[521]

Juliette S. Dowd, age 18, of North Branford applied for a widow's pension in the Connecticut Supreme Court of Errors on 26 January 1863 under the act of 14 July 1862. She was married to the soldier under the

---

517 Branford Vital Records, deaths, 1908. The sexton records call him Robert Stanley Dougherty.
518 Talcott, *Families of Guilford*, 304.
519 Letter, Medad D. Munson, at New Berne, N.C.; captain Co. K 15th CVI, 21 March 1864, in the pension file of Benjamin R. Dowd.
520 Albert B. Downs of New Haven, captain of Co. I 2nd Conn. Regiment was married to Celestia Ann Dowd.
521 Letter, Henry N. Stiles of North Haven, late captain Co. K 15th CVI, 30 December 1863, in the pension file of Benjamin R. Dowd.

name of Juliette Smith Gidney at Northford by Rev. Asa C. Pierce of the Northford Congregational Church on 20 March 1862. They had no children. She received a pension until her remarriage.

She was married second at North Branford by Rev. Asa C. Pierce on 15 June 1865 to Charles M. Ferguson of Woodbridge. They had one child Charles E. Ferguson and were divorced at New Haven on 11 December 1869. She asked the court to change her name back to Juliette Gidney. She was married third at Northford by Rev. William Howard on 12 April 1871 to Lynde Harrison Foote as his first wife. Foote died at Northford on 25 December 1903 and was buried in New Northford Cemetery. He was born at North Branford on 15 October 1834, son of Warham Williams Foote and Lucinda Harrison. Foote never served in the military.

She applied for a pension on 7 May 1908 under the act of 19 April 1908 as the widow of the soldier Benjamin R. Dowd. She had life use of a farm in Northford belonging to her daughter Flora Blakeslee by her husband Lynde H. Foote.

Juliette S. Gidney Dowd Ferguson Foote died at Northford on 20 April 1913 and was buried in New Northford Cemetery. She was born at Newburgh, New York on 24 June 1844, daughter of George Washington Gidney and Caroline Tyler of Northford.

DOUGLASS, JOSEPH P.
see Charles Johnson

DOWNEY, TIMOTHY alias TIMOTHY MURPHY
Co. G 117th New York Volunteers, private, enlisted 9 March 1864, discharged 13 August 1865, pension #563211 for the soldier and later for his widow Margaret

Timothy Murphy of New York enlisted on 9 March 1864 as a private in Co. G 117th New York Volunteer Infantry and was discharged at Raleigh, North Carolina on 1 September 1865.

He applied for an invalid pension on 7 April 1893 under the act of 27 June 1890 for exposure and rheumatism contracted during his service. His pension application was sent for special examination and was denied due to lack of proof of disability and he never reapplied. At the time of his enlistment he was described as five feet five inches tall, dark complexion, blue eyes, dark hair, occupation shoemaker and laborer. Before the war he had a shoemaker's shop on Hudson Avenue, Brooklyn, New York and lived there four years after his marriage and moved to Branford to work at the Branford Lock Works. Timothy Downey was mustered in as a member of the Mason Rogers Post No. 7 G.A.R. of Branford on 23 March 1882 and was dropped from membership on 25 September 1890. He moved to Stamford in 1891.

He was married at New York City by Rev. John Brady of St. Anthony's Church on Union Avenue on 19 April 1868 to Margaret Pine,[522] witnessed by William Pine. Timothy was age 29, born in Ireland, living at Brooklyn, son of William Downey and May Murphy. She was age 21, of Greenpoint, Brooklyn, New York; born in Ireland, daughter of John Pine and Catherine Hemly. Neither were previously married or divorced. They had four children, all living in 1898: Catherine "Kittie," born on 27 February 1868, married name Moore; William, born on 5 January 1870; Mary Alice, born on 1 January 1875; and John Thomas, born on 2 July 1877.

There are many affidavits and depositions in the file concerning his name and disability. His wife Margaret stated that when she met him he had a "short beard, was quite stout, and his face was slightly pitted from smallpox contracted when he was a baby." She knew him three months before they married and

---

522 The spelling Pine and Pyne are used in the file but she said Pine was correct.

never heard him called Timothy Murphy until the time of his pension application. She came to this country just before the war and he lived at Brooklyn, New York when he first came. He had four brothers, three of whom were dead; William was living at Brooklyn, New York. She had one sister Alice Walsh (Mrs. Lewis) of Guttenburg, New Jersey and one brother in Ireland. Other family members included David J. Downey of Brooklyn, age 60, son of John Downey deceased and his brother Dennis Downey of Brooklyn, age 62. Also mentioned is Catherine Downey, age 68, of Brooklyn, widow of Patrick Downey.[523]

His brother stated their real name was Downey, that he was also in the Civil War and was reported as shot dead but actually captured near City Point, Virginia on 16 September 1864. "Later my brother told me he enlisted as Timothy Murphy so their mother wouldn't know, her maiden name was Murphy." William Downey said he came to this country in 1859 to Brooklyn, New York.[524]

Timothy Downey died at Stamford on 16 September 1901 age 64 and was buried in Spring Grove Cemetery, Darien.[525] For the last two years of his life he lived at the Fitch's Soldier Home and accidently drowned while visiting his home at Stamford.

Margaret Downey of Stamford applied for and received a widow's pension on 14 October 1902. She died on 23 June 1915.

DUFFY, THOMAS
Co. I 14th CVI. private, enlisted 25 July 1863, wounded, to Co. C 2nd HA 30 May 1865, pension #543433 for the soldier, his widow and minor child

Thomas Duffy of Branford enlisted on 25 July 1863 and was mustered in at Hartford on 23 August 1863 as a private in Co. I 14th CVI for a term of three years. He was wounded at Spotsylvania, Virginia on 19 May 1864 and transferred to Co. C 2nd HA on 30 May 1865. He was discharged for disability on 10 June 1865. He does not appear in the 1860 or 1870 census at Branford or North Branford.

He applied for an invalid pension on 8 July 1865. His widow later applied for herself and a minor child.

EDGE, REUBEN D.
Co. G 11th CVI, private, enlisted 29 March 1864, died 31 October 1864, no pension

Reuben D. Edge of Branford enlisted on 29 March 1864 as a private in Co. G 11th CVI and died on 31 October 1864. He does not appear in the 1860 census at Branford.

EGAN, GEORGE M. or EAGAN
Co. C 3rd CVI, private, enlisted 24 April 1861, mustered out 12 August 1861, Co. B 1st Cavalry, private, enlisted 20 October 1861, prisoner, mustered out 2 August 1865, pension #1124725 for the soldier

George M. Egan[526] of Branford enlisted at New Haven on 24 April 1861 and was mustered in at Hartford on 14 May 1861 as a private in Co. C 3rd CVI for a term of three months. The Regiment fought at the first Battle

523 Deposition, Margaret Downey of Stamford, 14 November 1902; in the pension file of Timothy Downey.
524 Deposition, William Downey age 61 of Brooklyn, N. Y., 5 April 1902; in the pension file of Timothy Downey.
525 Fitch's Soldier Home, file 1740, buried as Timothy Murphy. His pension file states he died on 16 September 1901, his gravestone as 17 September, and the Fitch's Soldier Home record as 18 September.
526 For his biography see Wm. J. Pape, *History of Waterbury and the Naugatuck Valley Connecticut* (New York: S. J. Clarke Publishing Co., 1918), 21.

George Egan enlisted in the 3rd Connecticut which was a three month regiment that fought at the first Battle of Bull Run. (Photographic History of the Civil War, I:151)

of Bull Run. He was mustered out at Hartford on 12 August 1861 when his term expired. He reenlisted on 28 October 1861 and was mustered in at Meriden on 2 November 1861 as a private in Co. B 1st Calvary for a term of three years. He was promoted to corporal on 16 September 1862 and his rank was reduced to private on 24 May 1863. He was captured at Frederick, Maryland on 20 June 1863 and paroled in August 1863. He reenlisted as a veteran in Co. B on 1 January 1864. With his regiment he participated in many engagements in Virginia including the Battles of Cedar Mountain, the Second Bull Run, the Wilderness, Spotsylvania, Winchester, and Cedar Creek. Egan was mustered out with the rest of the 1st Connecticut Cavalry at Washington, D.C. on 2 August 1865 and discharged at New Haven on 18 August 1865.

He applied for an invalid pension on 31 October 1904. At the time of his enlistment he was described as five feet seven inches tall, dark complexion, dark eyes, black hair, occupation carpenter. Since his discharge he lived at Fair Haven August 1865 to December 1866; Meriden until May 1869; then Waterbury where he was still residing in 1915. He became a patrolman in the Waterbury police department on 8 April 1876 and was promoted to chief on 17 February 1884. He retired on 28 October 1905 and had an "enviable record as head of the department." He was married at Southington by Father Creighton on 28 October 1868 to Mary E. Garde. She was born on 1 December 1847 and died on 13 July 1926.[527] They had four children (all living in 1915): Katherine Ellen, born on 10 September 1869, married to H. P. McCarthy; Margaret Josephine, born on 3 June 1871; James R., born on 27 January 1873; and G. William, born on 28 November 1886.

George M. Egan died on 25 April 1928 and was buried in New St. Joseph's Cemetery in Waterbury.[528] He was born near Limerick, Ireland on 28 October 1842.

527 The Hale Collection, Waterbury, 191.
528 The Hale Collection, Waterbury, 191.

ELTON, GEORGE W.

Co. B 27th CVI, 1st lieutenant, enlisted 10 September 1862, prisoner, mustered out 27 July 1863, pension application #560341 for his widow Betsey Ann Monroe

George W. Elton, age 32, of Wallingford enlisted on 10 September 1862 and was mustered in on 3 October 1862 as 2nd lieutenant of Co. B 27th CVI for a term of nine months. He was the officer of Co. B issuing the order to fire on the enemy at Fredericksburg on 13 December 1862 during the attack up Marye's Height. "Lieut. Elton went into battle with us. He got knocked off or fell off from a stone wall, has had the rheumatism ever since."[529] "When I left the city, I had Lieut Elton leaning on my shoulder."[530] After the Battle of Fredericksburg "he was sick for a long time and unable to do duty for over a month, said he had trouble with his stomach. I was his tent mate while in winter quarters at camp near Falmouth, Va. in the winter of 1862 & 1863."[531] He was present but at times sick from November 1862 through February 1863. After the resignation of Daniel W. Field, he was promoted to 1st lieutenant on 1 April 1863. He commanded Co. B during the Chancellorsville campaign[532] and was captured on 3 May 1863, held prisoner at Libby Prison, Richmond, and paroled at City Point, Virginia on 15 May 1863. He reported to Camp Parole, Maryland on 18 May 1863 and was sent to Camp Convalescent, Virginia on 25 May 1863. On 10 June 1863 he was in charge of Par Prison. On 1 July 1863 he was at Camp Distribution in Alexandria and did not go to Gettysburg. Elton was mustered out with the rest of his regiment at New Haven on 27 July 1863. He was the brother-in-law of Capt. Medad D. Munson.

He was married first at Wallingford by Rev. E. R. Gilbert on 1 October 1850 to Cornelia Munson, daughter of Medad Ward Munson and Henrietta Dutton. She died at Wallingford on 8 March 1860 age 27.

George W. Elton died at Wallingford on 11 October 1881 age 52 and was buried there in Center Street Cemetery. He was the son of William Elton and Jerusha Hall. He worked in the electro - plating department of the Simpson, Hall, Miller & Co. in Wallingford.[533] He never applied for a pension.

His widow Betsey, now Betsey Monroe, applied for a pension on 22 September 1892 under the act of 27 June 1890. She was 56 years of age, living at Wallingford. She was married to the soldier under the name of Betsy Ann Linsley at Wallingford by Rev. Edwin R. Gilbert of the First Congregational Church on 23 April 1873. She was not previously married or divorced. She was married second on 22 October 1889 to Lyman Morse Monroe of Wallingford. The application was denied since Monroe was still living and George Elton's death was not caused by his military service.

There are depositions in the file from Jane S. Elton, sister-in-law of George W. Elton, and from his daughter Francis Wallace.[534] Francis states in 1895 that she is 41 years of age, the daughter of George W. Elton, late husband of Betsey A. Monroe. "I always lived in the same house at Wallingford with my father until after my marriage except for about one year in Titusville, Penn. and four months in Utica, NY. His death was sudden, less than a week."[535] Both women claimed he was a healthy man before his last illness and always worked, never complained that he had a disability from the war. Another deposition was from May J. Carrington, wife of G. K. Carrington and sister of the late George W. Elton. She lived in Wallingford except for six to eight years about 15 years ago in Philadelphia, Penn. "My brother always resided here

---

529 Letter, [George C. Baldwin], 15 December 1862.
530 Letter, 17 December 1862, Henry D. Boardman to his sister; see the chapter on Boardman.
531 Affidavit, Daniel Averill 2nd, 1 November 1892, in the pension file of George W. Elton.
532 Affidavit, Dr. Robert B. Goodyear of North Haven, 1 November 1892, in the pension file of George W. Elton.
533 Affidavit, Charles F. Harwood of Wallingford, no date, in the pension file of George W. Elton.
534 She was the only child of George Elton, born on 20 September 1853, married in 1875 to Henry L. Wallace.
535 Deposition, Francis (Elton) Wallace, 7 July 1895, in the pension file of George W. Elton.

[Wallingford], except for a short period at Utica, N. Y.; six months or so; and a year or so in Titusville, Pa. Both of these were after the war. About two years before his death he complained of periods of intense pain in his stomach with vomiting which lasted about a week. He was a large man and a heavy eater but always seemed very healthy. My brother Henry, my father and paternal grandfather all died of kidney disease. My brother George was the oldest brother."[536] There is a deposition from Douglas W. Hallenbeck of Wallingford, nephew of George Elton. Dr. Robert B. Goodyear of North Haven, a physician and comrade in Co. B states that "Elton was sick in camp at Falmouth during the winter of 1862 & 1863 and was excused from duty at different times between the 13th of December 1862 and the latter part of April 1863. The illness was gastric enteritis due to exposure from camping on the ground before suitable quarters could be provided."[537] There are many depositions in the file from co-workers and comrades.

In 1897 Betsy Ann Monroe writes to request that the case be reopened "I do not feel that the decision rendered was just." The case was reexamined and denied. She makes a third request in July 1913, her second husband Lyman M. Monroe died in 1903 and she supports herself with sewing. The request was denied on the same grounds, in addition, upon remarriage, she ceased to be the widow of the soldier and, hence, had no pensionable status under the act of 19 April 1908. She never received a pension.

Betsey Ann Linsley Elton Monroe died on 6 May 1917 and was buried in Center Street Cemetery, Wallingford.[538] She was born at Fair Haven on 2 August 1835, daughter of Alfred Linsley and Amarilla Mallory. She was the first cousin of soldiers Charles F. and Frederick A. Linsley.

ENNIS, EDWIN A.
see Charles Barry

ENNIS, JAMES
Co. B 27th CVI, private, enlisted 17 September 1862, prisoner, mustered out 27 July 1863, pension #717474 for the soldier and later for his widow Bridget

James Ennis, age 20, of Wallingford enlisted on 17 September 1862 and was mustered in on 3 October 1862 as a private in Co. B 27th CVI for a term of nine months. He fought at the Battle of Fredericksburg on 13 December 1862 with the rest of the company. He was charged with desertion on 20 December 1862 but was probably sick in the hospital. He was again charged with desertion from camp at Falmouth, Virginia on 20 January 1863 and returned to the company and was allowed to make up the duty. He was captured at the Battle of Chancellorsville, Virginia on 3 May 1863, held prisoner at Richmond, and paroled at City Point, Virginia on 14 May 1863. He reported to Camp Parole, Maryland on 16 May 1863, was sent to Washington, D.C. on 20 May 1863 and spent the remainder of his service at Camp Convalescent, Virginia. With the rest of the Chancellorsville paroled prisoners, he rejoined the Regiment at Baltimore on 20 July 1863. Ennis was mustered out with the rest of his regiment at New Haven on 27 July 1863.

He applied for an invalid pension on 17 July 1890 under the act of 27 June 1890. He stated he was a gold and silver plater until he was unable to work due to disability. He was a resident of the National Soldiers' Home at Togus, Kennebec, Maine in 1895. He may have at one time lived at New Bedford, Bristol Co. Massachusetts. In 1907 he was described as five feet six inches tall, light complexion, fair hair, blue eyes. He was

---

536 Deposition, May J. (Elton) Carrington, 7 July 1895, in the pension file of George W. Elton.
537 Affidavit, Dr. Robert B. Goodyear of North Haven, 1 November 1892, in the pension file of George W. Elton.
538 The Hale Collection, Wallingford, 83.

first admitted to the Fitch's Soldier Home[539] at Noroton Heights on 11 November 1886. He had multiple discharges and readmissions. His last admission was on 21 October 1903 and on 2 October 1908 he was transferred to the hospital in Norwich. On 19 June 1909 Andrew F. Ennis, Jr. was appointed his conservator by the Wallingford Probate Court.

James Ennis died at the Norwich State Hospital in Preston on 22 January 22, 1911 age 70 and was buried in Holy Trinity Cemetery, Wallingford. He was born in Ireland on 2 January 1832, son of James Ennis and Elizabeth Connor.

Bridget Ennis of 52 Church Street, Wallingford applied for a widow's pension on 4 February 1911 under the act of 19 April 1908. She was married to the soldier under the name of Bridget O'Neil at Meriden by Rev. Thomas Walsh on 9 October 1864. He was age 27, she was age 21, both born in Ireland and living at Meriden. They had two children living (in 1898): Mary Ennis, age 24: and Margaret Ennis, age 23.

EVANS, LEVERETT E.
Co. A 8th CVI, private, enlisted 25 September 1861, wounded, died 15 November 1862, no pension

Leverett E. Evans, age 21, of Branford enlisted at Hartford on 25 September 1861 and was mustered in on 5 October 1861 as a private in Co. A 8th CVI for a term of three years. He was wounded at Antietam, Maryland on 17 September 1862 and died at Fredericksburg, Maryland on 15 November 1862 from the wounds received at Antietam. He was living at Branford in 1860 with August and Julia Foot, a farm laborer, born in Connecticut.

EVANS, THOMAS H.
Co. B 27th CVI, private, enlisted 30 September 1862, mustered out 27 July 1863, pension #260813 for the soldier

Thomas H. Evans, age 44, of Wallingford enlisted on 30 September 1862 and was mustered in on 3 October 1862 as a private in Co. B 27th CVI for a term of nine months. He fought at the Battle of Fredericksburg on 13 December 1862 with the rest of the company. His comrades stated that he was sick and left behind before the Battle of Chancellorsville. On 11 April 1863 he entered Regimental Hospital with jaundice and was transferred to the hospital at Potomac Creek, a few miles from Fredericksburg, Virginia on 28 April 1863. By his own statement, he was in the hospital while the company fought at Gettysburg. Thomas Evans was mustered out with the rest of his regiment at New Haven on 27 July 1863.

He applied for an invalid pension on 22 November 1879. He was 62 years of age, living at Middletown. At the time of his enlistment he was as described as five feet three inches tall, dark complexion, black hair, dark eyes. He states, "that while in the line of duty, I was exposed to rain and snow, especially on picket duty shortly after the battle of Fredericksburg and contracted rheumatism. I was in the hospital near Fredericksburg, Virginia one month before my discharge. Upon discharge, I was confined to home for several months, unable to work. I never fully recovered and for the last seven years cannot even dress myself and am dependent on the charity of my nine children. I was well before the war, a harness maker, and able to make a comfortable living."[540] His CMSR does not have any record of hospitalizations during the war and his pension file has numerous depositions to support the disability claim. The pension was eventually

---

539 Fitch's Home for Soldiers, Deceased Veterans Discharge Files 1882-1932, box 1, file 90.
540 Sworn statement, Thomas H. Evans of Middletown, 22 November 1879, in his own pension file

granted. Comrades Byron Hill and Charles Paden stated that "shortly after the Battle of Fredericksburg, Evans was taken sick with rheumatism and had to be left behind when camp was broken up when we went to Chancellorsville."[541]

Evans further states that since his discharge he lived at Wallingford until about 1870 and since that time in Middletown.[542] His son James B. Evans, age 46 years in 1883, a carriage maker, lived in Middletown.[543] He states "I lived with him [Thomas Evans] about 6 years before he enlisted. I never knew him to be sick before the war. After he came home he was broken down. He lives with me and is unable to do any work." Another son P. H. Evans, age 47, lived in Middletown in 1883. Son Thomas B. Evans, Jr. was 46 years of age in 1881, also living in Middletown. A daughter, Mrs. Agusta A. Eaton lived at 61 Church Street, Middletown. There is no mention of his wife in the file.

Thomas H. Evans died on 1 September 1888 age 84 years & 5 months and was buried in Center Street Cemetery, Wallingford.[544] There was a Civil War marker at his gravesite in 1934.

FAIRCHILD, DOUGLAS

C. B 27th CVI, private, enlisted 10 September 1862, discharged disability 23 December 1862, pension #705884 for the soldier

Douglas Fairchild, age 35, of Wallingford enlisted on 10 September 1862 and was mustered in on 3 October 1862 as a private in Co. B 27th CVI for a term of nine months. On 1 December 1862 he was sick in the hospital. He was discharged on 23 December 1862 for disability by the U.S. Surgeon at Mt. Pleasant Hospital in Washington, D.C.

His CMSR has a copy of his discharge paper. He was 35 years of age, born at Stratford, described as five feet three inches tall, dark complexion, dark eyes and hair, a shoemaker, diagnosis of heart atrophy existing more or less three years.

He filed for an invalid pension on 23 June 1880. His pension file states he filed a claim on 27 May 1863 but he denies that he did. On 5 November 1881 Fairchild was living at 98 Lee Avenue, Brooklyn, Kings Co., New York. Before the war he was a shoemaker but is no longer able to work. He was claiming disability due to sun stroke for which he was discharged. "Within a day or two after I enlisted, Col. Woodward of my regiment made me his orderly, which position I held until the latter part of October when the regiment left for Washington, D.C. I was not able to sleep and ate little for several days. We stayed in Washington but a few days then went to camp at Chain Bridge or near there. I knew but few men in my company and was not with my own company after I enlisted. On our way to Virginia, a short distance after Long Bridge and going up the hill, I was taken with a violent headache and became unconscious. I awoke in a hospital tent. I was under the care of Dr. Treadway who is now dead. I was not able to go to Fredericksburg and was sent out to Mount Pleasant Hospital where I remained until I was discharged. After discharge I went to New Haven but could not work for several months. About September 1870 I was appointed superintendent of the State Hospital at New Haven. I left there in 1874 and went to Newtown and took charge of Grace Central Hotel as proprietor until December 1877. I moved to Danbury where I took charge of Turner house until April 1880. From 1854 to 1859 I lived at Freemont, Mich. I was a little while at Wallingford where I enlisted."[545]

---

541 Statements, Byron Hill and Charles Paden both of Wallingford, 4 March 1882, in the pension file of Thomas H. Evans.
542 Deposition, Thomas H. Evans of Middletown, 10 January 1884, in his own pension file.
543 Deposition, James B. Evans of Milddletown, 8 August 1883, in the pension file of Thomas H. Evans.
544 The Hale Collection, Wallingford, 18.
545 Deposition, Douglas Fairchild of Brooklyn, N. Y., 5 November 1881, in his own pension file.

There are many statements in his file concerning his health before and after the war. Most respondents stated he was not disabled and able to do a day's work. It appears his application of 1880 was denied. He reapplied on 9 July 1890 under the act of 27 June 1890. He was 63 years of age, living at Woodbury, Queens Co., New York; claiming disability due to a fall on 20 March 1881 at Hoboken, New Jersey. This application was granted.

He was married at 454 Greenwich Street, New York [City] by Rev. G. F. Katell on 22 October 1848 to Lydia Esther Hawley. She was born at Danbury on 17 May 1830, died on 30 March 1889 and was buried in Wooster Cemetery, Danbury. The pension board asked him "Does a record exist of your marriage? No, a Damn cuss at the N. J. Works stole my discharge papers and marriage certificate." They had only one child (living in 1898): Julian Douglas Fairchild, born at Stratford on 17 April 1850.

Douglas Fairchild died on 7 November 1898 and was buried in Wooster Cemetery, Danbury. He was born at Stratford on 17 June 1827, son of George Fairchild & Laura Gray.[546]

FERGUSON, CHARLES M.
Co. F 23rd CVI, corporal, enlisted 10 September 1862, discharged 31 August 1865, pension #843589 for the soldier

Charles M. Ferguson of Derby enlisted on 10 September 1862 and was mustered in on 14 November 1862 as a private in Co. F 23rd CVI for a term of ten months. He was promoted to corporal on 30 December 1862. The regiment served in New Orleans and the Mississippi Delta. Ferguson was discharged with the rest of his regiment at New Haven on 31 August 1863. He was a member of the Elias Howe Post G.A.R.

He applied for an invalid pension on 20 April 1892 under the act of 27 June 1890. He was living at Derby in 1862, Woodbridge in 1865 and Bridgeport in 1890.[547] He was admitted to the Fitch's Soldier Home[548] at Noroton Heights on 8 October 1897. The value of his possessions was out of the ordinary and included letters from the patent commission, a promissory note for $500, change in gold and bills worth $364 and a trunk.

He was married at North Branford by Rev. Asa C. Pierce of the Northford Congregational Church on 15 June 1865 to Juliette S., widow of the soldier Benjamin R. Dowd.[549] Ferguson and Juliette were divorced at New Haven on 11 December 1869.

Charles Munro Ferguson died at the Fitch's Soldier Home on 12 February 1906 age 69 and was buried there in Spring Grove Cemetery. He was the son of Erastus and Lydia Ferguson. The administrator of his estate was Charles Eugene Ferguson of Northford, his son by Juliette Gidney Dowd. The soldier left no widow or children under the age of sixteen.

FIELD, DANIEL W. or FIELDS
Co. B 27th CVI, 1st lieutenant, enlisted 25 August 1862, resigned, discharged 25 March 1863, pension #932797 for the soldier and later for his widow Kate R. Humphreys

Daniel W. Field, age 28, of Wallingford enlisted at New Haven on 25 August 1862 and was mustered in on 3 October 1862 as 1st lieutenant of Co. B 27th CVI for a term of nine months. "I recruited 42 men into the

546 Gilmore, Jean Fairchild, *Early Fairchilds in America and Their Descendants* (Baltimore: Gateway Press, Inc., 1991), 276.
547 The pension file has little personal information as to residence, birth, or parents. The 1900 census states he was born in Massachusetts to parents born in Connecticut.
548 Fitch's Home for Soldiers, Deceased Veterans Discharge Files 1882-1932, box 6, file 1562.
549 See entry under Benjamin R. Dowd. Ferguson's pension file is with Benjamin Dowd's.

27th."[550] In November and December 1862 he was present but sick. "Lieut. Field was not in the fight [at Fredericksburg], I believe he has got the dyspepsia."[551] On 11 March 1863 at the camp of the 27th Regiment near Falmouth, Virginia he tendered his resignation stating that he had no previous military experience and is wholly incompetent to fulfill the position he now occupies. He was honorably discharged on 25 March 1863 by Major General Couch, order No. 70.

He applied for an invalid pension on 19 September 1891 under the act of 27 June 1890, citing inability to work due to kidney disease. "On or about 12 December 1862 while on Picket duty at Fredericksburg, Virginia caught cold and had an attack of Jaundice, then Brights disease." He was described as six foot four inches tall, fair complexion, brown hair (now gray), blue eyes. After his discharge he lived at Wallingford; Anaheim, California about 1870; Los Angeles about 1872, and Hollywood, California about 1891 until 1908. Field was a member of the Stanton Post G.A.R. in Los Angeles.

He was married first at Wallingford by Rev. R. J. Adams on 13 December 1861 to Jennie A. Hall, age 24, daughter of Almer Hall of Wallingford. He was living at Durham, born at Madison. Neither were previously married or divorced. She died at Wallingford on 22 April 1873 and was buried there in Center Street Cemetery. After her death he moved to Southern California with his children. He had two children (living in 1898): Mrs. Annie S. Crickmore, born on 10 July 1863; and Benjamin F. Field, born on 24 November 1868. In 1923 Benjamin was living at Ocean Park, California. Other children were Fred and Almer, presumed to have died before 1898.

There is a copy of his death certificate in the pension file. He died at Los Angeles, California on 26 June 1910. There is a gravestone with his name at Center Street Cemetery, Wallingford but no dates. Daniel Webster Field was born at North Madison on 23 November 1833, son of Frederic Seymour Field and Dency Blatchley, both born in Connecticut. He lived in Los Angeles for two years and six months; and in California for forty years.

His widow, now Kate R. Humphreys of Los Angeles, California applied for a pension on 31 October 1922 under the act of 1 May 1920 after the death of her third husband. She was 56 years of age, born on 26 November 1865. She was married to the soldier as Kate Reed Elliott at Bakersfield, California by Rev. Edgar R. Fuller on 7 May 1902. She was previously married at Covington, Kentucky on 9 February 1884 to Frank L. Elliott. They were divorced at Cincinnati, Ohio on 19 October 1895. There is a copy of the divorce decree in the file. After the death of Daniel W. Field, she was married at Venice, California by Rev. Will A. Knighten on 5 March 1914 to John Ford Humphreys who never served in the military. Humphreys was married first on 21 February 1859 to Fannie C. Mathews who died on 18 May 1897. Humphreys was married second to Lyda R. B. Fritchey and divorced on 7 June 1913. Said Lyda Gritchey Humphreys died before 1922. There are statements in the file from Kate Humphrey's elder brothers Charles A. L. Reed of Cincinnati, Ohio and John G. Reed of Elmwood, Ohio.

There is a copy of the death certificate of John F. Humphreys in the file. He was born on 27 August 1839 in Missouri, son of Richard Humphreys, born in Maryland. John F. Humphreys died at Los Angeles, California on 12 August 1922.

Kate R. Humphreys was living at Los Angeles in 1930.

550 Deposition, Daniel W. Fields of Los Angeles, Cal., 4 March 1910, in the pension file of Alonzo F. Hubbell.
551 Letter, [George C. Baldwin] to home 15 December 1862; dyspepsia= indigestion, ulcer.

FIELD, GEORGE C.
see Barney Jennings

FISHER, ALBERT
Co. L 2nd HA, enlisted 8 February 1864, deserted 8 March 1864

Albert Fisher of Branford enlisted on 8 February 1864 as a private in Co. L 2nd HA and deserted on 8 March 1864. He does not appear in the 1860 or 1870 census at Branford or North Branford.

FLYNN, JOHN
Co. D 11th CVI, private, substitute, mustered in 26 November 1864, deserted, no pension

John Flynn, age 42, served as a substitute for Henry B. Lanphier of Branford. He was mustered in at New Haven on 26 November 1864 as a private in Co. D 11th CVI for a term of three years and deserted on 24 March 1865. He was described as five feet eight inches tall, blue eyes, black hair, ruddy complexion, unmarried, born in Ireland, occupation porter.[552] He does not appear in the 1860 or 1870 census at Branford or North Branford.

FOOTE, DELIZON B. or DENIZON
**Co. A 15th CVI, private, enlisted 18 July 1862, to 2nd Battalion VRC, discharged 19 July 1865,
pension #C2512260 for the soldier**

Delizon B. Foote, age 21, of Meriden enlisted at New Haven on 18 July 1862 and was mustered in on 25 August 1862 as a private in Co. A 15th CVI for a term of three years. He was sick in general hospital March through August 1863. He was transferred on 1 August 1863 to the 28th Company 2nd Battery Veteran Invalid Reserve Corps and served as a nurse. Delizon Foote was discharged at Portsmouth, Virginia on 19 July 1865.[553]

He applied for an invalid pension on 3 June 1904 which was rejected on 6 February 1907. He reapplied and received his pension on 22 May 1912. He claims he was discharged for disability. At the time of his enlistment he was described as five feet three inches tall, light complexion, blue eyes, brown hair, occupation factory employee. After his discharge he lived at Seymour for four years and since then at Meriden. He was married to Margaretta who died on 5 July 1892 age 41 and was buried in Walnut Grove Cemetery, Meriden.[554] He had no children living in 1904.

Delizon Brownwell Foote died at Meriden on 28 December 1913 and was buried there in Walnut Grove Cemetery. He was born at Yalesville, Wallingford on 13 May 1842, son of Luzerne Foote and Grace Fowler of Northford.

---

552 Muster & Payroll, List of Substitutes, RG 13, box 100, 2nd Congressional District, Connecticut State Library.
553 Discharge place from *Record of Service of Connecticut Men*; his CMSR says he was mustered out at New Bern, North Carolina on 27 June 1865 with the rest of the 15th CVI.
554 The Hale Collection, Meriden, 62.

FOOTE, FREDERICK
Co. B & C 14th Illinois Cavalry, drafted 8 February 1864, private, no pension

Frederick Foote, age 22, of LaSalle, Illinois was drafted on 8 February 1864 as a private in Co. C 14th Illinois Cavalry. "He was teaching school in Illinois when he joined and was promoted to 1st lieutenant of the cavalry."[555] With his regiment he saw action in Georgia and Tennessee including the Battle of Nashville in November 1864. He was transferred to Co. B and mustered out with the rest of his regiment at Nashville on 31 July 1865. He was the brother of Isaac Foote.

Frederick Foote died at North Branford on 22 February 1873,[556] probably unmarried. His name appears on the Northford Veterans' Monument. He was born at Northford on 24 April 1841, son of Frederick Foote and Sibyl Celestia Tuttle.[557]

FOOTE, ISAAC
Co. K 15th CVI, private, enlisted 12 August 1862, discharged disability 28 February 1863, pension #519118 for the soldier and later for his widow Mary

Isaac Foote, age 18, of North Branford enlisted at New Haven on 12 August 1862 and was mustered in on 25 August 1862 as a private in Co. K 15th CVI for a term of three years. He was admitted to the hospital at Fairfax Seminary, Virginia on 1 December 1862 and discharged for disability from Camp Convalescent, Virginia on 28 February 1863. He was the brother of Frederick Foote.

He applied for an invalid pension on 14 February 1879. At the time of his enlistment he was described as five feet eight inches tall, fair complexion, blue eyes, brown hair, occupation farmer. He suffered from a hernia caused by drilling and marching while in Camp Casey near Arlington, Virginia which was the cause of his discharge. "In late November or December 1862 I had malarial fever or chills and a hernia from severe drilling and marching below Arlington Heights, Virginia. When my command left for Fredericksburg I was left behind and taken to the Hospital on Bedloes Island & from there forwarded to Camp Convalescent, a camp of distribution at that time."

Isaac Foote died at Middletown, Ohio on 6 March 1896 and was buried there in Woodside Cemetery. He was born at North Branford on 17 October 1844, son of Frederick Foote and Sibyl Celestia Tuttle.[558] His name appears on the Northford Veterans' Monument.

Mary C. Foote of Middletown, Butler Co., Ohio applied for a widow's pension on 2 June 1896. She was infirmed requiring nursing care. She was married to the soldier under the name of Mary C. Neal at Eaton, Preble Co., Ohio by Rev. Charles W. Swain on 19 March 1867. Neither were previously married or divorced. In 1897 there were no children under the age of sixteen. She had a daughter Edith Foote who occupied part of her house. Mary C. Foote was born at Eaton, Ohio on 34 November 1844.[559] Her last pension payment was on 4 March 1905.

555 Foote, Abram W., *Foote Family Comprising the Genealogy and History of Nathaniel Foote of Wethersfield, Conn. and His Descendants* (Rutland, Vermont: The Tuttle Company, 1907), I:190. There is no indication in other records that he enlisted or was a lieutenant.
556 North Branfod Vital Records, I:126.
557 North Branford Vital Records, I:44.
558 North Branford Vital Records, 44B.
559 Foote, *Foote Family*, I:325.

Members of the First Connecticut Heavy Artillery manned the mortar guns at federal forts.
(Library of Congress, Prints & Photographs Division, LC-B815-377)

FOOTE, LOZELLE

Co. F 1st HA, private, enlisted 20 February 1862, discharged 2 March 1865, pension #596785 for the soldier and later for his widow Jennie

Lozelle Foote of New Haven enlisted at New Haven on 20 February 1862 and was mustered in on 3 March 1862 as a private in Co. F 1st HA for a term of three years. With his regiment he fought at Chickahominy and Malvern Hill, Virginia. Lozelle Foote was discharged at Battery Pruyn, Virginia on 2 March 1865 when his term expired. He was the brother of Philo B. Foote.

He applied for an invalid pension on 17 September 1890 under the act of 27 June 1890. At the time of his enlistment he was described as five feet nine inches tall, dark hair, light complexion, occupation oysterman. Since 1868 he lived at New Haven and was a member of the Admiral Foote Post No. 17 G.A.R.

He was married first at East Haven on 15 April 1867 to Isadore F. Russell. They were divorced on 20 October 1875 and he was given custody of their minor child Hattie C. Foote. He was married second at New Haven by Rev. Nathan Hubbell on 20 February 1876 to Jennie Elizabeth Johnson. He was age 38, born at Northford; she was age 24, born at Branford; both were living at New Haven. She was not previously married or divorced. He had two children living in 1903: Hattie C., born on 13 November 1868; and Frank L., born on 2 November 1876.

Lozelle Foote died at New Haven on 13 April 1905 and was buried there in Evergreen Cemetery. His name appears on the Northford Veterans' Monument. He was born at Northford on 13 February 1838, son of Warham Williams Foote and Lucinda Harrison.[560] A copy of his will dated 13 November 1904 is in the file. His wife Jennie E. Foote had life use of the house in New Haven and after her death it was bequeathed equally to his son Frank L. Foote and daughter Hattie C. Underhill.

Jennie E. Foote of New Haven applied for a widow's pension on 20 April 1905. She died on 14 July 1908 and was buried in Evergreen Cemetery, New Haven.[561] She was born at Branford on 5 May 1852, daughter of Sidney H. Johnson and Sarah Jane Shepard.

---

560 Foote, *Foote Family*, I:300.
561 The Hale Collection, New Haven, 920.

FOOTE, LYMAN H.
see Thomas Clark

FOOTE, PHILO B.
Co. K 15th CVI, private, enlisted 12 August 1862, died 10 December 1862, no pension

Philo B. Foote, age 19, of North Branford enlisted at New Haven on 12 August 1862 and was mustered in on 25 August 1862 as a private in Co. K 15th CVI for a term of three years. At the time of his enlistment he was described as five feet eight inches tall, fair complexion, brown eyes, brown hair, occupation farmer. Philo Foote died in the hospital at Fairfax Seminary, Virginia on 10 December 1862 of typhoid fever. His body "was removed home by his brother" and was buried in Northford Cemetery. A Civil War marker was on his gravesite in 1934 and his name appears on the Northford Veterans' Monument. Philo Beecher Foote was born at Northford on 16 January 1843, son of Warham Williams Foote and Lucinda Harrison.[562] He was the brother of Lozelle Foote.

FORBES, EDGAR L.
Co. E 1st HA, private, enlisted 23 May 1861, discharged 22 May 1864, Co. K 6th U.S. Veteran Corps, private, enlisted 20 April 1865, discharged 9 April 1866, pension #459882 for the soldier

Edgar L. Forbes of Branford was mustered in at Hartford on 23 May 1861 as a private in Co. E 4th CVI which became the 1st HA. With his regiment he fought at Chickahominy and Malvern Hill, Virginia. He was discharged from camp in Virginia on 22 May 1864 when his term expired. He reenlisted in New York as a private in Co. K 6th U.S. Veteran Hancock Corps on 20 April 1865. Edgar Forbes was discharged at Washington, D.C. as a corporal on 9 April 1866. He was the son of Levi Forbes.

He applied for an invalid pension on 30 June 1880. At the time of his enlistment he was described as five feet eleven inches tall, fair complexion, grey eyes, brown hair, occupation farmer and sailor. "In June 1861 we were on a forced march from Hagerstown, Maryland to Williamsport on Double Quick [time] with Knapsacks and 80 pounds of ammunition when I contracted varicous [sic] veins. We lay around in the Scorching Sun all day and returned to Camp again in the evening. We were then in the 4th Conn. inft. and afterwards transferred to 1st Conn. Heavy Arty." "I tented with him [Edgar Forbes] and on 20 June 1862 at Chickahominy River, Va. he had been on picket duty the night before and he lay in the Shelter tent sick all day. When the roll was called he was told he must fall in. He fell in line and then fell to the ground and was carried to the Surgeons Quarters and an ambulance sent him to Cold Harbor Hospital where he was taken Prisoner of War. I saw him again at Harrisons Landing after He got back to [the] Company. The next fall at Fort Scott he was detailed to take care of his Horse in deference to His previous suffering."[563] "We were

---

562 Foote, *Foote Family*, I:300.
563 Affidavit, George Phelps of Woodbury, in the pension file of Edgar L. Forbes. The hospital was abandoned by the Union army during the Battle of Cold Harbor on 27 June 1862 and the patients were captured. They were paroled at Haxall's Landing, Virginia on 25 July 1862.

A heavy artillery company at the Battle of Chancellorsville. (Photographic History of the Civil War, I:59)

A photograph taken about 1925 in front of the store at Short Beach, Branford shows in the back row (left to right) Ira B. Smith and Henry E. Johnson. In the front row are Albert P. Woodworth, Edgar L. Forbes, and Watson W. Stone. (Branford Historical Society photograph collection)

both sick in Cold Harbor Hospital and taken prisoner while in the Hospital on the 27 of June 1862 and were taken to Libby Prison in Richmond, Va. and were paroled July 25, 1862. From there we were sent back to Newport News under a flag of truce where we staid for some time in the hospital and from there to Harrison Landing where we joined our Regiment. When we were to be discharged [from 1st HA] we marched to Bermuda Hundred and about ten of us walked together, he [Forbes] could hardly walk."[564] There are many depositions in the file concerning his alleged disability.

He was born at Branford or Madison, he was not sure which,[565] on 5 September 1843. Since his discharge he lived at Bristol in 1866, then Branford since 1866 and winters at Seffner, Hillsboro Co., Florida since 1898.

He was married at Forestville by Rev. E. Marriner on 12 May 1866 to Esther Miner Cramer. Neither were previously married or divorced. They were long separated but not divorced and he provided some of her support. No further record was found of Esther Forbes and she did not apply for a widow's pension. He had the following children (living in 1915): Sarah Elizabeth, born at Branford on 21 February 1867; and Cora Lelia and Nora Delia twins, born at Branford on 24 January 1868. In 1922 one of his daughters was living at Philadelphia. He was a member of the Mason Rogers Post G.A.R. No. 7 of Branford and a charter member of Branford Battery A.

Edgar Levi Forbes died at Branford on 30 August 1926 and was buried there in Center Cemetery. His company and regiment are engraved on his stone. He was the son of Levi Forbes and Elizabeth Munder.

FORBES, LEVI
Co. B 12th CVI, sergeant, enlisted 1 November 1861, wounded 27 October 1862, discharged disability 27 March 1863, died 25 January 1866, pension #184081 for his widow Jane E. Forbes later Jane E. Cadwell

Levi Forbes, age 40, of Branford enlisted at New Haven on 1 November 1861 and was mustered in on 20 November 1861 as a sergeant in Co. B 12th CVI for a term of three years. He was wounded at Georgia Landing, Louisiana on 27 October 1862 and discharged for disability on 27 March 1863. Levi Forbes died on 25 January 1866. He was the father of Edgar L. Forbes.

He applied for an invalid pension on 6 June 1863. He was wounded in the left shoulder by a shell fired by the enemy during the battle of Labadieville, Louisiana 27 October 1862 and sent to the Hospital at Carlton, Louisiana until about the 1st of February 1863. As a consequence of the wound, he has been unable to do any manual labor. "After his discharge he was very much broken down in health suffering from bronchial afflictions and asthma and wholly unable to do any labor. He moved to Bristol in April 1864 for the purpose of trying to regain his health."[566] "After he was wounded he was taken down with a Severe cold that night and never recovered from its affect. The wound destroyed the use of his arm."[567] He died before receiving his pension.

564 Deposition, Henry Gardner of Piconniny Bay, Michigan, 27 October 1897, in the pension file of Edgar L. Forbes.
565 His place of birth on his death certificate is Madison, there is no record of his birth in Branford.
566 Affidavit, Samuel O. Plant and Sarah C. Shepard of Branford, 4 June 1869, in the pension file of Levi Forbes.
567 Affidavit, Samuel H. Granniss of New Haven, late Capt. Co. B 12th CVI, 21 May 1869, in the pension file of Levi Forbes.

He was married first to Elizabeth Munger who died at Branford on 19 November 1856 and was buried there in Center Cemetery.[568] He was married second at Branford by Rev. Timothy P. Gillett of the First Congregational Church on 11 July 1857 to Jane Elizabeth Coe.

Levi Forbes died at Bristol on 25 January 1866. A gravestone in Center Cemetery, Branford states he was buried in Forestville. His company and regiment are engraved on his stone and a G.A.R. marker was on his Branford gravesite in 1934. He was born at East Haven on 22 March 1821, son of Levi Forbes and Mary Redfield.[569]

Jane E. Forbes, age 28, of Bristol applied for a widow's pension on 3 June 1869. She had one child under the age of sixteen: Charles M. L. Forbes, born at Branford on 16 April 1858. She was married second at Southington by Rev. E. C. Jones on 14 January 1871 to Lucius C. Cadwell. He was age 25, born at Bristol, living at Plainville; she was age 28, born at Clinton, living at Forestville. Her pension was terminated upon her remarriage.

She reapplied for a pension on 23 June 1902, residing at Forestville, Hartford Co. after her divorce from Cadwell at Hartford on 13 June 1902. There is no record in the file of her pension payments or death. She was perhaps the Jane Cadwell living at Southington in 1910.

FORD, GEORGE
1st LA, private, enlisted 1 December 1864, mustered out 11 June 1865, no pension

George Ford[570] of North Branford enlisted and was mustered in on 1 December 1864 as a private in the 1st LA. With his regiment he saw action during the Siege of Richmond. He was mustered out with the rest of his regiment at Manchester, near Richmond, Virginia on 11 June 1865. He did not apply for a pension since his total service was less than nine months. After his discharge he lived at North Branford.

George Lewis Ford was married to Lois Rossiter Dudley. She was born at Guilford on 27 October 1839, daughter of Luther Frederic Dudley and Eliza A. Buck.[571] She died in 1924 and was buried in Bare Plain Cemetery, North Branford.[572] He died in 1919 and was buried in Bare Plain Cemetery. He was born at North Branford on 28 April 1839, son of William Ford and Sarah Rose.[573] He represented North Branford in the Connecticut General Assembly in 1893.

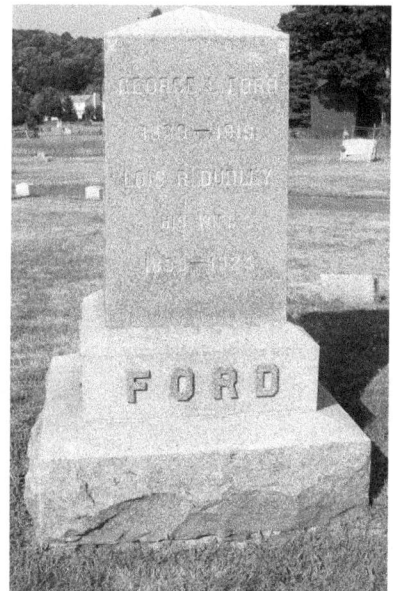

FORD, WILLIAM D.
see John Lamb

---

568 Branford Vital Records, 1852-1863, 5.
569 East Haven Vital Records, Town Meeting Book 3:170.
570 For his biography see Rockey, *History of New Haven County*, II:99.
571 Talcott, *Families of Guilford*, 359.
572 The Hale Collection, North Branford, 9.
573 North Branford Vital Records I:43.

FORRESTER, JULIUS F.
Co. C 10th CVI, private, substitute, mustered in 5 November 1864, mustered out 25 August 1865, no pension

Julius F. Forrester, age 24, served as a substitute for Ralph Blackstone of Branford. He was mustered in at New Haven on 5 November 1864 as a private in Co. C 10th CVI for a term of three years. He was described as five feet six inches tall, hazel eyes, brown hair, fair complexion, unmarried, born in Germany, occupation cigar maker. Forrester was mustered out with the rest of his regiment at Richmond, Virginia on 25 August 1865 and discharged at Hartford on 5 September 1865. He does not appear in the 1860 census at Branford.

FOSTER, ANDREW alias ANDREW FITZPATRICK
Co. G 82nd New York Infantry, enlisted 20 May 1861, Co. B 27th CVI, private, enlisted 16 October 1862, prisoner, mustered out 27 July 1863, pension #860545 for the soldier

Andrew Foster, age 28, enlisted at New Haven on 16 October 1862 and was mustered in on 18 October 1862 as a private in Co. B 27th CVI for a term of nine months. Shortly after arrival at Camp Seward on Arlington Heights, he was sent to the General Hospital in Washington, D.C. on 27 October 1862. He was sick in the hospital November and December 1862 but reported as deserted. He was probably in the hospital when the company fought at Fredericksburg and was still sick in the hospital in January 1863. He was captured at the Battle of Chancellorsville, Virginia on 3 May 1863, held prisoner at Richmond, and paroled at City Point, Virginia on 14 May 1863. He reported to Camp Parole, Maryland on 16 May 1863, was sent to Washington, D.C. on 20 May 1863 and spent the remainder of his service at Camp Convalescent, Virginia. With the rest of the Chancellorsville paroled prisoners, he rejoined the Regiment at Baltimore on 20 July 1863. Foster was mustered out at New Haven with the rest of the company on 27 July 1863.

His real name was Andrew Fitzpatrick or Andrew Foster Fitzpatrick. He had originally served in the 2nd Regiment New York militia under Captain Barry, which later became Co. G of the 82nd New York Infantry. The militia went to the first Battle of Bull Run. "I had enlisted about a month before that battle and the whole squad was sworn in by President Lincoln. We were never discharged from the service, we just went home."

Though a resident of New York City, he came to Connecticut and enlisted at New Haven in Co. B 27th CVI under the name of Andrew Foster. When he first applied for a pension, he failed to report his first enlistment, the reason of which he does not state. The examiner questioned whether he had deserted from the New York militia. The pension board states his enlistment in the militia was on 20 May 1861 and he deserted in August 1861.

He applied for an invalid pension on 19 February 1892 under the act of 27 June 1890. He was living at Brooklyn, Kings Co., New York. His occupation was as an umbrella frame maker.[574] In 1912 he was living at Ridgefield Park, Bergen Co., New Jersey for the last eighteen months. He was described as five feet seven inches tall, dark complexion, black eyes and hair. He was born at New York City on 14 July 1835 and had lived in New York since his birth; New York City until 1881, then Brooklyn, New York.[575] He was married at New York City by Rev. Dr. Hall on 1 August 1859 to Hannah E. Henderson. They had four children living (in 1898): Albert, born on 20 November 1870, Hannah, born on 4 April 1872, Caroline, born on 17 September

574 Deposition, Andrew Fitzpatrick of Brooklyn, N.Y., 27 September 1906, in his own pension file.
575 Pension application, Andrew Fitzpatrick, 4 June 1912, in his own pension file.

1874, and Gertrude, born on 17 December 1876. In 1912 his son Albert Fitzpatrick was living at Brooklyn, New York.

Andrew Fitzpatrick also known as Andrew Foster died on 4 December 1912.

FOWLER, DEGRASSE, JR.
Co. E 5th CVI, 2nd lieutenant, enlisted 22 June 1861, resigned 23 September 1861, died 8 March 1868, no pension

DeGrasse Fowler, Jr. of Seymour enlisted and was mustered in at Hartford on 22 June 1861 as a 2nd lieutenant in Co. E 5th CVI and resigned on 23 September 1861. He is on the draft list of 1863 for North Branford. He died on 8 March 1868 age 28 and was buried in Northford Cemetery, North Branford.[576] A Civil War marker was on his gravesite in 1934 and his name appears on the Northford Veterans' Monument. He was the brother-in-law of Ambrose L. Dayton.

DeGrasse Fowler, Jr. was the son of DeGrasse Fowler and Sophronia Austin. He was married to Grace Amorette Dayton, daughter of Jonathan Hezekiah Dayton & Polly Eliza Todd. She died on 30 March 1876 age 39 and was buried in Northford Cemetery.[577] They had one daughter Grace Helena born at North Branford on 13 March 1859.[578]

FOWLER, SAMUEL O.
Co. I 15th CVI, private, enlisted 12 August 1862, prisoner, mustered out 27 June 1865, pension #868596 for the soldier

Samuel O. Fowler, age 40, of Branford enlisted at New Haven on 12 August 1862 and was mustered in on 25 August 1862 as a private in Co. I 15th CVI for a term of three years. He saw action at the Battle of Fredericksburg, Virginia on 13 December 1862, during the Siege of Suffolk, Virginia in April 1863, and in the Peninsula Campaign of July 1863. He was captured with much of his regiment at the Battle of Kinston, North Carolina on 8 March 1865, confined at Libby Prison, Richmond on 23 March, and paroled at Boulware's & Cox's wharf on 26 March 1865. He reported to Camp Parole, Maryland on 30 March 1865, received a thirty day furlough and afterwards reported to Camp Convalescent, Virginia. Samuel Fowler was mustered out with the rest of his regiment at New Bern, North Carolina on 27 June 1865 and discharged at New Haven on 12 July 1865.

---

576 St. Andrews Episcopal Church Records, Northford, 3:118.
577 St. Andrews Church, 3:120.
578 St. Andrews Church, 3:31.

He applied for an invalid pension on 24 February 1891 under the act of 27 June 1890. At the time of his enlistment he was described as five feet seven inches tall, fair complexion, brown hair, gray eyes, occupation farmer. He contracted malarial fever while in the army in 1863 and deafness from shells flying over his head. He always lived at Branford and was unmarried. He was a member of the Mason Rogers Post No. 7 G.A.R.

Samuel Ozias Fowler died at Branford on 12 December 1906 and was buried there in Damascus Cemetery.[579] There was a G.A.R. marker on his gravesite in 1934. He was born at Branford on 31 August 1822,[580] son of Ozias Fowler and Esther Savage.

FOWLER, WALTER E.
Co. B 27th CVI, private, enlisted 9 September 1862, prisoner, mustered out 27 July 1863, pension #516002 for the soldier and later for his widow Jane

Walter E. Fowler, age 22, of Guilford enlisted on 9 September 1862 and was mustered in on 3 October 1862 as a private in Co. B 27th CVI for a term of nine months. He fought at the Battle of Fredericksburg on 13 December 1862 with the rest of the company. He was captured at the Battle of Chancellorsville, Virginia on 3 May 1863, held prisoner at Richmond, and paroled at City Point, Virginia on 14 May 1863. He reported to Camp Parole, Maryland on 16 May 1863, was sent to Washington, D.C. on 20 May 1863 and spent the remainder of his service at Camp Convalescent, Virginia. With the rest of the Chancellorsville paroled prisoners, he rejoined the Regiment at Baltimore on 20 July 1863. Walter Fowler was mustered out with the rest of his regiment 27 July 1863 at New Haven. He was the tent mate of George S. Rogers who named a son for him.

He applied for an invalid pension on 18 January 1892 under the act of 27 June 1890. It was granted due to disability not related to his service. After the war he lived at Branford. He was a charter member and second commander of the Mason Rogers Post No. 7 G.A.R. of Branford.

Walter E. Fowler died at Branford on 28 April 1901 and was buried there in Center Cemetery. A G.A.R. marker was on his gravesite in 1934 and 2011. A copy of his death certificate is in the file. He was born at Guilford on 26 October 1840, son of Harry Fowler and Caroline Williams, born at Guilford and Wallingford. His occupation was assistant judge of probate. A copy of his will is also in the file, his wife Jane was the sole heir. They had no children.

Jane E. Fowler filed for a widow's pension after his death. The application was initially denied due to the total value of the property she owned and a life insurance policy she received after the soldier's death. She reapplied under the act of 8 September 1916 and this ap-

Walter E. Fowler was the second commander of the Mason Rogers Post No. 7 G.A.R. of Branford.

---

579 Branford Vital Records, death, 1906.
580 Branford Vital Records, 1786-1840, 432.

plication was granted. She was married to the soldier under the name of Jane Elizabeth Palmer at Branford by Rev. David D. Bishop of the Trinity Episcopal Church on 26 December 1867. Neither were previously married or divorced.

Jane E. Fowler died at Branford on 20 June 1923 and was buried there in Center Cemetery. She was born at Branford on 29 September 1839, daughter of Isaac Hobart Palmer and Nancy Jane Carter.

FOWLER, WILLIAM N.
Co. G 29th CVI, private, enlisted 29 December 1863, died 14 October 1864, pension #86424 for his widow Amelia and minor son Silas C. Fowler

William N. Fowler of Branford enlisted at New Haven on 29 December 1863 and was mustered in at Fair Haven on 8 March 1864 as a private in Co. G 29th CVI for a term of three years. At the time of his enlistment he was described as age 18, five feet eight inches tall, dark complexion, brown eyes, black hair, born at Sag Harbor, New York; occupation farmer. His service was credited to Branford. A copy of his enlistment paper is in the pension file and he signed with his mark. While training at U.S. Rendezvous at Grapevine Point, Fair Haven he was admitted to Knight Hospital, New Haven on 23 January 1864 for a mild case of measles and released back to duty on 4 February 1864. He was present at muster roll through September 1864. He died at Camp Hospital, Bermuda Hundred, Virginia on 14 October 1864[581] from chronic diarrhea and left no personal belongings. He was buried at Jones Landing, Virginia. William N. Fowler does not appear in the 1860 census for Branford but is on the 1863 draft list for that town. His name appears on the Wall of Honor at Washington, D.C.

Amelia A. Fowler, age 16, of East Hampton, Suffolk Co., New York applied for a widow's pension on 21 February 1865. She was married under the name of Amelia A. Joseph to the soldier at East Hampton, New York by Henry B. Tuthill, JP on 24 December 1863. They had one child: Silas C., age 7 months, residing with her in East Hampton. On 29 October 1866 she was now Amelia A. Qenaw? and the court at Suffolk County, New York appointed Samuel N. Gardner, age 26, of East Hampton as guardian of Silas C. Fowler, born on 28 June 1864, and living in Suffolk County. She was married second at the home of Edward Disbury at East Hampton, New York by Henry B. Tuthill, JP on 1 October 1866 to Israel X. Qenaw? Her pension terminated upon her remarriage but continued for Silas until the age of sixteen.

---

581 His file gives the death date as both 13 and 14 October 1864.

FRANCISCO, CLIFFORD A.

Co. I 15th CVI, private, enlisted 13 August 1862, to 159th 2nd Battery VRC, died 25 April 1865, no pension

Clifford A. Francisco, age 22, of Branford enlisted at New Haven on 13 August 1862 and was mustered in on 25 August 1862 as a private in Co. I 15th CVI for a term of three years. "Clif Francisco from the 15th is here. Stayed in our tent last night - is very well."[582] He was present during muster roll March through June 1863. In July and August 1863 he was sick in quarters, was back on duty in September and October, and sick in general hospital November 1863 through April 1864 for bronchitis. He was transferred to the 159th Co. 2nd Battery VRC on 11 April 1864. He died at Branford on 25 April 1865 from disease.[583] He was the brother-in-law of George H. Rowland.

At the time of his enlistment he was described as fair complexion, blue eyes, brown hair, occupation farmer. He was listed as a "fallen hero" by the Mason Rogers Post No. 7 G.A.R. of Branford and his gravesite in Center Cemetery was decorated by the G.A.R. A Civil War marker was on his gravesite in 1934. He does not appear in the 1860 census at Branford but is on the 1863 draft list for that town. His death is recorded in Branford as 24 April 1865, age 24, born at Newark, New Jersey; a soldier, from disease, marital status not given.[584] He was living in 1850 at Newark, New Jersey and 1860 at Easton, Fairfield Co. with his father Thomas Francisco.

FRAZIER, JOHN

Co. A 13th CVI, private, enlisted 28 March 1864, to 13th Battery, mustered out 25 April 1866

John Frazier of Branford enlisted on 28 March 1864 as a private in Co. A 13th CVI and was transferred to the 13th Battery on 29 December 1864. He was mustered out at Fort Pulaski, Georgia on 25 April 1866. He does not appear in the 1860 census at Branford.

FREEMAN, WILBUR

Co. I 21st CVI, private, enlisted 20 August 1862, mustered out 16 June 1865, pension #909882 for the soldier

Wilbur Freeman of Haddam enlisted on 20 August 1862 and was mustered in at Norwich on 5 September 1862 as a private in Co. I 21st CVI for a term of three years. He was in the Battles of Cold Harbor, Fredericksburg and Drewry's Bluff, Virginia. His regiment entered Richmond with the victorious army with

---

582 Letter, Samuel Beach to home, 19 November 1862.
583 There is no discharge certificate in his CMSR.
584 Branford Vital Records, 1863-1895, 205; his CMSR states he was born at Elizabeth, New Jersey. His marital status on the 1863 draft list is listed as single.

General Grant when the confederate capitol was evacuated by General Lee.[585] Freeman was mustered out at Richmond, Virginia on 16 June 1865 and discharged at Norwich on 6 July 1865.

He applied for an invalid pension on 20 February 1896. He was described as five feet six inches tall, light complexion, black hair, blue eyes. He suffered from the effects of rheumatism and scurvy contracted during the war. He was married at Haddam by Rev. Rutherford on 20 March 1860 to Harriet A. Bushnell. They were divorced and she died by 1896. They had no children. There are very few documents in the pension file.

He was living at Westbrook in 1870 with his wife Harriet. He first appears at Branford in 1880, living in the Laura Blackstone Hobart household and boarded with her the rest of his life.[586]

Wilbur Freeman died at Branford on 20 April 1904 age 67 and was buried there in Center Cemetery.[587] His company and regiment are engraved on his stone and there was a G.A.R. marker was on his gravesite in 1934. In 2011 his gravesite had a Spanish American War marker. He was born at Higganum, son of Lyman Freeman.

FRISBIE, ALONZO P.
Co. K 15th CVI, private, enlisted 9 August 1862, mustered out 27 June 1865, pension application #400276 for the soldier and later filed by his widow Amelia

Alonzo P. Frisbie, age 40, of Wallingford enlisted at New Haven on 9 August 1862 and was mustered in on 25 August 1862 as a private in Co. K 15th CVI for a term of three years. He saw action at Fredericksburg, Virginia on 13 December 1862 and in the Peninsula Campaign of 1863. He was sick in his quarters during March and April 1863 and in general hospital from 30 April until 31 October 1864. He was on picket duty during the Battle of Kinston, North Carolina. His "Soldierly conduct was good." Alonzo Frisbie was mustered out with the rest of his regiment at New Bern, North Carolina on 27 June 1865 and discharged at New Haven on 12 July 1865. He was the father of Russell L. Frisbie of the same company and served under Capt. Medad D. Munson of Wallingford.

He applied for an invalid pension on 31 December 1886 but died shortly afterwards before receiving his pension. He claimed lung disease and injury to his legs during his service and was treated at Regimental Hospital. At the time of his enlistment he was described as five feet seven inches tall, light complexion, grey eyes, light hair, occupation tailor. He was married first at Branford by Rev. Frederick Miller of Trinity Episcopal Church on 25 December 1844 to Henrietta Linsley of Branford.[588] They were presumed divorced about October 1860. Henrietta died at Branford on 15 February 1875.[589]

---

585 Obituary, *The Branford Opinion*, 29 April 1904.
586 1880 and 1900 U.S. census, Branford; *The Branford Opinion*, 22 April 1904.
587 Branford Vital Records, deaths, 1904.
588 Branford Vital Records, Town Meeting book A, 157.
589 Branford Vital Records 1863-1895, 216; listed as a widow.

He was married second at Wallingford by Rev. R. J. Adams on 1 December 1860 to Lucy A. Crampton. He was age 38, born at Springfield, Massachusetts; she was age 24, born at Clinton. Lucy died at Wallingford on 22 October 1868 age 30 years & 2 months.

Alonzo Pharez Frisbie died at New York City on 3 March 1887 age 64 and was buried there in Cypress Hills Cemetery. He was the son of Pharez Frisbie and Caroline Bailey.

Amelia Frisbie of New Jersey Heights, New Jersey applied for a widow's pension in 1902. She was married to the soldier under the name of Amelia Brouwer at the home of W. Cook in Bristol by Rev. W. Swain of the Methodist Church on 20 December 1865. She was not previously married or divorced. Their marriage certificate was destroyed by a fire in 1878. They had four children all of whom were dead. She met the soldier on a visit to Meriden in 1865. Right after their marriage they moved Rockaway, New Jersey and stayed about one year; then Morristown until 1876; then Newark. His employer sent him to Somerville, New Jersey where they lived about two years. They were living there when he died in a New York hospital.

The application was sent for special examination to determine the legality of all the marriages of Alonzo Frisbie and conflicting information provided by Amelia. It appears from the examination that Alonzo P. Frisbie "married" Amelia before the death of his second wife whom he never divorced. He lived with Amelia as husband and wife until his death. Amelia becomes aware for the first time that she was not legally married to the soldier and asks "to drop me from the Pension Claim if I am not an Honorable wife. I thank God that my Dear Old Father and Step Mother thought I was an Honorable wife."[590]

FRISBIE, CHARLES H.
Co. E 15th CVI, private, enlisted 13 August 1862, prisoner, mustered out 27 June 1865, pension #7776640 for the soldier and later a pension application for his widow Dora

Charles H. Frisbie[591] of North Branford, age 25, enlisted at New Haven on 13 August 1862 and was mustered in on 25 August 1862 as a private in Co. E 15th CVI for a term of three years. He was detached as division teamster from October 1862 until the end of the war. Charles Frisbie was mustered out with the rest of his regiment at New Bern, North Carolina on 27 June 1865 and discharged at New Haven on 12 July 1865.

He applied for an invalid pension on 29 September 1890 under the act of 27 June 1890. At the time of his enlistment he was described as five feet nine inches tall, dark complexion, grey eyes, brown hair, occupation joiner. "He fought at the Battle of Fredericksburg and afterwards was placed on detached service in the quartermaster's department of the 2nd Division, 9th Corps Grand Army of the Potomac. Later he had charge, as wagon master, of all the transportation at Newbern, N.C.; over 1,000 horses and mules and one hundred men."[592] A statement in his obituary states that "During the war he was badly injured and suffered the loss of an arm"[593] was an incorrect. He lost his arm in an accident after the war. He was a member and commander for three consecutive terms of the Mason Rogers Post No. 7 G.A.R. of Branford and was active in the state's G.A.R. activities. He was parade marshal for the dedication of Branford's Soldier Monument in 1885.

He was married first at North Branford by Rev. Whitemore Peck of the North Branford Congregational Church on 31 December 1854 to Mary Foote. She died at Branford on 2 January 1907 and was buried there in Center Cemetery. He was married second at Branford by Rev. Theophilus S. Devitt of the First Congregational

---

590 Letter, Amelia Frisbie of New York, 30 July 1903, in the pension file of Alonzo P. Frisbie.
591 For his biography see Beers, *Biographical Record of New Haven County*, 712,
592 Beers, *Biographical Record of New Haven County*, 712.
593 Obituary, *The Branford Opinion*, 12 March 1909, 4; he lost his arm in a sawmill accident on 3 June 1874 not in the war.

Church on 28 October 1908 to Dora E. Allen. She was age 55, born at Middletown, living at Cromwell. In 1898 he had no children living.[594]

Charles Henry Frisbie died at Branford on 8 March 1909 and was buried there in Center Cemetery. His company and regiment are engraved on his stone and there was a G.A.R. marker was on his gravesite in 1934 and 2011. He was born at Stony Creek, Branford on 28 October 1836, son of Levi Frisbie and Betsey Beach.

Dora E. Frisbie Terhune of Bridgeport applied for a widow's pension on 12 March 1920. She was married first under the name of Dora E. Kelsey on 25 October 1867 to William J. Allen. He served in the U.S. Army under the name of John Jenett in Rhode Island. She was divorced from Allen at Bridgeport on 14 December 1888; she was living at Bridgeport; he at Berea, Ohio. In 1888 she had three minor children: Dora M. age 18, Rose M. age 16, and Willie C. Allen age 16. In 1907 she was living at New Haven and 1908 at Cromwell. Her pension claim was rejected because she married Charles H. Frisbie after 22 June 1890. She appealed through a letter to the President for a pension by a special act of Congress. This too was rejected under the pension act of 1 May 1920 requiring marriage to the soldier before 27 June 1905.

Dora Frisbie Terhune[595] was living at Bridgeport on 10 November 1923.

FRISBIE, JOHN R.
Co. F 25th Illinois Infantry, wounded, discharged disability 5 July 1864, died 25 October 1864, pension #335544 for the soldier and later for his mother Betsey Frisbie

John R. Frisbie of Onargo, Illinois enlisted on 4 August 1861 as a private in Co. F 25th Illinois Infantry. He was severely wounded at the storming of Missionary Ridge, Tennessee from a gunshot to the face and shoulder on 25 November 1863, rendering his right arm useless. He was in the hospital at Chattanooga until 30 April 1864 and afterwards was given a furlough. John Frisbie was sick at Springfield [Illinois] and discharged for disability at Camp Butler, Illinois on 2 July 1864.

He applied for an invalid pension on 30 July 1864. At the time of his enlistment he was described as five feet nine inches tall, dark complexion, hazel eyes, brown hair, occupation joiner. He died on 25 October 1864 from the effects of the wound and emaciation. He was born at North Branford on 30 July 1842.[596]

Above, Charles H. Frisbie was wagon master of the 15th CVI at New Bern, North Carolina and was commander of the Mason Rogers Post No. 7 of Branford. (Beers, Biographical Record of New Haven County, 712)

---

594 He had one adopted child Frank living in 1898.
595 Her presumed third marriage to Terhune is not referenced in the file.
596 Nora E. Frisbie, *Edward Frisbie of Branford And His Descendants* (Baltimore: Gateway Press, Inc., 1984), 306.

John R. Frisbie died as a result of wounds received during the storming of Missionary Ridge, near
Chattanooga, Tennessee on November 25, 1863. (Photographic History of the Civil War, 2:309)

His mother applied for and received a pension on 19 August 1890 under the act of 27 June 1890. Betsey Sheldon Frisbie died at Onargo, Iroquois Co., Illinois on 7 April 1893. Her husband Hervey Frisbie lived until 1903 but did not apply for a pension. Betsey was born at Branford on 5 January 1812, daughter of Jere Sheldon and Caty Lanfare.[597]

FRISBIE, RUSSELL L.

Co. K 15th CVI, enlisted 9 August 1862, discharged 15 July 1865, pension #726466 for the soldier and later for his widow Mary

Russell L. Frisbie, age 18, of Wallingford enlisted at New Haven on 9 August 1862 and was mustered in on 25 August 1862 as a private in Co. K 15th CVI for a term of three years. He saw action at Fredericksburg, Virginia on 13 December 1862, during the Siege of Suffolk, Virginia in the spring of 1863, and in the Peninsula Campaign of July 1863. During March 1864 he was in Regimental Hospital at New Bern, North Carolina for the mumps.[598] His "Soldierly conduct was good." Russell Frisbie was discharged from Fort Schuyler Hospital, New York on 15 July 1865. He was the son of Alonzo P. Frisbie of the same company and served under Capt. Medad D. Munson of Wallingford.

He applied for an invalid pension on 30 January 1888. At the time of his enlistment he was described as five feet six inches tall, fair complexion, light hair, blue eyes, occupation clerk. He contracted varicose veins in the winter of 1862/63 at Falmouth, Virginia during the march from Fairfax Seminary to Acquia Creek, Virginia. Also at Falmouth Plains near Fredericksburg he contracted rheumatism of the limbs, hips, and shoulders. While on provost guard at New Bern, North Carolina in February 1864 he was sick with small

---

597 Branford Vital Records, 1786-1840, 426.
598 Dr. H.V.C. Holcombe papers, Connecticut Historical Society, MS 92085, volume 3.

pox, affecting his eye sight, and was treated at the hospital in New Bern and McDougall Hospital. He returned to duty on 8 March 1864 and was detailed as a clerk in the Ordinance Department. He fell sick again and was admitted to the hospital steamer *A. R. Spaudling*; was sent to McDougall General Hospital and to Fort Schuyler Hospital in New York on 6 June 1865 where he was discharged for disability on 15 July 1865. After the war he removed to Terre Haute, Indiana. He was married first to Alice Vinyard and divorced from her on 19 February 1884 at Vigo County Court, Indiana.

Russell Linsley Frisbie died on 28 March 1911 at Terre Haute, Indiana and was buried there at Highland Lawn Cemetery. He was born at Branford on 14 September 1845, son of Alonzo Pharez Frisbie and Henrietta Linsley.[599]

Mary Frisbie, age 44, of Terre Haute, Indiana applied for a widow's pension on 6 April 1911. She was married to the soldier as his second wife under the name of Mary Frances Kelly at Terre Haute, Indiana by Rev. William G. Braeckly on 11 March 1887. She was not previously married or divorced. They had the following children (living in 1898): Herbert C., born on 20 August 1888; Harvey R., born on 27 March 1891; and Joseph F., born on 23 September 1893. The soldier left one minor child under the age of eighteen when he died: Mary L. Frisbie, born on 29 December 1900.

Mary Kelly Frisbie was born at Terre Haute, Indiana on 6 April 1866, daughter of Joseph Case Kelly and Laura Melinda Service.[600] She was married second at Terre Haute, Vigo County, Indiana by James P. Madigan, JP on 6 December 1923 to Harry Toney.

FROST, ALVA
Co. B 15th CVI, private, enlisted 7 August 1862, discharged 1 November 1862, pension #127811 for the soldier

Alva Frost of North Haven enlisted at New Haven on 7 August 1862 and was mustered in on 25 August 1862 as a private in Co. B 15th CVI for a term of three years. On or about 15 September 1862 he was injured and discharged for disability by Dr. H.V.C. Holcombe from Camp Chase, Virginia on 1 November 1862 for a ruptured hernia. His name appears on the North Haven Civil War Honor Roll.

He applied for an invalid pension on 31 August 1866 due to an injury to the stomach. It was determined that his injury was permanent and received in the line of duty. "He alleges this rupture was caused by heavy lifting and drawing a cart while undergoing punishment at Washington, D.C." He received a one half disability pension. In 1873 he was described as age 47, five feet nine inches tall, light complexion. He appears at North Haven during the 1850, 1860, and 1870 federal census, unmarried. He appears at Branford in 1880, age 53, born in Connecticut, unmarried, living by himself and his name appears in 1883 as a pensioner living at Branford. No further record of him in Branford was found.

Alva Frost died at the Soldiers' Home in Togus, Maine on 16 November 1890 and was buried there in the National Cemetery. He was born on 19 January 1823, son of Willard Frost and Miriam Ives.

599 Branford Vital Records, Town Meeting Book A, 236.
600 Frisbie, *Edward Frisbie of Branford*, 536.

FUCHS, CHARLES

Co. H 11th CVI, private, substitute, mustered in 25 November 1864, died 30 September 1865, no pension

Charles Fuchs, age 26, served as a substitute for Orrin H. Hoadley of Branford. He was mustered in at New Haven on 25 November 1864 as a private in Co. H 11th CVI for a term of three years. He was described as five feet seven inches tall, grey eyes, auburn hair, fair complexion, unmarried, born in Germany, occupation baker.[601] He died on 30 September 1865.

FUCHS, HENRY

Co. K 5th CVI, corporal, drafted 25 July 1863, mustered out 19 July 1865, no pension

Henry Fuchs of Branford served as a substitute or was drafted as a private in Co. K 5th CVI on 25 July 1863. He was promoted to corporal on 1 June 1865 and mustered out at Alexandria, Virginia on 19 July 1865.

GALLIGAN, WILLIAM J. also GALLAGHER

Co. B 27th CVI, private, enlisted 10 September 1862, mustered out 27 July 1863, pension #254960 for his widow Ann

William J Galligan, age 29, of Wallingford enlisted on 10 September 1862 and was mustered in on 3 October 1862 as a private in Co. B 27th CVI for a term of nine months. He fought at the Battle of Fredericksburg on 13 December 1862 with the rest of the company. He probably did not fight at Chancellorsville or Gettysburg due to illness. Galligan was mustered out with the rest of his regiment at New Haven on 27 July 1863.

William John Galligan died on 20 December 1872 as a result of disease contracted in the service and was buried in Holy Trinity Cemetery, Wallingford. There is no medical record in his CMSR. "He contracted diarrhea in Falmouth in the winter of 1862 after the Battle of Fredericksburg and in April 1863 was sent to the Hospital. Since discharge he was sick with diarrhea until he went to his Grave leaving a loving wife and five single girls."[602] "He was sick much of the time after Fredericksburg and unable to perform his duty as a soldier."[603] The disease and cause of death were supported by his physician's statements.

Ann Galligan filed for a widow's pension on 14 June 1887. She was married to the soldier under the name of Ann Raysen at Wallingford by Rev. Father Sheridan on 1 November 1859. Neither were previously married or divorced and she did not remarry after his death. They had the following children: Kate [Catherine], born on 30 July 1860; Mary, born on 3 July 1864; Maggie E., born on 24 September 1867; Jennie, born on 29 October 1871; and Ellen, born on 12 February 1873. Her attorney was Charles E. Galligan of Paw Paw, Michigan, no relation stated. A letter from her daughter Catherine F. Galligan of 53 Church Street, Wallingford states that Ann Galligan, widow of William J. Galligan, died on 18 December 1913.

---

601 Muster & Descriptive Rolls of Substitutes, RG 13, box 97, 2nd Congressional District, Connecticut State Library.
602 Statement, James Kennedy of Wallingford, 16 July 1888, in the pension file of William J. Galligan.
603 Affidavit, Charles Paden of Wallingford, 26 April 1888, in the pension file of William J. Galligan.

GALLOWAY, WILLIAM S.

3rd LA, private, enlisted 6 September 1864, mustered out 23 June 1865, pension #978891 for the soldier and later for his minor son George H. Galloway

William S. Galloway of Derby enlisted on 6 September 1864 as a private in the 3rd Battery LA for a term of nine months. Galloway was mustered out with the rest of his regiment at Richmond, Virginia on 23 June 1865 and discharged at New Haven on 3 July 1865.

He applied for an invalid pension on 16 August 1890 under the act of 27 June 1890. He was described as five feet six inches tall, light complexion, light hair, brown eyes, occupation laborer. After his discharge he lived at Ansonia and since September 1872 at Branford. He was admitted to the Fitch's Soldier Home[604] at Noroton Heights on 18 September 1906. He was a member of the Mason Rogers Post No. 7 G.A.R. of Branford.

He was married first to Josephine Durant and divorced at New Haven (no dates given). He was married second at Portchester, New York by Rev. William Hunt in April 1896 to Catherine "Katie" Williams. She was not previously married or divorced. They had one son: George H. Galloway, born at Branford on 5 March 1897. Catherine died at New Haven on 28 August 1908 and was buried in Center Cemetery, Branford. She was born on 12 July 1867 in England, daughter of David Williams and Charlotte Page.[605] In 1912 George W. Andrew of New Haven, brother-in-law of the soldier was guardian of George Henry Galloway, called Harry.

William S. Galloway died at the Fitch's Soldier Home on 7 January 1907 and was buried in Center Cemetery, Branford. His regiment is engraved on his stone and a G.A.R. marker was on his gravesite in 1934 and 2011. He was born at Brooklyn, New York on 4 February 1847.[606]

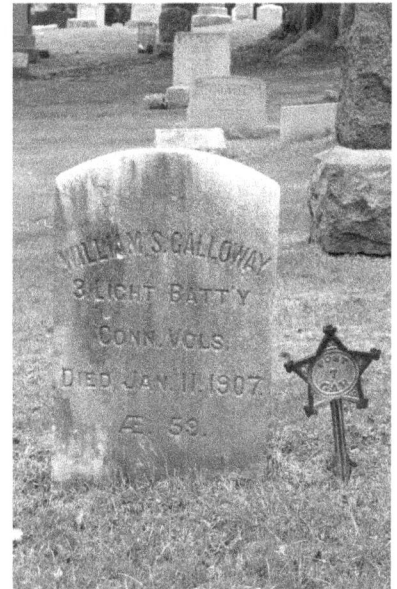

GALPIN, JOSEPH A.

Co. C 15th CVI, corporal, enlisted 14 August 1862, prisoner, discharged 23 June 1865, pension #366653 for his widow Caroline

Joseph A. Galpin, age 39, of Branford enlisted at New Haven on 14 August 1862 and was mustered in on 25 August 1862 as a private in Co. C 15th CVI for a term of three years. He was promoted to corporal on 1 December 1862. He saw action at the Battle of Fredericksburg, Virginia on 13 December 1862 and at the Siege of Suffolk, Virginia in 1863. In May or June 1863 he was left behind sick at camp near Portsmouth. "Joe Galpin is sick and has been for quite a while."[607] He was treated at Regimental Hospital, New Bern, North Carolina March and April 1864 for ulcers.[608] He was "slightly wounded" and captured with much of his regiment at Kinston, North Carolina on 8 March 1865, confined at Libby Prison, Richmond on 23 March, and paroled at Boulware's & Cox's wharf on 26 March 1865. He reported to Camp Parole, Maryland on 30 March 1865. He received a thirty day furlough and was discharged from Camp Parole, Maryland on 23 June 1865.

---

604 Fitch's Home for Soldiers, Deceased Veterans Discharge Files 1882-1932, box 10, file 2600.
605 New Haven Vital Records, deaths, 1908.
606 Branford Vital Records, deaths, 1907; his parents are not recorded.
607 Towner letter, 3 August 1863.
608 Dr. H.V.C. Holcombe papers, Connecticut Historical Society, MS 92085, volume 3.

Joseph Alleorp Galpin was killed at Suffield on 28 November 1876[609] by the fall of a derrick. At the time of his enlistment he was described as five feet ten inches tall, light complexion, grey eyes, grey hair, occupation manufacturer, born at Durham. He only appears in the 1860 census at Branford with his wife Caroline and seven children.[610]

Caroline W. Galpin of Milford applied for a widow's pension on 4 October 1890 under the act of 27 June 1890. She was married to the soldier under the name of Caroline W. Goddard at Granby by Rev. Pliney F. Sanborn of the East Granby Congregational Church on 17 May 1847, both were living at Granby. Neither were previously married or divorced and she did not remarry after his death. Her pension payments were dropped on 4 March 1895 because of her reported death.

GARLICK, SEYMOUR
Co. D 28th CVI, private, enlisted 30 August 1862, mustered out 28 August 1863, pension #325489 for the soldier

Seymour Garlick of Bridgewater enlisted on 30 August 1862 and was mustered in at Camp Terry, New Haven on 15 November 1862 as a private in Co. D 28th CVI for a term of nine months. Garlick was mustered out with the rest of his regiment at New Haven on 28 August 1863.

He was issued an invalid pension on 29 August 1863 for disease of the lungs. He applied for an increase in his pension on 20 April 1880 but the pension board discontinued his payments, "his disability having ceased." His pension was granted again on 24 April 1886. While at Ship Island, Mississippi on 20 December 1862 he was sick with lung fever and placed in the Regimental Hospital. "We were on the steamer Chekiang on our way to Ship Island when Garlick caught a severe cold when we were off Cape Hatteras during a storm and went into the hospital."[611] The steamer left New York on 3 December 1862; arrived at Ship Island on 11 December; left for New Orleans on 17 December for Camp Parapet; went back to New Orleans then to Pensacola, Florida arriving on 21 December where they were still stationed in February 1863. At the time of his enlistment he was described as five feet seven inches tall, dark hair, blue eyes, occupation farmer. After his discharge he lived at Waterbury, Bridgewater, and Branford. He first appears at Branford in the 1880 census.[612] He was a member of the Mason Rogers Post No. 7 G.A.R. of Branford.

He was married at South Britain by Rev. Butterfield on 6 January 1847 to Amaryllis Maria Ward. Neither were previously married or divorced. They had the following children (living in 1898): Sarah Maria, born on 16 June 1849; and Frederick E., born on 28 February 1853. She died at Branford on 20 March 1904 age 84 and was buried in Center Cemetery, New Milford; daughter of John Ward and Sarah Gilbert.[613]

Seymour Garlick died at Branford on 2 July 1909 and was buried in Center Cemetery, New Milford.[614] His company and regiment are engraved on his stone and there was a Civil War marker at his gravesite in 1934. He was born at New Milford on 29 December 1822, son of Daniel Garlick.

---

609 Death information from his pension file. It appears he may be the Joseph Galpin that died at Southwick, Massachusetts on 18 November 1876, son of George Galpin, born at Durham, Connecticut, station master, accident, www.ancestry.com, Massachusetts Deaths 1841-1915.

610 U.S. census 1860, Branford, New Haven County, Connecticut, population schedule, M653-85, dwelling 986, family 1098, page 913, www.heritagequest.com.

611 Deposition, Merritt Hunt of New Milford, 11 June 1884, in the pension file of Seymour Garlick.

612 U.S. census 1880, North Branford, New Haven County, Connecticut, population schedule, T9-107, dwelling 328, family 384, page 544; he was living by himself, www.heritagequest.com.

613 Branford Vital Records, deaths, 1904.

614 Branford Vital Records, deaths, 1909; The Hale Collection, New Milford, 68.

GATES, JOHN H.
see Peter Jones

GILBERT, FREDERICK A.
Co. G 17th CVI, private, enlisted 5 September 1864, mustered out 19 July 1865, pension #XC961507 for the soldier and later for his widow Julia

Frederick A. Gilbert of Branford enlisted and was mustered in on 5 September 1864 as a private in Co. G 17th CVI for a term of three years. After his enlistment his regiment served in Florida. Frederick Gilbert was mustered out with the rest of his regiment at Hilton Head, South Carolina on 19 July 1865 and discharged at New Haven on 31 August 1865. He does not appear in the 1860 census at Branford. He is probably the Frederick A. Gilbert, age 25, living at Southbury in the household of Hiram and Susan Gilbert. The same Frederick A. appears at Southbury in 1880, a widower, with children. He was living at Woodbury in 1900 and 1910 with his wife Julia and family.

He was married first at Plymouth, Litchfield Co. on 24 November 1870 to Katherine A. Carroll. She died at Woodbury on 27 December 1878[615].

He applied for an invalid pension on 20 July 1891 under the act of 27 June 1890. His pension is at the Veterans Administration. He died at Litchfield on 6 April 1920 and was buried in Pierce Hollow Cemetery, Southbury. He was born at Southbury on 6 January 1845, son of Hiram Gilbert and Huldah Ann Fogarty.

Julia A. Gilbert applied for a widow's pension on 28 February 1921. She was married to the soldier as his second wife under the name of Julia Petit at Woodbury on 29 June 1883. She was born at Roxbury on 19 March 1865 and died at Woodbury on 25 May 1951.

GILBERT, WELLS or WILLIS GILBERT
Co. K 6th CVI, private, enlisted 9 September 1861, discharged disability 21 December 1862, pension #26502 for the soldier and later for his widow Elizabeth

Willis Gilbert of Branford enlisted as Wells Gilbert at New Haven on 9 September 1861 and was mustered in on 12 September 1861 as a private in Co. K 6th CVI for a term of three years. He was discharged for disability on 21 December 1862.

He applied for an invalid pension on 1 July 1863[616]. He appears in the 1860 census at Branford, age 30, with his wife Elizabeth, age 30; both born in Connecticut. He is probably the Willis Gilbert, age 20, living in the household of Fanny Gilbert at Lyme in 1850. Elizabeth Gilbert applied for a widow's pension on 30 December 1863.

GILDE, JAMES
Co. D 7th CVI, private, enlisted 5 September 1861, mustered out 20 July 1865, pension application #537907 for the soldier

James Gilde of Trenton, New Jersey enlisted at New Haven on 5 September 1861 and was mustered in on 17 September 1861 as a private in Co. D 7th CVI for a term of three years. His regiment manned forts in

---

615 Carroll family tree, www.ancestry.com
616 His pension file at the NARA could not be located by the staff.

Georgia and South Carolina during the war. He reenlisted as a veteran in Co. D on 22 December 1863 and was mustered out with the rest of the regiment at Goldsboro, North Carolina on 20 July 1865. He was discharged at New Haven on 11 August 1865.

He applied for an invalid pension on 18 April 1885. At the Siege of Fort Pulaski, Georgia on 10 April 1862 while working upon the mortar battery he had buzzing with resulting deafness from the noise. In September and October 1862 he was sick in the hospital at Hilton Head, South Carolina. His application was rejected and in 1891 he writes a letter to the pension board asking why his application has not been acted on signing it "Your Respectfully Affected Friend and Soldier of the Late War." He reapplied on 2 January 1892 which was again rejected. The Board found no disability from the claimed ear injury. At the time of his discharge he was described as five feet eight inches tall, light complexion, brown hair, blue eyes. After the war he stated he lived at Branford but was living at North Branford in 1880.[617] He was a charter member of the Mason Rogers Post No. 7 G.A.R. of Branford. There is no mention of a wife or children in the file. The soldier made no further applications and the pension board abandoned the case. His death was not found in newspaper or vital records for Branford or North Branford or in the Fitch's Soldier Home index.

GOODRICH, HORACE W.
Co. G 20th CVI, corporal, enlisted 11 August 1862, discharged disability 10 May 1863, pension #638910 for the soldier and later for his widow Mary

Horace W. Goodrich of Branford enlisted at New Haven on 11 August 1862 and was mustered in on 8 September 1862 as a private in Co. G 20th CVI for a term of three years. He was promoted to corporal on 15 October 1862. He was admitted to the hospital on 16 January 1863 and discharged for disability from Finley Hospital, Washington, D.C. on 10 May 1863 for typhoid fever.

He applied for an invalid pension on 10 September 1889. At the time of his enlistment he was described as five feet ten inches tall, dark complexion, black eyes, black hair, occupation carriage trimmer. He lived at Branford after the war.

He was admitted to the Fitch's Home for Soldiers[618] at Noroton Heights on 3 November 1906. He stated that he had no children. Among his possessions at the time of his death were a handbag, one overcoat, one vest, three shirts, razor and strop, lather and brush.

Horace W. Goodrich died at the Fitch's Soldier Home in Noroton Heights on 15 June 1907 and was buried there in Spring Grove Cemetery. He was born at Branford on 6 January 1840, son of William Goodrich and Marian Whiting.

Mary M. Goodrich of Albany, New York applied for a widow's pension on 26 September 1907. She was married to the soldier under the name of Mary Maria Smith at Branford by Rev. Elijah C. Baldwin of the First Congregational Church on 22 April 1869. He was age 29, living at Branford; she was age 30, living at New York City. He was not previously married or divorced. She was married first under the name of Mary M. Sherman on 16 January 1864 to Henry P. Smith. Smith was a soldier in the 1st Connecticut LA and was killed at New Haven on 3 November 1868 in a railroad accident.

Mary M. Goodrich was living at 130 Lark Street, Albany, New York on 28 January 1908.

617 U.S. census 1860, North Branford, New Haven County, Connecticut, population schedule, M653-85, dwelling 71, family 76, page 517, www.heritagequest.com.
618 Fitch's Home for Soldiers, Deceased Veterans Discharge Files 1882-1932, box 10, file 2616.

GOODYEAR, ROBERT B.

Co. B 27th CVI, sergeant, enlisted 1 September 1862, prisoner, mustered out 27 July 1863, pension #XC2710436 for the soldier and later for his widow Ellen

Robert B. Goodyear[619] of North Haven, age 26, enlisted on 1 September 1862 and was mustered in on 3 October 1862 as a sergeant in Co. B 27th CVI for a term of nine months and served with the company throughout the war. He fought at the Battle of Fredericksburg on 13 December 1862. He was captured at the Battle of Chancellorsville, Virginia on 3 May 1863, held prisoner at Richmond, and paroled at City Point, Virginia on 14 May 1863. He reported to Camp Parole, Maryland on 16 May 1863, was sent to Washington, D.C. on 20 May 1863 and spent the remainder of his service at Camp Convalescent, Virginia. With the rest of the Chancellorsville paroled prisoners, he rejoined the Regiment at Baltimore on 20 July 1863. Goodyear was mustered out with the rest of his regiment at New Haven on 27 July 1863. He was one of six brothers who served in the war.

Robert B. Goodyear was a sergeant in Co. B 27th CVI and after the war a practicing physician in North Haven. (Rockey, History of New Haven County, I:278)

After the war he entered Medical School at Yale College and graduated in 1868. He was a practicing physician and surgeon at North Haven. He testified on behalf of many fellow soldiers for their pension claims. His name appears on the North Haven Civil War Honor Roll.

He applied for an invalid pension on 26 August 1904. He was married first on 19 May 1869 to Jane Lyman who died in March 1878 and was buried in Center Cemetery, North Haven. He was married second on 26 June 1884 to Ellen Maria Hotchkiss, daughter of Stephen Hotchkiss and Maria Goodyear.[620]

Dr. Robert Beardsley Goodyear died at North Haven on 21 February 1923 and was buried there in Center Cemetery.[621] He was born at North Haven on 4 November 1836, son of Bela Goodyear and Lucy Foote.[622]

Ellen Maria Goodyear of North Haven applied for widow's pension on 15 March 1923. She was living at North Haven in 1930. The pension is at the Veterans Administration.

GRAHAM, WILLIAM F.

U.S. Navy, landsman, enlisted 8 January 1864, discharged 18 March 1865, pension #7292 for his widow Julia

William F. Graham enlisted at New York on 8 January 1864 as a landsman in the U.S. Navy and served on the U.S.S. *Savannah* and U.S.S. *Wanderer*. He was discharged at the Brooklyn Navy Yard, New York on 18 March 1865.

---

619 For his biography see Rockey, *History of New Haven County*, I:277; Sheldon B. Thorpe, *North Haven Annals* (New Haven: Price, Lee & Adkins Co., 1892), 322.

620 Rockey, *History of New Haven County*, I:278; Grace Goodyear Kirkum, *Genealogy of the Goodyear Family* (San Francisco: Simeon & Co., 1899).

621 The Hale Collection, North Haven, 10.

622 Rockey, *History of New Haven County*, I:278; *Genealogy of the Goodyear Family*, 96.

William Franklin Graham died at Branford on 2 January 1889 age 44 and was buried there in Center Cemetery. A G.A.R. marker was on his gravesite in 1934. He was born at Durham and was a member of the Mason Rogers Post No. 7 G.A.R. of Branford.

Julia Elizabeth Graham applied for a widow's pension after his death. She was married to the soldier under the name of Julia E. Rogers at Stony Creek, Branford by Rev. Alpha H. Simonds of the First Baptist Church on 5 August 1866. She received a pension until her second marriage to Branford Civil War soldier Ammi B. Barker in 1893 (see Barker above).

GRAY, SAMUEL N.
Co. H 1st Cavalry, private, enlisted 30 November 1863, prisoner, discharged 5 August 1865, pension application #743877 for the soldier and later for his widow Harriet

Samuel N. Gray & family probably about December 1883. Left to right John?, Samuel, son Samuel, and wife Rosa. (Courtesy of Charles A. Allen)

Samuel N. Gray, age 19, of Wilton enlisted and was mustered in at Bridgeport on 30 November 1863 as a private in Co. H 1st Calvary for a term of three years. There was a question about his age, Edgar A. Finney of Norwalk was appointed guardian and approved Gray's enlistment. He was sick in July and August 1864 and treated at Dismounted Camp, Germantown, Pennsylvania, and Point Giesboro, Maryland. He was sick at G. H. Patterson Park, Baltimore, Maryland in September and October 1864. He was captured on 16 March 1865 near Ashland, Hanover Co., Virginia and confined at Richmond. He was paroled at Boulware's & Cox's wharf on 26 March 1865. He reported to Camp Parole, Maryland on 30 March 1865 and received a thirty day furlough. Gray was mustered out with the rest of his regiment at Washington, D.C. on 2 August 1865 and discharged at New Haven on 18 August 1865. He married the daughter of Sergeant George G. Bradley of the 10th CVI.

He applied for an invalid pension on 30 August 1890 under the act of 27 June 1890 but the application was denied due to failure to show the disability was due to his military service. He never received a pension. At the time of his enlistment he was described as five feet four inches tall, dark complexion, brown eyes, brown hair, occupation farmer. There are many documents in the file attesting to his illness. After his discharge he lived at Branford, Iowa, Nebraska, and returned to Branford. He was mustered in on 28 June 1892 and was later commander of the Mason Rogers Post No. 7 G.A.R. of Branford.

He was married first at Branford by Rev. John Ripper on 19 March 1870 to Rosa Lois Bradley. He was age 23, born at Wilton, living at Branford; she was age 18, born and living at Branford. She died at Bellevue,

Sarpy Co., Nebraska on 15 September 1891 age 39 and was buried in the Bellevue Cemetery. She was born at Branford on 12 February 1852, daughter of George Granniss Bradley and Lois Elizabeth Rowland.

Samuel Nichols Gray died at Branford on 16 November 1896 and was buried there in Center Cemetery. His company and regiment are engraved on his stone and a G.A.R. marker was on his gravesite in 1934. He was born at Wilton, son of John Archer Gray and Sarah Ann Nichols.

Harriet J. Gray of Branford applied for a widow's pension on 8 March 1898. She was married to the soldier under the name of Harriet Jane Baldwin at New Haven by Rev. Eben C. Sage of the Baptist Church on 20 January 1896. He was age 45, living at Branford; she was age 36, living at New Haven. She was not previously married or divorced and did not remarry after his death. She applied for a pension as guardian of his minor children by his first wife: John Archer, born on 4 October 1883; Harriet Rosella "Hattie," born on 29 May 1885; and Pauline Ellen, born on 1 September 1887 all born in Nebraska. Harriet claims they were baptized at the Presbyterian Church in Bellevue, Nebraska but there is no record. Harriet was not eligible for a pension since she married the soldier after 1890. Her application for the children was rejected since he was not a pensioner during his lifetime. The case was reopened on 11 January 1902. She writes claiming a grave injustice is being done to these minor children who should be entitled to a pension. It does not appear the children ever received one.

Harriet J. Gray of Branford, age 55, applied for and finally received a pension under the act of 8 September 1916. Harriet Baldwin Gray was buried in Center Cemetery, Branford on 7 March 1932.[623] She was born at Orange on 21 December 1860.

GREEN, CHARLES H.
Co. G 29th CVI, private, enlisted 29 December 1863, died 24 September 1864, pension #56853 for his mother Esther

Charles H. Green of Branford enlisted at New Haven on 29 December 1863 and was mustered in on 8 March 1864 as a private in Co. G 29th CVI for a term of three years. His service was credited to Branford. He was sick in Knight Hospital and returned to duty on 3 March 1864. During July and August 1864 he was sick at General Hospital, Bermuda Hundred, Virginia and died on 24 September 1864. His name appears on the Wall of Honor at Washington, D.C. His mother Esther Jane Green applied for a pension on 2 November 1864.

GREEN, JOHN
Co. K 14th CVI, private, drafted 25 July 1863, deserted 18 August 1863

John Green of Branford served as a substitute or was drafted on 25 July 1863 as a private in Co. K 14th CVI and deserted on 18 August 1863. He does not appear in the 1860 census at Branford.

---

623 Branford Sexton Records, 1884-1932, 136. She was living at Branford in 1930 but her death was not found in the Branford Vital Records.

A sketch of a Negro soldier at ease by Alfred R. Waud. (The Battle-Pieces of Herman Melville, 130)

GRIFFIN, ALEXANDER or GRIFFING
Co. I 29th CVI, private, enlisted 2 January 1864, mustered out 24 October 1865, no pension

Alexander Griffin of Branford enlisted at New Haven on 2 January 1864 and was mustered in on 8 March 1864 as a private in Co. I 29th CVI for a term of three years.[624] His service was credited to Branford. At the time of his enlistment he was described as age 28, five feet one inch tall, black complexion, black hair and eyes; born at Philadelphia, Pennsylvania; occupation steward. A copy of his enlistment paper is in the file, signed with his mark. Griffin was mustered out at Browns-ville, Texas on 24 October 1865. His name appears on the Wall of Honor at Washington, D.C.

GRIMES, JOHN R.
Co. H 29th CVI, corporal, enlisted 30 December 1863, discharged 1 September 1865, died 31 August 1865, pension #80875 for his mother Clarissa Grimes

John R. Grimes[625] of Branford enlisted at New Haven on 30 December 1863 and was mustered in on 8 March 1864 as a private in Co. H 29th CVI for a term of three years. At the time of his enlistment he was described as age 21, five feet six inches tall, black complexion, black eyes and hair, born at New Haven, occupation steward. His service was credited to Branford. A copy of his enlistment paper is in the file, signed with his mark. He was reported as deserted on 4 February 1864 but was present for muster roll on 29 February. He was promoted to corporal on 1 January 1865. He was sick in the hospital beginning 3 July 1865 and died at Corps d'Afrique U.S. General Hospital, New Orleans on 31 August 1865 from scurvy and was buried at New Orleans. His belongings included a great coat, one pair of trousers, one blanket, one knapsack, and one rubber blanket. His name appears on the Wall of Honor at Washington, D.C.

His mother Clarissa Grimes, age 66, of New Haven applied for a pension on 4 December 1865. She was the widow of William Grimes who died at New Haven on 21 August 1865. The soldier furnished his mother with money for food, clothing, and fuel. The soldier left no wife or children and was never married. The Grimes family was living at New Haven in the 1830, 1840, 1850 and 1860 census. In 1860 the head of household was William Grimes age 78, born in Virginia; Clarissa age 61, born in Connecticut and their family.[626] Clarissa Grimes died on 16 December 1869 age 73 and was buried in Grove Street Cemetery, New Haven.[627]

---

624 His CMSR lists him as Co. G; the *Record of Service of Connecticut Men* as Co. I.
625 Complied Military Service Records of Volunteer Union Soldiers Who Served with the United States Colored Troops Infantry Organizations 26th through 30th (including the 29th Connecticut), NARA M1824, www.ancestry.com.
626 U.S. census 1860, New Haven Ward 3, population schedule M653-86, dwelling 83, family 37, page 428, www.ancestry.com.
627 The Hale Collection, New Haven, 136; her husband William Grimes and six of their children are buried in Grove Street Cemetery.

GUTERSLOH, CHRISTIAN
Co. B 15th CVI, private, enlisted 6 August 1862, deserted 6 October 1862, no pension

Christian Gutersloh of Branford enlisted on 6 August 1862 as a private in Co. B 15th CVI for a term of three years. He deserted on 6 October 1862. He was living at New Haven in 1860, age 33, born in Hanover, Germany with a wife and family.[628] He appears on the 1863 draft list for Branford.

HALL, BILLIOUS C.
Co. B 27th CVI, sergeant, enlisted 10 September 1862, prisoner, mustered out 27 June 1863, pension #1082531 for the soldier

Billious C. Hall [629] of Wallingford, age 28, enlisted on 10 September 1862 and was mustered in on 3 October 1862 as a sergeant in Co. B 27th CVI for a term of nine months. He fought at the Battle of Fredericksburg on 13 December 1862 with the rest of his regiment. He was captured at the Battle of Chancellorsville, Virginia on 3 May 1863, held prisoner at Richmond, and paroled at City Point, Virginia on 14 May 1863. He reported to Camp Parole, Maryland on 16 May 1863, was sent to Washington, D.C. on 20 May 1863 and spent the remainder of his service at Camp Convalescent, Virginia. With the rest of the Chancellorsville paroled prisoners, he rejoined the Regiment at Baltimore on 20 July 1863. Billious Hall was mustered out with the rest of his regiment at New Haven on 27 July 1863.

He applied for a pension on 21 April 1904 under the act of 27 June 1890. In 1907 he was age 75, occupation farmer and post master. He was described as five feet eleven inches tall, dark complexion, blue eyes, dark hair. Before his enlistment he lived at Wallingford and came to Naugatuck in 1859. After his discharge he returned to Naugatuck, post office Union City. He was married first at Naugatuck on 7 December 1859 to Grace Ann Evans who died on 25 April 1861, daughter of Oliver and Harriet Evans. He was married second at Naugatuck by Rev. Charles Sherman on 5 April 1862 to Adelaide E. Smith, daughter of Asahel and Elizabeth Smith. She died before 1904. He had three children living (in 1915): Clarence Dwight, born on 18 January 1867; Edward Clinton, born on 2 August 1870; and Louis Harrison born on 5 June 1875.

Billious Cook Hall died at Naugatuck on 14 October 1916 and was buried there in Grove Cemetery. He was born at Wallingford on 5 September 1833, son of Edward L. Hall and Mary K. Cook. No record of his birth was recorded at Wallingford but the town clerk certified that Hall showed him a page from the family bible showing his birth and those of his siblings.

---

628 U.S. census 1860, New Haven, population schedule M653-87, page 849, www.ancestry.com.
629 For his biography see Beers, *Biographical Record of New Haven County*, 1470; Rockey, *History of New Haven County*, II:741.

HALL, ISAAC K.
Co. B 27th CVI, corporal, enlisted 10 September 1862, discharged disability 22 February 1863, pension #260097 for his widow Ellen

Isaac K. Hall[630] of Wallingford, age 27, enlisted on 10 September 1862 and was mustered in on 3 October 1862 as a corporal in Co. B 27th CVI for a term of nine months. He was sick in the hospital beginning 1 December 1862 through February 1863. He did not fight at the Battle of Fredericksburg. He was discharged for disability on 22 February 1863 by the surgeon at Satterlee General Hospital at West Philadelphia, Pennsylvania. At the time of his enlistment he was described as five feet ten inches tall, light complexion, brown eyes, brown hair, occupation farmer and at discharge had been unfit for duty for 60 days due to incipient phthisis.

"The Regiment was at Chain Bridge. Hall was detailed for Picket duty and contracted a cold and came into camp sick. He was cared for by the Surgeon. Several weeks later he had an attack of malaria. He was unfit for duty when we marched to Fredericksburg and was sent to the hospital from Camp Tuttle. He was not again with our company."[631]

His death was attributed to his illness in the service including rheumatism and malaria resulting in apoplexy and meloncholia. The soldier's sister Mrs. David M. Stone of Brooklyn, New York visited him while he was in the hospital at Philadelphia and the soldier stayed with her after his discharge. He spent periods of time in sanitariums and asylums after the war. Statements from physicians confirm the disability acquired during service; that he was never well after his discharge and unable to work. He never applied for a pension.

Comrade Billious C. Hall was in Co. B and a distant cousin claims that Isaac Hall was a well, robust man before his enlistment, in the prime of his life. The men in his family all lived to be old men.[632]

Isaac Kirtland Hall died on 22 April 1886 at a hospital in Hartford and was buried In Memoriam Cemetery, Wallingford. He was born at Wallingford on 7 November 1834, son of Peter Hall and Delight Kirtland. He was a member of the Arthur Dutton Post G.A.R. No. 36.

Ellen M. Hall of East Wallingford applied for a widow's pension on 1 November 1886. She made several applications which were rejected. She was married to the soldier under the name of Ellen M. Hart at Durham on 29 April 1861. She had known him five months before their marriage and was a school teacher in the neighborhood. Neither were previously married or divorced. She lived in the same house since her marriage and they did not have children. Her sister was Mary E. Hart of Bridgeport, Fairfield County.

Ellen M. Hall died on 24 January 1891 and was buried In Memoriam Cemetery, Wallingford. She was born on 11 March 1841.[633]

HALL, JAMES
Co. A 11th CVI, private, enlisted 8 February 1864, to U.S. Navy, deserted 2 May 1865

James Hall of Branford enlisted on 8 February 1864 as a private in Co. A 11th CVI. He was transferred to the U.S. Navy on 30 April 1864 and served on the U.S.S. *Florida* and the U.S.S. *Quaker City*. He deserted on 2 May 1865. He does not appear in the 1860 census at Branford.

---

630 For his biography see Rockey, *History of New Haven County*, I:422.
631 Deposition, Robert B. Goodyear, 11 May 1889, in the pension file of Isaac K. Hall.
632 Deposition, Billious C. Hall of Union City, 20 September 1889, in the pension file of Isaac K. Hall.
633 The Hale Collection, Wallingford, 205.

HALL, JOHN G.
Co. C 17th New York Infantry, private, died 6 October 1865, pension #88420 for his widow Rachel

John G. Hall enlisted at New York City on 26 September 1863 and was mustered in at Camp Sprague on 6 October 1863 as a private in Co. C 17th New York Infantry for a term of three years. He died at DeCamp General Hospital, Davids' Island, New York Harbor on 6 October 1865 from chronic diarrhea.

Rachel Hall of Branford applied for a widow's pension on 8 August 1865. She was married to the soldier under the name of Rachel Walston at Wallingford by Augustus Hall, JP on 16 May 1857. He was living at Branford and she at Wallingford. They had no children. She was age 45, a widow, living at Branford in 1870 with Eliza Wilson, another Civil War widow. In 1880 she was a servant for Davis Towner of Branford, a widow, age 58 [sic 55], born in Connecticut and appears as a pensioner at Branford in 1883.

Rachel Hall died at the Poor Farm in Branford on 21 December 1890 age 65. She was born at Guilford, daughter of David Walston and Ruth Dowd.[634]

HALL, ROGER
Co. B 27th CVI, private, enlisted 8 September 1862, mustered out 27 July 1863, pension #598184 for the soldier and later for his widow Eliza

Roger Hall, age 37, of Branford enlisted on 8 September 1862 and was mustered in on 3 October 1862 as a private in Co. B 27th CVI for a term of nine months. He was sick in the hospital in November and December 1862. On 1 December 1862 he was sick in McDougall General Hospital at Fort Schuyler, New York with acute rheumatism. February and March 1863 he was again reported as sick in the hospital. From 10 April to 21 April 1863 he was reported absent without leave, having overstayed his furlough. He probably did not go to Fredericksburg or Chancellorsville. Roger Hall was mustered out with the rest of his regiment at New Haven on 27 July 1863. He was the brother-in-law of Richard J. Paine.

He applied for an invalid pension on 5 June 1891 under the act of 27 June 1890. His application states he still suffers from an abscess in his right hip contracted while in the service and other ailments, preventing him from working. He was described as five feet ten inches tall. He was married at Branford by Rev. Henry Olmstead in the Trinity Episcopal Church parsonage on 26 August 1852 to Eliza Fanny Page. Neither were previously married or divorced. They had two children living (in 1898): Harriet R., born on 1 December 1852; and Frank R., born on 23 April 1868.

Roger Hall died at Stony Creek, Branford on 29 January 1905 and was buried in Stony Creek Cemetery. A G.A.R. marker was on his gravesite in 1934 and 2011 and his name appears on the Stony Creek Veterans' Monument. A copy of his death certificate is in the file. He was born at Stony Creek on 20 February 1831, son of Alanson Hall and Martha R. Walker, born at Wallingford and Branford. He was a member of the Mason Rogers Post No. 7 G.A.R. of Branford.

---

634 Branford Vital Records, 1863-1895, 243; no parents given; Talcott, *Families of Guilford, Connecticut*, 1186. Talcott calls her husband John Giles Hall; the marriage record in the pension file calls him John Gilbert Hall. She gave his name as Gilbert Hall on a deposition dated 18 December 1866.

Eliza F. Hall of Stony Creek applied for a widow's pension on 25 February 1905. She died at Stony Creek on 6 March 1908 and was buried in Stony Creek Cemetery.[635] She was born at Stony Creek on 30 June 1831, daughter of Dennis Smith Page and Almira Louisa Hull.[636]

HALLING, WILLIAM
Co. D 5th CVI, private, drafted 25 July 1863, deserted, no pension

William Halling of Branford served as a substitute or was drafted on 25 July 1863 as a private in Co. D 5th CVI. He deserted on 16 October 1863. He does not appear in the 1860 census at Branford.

HANSON, PETER
Co. K 6th, private, enlisted 22 February 1864, possibly to U.S. Navy, no pension

Peter Hanson of Branford enlisted on 22 February 1864 as a private in Co. K 6th CVI. He was on detached duty 30 July 1864 awaiting transfer to the U.S. Navy. There is no further military record. He does not appear in the 1860 census at Branford.

HARGENT, JOHN
Co. M 2nd HA, private, enlisted 11 February 1864, deserted 21 February 1864, no pension

John Hergent of Branford enlisted on 11 February 1864 as a private in Co. M 2nd HA and deserted on 21 February 1864. He does not appear in the 1860 census at Branford.

HARLOW, HENRY P.
Co. K 11th CVI, private, enlisted 11 October 1861, discharged disability 14 June 1862, pension #344050 for the soldier

Henry P. Harlow of Killingworth enlisted on 11 October 1861 and was mustered in at Hartford on 27 November 1861 as a private in Co. K 11th CVI for a term of three years. He was discharged for disability at New Bern, North Carolina on 14 June 1862.

He applied for an invalid pension on 16 February 1881. He was described as five feet three inches tall, light complexion, brown hair, blue eyes, occupation farmer. On 4 February 1862 at Hatteras Island while drilling he fell over a tree stump and injured his left knee. On 24 December 1863 at Annapolis, Maryland while building sheds for the officer's horses his left knee was injured again by a falling timber and

635 Branford Vital Records, deaths, 1908.
636 Branford Vital Records, 1786-1840, 378.

was discharged due to the injury. He appears in the 1880 census at Branford, age 47, with his wife Laura P., age 47, daughter Henrietta age 18; all born at Connecticut.[637] From 1883 until 13 September 1890 he lived at Wethersfield. His pension file provides no further information as to his marriage or children. It appears his wife was Laura R. Crossley who was married first to Stephen P. Harlow.

Henry P. Harlow died at Branford on 19 October 1890 and was buried there in Center Cemetery.[638] His company and regiment are engraved on his stone and there was a Civil War marker was on his gravesite in 1934.

HARLOW, STEPHEN P.
Co. K 2nd HA, private, enlisted 6 August 1862, wounded, to Co. K 22nd VRC, discharged 4 July 1865, pension #102142 for the soldier

Stephen P. Harlow of Morris enlisted at Washington, Connecticut on 6 August 1862 and was mustered in at Litchfield on 11 September 1862 as a private in Co. K 2nd HA for a term of three years. He was wounded at Cold Harbor, Virginia on 1 June 1864 and was treated in the field hospital. He was admitted to Sickle General Hospital, Alexandria, Virginia on 7 June 1864. He was transferred to Blackwell's Island General Hospital, New York on 31 July 1864 and to Knight Hospital, New Haven on 16 September 1864. He deserted on 4 October 1864 but returned on October 16th and entered the hospital at Readville, Massachusetts on 18 October. He was transferred to Co. K 22nd VRC on 3 February 1865. Stephen Harlow was mustered out at Camp Dennison, Cleveland, Ohio on 4 July 1865 when his term expired.

He applied for an invalid pension on 21 January 1869 for a gunshot wound to the right shoulder and thigh. He states he was wounded at the Battle of Cold Harbor, Virginia taking a ball through his right shoulder, another in the arm and one in the leg. His arm was still very weak and could only be lifted slightly, the shoulder blade was out of place and never healed properly, and the arm feels dumb all the time. He was also wounded in the left arm below the elbow leaving that arm weak and painful. The gunshot wound to his right leg above the knee has left him lame and he is unable to perform only light manual labor for short periods of time. At the time of his discharge he was described as age 32, five feet six inches tall, light complexion, blue eyes, light hair, occupation farmer. On 29 December 1868 he was a resident of New Preston and 1877 of Salem, New London Co. He appears at Branford in 1883 as a pensioner and in 1887 was living at Clinton. His pension payment was $4.00 per month for a one half disability and he tried for many years to have the rate increased. A physician in 1875, hired by the pension board, upon examination of the soldier determined Harlow was three fourths disabled and recommended a monthly rate of $6.00 but the request was denied.

In 1898 he states he was a widower, married to Egin? Wallace at Hadlyme (no date given) and was not previously married. He had two children living (in 1898): Stephen A., born on 5 January 1854; and Julia, born on 3 January 1856.

It appears he was married at Lyme by John S. Welles, JP on 26 September 1848 to Laura R. Crossley.[639] He was living at Wethersfield, she at Lyme. They were probably divorced and Laura married second Henry P. Harlow, perhaps Stephen's nephew.[640] By 1860, Stephen's son Stephen A. is living with Henry and Laura at Hartford.

---

637 U.S. census 1880, Branford, New Haven County, Connecticut, population schedule, T9-107, dwelling 252, family 298, page 540, www.heritagequest.com.
638 Branford Vital Records, 1863-1895, 242.
639 Barbour Collection, Lyme Vital Records 3:191.
640 Henry P. Harlow is perhaps the son of John Harlow and Emeline Goodrich; Stephen is perhaps the son of John Harlow and Ruth Vibbert. Further research is needed on Laura R. Crossley of Lyme, see Vicki S. Welch, *The Connecticut Nutmegger*, Dec. 2002, 381.

Stephen P. Harlow died at Rocky Hill on 19 July 1898 and was buried there in Rocky Hill Cemetery.[641] His company and regiment are engraved on his stone and there was a Civil War marker on his gravesite in 1934. He was born at Wethersfield.

HARRIS, THEODORE
Co. E 1st HA, private, enlisted 5 December 1864, mustered out 25 September 1865, pension #842146 for the soldier

Theodore Harris of Branford enlisted on 5 December 1864 as a private in Co. E 1st HA and served with his regiment at the Siege of Petersburg and Richmond, Virginia. He was mustered out with the rest of his regiment at Washington, D.C. 25 September 1865 and discharged at Hartford on 1 October 1865. He does not appear in the 1860 census at Branford. He applied for an invalid pension on 4 December 1891 under the act of 27 June 1890.

HARRISON, BENJAMIN F.
Independent Corps, New York Infantry, surgeon, commissioned 1 August 1862, mustered out 7 February 1864, no pension

Benjamin F. Harrison, a physician from Wallingford, served as surgeon of the New York Volunteer Light Infantry and was on the Sanitary Commission. (Rockey, History of New Haven County, I:426)

Benjamin F. Harrison[642] attended Yale University Medical School and graduated in 1836. Before the war he practiced in New York City, Milford, Cincinnati, Ohio, and Wallingford. He was commissioned by Governor Morgan of New York on 1 August 1862 as surgeon of the Independent Corps, New York Volunteer Light Infantry, already in the field at Yorktown, Virginia. The corps served in South Carolina at Beaufort, St. Helena, Folly Island, and Morris Island. Benjamin F. Harrison was mustered out with the rest of his regiment on 7 February 1864. He then entered the service of the Sanitary Commission and was assigned to South Carolina and Florida. At the close of 1864 he returned to Wallingford where he remained the rest of his life.[643] He received an honorary A. M. degree from Yale University in 1872.

He was married first on 8 June 1837 to Susan Lewis of Wallingford who died on 10 September 1839, daughter of Frederick Lewis. He was married second on 20 June 1868 to Virginia Victoria Abell of Franklin, Connecticut who died on 27 December 1869. He was married third in 1885 to Sarah Electa Hall of Wallingford. She was born on 19 November 1839, daughter of Joel Hall and Hannah Beach. Sarah Hall Harrison died on 9 January 1916 and was buried In Memoriam Cemetery, Wallingford.

Dr. Benjamin Franklin Harrison died at Wallingford on 23 April 1886 and was buried there In Memoriam Cemetery. There was a Civil War marker on the gravesite in 1934. He was born at Northford on 19 April 1811, son of Elizur Harrison and Rebecca Bartholomew.

---

641 The Hale Collection, Rocky Hill, 67.
642 For his biography see Rockey, *History of New Haven County*, I:424; Hart, *Representative Citizens of Connecticut*, 366.
643 Rockey, *History of New Haven County*, I:425.

HARRISON, C. ALBERT or CHARLES ALBERT
Co. B 27th CVI, corporal, enlisted 20 August 1862, discharged 30 July 1863, pension #XC2999559 for the soldier and later for his widow Ann

C. Albert Harrison[644] of North Branford, age 20, enlisted on 20 August 1862 and was mustered in on 3 October 1862 as a corporal in Co. B 27th CVI for a term of nine months. He fought at the Battle of Fredericksburg on 13 December 1862 with the rest of the company. He probably fought at the Battle of Chancellorsville[645] on 3 May 1863 or was on picket duty. On 27 May 1863 he was charged with neglect of duty near Falmouth for allowing a Rhode Island soldier to swim across the Rappahannock River and hold communication with the enemy. On 15 June 1863 while marching he was taken with a severe headache and admitted on 18 June 1863 to General Hospital at Alexandria, Virginia. On 28 June 1863 he was transferred to Knight Hospital, New Haven where he was discharged on 30 July 1863. He was the brother of Nathan A. Harrison also of Co. B 27th CVI. Before the war he attended the Mills Military School in New Haven.[646]

Following the war, C. Albert Harrison moved to Paw Paw, Michigan and was a practicing attorney. He lived in Paw Paw from August 1863 until July 1883. He moved to Wallingford in 1883 and maintained a summer home in North Branford. He was a member and commander of the Arthur H. Dutton Post No. 36 G.A.R. of Wallingford and judge advocate of the Connecticut G.A.R. He represented Co. B on the committee to erect a monument in honor of the 27th CVI at Gettysburg.

He applied for an invalid pension on 30 April 1896 under the act of 27 June 1890. He was described as five feet eight inches tall, light complexion, gray eyes, black hair.

He was married first at Paw Paw, Van Buren Co., Michigan by Rev. A. E. Hastings of the Presbyterian Church on 29 April 1867 to Emma I. Southwell. He was age 23, living at Paw Paw, she was age 17 living at Decatur, Van Buren County. She was born in New York, daughter of Enoch Southwell and Mary Bryant. They were divorced in 1874. She was married second to Mr. Longwell. Emma Isabella Harrison Longwell died on 12 May 1909 age 58 years, 4 months & 22 days at Paw Paw, Michigan.

He was married second at North Branford by Rev. Edson L. Clark of the North Branford Congregational Church on 5 September 1876 to Anna Isabelle Munger of North Branford. They had two children: Lillian M., born on 28 July 1877 and Blanche E., born on 28 February 1879. In 1906 he names another daughter by his first marriage, Helen E., born in 1872.

Charles Albert Harrison died at North Branford on 28 April 1927 and was buried there in Bare Plain Cemetery. A G.A.R. marker was on the gravesite in 1934 and 2011. A copy of his death certificate is in his file. He was born at North Branford on 28 July 1842, son of Albert Harrison and Anna Foote, born at North Branford and Northford.

---

644 For his biography, see William Richard Cutter, *Genealogical and Family History of the State of Connecticut* (New York: Lewis Historical Society Co., 1911), I:119.

645 His biography in Cutter states he took part in the battles of Fredericksburg and Chancellorsville, he was not taken prisoner with the rest of the 27th.

646 Cutter, *Family History of Connecticut*, 119.

Anna Isabelle Harrison filed for a widow's pension on 22 June 1927. She died at North Branford on 11 March 1945 and was buried there in Bare Plain Cemetery. She was born at North Madison on 30 March 1857, daughter of George Hubbard Munger and Susan Torrey.

HARRISON, ELIZUR H.
Co. F 1st HA, private, enlisted 26 March 1862, wounded 6 August 1864, discharged 25 March 1865, no pension

Elizur H. Harrison of North Branford enlisted on 26 March 1862 as a private in Co. F 1st HA for a term of three years. With his regiment he fought at Chickahominy and Malvern Hill, Virginia. He was wounded at Petersburg, Virginia on 6 August 1864 and discharged on 25 March 1865 when his term expired. He was the son of Sylvanus Harrison of the 10th CVI. He never applied for a pension.

Elizur Henry Harrison he died at North Branford on 9 April 1873 age 27 and was buried there in Northford Cemetery. [647] A Civil War marker was on his gravesite in 1934 and his name appears on the Northford Veterans' Monument. He may have been married to Jane E. or Jennie who was married on 23 September 1874 to Francis Cook Bartholomew as his second wife.[648] She had a daughter Lulu May born c. 1870 who was adopted by Bartholomew.[649]

HARRISON, FRANKLIN M.
Co. A 15th CVI, private, enlisted 17 July 1862, discharged disability 8 January 1863, Co. H 3rd Veterans Corps, enlisted 1 March 1865, discharged 1 September 1865, pension #354076 for the soldier

Franklin M. Harrison, age 21, of Meriden enlisted at New Haven on 17 July 1862 and was mustered in on 25 August 1862 as a private in Co. A 15th CVI for a term of three years. He was left at Camp Casey near Fairfax Seminary, Virginia on 1 December 1862 due to sickness. He was discharged for disability from General Hospital, Chestnut Hill, Philadelphia, Pennsylvania on 8 January 1863 for lung disease. He reenlisted at Hartford on 1 March 1865 as a private in Co. H 3rd Veterans Corps and did office work at Hartford. He was discharged at Hartford on 1 September 1865.

He applied for an invalid pension on 27 May 1863. At the time of enlistment he was described as five feet six inches tall, light complex-

Gravestones for Elizur Harrison at Northford Cemetery.

647 The Hale Collection, North Branford, 73.
648 Bartholomew, *Record of Bartholomew Family*, I:291.
649 U.S. census 1880, North Branford, New Haven County., roll 107, Francis C. Bartholomew household, dwelling 242, family 262, page 525B, www.heritagequest.com.

ion, brown hair, blue eyes, occupation farmer. He was injured at Fairfax, Virginia about 1 November 1863 by falling on his right side while crossing a stream, resulting in lung disease. He was treated in a hospital at Washington, D.C. and then at a hospital in Philadelphia where he was discharged. He received a pension but was dropped from the rolls on 14 July 1886 due to recovery of his illness. He reapplied for a pension on 29 September 1894 which was sent for special examination and rejected. There are many documents in the file concerning his lung disease. In 1905 he received a partial disability pension and later a full pension as his lung disease progressed.

After his discharge he lived at North Branford and in 1868 moved to Iowa with his parents. He lived in Polk County near Des Moines; 1879 moved to Boone, Dallas County; and in the Fall of 1886 moved to Waukee, Dallas Co., Iowa. He was a resident of the Solder's Home in Marshall County in 1895. He returned to Polk County living at Valley Junction and Campbell, Iowa.

He was married on 27 October 1890, the name of his wife is not given in the pension file.[650] She was previously married and had a son William P. Bennett of Des Moines and a son-in-law William Fuller of Valley Junction. She never applied for a pension.[651]

Franklin M. Harrison died at Campbell, Iowa on 26 February 1915. He was born at North Branford on 7 April 1841, son of Lyman Harrison and Emily Rogers.

HARRISON, HART LIND or H. LYNDE HARRISON
27th CVI, quartermaster, enlisted, 25 September 1862, resigned 20 January 1863, no pension

Hart Lind Harrison[652] of Branford enlisted on 25 September 1862 as quartermaster of the 27th CVI and was commissioned as an officer on 6 October 1862. He was sick in the hospital in December 1862 and January 1863. On 14 January 1863 he was back in Branford and writes a letter of resignation. He states that since camp at Falmouth he has been quite sick with bronchial hemorrhage. His resignation was accepted at New Haven on 20 January 1863 and he was honorably discharged. "There is probably no harm in saying now that he greatly desired to go out as adjutant of the Twenty-seventh C. V. and was thoroughly disgusted when he was appointed quartermaster and resigned his commission three months later. One cannot but wonder what would have happened had he secured the place he coveted."[653] In 1864 he provided a substitute since he did not serve a full term. He was the brother of William H. Harrison.

H. Lynde Harrison was born at New Haven on 15 December 1837, son of James Harrison and Charlotte Nicoll Lynde. He graduated from Yale Law School in 1860. He was an attorney, judge, state senator, and Connecticut speaker of the house with a long career in public service.

H. Lynde Harrison of Branford was quartermaster of Co. B 27th CVI but resigned due to illness. He had a long career in public service as an attorney, state senator, and judge. (Hart, Encyclopedia of Connecticut Biography, 41)

---

650 U.S. census 1900, Des Moines, Polk Co., Iowa, her name is given as Susan C. age 53, population schedule, T624-419, dwelling 559, family 584, page 227, www.heritagequest.com.

651 Franklin Harrison is living alone in the 1910 census at Des Moines.

652 For his biography see Beers, *Biographical Record of New Haven County*, 688; William T. Davis, *The New England States* (Boston: D. H. Hurd & Co., 1902), 1101; Hart, *Representative Citizens of Connecticut*, 360; Samuel Hart, *Encyclopedia of Connecticut Biography, Genealogical Memorial Representative Citizens* (New York: the American Historical Society 1917), 41.

653 Obituary, *Shore Line Times*, 14 June 1906, 1.

After the war he lived at Branford and Guilford. He was a charter member and commander of the Parmelee Post No. 42 G.A.R. of Guilford and a member of the Admiral Foote Post No. 17 G.A.R. of New Haven.

He was married first at Branford by Rev. David D. Bishop of Trinity Episcopal Church on 7 May 1866 to Sarah Frisbie Plant of Branford.[654] She died at Guilford on 10 March 1879 and was buried in East Cemetery, Guilford.[655] He was married second on 30 September 1886 to Harriet Sage White of Waterbury, daughter of Luther C. White.[656] She died on 7 June 1922 and was buried in Grove Street Cemetery, New Haven.

H. Lynde Harrison died at Guilford on 8 June 1906 and was buried in Grove Street Cemetery, New Haven.

HARRISON, JOHN C.
see James Morse

HARRISON, JOHN H.
see Joseph Dietrich

HARRISON, LORENZO E.
Co. K 15th CVI, private, enlisted 6 August 1862, mustered out 27 June 1865, pension #852815 for the soldier and later for his widow Mary

Lorenzo E. Harrison, age 42, of North Branford enlisted at New Haven on 6 August 1862 and was mustered in on 25 August 1862 as a private in Co. K 15th CVI for a term of three years. He was in the hospital at New Bern and Moorehead City, North Carolina from April until December 1864 with remittent fever. Harrison was mustered out with the rest of his regiment at New Bern, North Carolina on 27 June 1865 and discharged at New Haven on 12 July 1865. He was the brother of Sylvanus Harrison and served under Capt. Medad D. Munson of Wallingford.

He applied for an invalid pension on 30 April 1888. At the time of his enlistment he was described as five feet eight inches tall, dark complexion, blue eyes, brown hair, occupation farmer. At Fredericksburg, Virginia on 11 December 1862 he severely sprained his left ankle while under fire from the enemy. He was brought back to camp and did not fight at the battle two days later. For about three months he was unable to perform duty in the ranks and was detailed as a cook. At New Bern, North Carolina in the Fall of 1864 he contracted malarial poisoning and was treated in the hospital. Since his discharge he lived at Northford, 1879 to Wallingford and May 1883 he returned to Northford. He summered in Branford. A letter from Henry N. Pardee about his injury is in his pension file.

654 Branford Vital Records, 1863-1895, 135.
655 *Branford Gleaner*, 12 March 1879; a gravestone for her is also at Center Cemetery, Branford in the Plant plot and at Grove Street Cemetery, New Haven.
656 Beers, *Biographical Record of New Haven County*, 689.

camp Mud Falmouth Va. I think the
12th of Dec 1862 and marched Towards Fredericksburgh.
We was Halted on Top of The Hill before reaching The River.
while There The Enemy dropped several
Shills [shells] in amongst The Regt. we was formed in
line and marched To The Rear to get out of the
range of the Shells and it was in this rear
March that L. E. Harrison Spraned his Ankle
he made a misstep in crossing a ditch and
fell being assisted to rise he found that
his Ankle was badly Sprained so much
so that when we was formed in line
again within an hour or So to March to
Fredericksburgh he was unable to go with us
but was helped back to Camp Mud which we
had left in the Morning. I did not see him
again for two or three days or until the Regt.
was marched back to camp Mud. at that time
his Ankle was badly swollen and he was
unable to walk.

He was married first on 17 December 1846 to Antoinette Todd of Northford. They were divorced on 16 March 1874. He had three children (living in 1898): Ella A., born on August 1849; Louise A., born on June 1851, and Urban T., born on 3 May 1855. He was a member of the Arthur Dutton Post No. 36 G.A.R. of Wallingford.

Lorenzo Elizur Harrison died at Branford on 15 June 1906 and was buried in Northford Cemetery, North Branford. His company and regiment are engraved on his stone and a Civil War marker was on his gravesite in 1934. His name appears on the Northford Veterans' Monument. He was born at Northford on 10 April 1820, son of Elizur Harrison and Rebecca Bartholomew, both born at Northford.

Mary J. Harrison applied for a widow's pension on 25 July 1906 but died before receiving her pension. She was married to the soldier under the name of Mary J. Doolittle at Northford by Rev. George D. Folsom on 8 August 1878. He was age 58, living at North Branford; she was age 49, born at North Haven, living at Wallingford. She was the widow of Albert B. Doolittle of Wallingford. Albert B. Doolittle died at Wallingford on 22 August 1877 age 49; son of Enos and Charity Doolittle.

Mary J. Harrison died at Northford on 4 December 1906 age 76 and was buried in Northford Cemetery.[657] She was the daughter of Anson Bassett and Phebe Barnes.

---

657 North Branford Vital Records, deaths, 1906.

HARRISON, NATHAN A.
Co. B 27th CVI, private, enlisted 9 September 1862, prisoner, mustered out 27 July 1863, pension #736091 for the soldier and later for his widow Anna

Nathan A. Harrison[658] of North Branford, age 26, enlisted on 9 September 1862 and was mustered in on 3 October 1862 as a private in Co. B 27th CVI for a term of nine months. He was on picket duty during the Battle of Fredericksburg. He was captured at the Battle of Chancellorsville, Virginia on 3 May 1863, held prisoner at Richmond, and paroled at City Point, Virginia on 14 May 1863. He reported to Camp Parole, Maryland on 16 May 1863 and spent the remainder of his service at Camp Convalescent, Virginia. With the rest of the Chancellorsville paroled prisoners, he rejoined the Regiment at Baltimore on 20 July 1863. Nathan A. Harrison was mustered out with the rest of his regiment at New Haven on 27 July 1863. He was the brother of C. Albert Harrison also of Co. B 27th CVI.

He filed an invalid pension on 26 June 1880. He was described as five feet nine inches tall, light complexion, brown hair, blue eyes, occupation farmer. "In December 1862 I was placed on the picket line and remained there through the Battle of Fredericksburg. I was deafened by the cannonading and had my forefinger on my left hand struck with what I suppose was a splinter of a shell. After the battle they removed the fragment. Afterwards I suffered from a throbbing sensation in my ears. I was not well after the battle, sick with a severe attack of fever which rendered me unconscious. I was placed in the hospital at Falmouth. Since that time I have been very deaf."[659] There is no medical record in his CMSR. The Surgeon General's Office did report that he was admitted to Regimental Hospital on 27 December 1862 and again on 29 January 1863, released on 16 February 1863.

His pension file is large with many depositions from fellow soldiers and physicians concerning his disability. The pension board wanted proof that he was not deaf before his enlistment. His mother "was deaf from my earliest recollection." He did not claim a disability for the injured finger which other soldiers said "was crooked." He received a partial disability pension. There are more depositions, mostly from family and neighbors in 1896, proving that his deafness now prevents him from working. "His hearing was greatly impaired throughout his remaining days."[660] He was a member of the Mason Rogers Post No. 7 G.A.R. of Branford and the Admiral Foote Post No. 17 G.A.R. of New Haven.

Nathan A. Harrison died at North Branford on 26 November 1911 and was buried there in Bare Plain Cemetery. His regiment is engraved on his stone and he had a G.A.R. marker on his gravesite in 1934. A copy of his death certificate is in the file. He was born at North Branford on 27 June 1836, son of Albert Harrison and Anna Hall Foote, born at North Branford and Northford.

Anna Louise Harrison of North Branford applied for a widow's pension on 5 December 1911. She was married to the soldier under the name of Anna Louise Strickland at New Haven by Rev. Edward L. Drown of St. Paul's Church on 24 September 1862. They were ages 26 and 18, both living in New Haven. Neither were previously married or divorced. They had five sons: Nathan Irving, born on 24 July 1864; Albert Eu-

---

658 For his biography see Rockey, *History of New Haven County*, II:100; Hill, *Modern History of New Haven*, II:156.
659 Pension application, Nathan A. Harrison, 26 June 1880, in his own pension file.
660 Hill, *Modern History of New Haven*, II:156.

gene, born on 8 October 1866; Lewis Strickland, born on 6 December 1868; Royal Nelson, born on 6 March 1871; and John Rose, born on 10 March 1882.

Anna L. Harrison died at Branford on 6 March 1926 and was buried in Bare Plain Cemetery, North Branford. She was born at New Haven on 3 February 1844, daughter of Royal Nelson Strickland and Mary Louise Hayden.[661]

HARRISON, SYLVANUS
Co. C 10th CVI, private, enlisted 28 September 1861, discharged 21 October 1864, pension #371207 for his widow Caroline

Sylvanus Harrison of North Branford enlisted at Hartford on 28 September 1861 and was mustered in on 22 October 1861 as a private in Co. C 10th CVI for a term of three years. On 8 February 1862 he had to lie on the ground in a cornfield in a drenching rain and contracted a hard cold and rheumatism. He was sent to the hospital and never returned to his regiment. He was on detached duty in March and April 1862 at Regimental Hospital in New Bern, North Carolina. In July and August 1863 he was on detached service on the convalescent ship *Cosmopolitan* at St. Augustine, Florida. In March and April 1864 he was sick at Knight General Hospital, New Haven and from May until August working there as a nurse. He was transferred to the 159th 2nd Battery Veteran's Invalid Corps on 7 May 1864. He was discharged at Hartford on 21 October 1864 when his term expired. He was the father of Elizur H. Harrison of the 1st HA and brother of Lorenzo Harrison.

Sylvanus Harrison died at North Branford on 26 May 1878 age 62 and was buried there in Northford Cemetery. His company and regiment are engraved on his stone and Civil War marker was on his gravesite in 1934. His name appears on the Northford Veterans' Monument. He was born at North Branford, son of Elizur Harrison and Rebecca Bartholomew. He was not a pensioner.

Caroline C. Harrison, age 68, of New Haven applied for a widow's pension on 19 April 1888. She was married to the soldier under the name of Caroline C. Jones at Durham by Rev. Henry Gleason of the Durham Congregational Church on 16 February 1837. Neither were previously married or divorced. In 1889 she moved to Springfield, Hampton Co., Massachusetts to live with her daughter Delia Andrews.

HARRISON, WILLIAM H.
Co. A 7th CVI, private, enlisted 19 August 1861, died 26 October 1862, pension #41820 for his widow Sarah

William Holton Harrison of Southington enlisted at New Haven on 19 August 1861 and was mustered in as a private in Co. A 7th CVI for a term of three years. He died at Regimental Hospital in Hilton Head, South Carolina on 26 October 1862 of typhoid fever.[662] His company and regiment are engraved on his gravestone

---

661 Branford Vital Records, deaths, 1926.
662 The Frisbie Genealogy gives his death as 12 October 1862 at Port Royal, South Carolina.

at Oak Hill Cemetery, Southington and there was a Civil War marker on his gravesite in 1934.[663] He was the son of James Harrison and Charlotte Nicholl Lynde of Branford and was the brother of H. Lynde Harrison.

Sarah L. Harrison, age 25, of Southington applied for a widow's pension on 16 September 1864. She was married to the soldier under the name of Sarah Louisa Frisbie at Southington by Rev. Elisha C. Jones of the Congregational Church on 31 May 1858. No children are named in the file. She was born at Southington on 8 March 1839, daughter of Martin Frisbie and Sarah Moore. She was married second at Southington on 17 October 1866 to Edward William Twitchell who served in the Civil War.[664]

HART, HENRY T.
Co. B 27th CVI, private, enlisted 19 August 1862, mustered out 27 July 1863, pension #403636 for his widow Ellen

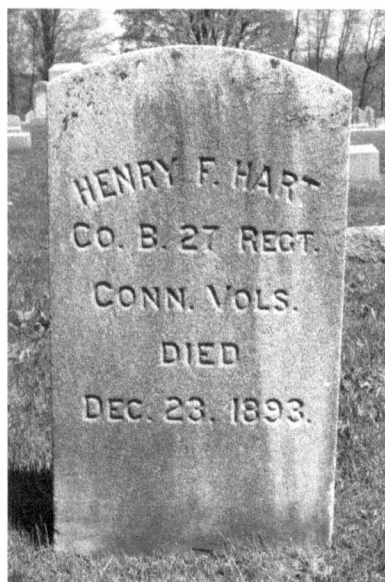

Henry T. Hart of Branford enlisted on 19 August 1862 and was mustered in on 3 October 1862 as a private in Co. B 27th CVI for a term of nine months. It appears he served throughout the war with the company and fought at the Battles of Fredericksburg on 13 December 1862, Chancellorsville on 3 May 1863, and Gettysburg 1-3 July 1863. Hart was mustered out with the rest of his regiment at New Haven on 27 July 1863.

Henry Timothy Hart died at Branford on 26 December 1893 age 52 and was buried there in Center Cemetery. His company and regiment are engraved on his stone and there was a Civil War marker was on his gravesite in 1934. He never applied for a pension. He was living at Branford in 1860.[665] He is probably the Henry Hart, age 9, living with George and Lavia Hart at Guilford in 1850.[666]

Ellen Hart of 352 Edgewood Avenue, New Haven applied for a widow's pension on 11 May 1894 receiving an additional $2.00 per month for her daughter Minnie E. who was under the age of sixteen. Minnie was born at South Water Street, New Haven on 25 November 1878, daughter of Henry T. Hart, age 38, born at Guilford, a teamster; and Ellen Page, age 27, born at Branford, their 3rd child.

She was married to the soldier under the name of Ellen Page at Branford by Rev. Elijah C. Baldwin of the First Congregational Church on 19 November 1866. He was age 23, born at Guilford; she was age 18, born at Branford. She lived in the same neighborhood as him at New Haven and married him after the war. Neither were previously married or divorced. Ellen Hart was dropped from the pension rolls on 29 June 1895 due to her marriage to Mr. Mills. She died at Oneonta, New York on 20 October 1900 and was buried in Center Cemetery, Branford.[667] She was the daughter of Charles Page and Caroline Roberts of Branford.

663 The Hale Collection, Southington, 72.
664 Frisbie, *Edward Frisbie of Branford*, I, 551.
665 U.S. census *1860*, Branford, New Haven County, Connecticut, population schedule, M653-85, dwelling 862, family 964, page 898; age 18, a farm laborer living with Malachi Linsley, www.heritagequest.com.
666 U.S. census 1850, Guilford, New Haven County, Connecticut, population schedule, M432-45, dwelling 222, family 274, page 118A, www.ancestry.com.
667 *The Branford Opinion*, 27 October 1900.

HARTSON, ISAAC Y.
Co. K 25th CVI, private, enlisted 26 August 1862, discharged 26 August 1863, pension #A1-12-27 for the soldier and later for his widow R. Lena

Isaac Y. Hartson of Farmington enlisted at Hartford on 9 September 1862 and was mustered in on 11 November 1862 as a private in Co. K 25th CVI for a term of nine months. The regiment served in New Orleans, Louisiana. He was wounded at the Battle of Irish Bend, Louisiana on 14 April 1863 and mustered out with the rest of his regiment at Hartford on 26 August 1863.

He applied for an invalid pension on 24 February 1868. He received a severe gunshot wound at Irish Bend, Louisiana on 14 April 1863 to the left leg below the knee resulting in damage to the tendons, knee, and muscles leaving the entire leg weak. He was admitted to University General Hospital at New Orleans on 17 April 1863. At the time of his enlistment he was described as five feet nine inches tall, light complexion, blue eyes, light hair, occupation carriage trimmer. After his discharge he lived at Plainville and moved to Branford in 1903. He was transferred from the Newton T. Monross Post No. 27 G.A.R. of Forestville and became a member and commander of the Mason Rogers Post No. 7 of Branford. There are several pension applications for increased benefits and communications with the pension board regarding his payments. There are a number of depositions concerning his marriages.

He was married first at Plainville on 28 November 1860 to Annette Winston Dealing who died at Plainville on 12 September 1889 age 47, daughter of Benjamin and Eunice Dealing. He was married second at Plainville on 12 November 1890 to Julia Johnson who died two months later at Plainville on 13 January 1891 age 48, daughter of Jerome Johnson. He was married third at Plainville by Rev. J. W. Simpson on 24 November 1892 to Lena Peck of Plainville. She was not previously married or divorced. He had the following children: by his first marriage - Frederick D., born on 10 September 1861, died on 26 April 1903; Chas. M., born on 1 January 1870; and by his third marriage - Merritt I., born on 31 March 1894. Merritt enlisted on 14 December 1917 as a private first class in the 11th Company 152 Depot Base Hospital 48 A.E.F. during the World War and was discharged on 7 May 1919. Merritt Hartson was living at Branford in 1932.

Isaac Yale Hartson died at Short Beach, Branford on 18 May 1926 and was buried in West Cemetery, Plainville. He was born at Meriden on 20 September 1839, son of Merritt E. Hartson and Emeline Yale.

R. Lena Hartson of Branford applied for a widow's pension on 25 May 1926. Rosa Lena Hartson died at Branford on 3 June 1932 age 65 and was buried in West Cemetery, Plainville. She was born at Burlington, daughter of Seth Peck and Rosa Moses.[668]

HENRY, JAMES H.
Co. G 1st HA, private, enlisted 16 November 1863, deserted 27 December 1863, no pension

James H. Henry of North Branford enlisted on 16 November 1863 and was mustered in on 6 December 1863 as a private in Co. G 1st HA. He deserted on 27 December 1863.

---

668 *The Branford Review*, 9 June 1932, 1.

HICKMAN, JOHN T.

Navy, 2nd lieutenant Co. E 1st Maryland Cavalry, pension #815805 for the soldier and later for his wife Virginia

John T. Hickman of Maryland served in the Navy before the Civil War from 1858 until 1860 as a landsman on the ships *Alleghany*, *Bainbridge*, and *Pennsylvania*. He enlisted as a 2nd lieutenant during the Civil War in Co. E 1st H. B. Maryland Cavalry.

He applied for an invalid pension on 19 November 1890 under the act of 27 June 1890. He was mustered into the Mason Rogers Post No. 7 G.A.R. of Branford on 23 June 1892.[669] He does not appear in the 1880 census at Branford or in the 1895 city directory.

He was born in Maryland, and died on 7 April 1906. Virginia B. Hickman of Maryland applied for a widow's pension on 10 April 1906.

HIGGS, ISRAEL

Co. B 27th CVI, private, enlisted 8 September 1862, discharged disability 5 March 1863, pension #1029506 for the soldier

Israel Higgs, age 27, of New Haven enlisted on 8 September 1862 and was mustered in on 3 October 1862 as a private in Co. B 27th CVI for a term of nine months. He was sick in the hospital November and December 1862. On 23 February 1863 he was discharged from Mt. Pleasant Hospital in Washington, D.C. where he been since 1 December 1862. He was discharged from service on 5 March 1863 from Satterlee General Hospital, Philadelphia due to disability. His discharge paper is in his CMSR. He was described as five feet six inches tall, gray eyes, black hair, dark complexion, occupation blacksmith. He had been unfit for duty for 60 days, cause anemia with enlargement of the liver and general debility. Capt. Ely stated "Israel Higgs was a man of good character. I saw him often in camp near Falmouth and thought he looked very much down in health."[670]

He applied for a pension on 26 February 1899 under the act of 27 June 1890. He received a partial pension, was unable to connect his present physical condition to his service. He received a full pension when he reached 70 years of age.

He was born at Mattewan, Dutchess Co., New York on 27 March 1836. He was married first to Miss Martha M. Hubbell at Naugatuck.[671] She died at Bridgeport on August 1861. He was married second at Mount Vernon, Westchester Co., New York by Rev. James M. Carrol of the First Methodist Episcopal Church on 20 November 1871 to Catherine Cecelia Cole. Neither of his wives had previous marriages. He had one child living (in 1899); Albert Lester Higgs, born on 19 February 1883 at Mount Vernon, New York. In 1915 he states that he does not have the dates for the births of his children but they are all dead. During the 1880 census he was living at Eastchester, Westchester Co., New York; age 44, born in New York, a blacksmith; wife Cecelia age 33, born in New York; sons Alonzo F. age 18, born in Connecticut; and Arthur L. age 3, born in New York.[672]

---

669 The Mason Rogers Post records confirm he is the John T. Hickman of Maryland.
670 Affidavit, Calvin L. Ely, 15 March 1900, in the pension file of Israel Higgs.
671 Martha Hubbell was from Naugatuck or they were married there. His writing is poor.
672 U.S. census 1880, Eastchester, Westchester Co., NY; population schedule T9, Roll 945, dwelling 433, family 504, page 208, www.heritagequest.com.

At the time of his enlistment he was living at New Haven. Since his discharge he lived at Bridgeport; Mount Vernon, New York; Utica, New York from 1876 until 1907, and the Soldiers' Home at Bath, Steuben Co., New York by 1912. Israel Higgs died on 19 April 1918, and was buried in the Bath National Cemetery.

HILL, BRYON
Co. B 27th CVI, musician, enlisted 28 August 1862, mustered out 27 July 1863, pension #769942 for the soldier and later for his widow Emma

Bryon Hill, age 21, of Wallingford enlisted on 28 August 1862 and was mustered in on 3 October 1862 as a musician in Co. B 27th CVI for a term of nine months. It appears he was with the company throughout the war and would have fought at the Battles of Fredericksburg on 13 December 1862, Chancellorsville on 3 May 1863, and Gettysburg 1-3 July 1863. Hill was mustered out with the rest of his regiment at New Haven on 27 July 1863.

He applied for an invalid pension on 22 October 1888. He claimed he contracted disease of the lungs from exposure during his service and has suffered ever since and is unable to do manual labor. He was treated at camp by the surgeon in his quarters. "He was often unable to perform duty."[673] There is no medical record in his CMSR. He was described as five feet three inches tall, light complexion, grey eyes, brown hair, occupation farmer. He returned to Wallingford after his discharge and in 1890 was employed at Simpson Hall Millers & Co. as a carton trimmer in room No. 6.

Bryon Hill died at Wallingford on 11 December 1913 and was buried there in Center Street Cemetery. He was born at Wallingford on 28 April 1841, son of William Hill and Susan Hull, born at Guilford and Wallingford.

Emma A. Hill of North Elm Street, Wallingford applied for a widow's pension on 18 December 1913. She was married to the soldier under the name of Emma Augusta Howd by Rev. R. J. Adams of the Baptist Church at Wallingford on 8 October 1868. Neither were previously married or divorced and she did not remarry after his death. They had two children living (in 1898): Frederick B., born on 27 November 1871; and Linus A., born on 5 February 1875. They had another son Elmer, born on 9 February 1873.[674]

Emma A. Hill died on 2 March 1928 age 78 and was buried in Center Street Cemetery, Wallingford.[675] She was born at Wallingford on 11 January 1850, daughter of William Howd and Lucinda Rice.

HILLINE, EDWARD
Co. F 1st HA, private, drafted 7 December 1864, deserted 31 July1865, no pension

Edward Hilline of Branford served as a substitute or was drafted on 7 December 1864 as a private in Co. F 1st HA and deserted on 31 July 1865. He does not appear in the 1860 census at Branford.

HILLINER, JOHN
John Hilliner, age 27, served as a substitute for John Higgins of Branford. He was mustered in at New Haven on 7 December 1864 , unassigned for a term of three years. He was described as five foot six inches tall, hazel eyes, brown hair, fair complexion, unmarried, born in Germany, occupation merchant.[676] No pension was found.

673 Statement, D. W. Field of Los Angeles, 16 September 1889, in the pension file of Byron Hill.
674 Talcott, *Families of Guilford, Connecticut*, 639.
675 The Hale Collection, Wallingford, 55.
676 Muster & Descriptive Rolls of Substitutes, RG 13, box 97, 2nd Congressional District, Connecticut State Library.

HIPWELL, JOHN H. R.
Co. K 2nd HA, private, enlisted 30 December 1863, killed 19 October 1865, no pension

John H. R. Hipwell of Branford enlisted on 30 December 1863 as a private in Co. K 2nd HA for a term of three years. He was killed at Cedar Creek, Virginia on 19 October 1865. There is no pension. He does not appear in the 1860 census at Branford or North Branford.

HITCHCOCK, OLIVER A.
Co. I 25th CVI, private, enlisted 31 October 1862, mustered out 26 August 1863, pension #343921 for the soldier and later for his widow Cornelia

Oliver A. Hitchcock of Southington enlisted at Hartford on 31 October 1862 and was mustered in on 11 November 1862 as a private in Co. I 25th CVI for a term of nine months. He was detailed as a musician and later returned to the ranks. His regiment served in New Orleans, Louisiana and fought at the Battle of Irish Bend on 14 April 1863. Hitchcock was mustered out with the rest of his regiment at Hartford on 26 August 1863.

He applied for an invalid pension on 13 May1879 and was living at Plantsville, Southington. While loading a cannon at Simo Port in May 1863 he contracted a hernia and chronic diarrhea which still affects him. He was in the hospital at Louisiana in July and August 1863. After his discharge he lived at Burlington and Southington. He was married first to Betsey who died on 10 June 1852 age 40.

Oliver A. Hitchcock died at New Haven on 8 July 1891 age 75 and was buried in Quinnipiac Cemetery, Southington. He was the son of Dr. Aaron Hitchcock and Melita Mann; born at Wolcott and Vermont.

Cornelia S. Hitchcock, age 57, of New Haven applied for a widow's pension on 27 July 1891. She was married to the soldier under the name of Cornelia Smith at New Britain by Rev. Horace Winslow on 6 September 1855. He was age 35, born at Burlington; she was age 21, born at Plymouth. She later lived at Short Beach, Branford.

HOADLEY, ORRIN H.
see Charles Fuchs

HOGAN, MICHAEL
Michael Hogan, age 23, served as a substitute for George H. Page of Branford. He was mustered in at New Haven on 29 November 1864 as a private for a term of three years. He was described as six feet tall, blue eyes, dark brown hair, dark complexion, unmarried, born in Ireland, occupation seaman.[677]

---

677 Muster & Descriptive Rolls of Substitutes, RG 13, box 97, 2nd Congressional District, Connecticut State Library; his
       service is not found in *Record of Service of Connecticut Men.*

William W. Holmes of Co. B 27th Connecticut Volunteers was on detached duty in the ambulance corps. (Photographic History of the Civil War, 7:313)

HOLMES, WILLIAM W.

Co. B 27th CVI, private, enlisted 10 September 1862, mustered out 27 July 1863, pension #942599 for the soldier

William W. Holmes, age 24, of Wallingford enlisted on 10 September 1862 and was mustered in on 3 October 1862 as a private in Co. B 27th CVI for a term of nine months. "December 1862 I was detailed in the Ambulance Corp and visited the Regiment occasionally."[678] He fought at the Battle of Fredericksburg on 13 December 1862. In April 1863 he was still detached as a stretcher carrier. In May and June 1863 he was at Mower General Hospital, Chestnut Hill, Philadelphia in Ward 42 and on 14 June 1863 at Emory General Hospital in Washington, D.C. On 3 July 1863 he was admitted to the Lovell General Hospital, Portsmouth, Rhode Island; probably was on duty at the hospitals, not as a patient. There is no record in his CMSR or pension file of medical illness or treatment during the war. Holmes was mustered out with the rest of his regiment at New Haven on 27 July 1863.

He applied for a pension on 15 December 1891 under the act of 27 June 1890. He had fractured his right leg at Glastonbury in 1855 and his right hand in 1866. He was described as five feet nine inches tall, light complexion, hazel eyes, brown hair, occupation mechanic.

He was married at Branford by Rev. Elijah C. Baldwin of the First Congregational Church on 29 October 1865 to Cornelia Augusta Johnson. They had the following children: Nellie A., born on 24 August 1866; William Herbert, born on 19 December 1867; Lelia May, born on 13 October 1869; Eva A., born on 23 April 1872, died before 1898; LeRoy Johnson, born on 27 December 1873; and Nellie Augusta, born on 21 March 1877. Cornelia Holmes died on 18 December 1917, daughter of Frederick W. Johnson and Nancy Linsley. Since his discharge he lived at Wallingford until 1882, New Haven from 1900 until 1902, and Meriden since 1902. In 1913 his eldest brother, James H. Holmes, age 81, was living at Yalesville. James states there is no record of their births but he was always told that William was six years younger than he and born on 12 March 1838.

William Wallace Holmes died at Meriden on 9 December 1918. He was born at Glastonbury, son of Alvah V. Holmes and Mary Alger.

---

678 Deposition, William W. Holmes, 7 March 1885, in the pension file of Nathan A. Harrison

HOPKINS, ALBERT F.

Co. G 13th CVI, corporal, enlisted 16 December 1861, wounded, to Co. D 13th CVI, discharged 25 January 1866, no pension

Albert F. Hopkins of Branford enlisted at New Haven on 16 December 1861 and was mustered in on 22 December 1861 as a private in Co. G 13th CVI for a term of three years. He reenlisted as a veteran in Co. G on 8 February 1864 and was promoted to corporal. With his regiment he served at New Orleans and the Virginia campaign of 1864. He was wounded at Cedar Creek, Virginia on 19 October 1864 and transferred to Co. D 13th CVI and his rank reduced to private. He was discharged on 25 January 1866. He does not appear in the 1860 census at Branford but is on the 1863 draft list; age 20, born in Connecticut, single, occupation farmer.

Albert Hopkins of Branford enlisted in the 13th Connecticut Volunteer Infantry and was wounded at the Battle of Cedar Creek, Virginia. (E. F. Ely's Gallery, Rockville; Branford Historical Society Collection)

HOSLEY, LORING D.

Co. B 26th Mass. Vols, private, enlisted 14 September 1861, mustered out 7 November 1864, pension application #632589 for the soldier

Loring D. Hosley[679] of Townsend, Massachusetts enlisted on 14 September 1861 and was mustered in at Camp Chase, Lowell, Massachusetts on 18 October 1861 as a private in Co. B 26th Massachusetts Volunteers for a term of three years. His regiment saw service in the New Orleans area and in the Shenandoah Valley including the Battles of Bermuda Hundred and Cedar Creek, Virginia. Loring Hosley was mustered out on 7 November 1864. He was the brother of William B. Hosley and first cousin of Samuel Beach.

Loring Davis Hosley was born at Branford on 3 September 1827, son of Loring Dwight Hosley and Anna Aritta Beach.[680] By 1860 he was living at Springfield, Masachusetts. He was married to Margaret Allen who died on 29 May 1892 age 69.[681]

He applied for a pension on 25 April 1896 but died before receiving one. Loring D. Hosley died at Springfield, Massachusetts 7 November 1897.[682]

HOSLEY, WILLIAM B.

Co. K 27th Mass. Vols, private, enlisted 20 August 1862, died 24 October 1862, pension #8993 for his widow Jane and minor son

William B. Hosley of Springfield, Massachusetts enlisted and was mustered in on 20 August 1862 as a private in Co. K 27th Massachusetts Volunteers for a term of three years. He died of typhoid fever at New

---

679   Various spellings - Loring, Loren, Lorin.
680   Branford Vital Records, Town Meeting Book A, 232.
681   Massachusetts deaths 1841-1915 referencing Deaths at Springfield, 427:672, www.familysearch.org.
682   *The Branford Opinion*, 13 November 1897.

Bern, North Carolina on 24 October 1862. "I am sorry to hear of the death of Wm B Hosley, hope it will prove not true. if you should learn any more particulars - write more about it. I suppose he was driven into the Army by force of circumstances."[683] He was the brother of Loring D. Hosley and first cousin of Samuel Beach.

William Beach Hosley was born at Branford on 14 February 1823, son of Loring Dwight Hosley and Anna Aritta Beach.[684] He was living with his parents at Branford in 1850 but appears at Springfield, Massachuetts in 1860 with his wife and family.

Jane M. Hosley applied for a widow's pension on 24 December 1862 and received $8 per month. She was married to the soldier under the name of Jane M. Phelps at Springfield, Massachusetts by Rev. George B. Ide on 27 June1853. He was living at Springfield, age 31, born in Connecticut, his first marriage, a tailor. She was living at Meriden, born at Windsor [Connecticut], age 41, her second marriage. She was the daughter of Phineas Griswold.[685] She received an additional $2 per month under the act of 25 July 1866 for her minor son until he turned age sixteen. Her son Charles O. Hosley was born on 21 February 1855. There is no further record in the pension file after 1866.

HOTCHKISS, JOHN
Co. B 27th CVI, private, enlisted 25 August 1862, discharged 17 June 1863, died 11 February 1864, pension #148262 for his widow Georgianna Cook and his minor children

John Hotchkiss, age 44, of Branford enlisted on 25 August 1862 and was mustered in on 3 October 1862 as a private in Co. B 27th CVI for a term of nine months. He was present at roll call in November and December 1862 and probably fought at the Battle of Fredericksburg on 13 December 1862 with the rest of the company. "Among the number sick is John Hotchkiss."[686]

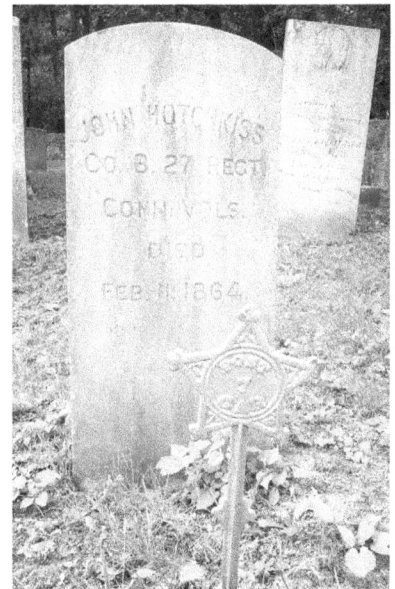

He was sick at Regimental Hospital near Falmouth, Virginia in January and February 1863. In March and April 1863 he was a patient at Stanton General Hospital, Washington, D.C. In May and June 1863 he was at McDougall General Hospital, Fort Schuyler, New York Harbor. He was discharged on 17 June 1863 from Fort Schuyler Hospital and mustered out at New Haven on 27 July 1863 with the rest of the company.

He contracted diarrhea and rheumatism in the service, was sick when he was discharged and died as a result. Capt. Ely stated "while in camp at or near Falmouth in the state of Virginia on or about the 15th day of December 1862 and in the line of his duty, he contracted the disease, continued to suffer from said disease until discharge and died having never recovered."[687]

---

683 Letter, Samuel Beach to home, 18 November 1862.
684 Branford Vital Records, Town Meeting Book A, 232.
685 Marriage data from the pension file and Massachusetts marriages 1841-1915 referencing Springfield marriages for 1853, #110, www.familysearch.org.
686 Letter, Samuel Beach to home, 28 December 1862.
687 Statement, Calvin L. Ely of Branford, 31 May 1865, in the pension file of John Hotchkiss.

He died at Branford on 11 February 1864 and was buried there in Damascus Cemetery. His company and regiment are engraved on his stone and there was a G.A.R. marker on his gravesite in 1934 and 2011. His name appears on the Stony Creek Veterans' Monument. He was born at Branford on 20 September 1816, son of Lancelot Hotchkiss and Lucretia Cook.[688] He was the brother-in-law of Lewis Tucker.

Georgianna Hotchkiss of Stony Creek, Branford applied for a pension on 8 December 1864 under the act of 14 July 1862 as the guardian of his minor children. She was married to the soldier as Georgianna Tucker at Branford by Rev. A. C. Wheat of the First Baptist Church on 2 August 1846. Five children were born at Branford: Alice Mary, born on 8 October 1852; Minnie A., born on 12 January 1855; James Henry, born on 10 October 1857; John S., born on 19 April 1860; and Lewis M., born on 20 May 1864 three months after his father died. She received a pension for her son Lewis on 10 December 1869 which ended on 19 May 1880 when he turned sixteen.

She was married second at Branford by Rev. L. D. Phelps on 9 December 1869 to Samuel S. Cook. He was age 40, born at Branford, an oysterman; she was age 38, born at Branford. Samuel Cook died at Branford on 9 October 1893 age 64[689] and was buried there in Damascus Cemetery.

Georgianna Tucker Hotchkiss Cook died at Branford on 39 July 1898[690] and was buried in Stony Creek Cemetery. She was born at Stony Creek on 19 June 1831, daughter of Nelson Nathan Tucker and Betsey Griswold.

HOUGHTLING, WILLIAM
Co. D 61st Massachusetts Infantry, private, enlisted 3 September 1864, killed 2 April 1865, no pension

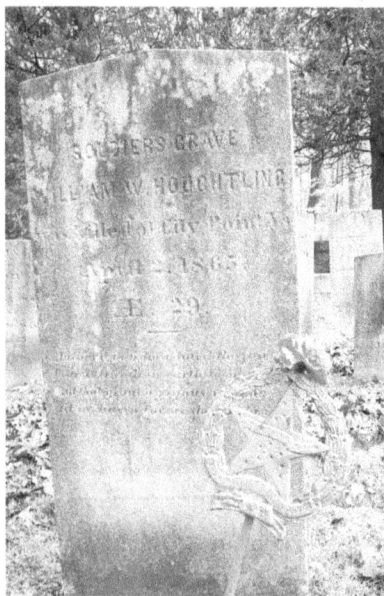

William Houghtling, age 29, of Adams, Berkshire Co., Massachusetts enlisted on 3 September 1864 as a private in Co. D 61st Massachusetts Infantry. At the time of his enlistment he was described as five feet seven inches tall, light complexion, blue eyes, dark hair, occupation carder. He was killed in the Battle at City Point, near Petersburg, Virginia on 2 April 1865. There is a gravestone for him in Damascus Cemetery, Branford with a patriot's maker.

He was born at Schodrack, New York and was married to Elizabeth Walker of Branford. They had four children baptized at Trinity Episcopal Church, Branford in April 1867, the children of Mrs. William Houghtling: Annette Elizabeth, Ida Jane, Hettie Viola, and William Willard.[691] She removed to Big Rock, Kane Co., Illinois and was married second on 10 September 1870 to Henry Like.[692] Though eligible, she never applied for a pension for herself or her minor children. From his gravestone at Damascus Cemetery, Branford:

---

688 Talcott, *Families of Guilford*, 658 & 660.
689 Branford Vital Records, 1863-1895, 251.
690 Branford Vital Records, deaths, 1898.
691 Branford Trinity Episcopal Church Records, 46.
692 Correspondence, with Judy Tighe (a descendant) with the author, 16 March 2005.

SOLDIER'S GRAVE

HUSBAND DEAR HOW HARD THE PARTING

DEAREST FRIEND ON EARTH TO ME.

BUT GOD GRANT A JOYOUS MEETING

YET IN HEAVEN FOR US THERE'LL BE.

HOWD, GEORGE W.
Co. K 15th CVI, private, enlisted 6 August 1862, mustered out 27 June 1865, pension #287075 for the soldier and later for his widow Alice L.

George W. Howd, age 24, of Wallingford enlisted at New Haven on 6 August 1862 and was mustered in on 25 August 1862 as a private in Co. K 15th CVI for a term of three years. He saw action at Fredericksburg, Virginia on 13 December 1862, during the Siege of Suffolk, Virginia in the spring of 1863, and in the Peninsula Campaign of July 1863. He was on picket duty during the Battle of Kinston, North Carolina. He was in the hospital at New Bern, North Carolina in April 1864 for remittent fever. George Howd was mustered out with the rest of his regiment at New Bern, North Carolina on 27 June 1865 and discharged at New Haven on 12 July 1865. His "Soldierly conduct was good." He served under Capt. Medad D. Munson of Wallingford.

He applied for an invalid pension on 19 May 1880 but died shortly afterwards. At the time of his enlistment he was described as five feet six inches tall, light complexion, blue eyes, brown hair, occupation mechanic. At Portsmouth, Virginia and New Bern, North Carolina he was sick with lung and stomach trouble and treated in General Hospital at Acquia Creek, Virginia. He was never well again after his discharge. Since his discharge he lived at Meriden and New Haven.

George W. Howd died at New Haven on 22 March 1881 and was buried there in Evergreen Cemetery. He was the son of Edwin and Mary Howd, born at Northford and Wallingford.

Alice L. Howd of New Haven applied for a widow's pension on 26 October 1881. She was married to the soldier under the name of Alice L. Kidder at New Haven by Rev. Edward S. Lines of St. Paul's Church on 25 November 1880. He was age 42, born at Wallingford; she was age 23, born at New Haven; both were living at New Haven. Neither were previously married or divorced.

She was married second at New Haven by Rev. Thomas Samson of the Calvary Baptist Church on 25 November 1886 to William D. Short. He was age 30, born at Derby, not previously married; both living at New Haven. Her pension was terminated upon her second marriage. She reapplied for a pension on 19 November 1889. The death of her second husband is not noted and there is no further record in the file.

HOWD, WILLIAM T.
Co. K 6th CVI, private, enlisted 9 September 1861, to Co. B 1st U.S. Artillery, discharged 12 September 1864, pension #C2-502-108 for the soldier

William T. Howd, age 19, of Branford enlisted at New Haven on 9 September 1861 and was mustered in on 12 September 1861 as a private in Co. K 6th CVI for a term of three years. He was transferred to Co. B 1st U.S. Infantry at Beaufort, South Carolina on 12 September 1864 and discharged the same day near Point of Rocks, Virginia.

He applied for an invalid pension on 20 November 1904. At the time of his enlistment he was described as five feet nine inches tall, fair complexion, hazel eyes, brown hair, occupation farmer. He always lived

at Stony Creek, Branford. He was married at Branford by Rev. Alpha H. Simonds of the First Baptist Church in 1869 to Carrie Brainerd. They were divorced about 1884 and he never remarried. They had one daughter (living in 1904): Ettie May, born on 8 May 1880. He was a charter member of the Branford Battery A. He was admitted to the Fitch's Soldier Home[693] at Noroton Heights on 1 July 1909. His conservator was Thomas D. Williams of Branford.

William Theodore Howd died at the Fitch's Soldier Home on 8 July 1918[694] and was buried in Stony Creek Cemetery, Branford. His name appears on the Stony Creek Veterans' Monument. A government issued stone was placed at the gravesite in 2005. He was born at Stony Creek on 25 January 1842,[695] son of Nelson Howd and Cornelia Rogers.

HOYT, GEORGE E.
Co. E 1st HA, private, enlisted 18 December 1863, mustered out 25 September 1865, pension #504474 for the soldier

George E. Hoyt of North Branford enlisted and was mustered in at New Haven on 18 December 1863 as a private in Co. E 1st HA for a term of three years. With his regiment he fought at Chickahominy and Malvern Hill, Virginia. Hoyt was mustered out with the rest of his regiment at Washington, D.C. on 25 September 1865 and discharged at Hartford on 1 October 1865.

He applied for an invalid pension on 3 November 1883. At Fort O'Rourke, New Alexandria, Virginia in the summer of 1865 he had chills, malaria, and rheumatism. He had further attacks after his discharge and was unable to work. His application was sent for special examination to determine the claim of disability. The examiner stated "he was a large, fine looking man" and found little or no indication of disability by appearance. His pension application was rejected. He reapplied on 30 July 1895 under the act of 27 June 1890 which was granted. In 1895 he was described as age 47, five feet eleven inches tall, light complexion, light gray hair, blue eyes. Ten years before the war he lived at Poundridge, Westchester Co., New York. He enlisted from North Branford but does not appear in the census there in 1860, probably came to Connecticut only to enlist. After his discharge he lived at Poundridge with his parents, in 1866 worked at a lock factory in Norwalk, and in 1871 came to New Canaan, Fairfield Co. (his mail was sent to P. O. Box Vista, Westchester Co., New York). No wife, children, or death are mentioned in the file.

---

693 Fitch's Home for Soldiers, Deceased Veterans Discharge Files 1882-1932, box 12, file 2922.
694 Branford Vital Records, deaths, 1918.
695 On his pension applications he gives conflicting birth dates of 21 January 1841 and 25 January 1842. Apparently no public record could be found.

HUBBARD, HENRY W.

Co. B 27th CVI, private, enlisted 22 August 1862, prisoner, mustered out 27 July 1863, pension #823484 for the soldier and later for his widow Emma

Henry W. Hubbard[696] of Branford, age 29, enlisted at New Haven on 22 August 1862 and was mustered in on 3 October 1862 as a private in Co. B 27th CVI for a term of nine months. He fought at the Battle of Fredericksburg on 13 December 1862 with the rest of the company. He was captured at the Battle of Chancellorsville, Virginia on 3 May 1863, held prisoner at Castle Thunder, Richmond, and was paroled at City Point, Virginia on 14 May 1863. He reported to Camp Parole, Maryland on 16 May 1863, was sent to Washington, D.C. on 20 May 1863 and spent the remainder of his service at Camp Convalescent, Virginia. "He was promoted to corporal after Chancellorsville."[697] With the rest of the Chancellorsville paroled prisoners, he rejoined the Regiment at Baltimore on 20 July 1863. Hubbard was mustered out with the rest of his regiment at New Haven on 27 July 1863. He was the brother-in-law of Harvey W. Beach of the same company and regiment. After the war he served in Co. K 2nd Connecticut National Guard for five years, first as orderly sergeant, was promoted to 2nd lieutenant, and discharged as 1st lieutenant.[698] In 1884 he was captain and commander of the Colonel Allen Guards.[699]

Henry W. Hubbard of Branford served in Co. B 27th CVI and was taken prisoner at Chancellorsville in 1863. (Beers, Biographical Record of New Haven County, 956)

He applied for an invalid pension on 18 January 1892 under the act of 27 June 1890. He was described as five feet five inches tall, brown eyes, brown hair, light complexion. He had a small scar on his forehead caused by a fire when he was a child. Before his enlistment he lived at Middletown and came to Branford in 1855 where he returned after the war. He was married at Branford by Rev. Davis L. Shailer of the First Baptist Church on 3 June 1858 to Emma Phelps Linsley. Neither were previously married or divorced. They had three children living (in 1904): Ida Augusta Jerrolds, born on 28 August 1859; Henrietta

Wilhelmina Hubbard, born on 7 June 1862; and Luella Linsley Moore, born on 22 May 1863. He was a charter member, commander, and chaplain of the Mason Rogers Post No. 7 G.A.R of Branford.

Henry William Hubbard died at Branford on 26 May 1916 and was buried there in Center Cemetery. His company and regiment are engraved on his stone and there was a Civil War marker was on his gravesite in 1934. He was born at Durham on 27 June 1833, son of Richard Hubbard and Rhoda Andrews.

---

696 For his biography see Rockey, *History of New Haven County*, II:67; and Beers, *Biographical Record of New Haven County*, 956.

697 Beers, *Biographical Record of New Haven County*, 956; there is no record in his pension file of this promotion.

698 Beers, *Biographical Record of New Haven County*, 956.

699 *Shore Line Times*, 31 October 1884.

*After his capture at
Chancellorsville, Henry Hubbard
was held at a prison in Richmond
called Castle Thunder.
(Library of Congress, Prints &
Photographs Division, LC-DIG-
cwpb-02506)*

Emma P. L. Hubbard of 9 Wilford Avenue, Branford applied for a widow's pension on 6 October 1916. She died at Branford on 7 June 1918 and was buried there in Center Cemetery. She was born at Branford on 15 August 1839, daughter of James L. Linsley and Henrietta Munger.[700] She was the first cousin of soldiers Charles E. and William H. Linsley. She was a member of the Mason Rogers Women's Relief Corps No. 46 of Branford.

HUBBELL, ALONZO F.
Co. B 27th CVI, sergeant, enlisted 25 August 1862, mustered out 27 July 1863, pension #700473 for his widow Emma

Alonzo F. Hubbell, age 23, of Branford enlisted at New Haven on 25 August 1862 and was mustered in on 3 October 1862 as a sergeant in Co. B 27th CVI for a term of nine months. He was present at roll call from 3 October to 1 November 1862. "He left the camp for the hospital about Dec. 1, 1862 just before we broke camp at Chain Bridge."[701] In November and December 1862 and January through March 1863 he was sick at the Citizens General Hospital at Broad and Prime Streets, Philadelphia. "He never returned to the Regiment but joined us at Baltimore when the Regiment was on the way home and [he] came home with us."[702] Hubbell was mustered out with the rest of his regiment at New Haven on 27 July 1863 but was not present.

---

700 Branford Vital Records, deaths, 1918.
701 Deposition, Robert B. Goodyear of North Haven, 10 December 1909, in the pension file of Alonzo F. Hubbell.
702 Deposition, Robert B. Goodyear of North Haven, 10 December 1909, in the pension file of Alonzo F. Hubbell.

He never applied for a pension. At the time of his enlistment he was described as five feet seven inches tall, fair complexion, blue eyes, light hair. He was married at Milford on 20 September 1869 to Emma Pond at the home of Mrs. William Smith, the aunt of the bride, by Rev. George C. Griffith of the Plymouth Congregational Church. He was living at Sandusky, Ohio and she at Milford. Neither were previously married or divorced.

Alonzo Frederick Hubbell died at Chicago, Illinois on 8 May1894 and was buried in Mountain House Cemetery, Kalamazoo, Michigan. He was born at New Haven or Wallingford on 7 July 1839.

Emma Hubbell of Pasadena, California applied for a pension on 8 September 1908 under the act of 19 April 1908. There are lengthy depositions to prove she was married and that her husband was the soldier in the 27th CVI. The examiner states that "she is a refined and intelligent woman of good reputation for the truth."[703] She states "my husband kept his discharge and other important papers in the safe at the Wheel Company at Sandusky, Ohio which was destroyed in a fire." She also states, that "her husband's mother died when he was two years old and he had a step mother. He left home and lived with an older couple. He had two brothers and two sisters. I only knew the name of one of the brothers, Levi Hubbell and one of the sisters Jane Tuttle,[704] both of whom I met. She lived with us a year after our marriage then went to New Haven. I last heard she was still there, a widow. I never met the other brother or sister but they are dead. Levi Hubbell died in Bridgeport and I attended his funeral. I was born and raised in Milford. My sister Mrs. Grace Cobb of West Haven may still be alive. It has been many years since I heard from her. I have no other living relatives. My husband was born in New Haven and lived there until he was 12 years of age when he went to Wallingford to live for 2 or 3 years, working for his board and attending school. He learned the trade of carriage making in Branford or Wallingford. He was working at the Wheel Works Company in Sandusky, Ohio and we met at a wedding in Danbury. It is my understanding that he returned to Branford after his discharge; then went to Coldwater, Michigan with Mr. Latin. I don't know how long he was there but he did tell me he and Mr. Latin patented a wagon seat. Afterwards my husband went to Sandusky and met Mr. Barney, President of the Sandusky Wheel Company and they began to manufacture the wagon seat. He was superintendent of the company. After our marriage we lived there 16 years. Afterwards he became a travelling salesman, selling wheels and wood works pertaining to carriages. He may have been in Kalamazoo, Michigan after his discharge, also."

"During the war he was treated at a hospital in Philadelphia for jaundice. He said the surgeon that treated him was very kind to him and we named our first baby Robert after him. I don't remember the surgeon's last name. After my husband and I left Sandusky, Ohio we went to Syracuse, New York and lived there five years; then we went to Kalamazoo, Michigan for 3 or 4 years; then to Chicago, Illinois for only 2 or 3 months when he came down with La Grippe which developed into Bright's Disease which caused his death."

"After his death I went back to Kalamazoo until 1900 and came here to Pasadena, remained 2 years; returned to Kalamazoo for 2 years; then returned here again in May 1904 where I have remained since."

"He told me he had only been in the army a short time when he was taken with a terrible cold due to exposure to heavy rain storms and he came down with jaundice and was sent to the hospital where most of his service was spent. He spoke mostly of his hospital experience. He and his sister both said that was his only military service."[705]

It appears Emma Hubbell finally received her pension. Key factors were fellow soldiers identifying him from a photograph taken during the war that was in her possession and others identifying his signature.

---

703 Alfred L. Leonard, special examiner, 6 November 1909, in the pension file of Alonzo F. Hubbell.
704 Jane Tuttle died September 1909, report of examiner W. B. Robinson, 17 December 1909.
705 Deposition, Emma Hubbell of Pasadena, Cal., 3 November 1909, in the pension file of Alonzo F. Hubbell.

Only one witness could be found that attended their marriage ceremony. Alonzo and Emma Hubbell had a son Robert, and a daughter who was an invalid; perhaps other children.

Emma Pond Hubbell died at Pasadena, California on 13 November 1922. She was born at Milford on 23 December 1829.

HULL, ELI
Co. F 20th CVI, private, enlisted 15 August 1862, mustered out 13 June 1865, pension #796422 for the soldier

Eli Hull of Branford enlisted on 15 August 1862 and was mustered in on 8 September 1862 as a private in Co. F 20th CVI for a term of three years. His regiment served at the Battle of Gettysburg, in Georgia during 1864 and saw action in North Carolina in 1865. They were present at the Grand Review in Washington, D.C. on 23 May 1865. Eli Hull was mustered out with the rest of his regiment at New Haven on 13 June 1865. He was the brother of James C. Hull.

He applied for an invalid pension on 26 September 1891 under the act of 27 June 1890. There are very few documents in his pension file. He was married to Nancy Ann Boylan who was born in Ireland and died at Branford on 31 December 1892 age 76 years & 8 months.[706] After his discharge he lived at Guilford and Stony Creek, Branford. He was admitted to Fitch's Soldier Home[707] on 1 November 1901 and discharged on 26 March 1903. He was readmitted on 29 September 1903.

Eli Hull died at Stony Creek on 30 June 1906 while visiting his daughter and was buried in Damascus Cemetery.[708] He was the son of James Chauncey Hull and Wealthy Ann Frisbie.

HULL, JAMES C.
Co. H 15th CVI, enlisted 14 August 1862, died 25 March 1863, pension #16527 for his widow Eliza

James Chauncey Hull, age 45, of Branford enlisted at New Haven on 14 August 1862 and was mustered in on 25 August 1862 as a private in Co. H 15th CVI for a term of three years. He was sick in the hospital beginning January 1863. He died at Lincoln General Hospital, Washington, D.C. on 25 March 1863 of typhoid fever.[709] There is gravestone for him in Center Cemetery, Branford. His company and regiment are engraved on his stone and there was a G.A.R. marker on his gravesite in 1934 and 2011. He was born on 2 April 1816,[710] son of James Chauncey Hull and Wealthy Ann Frisbie and was the brother of Eli Hull. At the time of his enlistment he was described as five feet seven inches tall, fair complexion, blue eyes, light hair, occupation farmer, born at Branford.

---

706 Branford Vital Records, 1863-1895, 249.
707 Fitch's Home for Soldiers, Deceased Veterans Discharge Files 1882-1932, box 8, file 2049.
708 *The Branford Opinion*, 6 July 1906, 4; there is no gravestone.
709 His CMSR states he died of tuberculosis and diarrhea.
710 Gravestone at Center Cemetery.

Eliza E. Hull, age 39, of Branford applied for a widow's pension on 31 December 1863. She was married under the name of Eliza E. Hart at Guilford by Rev. Lorenzo T. Bennett of the Guilford Episcopal Church on 11 October 1845. She had five children with the soldier: Fanny E., born on 31 July 1845; Anna Lewia, born on 5 November 1850; Sarah Hart Hull, born on 1 September 1852; Alzarah Emeline, born on 29 October 1855; and George C., born on 28 August 1863. They all resided with their mother in Branford. It would appear her son George died young, she only received a pension allowance for the minor children Anna, Sarah, and Alzarah. She lived at Branford until at least 1883, then New London, and Orange. Eliza E. Hull never remarried.

Eliza Hart Hull died at Orange on 22 August 1910 and was buried in Center Cemetery, Branford. She was born at Southington on 15 January 1824, daughter of George Hart and Lewia Page, born at Southington and Guilford.

HUNTLEY, WILLIAM H.
Co. H 13th CVI, sergeant, enlisted 23 January 1861, discharged 25 April 1866, pension #826326 for the soldier

William H. Huntley of New Haven enlisted on 23 January 1862 and was mustered in on 28 January 1862 as a corporal in Co. H 13th CVI for a term of three years. He was promoted to sergeant on 17 May 1862 and his rank was reduced to private on 11 June 1862. He was again promoted to corporal on 6 September 1862 and to sergeant on 1 February 1863. With his regiment he served in the New Orleans area including the Battle of Irish Bend on 14 April 1863 and the Siege of Port Hudson. He was discharged at Thibodaux, Louisiana on 29 February 1864 and reenlisted the same day as a veteran in Co. H. During the Virginia campaign he fought at the Battles of Winchester, Fisher's Hill, and Cedar Creek. He was promoted to 1st sergeant on 1 October 1864 and transferred to Co. E 13th Battalion C. V. on 29 December 1864. He was discharged at Fort Pulaski, Georgia on 25 April 1866.[711]

He applied for an invalid pension on 11 September 1888. He was born at Ellington and was a member and adjutant of the Admiral Foote Post No. 17 G.A.R. of New Haven and the Mason Rogers Post No. 7 G.A.R. of Branford. He lived at New Haven, served on the pension board, and was a special examiner.

William H. Huntley died on 22 January 1925 and was buried in Evergreen Cemetery, New Haven. His rank, company, and regiment are engraved on his stone and there was a Civil War marker on his gravesite in 1934. He was born on 24 Nov 1838, probably the son of William R. and Minnie L. Huntley.[712]

---

711 The records of the Mason Rogers Post No. 7 G.A.R. confirms this is the right soldier.
712 The Hale Collection, New Haven, 585; his death is not in the New Haven Vital Records.

HUTCHINSON, JOHN
U.S. Navy, no pension[713]

John Hutchinson died at Branford on 17 September 1898 and was buried there in Center Cemetery. He was born at Guilford, Ireland, son of Christopher and Ann Hutchinson[714] and lived at Branford for twenty years previously living at Grosvenordale.[715] He was married to Charlotte Kimball who died at Branford on 21 May 1888.[716]

He was a charter member and first quartermaster of the Mason Rogers Post No. 7 G.A.R. of Branford which met on the second floor of his store. He was active in the organization and was on the committee for the Branford Soldiers' Monument.

HYDE, JAMES R.
Co. F 1st Cavalry, private, enlisted 12 September 1864, discharged 21 June 1865, no pension

James R. Hyde of Branford enlisted on 12 September 1864 as a private in Co. F 1st Connecticut Cavalry and was discharged on 21 June 1865. He does not appear in the 1860 census at Branford.

William B. Ives served in the 1st Light Battery and was discharged for disability in 1864. (Beecher, First Light Battery, II:781)

IVES, WILLIAM B.
1st LA, private, enlisted 21 October 1861, discharged disability 19 April 1864, pension #619594 for the soldier and later for his widow Catherine

William B. Ives, age 31, of Branford enlisted at Meriden on 21 October 1861 and was mustered in on 14 November 1861 as a private in the 1st LA for a term of three years. His regiment served in South Carolina including the Siege of Charleston. He was transferred to the invalid corps and was unassigned in the VRC on 25 February 1864. He was discharged for disability caused by exposure on 19 April 1864. He does not appear in the 1860 census at Branford but does appear on the 1863 draft list. He stated he lived at Cheshire when he enlisted.

He applied for an invalid pension on 28 January 1879. At Camp Pigeon Point in Beaufort, South Carolina he developed piles which grew worse and from which he was disabled from performing further duty. At the time of his enlistment he was described as five feet ten inches tall, light complexion, grey eyes, light brown hair, occupation mechanic, born at Cheshire. Before the war he lived in many places:

---

713 There are a number of John Hutchinsons in the Navy during the Civil War, a connection to the one from Branford could not be made.
714 Branford Vital Records, deaths, 1898.
715 Obituary, *Shore Line Times*, 23 September 1898.
716 Branford Vital Records, 1863-1895, 238.

Cheshire 1855; New Haven 1856 for two months; Worcester, Massachusetts June to November 1856; New Orleans Spring 1857 where he worked as a fireman and deck hand on the steamers *Elephant* and *Antelope* on the Mississippi River and docks; April 1857 back to Cheshire; Fair Haven 1858; and returned to Cheshire 1859. After his discharge he lived at Cheshire; East Haven June 1864 until June 1867; back to Cheshire; three months in Chicago; since then in Southington except three months in Chicago during 1872.

He was married at Pine Orchard, Branford by Rev. Henry Olmstead of Trinity Episcopal Church on 30 June 1857 to Catherine Costello of Branford. They had the following children (living in 1898): George H., born on 12 November 1860; Samuel E., born on 20 December 1864; Frances L., born on 19 January 1866; William B., born on 19 March 1869; and Charles N., born on 3 February 1871.

William Bruce Ives died at Fannie Paddock Hospital in Tacoma, Pierce Co., Washington on 13 May 1906 age 75 where he had been treated for one year. He was buried there in Oakwood Cemetery.

Catherine Ives, age 68, of New Britain applied for a widow's pension on 30 June 1906.

JACOBS, EGBERT
Co. B 15th CVI, private, enlisted 4 August 1862, mustered out 27 June 1865, pension #348821 for the soldier

Egbert Jacobs[717] of East Haven, age 19, enlisted at New Haven on 4 August 1862 and was mustered in on 25 August 1862 as a private in Co. B 15th CVI for term of three years. He deserted on 3 December 1862 during the march from Washington, D.C. to Acquia Creek. The Provost Marshall for the State of Connecticut on 6 January 1863 authorized Jonathan L. Harrison of North Branford to "arrest the body of Egbert Jacobs of East Haven for desertion." On 20 February 1863 Jonathan L. Harrison of North Branford turned "the body of Egbert Jacobs, a prisoner, over to the authorities." He was returned to Newport News, Virginia on 22 February 1863 and in April 1863 was confined in jail at Suffolk, Virginia awaiting trial. He was tried by General Court Martial by order of General Getty, released from confinement on 21 June 1863 and returned to duty with the regiment but forfeited his pay. He saw action at the Battle of Kinston, North Carolina on 8 March 1865 but was not taken prisoner. Jacobs was honorably discharged with the rest of the regiment at New Bern, North Carolina on 27 June 1865 and discharged at New Haven on 12 July 1854 but his file states he was a "Poor Soldier."

He applied for an invalid pension on 22 December 1885. At the time of his enlistment he was described as five feet six inches tall, light complexion, light hair, blue eyes, occupation farmer, born at North Haven. On 30 August 1864 at New Bern, North Carolina he contracted malaria fever and rheumatism and was admitted to the Regimental Hospital. "He was in bad health the day the regiment got paid off and had to be taken by carriage to the conscript camp to receive his pay at Grapevine Point, Fair Haven."[718] At the time of his pension application he was under a doctor's care for progressive debility from chronic malarial poison-

---

717 Correspondence concerning his pension can be found in the *Noble Pension Records*, RG 13, box 39, case 778, Connecticut State Library.

718 Affidavit, A. Frederick Humie of New Haven, 21 November 1885, in the pension file of Egbert Jacobs.

ing resulting in numerous hospital admissions. Since his discharge he lived from 1865 until 1868 at North Haven; then East Wallingford; 1890 at Durham and died at North Branford. He did receive a pension minus the time he was absent from the regiment. There is no other biographical information in his pension file.

Egbert Jacobs died at North Branford on 7 May 1895, unmarried, and was buried in Bare Plain Cemetery, North Branford.[719] A Civil War marker was on his gravesite in 1934 and 2011. He was born at North Haven, son of DeForest Jacobs.[720] His name appears on the North Haven Civil War Honor Roll.

JENNINGS, BARNEY
Co. G 10th CVI, private, substitute, mustered in 8 October 1864, wounded, discharged 8 July 1865, pension #358811 for the soldier

Barney Jennings[721] served as a substitute for George C. Field of Branford. He was mustered in at New Haven on 8 October 1864 as a private in Co. G 10th CVI for a term of three years. He was wounded at Fort Gregg, Virginia on 2 April 1865 and discharged from the U.S. General Hospital at Fortress Monroe, Virginia on 8 July 1865.

He applied for an invalid pension on 14 October 1886 which was granted on 7 May 1887. He received a severe gunshot wound to his right leg near Richmond, Virginia while in action at Fort Gregg on 2 April 1865 during the Siege of Petersburg. He was sent to the field hospital then to Point of Rocks Hospital and finally to Fort Monroe where he was discharged. He also suffered from rheumatism, malarial poisoning, and chronic diarrhea. After his discharge he had a number of hospital admissions and claimed at the time of his application that he was unable to work and "was in bad shape." At the time of his discharge he was described as age 24, five feet four inches tall, fair complexion, gray eyes, dark hair, occupation boatman. Six years before his enlistment he was a boatman on the Erie Canal. After his discharge he lived at Buffalo, Rochester and Syracuse, New York for six or seven years; about 1872 to Louisville, Kentucky; three years at New Albany, Indiana; Columbus, Ohio; and Connecticut.[722] He was employed after the war as a boatman or sailor. From 1886 until 1892 he was living at Bridgeport and was often in Bridgeport Hospital. By 1900 he was a resident at Fitch's Home for Soldiers in Noroton.

He was married first at Louisville, Kentucky by Squire Martin in August 1869. Her name was not given and they were divorced. He was married second at New Albany, Indiana in 1873 to Lena Drybread. She was living in 1898 and the soldier had no children. She did not apply for a widow's pension.

He stated he was born at Branford on 28 May 1831 but says there is no public record of his birth.[723] The pension office stated he was born in New York. He does not appear in the 1860 census at Branford or North Branford.

Barney Jennings died at Fitch's Soldier Home on 4 June 1907 age 76 and was buried there in Spring Grove Cemetery.[724] His company and regiment are engraved on his stone.

719 The Hale Collection, North Branford, 14.
720 North Branford Vital Records, deaths, 1895; his mother is possibly Celia Brockett.
721 Correspondence concerning his pension can be found in the *Noble Pension Records*, RG 13, box 40, case 784, Connecticut State Library.
722 He provides different information on different pension applications, also mentions living in Pennsylvania, Illinois, and Mississippi.
723 No birth record was found at Branford or North Branford.
724 Fitch's Home for Soldiers, Deceased Veterans Discharge Files 1882-1932, box 8, file 116.

JEPSON, BENJAMIN

Co. A & Co. K 10th CVI, captain, enlisted 29 August 1861, wounded, resigned 1 June 1864, pension #C2514437 for the soldier

Benjamin Jepson[725] of New Haven enlisted on 29 August 1861 and was mustered in at Hartford on 25 September 1861 as 1st lieutenant of Co. A 10th CVI for a term of three years. He was promoted to captain of Co. K 10th CVI on 14 December 1861. He was wounded at Roanoke Island, North Carolina on 8 February 1862 and resigned on 1 June 1864. When the war first began, Benjamin Jepson had issued a circular in which he urged that "all our children have early instruction in our national songs and a thousand children assembled on the Fourth."[726]

He applied for an invalid pension on 16 April 1904. At the time of his enlistment he was described as five feet five inches tall, light complexion, gray eyes, black hair, occupation teacher of music. At Roanoke Island, North Carolina on 8 February 1862 he received a bullet wound to the left side of the head which took off a small piece of his ear and was sent home on 12 February on furlough. From July 1863 until June 1863 he was detached to the recruiting service at New Haven but by September 1863 was under arrest by order of the Secretary of War. His length of service for the calculation of his pension was reduced by three months for an absence in violation of military service. He was arrested on two charges; one, conduct unbecoming an officer and a gentleman; and second, conduct prejudicial to good order and military discipline. While under arrest he continued in the New Haven recruiting office and during his suspension was in charge of volunteer recruits at Fort Trumbull, New London. He was found not guilty of the first charge but guilty of the second by a general court martial convened at New

PROF. BENJAMIN JEPSON.

Benjamin Jepson of New Haven and a summer resident of Stony Creek was promoted to captain of Co. K 10th CVI. (The Saturday Chronicle, 7 February 1918, 8)

Haven by virtue of special orders from Headquarters, Department of the East, dated 9 October 1863. The exact misdemeanor is not stated. He was sentenced to suspension of rank, pay, and emoluments for three months. The sentence was approved on 2 March 1864. He received an honorable discharge after submitting his resignation on 1 June 1864. After his discharge he lived at New Haven and summered in Stony Creek, Branford for many years.

Before the Civil War he was elected lieutenant of the Independent Rangers in 1855, a volunteer company organized under Governor William T. Miner of Connecticut. In 1857 he joined the Henry Ward Beecher Sharp Rifle Co. organized at the North church (United church) in New Haven. He was promoted from orderly sergeant to captain and advocated making Kansas a free state.[727]

He was an active member and commander of the Admiral Foot Post No. 17 G.A.R. of New Haven. He held many posts in the G.A.R.; organist, music director, and patriotic instructor. He was also a charter mem-

---

725 For his biography see *The Saturday Chronicle*, New Haven, 7 February 1914, 8.

726 Crofut and Morris, *Military & Civil History of Connecticut*, 82. Benjamin Jepson was the instructor of music for the New Haven school system for fifty years and the author of the standard text for elementary school music instruction. He received an honorary degree from Yale College.

727 *The Saturday Chronicle*, New Haven, 7 February 1914, 8.

ber and captain of the Second Company Governor's Foot Guard of New Haven when it was organized after the war.

Benjamin Jepson was married at New Haven by Rev. George Washington Woodruff on 9 September 1858 to Mary Louise Wiswell. She was born on 3 August 1839, died on 13 February 1910 and was buried in Evergreen Cemetery, New Haven.[728] They had the following children: Arthur Wiswell, born on 21 October 1866; Harry Benjamin, born on 16 August 1870; and Clara Louise, born on 20 December 1874.

Benjamin Jepson died at New Haven on 7 June 1914 and was buried there in Evergreen Cemetery. At the time of his death he was last surviving officer of the 10th CVI. He was born at Sheffield, England on 22 May 1832, son of John Jepson and Emelia Bromhead.

JERGENSON, EMANUAL
Co. E 1st HA, sergeant, enlisted 26 December 1863, mustered out 25 September 1865, no pension

Emanual Jergenson of North Branford enlisted on 26 December 1863 as a private in Co. E 1st HA. He participated in the Siege of Petersburg and Richmond, Virginia with his regiment and was promoted to sergeant on 24 May 1864. Jergenson was mustered out with the rest of the regiment at Washington, D.C. on 25 September 1865 and discharged at Hartford on 1 October 1865. He does not appear in the 1860 census at North Branford.

JOHNSON, CAMPBELL

Campbell Johnson served as a substitute for John Spencer of Branford. He was mustered in at New Haven on 30 November 1864 as a private in the 7th CVI for a term of three years.[729] His name does not appear in the Record of Service of Connecticut Men or in the Branford or North Branford 1860 census.

JOHNSON, CHARLES
Co. I 10th CVI, private, substitute, mustered in 22 November 1864, discharged 6 June 1865, no pension

Charles Johnson, age 23, served as a substitute for Joseph P. Douglass of Branford. He was mustered in at New Haven on 22 November 1864 as a private in Co. I 10th CVI for a term of three years. He was described as five feet nine inches tall, grey eyes, brown hair, fair complexion, unmarried, born in Ireland, occupation clerk.[730] He was sick in April 1865 and discharged at Patterson Park, Baltimore, Maryland on 6 June 1865.

---

728 The Hale Collection, New Haven, 555.
729 Muster & Payroll, List of Substitutes, RG 13, box 100, 2nd Congressional District, Connecticut State Library.
730 Muster & Descriptive Rolls of Substitutes, RG 13, box 97, 2nd Congressional District, Connecticut State Library.

JOHNSON, DAVIS S.

Co. A 10th CVI, corporal, enlisted 18 September 1861, reenlisted 1 January 1864, promoted 25 June 1865, mustered out 25 August 1865, pension #334609 for his widow Margaret

Davis S. Johnson of Branford enlisted at Hartford on 18 September 1861 and was mustered in on 25 September 1861 as a private in Co. A 10th CVI for a term of three years. With the rest of the regiment he fought at the Battle of Roanoke Island, North Carolina on 8 February 1862. He was sick in General Hospital, Beaufort, North Caolina in May and June 1862. He reenlisted at St. Augustine, Florida as a veteran in Co. A on 1 January 1864 and was promoted to corporal on 25 June 1865. During 1864 and 1865 the regiment served in the Virginia campaigns and was present at the surrender at Appomattox Court House. Davis Johnson was mustered out with the rest of his regiment at Richmond, Virginia on 25 August 1865 and discharged at Hartford on 5 September 1865. He was the brother of Elizur C. Johnson of the same company.

After his discharge he lived at Branford. He was a charter member of the Mason Rogers Post No. 7 G.A.R. of Branford and a charter member of the Branford Battery A. He never applied for a pension.

Davis S. Johnson died at Branford on 28 March 1890 age 46 and was buried there in Center Cemetery. His rank, company, and regiment are engraved on his stone. He was born at Branford, son of George William Johnson and Maria Cook.

Margaret Johnson of Branford applied for a widow's pension on 17 July 1890 under the act of 27 June 1890. She was married to the soldier under the name of Mrs. Margaret Hobbs at Branford by Rev. Henry Olmstead of the Trinity Episcopal Church on 21 April 1881. She was married first on 22 April 1871 to Thomas Hobbs who died at County Cork, Ireland on 1 June 1872. She had a son William E. Hobbs.

Margaret Johnson died at Branford on 1 September 1917 and was buried there in Center Cemetery. She was born at Sligo, Ireland on 27 August 1846, daughter of James McNulty and Margaret Craig.

JOHNSON, ELIZUR C.

Co. A 10th CVI, private, enlisted 21 September 1861, wounded, reenlisted 1 January 1864, mustered out 25 August 1865, pension #679269 for the soldier

Elizur C. Johnson of Branford enlisted and was mustered in at Hartford on 21 September 1861 as a private in Co. A 10th CVI for a term of three years. He was wounded in the arm at the Battle of Roanoke Island, North Carolina on 8 February 1862, placed in the hospital, and sent home on furlough. He was discharged at St. Augustine, Florida on 1 January 1864 and reenlisted the same day as a veteran in Co. A. During 1864 and 1865 he served with his regiment in the Virginia campaigns and was present at the surrender at Appomattox Court House. Elizur Johnson was mustered out with the rest of his regiment at Richmond, Virginia on 25 August 1865 and discharged at Hartford on 5 September 1865. He was the brother of Davis S. Johnson of the same company and brother-in-law of Loring and William Hosley.

He applied for an invalid pension on 24 September 1890 under the act of 27 June 1890. At the time of his enlistment he was described as six feet tall, brown eyes, brown hair, occupation farmer. He was married at Branford by Rev. Palmer G. Wightman of the First Baptist Church on 31 August 1859 to Abigail

Anna Hosley. She died at Branford on 21 July 1910 and was buried there in Center Cemetery. They had the following children: Frank S., born on 13 March 1860. died before 1898; Lillie A., born on 23 May 1862; Lottie H., born on 14 August 1866, died before 1898; Edna, born on 30 April 1868; Bertha M., born on 1 November 1870; Jennie G., born on 27 November 1873; Ida F., born on 21 August 1877; and Elizabeth H., born on 12 December 1879. He was a charter member and commander of the Mason Rogers Post No. 7 G.A.R. of Branford.

Elizur C. Johnson died at Branford on 12 April 1917 and was buried there in Center Cemetery. His company and regiment are engraved on his stone. He was born at Branford on 10 July 1838, son of George William Johnson and Maria Cook.[731]

JOHNSON, GEORGE
Co. I 10th CVI, corporal, substitute, mustered in 8 December 1864, mustered out 25 August 1865, no pension

George Johnson, age 28, served as a substitute for Henry Palmer of Branford. He was mustered in at New Haven on 8 December 1864 as a private in Co. I 10th CVI for a term of three years.[732] He was described as five feet nine inches tall, blue eyes, dark hair, fair complexion, born in Canada, occupation painter. He was sick in the hospital from 14 January 1865 until April and was promoted to corporal on 1 July 1865. George Johnson was mustered out at the rest of his regiment at Richmond, Virginia on 25 August 1865 and discharged at Hartford on 5 September 1865.

JOHNSON, HENRY
Co. B 12th CVI, corporal, enlisted 1 November 1861, prisoner, mustered out 12 August 1865, pension # 350703 for his widow Sarah

Henry Johnson of Branford enlisted on 1 November 1861 as a private in Co. B 12th CVI for a term of three years. He reenlisted in Co. B at New Iberia, Louisiana on 31 December 1863 and was promoted to corporal on 4 August 1864. He was captured at Cedar Creek, Virginia on 19 October 1864 and possibly wounded. He was transferred to Co. B 12th Battalion Connecticut Volunteers on 26 November 1864 as a private. Henry Johnson was mustered out with the rest of his regiment at Savannah, Georgia on 12 August 1865 and discharged at Hartford on 22 August 1865.

---

731   Branford Vital Records, deaths, 1917.
732   There were two George Johnsons in Co. I 10th CVI; the other was a substitute for S. V. Everitt and deserted on 2 May 1865.

At the time of his enlistment he was described as age 29, six feet one inch tall, light complexion, blue eyes, brown, hair, occupation farmer, born at Branford. [733] After his discharge he lived at Branford and never applied for a pension. He was a member of the Mason Rogers Post No. 7 G.A.R. of Branford.

Henry Johnson died at Branford on 13 April 1890 and was buried there in Center Cemetery. His company and regiment are engraved on his stone. He was born at Branford on 15 April 1835, son of Charles Johnson and Henrietta Page.[734] He was married first at Branford on 7 December 1857 to Jane Elizabeth Hotchkiss who died on 30 March 1865.[735]

Sarah J. Johnson, age 50, of Branford applied for a widow's pension on 15 August 1890. She was married to the soldier under the name of Sarah J. Mallory at Branford by Rev. Timothy P. Gillett of the First Congregational Church on 25 September 1865. She was married first to George Walter Mallory, a Civil War soldier. Mallory was a private in Co. E, later Co. H 43rd New York Infantry and was killed in action at the Battle of the Wilderness on 12 May 1864 and buried in the field. She had no children with Henry Johnson and had life use of a small property.

Sarah Jane Mallory Johnson was born at New Haven and died at Branford on 17 May 1893.[736]

JOHNSON, HENRY E.
Co. B 12th CVI, private, enlisted 7 April 1864, mustered out 12 August 1865, pension #C2480011 for the soldier

Henry E. Johnson of East Haven enlisted or was drafted on 7 April 1864 as a private in Co. B 12th CVI. He was transferred to Co. B 12th Battalion on 26 November 1864 and was mustered out on 12 August 1865. The T-289 pension card for Henry of East Haven calls him a corporal, confusing him with Henry of Branford. He was living at East Haven in 1860, probably the son of Samuel and Clarissa Johnson.

Henry E. Johnson of East Haven applied for a pension on 28 December 1891 under the act of 27 June 1890. After his discharge he lived at New Haven and by 1925 was living at Branford.

Henry E. Johnson died at Branford on 21 December 1928, a widower, and was buried in East Lawn Cemetery, East Haven.[737] He was born on 24 November 1825 in New Jersey.[738]

JOHNSON, HOMER R.
Co. B 27th CVI, private, enlisted 10 September 1862, prisoner, mustered out 27 July 1863, pension #485372 for the soldier and later for his widow Mary

Homer R. Johnson, age 25, of Wallingford enlisted on 10 September 1862 and was mustered in on 3 October 1862 as a private in Co. B 27th CVI for a term of nine months. He fought at the Battle of Fredericksburg on 13 December 1862 with the rest of the company. He was in the infirmary from 31 January until 3 February 1863 and released back to duty. He was captured at the Battle of Chancellorsville, Virginia on 3 May 1863, held prisoner at Richmond, and was paroled at City Point, Virginia on 14 May 1863. He reported to Camp Parole, Maryland on 16 May 1863, was sent to Washington, D.C. on 20 May 1863 and spent the remainder

---

733   His discharge papers can be found in the Branford Historical Society archives, RG 1, box 12, folder 5.
734   Branford Vital Records, 1786-1840, 372.
735   Branford Vital Records, 1852-1863, 10.
736   Branford Vital Records, deaths, 1893; her parents are not recorded.
737   Branford Vital Records, deaths, 1898; no stone is listed in the Hale Collection.
738   Branford Vital Records, deaths, 1928; his parents are recorded as unknown.

of his service at Camp Convalescent, Virginia. With the rest of the Chancellorsville paroled prisoners, he rejoined the Regiment at Baltimore on 20 July 1863. Homer Johnson was mustered out with the rest of his regiment at New Haven on 27 July 1863 but was absent. In his pension application, he states he was discharged at Hartford.

He applied for an invalid pension on 3 March 1891 under the act of 27 June 1890. He was married at Wallingford by Rev. R. J. Adams of the Baptist Church on 25 October 1863 to Mary E. Bradley. He was living at Wallingford, age 26; she was age 25, living at Hamden. Neither were previously married or divorced. They had four children born at Wallingford: Franklin, born on 13 June 1865; Charles E., born on 11 February 1868; Adella A., born on 3 January 1873, died on 27 March 1873; and Daisy May, born on 1 July 1876. He owned a 180 acre farm in Wallingford with a dwelling house and barn.

Homer R. Johnson died at Wallingford on 8 July 1893 age 56 and was buried there in Center Street Cemetery. He was the son of Franklin Johnson. A copy of his will, dated 20 July 1891, is in the file, his wife had life use of part of the farm. There is a copy of the inventory of his estate and a list of expenditures.

Mary E. Johnson applied for a widow's pension on 30 August 1893. After the soldier's death she leased the farm for $175 per year. There are statements in the file concerning the value of the property and her income. Mary E. Johnson died on 17 March 1926 age 87 and was buried in Center Street Cemetery, Wallingford.[739] She was born at Hamden on 25 October 1863.

JOHNSON, JOSIAH
Co. B 27th CVI, private, enlisted 9 September 1862, died 5 January 1863 from wounds received at Fredericksburg, pension #22953 for his mother Julia A. Johnson

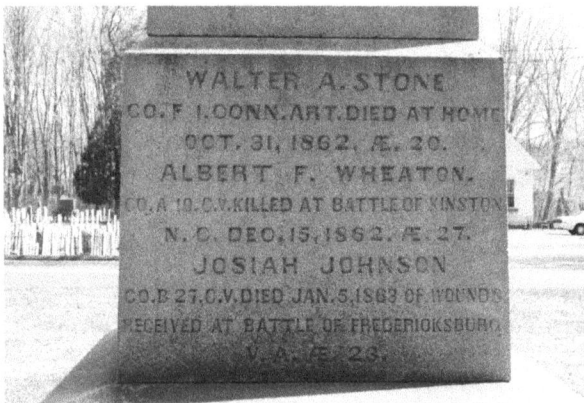

Josiah Johnson, age 21, of North Branford enlisted on 9 September 1862 and was mustered in on 3 October 1862 as a private in Co. B 27th CVI for a term of nine months. He was wounded at Fredericksburg on 13 December 1862. "Josiah Johnson was behind me in the ranks, he got a ball through his leg, will probably have to have it amputated."[740] "I did not get off that field until 10 o'clock in the evening for I was looking for Josiah."[741] "Josiah Johnson was brought in last night, wounded in the leg below the knee by a ball. We carried Josiah Johnson across the river without his leg being dressed."[742] On 4 January 1863 Johnson was listed as deserted but was in the hospital. He died at Harwood Hospital, Washington, D.C. on 5 January 1863 from wounds received at Fredericksburg, following a right thigh amputation. Among his personal effects were one pistol, one silver watch, and two memorial books. On 31 January 1874 the charge of desertion was removed from his record. His name is inscribed on the North Branford Soldiers' Monument. He was the brother-in-law of Merwin Wheaton of the same company and regiment.

739   The Hale Collection, Wallingford, 90.
740   Letter, 17 December 1862, Henry D. Boardman to his sister; see the chapter on Boardman.
741   Letter, Merwin Wheaton, in the pension file of Josiah Johnson.
742   Letter, [George C. Baldwin] to home, 15 December 1862.

A pension was granted to his mother Julia A. Johnson on 31 March 1863 under the act of 14 July 1862. She was married under the name of Julia Ann Murray at New Haven on 14 September 1837 to Chauncey Johnson.[743] Julia A. Johnson died on 12 March 1883 at Cadillac, Mexford Co., Michigan where she was buried. She died suddenly at the home of her son-in-law and daughter Merwin and Carrie Wheaton with whom she resided.

There are letters in the file, dated 1887, demanding the return of the pensioner's last check, which was never cashed, and proof her death. The last pension check was never found.

JONES, ELIJAH B.
Co. E 5th CVI, sergeant, enlisted 22 June 1861, killed 9 August 1862, pension #71186 for his widow Mary Jones and minor son

Elijah B. Jones of Wilton enlisted at Hartford on 22 June 1861 and was mustered in on 22 July 1861 as a sergeant in Co. E 5th CVI for term of four years. He was killed instantly from a gunshot to the head at the Battle of Cedar Mountain, Virginia on 9 August 1862. "As the line advanced into the field, the fire of the enemy became hotter and Color Sergeant Jones carrying the stars and stripes, fell on his face, killed outright."[744] He was buried by men from his company immediately after the battle. He had previously served in the Navy on the ship S.S. *Philadelphia*.

Mary E. Jones of Westport, Fairfield Co. applied for a widow's pension on 10 September 1862. She received her husband's $100.00 bounty on 21 August 1863. She was married to the soldier under the name of Mary E. Gray at New Canaan by Rev. John L. Gilder on 29 November 1860. He was age 23, born at Williamsburg, New York; she was age 19, born at Wilton. They had one son, Elijah B. Jones, born at Wilton on 12 February 1861. She was the sister of Samuel N. Gray of the 1st Connecticut Cavalry.

She was married second at Westport by Rev. George Hollis on 25 September 1864 to Henry D. Linsley. He was age 22, born and living at Branford; she was age 22, born and living at Westport.[745] He was not previously married or divorced. Her pension terminated upon her remarriage but she continued to receive an allowance of $8.00 per month commencing 25 September 1864 until 12 February 1877 as guardian for her minor son Elijah Bradley Jones.

Mary Jones Linsley moved to Branford after her marriage to Henry D. Linsley and her son Elijah B. Jones lived in their household. Henry D. Linsley died at Branford on 7 June 1915 and was buried there in Center Cemetery. A copy of his will is in the pension file.

She reapplied for a pension on 25 April 1916 after the death of Henry D. Linsley based on the service of her first husband. Mary Gray Jones Linsley died at Branford on 21 November 1921 and was buried there in Center Cemetery. She was born at Wilton on 10 April 1842, daughter of John Archer Gray and Sarah Ann Nichols.[746]

---

743 Connecticut Marriages 1726-1867, www.familysearch.org; the names of Carrie Johnson Wheaton's parents are confirmed by her death in the Michigan Death Index.
744 Marvin, *Fifth Regiment Volunteers*, 159.
745 Note the discrepancy in the records of her birth place.
746 Branford Vital Records, deaths, 1921.

JONES, PETER
Co. E 1st Cavalry, private, substitute, enlisted 10 August 1864, mustered out 2 August 1865, no pension

Peter Jones, age 21, served as a substitute for John H. Gates of North Branford. He enlisted at New Haven on 10 August 1864 and was mustered in on 19 August 1864 as a private in Co. E 1st Connecticut Cavalry for a term of three years. At the time of his enlistment he was described as five feet seven inches tall, brown eyes, black hair, light complexion, unmarried, born in England, occupation seaman.[747] Peter Jones was mustered out at Washington, D.C. on 2 August 1865 and discharged with the rest of the regiment at New Haven on 18 August 1865. He does not appear in the 1860 census at North Branford.

JONES, WILLIAM S.
Co. G 14th CVI, private, enlisted 8 August 1862, discharged disability 8 December 1862, pension #586746 for the soldier and later for his widow Nellie

William S. Jones[748] of Madison enlisted at Hartford on 8 August 1862 and was mustered in on 23 August 1862 as a private in Co. G 14th CVI for a term of three years. He was discharged for disability from Mt. Pleasant Hospital, Washington, D.C. on 8 December 1862.

He applied for an invalid pension on 30 June 1880. At the time of his enlistment he was described as five feet eight inches tall, light complexion, brown hair, black eyes, occupation farmer. At the Battle of Antietam he developed bleeding of the lungs and was sent by ambulance to Mt. Pleasant Hospital in Washington, D.C. where he was discharged. After his discharge he lived at Branford in 1863, New Haven from 1864 to 1876, then at East Haven. There are many depositions in his file.

William S. Jones died at East Haven on 7 November 1904 and was buried in Bare Plain Cemetery, North Branford.[749] He was born at Northford on 13 April 1839, son of Edwin L. Jones and Emily C. Johnson, both born at North Madison.

Ellen C. (Nellie) Jones of East Haven applied for widow's pension on 16 November 1904. She was married to the soldier under the name of Nellie Cornelia Russell at the North Branford Congregational Church by Rev. William H. Curtiss on 5 June 1862. Neither were previously married or divorced. They had no children living in 1898. She owned two pieces of property in East Haven, one at Indian Neck, Branford and one piece in Madison.

Nellie Russell Jones died on 16 July 1918 and was buried in Bare Plain Cemetery, North Branford. She was born at North Branford on 22 March 1843, daughter of Richard Russell and Lucretia Bradley Moulthrop.

---

747   Muster & Descriptive Rolls of Substitutes, RG 13, box 97, 2nd Congressional District, Connecticut State Library.
748   For his biography see Rockey, *History of New Haven County*, I:242.
749   The Hale Collection, North Branford, 7.

JOST, JACOB
Co. A 29th New York Volunteers, private, enlisted 7 May 1861, discharged 27 August 1865, pension #904050 for the soldier

Jacob Jost enlisted on 7 May 1861 as a private in Co. A 29th New York Volunteers for a term of three years and was discharged on 20 June 1863. He reenlisted on 29 July 1863 in Co. I 15th New York Volunteers and was discharged on 27 August 1865. He also served in Co. D 19th and Co. H 28th U.S. Infantry.

He was mustered into the Mason Rogers Post No. 7 G.A.R. of Branford on 23 November 1882, no muster out or transfer date is given. He applied for an invalid pension on 20 August 1890 under the act of 27 June 1890, by then living in Iowa. He is probably the Jacob Jost living at Dayton, Butler Co., Iowa in 1910, age 65, with his wife Melenta. Jacob Jost died at Clarksville, Iowa on 11 February 1916. He was born in Germany.

KELSEY, GILBERT I.
Co. G 20th CVI, private, enlisted 19 August 1862, died 3 November 1862, pension #137020 for his widow Eliza

Gilbert Isaiah Kelsey of North Branford enlisted at New Haven on 19 August 1862 and was mustered in on 8 September 1862 as a private in Co. G 20th CVI for a term of three years. He died at Camp Pleasant Valley, Maryland on 3 November 1862 from scurvy. There is a gravestone for him at Clinton Cemetery. He was the son of Albert Kelsey and Ann J. Post.[750]

Eliza A. Kelsey of Clinton applied for a widow's pension on 5 December 1863. She was married to the soldier under the name of Eliza Ann Hurd at Clinton by Rev. Samuel N. Smith on 28 October 1860. She was age 17, he was age 24; both living at Clinton. They had no children.

KELSEY, RICHARD T.
Co. B 27th CVI, private, enlisted 21 August 1862, prisoner, mustered out 27 July 1863, pension #892253 for the soldier and later for his widow Antoinette

Richard T. Kelsey[751] of Guilford, age 21, enlisted on 21 August 1862 and was mustered in on 3 October 1862 as a private in Co. B 27th CVI for a term of nine months. He fought at the Battle of Fredericksburg on 13 December 1862 with the rest of the company. He was captured at the Battle of Chancellorsville, Virginia on 3 May 1863, held prisoner at Richmond, and was paroled at City Point, Virginia on 14 May 1863. He reported to Camp Parole, Maryland on 16 May 1863, was sent to Washington, D.C. on 20 May 1863 and spent the remainder of his service at Camp Convalescent, Virginia. With the rest of the Chancellorsville paroled prisoners, he rejoined the Regiment at Baltimore on 20 July 1863. Richard Kelsey was mustered out with the rest of his regiment at New Haven on 27 July 1863.

He applied for an invalid pension on 19 January 1892 under the act of 27 June 1890. He was described as five feet seven inches tall, light complexion, blue eyes, brown hair, occupation farmer. Since his discharge he lived at Guilford. After the war he was in the Guilford 1st Light Battery for about nine years. He was a member of the Parmelee Post No. 42 G.A.R. of Guilford.

---

750   Edward A. Claypool and Azalea Clizbee, *A Genealogy of the Descendants of William Kelsey* (Bridgeport: The Marsh Press, Inc., 1947), III:65.

751   For his biography see Hill, *Modern History of New Haven*, I:893; Cutter, *Family History of Connecticut*, II:1072.

He was married at his home in Guilford by Rev. Pascal Gallup Wightman pastor of the First Baptist Church of Groton on 18 October 1869 to M. Antoinette Baldwin of Guilford. Neither were previously married or divorced. They had four children living (in 1904): Gustave Baldwin, born on 2 November 1870; Ernest Russell, born on 17 August 1873; Agnes Fayette, born on 14 June 1876; and Richard Percy, born on 6 March 1882. They were members of the First Baptist Church at Branford. Their son Ernest R. Kelsey, a physician, served in the World War as Captain in the Medical Corps, entering the service on 26 October 1918 and was discharged on 12 August 1919 at Camp Greenleaf, Georgia.

Richard Taylor Kelsey of Guilford died at St. Raphael's Hospital, New Haven on 2 April 1920. He was buried in Center Cemetery, Branford and there was a Civil War marker was on his gravesite in 1934.[752] He was born at Guilford on 2 October 1841, son of Alvah Kelsey and Mary Almira Higgins.

Antoinette B. Kelsey of Guilford applied for a widow's pension on 12 June 1920. She was buried on 1 November 1929 in Center Cemetery, Branford.[753] She was born at Carmel, Putnam Co., New York, daughter of Arva Baldwin and Harriet Carpenter. She was the sister of George W. Baldwin.

KENNEDY, JAMES
Co. B 27th CVI, private, enlisted 10 September 1862, prisoner, mustered out 27 July 1863, pension #399293 for his widow Mary

James Kennedy, age 36, of Wallingford enlisted on 10 September 1862 and was mustered in on 3 October 1862 as a private in Co. B 27th CVI for a term of nine months. He fought at the Battle of Fredericksburg on 13 December 1862 with the rest of the company. He was captured at the Battle of Chancellorsville, Virginia on 3 May 1863, held prisoner at Richmond, and was paroled at City Point, Virginia on 14 May 1863. He reported to Camp Parole, Maryland on 16 May 1863, was sent to Washington, D.C. on 20 May 1863 and spent the remainder of his service at Camp Convalescent, Virginia. With the rest of the Chancellorsville paroled prisoners, he rejoined the Regiment at Baltimore on 20 July 1863. Kennedy was mustered out with the rest of his regiment at New Haven on 27 July 1863.

He filed for an invalid pension on 13 October 1886 and began receiving payments on 1 November 1886. He was described as 56 years of age, five feet five inches tall, light complexion, brown hair, gray eyes, occupation farmer. He lived at Wallingford since his discharge. "My disability occurred while taken prisoner at the battle of Chancellorsville while in the hands of the enemy while en-route to Richmond. Near Guinea Station there [was] a severe storm which lasted all night and into the next day. We had to lay on the ground with no shelter. I caught a severe cold which resulted in asthma, from which I have never recovered. I was finally released on parole and remained at camp convalescent at Alexandria, Va. until my discharge." In an affidavit dated 1892 he states "about two years ago there was an accident on the track of the New York, New Haven and Hartford Rail Road. He with others walked down toward the place, he tripped and fell on

---

752   Branford Sexton Records, 1884-1932, 95; The Hale Collection, 4.
753   Branford Sexton Records, 1884-1932, 128.

his left side on the iron rail breaking several ribs and his breast was severely bruised. [He] has not recovered and has not been able to work since."[754]

He was married first at New Britain by Rev. L. O. Daly on 16 February 1858 to Margaret Hayes, both of New Britain. He was age 27, she was age 21, both born in Ireland. Margaret died at Wallingford on 14 April 1861 age 25 years & 1 month during child birth.

James Kennedy died at Wallingford on 18 June 1893 age 60 and was buried there in Holy Trinity Cemetery. He left one daughter Mary, born on 2 April 1875.

Mary Kennedy of Wallingford applied for a widow's pension on 28 August 1893. She was married to the soldier under the name of Mary Shanahan at the Church of the Holy Cross, New York City by Rev. Patrick Egan on 5 August 1863.

Mary Kennedy died on 25 November 1904. She left one daughter living at Bridgeport.

KERR, JOHN
Co. B & D 12th CVI, private, enlisted 1 November 1861, discharged 2 December 1864, pension #312886 for his widow Mary

John Kerr of Branford enlisted on 1 November 1861 and was mustered in on 20 November 1861 as a private in Co. B 12th CVI for a term of three years. With his regiment he served at New Orleans and in the Battles of Winchester and Cold Harbor, Virginia. He was discharged at Hartford on 2 December 1864. He was listed as a wagoner of the 12th CVI on the 1863 Branford draft list.

"I was personally acquainted with John Kerr who formerly resided at Drummond in the County of Tyrone in Ireland. I was also acquainted with Rebecca Kerr otherwise Haydock the first wife of said John Kerr. She died at Drummond on or about the 18th day of August 1848 and was interred at the burial place attached to the Friends Meeting house at Grange in said County of Tryone."[755]

John Kerr died at Branford on 28 April 1888 age 57 years, 5 months & 4 days and was buried there in Center Cemetery. A Civil War marker was on his gravesite in 1934. He first appears at Branford in 1858.[756] He was a member of the Mason Rogers Post No. 7 G.A.R. of Branford and never applied for a pension.

Mary Kerr of Branford applied for a widow's pension on 17 July 1890 under the act of 27 June 1890. She was married to the soldier under the name of Mary Barr at the house of Richard Powell in Hudson, New York by James Algier, JP on 28 November 1850. There are very few documents in the pension file.

Mary Kerr died at Branford on 13 January 1892 age 62 and was buried there in Center Cemetery.[757] She was born in Ireland, daughter of Thomas and Mary Ann Barr.

---

754 Affidavit, James Kennedy, 19 September 1892, in his own pension file.
755 Affidavit, John Shillington of Ireland, received 22 August 1891, in the pension file of John Kerr.
756 Death of son John in November 1858, Branford Vital Records, 1852-1863, 8.
757 Branford Vital Records, deaths, 1892.

DEFENSES OF WASHINGTON – CAMP OF THE FIRST CONNECTICUT HEAVY ARTILLERY

The 1st Connecticut Heavy Artillery was among the troops in the defense of
Washington, D.C. (First Connecticut Artillery, 17)

KINNEEN, JAMES also KINNEY
Co. B 12th CVI, corporal, enlisted 22 November 1861, reenlisted 1 January 1864, prisoner, discharged 12 August 1865, pension #361631 for the soldier

James Kinneen of Branford enlisted on 22 November 1861 and was mustered in on 25 November 1861 as a private in Co. B 12th CVI for a term of three years. He was wounded at Port Hudson, Louisiana on 10 June 1863. He reenlisted in Co. B as a veteran on 1 January 1864 and was promoted to corporal on 4 August 1864. He was captured at Cedar Creek, Virginia on 19 October 1864 and confined at Richmond on 23 October. He was sent to Salisbury Prison, North Carolina on 4 November 1864 and was paroled at N. E. Ferry, North Carolina on 22 February 1865. James Kinneen was mustered out at Savannah, Georgia on 12 August 1865 and discharged at Hartford on 22 August 1865.

While at Camp Parapet, New Orleans, Louisiana about 15 June 1862 he suffered from sun stroke while on guard duty and was in the hospital for six weeks. Since that time he has had pain in his head and cannot work in the hot sun. About October 1862 near Donaldsville, Louisiana he incurred a strain of his left side from rigorous marching and while a prisoner in Salisbury, North Carolina prison in January 1865 his feet froze. He initially received a partial disability.

About nine years before his enlistment he lived at Branford and returned there after his discharge. In 1871 he moved to New Britain for six years, to Meriden about one year, to Mansfield Valley, Pennsylvania about six years, lastly to Cleveland, Ohio about 1885. By 1894 he was living at the Soldiers' Home in Sandusky, Eric Co., Ohio, a widower.

He was married at Branford by Rev. Lynch on 19 October 1856 to Mary McQueeney.[758] They had the following children (living in 1898): Mary Ann, born on 21 September 1857; James Henry, born on 1 September 1861; William, born on 9 January 1870; Thomas, born on 28 June 1872; and Joseph, born on 18 September 1880.

---

758   Branford Vital Records, 1852-1863, 7; also spelled McQuinney.

KINNEEN, MICHAEL also KINNEY
Co. K 1st HA, private, enlisted 23 May 1861, discharged 22 May 1864, pension #842924 for the soldier and later for his widow Catherine

Michael Kinneen of Branford enlisted and was mustered in at Hartford on 23 May 1861 as a private in Co. K 4th CVI which became the 1st HA. With his regiment he fought at Chickahominy and Malvern Hill, Virginia. He was discharged at Bermuda Hundred, Petersburg, Virginia on 22 May 1864 when his term expired. "I was in the same company as Edgar L. Forbes. We came home together and could not get a train so [we] walked from New Haven to Branford."[759]

He applied for an invalid pension on 13 December 1876. At the time of his enlistment he was described as five feet five inches tall, light complexion, brown eyes, black hair, occupation mechanic. At Fort Richardson, Arlington Heights, Virginia in November 1861 he sustained an injury to his right arm by a fall in front of his tent which removed him from duty. He was in Regimental Hospital over a month. His application was sent for special examination to determine if the injury to his right arm was during his service. It was difficult to find evidence but his tent mate attested to the injury. The surgeon at Regimental Hospital also remembered the injury and stated the arm was broken and would never heal properly. It appears Kinney withdrew his pension application upon advice of his attorney, a decision he later regretted.

He reapplied for a pension on 28 November 1890 under the act of 27 June 1890. He lived one year at South Norwalk before removing to Branford. A record of his birth or baptism in Ireland could not be found. He was a charter member and commander of the Mason Rogers Post No. 7 G.A.R. of Branford.

Michael Kinney died at Branford on 6 June 1914 and was buried there in St. Agnes Cemetery. He was born on 29 March 1843, son of John Kinney and Hannah Greeley, all born in Leitrim, Ireland.

Catherine Kinney applied for a widow's pension on 17 June 1914. She was married to the soldier under the name of Catherine McGowan at Norwalk by Rev. Peter A. Smith of St. Mary's Church on 24 April 1867. They came to Branford the same day and lived there ever since. Neither were previously married or divorced. In 1917 she still had not received her pension due to inactivity on the part of the pension board apparently due to variations in the spelling of the soldier's name. She states the only time the name was spelled Kinneen was when he enlisted and on his military records. The family uses Kinney. They had the following children (living in 1898): John F., born on 16 January 1868; Mary Jane, born on 27 February 1869; and Francis J., born on 11 December 1874; all born at Branford.

Catherine Kinney died at Bridgeport on 21 March 1930 age 86 and was buried in St. Agnes Cemetery, Branford.[760]

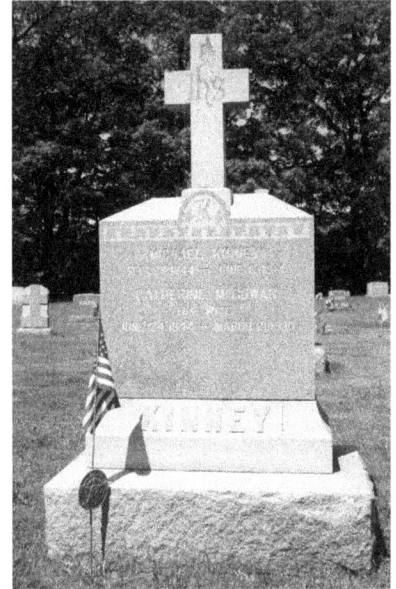

---

759   Deposition, Michael Kinneen of Branford, 1 February 1897, in the pension file of Edgar L. Forbes.
760   *The Branford Review*, 27 March 1930, 8.

KNERINGER, MATTHIAS

Co. B 27th CVI, private, enlisted 22 August 1862, mustered out 27 July 1863, pension #323885 for the soldier and later for his widow Hannah

Matthias Kneringer, age 43, of Branford enlisted on 22 August 1862 and was mustered in on 3 October 1862 as a private in Co. B 27th CVI for a term of nine months. From November 1862 until the end of his service he was detailed to the Quarter Master Department. Kneringer was mustered out with the rest of his regiment at New Haven on 27 July 1863.

He applied for an invalid pension on 20 March 1883. He was described five feet eight inches tall, light complexion, gray hair, hazel eyes, occupation tailor. He states that while in the line of duty "at Throughfare Gap, Virginia in June 1863, our Regiment received orders to load up the trains. I being detailed in [the] Q. M. Dept. became ill and strained my back which finally resulted in general debility."

Matthias Kneringer was admitted to the Soldiers' Home at Togus, Maine on 3 April 1891 and died there on 10 April 1891. He was buried in the National Cemetery, Togus, Maine. He was born in New York.[761]

Hannah E. Kneringer of New Haven applied for a widow's pension on 2 October 1891. She was married to the soldier under the name of Hannah E. Mitchell at New York City by Rev. Charles Chase on 6 January 1846. They were living at Branford during the 1860 census as Mattheus Knernager age 44, born New York, a tailor; wife Hannah E. age 36, born New Jersey; children Adele age 13, Harry age 6, Reuben age 4, and Jane age 2, all born in Connecticut.[762]

KNIGHT, WINTHROP

Winthrop Knight is listed on the Branford selectman's report for men "belonging to Branford" who enlisted in 1862 to fill the town's quota. The selectman noted he was living at Stony Creek, enlisted in the 13th CVI and died in camp. He appears at Branford in 1860, age 49, born in Maine with his wife Susan age 33, born in Connecticut.[763] No other record was found.

LAMB, JOHN

John Lamb, age 21, served as a substitute for William D. Ford of North Branford. He enlisted on 11 August 1864 at the Brooklyn Navy Yard.[764]

LAMM, ADAM or LAMB

Co. B 27th CVI, private, enlisted 1 September 1862, prisoner, mustered out 27 July 1863, no pension

Adam Lamm, age 35, of North Haven enlisted on 1 September 1862 and was mustered in on 3 October 1862 as a private in Co. B 27th CVI for a term of nine months. He fought at the Battle of Fredericksburg on 13 December 1862 with the rest of the company. He was captured at the Battle of Chancellorsville, Virginia on 3 May 1863, held prisoner at Richmond, and was paroled at City Point, Virginia on 14 May 1863. He reported

---

761   Draft Enrollment 1863, 2nd Congressional District, Branford.

762   U.S. census 1860, Branford, New Haven County, Connecticut, population schedule, M653-85, dwelling 743, family 835, page 883, www.heritagequest.com.

763   U.S. census 1860, Branford, New Haven County, Connecticut, population schedule, M653-85, dwelling 1006, family 1119, page 916, www.heritagequest.com.

764   Statements of Navy substitutes, RG 13, box 96, 2nd Congregational District, Connecticut State Library.

to Camp Parole, Maryland on 16 May 1863 and spent the remainder of his service at Camp Convalescent, Virginia. With the rest of the Chancellorsville paroled prisoners, he rejoined the Regiment at Baltimore on 20 July 1863. Adam Lamm was mustered out with the rest of his regiment at New Haven on 27 July 1863. His name appears on the North Haven Civil War Honor Roll.

LANPHIER, HENRY B.
see John Flynn

LAY, JAMES W.
Co. F 3rd Illinois Cavalry, captain, enlisted 5 August 1861, discharged 5 September 1864, pension #623189 for the soldier

James W. Lay enlisted at Quincy, Illinois on 5 August 1861 and was mustered at Camp Butler on 27 August 1861 as a sergeant in Co. F 3rd Illinois Cavalry. He was promoted to 2nd lieutenant in September 1862 and to 1st lieutenant on 21 June 1862. The regiment served in Arkansas and Mississippi including the Siege of Vicksburg and the Battle of Nashville. He was promoted to captain of Co. F on 29 August 1863 and discharged on 5 September 1864.

He applied for an invalid pension on 22 May 1888. He was described as five feet eight inches tall, light complexion, dark hair, dark eyes. While on a march from Jackson, Tennessee to Meridian, Alabama he was injured by another horse running into his own, causing him to fall and his horse stepping onto him. Since his discharge he lived at Branford, the native home of his parents. He was a charter member and commander of the Mason Rogers Post No. 7 G.A.R. of Branford. He was on the committee for the Branford Soldiers' Monument.

His wife Charlotte Mason, born at Westford, New York, died at Branford on 29 September 1888 and was buried there in Center Cemetery.[765]

He was admitted to the Fitch's Soldier Home at Noroton Heights on 11 August 1896. As a captain he received a larger than usual pension and his admittance had to be reviewed by the Home's board. He agreed to turn over his pension except for one dollar per week. His possessions included food, clothing, tobacco, stamps, newspapers, and periodicals.

James Willoughby Lay died at the Fitch's Soldier Home on 23 September 1896 and was buried in Center Cemetery, Branford.[766] His rank, company, and regiment are engraved on his stone. He was born at Branford on 16 November 1829, son of Dr. Willoughby Lynde Lay and Anna Maria Harrison.[767]

---

765 Branford Vital Records, 1863-1895, 239.
766 *Shore Line Times*, 25 September 1896.
767 Branford Vital Records, 1786-1840, 352.

LEE, FREDERICK W.

Co. K 10th CVI, private, enlisted 8 October 1861, discharged disability 20 December 1861, Co. G 20th CVI, sergeant, enlisted 15 August 1862, discharged disability 10 December 1862, pension #689126 for the soldier

Frederick W. Lee of Guilford enlisted at Hartford on 8 October 1861 and was mustered in on 22 October 1861 as a private in Co. K 10th CVI and was discharged for disability at Annapolis, Maryland on 20 December 1861. He reenlisted, now of Branford, at New Haven on 15 August 1862 and was mustered in on 8 September 1862 as a sergeant in Co. G 20th CVI. Frederick Lee was discharged for disability at Loudon Heights, Virginia on 10 December 1862 for disease of the lungs.

He applied for an invalid pension on 25 July 1890 under the act of 27 June 1890. At the time of his enlistment he was described as five foot six inches tall, light complexion, blue eyes, brown hair, occupation painter. He was married at East Haddam by Rev. Nelson Goodrich on 19 October 1856 to Lucy Ann Abell of East Haddam. She died on 10 January 1904. They had the following children: Sarah Rebecca, born on 26 June 1858, died before 1915; Grace Marilla, born on 3 April 1860, married name Fitch; Addie Abell, born on 3 July 1862, married name Campbell; Charles Frederick, born on 7 June 1867; Ernest Walter, born on 9 November 1869; Mary Deming, born on 6 December 1871; Kitty Clover, born on 7 May 1875; and Sadie Young, born on 17 February 1879, died before 1915. After his discharge he lived at Harinan, Illinois and moved to Tiskilwa, Bureau Co., Illinois in November 1880.

Frederick W. Lee died at Tiskilwa, Illinois on 10 May 1916. He was born at Guilford on 10 June 1834, son of Frederick W. and Rebecca Lee.

Joseph Lee of Massachusetts came to Branford in 1883 and was a member of the Mason Rogers Post No. 7 G.A.R. (Photograph by Ramsdell Studio, New Haven; Branford Historical Society photograph collection)

LEE, JOSEPH

Co. E & Co. F 1st Massachusetts Cavalry, private, enlisted 26 December 1863, reenlisted, discharged 17 June 1865, pension #XC3021979 for the soldier and later for his widow Susan

Joseph Lee, age 26, enlisted at Chicopee, Massachusetts on 26 December 1863 as a private in Co. E. 1st Massachusetts Cavalry for a term of three years. He was on detached service in April 1863 at Cedar Mountain, Virginia. He was captured at Rapidan, Virginia on 3 May 1863 and confined at Richmond. He reported to Camp Parole, Maryland on 22 September 1863 and was sent to Cavalry Depot, Washington, D.C. on 6 October 1863. Joseph Lee was mustered out at Warrentown, Virginia on 25 December 1863 and reenlisted on 26 December 1863 as a veteran in Co. F. 1st Massachusetts Cavalry. He was discharged from Dale General Hospital at Worcester, Massachusetts on 17 June 1865 where he was sent for rheumatism on 28 January 1865.[768]

He applied for an invalid pension on 3 May 1892 under the act of 27 June 1890. At the time of his enlistment he was described as five feet seven inches tall, grey eyes, dark hair. He moved to Branford in 1883 and lived there until 1905; lived at Spencer, Massachusetts from 1905

---

768   A copy of his discharge and military service papers are in the Branford Historical Society Archives, RG 1, box 27, folder 1.

until 1909; then returned to Branford.[769] He was married first at Worcester, Massachusetts in 1861 to Sarah Louise Cook who died there in 1877.[770] He was married second at Branford on 30 October 1890 to Susan Maria Walsh Oesterle, a widow.[771] He was a member and commander of the Mason Rogers Post No. 7 G.A.R. of Branford. He was on the committee for the Branford Soldiers' Monument. His pension is at the Veteran's Administration.

JOSEPH LEE
CO. F 1st REGT. MASS. CAVALRY
1836 — 1928

Joseph Lee died at Branford on 19 May 1928 in his 93rd year and was buried there in Center Cemetery.[772] His company and regiment are engraved on his stone and there was a G.A.R. marker on his gravesite in 1934 and 2011. He was born at Williston, Vermont, son of John and Ann Lee.

Susan W. Lee of Branford applied for a widow's pension on 27 June 1928. She died at Branford on 23 July 1946 and was buried there in Center Cemetery.[773] She was born at New York City,[774] daughter of George Walsh and Mary Connors.[775]

LESTER, THOMAS
Co. F 11th CVI, private, enlisted 11 March 1864, prisoner, discharged 21 December 1865, pension #120202 for the soldier and later for his widow Harriet

Thomas Lester of Branford enlisted and was mustered in on 11 March 1864 as a private in Co. F 11th CVI. He was captured at Drewry's Bluff, Virginia on 16 May 1864. He was released from prison by U.S. troops on 4 May 1865 and discharged on 21 December 1865. He applied for an invalid pension on 21 November 1866 and his widow Harriet Lester applied for a pension on 16 March 1868. He does not appear in the 1860 census at Branford.

LINSLEY, ATWOOD or J. ATWOOD
Co. E 5th CVI, corporal, enlisted 22 June 1861, reenlisted, mustered out 19 July 1865, pension #846385 for the soldier and later for his widow Julia

LINSLEY

J. ATWOOD LINSLEY
Co. E. 5. Reg't Conn Vols
BORN MARCH 4. 1845
DIED JUNE 6, 1917
JULIA E. REYNOLDS
HIS WIFE
BORN FEBRUARY 4. 1846
DIED DECEMBER 6. 1933

J. Atwood Linsley of Branford enlisted at Hartford on 22 June 1861 and was mustered in on 22 July 1861 as a private in Co. E 5th CVI. He was discharged at Tracy City, Tennessee on 21 December 1863 and

769 Obituary, *The Branford Review*, 24 May 1928, 1.
770 Obituary, *The Branford Review*, 24 May 1928, 1.
771 Branford Vital Records, 1863-1895, 176; she was the widow of Charles Oesterle or Osterle.
772 Branford Vital Records, deaths, 1928.
773 Branford Vital Records, deaths, 1946.
774 Branford Vital Records, deaths, 1946, her parents are not recorded.
775 Branford Vital Records, deaths, 1936, for her brother George Walsh.

Benjamin Maltby Linsley of North Branford was missing in action after the
Battle of the Wilderness. (Harper's Weekly, 28 May 1863)

reenlisted the same day as a veteran in Co. E for a term of four years. He was promoted to corporal on 1 September 1864. With his regiment he fought at the Battles of Cedar Mountain, Chancellorsville, and Gettysburg and took part in the campaigns of Atlanta, the Carolinas and with General Sherman on the march to Savannah. Atwood Linsley was mustered out with the rest of his regiment near Alexandria, Virginia on 19 July 1865.

He applied for an invalid pension on 21 December 1891 under the act of 27 June 1890 for age related illness. At the time of his enlistment he was described as five feet seven inches tall, light complexion, blue eyes, light hair. He was married first at Branford on 3 October 1867 to Emma Tomlinson. She died at Branford on 25 December 1871. Since his discharge he lived at Branford except three months in Waterbury. He was a charter member and commander of the Mason Rogers Post No. 7 G.A.R. of Branford.

John Atwood Linsley died at Branford on 6 June 1917 and was buried there in Center Cemetery. His company and regiment are engraved on his stone. He was born at Branford on 4 March 1845, son of Elias Linsley and Mary Bradley, born at North Branford and Branford.

Julia Elizabeth Linsley of Branford applied for a widow's pension on 21 July 1917. She was married to the soldier under the name of Julia E. Reynolds at Seymour by Rev. George Seabury of the Seymour Episcopal Church on 8 January 1873. She was not previously married or divorced. She was unable to find a public record of her birth, her papers were destroyed by a fire in 1904 or 1905. Her sister, Sarah L. Reynolds Howard of New Haven testified on her behalf in 1917. She had one daughter Mildred Eugenia, born at Branford on 1 June 1874 who died there on 5 October 1892.

Julia E. Linsley died at Branford on 6 December 1933 and was buried there in Center Cemetery.[776] She was born at Seymour on 4 February 1843, daughter of Charles Reynolds and Mary Short.[777]

LINSLEY, BENJAMIN M.
10th CVI, private, enlisted 14 August 1862, to Co. A 14th Regiment U.S. Infantry, killed 12 May 1864, no pension.

Benjamin Maltby Linsley of New Haven enlisted on 14 August 1862 in the 10th CVI, unassigned. He was transferred to Co. A 1st Battalion 14th Regiment U.S. Infantry. At the time of his enlistment he was described as five feet seven inches tall, hazel eyes, dark hair, fair complexion, occupation teacher. "He was promoted to lieutenant and sent out on a scouting trip at the Battle of the Wilderness and was never heard from again. His brothers and comrades searched but never found him."[778] He was reported as missing in action on 12 May 1864 and presumed killed after the Battle of the Wilderness, Virginia. There is a gravestone for him in Northford Cemetery. His gravestone reads "member Co. A 14th United States Inf. missing after Battle of Wilderness May 9, 1864 AE 22---Appointed 1st Lieut. 108th United States C.T. by Special Order No. 216---War Department 1864." There was a Civil War marker on his gravesite in 1934. His name is on the New Haven Soldiers and Sailors Monument on East Rock and on the Northford Veterans' Monument. He was born at Northford on 2 November 1841, son of John Stephen Linsley and Eliza Ann Halsey.[779] He was the brother of James H. and John S. Linsley.

LINSLEY, CHARLES E.
U.S. Navy, enlisted 1 September 1864, discharged 1 September 1865, pension #33476 for the sailor

Charles E. Linsley of Branford enlisted at the Brooklyn, New York Navy Yard on 1 September 1864. He served as a landsman on the U.S.S. *Vermont* until 18 September 1864, the U.S.S. *Grand Gulf* until 2 August 1865, the U.S.S. *Portsmouth* until 31 August 1865, and the U.S.S. *North Carolina* from which he was discharged at the Brooklyn Navy Yard on 1 September 1865. He was the first cousin of William H. Linsley.

He applied for an invalid pension on 24 September 1890 under the act of 27 June 1890. At the time of his enlistment he was described as five feet five

---

776 Branford Vital Records, deaths, 1933.
777 Branford Vital Records, deaths, 1933.
778 Ray Linsley, *Connecticut Linsleys,* 109.
779 Ray Linsley, *Connecticut Linsleys,* 109.

(Photographic History of the Civil War, 6:63)

inches tall, florid complexion, grey eyes, brown hair, occupation seaman. "I was on the Steamer USS Grand Gulf, transferred from her at New Orleans to the ship Portsmouth; from her to the North Carolina and from her discharged at the Brooklyn Ship Yard." He always lived at Branford and was a member of the Mason Rogers Post No. 7 G.A.R. of Branford.

He was married at Branford by Rev. Elijah C. Baldwin of the First Congregational Church on 26 December 1868 to Susan Frances Bartlett. Neither were previously married or divorced. She died at Branford on 2 March 1915 and was buried there in Center Cemetery. Their only child Arthur Sherwood, was born on 23 July 1875 and died soon after.

Charles Edward Linsley died at Branford on 9 October 1924 and was buried there in Center Cemetery. A G.A.R. marker was on his gravesite in 1934. He was born at Branford on 28 January 1843, son of John Linsley and Lucinda Monroe.

LINSLEY, CHARLES F.
Co. F 15th CVI, quartermaster, enlisted 13 August 1862, promoted 1 June 1863, mustered out 27 June 1865, no pension

Charles F. Linsley[780] of Branford enlisted at New Haven on 13 August 1862 and was mustered in on 25 August 1862 as a private in Co. F 15th CVI for a term of three years. He was promoted to quartermaster sergeant of the regiment on 1 June 1863 as a non-commissioned officer and detailed to the commissary department

---

780   For his biography see C. Bancroft Gillespie, *A Century of Meriden* (Meriden: Journal Publishing Co., 1906), III:74 and *History of Connecticut In Monographic Form, Biographical Volume* (New York: Lewis Historical Publishing Co., Inc., no date), 9.

for the remainder of the war. Charles F. Linsley was mustered out with the rest of his regiment at New Bern, North Carolina on 27 June 1865 and discharged at New Haven on 12 July 1865. He was the first cousin of Frederick A. Linsley.

After his discharge he lived at Meriden and never applied for a pension. He was secretary and director of Bradley & Hubbard Manufacturing Co. of Meriden. He was married on 26 January 1871 to Georgianna Emily Gay, daughter of George E. Gay and Martha Delia Waters. She died on 9 March 1922 and buried in Walnut Grove Cemetery, Meriden. They had one daughter Bessie Gay, born on 31 January 1878, later Mrs. James H. Hinsdale. He was a member of the Mason Rogers Post No. 7 G.A.R. of Branford. He was on the committee to erect a monument at Gettysburg for Major-General John Sedgwick, commander of the Sixth Corps and attended the dedication ceremonies on 19 June 1913.[781]

Charles Foote Linsley died at Meriden on 28 March 1932 and was buried there in Walnut Grove Cemetery.[782] He was born at Branford on 29 March 1843, son of Frederic Linsley and Harriet Foote.

Charles F. Linsley of Branford was quartermaster sergeant of the 15th CVI. After the war he lived at Meriden. (Gillespie, A Century of Meriden, III:74)

LINSLEY, FRANKLIN D.
see Joseph Willis

LINSLEY, FREDERICK A.
Co. E 2nd E. S. Maryland Volunteers, enlisted 25 December 1861, discharged 27 December 1864, pension #419524 for the soldier and later for his widow Elizabeth

Frederick A. Linsley of Branford enlisted at Chestertown, Kent Co., Maryland on 25 December 1861 as a private in Co. E 2nd East Shore Maryland Volunteers for a term of three years.[783] The regiment served in Maryland and Virginia along the Potomac. Frederick Linsley was discharged at Harper's Ferry, Virginia on 27 December 1864 as a 3rd corporal. He was the first cousin of Charles F. Linsley.

He applied for an invalid pension on 7 July 1890 under the act of 27 June 1890. At the time of his enlistment he was described as five feet eight inches tall, dark complexion, dark hair, blue eyes, occupation carpenter and farmer. While at Fort Lookout, Maryland on 1 February 1863 he contracted lung fever after wading in a creek and was in Cockoysville Hospital, Maryland until 1 May 1863. He came home sick on furlough for 30 days then returned to duty. While fighting under General Sheridan of the 8th Corps near Winchester, Virginia he sprained his ankle on 19 September 1864 falling off a ledge. Nicholas R. Terhune, sergeant of the company stated he was surprised Linsley survived the lung

---

781   *History of Connecticut*, 13.
782   *The Branford Review*, 31 March 1932; The Hale Collection, Meriden, 53.
783   It is not known why he enlisted in a Maryland regiment. Nicholas Terhune was sergeant of the same company.

The 2nd East Shore Maryland Volunteers served under General Joseph Hooker at Lookout Mountain, Tennessee in 1863.
(Photographic History of the Civil War, 2:303)

fever, after his return was often on light duty, and has not been well since his discharge.[784] There are many affidavits in the file about his disability. Since his discharge he lived at Branford.

Frederick Alden Linsley died at Branford on 27 November 1894 and was buried there in Center Cemetery. His company and regiment are engraved on his stone and a G.A.R. marker was on his gravesite in 1934 and 2011. He was born at Branford on 6 March 1842, son of Benjamin C. Linsley and Lydia Bradley.[785]

Elizabeth A. Linsley of Branford applied for a widow's pension on 21 February 1895. She was married to the soldier under the name of Elizabeth Adelaide Stent at East Haven by Rev. E. Edwin Hall on 25 February 1880, both were living at Branford. Neither were previously married or divorced. They had one child Philo J., born on 25 March 1883. Her property included a small house and thirteen acres. Elizabeth Stent Linsley died at Branford on 29 August 1906 and was buried there in Center Cemetery. She was born at Branford on 23 May 1844, daughter of John Stent and Polly A. Dowd.[786]

LINSLEY, JACOB F.
Co. K 15th CVI, private, died 1 March 1863, no pension

Jacob Frisbie Linsley, age 18, of North Haven enlisted on 9 August 1862 and was mustered in on 25 August 1862 as a private in Co. K 15th CVI for a term of three years. Soon after his enlistment he was sick in his quarters and was admitted to Windmill Point Hospital near Acquia Creek, Virginia on 24 January 1863. He died at Finley Hospital in Washington, D.C. on 1 March 1863 of typhoid fever where he was admitted on 8 February. His sister was present at the time of his death and his effects released to her. He was buried in Center Cemetery, North Haven. He was born at North Haven on 20 June 1846, son of Alfred Linsley and

784   Affidavit, Nicholas R. Terhune of Branford, 8 May 1893, in the pension file of Frederick A. Linsley.
785   Branford Vital Record, Town Meeting Book A, 237.
786   Branford Vital Record, Town Meeting Book A, 234.

Polly Frisbie of North Branford. At the time of his enlistment he was described as five feet eight inches tall, fair complexion, blue eyes, black hair, occupation farmer. He was the brother of Samuel M. Linsley and the first cousin of Marcus M., Joseph F., and Solomon F. Linsley. His name appears on the North Haven Civil War Honor Roll.

LINSLEY, JARED, JR.
U.S. Navy paymaster, no pension

Jared Linsley, Jr. served as a paymaster in the U.S. Navy during and after the Civil War. He was acting assistant paymaster 11 July 1864, named assistant 23 July 1866, and promoted to paymaster on 24 February 1872. On 10 May 1875 he was ordered onto the *U.S.S. Minnesota* at New York Harbor.[787] He was born at New York City on 30 July 1842, son of Jared Linsley and Catherine Fisher Baldwin of New York City and North Branford.

Jared Linsley, Jr. died at New York City on 24 January 1878 and was buried in Northford Cemetery.[788] His gravestone reads "Paymaster United States Navy." A Civil War marker was on his gravesite in 1934.

LINSLEY, JOSEPH F.
Co. H 33rd Wisconsin Volunteers, captain, enlisted 18 October 1862, killed 19 April 1863, pension #11932 for his widow Betsey and minor child

Joseph Foote Linsley enlisted at Racine, Wisconsin and was mustered in at Camp Utley, Wisconsin on 18 October 1862 as captain of Co. H 33rd Wisconsin Volunteer Infantry for a term of three years. He was a resident of New Haven but enlisted in Wisconsin where his parents were living. The regiment proceeded to Memphis, Tennessee and Vicksburg, Mississippi. Joseph Linsley was killed at Perry's Ferry on the Coldwater River near Hernando, Mississippi from a gunshot wound to the head. He was born on 22 June 1837, son of Marcus Linsley and Clarissa Fowler. He was the brother of Solomon F. and Marcus M. Linsley and the first cousin of Jacob F. and Samuel M. Linsley.

Betsey Linsley of Paris, Kenosha Co., Wisconsin applied for a widow's pension on 13 June 1863. She was living with the soldier's parents. She was married to the soldier under the name of Betsey Sperry on 17 November 1861 at New Haven by Rev. Edward A. Strong of the College Street Congregational Church in the home of E. H. and Carrie

Joseph Foote Linsley of New Haven was captain of Co. H 33rd Wisconsin Volunteers and was killed at Perry's Ferry, Mississippi. (Branford Historical Society photograph collection)

---

787 *Commercial Advertiser*, 10 May 1875, www.genealogybank.com.
788 The Hale Collection, North Branford, 67.

Sperry. Neither were previously married or divorced. By 1873 she returned to New Haven. They had one child, James Frank Linsley born at New Haven on 10 July 1862 who received a pension until the age of sixteen. He was living at New Haven in 1928. She was married second at New Haven on 5 July 1894 by Rev. G. B. Morgan of Christ Church to William T. Northrop as his second wife. He was born at Roxbury on 20 April 1835, died at New Haven on 24 August 1915 and was buried in Evergreen Cemetery, New Haven.

After the death of her second husband she reapplied for a pension on 26 September 1916. Betsey Sperry Linsley Northrop died at New Haven on 7 October 1928 and was buried in Evergreen Cemetery. She was born at Naugatuck or Bethany on 24 January 1839,[789] daughter of Marvin Sperry and Lavinia Gaylord.

LINSLEY, MARCUS M.
Co. A & E 15th CVI, sergeant, enlisted 20 August 1862, to U.S. Navy 17 May 1864, discharged 14 June 1865, no pension

Marcus M. Linsley[790] of New Haven enlisted on 20 August 1862 and was mustered in on 25 August 1862 as a private in Co. E 15th CVI for a term of three years and was promoted to corporal on 20 May 1863. He was transferred to Co. A 15th CVI on 20 August 1863 and promoted to sergeant at Portsmouth, Virginia. During November and December 1863 he was assigned to the recruiting service at New Haven and returned to duty with his regiment on 31 March 1864. At New Bern, North Carolina on 17 May 1864, he was transferred to the U.S. Navy as a Master's Mate and served on the *U.S.S. Ino*. Marcus Linsley was discharged on 14 June 1865. He was a member of the Robert O. Tyler Post No. 50 G.A.R. of Hartford. He was the brother of Joseph F. and Solomon F. Linsley and the first cousin of Jacob F. and Samuel M. Linsley.

Marcus M. Linsley was a corporal in Co. E 15th CVI. (Branford Historical Society photograph collection)

He was married on 25 November 1857 to Francis Louisa Bradley. At the time of his enlistment he was described as five feet nine inches tall, florid complexion, blue eyes, brown hair, occupation mechanic, age 30, born at Meriden, married with one child. After his discharge he lived at New Haven, Middletown, and Hartford.

Marcus Munson Linsley died on 13 January 1904 and was buried in Walnut Grove Cemetery, Meriden. He was born at North Haven or Meriden on 15 August 1832, son of Marcus Linsley and Clarissa Fowler.

LINSLEY, SAMUEL M.
Co. K 15th CVI, private, enlisted 9 August 1862, died 19 November 1862, no pension

Samuel Munson Linsley, age 22, of North Haven enlisted at New Haven on 9 August 1862 and was mustered in on 25 August 1862 as a private in Co. K 15th CVI for a term of three years. He died at Camp Casey near Fairfax Seminary, Virginia on 19 November 1862 of typhoid fever and was buried in Center Cemetery, North Haven. His father was present at the time of his death. He was born at North Haven on 12 September

---

789   Her birth place on her marriage certificate in the pension file is listed as Naugatuck, on her pension application in 1916 as Bethany.
790   For his biography see Beers, *Biographical Record of New Haven County*, 107.

1839, son of Alfred Linsley and Polly Frisbie of North Branford. He was the brother of Jacob F. Linsley and the first cousin of Marcus M., Joseph F., and Solomon F. Linsley. At the time of his enlistment he was described as five feet seven inches tall, fair complexion, blue eyes, brown hair, occupation butcher. His name appears on the North Haven Civil War Honor Roll.

LINSLEY, SOLOMON F.

Co. G 6th CVI, corporal, enlisted 26 August 1861, discharged 14 March 1862, reenlisted 9 August 1862, Co. K 15th CVI, 1st lieutenant, prisoner, mustered out 27 June 1865, pension #548089 for his widow Lucy

Solomon F. Linsley[791] of New Britain, age 32, enlisted at New Haven on 26 August 1861 and was mustered in on 4 September 1861 as a private in Co. G 6th CVI. At the time of his enlistment he was described as five feet eight inches tall, light complexion, blue eyes, black hair, occupation carpenter. He was promoted to corporal on 4 October 1861 and discharged for disability at Port Royal, South Carolina on 14 March 1862.

He reenlisted on 9 August 1862 as a 2nd lieutenant in Co. K 15th CVI for a term of three years. He saw action at the Battle of Fredericksburg, Virginia on 13 December 1862, the Siege of Suffolk in the spring of 1863, and in the Peninsula Campaign July 1863. He was promoted to 1st lieutenant on 16 November 1863. He was instrumental in the forming of Co. K and was in command of the Brigade Pioneer Corps. He was captured with much of his regiment at the Battle of Kinston, North Carolina on 8 March 1865, escaped on 12 March, was recaptured several days later, sent by train to Richmond arriving at Libby Prison,

Solomon F. Linsley was 1st lieutenant of Co. K 15th CVI and was captured at the Battle of Kinston, Virginia; escaped but was recaptured several days later. (Beers, Biographical Record of New Haven County, 185)

Richmond on 21 March two days before the rest of the regiment arrived. He was paroled at Boulware's & Cox's wharf on 26 March 1865. He reported to Camp Parole, Maryland on 30 March 1865, received a thirty day furlough and afterwards reported to Camp Convalescent, Virginia. Solomon Linsley was mustered out with the rest of his regiment at New Bern, North Carolina on 27 June 1865 and discharged at New Haven on 12 July 1865. "He was in the battles of Fredericksburg, Edenton Road, Providence Church Road, the Siege of Suffolk and Kinston, and was through the scourge of yellow fever at Newbern, North Carolina." He was one of three brothers and one of twenty-two first cousins to serve in the Civil War. He was a member of the Admiral Foote Post No. 17 G.A.R. of New Haven. He never applied for a pension.

After the war he was an architect and builder at North Haven. He designed the North Haven Town Hall which was dedicated to the town's Civil War soldiers. His name appears on the North Haven Civil War Honor Roll.

Solomon Fowler Linsley died at North Haven on 13 March 1901 and was buried in Fairview Cemetery, New Britain. He was born at Northford or Wallingford on 25 May 1830, son of Marcus Linsley and Clarissa Fowler, both born at North Branford. He was the brother of Marcus M. and Joseph F. Linsley and the first cousin of Jacob F. and Samuel M. Linsley.

---

791   For his biography see Beers, *Biographical Record of New Haven County*, 185; and Marvin, *Fifteenth Regiment Volunteers*; 140, 206, 220 & 351.

Lucy A. Linsley of North Haven applied for a widow's pension on 26 March 1901. She was married to the soldier under the name of Lucy A. Tracy at Windsor by Thomas H. Rouse on 28 February 1855. Neither were previously married or divorced. She died in 1921 and was buried in Fairview Cemetery, New Britain.[792] She was born on 19 May 1834, daughter of Solomon F. Tracy and Almira Nichols.[793]

LINSLEY, WILLIAM H.
Co. B 15th CVI, private, enlisted 6 August 1862, mustered out 27 June 1865, pension #519537 for the soldier

William H. Linsley, age 19, of Branford enlisted at New Haven on 6 August 1862 and was mustered in on 25 August 1862 as a private in Co. B 15th CVI for a term of three years. He was left sick at Regimental Hospital, Camp Casey near Fairfax Seminary, Virginia from 25 August until 31 December 1862. He saw action at the Siege of Suffolk, Virginia in the spring of 1863 and in the Peninsula Campaign of July 1863. Linsley was sick with yellow fever during the plague at New Bern, North Carolina. "I left Wm. Linsley in the Hospital, he is getting better. He had a narrow escape. He was put in the death room once."[794] He was arrested for "conduct to the prejudice of good order and military discipline." While on picket duty at the Rail Road Crossing on the Deep Creek Road, he left his post without any Authority and when found was arrested at a "House of Ill fame" near Portsmouth, Virginia on 4 November 1863. He was confined in jail for two months and released. During the summer of 1864 he had daily duty at the Provost Marshall's office and in 1865 had daily duty as a railroad guard. He was termed a "Good soldier." William Linsley was mustered out with the rest of his regiment at New Bern, North Carolina on 27 June 1865 and honorably discharged at New Haven on 12 July 1865. He was the first cousin of Charles E. Linsley.

He applied for an invalid pension on 7 July 1890 under the act of 27 June 1890 and was living at the National Military Home in Leavenworth, Kansas. At the time of his enlistment he was described as five feet ten inches tall, light complexion, gray eyes, brown hair, occupation carpenter. After the war he lived at Branford from June 1865 until 1868; St. Paul, Minnesota from 1868 until November 1873; Cincinnati, Ohio until November 1878; New Britain, Connecticut until 1881; San Francisco, California from 1881 until October 1886; Texarkana, Texas until 1888; National Soldiers' Home, Leavenworth, Kansas from 1888 until 1904; and Los Angeles, California since 1907.[795]

William H. Linsley died on 24 February 1913, probably at Los Angeles, unmarried. He was born at Branford on 22 December 1843, son of Joseph Nelson Linsley and Harriet M. Whiting. The pension mentions his sister Mrs. Mary L. Newell of Branford.

LOGAN, MICHAEL
Co. G 12th CVI, private, enlisted 12 March 1864, to Co. D 12th Battalion 26 November 1864, mustered out 12 August 1865, pension #957381 for the soldier

Michael Logan of Branford enlisted and was mustered in on 12 March 1864 as a private in Co. G 12th CVI and was transferred to Co. D 12th Battalion on 26 November 1864. He was mustered out at Savannah, Georgia on 12 August 1865 and discharged at Hartford on 22 August 1865.

792 The Hale Collection, New Britain.
793 *Connecticut Linsleys*, 100.
794 Towner letter, 22 October 1864.
795 On another pension application in the file he gives his residence as Branford 1865-1875; Leavenworth, Kansas 1875-1888; San Antonio, Texas 1888-1902; Los Angeles since 1912.

He applied for a partial invalid pension on 13 April 1889. During the summer of 1864 while at Camp Carrollton, Louisiana he contracted chronic diarrhea and rheumatism from exposure and hardships. He was treated at the Universal Hospital, New Orleans about three months and rejoined his regiment at Winchester, Virginia in September 1864. Since his discharge he lived in Rhode Island and Connecticut, occupation farmer. After the war he reenlisted as a private in Co. E 3rd Regiment Connecticut National Guard and was discharged in 1871 as a sergeant. From 1889 until 1900 he was living at Hampton, Windham County. In 1902 he was described as five feet five inches tall, light complexion, blue eyes, brown hair, born at Pittsburg, Massachusetts. There is no mention in his file of a wife or children.

Michael Logan was admitted to Fitch's Home for Soldiers on 3 March 1906 and died there on 13 April 1906 age 57. He was buried in Spring Grove Cemetery, Darien.

LULL, OSCAR S.
Co. E 12th CVI, enlisted 20 December 1861, discharged disability 12 September 1862, Co. B 11th VRC, enlisted 28 July 1863, discharged 25 July 1865, no pension

Oscar S. Lull of Branford enlisted on 20 December 1861 and was mustered in on 28 December 1861 as a private in Co. E 12th CVI for a term of three years. He was discharged for disability on 12 September 1862. He reenlisted, now of Ledyard, on 28 July 1863 as a private in Co. B 11th V.R.C. and was discharged on 25 July 1865. He does not appear in the 1860 census at Branford or North Branford.

LYNCH, DANIEL H.
Co. A 15th, private, substitute, mustered in 19 August 1864, to Co. A 7th CVI, prisoner, promoted, mustered out 20 July 1865, no pension

Daniel Lynch, age 23, served as a substitute for Reuben N. Augur of Northford. He was mustered in at New Haven on 19 August 1864 as a private in Co. A 15th CVI for a term of three years. He was described as five feet ten inches tall, light complexion, brown eyes, light hair, unmarried, born in England, occupation seaman. His nearest relative was Mrs. Lynch of London, England. He joined the regiment at New Bern, North Carolina on 25 August 1864. He was captured with much of his regiment at the Battle of Kinston, North Carolina on 8 March 1865, confined at Libby Prison, Richmond on 23 March, and paroled at Boulware's & Cox's wharf on 26 March 1865. He reported to Camp Parole, Maryland on 30 March 1865, received a thirty day furlough and afterwards reported to Camp Convalescent, Virginia. He was transferred to Co. A 7th CVI at Goldsboro, North Carolina on 23 June 1865 and promoted to corporal on 1 July 1865. Daniel Lynch was mustered out at Goldsboro, North Carolina on 20 July 1865.

He does not appear in the 1860 or 1870 census at Branford or North Branford.

LYNHAN, JAMES
Co. I 11th CVI, private, enlisted 12 March 1864, wounded, deserted 19 July 1864, no pension

James Lynhan of Branford enlisted and was mustered in on 12 March 1864 as a private in Co. I 11th CVI. He was wounded at Petersburg, Virginia on 16 June 1864 and deserted on 19 July 1864. He does not appear in the 1860 census at Branford.

MAHER, JOHN
Co. G 15th CVI, private, enlisted 30 December 1863, to Co. G 7th CVI, mustered out 20 July 1865, no pension

John Maher, age 38, of Branford enlisted on 30 December 1863 as a private in Co. G 15th CVI for a term of three years. He was in action at Kinston, North Carolina on 8 March 1865 but was not taken prisoner. He was transferred to Co. G 7th CVI on 23 June 1865 and mustered out at Goldsboro, North Carolina on 20 July 1865. At the time of his enlistment he was described as five feet two inches tall, fair complexion, blue eyes, brown hair, occupation blacksmith, born in Ireland. He appears in the 1860 census at North Branford with a wife and children.

MALTBY, CHARLES D.
Co. K 15th CVI, private, enlisted 6 August 1862, discharged disability 1 March 1863, pension #300456 for his widow Mary

Charles D. Maltby, age 40, of North Branford enlisted at New Haven on 6 August 1862 and was mustered in on 25 August 1862 as a private in Co. K 15th CVI for a term of three years. At the time of his enlistment he was described as six feet one inch tall, dark complexion, brown eyes, black hair, occupation mechanic. "It was at long bridge that comrade Maltby was first taken with chills and fevers about the middle of Sept 1862. The attack of chills were frequent and severe so much so that in two months he was reduced to a mere skeleton."[796] "In the latter part of Nov 1862 when [the] Reg't had Marching Orders he was unfit for duty & was left in Camp to be taken to the Hospital and never returned to the Regt."[797] He was discharged for disability from the hospital at Fairfax Seminary, Virginia on 1 March 1863.[798]

Charles DeWitt Maltby died at Northford on 1 March 1881 age 59 and was buried in Northford Cemetery. His name appears on the Northford Veterans' Monument. He was born at North Branford on 17 April 1822 son of Samuel Maltby and Charlotte DeWitt. He was not a pensioner.

Mary A. Maltby of Northford applied for a widow's pension on 5 August 1890 under the act of 27 June 1890. She was married to the soldier under the name of Mary Augusta Linsley at Northford by Rev. John Maltby on 18 September 1845. Neither were previously married or divorced. She died at Northford on 19 March 1895 and was buried in Northford Cemetery.[799] She was born on 5 September 1824, daughter of Eliakim Linsley and Jennette Hall. She was the first cousin of Jared Linsley, Jr.

MARTIN, JAMES
Co. E 15th CVI, private, substitute, mustered in 7 August 1864, prisoner, to Co. E 7th CVI. no pension

James Martin, age 25, of North Branford served as a substitute for Merrick M. Russell of North Branford. He was mustered in at New Haven on 7 August 1864 and assigned on 25 August 1864 as a private in Co. E 15th CVI for a term of three years. He was described as five feet two inches tall, black eyes, black hair, light complexion, unmarried, occupation shoemaker, born in Ireland. He joined the regiment at New Bern, North Carolina. He was captured with much of his regiment at the Battle of Kinston, North Carolina on 8

---

796   Affidavit, Lorenzo E. Harrison of Northford, 8 December 1891, in the pension file of Charles D. Maltby.
797   Affidavit, George W. Talmadge of Northford, 5 December 1891, in the pension file of Charles D. Maltby.
798   His CMSR states he was discharged from Fort Schuyler Hospital, New York.
799   North Branford Vital Records, deaths, 1895.

March 1865, confined at Libby Prison, Richmond on 23 March, and paroled at Boulware's & Cox's wharf on 26 March 1865. He reported to Camp Parole, Maryland on 30 March 1865, received a thirty day furlough and afterwards reported to Camp Convalescent, Virginia. He was transferred to Co. E 7th CVI on 24 June 1865 and joined that regiment at Goldsboro, North Carolina on 28 June 1865. James Martin was mustered out at Goldsboro, North Carolina on 20 July 1865. He does not appear in the 1860 or 1870 census at Branford or North Branford.

MARTIN, JOHN
Co. M 1st Cavalry, private, enlisted 25 November 1864, mustered out 2 August 1865, no pension

John Martin of Branford enlisted and was mustered in on 25 November 1864 as a private in Co. M 1st Connecticut Cavalry. He was mustered out with the rest of his regiment at Washington, D.C. on 2 August 1865 and discharged at New Haven on 18 August 1865. He does not appear in the 1860 or 1870 census at Branford or North Branford.

MASON, CHARLES
Co. H 29th CVI, private, enlisted 31 December 1863, mustered out 24 October 1865, no pension

Charles M. Mason, age 21, of Branford enlisted at New Haven on 31 December 1863 and was mustered in on 8 March 1864 as a private in Co. H 29th CVI for a term of three years. His service was credited to Branford and he appears on the 1863 draft list for that town. At the time of his enlistment he was described as five feet six inches tall, black complexion, eyes, and hair; born at Hartford, occupation sailor. A copy of his enlistment paper is in the file and signed with his mark. He was on duty with the regiment in 1864. Beginning 8 December 1864 he was detailed to the 2nd Brigade, 3rd division, 25th Ambulance Corps in the field in Virginia. He continued to serve in the ambulance corps while the regiment was in Texas. Mason was mustered out with the rest of his regiment at Brownsville, Texas on 24 October 1865. His name appears on the Wall of Honor at Washington, D.C.

McDERMOTT, JAMES
Co. G 15th CVI, private, enlisted 4 August 1862, discharged disability 11 May 1864, pension #263057 for the soldier and later for his widow Jane

James McDermott, age 44, of Guilford enlisted at New Haven on 4 August 1862 and was mustered in on 25 August 1862 as a private in Co. G 15th CVI for a term of three years. He was wounded, no date given and was discharged for disability from New Haven Hospital on 11 May 1864.

He applied for an invalid pension on 5 April 1879. At the time of his enlistment he was described as five feet nine inches tall, florid complexion, blue eyes, brown hair, born in Ireland. While on the march to Fredericksburg about 4 December 1862 he sprained his left foot. "He continued on duty until after the battle of Fredericksburg when he was relieved from active duty. When the Reg't went to Newport News about Feb. 1st [1863], he was sent to Hampton General Hospital to be treated.[800] He was then sent to the hospital at New Haven where he stayed about six months. "His foot and ankle were always bad since he came home…He was not a drinking man. He was one of the best of men…In 1877 he was sent to Fitch's Soldier Home at Noroton Heights and they sent him to Bridgeport Hospital where he died."[801] He stated in his application he lived at Guilford from 1849 until he enlisted and returned to Guilford after his discharge.

James McDermott died at Bridgeport Hospital on 14 November 1887 and was buried in St. Mary's Cemetery, Branford.

Jane McDermott, age 67, of Guilford applied for a widow's pension on 14 September 1888. She was married to the soldier at Jersey City, New Jersey by Father Kelley in November 1846 (her maiden name is not given). Neither were previously married or divorced and she could not find a public record of their marriage. After their marriage they lived in Boston for two years; to Poughkeepsie, New York a couple of years; to Stony Creek until he went to war; and since the war at Guilford. They had seven children, all living in 1889 and over the age of sixteen. There is no record of her burial in Branford.

McGINLEY, JAMES
Co. K 11th CVI, private, drafted 25 November 1864, deserted 15 December 1864, no pension

James McGinley of Branford served as a substitute or was drafted on 25 November 1864 as a private in Co. K 11th CVI and deserted on 15 December 1864. He does not appear in the 1860 census at Branford.

McGINNIS, JOHN
Co. B 20th CVI, private, substitute, mustered in 30 November 1864, failed to report, no pension

John McGinnis, age 23, served as a substitute for Jarvis Averill of Branford. He was mustered in at New Haven on 30 November 1864 as a private in Co. B 20th CVI for a term of three years. He was described as five feet six inches tall, blue eyes, brown hair, dark complexion, born in Ireland, occupation laborer.[802] He was transferred from New Haven to the company on 7 January 1865 but failed to report. He does not appear in the 1860 census at Branford.

McGOWAN, JAMES
Co. B 27th CVI, private, enlisted 1 September 1862, prisoner, mustered out 27 July 1863, reenlisted U.S. Navy; reenlisted Co. D 15th CVI, transferred to Co. D 7th CVI, pension #529115 for the soldier and later for his widow

James McGowan, age 18, of Wallingford enlisted on 1 September 1862 and was mustered in on 3 October 1862 as a private in Co. B 27th CVI for a term of nine months. He fought at the Battle of Fredericksburg on 13 December 1862 with the rest of the company. He was captured at the Battle of Chancellorsville, Virginia on 3 May 1863, held prisoner at Richmond, and was paroled at City Point, Virginia on 14 May 1863. He reported to Camp Parole, Maryland on 16 May 1863, was sent to Washington, D.C. on 20 May 1863 and spent the remainder of his service at Camp Convalescent, Virginia. With the rest of the Chancellorsville paroled

800   Affidavit, William Ronald of New Haven, no date, in the pension file of James McDermott.
801   Affidavit, Jane McDermott of Guilford, 8 November 1889, in the pension file of James McDermott.
802   Muster & Descriptive Rolls of Substitutes, RG 13, box 97, 2nd Congressional District, Connecticut State Library.

prisoners, he rejoined the Regiment at Baltimore on 20 July 1863. McGowan was mustered out with the rest of his regiment on 27 July 1863 at New Haven.

After his discharge he enlisted in the U.S. Navy.[803] He reenlisted again, now living at Salisbury, on 24 January 1865 as a private in Co. D 15th CVI. With the 15th he fought at the Battle of Wise's Forks on 8-10 March 1865 and the regiment occupied Kinston, North Carolina on 14 March 1865. He was transferred to Co. D 7th CVI on 23 June 1865 and was mustered out at Goldsboro, North Carolina on 20 July 1865.

He applied for an invalid pension on 13 January 1891 under the act of 27 June 1890. His widow applied for a pension after his death.

McGUIRE, THOMAS
Co. A & E 9th CVI, musician, reenlisted, mustered out 3 August 1865, no pension

Thomas McGuire of Branford enlisted and was mustered in on 24 April 1862 as a private in Co. E 9th CVI for a term of three years. He was transferred to Co. A 9th CVI on 28 February 1863 and detailed as a musician on 27 April 1863. He reenlisted on 6 January 1864 in Co. A 5th Battalion and returned to the ranks on 12 October 1864. McGuire was mustered out at Savannah, Georgia on 3 August 1865 and discharged at New Haven on 8 August 1865. He does not appear in the 1860 census at Branford or North Branford.

McKEON, FRANCIS or FRANK
Co. E 9th CVI, lieutenant, enlisted 5 September 1861, wounded, discharged 26 October 1864, pension #264969 for the soldier and later for his widow Mary

Francis McKeon of New Haven enlisted on 5 September 1861 and was mustered in on 30 October 1861 as 2nd lieutenant of Co. E 9th CVI for a term of three years. He was promoted to 1st lieutenant on 25 February 1863. He was wounded at Grand Gulf, Mississippi and discharged at New Haven on 26 October 1864. Before the war he served in a New Haven military company known as the Emmett Guards.

He applied for an invalid pension on 19 November 1883. He was described as five feet six inches tall, light complexion, brown hair, blue eyes. About 23 June 1862 he injured his left leg at Grand Gulf, Mississippi resulting in blood poisoning. Later in the Shenandoah Campaign in September 1864 he contracted rheumatism. It is unclear whether he received a pension.

Francis McKeon died at Branford on 30 August 1888 and was buried there in St. Agnes Cemetery. A G.A.R. emblem is engraved on his stone. He was born at County Cavan, Ireland on 28 December 1834,[804] son of Frank McKeon and Katherine Gaffey.

Francis McKeon was a 1st lieutenant in the 9th CVI and came to Branford in 1877. Pictured from left to right are Capt. Terence Sheridan, Lt. Francis McKeon, and Lt. Michael Mullins. (Murray, History of Ninth Regiment, 65)

803 There are a number of James McGowans in the Navy and his pension could not be determined; his pension as listed on the T289 could not be found by the National Archives staff.
804 Murray, *History of Ninth Regiment*, 344.

Mary McKeon applied for a widow's pension on 3 November 1888. The application was sent for special examination to determine if the soldier's cause of death was related to his military service. There are many affidavits in the file. She was married to the soldier under the name of Mary Reilly at St. Patrick's Church, New Haven by Rev. Matthew Hart on 28 April 1864. Neither were previously married or divorced. They lived at New Haven and moved to Branford in 1877. They had six children: Catherine E., born on 7 October 1865; Mary, born on 23 February 1867; Francis P., born on 1 July 1869; Philip, born on 16 February 1862; and Anna, born on 10 December 1875.

Mary Reilly McKeon died at Branford on 15 March 1911 and was buried there in St. Agnes Cemetery. She was born at Caren, Ireland on 15 August 1839, daughter of Michael and Katherine Reilly.[805]

MERRING, LEVI
Co. G 1st HA, enlisted 16 December 1863, deserted, no pension

Levi Merring of North Branford enlisted on 16 December 1863 as a private in Co. G 1st HA and deserted on 27 December 1863. He does not appear in the 1860 census at Branford or North Branford.

MIX, STEPHEN
Co. K 15th CVI, private, enlisted 6 August 1862, mustered out 27 June 1865, pension #339588 for his widow Sarah

Stephen Mix, age 40, of Durham enlisted at New Haven on 6 August 1862 and was mustered in on 25 August 1862 as a private in Co. K 15th CVI for a term of three years. He saw action at Fredericksburg, Virginia on 13 December 1862, during the Siege of Suffolk, Virginia in the spring of 1863, and in the Peninsula Campaign of July 1863. He was on picket duty during the Battle of Kinston, North Carolina. Mix was mustered out with the rest of his regiment at New Bern, North Carolina on 27 June 1865 and discharged at New Haven on 12 July 1865. His "Soldierly conduct was good." He served under Capt. Medad D. Munson of Wallingford.

At the time of his enlistment he was described as five feet five inches tall, fair complexion, blue eyes, black hair, occupation mechanic, born at Wallingford. He appears at Durham in 1860, Wallingford in 1870, and North Branford in the 1880 census. He did not apply for a pension. Stephen Mix died at North Branford on 22 March 1887 and was buried in Northford Cemetery.[806]

---

805   Branford Vital Records, deaths, 1911.
806   The Hale Collection, North Branford, 64.

Sarah Mix, age 50, of Northford applied for a widow's pension on 24 July 1890 under the act of 27 June 1890. She was married to the soldier under the name of Sarah M. Brainard at Wallingford by Rev. A. E. Denison on 4 November 1850, both of Wallingford.[807] They had no children. Sarah Brainard Mix died on 6 August 1911 age 92 and was buried in Northford Cemetery.[808]

MOONEY, MICHAEL
Co. G 20th CVI, private, enlisted 14 August 1862, discharged disability 14 April 1863, pension #222451 for the soldier

Michael Mooney of Branford enlisted at New Haven on 14 August 1862 and was mustered in on 8 September 1862 as a private in Co. G 20th CVI for a term of three years. He was discharged for disability at Stafford Court House, Virginia on 14 April 1863.

He applied for an invalid pension on 17 February 1879 for chronic rheumatism and defective eye sight contracted during his service. At the time of his enlistment he was described as five feet six inches tall, light complexion, brown hair, blue eyes. On 5 November 1862 near Keyes Ford, Virginia while on the march to the Loudon Valley along the Shenandoah River in the rain and mud, he contracted rheumatism of both legs, erysipelas of the face, and was sick in quarters for two weeks with resulting partial blindness. He was discharged by order of the Regimental Surgeon Dr. Carey. There is no information in the file about his family or a death date. He appears on the 1863 draft list for Branford, age 43, born in England, occupation farmer, married. In June 1880 he was living at Fair Haven, age 60.

MORAN, JOHN
Co. B 1st Cavalry, private, enlisted 16 November 1861, reenlisted, prisoner, mustered out 2 August 1865, no pension

John Moran of Branford enlisted and was mustered in on 16 November 1861 as a private in Co. B 1st Connecticut Cavalry for a term of three years and reenlisted as a veteran in Co. B on 1 January 1864. With his regiment he participated in many engagements in Virginia including the Battles of Cedar Mountain, the Second Bull Run, The Wilderness, Spotsylvania, and Winchester. He was captured at Cedar Run Church, Virginia on 17 October 1864. Moran was mustered out at Washington, D.C. on 2 August 1865 and discharged with the rest of his regiment at New Haven on 18 August 1865.

He appears in the 1860 census at Branford, age 28, born in Ireland, a farm laborer living in the household of Samuel Griffin.[809] After his discharge he lived at Branford. He did not apply for a pension.

John Moran died at Branford on 12 September 1910 and was buried there in St. Agnes Cemetery. He was born at County Leitrim, Ireland, son of Bernard and Catherine Moran.[810] He was married at Branford by Rev. Campbell on 15 April 1866 to Bridget McWeeney or McQueeny.[811] She died on 28 October 1927 and was buried in St. Agnes Cemetery, Branford.[812] She did not apply for a widow's pension.

807   The Barbour Collection, Wallingford, V-1:270.
808   The Hale Collection, North Branford, 64.
809   U.S. census 1860, Branford, New Haven County, Connecticut, population schedule, M653-85, dwelling 991, family 1103, page 914, www.heritagequest.com.
810   Branford Vital Records, deaths, 1910.
811   Branford Vital Records, 1863-1895, 134.
812   The Hale Collection, Branford, 121; the stone was not found. Her death is not in the Branford Vital Records.

MORRIS, WILLIAM H.
Co. I 29th CVI, private, enlisted 2 January 1864, mustered out 24 October 1865, no pension

William H. Morris of Branford enlisted at New Haven on 2 January 1864 as a private in Co. I 29th CVI. His service was credited to Branford. He was sent to Knight Hospital from conscript camp on 13 February 1864 and returned to duty on 11 March 1864. Morris was mustered out with the rest of the regiment at Brownsville, Texas on 24 October 1865. His name appears on the Wall of Honor at Washington, D.C.

MORSE, JAMES or MOORE
Co. E 15th CVI and Co. E 7th CVI, private, substitute, mustered in 18 August 1864, prisoner, mustered out 20 July 1865, no pension

James Morse, age 29, of North Branford served as a substitute for John C. Harrison. He was mustered in at New Haven on 18 August 1864 and assigned as a private in Co. E 15th CVI for a term of three years. He was described as five feet seven inches tall, light complexion, grey eyes, light hair, unmarried, occupation seaman, born in England. He joined the regiment at New Bern, North Carolina on 25 August 1864. He was captured with much of his regiment at the Battle of Kinston, North Carolina on 8 March 1865, confined at Libby Prison, Richmond on 23 March, and paroled at Boulware's & Cox's wharf on 26 March 1865. He reported to Camp Parole, Maryland on 30 March 1865, received a thirty day furlough and afterwards reported to Camp Convalescent, Virginia. He was transferred to Co. E 7th CVI on 23 June 1865 and mustered out at Goldsboro, North Carolina on 20 July 1865. He does not appear in the 1860 census at North Branford.

MORTON, HENRY or JOHN HENRY
Co. A 13th CVI, private, enlisted 1 January 1862, reenlisted 27 August 1864, wounded, no pension

John Henry Morton of New Britain enlisted on 1 January 1862 and was mustered in on 6 January 1862 as a private in Co. A 13th CVI. With his regiment he served in the New Orleans area including the Battle of Irish Bend on 14 April 1863 and the Siege of Port Hudson. He reenlisted as a veteran in Co. A on 8 February 1864.[813] During the Virginia campaign he fought at the battles of Winchester, Fort Fisher, and Cedar Creek. "He enlisted in the 13th Connecticut Volunteers and served throughout the war. He was wounded twice, once in the leg, and once in the back."[814] He was living at Branford at the time of his enlistment. He never applied for a pension.

Henry Morton died at Branford on 16 May 1901 and was buried there in Center Cemetery.[815] He was born at Belturbet, Cavan Co., Ireland on 27 November 1843, son of John Morton.[816] He was married at New York City on 19 April 1866 to Margaret Clifford.

---

813   The *Record of Service of Connecticut Men* states he deserted on 27 August 1864. The history of the 13th does not list him among those that deserted.
814   Obituary, *The Branford Opinion*, 18 May 1901, 3.
815   Branford Vital Records, deaths, 1901.
816   Branford Vital Records, deaths, 1901.

Margaret Clifford Morton died at Branford on 3 February 1929 and was buried there in Center Cemetery. She was born at Beltrame, Sligo, Ireland on 11 September 1839, daughter of William Clifford and Sarah Ferguson.[817] She never applied for a widow's pension.

MUNSON, MEDAD D.
Co. K 15th CVI, captain, mustered in 25 August 1862, mustered out 27 June 1865, pension #C2523516 for the soldier

Medad D. Munson[818] of Wallingford enlisted at New Haven on 6 August 1862 and was commissioned on 25 August 1862 as 1st lieutenant of Co. K 15th CVI for a term of three years. He was the first man from Wallingford to enlist in the 15th. He was promoted to captain of Co. K on 16 November 1863 and served throughout the war. With the regiment he served at Fredericksburg and Portsmouth, Virginia. He was in command of Co. K which had provost duty in New Bern, North Carolina when the regiment fought at the Battle of Kinston on 8 March 1865. Medad Munson was mustered out with the rest of his regiment at New Bern, North Carolina on 27 June 1865 and discharged at New Haven on 12 July 1865. A number of North Branford men served under him. His brother Oliver S. Munson, a sergeant in Co. K, died of disease on 26 November 1862. He was the brother-in-law of George W. Elton.

Medad D. Munson of Wallingford was captain of Co. K 15th CVI and returned to Wallingford after the war. (Marvin, Fifteenth Regiment Vols, 104)

He was married at North Branford by Rev. Whitmore Peck of the Congregational Church on 3 October 1853 to Laura S. Gordon of North Branford.[819] She was age 28, born at Plymouth, Connecticut, living at North Branford, daughter of Washington Gordon and Tryphena Augur. After the war he returned to Wallingford.

Medad Douglass Munson died at Wallingford July 1907. He was born at Wallingford on 22 August 1830, son of Medad Ward Munson and Henrietta Dutton.[820]

MUNSON, WILLIAM W.
Co. E 27th CVI, corporal, enlisted 19 August 1862, prisoner, reenlisted, wounded, discharged disability 8 August 1865, pension #914571 for the soldier and later for his widow Nellie

William W. Munson, age 18, of North Branford enlisted at New Haven on 19 August 1862 and was mustered in on 3 October 1862 as a private in Co. E 27th CVI for a term of nine months. He was captured at the Battle of Chancellorsville, Virginia on 3 May 1863, held prisoner at Richmond, and was paroled at City Point, Virginia on 14 May 1863. He reported to Camp Parole, Maryland on 16 May 1863, was sent to Washington, D.C. on 20 May 1863 and spent the remainder of his service at Camp Convalescent, Virginia. With

---

817 Branford Vital Records, deaths, 1929.
818 For his biography see Thorpe, *History of the Fifteenth*, 350.
819 North Branford Vital Records, I:113B.
820 Myron A. Munson, *The Munson Record, Captain Thomas Munson and His Descendants* (New Haven: The Munson Association, 1895), I:435 and IV:1855.

the rest of the Chancellorsville paroled prisoners, he rejoined the Regiment at Baltimore on 20 July 1863. William Munson was mustered out with the rest of his regiment at New Haven on 27 July 1863.

He reenlisted on 11 February 1864, now living at New Haven, as a private in Co. M 2nd HA. He was promoted to corporal on 11 March 1864 and was shot through the right leg below the knee at Fisher's Hill, Virginia on 22 September 1864. He was first taken to the Field Hospital at the Taylor House, Winchester, Virginia; then to Baltimore; to Philadelphia, and finally to Knight Hospital, New Haven. He was transferred to Co. C 2nd HA on 20 July 1865 and discharged for disability as a result of his wound on 8 August 1865.

He applied for a disability pension on 15 September 1865. At the time of his enlistment he was described as five feet four inches tall, light complexion, blue eyes, born hair, occupation joiner. His leg remained severely damaged from the gunshot wound which fractured the tibia. In 1860 he was living in the household of George Baldwin of North Branford but since his discharge lived at Waterbury.

William Wilson Munson died at Waterbury on 13 February 1921 and was buried there in Riverside Cemetery. He was born at Philadelphia, Pennsylvania on 24 April 1846, son of Charles Munson and Elizabeth Falloneh.

Nellie L. Munson of Waterbury applied for a widow's pension on 18 March 1921. She was married to the soldier under the name of Nellie Louisa Seymour at Waterbury by Rev. William H. Wardell of the First Methodist Episcopal Church on 12 September 1869. Neither were previously married or divorced. They had one child (living in 1898): Lilla Wardell Munson, born on 5 December 1871, married name Crane. After one year Nellie still had not received her pension. The pension board claimed both she and the soldier said they were married before which she denied.

Nellie L. Munson died on 23 March 1923 and was buried in Riverside Cemetery, Waterbury.[821] She was born at Waterbury on 15 April 1849, daughter of Robert S. Seymour and Abigail Bronson.

MURPHY, JOHN
Co. A 11th CVI, private, enlisted 8 February 1864, to the Navy, deserted 11 September 1864, no pension

John Murphy of Branford enlisted and was mustered in on 8 February 1864 as a private in Co. A 11th CVI. He was transferred to the U.S. Navy, served on the U.S.S. *Roanoke* and deserted on 11 September 1864. He does not appear in the 1860 census at Branford.

MYER, WILLIAM
Co. L 2nd HA, private, enlisted 8 February 1864, deserted 24 February 1864, no pension

William Myer of Branford enlisted on 8 February 1864 as a private in Co. L 2nd HA and deserted on 24 February 1864. He does not appear in the 1860 census at Branford.

---

821   The Hale Collection, Waterbury, 371.

MYERS, GEORGE W.

Co. C 5th CVI, private, drafted 28 July 1863, deserted 1 July 1864, no pension

George W. Myers of Branford served as a substitute or was drafted on 28 July 1863 as a private in Co. C 5th CVI and deserted on 1 June 1864. He does not appear in the 1860 census at Branford.

NEALE, DANIEL or NEALL

Co. E 37th Massachusetts Volunteers, corporal, enlisted 14 August 1862, discharged 21 June 1865, pension #XC2686602 for the soldier and later for his widow Matilda

Daniel Neale enlisted at Pittsfield, Massachusetts on 14 August 1862 as a private in Co. E 37th Massachusetts Volunteer Infantry for a term of three years and was promoted to corporal. The regiment fought at the Battles of Fredericksburg, Chancellorsville, and Gettysburg. In 1864 and 1865 they served during the Virginia campaign fighting in the Battles of The Wilderness, Cold Harbor, and Petersburg. He was discharged at Washington, D.C. on 21 June 1865.[822]

He applied for an invalid pension on 29 May 1874 for a gunshot wound to the left forearm. He became a member of the Mason Rogers Post No. 7 G.A.R. of Branford, transferred in from another post on 25 January 1883, age 45, born in England. He is probably the Daniel Neale living at Manchester in 1880 with his wife Lydia and children. He was married second about 1888 to Matilda. He appears at Springfield, Massachusetts in 1890.

Daniel Neale died at Springfield, Massachusetts on 10 March 1913 and is buried in Buckland Cemetery, Manchester, Connecticut. He was born at Bradford, England on 15 March 1835.[823]

Matilda L. Neale applied for a widow's pension on 9 April 1913. She was married to the soldier as his second wife under the name of Matilda L. Weissenborn. She was living at Springfield in 1920 and Wilbraham, Hampden Co., Massachusetts in 1930 and 1940. His pension is at the Veterans Administration.

NELSON, WILLIAM

Co. M 1st Cavalry, enlisted 24 December 1863, deserted 21 January 1864, no pension

William Nelson of North Branford enlisted and was mustered in on 24 December 1863 as a private in Co. M 1st Connecticut Cavalry and deserted on 21 January 1864. He does not appear in the 1860 census at North Branford.

NETTLETON, JOSEPH F.

Co. D 2nd CVI, private, enlisted 23 April 1861, mustered out 7 August 1861, pension #788238 for the soldier and later for his widow Amaritta

Joseph F. Nettleton of Derby enlisted at New Haven on 23 April 1861 and was mustered in on 7 May 1861 as a private in Co. D 2nd CVI for a term of three months. He was discharged for disability at Camp Mansfield, Virginia on 4 July 1861 and mustered out with the rest of the regiment on 7 August 1861 when his term expired. He was drafted on 18 July 1863 but refused admission into the Army on the grounds of permanent disability from sunstroke.

---

822 A copy of his discharge paper is in the Branford Historical Society archives.
823 Thompson family tree , www.ancestry.com

Joseph F. Nettleton (History of Widow's Son Lodge No. 66 of Branford, 1976, 50)

He applied for an invalid pension on 24 September 1888 under the acts of 14 July 1862 and 3 March 1873. While marching through Washington, D.C. to the Capital grounds from a boat on 12 May 1861 he suffered from sunstroke, fainted on the street, and was carried to a temporary hospital in the Patent office building where he stayed two weeks. He returned to duty, was again taken sick and discharged for "general debility and pulmonary hemorrhage." At the time of his discharge he was described as age 22, born at Newtown, five feet seven inches tall, light complexion, blue eyes, dark brown hair, occupation mechanic. After the war he lived at Branford and was a charter member of the Mason Rogers Post No. 7 G.A.R. He moved to Redlands, San Bernadino Co., California in 1891 for his health.

He was married at New Haven by Rev. John T. Huntington on 29 April 1861 to Amaritta Barker of Branford. A daughter Miss Lucy B. Nettleton was living at Redlands, California in 1923 and appears to be his only child.

Joseph Foster Nettleton died at Redlands, California on 1 September 1903 and was buried there in Hillside Memorial Park. He was born at Newtown on 25 June 1840, son of Joseph Nettleton and Phoebe Curtis.

Amaritta Nettlton applied for a widow's pension on 9 May 1905. She had difficulty getting a pension based on the 27 June 1890 pension act which stated the soldier had to serve ninety days and the board claimed he did not die from the disability attributed to his service. She finally received a pension under a special act of Congress on 2 March 1915.

Amaritta Barker Nettleton died at Redlands, California on 19 June 1923. She was born at Columbus, Ohio on 12 April 1842, daughter of Eliphalet Barker and Martha McCoy of Branford.

NICHOLS, HENRY Z.
Co. B 27th CVI, musician, enlisted 10 September 1862, mustered out 27 July 1863, pension #652501 for the soldier and later for his widow Eliza

Henry Z. Nichols, age 35, of Branford enlisted on 10 September 1862 and was mustered in on 3 October 1862 as a musician in Co. B 27th CVI for a term of nine months. He fought at the Battle of Fredericksburg on 13 December 1862 with the rest of the company. "I left the Regiment in Dec. 1862 soon after the battle of Fredericksburg. I was sent to the Hospital in Washington, D.C. and did not rejoin the Regiment until it was mustered out in New Haven."[824] Nichols was mustered out with the rest of his regiment at New Haven on 27 July 1863.

He applied for an invalid pension on 18 January 1892 under the act of 27 June 1890 which was rejected for lack of disability though he had numerous age related illnesses. He was a charter member and third commander of the Mason Rogers Post No. 7 G.A.R. of Branford. A snare drum was presented to Nichols by the Widow's Son Masonic Lodge No. 66 of Branford when he enlisted. The drum was given to the Lodge after Nichols' death and is still on display.

---

824   Deposition, Henry Z. Nichols, March 1885, in the pension file of Nathan A. Harrison.

Henry Z. Nichols died at Branford on 14 May 1894 age 66 and was buried there in Center Cemetery. A G.A.R. marker was on his gravesite in 1934 and 2011. He was born at Branford on 18 August 1827, son of Darius Nichols and Silvia Fox.[825]

Eliza A. Nichols of Branford applied for a widow's pension on 15 November 1894. She was married to the soldier under the name of Eliza Ann Pond at Branford by Rev. William Henry Rees of Trinity Episcopal Church on 13 June 1850. Neither were previously married or divorced. Their son Charles H. Nichols was living at New York City in 1925. Charlotte M. Crowe, age 76 and Sarah M. Burritt, age 74, sisters of Henry Z. Nichols were living at New Haven in 1908.

Eliza A. Nichols was living at New Haven from 1908 to 1925. She died on 25 September 1925 and was buried in Center Cemetery, Branford. She was born at Branford on 15 September 1832, daughter of Harvey Pond and Betsey Linsley.

Henry Z. Nichols enlisted in Co. B 27th CVI at the age of thirty-five. (History of Widow's Son Lodge No. 66 of Branford, 1976, 50)

O'BRIEN, EDWARD

Co. B 27th CVI, private, enlisted 10 September 1862, prisoner, mustered out 27 July 1863, pension #359530 for his widow Margaret

Edward O'Brien, age 26, of Wallingford enlisted on 10 September 1862 and was mustered in on 3 October 1862 as a private in Co. B 27th CVI for a term of nine months. He fought at the Battle of Fredericksburg on 13 December 1862 with the rest of the company. He was captured at the Battle of Chancellorsville, Virginia on 3 May 1863, held prisoner at Richmond, and was paroled at City Point, Virginia on 14 May 1863. He reported to Camp Parole, Maryland on 16 May 1863, was sent to Washington, D.C. on 20 May 1863 and spent the remainder of his service at Camp Convalescent, Virginia. With the rest of the Chancellorsville paroled prisoners, he rejoined the Regiment at Baltimore on 20 July 1863. Edward O'Brien was mustered out with the rest of his regiment at New Haven on 27 July 1863.

"Edward O'Brien was my comrade and I knew him before the war, he was in perfect health. Sometime after his return from the war he became more delicate and seemed to fade away to the time of his death."[826]

The Masons of Branford presented this drum to Nichols which he carried at the Battle of Fredericksburg.

---

825 Branford Vital Records, Town Meeting Book A, 233.
826 Affidavit, James Kennedy of Wallingford, 11 December 1890, in the pension file of Edward O'Brien.

Gravestone of Henry Z. Nichols at Center Cemetery

Edward O'Brien died on 19 February 1882 and was buried in Holy Trinity Cemetery, Wallingford. He never applied for a pension.

Margaret O'Brien, age 49, of Wallingford applied for a widow's pension 17 November 1890 under the act of 27 June 1890. She was in poor health and receiving assistance from the town. She received an additional $2.00 per month for her daughter Margaret, born on 31 August 1877, who would reach the age of 16 in 1893. She was married to the soldier under the name of Margaret McCarty at Wallingford by Father Sheriden of the Holy Trinity Church on 8 January 1860. Both were born in Ireland and neither were previously married or divorced. Their children were: Dennis, born on 21 March 1866; Ellen, born on 19 May 1869; Catherine, born on 17 October 1873; Mary, born on 5 July 1870, died on 29 October 1890; and Margaret, born on 31 August 1877.[827]

Margaret O'Brien died on 19 March 1900.

O'BRIEN, JOHN
Co. B 27th CVI, private, enlisted 8 September 1862, prisoner, mustered out 27 July 1863, no pension

John O'Brien, age 21, of Branford enlisted on 8 September 1862 and was mustered in on 3 October 1862 as a private in Co. B 27th CVI for a term of nine months. He fought at the Battle of Fredericksburg on 13 December 1862 with the rest of the company. He was captured at the Battle of Chancellorsville, Virginia on 3 May 1863, held prisoner at Richmond, and was paroled at City Point, Virginia on 14 May 1863. He reported to Camp Parole, Maryland on 16 May 1863, was sent to Washington, D.C. on 20 May 1863 and spent the remainder of his service at Camp Convalescent, Virginia. With the rest of the Chancellorsville paroled prisoners, he rejoined the Regiment at Baltimore on 20 July 1863. John O'Brien was mustered out with the rest of his regiment at New Haven on 27 July 1863 but was absent.

---

827   Records of the Holy Trinity Catholic Church at Wallingford, copy in the pension file.

He never applied for a pension. He is probably the John O'Brien, age 20, a farm laborer living in the household of John Blackstone of Branford in 1860.[828] He is on the 1863 draft list for Branford, Class 3, age 21, born Ireland, single, occupation farmer. He does not appear in the 1870 census at Branford.

O'CALLAHAN, PHILIP
Co. E 11th CVI, private, substitute, mustered in 1 December 1864, no pension

Philip O'Callahan served as a substitute for Martin C. Bishop of North Branford. He was mustered in at New Haven on 1 December 1864 as a private in Co. E 11th CVI for a term of three years. He was detailed to Headquarters 2nd Independent Brigade District of Southwest Virginia on 1 August 1865. There was no further military record from the adjutant general.

O'NEAL, JOHN
John O'Neal served as a substitute for Edmund M. Averill of Branford. He was mustered in at New Haven on 30 November 1864 as a private for a term of three years.[829] He does not appear in the 1860 census at Branford or North Branford.

PACKARD, CHARLES H.
Co. I 2nd CVI, enlisted 22 April 1861, mustered out 7 August 1861, reenlisted Co. A 10th CVI, wounded twice, discharged disability 31 July 1865, pension #53597 for the soldier

Charles H. Packard of New Haven enlisted at New Haven on 22 April 1861 and was mustered in on 7 May 1861 as a private in Co. I 2nd CVI, also known as Rifle Co. F. He was mustered out at New Haven on 7 August 1861 when his term expired. He reenlisted at Hartford on 26 October 1861, then of Branford, as a private in Co. A 10th CVI for a term of three years. With the rest of the regiment he fought at the Battle of Roanoke Island, North Carolina on 8 February 1862. He was sick from 31 October 1862 until April 1863 in Regimental Hospital at New Bern and in General Hospital at Portsmouth, North Carolina. Packard was mustered out on 31 December 1863 and reenlisted at St. Augustine, Florida on 1 January 1864 as a veteran in Co. A, then a resident of East Haven. He was wounded at Petersburg, Virginia on 13 September 1864 by a gunshot through the calf of his leg and treated in General Hospital, Fort Monroe, Virginia. He was wounded a second time at Darbytown Road, Virginia on 13 October 1864 with a gunshot wound of his right thigh causing a compound fracture. He was treated at Richmond and sent to Knight Hospital at New Haven where he was discharged for disability on 31 July 1865.

---

828   U.S. census 1860, Branford, New Haven County, Connecticut, population schedule, M653-85, dwelling 671, family 752, page 874, www.heritagequest.com.

829   Muster & Payroll, List of Substitutes, RG 13, box 100, 2nd Congressional District, Connecticut State Library; his service is not found in *Record of Service of Connecticut Men*.

He received a pension commencing on 27 November 1865 under the act of 14 July 1862 for the gunshot wound to his right thigh which caused permanent disability. At the time of his enlistment he was described as five feet seven inches tall, light complexion, blue eyes, light hair. Before the war he lived with his grand-father Charles Packard at Harpersfield, Delaware Co., New York from 1850-1852 and from 1852-1860 with Thomas Granniss at New Haven. After his discharge he returned to New Haven for one month; lived at Helena, Montana from 1865-1867; Baker City, Oregon 1867-1870; and Philadelphia since 1870.

He was married at New Haven by Rev. G. E. Havens on 31 March 1864 to Mary A. Granniss. In 1898 he had not seen her for thirty-one years but was never divorced and had no children or living relatives. He stated there was no one to prove his birth date.

Charles H. Packard died at Philadelphia, Pennsylvania on 30 July 1914 and was buried there in the National Cemetery. He was born on 20 April 1840.[830]

PADEN, CHARLES alias CHARLES PAXTON or PAYTON
Co. B 27th CVI, private, enlisted 10 September 1862, wounded, discharged 30 July 1863, pension #911931 for the soldier

Charles Paden, age 28, of Wallingford enlisted on 10 September 1862 and was mustered in on 3 October 1862 as a private in Co. B 27th CVI for a term of nine months. He fought at the Battle of Fredericksburg on 13 December 1862 with the rest of the company. He was on picket duty during the Battle of Chancellorsville on 3 May 1863 and was not captured with the rest of the company.[831] He fought at the Battle of Gettysburg and was slightly wounded on 2 July 1863 in the afternoon from a gunshot to his left hand. He was treated in the hospital at Baltimore and Philadelphia. He was admitted to Knight General Hospital, New Haven on 10 July 1863 and discharged on 30 July 1863.

He applied for an invalid pension on 30 June 1880. At the time of enlistment he was described as five feet seven inches tall, light complexion, light brown hair, blue eyes. "I am a shoemaker, age 55, of Wallingford. I worked in the spoon factory before enlisting."[832] Charles Paden often testified on behalf of other soldiers.

He was married at New Haven by Rev. Matthew Hart of St. Peter's Church about the middle of April 1856 to Ann Leavey. She died on 23 August 1880. He had the following children (living in 1897): Thomas F., born on 18 October 1857; Ann, born on 4 September 1861; Charles, born on 4 May 1863; James, born in 1865; Patrick Henry, born on 24 June1869; Margaret G., born on 21 April 1871; Mary Jane, born on 28 August 1873; and Martin, born on 13 November 1875.

Charles Paden died on 5 January 1907 age 73 and was buried in Holy Trinity Cemetery, Wallingford.[833]

PAGE, BENJAMIN, JR.
see James Stewart

---

830   His reenlistment paper dated 4 January 1864 gives his birth place as Albany, New York; on his pension application he states he was born at New Haven.
831   Deposition, Charles Paden of Wallingford, in the pension file of Henry A. Camp.
832   Deposition, Charles Paden of Wallingford, 12 November 1889, in the pension file of John Condon.
833   The Hale Collection, Wallingford, 140.

PAGE, ELIZUR E.

Co. F 27th CVI, private, enlisted 9 September 1862, prisoner, mustered out 27 July 1863, pension #400624 for the soldier and later for his widow Maria

Elizur E. Page, age 32, of North Branford enlisted on 9 September 1862 and was mustered in on 3 October 1862 as a private in Co. F 27th CVI for a term of nine months. He fought at the Battle of Fredericksburg on 13 December 1862 with the rest of the company. He was captured at the Battle of Chancellorsville, Virginia on 3 May 1863, held prisoner at Libby Prison, Richmond, and was paroled at City Point, Virginia on 14 May 1863. He reported to Camp Parole, Maryland on 16 May 1863, was sent to Washington, D.C. on 20 May 1863 and spent the remainder of his service at Camp Convalescent, Virginia. With the rest of the Chancellorsville paroled prisoners, he rejoined the Regiment at Baltimore on 20 July 1863. Elizur Page was mustered out with the rest of his regiment at New Haven on 27 July 1863. He was in Co. F 27th CVI Pioneer Corps.[834] He was the first cousin of John B. and Joel C. Page.

He applied for an invalid pension on 12 September 1889. At the time of his enlistment he was described as five feet eleven inches tall, light complexion, dark hair, brown eyes, occupation farmer. He claimed a number of disabilities resulting from his capture at Chancellorsville. After his discharge he lived at North Branford. He was a member of the Mason Rogers Post No. 7 G.A.R. of Branford.

Elizur E. Page died at North Branford on 19 February 1894 age 65 years & 10 months and was buried there in the Episcopal Cemetery. His company and regiment are engraved on his stone and there was a G.A.R. marker on his gravesite in 1934. He was born at North Branford, son of David Page and Nancy Rose.

Maria F. Page applied for a widow's pension on 3 March 1894. She was married to the soldier under the name of Maria F. Allen at Birmingham, Derby by Rev. George A. Hubbell on 10 October 1856. She was born at Huntington (Shelton). She had been married first to George Wheeler. She received a divorced and annulment from Wheeler on 13 September 1852 and changed her name back to Allen. She had no children.

Maria F. Page died at North Branford on 30 January 1908 age 81 and was buried there in the Episcopal Cemetery.[835]

PAGE, GEORGE H.

see Michael Hogan

PAGE, HENRY

Co. G 7th CVI, musician, enlisted 28 August 1861, mustered out 20 July 1865, pension #843673 for the soldier

Henry Page of Branford enlisted at New Haven on 28 August 1861 and was mustered in on 7 September 1861 as a private in Co. G 7th CVI, detailed as a musician. He was discharged at St. Helena Island, South

---

834   Sheldon, *History of Twenty-seventh*, 122.
835   North Branford Vital Records, deaths, 1908.

Carolina on 21 December 1863 and reenlisted the next day as a veteran in Co. G. He was wounded at Drewry's Bluff, Virginia on 14 May 1864. Henry Page was mustered out with the rest of his regiment at Goldsboro, North Carolina on 20 July 1865 and discharged at New Haven on 11 August 1865.

He applied for an invalid pension on 30 April 1892 under the act of 27 June 1890. He received a gunshot wound to the left shoulder at Drewry's Bluff on 14 May 1864 by a rifle ball fired by a rebel sharpshooter. At the time of his enlistment he was described as five feet five inches tall, light complexion, blue eyes, light hair, occupation boatman. Since his discharged he lived at Stony Creek, Branford. He was married at Boston, Massachusetts by H. F. Gardner, JP on 19 December 1871 to Emily L. Clark. She died at Branford on 10 March 1927 age 84 and was buried in Old North Cemetery, Hartford.[836] They had one child: Irving Washington Page, born on 15 May 1873, living in 1898. He was a charter member of the Mason Rogers Post No. 7 G.A.R. of Branford.

Captain Henry W. Page died at Stony Creek on 4 September 1927[837] and was buried in Old North Cemetery, Hartford. His company and regiment are engraved on his stone and there was a Civil War marker on his gravesite in 1934. His name appears on the Stony Creek Veterans' Monument. He was born at Guilford on 20 February 1842, son of Stephen Page and Margaret Crooks.

PAGE, HENRY B.
Co. G 14th CVI, enlisted 4 August 1862, discharged disability, died 12 February 1863, pension #9664 for the soldier

Henry B. Page, age 22, of Old Saybrook enlisted at Hartford on 4 August 1862 and was mustered in on 20 August 1862 as a private in Co. G 14th CVI for a term of three years. He was discharged for disability from Armory Hospital, Washington, D.C. on 15 January 1863. He died on 12 February 1863 and was buried in Center Cemetery, Branford. His company and regiment are engraved on his stone and there was a G.A.R. marker on his gravesite in 1934 and 2011.[838]

He applied for an invalid pension on 4 February 1863 and died eight days later. At the time of his enlistment he was described as five feet seven inches tall, dark complexion, hazel eyes, dark hair, occupation farmer, born at Branford. He had been unfit for duty for sixty days due to gangrene of his feet and resultant amputation. He enlisted from Old Saybrook but he was probably living at Branford. At the time of his pension application he was living at Southington.

Henry Brooks Page was born at Branford on 6 July 1842, son of Woodward Page and Irene Goodrich.[839]

---

836   Branford Vital Records, deaths, 1927.
837   Obituary, *Shore Line Times*, 9 September 1927 states he died at Guilford; he was a captain of tour boats at Stony Creek.
838   The Hale Collection, Branford, 92.
839   Branford Vital Records, Town Meeting Book A, 229.

PAGE, JAMES B.
Co. B 27th CVI, private, enlisted 10 September 1862, prisoner, mustered out 27 July 1863, pension #675846 for the soldier and later for his widow Antoinette

James B. Page, age 26, of Guilford enlisted on 10 September 1862 and was mustered in on 3 October 1862 as a private in Co. B 27th CVI for a term of nine months. He fought at the Battle of Fredericksburg on 13 December 1862 with the rest of the company. He was captured at the Battle of Chancellorsville, Virginia on 3 May 1863, held prisoner at Richmond, and was paroled at City Point, Virginia on 14 May 1863. He reported to Camp Parole, Maryland on 16 May 1863, was sent to Washington, D.C. on 20 May 1863 and spent the remainder of his service at Camp Convalescent, Virginia. With the rest of the Chancellorsville paroled prisoners, he rejoined the Regiment at Baltimore on 20 July 1863. James Page was mustered out with the rest of his regiment at New Haven on 27 July 1863. He was the brother of Joel C. Page and first cousin of Elizur E. Page.

He applied for an invalid pension on 27 September 1889 for age related diseases contracted while in the Army. "While a prisoner in Richmond I contracted a severe cold. Directly after coming home I took to my bed with a Fever and have since suffered with chronic rheumatism." He was described as five feet eight inches tall, light complexion, blue eyes, brown hair, occupation farmer.

He was married first at Guilford on 18 October 1854 to Sally Parmelee Snow. They were divorced on 1 January 1881. The family bible located at his home at Brooksvale, Cheshire was examined by the pension board representative. It was presented to James Baldwin Page by his mother in January 1856, published by Silas Andrus and Son, Hartford, 1856. The bible lists the following births: James B. Page, born on 14 February 1835; Sally P. Snow, born on 13 December 1839; Frank H. Page, born on 2 April 1856; Nellie R., born on 6 November 1858; Willie E., born on 13 February 1861, died on 27 December 1861; Jennie E., born on 19 November 1862; Freddie W., born on 26 April 1864; Rosa E., born on 28 August 1869; Lovell H., born on 16 January 1872; Rose D., born on 8 June 1883. Marriages from the bible: James B. Page and Sally P. Snow were married on 18 October 1854. James B. Page and Anettee [Antoinette] Doolittle were married on 19 May 1881. Deaths from the bible: Edmond Page, died on 11 January 1881; Nannice [Nancy] Page, died on 22? February [no year given]; and Eli F. Page, died on 10 November 1897.

James B. Page had three minor children in 1881 by his first marriage: Burton H. age 12, Ross E. [Rosa] age 11, and Scovill U. [Lovell] age 8. In 1898 the following children were living: Franklin H., born on 1 April 1856; Nellie R., born on 6 November 1858; Jennie E., born on 19 November 1862; Burton H., born on 11 September 1866; Rosa E., born on 28 August 1869[840]; Lovell H., born on 16 January 1872; and Rosie S. Page, born on 8 June 1883.

He was married second at East Haven by Rev. E. Edwin Hall on 19 May 1881 to Antoinette Sophronia Doolittle.[841] He was age 46, born at Guilford; she was age 38, born at Wallingford; both were living at North Haven. She was not previously married or divorced.

---

840 Another daughter with the same birth date is listed in the Branford Vital Records as Ida Belle. She died 13 December 1872.
841 East Haven Vital Records, copy in the file. Antoinette Page states they were married in the village of Fair Haven.

James Baldwin Page died at Cheshire on 2 August 1906 and was buried in West Side Cemetery, Guilford. He was born at Guilford on 17 February 1935, son of Edmund Page and Nancy Gordon of Branford.

Antoinette Page applied for a widow's pension on 25 August 1906. She was born at Wallingford on 27 May 1843. In 1906 she was living at Cheshire and in 1916 at Wallingford with her daughter Mrs. Rose Page Snow. Antoinette Page died on 26 January 1919.

PAGE, JOEL C.
Co. E 15th CVI, private, enlisted 6 August 1862, discharged disability 20 November 1863, pension #837850 for the soldier

Joel C. Page, age 22, of Guilford enlisted at New Haven on 6 August 1862 and was mustered in on 25 August 1862 as a private in Co. E 15th CVI for a term of three years. Upon arriving in Virginia he was detailed as an ambulance driver. He was hospitalized for two months for phthisis pulmonalis and discharged for disability from Balfour Hospital, Portsmouth, Virginia on 20 November 1863. He was the brother of James B. Page and first cousin of Elizur E. Page.

He applied for an invalid pension on 27 January 1869. At the time of his enlistment he was described as five feet ten inches tall, fair complexion, blue eyes, occupation farmer. In October 1863 he was sent to Balfour Hospital near Portsmouth, Virginia for about three months. He was discharged for chronic diarrhea and was unfit for the invalid corps. There are affidavits in his file attesting to his inability to work. After his discharge he returned to Guilford. He was admitted to the Fitch's Soldier Home[842] at Noroton Heights on 14 January 1903. At the time of his death his possessions included an overcoat, one vest, one pair of trousers (badly moth eaten), two handkerchiefs, one watch and metal chain, and sixty-three cents in cash. He was a member and commander of the Parmelee Post No. 42 G.A.R. of Guilford and a member of the Admiral Foote Post G.A.R. No. 17 of New Haven.

Joel Canfield Page died at the Fitch Soldiers' Home in Noroton Heights on 30 January 1917, unmarried, and was buried in West Side Cemetery, Guilford. He was born at Guilford on 10 February 1840, son of Edmund Page and Nancy Gordon of Branford.

PAINE, RICHARD J.
Co. K 6th CVI, sergeant, enlisted 9 September 1861, discharged 11 September 1864, pension #342606 for the soldier and later for his widow Maria

Richard J. Paine of Branford enlisted at New Haven on 9 September 1861 and was mustered in on 12 September 1861 as a private in Co. K 6th CVI for a term of three years. He was promoted to corporal on 20 November 1862 and to sergeant on 6 March 1863. He was discharged at Petersburg, Virginia on 11 September 1864 when his term expired. He was in the Connecticut Second Company Governor's Foot Guard from 1859 until his enlistment. He was the brother-in-law of Roger Hall.

---

842   Fitch's Home for Soldiers, Deceased Veterans Discharge Files 1882-1932, box 8, file 2171.

He applied for an invalid pension on 7 May 1884. At the time of his enlistment he was described as five feet eleven inches tall, dark complexion, brown hair, hazel eyes, occupation engraver. He suffered from several ailments contracted during the war including malarial poisoning at Petersburg, Virginia in August 1864. He was treated at Davids' Island, New York and transferred to Knights Hospital, New Haven. He returned briefly to his regiment until his discharge. There are detailed affidavits from the soldier concerning his regiment and illnesses. Since his discharge he lived at Stony Creek, Branford. He was a member of the Mason Rogers Post No. 7 G.A.R. of Branford.

Richard J. Paine died at Stony Creek on 24 November 1891 and was buried in Stony Creek Cemetery. A G.A.R. marker was on his gravesite in 1934 and 2011 and his name appears on the Stony Creek Veterans' Monument. He was born at Canton, Massachusetts on 17 July 1839, son of Richard Paine and Avis W. Kingsley.[843]

Maria L. Paine of Stony Creek applied for a widow's pension on 15 January 1892 under the act of 27 June 1890. She was married to the soldier under the name of Maria Louisa Page at Branford by Rev. Timothy P. Gillett of the First Congregational Church on 15 September 1861. Neither were previously married or divorced. Three days after their marriage he enlisted and fell ill during the war from which he never fully recovered.[844] They had two children under the age of sixteen in 1892: Rollins S., born on 18 November 1877; and Essie E., born on 30 April 1880. She received an additional two dollars each month for each child until the age of sixteen.

Richard J. Paine of Stony Creek, Branford served in the 6th CVI and returned to Stony Creek after the war. The photograph was taken about 1868 with his son Joseph. (courtesy of Joan Paine Johnson)

Maria L. Paine died at Stony Creek on 30 October 1935 and was buried in Stony Creek Cemetery. She was born at Stony Creek on 30 August 1838, daughter of Dennis S. Page and Almira Louisa Hull.

---

843   Branford Vital Records, deaths, 1891.
844   Maria Page Paine Passes 95th Year, *New Haven Sunday Register*, 10 September 1933.

PALMER, AMMI B.
Co. B 15th CVI, corporal, enlisted 6 August 1862, prisoner, mustered out 27 June 1865, pension #388403 for the soldier and later for his widow Annice

Ammi B. Palmer, age 19, of Branford enlisted at New Haven on 6 August 1862 and was mustered in on 25 August 1862 as a corporal in Co. B 15th CVI for a term of three years. His rank was reduced by his own request on 1 December 1863. He saw action at the Battle of Kinston, North Carolina on 8 March 1864 and was wounded.[845] He was in the hospital with yellow fever at New Bern, North Carolina in October 1864. For most of the war he was detached to the Brigade Commissary Department. Ammi Palmer was mustered out with the rest of his regiment at New Bern, North Carolina on 27 June 1865 and discharged at New Haven on 12 July 1865. He was described as a "Good Soldier."

He applied for an invalid pension on 30 December 1891 under the act of 27 June 1890 for a variety of illnesses not related to his service. At the time of his enlistment he was described as five feet ten inches tall, dark complexion, blue eyes, brown hair, occupation farmer. He fractured his right leg on 27 April 1886 when thrown from his wagon by the running away of a horse. After his discharge he lived at Branford except about 1872 to 1879 at Hartford. He was a charter member and adjutant of the Mason Rogers Post No. 7 G.A.R. of Branford.

Ammi Barker Palmer died at Branford on 16 October 1893 and was buried there in Mill Plain Cemetery. He was born at Branford on 17 January 1843, son of Timothy Palmer and Louisa Beach.[846]

Annice E. Palmer of Branford applied for a widow's pension on 24 November 1893. She was married to the soldier under the name of Annice Estelle Bartholomew by Rev. Elijah C. Baldwin of the First Congregational Church on 2 June 1868. They had four children: Caroline P., born February 1872; Frederick H., born on 3 January 1875; Charlotte A., born on 9 May 1880; and Sydney J., born on 21 December 1883.

Annice E. Palmer died on 17 October 1921 and was buried in Mill Plain Cemetery. She was born at Branford on 29 December 1845, daughter of John Jerome Bartholomew and Charlotte Ann Squire.

PALMER, HENRY
see George Johnson

---

845   Thorpe, *History of the Fifteenth*, 97. There is no record of him seeing action or being wounded at Kinston in his CMSR or pension file.
846   Branford Vital Records, Town Meeting book A, 234.

PALMER, JOHN HENRY

Co. K 10th CVI, corporal, enlisted 23 September 1862, wounded, died 11 April 1865, pension #137021 for his father Charles Palmer

John Henry Palmer of North Branford enlisted and was mustered in at New Haven on 23 September 1862 as a private in Co. K 10th CVI for a term of three years. He was sick in General Hospital at Hilton Head, South Carolina from July to October 1863 and at General Hospital, Fort Schuyler, New York in July and August 1863. He served with the regiment in 1864 in the Virginia campaigns and was promoted to corporal on 1 January 1865. He received a gunshot wound to the head in action at Petersburg, Virginia on 2 April 1865. He was admitted to General Hospital, Fort Monroe, Virginia from the field on 5 April 1865 and died there from his wounds on 11 April 1865. His name is inscribed on the North Branford Soldiers' Monument. He was born at North Branford on 10 November 1838 and was never married. At the time of his enlistment he was described as five feet seven inches tall, light complexion, blue eyes, light hair, occupation farmer. He was the first cousin of Theodore Palmer.

His father Charles Palmer applied for a pension on 8 June 1868. He was disabled for fifteen years and the soldier had contributed towards his support. His wife, Mary Granniss Palmer died on 15 February 1861 age 52. Charles Palmer died at North Branford on 19 March 1876 age 69 and was buried in the North Branford Congregational Cemetery.[847] He was the son of David Palmer and Mary Russell.

PALMER, LUZERNE A.

Co. C & I 5th CVI, lieutenant, enlisted 21 June 1861, wounded, resigned 1 April 1863, pension #179448 for the soldier and later for his widow Emma

Luzerne A. Palmer of Branford enlisted at Hartford on 21 June 1861 and was mustered in on 22 June 1861 as a sergeant of Co. C 5th CVI for a term of four years. He was wounded at the Battle of Cedar Mountain, Virginia on 9 August 1862 and promoted the same day at Kelly's Ford, Virginia as 2nd lieutenant of Co. I 5th CVI. "Sergeant Luzern A. Palmer bore it [the stars and stripes] to the front again until he fell."[848] He was brought to General Hospital at Alexandria, Virginia on 16 August 1862 and transferred to General Hospital at Davids' Island, New York harbor on 6 September 1862. He resigned on 1 April 1863 on a surgeon's certificate.

He applied for an invalid pension on 9 January 1865. He was struck in the chest with a musket ball hitting his watch in his vest pocket which probably saved his life. He was also wounded in the forearm, knee, groin, and leg. He forearm was broken. He contracted a cold and cough while lying on the ground in the rain for two days after the battle. There are many affidavits in the file attesting to his injuries and illness.

Luzerne Augustus Palmer died at Branford on 21 September 1873. He died from pulmonary disease caused by exposure while in the service. He was born at Branford on 6 June 1839, son of Jonathan Palmer and Elizabeth Beach.[849]

---

847   The Hale Collection, North Branford, 32.
848   Marvin, *Fifth Regiment Volunteers*, 159; he carried the flag after Elijah B. Jones was killed.
849   Branford Vital Records, Town Meeting Book A, 234.

Emma C. Palmer of Branford applied for a widow's pension on 8 October 1873. She was married to the soldier under the name of Emma C. Patten at Branford by Rev. Jacob G. Miller of the First Congregational Church on 26 November 1862. She was age 18, born at Green Village, New Jersey, living at Branford. Neither were previously married or divorced and she did not remarry after his death. They had three children: Elizabeth A., born on 5 November 1863; William H., born on 22 December 1865; and Frank S. born on 1 July 1869. She moved to Weld County, Colorado with her children between 1877 and 1880.

Emma C. Palmer died at Greeley, Weld Co., Colorado on 27 February 1915.

PALMER, NATHAN A.
Co. B 27th CVI, to Co. I 14th CVI, private, enlisted 10 September 1862, deserted, wounded, discharged 11 February 1865, pension #926428 for the soldier and later for his widow Emma

Nathan A. Palmer, age 18, enlisted at North Haven on 10 September 1862 and was mustered in on 3 October 1862 as a private in Co. B 27th CVI for a term of nine months. On 3 December 1862 he deserted from camp in Maryland on the march between Washington, D.C. and Port Tobacco, Maryland. He had in his possession one Enfield and 100 rounds of ammunition. On 6 January 1864 he surrendered to the provost marshal in Connecticut. He was held on arrest at Fort Trumbull, was received at Camp Distribution, Alexandria, Virginia on 20 January 1864 from Fort Columbia, New York. He was assigned on 25 April 1864 to Co. I 14th CVI to "make good the loss by desertion." On 10 May 1864 "he shot off his own finger (right hand forefinger) as his regiment was about to engage in the Battle of Spotsylvania Court House, Virginia during which time he was treated in the hospital until 16 August 1864 for said intentionally self-inflicted wound." Nathan Palmer was honorably discharged from Camp near Hatchers Run, Virginia on 11 February 1865.

He applied for a pension on 27 March 1906. At the time of his enlistment he was described as five feet ten inches tall, fair complexion, blue eyes, dark hair, occupation farmer. His pension was originally calculated as 1 year, 4 months, and 23 days minus 3 months and 6 days for the self-inflicted gunshot wound. His total service was actually 9 months and 3 days. There are a number of documents concerning the amount of his pension based on the days he actually served.

Since his discharge he lived at North Haven for about 20 years, New Haven 1908, and East Haven. He was married at New Haven by Rev. Charles W. Drake on 1 May 1873 to Emma A. Palmer. He was age 29, born at North Haven, living at New Haven. She was age 24, born and living at North Haven. He was not previously married or divorced.

Nathan A. Palmer of East Haven died on 8 August 1922 and was buried in Center Cemetery, North Haven.[850] He was born at North Haven on 8 March 1844, son of Jasper Palmer and Maria Wolcott, both born at North Haven. His only child, Gertrude A. Palmer was born on 17 May 1877 and died on 17 May 1887. His name appears on the North Haven Civil War Honor Roll.

Emma A. Palmer of 466 Main Street, East Haven applied for a widow's pension on 19 August 1922. Her maiden name was Emma Augusta Page. She had been previously married on 27 November 1861 to Charles M. Palmer and he was granted a divorce on 1 March 1873. They had one child Eva A. Palmer, age 5 years in 1873. Her first husband never served in the military.

Emma A. Palmer died on 11 December 1929 and was buried in Center Cemetery, North Haven.

---

850   The Hale Collection, North Haven, 3.

PALMER, THEODORE
Co. G 13th CVI, sergeant, reenlisted, mustered out 25 April 1866, pension #318083 for the soldier and later for his widow Emma

Theodore Palmer of North Branford enlisted at New Haven on 25 October 1861 and was mustered in on 28 January 1862 as a corporal in Co. G 13th CVI for a term of three years. His rank was reduced on 15 June 1863 but he was promoted to sergeant on 2 October 1863. With his regiment he served in the New Orleans area and fought at the Battle of Irish Bend on 14 April 1863 and in the Siege of Port Hudson. He reenlisted as a veteran in Co. G with the rank of sergeant on 8 February 1864 and was transferred to Co. D 13th Battalion. He served during the Virginia campaign at the Battles of Winchester, Fisher's Hill, and Cedar Creek. Theodore Palmer was mustered out at Fort Pulaski, Georgia on 25 April 1866 and released at Hart Island, New York on May 5-7, 1866. He was the brother-in-law of Albert U. Platts and first cousin of John Henry Palmer.

He applied for an invalid pension on 29 July 1890 under the act of 27 June 1890. He was married first to Jane E. Baldwin who died at North Branford on 1 April 1875. He was married second at New Haven by Rev. George Lansing Taylor of the Third Methodist Episcopal Church on 11 March 1876 to Emily Wolcott. He was age 42, born and living at New Haven; she was age 25, born at East Haven, living at New Haven. After his discharge he lived at North Branford and New Haven. He was a member of the Admiral Foote Post No. 17 G.A.R. of New Haven.

Theodore A. Palmer died at New Haven on 22 May 1891 age 57 and was buried there in Evergreen Cemetery. He was the son of Timothy Russell Palmer and Adeline Stone of North Branford.

Emma A. Palmer of New Haven applied for a widow's pension on 28 May 1891. She was married first to David P. Burrell of East Haven on 21 May 1866. She obtained a divorce on 1 March 1876 and changed her name back to Emily Wolcott. Emma A. Palmer died on 4 September 1899.

PALMER, W. BRADLEY or WILLIAM B. PALMER
Co. B 27th CVI, private, enlisted 21 August 1862, prisoner, mustered out 27 July 1863, pension #654995 for the soldier and later for his widow Bessie

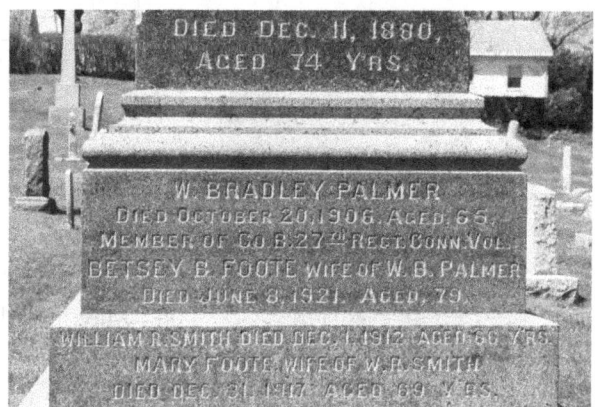

William Bradley Palmer, age 21, of Branford enlisted on 21 August 1862 and was mustered in on 3 October 1862 as a private in Co. B 27th CVI for a term of nine months. "Bradley Palmer was not at the battle [of Fredericksburg], was left behind sick."[851] In January and February 1863 he was sick in Regimental Hospital. He was captured at the Battle of Chancellorsville, Virginia on 3 May 1863, held prisoner at Richmond, and was paroled at City Point, Virginia on 14 May 1863. He reported to Camp Parole, Maryland on 16 May 1863, was sent to Washington, D.C. on 20 May 1863 and spent the remainder of his service at Camp Convalescent, Virginia. With the rest of the Chancellorsville paroled prisoners, he rejoined the Regiment at Baltimore on 20 July 1863. Bradley Palmer was mustered out with the rest of his regiment at New Haven on 27 July 1863. After the war he served three years in the 2nd Connecticut National Guard. He was the brother-in-law of Samuel G. Cooke.

---

851   Letter, [George C. Baldwin] to home, 15 December 1862.

W. Bradley Palmer of Branford, holding his kepi, had his photograph taken two days before he was mustered in as a private in Co. B 27th CVI. He returned to Branford after the war and died in the house where he was born on Paved Street. (Branford Historical Society photograph collection)

He applied for an invalid pension on 18 September 1890 under the act of 27 June 1890. "He was crippled in the feet for about a month at Falmouth on or about 20 January 1863. His feet froze due to extreme marching and exposure."[852] "I was treated at the Camp hospital and at Windmill Point Hospital, Va." At the time of his enlistment he was described as five feet ten inches tall, dark complexion, dark hair, grey eyes. He was a member of the Mason Rogers Post No. 7 G.A.R. of Branford. "For the past year or two he had missed the post meetings where his presence always added to the coming together of the veterans of the war."[853]

Bradley Palmer died at Branford on 20 October 1906 in the house where he was born and was buried in Center Cemetery. His company and regiment are engraved on his stone and a G.A.R. marker was on his gravesite in 1934. His name appears on the Stony Creek Veterans' Monument. He was born at Branford on 30 October 1840, son of Wilman Palmer and Susan Cornelia Bradley, born at Branford and New Haven.

Bessie B. Palmer applied for a widow's pension on 6 November 1906. In the file is a list of her assets and income. She was married to the soldier under the name of Bessie Blackstone Foote at Branford by Rev. Elijah C. Baldwin of the First Congregational Church on 24 November 1869. He was age 29, she was age 27, both born and living at Branford. Neither were previously married or divorced. They had no children.

Bessie Foote Palmer died at Branford on 8 June 1921 and was buried there in Center Cemetery.[854] She was born at Branford on 3 April 1842, daughter of John Foote and Fanny Blackstone.[855]

PARDEE, HENRY N.
Co. K 15th CVI, sergeant, enlisted 13 August 1862, mustered out 27 June 1865, pension #903267 for the soldier

Henry N. Pardee of North Branford enlisted at New Haven on 13 August 1862 and was mustered in on 25 August 1862 as a corporal in Co. K 15th CVI for a term of three years. He was promoted to sergeant on 1 May 1864. He saw action at the Battle of Fredericksburg, Virginia on 13 December 1862, during the Siege of Suffolk, Virginia in April 1863, and in the Peninsula Campaign of July 1863. He was a patient in Mansfield General Hospital, Morehead City, North Carolina from September 1864 until 1 January 1865 for fever. He was on picket duty

Foote-Palmer monument at Center Cemetery

---

852   Affidavit, Richard. T. Kelsey of Branford, 22 April 1891, in the pension file of W. Bradley Palmer.
853   Obituary, *Shore Line Times*, 25 October 1906.
854   Branford Vital Records, deaths, 1921.
855   Branford Vital Records, Town Meeting Book A, 238.

during the Battle of Kinston, North Carolina. Pardee was mustered out with the rest of his regiment at New Bern, North Carolina on 27 June 1865 and discharged at New Haven on 12 July 1865. He served under Capt. Medad D. Munson of Wallingford. One of his letters is in the pension file of Lorenzo Harrison.

He applied for an invalid pension on 17 June 1892 under the act of 27 June 1890 for a variety of age related illnesses. He was married to Emma Jerusha Cook, daughter of Leverett Cook and Thankful Stevens. She died at Northford on 8 February 1887 age 46 and was buried in Northford Cemetery.[856] They had two children born at Northford: Leroy Cook, born on 29 January 1861; and Frank Porter, born on 20 April 1863, died on 4 May 1888.[857] After the war he lived at Northford.

Henry Newton Pardee died at Northford on 6 April 1898 age 64 and was buried in Northford Cemetery. His rank, company, and regiment are engraved on his stone and a Civil War marker was on his gravesite in 1934. His name appears on the Northford Veterans' Monument. He was born at Durham, son of David Pardee and Althea Newton.[858]

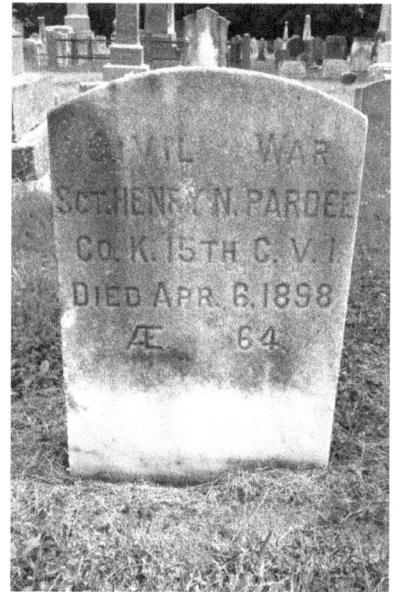

PARKER, WILLIAM H.
Co. K 29th CVI, enlisted 2 January 1864, discharged 1 June 1865, no pension

William H. Parker of Branford enlisted at New Haven on 2 January 1864 and was mustered in on 8 March 1864 as a private in Co. K 29th CVI for a term of three years. His service was credited to Branford. He was sick at Knight Hospital from August 1864 through April 1865 and it does not appear he rejoined his regiment. He was discharged on 1 June 1865. His name appears on the Wall of Honor at Washington, D.C.

PARSONS, EDWIN W.
Co. B 27th CVI, private, enlisted 9 September 1862, mustered out 27 July 1863,, pension #433633 for the soldier

Edwin W. Parsons, age 44, of Branford enlisted on 9 September 1862 and was mustered in on 3 October 1862 as a private in Co. B 27th CVI for a term of nine months. He did not fight at the Battle of Fredericksburg.[859] From 23 December 1862 through 2 March 1863 he was sick at the Campbell General Hospital, Washington, D.C. In March and April 1863 he was a patient at the General Hospital, Portsmouth Grove, Rhode Island. On 3 April 1863 he was transferred to Knight General Hospital, New Haven and remained there until his discharge. On 14 July 1863 he was transferred to the invalid corps at the hospital. He

---

856 The Hale Collection, North Branford, 67.
857 St. Andrews Church Records, Northford, 3:44 & 122.
858 Donald Lines Jacobus, *The Pardee Genealogy* (New Haven Colony Historical Society, 1927), 274.
859 Letter, Samuel Beach to home, 4 January 1863.

was described as five feet six inches tall, hazel eyes, black hair, dark complexion, occupation bell agent in the hospital, disabled for 3 months & 11 days, general debility, good character. Parsons was mustered out with the rest of his regiment at New Haven on 27 July 1863. "I was only with the Regiment a short time being in the Hospital."

He applied for an invalid pension on 22 October 1888. While at Falmouth, Va. about December 1862, he contracted inflammatory rheumatism resulting in disease of the kidney and general debility. "About the 8th day of December 1862 a few days before the battle of Fredericksburg where the company was on a forced march, the weather being very wet and Stormy. Said Parsons contracted Rheumatism and was in a very bad condition. After the war I saw him often and he was a constant sufferer caused no doubt by his exposure."[860] Since his discharge he lived at Branford and worked as a high school janitor. He was a member of the Mason Rogers Post No. 7 G.A.R. of Branford.

He was married at Branford by Rev. Timothy P. Gillett of the First Congregational Church on 18 February 1840 to Antoinette Bartholomew of Branford.[861] She died at Branford on 2 June 1881.[862] They had nine children, several of whom died young.

Edwin White Parsons died at Branford on 12 April 1897 and was buried there in Center Cemetery. His company and regiment are engraved on his stone. He was born at Granville, Massachusetts on 11 February 1818, son of Levi Parsons and Abigail Ward.[863]

PHELAN, THOMAS
Co. M 1st HA, Co. G 24th VRC, private, enlisted 1 February 1862, discharged 1 February 1865, pension #263937 for his widow Mary

Thomas Phelan of New Haven enlisted on 21 January 1862 and was mustered in on 1 February 1862 as a private in Co. M 1st HA for a term of three years. He was with the siege train at Yorktown, Virginia in April and May 1862 and assisted in the reply to the midnight attack by the enemy at Harrisons Landing 30 July 1862. He saw action at Fredericksburg, Virginia on 11 December 1862 and 3 May 1863. He was transferred to Co. G 24th VRC on 12 February 1864 for a "broken down constitution" and evidently over fifty years of age. He endured much hard service until February 1863 when he rapidly broke down and was subsequently on the sick list or on light duty. He was reported absent without authority on 13 April 1864 but returned to duty on 4 May 1864 and was arrested for desertion. He was honorably discharged at Washington, D.C. on 1 February 1865. He lived at North Branford and Wallingford after his discharge.

Thomas Phelan died on 28 February 1886 age 73 and was buried in Holy Trinity Cemetery, Wallingford.[864] His company and regiment are engraved on his stone and there was a Civil War marker on his gravesite in 1934. His name appears on the Northford Veterans' Monument.

Mary Phelan, age 62, of Wallingford applied for a widow's pension on 2 October 1886. She was married to the soldier under the name of Mary Garvin at the Church of the Transfiguration on 25 Mott Street, New York City by Rev. William McClellan on 26 June 1847. Her last pension payment was on 4 December 1898 and her death occurred on 24 January 1899.

---

860   Affidavit, Henry D. Boardman of Great Barrington, Mass., 26 December 1888, in the pension file of Edwin W. Parsons.
861   Branford Vital Records, 1786-1840, 378.
862   Branford Vital Records, 1863-1895, 226.
863   Branford Vital Records, deaths, 1897.
864   The Hale Collection, Wallingford, 131.

PLATTS, ALBERT U.
Co. C 20th CVI, corporal, enlisted 28 July 1862, mustered out 13 June 1865, pension #782905 for the soldier and later for his widow Clara

Albert U. Platts of Essex enlisted on 28 July 1862 and was mustered in on 8 September 1862 as a corporal in Co. C 20th CVI for a term of three years. His regiment saw action at the Battle of Chancellorsville, Virginia on 1 May 1863 and were among the first to arrive at Gettysburg and defended Culp's Hill. They were stationed in Georgia in 1864 and fought at the Battle of Peach Tree Creek on 20 July 1864. During 1865 they marched to Atlanta and saw action in North Carolina. Platts was mustered out near Washington, D.C. on 13 June 1865. He was the brother-in-law of Theodore Palmer.

Albert U. Platts of Essex served in the 20th CVI and came to North Branford after the war. He is buried in the North Branford Congregational Cemetery. (Photograph by Janet Gregan, 1985, Totoket Historical Society)

He applied for an invalid pension on 1 April 1902. At the time of his enlistment he was described as five feet nine inches tall, florid complexion, black eyes, brown hair, occupation clerk. He was married at North Branford by Rev. William B. Curtiss of the North Branford Congregational Church on 22 February 1877 to Clara Watson Palmer. Neither were previously married or divorced. They had one child: Eunice A., born on 8 January 1878. Since his discharge he lived at North Branford.

Albert Uriah Platts died at North Branford on 3 August 1914 and was buried there in the Congregational Cemetery. He was born at Winthrop, Saybrook on 28 June 1842, son of Asa Platts and Julia Amelia Jones.

Clara W. Platts applied for a widow's pension on 14 August 1914. She died on 25 December 1929 and was buried in the North Branford Congregational Cemetery. She was the daughter of Timothy Russell Palmer and Adeline Stone.

POTTER, ELIAS E.
see Edward Donnelly

POWELL, JOHN
Co. B 12th CVI, wagoner, enlisted 18 February 1862, prisoner, died 11 January 1865, no pension

John Powell of Branford enlisted and was mustered in on 18 February 1862 as a wagoner in Co. B 12th CVI for a term of three years. He was captured on 19 October 1864 near Cedar Creek, Virginia and died at Salisbury Prison, North Carolina on 11 January 1865. He appears in the 1860 census at Branford, age 32, born in Ireland, living in the household of John Kerr.[865]

---

865   U.S. census 1860, Branford, New Haven County, Connecticut, population schedule, M653-85, dwelling 723, family 810, page 881, www.heritagequest.com.

PRATT, EUGENE H.
9th Regiment band, enlisted 18 September 1861, discharged 17 September 1862, pension #307075 for the soldier and later for his widow Lucy

Eugene H. Pratt of Meriden enlisted at New Haven on 18 September 1861 and was mustered in on 4 October 1861 as a musician in the 9th Regiment band. He was discharged for disability at Camp Parapet, Louisiana on 17 September 1862.

He applied for an invalid pension on 14 June 1880. At New Orleans in January 1862 from the climate and drinking water, he contracted diarrhea and was excused from duty for nearly five months. He was treated in quarters, was never in the hospital and discharged for disability by general order. At the time of his discharge he was described as five feet eight inches tall, dark complexion, dark hair, brown eyes, occupation farmer. After the war he lived at Meriden until May 1866, then Wallingford until at least 1880 and died at North Branford.

Eugene H. Pratt died at Northford on 18 November 1887 age 53 and was buried in Northford Cemetery. His regiment is engraved on his stone and a Civil War marker was on his gravesite in 1934. He was born at East Haddam, son of Nathan and Orpha A. Pratt, born at Essex and Haddam.

Lucy A. Pratt of Northford applied for a widow's pension on 2 May 1888. She was married first under the name of Lucy Ann Andrews at Southington by Rev. Elisha C. Jones of the Congregational Church to George W. Andrews. He was living at Prospect and she at Cheshire. Andrews died in the Civil War on 25 July 1864. She was married second at Springfield, Massachusetts by Rev. Richard G. Greene on 2 July 1866 to Eugene H. Pratt. No children are listed in the pension file or census records.

Lucy Andrews Pratt died on 22 February 1913 and was buried in Northford Cemetery.

PROUT, GEORGE M.
Co. B 27th CVI, corporal, enlisted 10 September 1862, mustered out 27 July 1863, pension #534505 for the soldier and later for his widow Harriet

George M. Prout, age 37, of Branford enlisted on 10 September 1862 and was mustered in on 3 October 1862 in Co. B 27th CVI for a term of nine months. He enlisted as a private and was soon promoted to corporal. "General Prout we call him…If I were to express idea of things that way I should say that Prout follows QM around with [his] nose all the time."[866] In November and December 1862 he was sick in the hospital at New Haven and in January and February 1863 sick in Regimental Hospital at Falmouth, Virginia. He contracted typhoid fever and malarial poisoning and rheumatism at Falmouth, Virginia in January 1863 resulting in

---

866   Letter, Samuel Beach to home, 16 November 1862; QM refers to H. Lynde Harrison.

deafness of his left ear. From Regimental Hospital he was sent to Windmill Point Hospital, Virginia for some four weeks, then to Potomac Creek Hospital, Virginia on 21 April 1863 where he remained until June 1863. He never returned to the Regiment for duty. Prout was mustered out with the rest of his regiment at New Haven on 27 July 1863. George M. Prout secured a substitute, Willoughby Arlington, who enlisted on 3 September 1864 at the Brooklyn Navy Yard.[867]

He applied for an invalid pension on 28 September 1888. "When I saw him after his return, he looked pretty bad and has not been an able bodied man since."[868] At the time of his enlistment he was described as five feet ten inches tall, light complexion, grey hair, grey eyes.

He was married at Fair Haven by Rev. William Vibbert of St. James Church on 9 January 1854 to Harriet Elizabeth Collins. Neither were previously married or divorced.

George Minott Prout died at Branford on 13 November 1901 and was buried there in Center Cemetery. His rank, company, and regiment are engraved on his stone. He was born at Middletown on 1 May 1831, son of Oliver Prout and Susan Spencer, born at Middletown and Haddam.

Harriet Elizabeth Prout applied for a widow's pension on 13 December 1901. She owned an eighty-three acre farm and lived with her son George S. Prout. She died at Branford on 11 March 1904 and was buried there in Center Cemetery. She was born at Branford on 28 November 1831, daughter of Jonathan Collins and Betsey Johnson.[869]

RAPP, WILLIAM

Career army officer, Mexican War, wounded, Civil War, pension #636422 for the soldier and later for his widow Clara

William Rapp was a sergeant major in the U.S. Army and spent the end of his life at Branford. He enlisted at New York City on 1 April 1850 as a corporal in Co. K 2nd Dragoons under Capt. William Steele stationed at Fort Conrad, territory of New Mexico. The company served during the Mexican War in the 2nd U.S. Artillery. At Goruadad el Muerte, territory of New Mexico, he was shot and wounded by a concealed foe resulting in partial loss of sight in his right eye. He was treated at Fort Fillmore and Fort Conrad and discharged at Fort Leavenworth on 1 April 1855.

He reenlisted in May 1856 and served as 1st sergeant of Co. I 2nd U.S. Artillery at Fort McHenry, Maryland. He was discharged in May 1861. He reenlisted in Co. F 4th U.S. Artillery on 1 October 1861 at Fort Washington, Maryland, received his commission as sergeant major of the 4th U.S. Artillery and was discharged on 20 December 1862 to accept a commission in the 3rd New York Volunteer Artillery. He was on his way to join the 3rd New York in North Carolina when he fell ill in Baltimore and had to resign his commission in January 1863, never having been mustered in.

After the Civil War he reenlisted at Fort Monroe, Virginia on 21 March 1868 in the 4th U.S. Artillery for a term of three years. In 1870 he was described as age 50, five feet eleven inches tall, ruddy complexion, light hair, blue eyes. He was discharged and retired on 21 March 1871 after serving as hospital steward at Fort Totten, Washington, D.C.

867   Statements of Navy substitutes, RG 13, box 96, 2nd Congregational District, Connecticut State Library.
868   Affidavit, George R. Spinks of Branford, 23 April 1889, in the pension file of George M. Prout.
869   Branford Vital Records, deaths, 1904.

He applied for an invalid pension on 10 February 1892 under the act of 27 June 1890. After the war he lived in Minnesota and Omaha, Douglas Co. Nebraska where he owned an apothecary. In 1892 he was living at North Denver, Colorado. His pension file is large with much detail.

He was married at Albany, New York while stationed there as a recruiting sergeant by Rev. John Miles on 23 May 1858 to Clara Theresa VonBaczka. They had one son John Henry Alvero Rapp, born on 20 September 1862, living in 1898; and one daughter Helen Catherine Theodora Rapp, born on 9 September, 1865, married to Richard M. Lewis. By 1914 she was Mrs. Helen Rapp Hasse of Branford.

William Rapp died in 1906 and was buried in Center Cemetery, Branford. There was a Civil War marker on his gravesite in 1934. He was born at Frankfort, Germany in 1820.

Clara T. Rapp of Branford applied for a widow's pension on 7 March 1907. She died at Branford on 8 February 1914 and was buried there in Center Cemetery.

RATH, GOTTFRIED or GODFREY
Co. C 15th CVI, enlisted 11 August 1862, discharged disability 29 December 1862, pension #356662 for the soldier and later for his widow Josephine

Gottfried Rath, age 43, of Branford enlisted at New Haven on 11 August 1862 and was mustered in on 25 August 1862 as a private in Co. C 15th CVI for a term of three years. He was soon sick in his quarters and left behind at a hospital at Fairfax Seminary, Virginia on 1 December 1862. He was discharged for disability at Fairfax Seminary, Virginia on 29 December 1862 for dysentery. He was then sent to the hospital at Fort Schuyler, New York and discharged from there on 5 January 1863.

He applied for and was granted a partial invalid pension on 15 December 1876. At the time of his enlistment he was described as six feet tall, light complexion, brown hair, grey eyes, occupation shoemaker. He also claimed that while guarding a well on Arlington Heights he was struck by a blow to the forehead and rendered unconscious. Since his discharge he lived at Branford and Derby.

Gottfried Rath died at Derby on 2 June 1886 and was buried in St. Mary's Cemetery, Ansonia. He was born at Hesse Cassel, Germany (Prussia).

Josephine Rath of Derby applied for a widow's pension on 27 October 1891. She was married to the soldier under the name of Josephine Becker[870] at New York City on 24 December 1855. Neither were previously married or divorced. They had the following children born at Branford: Charles, born on 18 February 1860; Sophia, born on 7 May 1862; Frederica, born on 20 December 1863; Albert, born on 3 November 1865; and Emma Caroline, born on 15 February 1868.

Josephine Rath died on 8 March 1915 and was buried in St. Mary's Cemetery, Ansonia.[871] She was born on 26 December 1837 at Hesse Cassel, Germany.

---

870   Her name is given as Becker in the pension file and Kuntensturf in the Branford Vital Records at the time of the children's births.
871   The Hale Collection, Ansonia.

REIF, CHRISTIAN or GEORGE C.

Co. C 11th CVI, sergeant, enlisted 25 September 1861, discharged 24 October 1864, pension #745505 for the soldier and later for his widow Emma

Christian Reif of North Branford enlisted at Hartford on 25 September 1861 and was mustered in on 27 November 1861 as a sergeant in Co. C 11th CVI for a term of three years. His rank was reduced on 25 June 1862. He was transferred to the 41st Company 2nd Regiment VRC on 30 September 1863 and discharged at Hartford on 24 October 1864.

He applied for an invalid pension on 26 April 1880 due to lung disease acquired while in the service. At New Bern, North Carolina on 14 March 1862 he had to wade ashore in the rain from the transports and caught a severe cold which still disables him. He was treated at Knight Hospital, New Haven from 1 October 1862 until 30 September 1863. At the time of his enlistment he was described as five feet five inches tall, light complexion, brown hair, grey eyes, occupation tinner. Before his enlistment he lived at Northford and New Haven and after the war at New Haven.

He was married at New Haven by Rev. C. J. Bendel on 5 April 1863 to Emma Lutters. He was age 26, born in Germany, living at New Haven; she was age 18, born in Germany, living at Long Island. They had the following children: George F., born on 12 July 1865; Lorenz E., born on 10 April 1869, living at New Haven in 1912; Carrie R., born on 15 Aug 1872; May L., born on 16 February 1878, living at New Haven in 1915, unmarried; Frederick W., born on 14 August 1882; and Robert B., born on 13 January 1884.

George Christian Reif died at New Haven on 29 May 1912 and was buried there in Evergreen Cemetery. His name appears on the Northford Veterans' Monument. He was born in Saxony, Germany on 25 December 1836, son of George Reif and Sophia Mueller.[872]

Emma Reif applied for a widow's pension on 8 June 1912. She died at New Haven on 20 April 1917 and was buried there in Evergreen Cemetery. She was born on 28 April 1845, daughter of Ferdinand Lutters and Antoinette Keuchman.[873]

REIF, LORENZ

Co. C 11th CVI, sergeant, enlisted 25 September 1861, discharged 24 October 1864, pension #243670 for his widow Louisa

Lorenz Reif of North Branford enlisted on 25 September 1861 and was mustered in at Hartford on 27 November 1861 as a corporal in Co. C 11th CVI for a term of three years. He was promoted to sergeant on 14 November 1862 and discharged on 24 October 1864. "While on duty at Slocum Creek near Newberne on 13 March 1862, the company had to jump in the water above their waists to wade ashore. They then marched five or six miles in wet clothes and barracked in the woods for the night in a heavy rain storm without shelter. Reif contracted a severe cold in his lungs resulting in typhoid fever. Afterwards he was not well and placed on light duty."[874]

Lorenz Reif died of lung disease at New Haven on 7 November 1874 age 35 and was buried there in Evergreen Cemetery. His company and regiment are engraved on his stone and his name appears on the Northford Veterans' Monument. He never applied for a pension.

---

872 The town of birth is given in the file as Grub? and in another place Mericengea?
873 New Haven Vital Records, deaths, 1917.
874 Deposition, Fred D. Schlachler, age 55 of New York City, 17 January 1887, in the pension file of Lorenz Reif.

Louisa Reif applied for a widow's pension on 20 August 1886. She was married to the soldier under the name of Louisa Heausmann at New Haven by Rev. William Henry Rice of the Moravian Church on 6 December 1863. He was age 24, born in Saxony, Germany and she was age 26, born in County Bern, Switzerland; both were living at New Haven. They had the following children: Ida Louisa, born on 14 August 1866; and Louisa Mina, born on 21 August 1872 who received a pension until the age of sixteen.

Louisa Reif died at New Haven[875] on 27 February 1921.

REYNOLDS, PETER F.
Co. C 9th CVI, private, enlisted 6 November 1862, discharged disability 27 November 1862, reenlisted 28 October 1863 Co. L 1st HA, corporal, mustered out 25 September 1865, pension #365944 for his widow Margaret

Peter F. Reynolds of New Haven first enlisted at New Haven on 6 November 1862 as a private in Co. C 9th CVI. He was discharged for disability at St. James Hospital, New Orleans on 27 November 1862 for typhoid fever. He reenlisted on 28 October 1863 and was mustered in on 28 November 1863 as a private in Co. L 1st HA for a term of three years. He participated in the Siege of Petersburg and Richmond, Virginia with the rest of his regiment and was promoted to corporal on 10 August 1865. Peter Reynolds was mustered out with the rest of his regiment at Washington, D.C. on 25 September 1865 and discharged at Hartford on 1 October 1865. He was a member of the Mason Rogers Post No. 7 G.A.R. of Branford.

Peter F. Reynolds died at Branford on 10 May 1889 age 48 years, 3 months & 28 days and was buried there in St. Mary's Cemetery. His company and regiment were engraved on his stone and there was a Civil War marker on his gravesite in 1934. He was born at New Haven, probably the son of Patrick and Catherine Reynolds. He never applied for a pension.

Margaret Reynolds of Branford applied for a widow's pension on 27 August 1890 under the act of 27 June 1890. She was married to the soldier under the name of Margaret O'Neil at New Haven by Rev. Matthew Hart of St. Patrick's Church on 30 October 1860. Neither were previously married or divorced. They had the following children under the age of sixteen at the time of his death: James Bernard, born on 25 September 1875; and Steven Vincent, born on 19 March 1881.

Margaret Reynolds died at Branford on 16 October 1901 and was buried there in St. Mary's Cemetery.[876] She was born in Ireland on 10 April 1841.[877]

REYNOLDS, STEPHEN
Co. C 5th CVI, private, enlisted 7 December 1864, discharged 17 May 1865, no pension

Stephen Reynolds of Branford enlisted and was mustered in on 7 December 1864 as a private in Co. C 5th CVI and was discharged on 17 May 1865. He does not appear in the 1860 census at Branford.

---

875 Information from the pension record; her death is not in the New Haven Vital Records.
876 Sexton Record 1884-1932, 66; there is no stone.
877 Her parents are not recorded on her death certificate.

RICH, JAMES S.
Co. C 12th CVI, private, enlisted 9 December 1861, prisoner, discharged 25 February 1865, pension #413119 for the soldier

James S. Rich of Chatham enlisted at Hartford on 9 December 1861 and was mustered in on 27 December 1861 as a private in Co. C 12th CVI for a term of three years. He was sick with malarial fever in hospitals at New Orleans and Franklin, Louisiana during the fall and winter of 1862. He was discharged at New Iberia, Louisiana on 31 December 1863 and re-enlisted the next day as a veteran in Co. C for a term of three years. He was captured at Cedar Creek, Virginia on 19 October 1864 with much of his regiment. He was brought from Lynchburg, Virginia and confined at Richmond on 23 October 1864 and moved to Andersonville Prison on 4 November 1864. He was transferred to Co. F 12th Battalion on 26 November 1864. He was paroled at Charleston, South Carolina on 16 December 1864 and reported to College Green Barracks, Maryland on 19 December. After a thirty day furlough, he returned to duty on 3 February 1865 and was in the hospital during February suffering from diarrhea contracted during his time in prison. He was released at Savannah, Georgia on 25 February 1865. He states he came home sick.

He applied for an invalid pension on 12 March 1888. At the age of eighty-six he was denied an increase in his pension because the pension board said "he was not totally blind." At the time of his enlistment he was described as five feet six inches tall, dark complexion, hazel eyes, brown hair, occupation farmer. He was married at East Hampton by Rev. B. B. Hopkinson of Middle Haddam on 28 November 1867 to Almyra E. Butler. Neither were previously married or divorced. She died at Branford on 15 December 1929 and was buried there in Center Cemetery.[878] They had the following children: Carrie (McMillan) born on 26 April 1869, living at Branford in 1929; Willie, born February 1871, died 1875; Anna, born March 1874, died 1875; and Albert S., born on 1 May 1878, living at New Haven in 1932. Since his discharge he lived at East Hampton (Chatham) from November 1865 until April 1881, Wethersfield from April 1881 until April 1885, New London from April 1885 until 1889 when he moved to Branford. He was a member and commander of the Mason Rogers Post No. 7 G.A.R. of Branford.

James Samuel Rich died at New Haven on 28 November 1932 and was buried in Center Cemetery, Branford.[879] He was born at Kinston, New York on 29 June 1842, son of Oliver Rich and Malantha Oliver.[880] When he died he was one of two remaining members of the Mason Rogers Post No. 7 G.A.R. of Branford.

---

878 Branford Vital Records, deaths, 1929.
879 Branford Sexton Records, 1884-1932, 139; Obituary, *The Branford Review*, 1 December 1932, 1. A G.A.R. marker on the gravesite of William Dutton nearby is probably his.
880 Branford Vital Records, deaths, 1932; his pension record states he was born on 12 June 1842 at Haddam. There is a record of the births of his siblings in the file.

Amos Roberts, Jr. served in the Civil War from Maine and came to New Haven and Branford after the war. He died at Stony Creek in 1926. He was active in the Branford, state and national G.A.R. and is shown here in his Grand Army of the Republic uniform. (Branford Historical Society photograph collection)

RILEY, THOMAS
Co. I 1st Cavalry, private, enlisted 9 October 1864, deserted 20 February 1865, no pension

Thomas Riley of Branford enlisted on 9 December 1864 as a private in Co. I 1st Connecticut Cavalry and deserted on 20 February 1865. He does not appear in the 1860 census at Branford.

ROBERTSON, ALEXANDER
Alexander Robertson, age 28, served as a substitute for Leverett Chidsey of North Branford. He was mustered in at New Haven on 18 August 1864 as a private in the 1st HA for a term of three years.[881] He was described as five foot three inches tall, grey eyes, dark hair, light complexion, married, born in Ireland, occupation bolt maker. His name does not appear in the 1860 census at Branford or North Branford.

ROBERTS, AMOS, JR.
Co. D 20th Maine Infantry, private, enlisted 29 August 1862, discharged disability 9 February 1864, reenlisted Maine 3rd Light Battery, enlisted 21 October 1864, discharged 17 June1865, pension #945675 for the soldier and later an application for his widow Kittie

Amos Roberts, Jr. of Gray, Maine, age 23, enlisted at Portland, Maine on 29 August 1862 as a private in Co. D 20th Maine Infantry. With his regiment he fought at the Battle of Gettysburg on 2 July 1863. He was discharged for disability from Finley Hospital, Washington, D.C. on 9 February 1864. He reenlisted at Bangor, Maine on 21 October 1864 as a private in the Maine 3rd Battery Light Artillery. The regiment was assigned to the defenses of Washington, D.C. and participated in the Siege of Petersburg, Virginia in 1865. He was discharged with the rest of his regiment at Augusta, Maine on 17 June 1865.

He applied for an invalid pension on 14 December 1896 under the act of 27 June 1890. At the time of his enlistment he was described as five feet six inches tall, dark complexion, grey eyes, dark hair, occupation shoemaker. On 25 September 1864 at Antietam, Maryland he contracted rheumatism and fever. He was discharged for disability due to a fall from an ambulance injuring his back and was transferred to the Invalid Corps. He was married first to Rebecca Pullin who died at Dexter, Maine. He could not remember the date of her death.[882] It appears he was married to Ella R. and

---

881   His service was not found in the *Record of Service of Connecticut Men*.
882   Family record, typescript, Jerald Greenvall 2011 - Rebecca J. Pullen was born in 1839 and died in 1887, buried in Mt. Pleasant Cemetery, Dexter, Maine.

lived at Haddam, Middlesex Co., Connecticut in 1870.[883] He had children by his first two wives. He states on his pension application that since his discharge he lived at Dexter, Maine until about 1868 and moved to New Haven. He was a member and commander for ten years of the Mason Rogers Post No. 7 G.A.R. of Branford. He was active in G.A.R. activities and was an aide de camp for the national organization in 1913 and 1916.

Amos B. Roberts, Jr. died at Stony Creek, Branford on 22 October 1926 and was buried there in Damascus Cemetery. "The passing of Commander Roberts takes away another old friend from our midst and a member of the G.A.R. which there are but a few left now."[884] His company and regiment are engraved on his stone and there was a G.A.R. marker on his gravesite in 1934 and 2011. He was born at Sangerville, Piscataquis Co., Maine on 8 October 1838, son of Amos Roberts and Christina Rising.[885]

Kittie A. Roberts of Branford applied for a widow's pension on 21 January 1927. She was married to the soldier under the name of Kittie A. Record[886] at New Haven by Rev. A. H. Weld on 13 March 1887. Kittie Roberts received a divorce from Amos Roberts, Jr. "through no fault of her own." She did not remarry after their divorce. They had two children (living in 1927): Sadie W., born on 16 August 1887; and Hazel M., born on 10 June 1890. There is no evidence in the file that Kittie received a pension and she was not given a certificate number.

Kittie A. Roberts died at Branford on 5 July 1952 and was buried there in Damascus Cemetery.[887] She was born at Poughkeepsie, New York on 23 July 1862; daughter of William Henry Record and Marguerite Ayers.

ROBINSON, HENRY P.
Co. D 15th CVI, private, enlisted 11 August 1862, to Co. A 13th VRC, discharged disability 19 April 1864, pension #XC968833 for the soldier and later for his widow Minnie

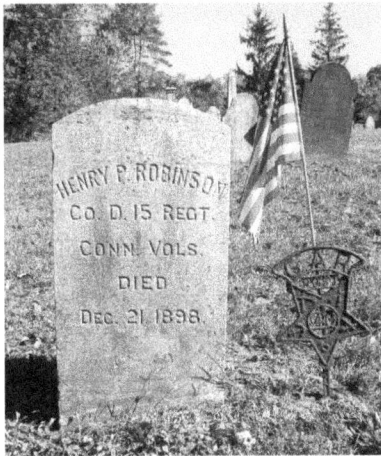

Henry P. Robinson, age 22, of Branford enlisted at New Haven on 11 August 1862 and was mustered in on 25 August 1862 as a private in Co. D 15th CVI for a term of three years. During 1862 he was detailed as a hospital nurse. He was sent to the hospital sick at Acquia Creek, Virginia on 24 January 1863 and later to a hospital in Washington, D.C. He was transferred to Co. A 13th VRC on 9 July 1863 and discharged for disability on 19 April 1864. His pension is at the Veterans Administration.

He applied for an invalid pension on 20 February 1893 under the act of 27 June 1890. At the time of his enlistment he was described as five feet nine inches tall, dark complexion, brown eyes, black hair, occupation farmer, born at North Haven. He does not appear in the 1860 census at Branford but is probably the Henry P. Robinson living

---

883 U.S. census 1870, Haddam, Middlesex Co., population schedule M593-107, dwelling 275, family 280, page 181A; she was born in Conn., www.ancestry.com.

884 Obituary of Amos Roberts, *The Shore Line Times*, 28 October 1926, 8.

885 As recorded in the Roberts bible; in 1907 owned by Simeon R. Roberts of Corinna, Maine; in the pension file of Amos B. Roberts, Jr.

886 His pension application gives her name as Kittie Kimball. All other records and her family confirm her name was Kittie (Kittendean) Record, daughter of William Henry Record and Marguerite Ayers.

887 Branford Vital Records, deaths, 1952.

at Derby in 1850 with Charles F. and Mary C. Robinson. Henry appears at Oxford with the same family in 1870 and with Mary C. Robinson at Guilford in 1880.

Henry P. Robinson died at Oxford on 21 December 1898 and was buried there in Jack's Hill Cemetery. His company and regiment are engraved on his stone and there was a Civil War marker at the gravesite in 1934.

Minnie Robinson applied for a widow's pension on 28 February 1899. She is perhaps the Minnie Robinson of Prospect who died at Naugatuck on 15 February 1954 age 89, widow of Henry.[888]

JOHN S. ROBINSON
CO. F 27. C.V. DIED AT BALTIMORE M.D.
JUNE 19. 1863. Æ. 27.
DAYTON R. SCRANTON
CO. F 12 C.V. DIED IN L. A. DEC. 15. 1863. Æ.

ROBINSON, JOHN S.
Co. F 27th CVI, private, enlisted 10 September 1862, died 18 June 1863, pension #116227 for his mother Almira Robinson

John S. Robinson of North Branford enlisted at New Haven on 10 September 1862 and was mustered in on 3 October 1862 as a private in Co. F 27th CVI for a term of nine months. He was on picket duty during the Battle of Chancellorsville. John Robinson died at McKinns General Hospital, Baltimore, Maryland on 18 June 1863 age 27 of sickness. There is gravestone for him at Bare Plain Cemetery and Civil War maker was on his gravesite in 1934. His name is inscribed on the North Branford Soldiers' Monument.

His mother Almira Robinson of North Branford applied for a pension on 6 June 1868 under the act of 14 July 1862. Her husband and father of the soldier, Salmon Robinson was an invalid for many years. Salmon Robinson died at North Branford on 29 September 1870 age 76 and Almira Robinson died on 26 December 1888.

ROBINSON, LORENZO
Co. D 27th CVI, private, enlisted 1 September 1862, reenlisted Co. F 6th CVI, discharged 17 August 1865, pension #453693 for the soldier and later for his widow Eunice

Lorenzo Robinson, age 37, of New Haven enlisted at New Haven on 1 September 1862 and was mustered in on 3 October 1862 as a private in Co. D 27th CVI for a term of nine months. He was discharged for disability at General Hospital Summit House, Philadelphia on 21 April 1862 due to a gunshot wound to his left hand. He reenlisted on 13 August 1863 in Co. F 6th CVI and was discharged on 17 August 1865. After the war he enlisted on 28 August 1867 in Co. I 8th U.S. Infantry. He was reported as deserted in July 1868, was apprehended on 9 December 1871, tried and sentenced to confinement. Lorenzo Robinson was retained in the service to make good the time lost and was discharged on 10 January 1874.

---

888   Connecticut Death Index 1949-2001, www.familysearch.com.

He applied for an invalid pension on 10 January 1891 under the act of 27 June 1890. At the time of his enlistment he was described as five feet eight inches tall, light complexion, dark eyes, brown hair, occupation farmer, born at North Branford. He received a gunshot wound to his left hand while on duty near Chain Bridge in November 1862 from an accidental discharge of a gun. After his discharge he lived at Branford, North Haven, New Haven, and moved to Durham in 1893. He was married first at Branford by Rev. Timothy P. Gillett of the First Congregational Church on 26 January 1857 to Mary Rogers.[889] They were divorced in May 1866.

Lorenzo D. Robinson died at New Haven on 30 September 1896. He was living at Durham but was in New Haven looking for work.

Eunice L. Robinson of Durham applied for a widow's pension on 13 November 1896. She was married first at Roxbury by Rev. A. Isham under the name of Eunice L. Harris to Elsworth A. Blakeley [Blakeslee] on 2 April 1871. He was age 23, living at Hamden; she was age 22, living at Roxbury. Blakeslee died at Wallingford on 17 January 1882. She was married to the soldier under the name of Eunice Laura Blakeslee at Hartford by Rev. George Leon Walker on 20 October 1887. He was age 50, a widower, living at South Glastonbury, born at North Branford; she was age 38, a widow, living at East Hartford, born at Roxbury. They had no children.

Her application was sent for special examination because Lorenzo Robinson's death record at New Haven stated he was divorced. Affidavits in the file confirm the divorce referred to his first marriage only. Lydia E. Babson of New Haven testified that she knew Robinson was divorced from his first wife Mary. That she (Babson) "was engaged to him for 15 years and he always said he was divorced. I didn't marry him because he was a wild, drinking man."[890]

Eunice L. Robinson was killed on 3 October 1917 in an automobile accident.

ROGERS, ALBERT T.
31st Virginia Artillery, drafted 11 September 1861, ambulance corps

Albert T. Rogers was born at Branford on 15 April 1833, son of Henry Rogers and Nancy Towner.[891] He moved to Virginia in 1857 for his health and owned a farm near Lynchburg. He was drafted into the Confederate Army at Richmond on 11 September 1861 for a term of three years and was a member of Capt. Kirkpatrick's Company of the 31st Virginia Light Artillery serving under Stonewall Jackson. He was detailed for work in the hospitals and as an ambulance driver serving at Antietam and in twenty-one other engagements.

He was married in Virginia on 4 July 1860 to Jane Malone Drumheller. The family returned to Branford in September 1865. They had nine children born in Virginia and Branford. She died at Branford on 2 March 1908 and was buried there in Center Cemetery. She was born at Amherst, Virginia on 24 July 1836, daughter of John Drumheller and Susan Heaster.[892]

---

889 Branford Vital Records, 1852-1863, 9.
890 Affidavit, Lydia E. Babson of New Haven, 23 September 1897, in the pension file of Lorenzo Robinson.
891 Branford Vital Records, 1786-1840, 368.
892 Branford Vital Records, deaths, 1908.

Mason Rogers of Branford was a sergeant in Co. B 15th CVI and was the first soldier of the 15th to die of yellow fever at New Bern, North Carolina in 1864. The Branford G.A.R. post was named for him. (Photographs: a. Burwell & Homan Studio, New Haven; b. Filley & Gilbert Studio, New Haven; all from Branford Historical Society photograph collection.)

Albert Towner Rogers died at Branford on 4 October 1911 and was buried there in Center Cemetery. His gravestone reads "31st Va. Lt. Art. C.S.A." and a G.A.R. marker was on his gravesite in 1934.

ROGERS, HENRY
see Peter Sundelas

ROGERS, MASON
Co. B 15th CVI, sergeant, enlisted 28 July 1862, died 9 September 1864, no pension

Mason Rogers, age 18, of New Haven enlisted on 28 July 1862 and was mustered in on 25 August 1862 as 3rd sergeant in Co. B 15th CVI for a term of three years. He was sick in his quarters and left sick in the hospital at Camp Casey near Fairfax Seminary, Virginia in 1862. He was transferred to Fort Wood General Hospital, Bedloe's Island, New York Harbor and returned to his regiment on 3 February 1863. On 16 July 1863 he was on detached service at the Draft Rendezvous Station in New Haven and returned to his regiment on 22 April 1864. He was on guard duty at the Pollock Street jail from May until August 1864. Mason Rogers died at Regimental Hospital in New Bern, North Carolina on 9 September 1864 of yellow fever, the first of the 15th CVI to die of the disease that decimated the ranks. He was buried in Union Cemetery, New Bern.[893] His effects, consisting of a cap, great coat, trousers, blanket, haversack, knapsack, canteen, and rubber blanket were turned over to his friends. "Doctor Holcomb took care of Mason Rogers but Mason was taken sick down town and the doctor did not get to him soon enough perhaps."[894] Rogers was described as a "Good Soldier."

---

893   *The Connecticut War Record*, December 1864, 2:5:336.
894   Towner letter, 25 September 1864.

He was born at Branford on 25 April 1844, son of Elizur Rogers and Sally Foote.[895] At the time of his enlistment he was described as five feet four inches tall, light complexion, hazel eyes, dark hair, occupation printer. Before the war he was a member of the New Haven Grays. "Mason, a youth of much promise, enlisted in the 15th regiment of Connecticut volunteers, and having secured the affection and esteem of all his associates, died of fever at Newbern, North Carolina."[896]

The Grand Army of the Republic Post No. 7 of Branford was named for him. His name is on the New Haven Soldiers and Sailors Monument on East Rock.

ROGERS, WALTER
Co. B 1st Cavalry, private, enlisted 28 October 1861, to Co. C & F U.S. 4th Infantry, discharged 2 November 1864, reenlisted 22 November 1875, died 14 July 1878, pension #196400 for his widow Esther

Walter Rogers of Branford enlisted on 28 October 1861 and was mustered in at Meriden on 2 November 1861 as a private in Co. B 1st Connecticut Cavalry. In March and April 1862 he was sick on furlough at home in Stony Creek. He was transferred to Co. C 4th U.S. Infantry at Washington, D.C. on 24 November 1862 and the company was reorganized in 1864 as Co. F. He was a private select recruit working in the general mounted service and was discharged at City Point, Virginia on 2 November 1864. He reenlisted in the regular army at New York City on 22 November 1875 for a term of three years. Walter Rogers died at Jefferson Barracks, Missouri on 14 July 1878 of sun stroke. He was on a day's pass and the cause of his death was debated in the pension file, possibly attributed to drinking. He was the son of Isaac Rogers and Sally Franklin of Branford.

Esther Rogers received a widow's pension on 8 March 1879. She was married to the soldier under the name of Esther Shanley at St. Patrick's Church, New Haven by Rev. Hart on 12 August 1868. He was age 24, born at Branford; she was age 21, born in Ireland; both were living at New Haven. She was married second at New York City on 16 July 1884 to Mr. Redmonds as his first wife. He was born in Ireland, son of Michael Redmonds and Sarah Murphy and died at New Haven on 5 December 1896 age 43. She was married third at St. Mary's Church, New Haven by Rev. H. F. Lilly on 28 August 1900 to David J. Shields. He was a widower; born in Ireland and died at New Haven on 26 January 1903 age 62 years, 11 months & 24 days. She had several pension applications and rejections due to her remarriages and was finally granted a pension under a Special Act of Congress on 11 July 1918; she was a cripple, living at the Hospital of St. Raphaels in New Haven. There are letters in the file from her sister-in-law Mrs. Bernard J. Shanley; from John F. Shanley of New Haven; a cousin Esther Shanley; and Walter Roger's brother Frederick Rogers of Branford.

Esther Shanley Shields died at New Haven on 28 February 1923 and was buried there in St. Bernard's Cemetery. She was born in Ireland, daughter of John Shanley and Esther Reynolds.

ROSE, VIRGIL H.
see Lawrence Brown

---

895   Branford Vital Records, Town Meeting Book A, 231.
896   Obituary for his brother Frank A. Rogers, *New Haven Daily Palladium*, 23 January 1866.

The 1st Connecticut Heavy Artillery fought at the Battle of Chickahominy, Virginia on 27 June 1862. (Library of Congress, Prints & Photographs Division, LC-DIG-cwpb-03792)

ROWLAND, GEORGE H.

Co. F 1st HA, private, enlisted 23 May 1861, mustered out 26 September 1865, pension #670393 for his minor child Pearl

George H. Rowland of Branford enlisted and was mustered in at Hartford on 23 May 1861 as a private in Co. F 4th CVI which became the 1st HA. With his regiment he fought at Chickahominy and Malvern Hill, Virginia. He was mustered out on 2 February 1864 and reenlisted the same day as a veteran in Co. F. He deserted on 19 March 1865 while on furlough but reported back to duty on 8 April 1865. He participated in the Siege of Petersburg and Richmond, Virginia with the rest of his regiment. Rowland was mustered out at Washington, D.C. on 25 September 1865 and discharged at Hartford on 1 October 1865. He was the brother-in-law of George G. Bradley and Clifford Francisco.

Since his discharge he lived at Branford and New Haven. He was married at Branford by Rev. Elijah C. Baldwin of the First Congregational Church on 14 November 1866 to Ann A. Francisco. He was age 27, born at New York City; she was age 24, born at Williamsport, New Jersey; both living at Branford.[897] She died on 13 February 1894 and was buried in Evergreen Cemetery, New Haven.[898] She was born on 3 July 1843, daughter of Thomas Francisco and was the sister of soldier Clifford Francisco. Rowland was a member of the Admiral Foote Post No. 17 G.A.R. of New Haven.

George Henry Rowland died at New Haven on 27 January 1898 and was buried there in Evergreen Cemetery.[899] There was a Civil War marker on his gravesite in 1934. He was born at New York City on 7 December 1838, son of John Rogers Rowland and Mary Ann Lanfare of Branford. John Rowland of New Haven, guardian of George Rowland's minor child Pearl applied for a pension on 10 February 1898. Pearl V. Rowland was born on 2 October 1885.

---

897   Branford Vital Records, 1863-1895, 135.
898   The Hale Collection, New Haven, 886.
899   *The Branford Opinion,* 5 February 1898.

ROWLEY, AUGUSTUS R.
see Alfred DeBacque

RUSSELL, ALFRED
Co. H 13th CVI, sergeant, enlisted 18 January 1862, wounded, discharged 6 January 1865, pension #473703 for the soldier and later for his widow Sophia

Alfred Russell of North Branford enlisted and was mustered in at New Haven on 18 January 1862 as a private in Co. H 13th CVI for a term of three years. He was promoted to sergeant on 21 June 1862 and to first or orderly sergeant on 1 January 1863. He was "dangerously" wounded by a gunshot to the shoulders and neck at the Battle of Irish Bend, Louisiana on 14 April 1863. After the battle he was treated in a converted sugar-house used as the field hospital and transferred to the University Hospital at New Orleans. "The night was very dark and cold. Groping in the dark I found my first-sergeant. He had been shot through the neck; yet as if by some miracle, the wound was not fatal. He was suffering from cold and thirst, and faint from the loss of blood. Throwing my blanket over the poor fellow, I returned to camp and brought him a canteen of hot coffee and some food for him and for my other wounded."[900] "He was severely wounded at the battle of Irish Bend and was left for dead on the battlefield, but was later found by Colonel Homer B. Sprague and cared for."[901] He was in a hospital in Connecticut December 1863. His rank was reduced to sergeant on 1 October 1864 and he was in the hospital or on detached duty for the rest of his enlistment. Alfred Russell was mustered out at New Haven on 6 January 1865. He was the brother of Martha Russell, a Civil War correspondent.

He applied for an invalid pension on 18 March 1865 due to his wounds. Also, at Cedar Creek, Virginia on 1 October 1864 he contracted rheumatism. He was married first at North Branford by Rev. John

(Photograph from the author's collection)

---

900 Sprague, *History of the 13th Regiment*, 120.
901 Hill, *Modern History of New Haven*, II:681.

Baldwin of the Congregational Church on 6 March 1845 to Caroline M. Harrison.[902] She died at North Branford on 15 August 1867 and was buried there in the Congregational Cemetery. He was married second at North Branford on 10 December 1878 to Sophie T. Abbot. She was divorced from her first husband in September 1878.

Alfred Russell died at North Branford on 7 October 1895 and was buried there in the Congregational Cemetery. He was born on 22 July 1818, son of Augustus Russell and Lydia Rose.[903]

Sophia T. Russell applied for a widow's pension on 7 November 1895. She was born at St. Johns, New Brunswick, Canada on 14 February 1844. In 1899 she was living at Guilford and 1916 at New Haven. She died at New Haven on 5 June 1917 and was buried in Alderbrook Cemetery, Guilford.[904]

RUSSELL, CHARLES
Co. L 2nd HA, private, enlisted 8 February 1864, deserted 25 February 1864, no pension

Charles Russell of Branford enlisted on 8 February 1864 as a private in Co. L 2nd HA and deserted on 25 February 1864. He was perhaps Charles William Russell, born on 10 July 1836, son of Richard Russell and Lucretia Bradley Moulthrop of North Branford. Charles William Russell went to Mobile, Alabama.[905]

RUSSELL, JOHN B.
see Charles Ames

RUSSELL, MERRICK M.
see James Martin

SANFORD, DANIEL
Co. F 9th CVI & Co. C 9th Battalion, private, enlisted 12 April 1864, no pension

Daniel Sanford of Guilford enlisted on 12 April 1864 as a private in Co. C 9th Battalion. He was transferred on 22 April 1864 to Co. F 9th CVI. There is no further record in the file. He does not appear in the 1860 census at Branford at North Branford. His name is on the Northford Veterans' Monument.

SCHAFFER, HENRY L. alias JOHN H. SCHAFFER
Co. D 5th CVI, private, drafted 25 July 1863, wounded, mustered out 19 July 1865, pension #927706 for the soldier and later for his widow Wilhelmina

Henry L. Schaffer of Branford served as a substitute or was drafted on 25 July 1863 as a private in Co. D 5th CVI. He was wounded on the skirmish line at Marietta, Georgia on 19 June 1864 and mustered out with the rest of the regiment at Alexandria, Virginia on 19 July 1865. He does not appear in the 1860 census at Branford.

He applied for an invalid pension on 28 August 1890 under the act of 27 June 1890.

---

902   North Branford Vital Records, I:36B.
903   Alfred Lovell Russell, *Ancestry of Alfred Russell and Caroline Harrison*, privately printed, 1928.
904   New Haven Vital Records, her maiden name is given as Traer.
905   Talcott, *Families of Guilford*, 1033.

Henry L. Schaffer, alias John H., died at Brooklyn, New York on 24 August 1922. Wilhelmina Schaffer applied for a widow's pension on 1 September 1922.

SCHENCK, PAUL
Co. K 27th CVI, enlisted 15 September 1862, mustered out 27 July 1865, pension #758827 for the soldier and later for his widow Jennette

Paul Schenck of Branford enlisted at New Haven on 15 September 1862 and was mustered in on 3 October 1862 as a private in Co. K 27th CVI for a term of nine months. It appears he fought at the Battles of Fredericksburg, Chancellorsville, and Gettysburg. Schenck was mustered out with the rest of his regiment at New Haven on 27 July 1865.

He applied for an invalid pension on 26 April 1901 for age related illnesses. He was described as five feet seven inches tall, brown eyes, black hair, dark complexion, occupation blacksmith. He was married at Branford by Rev. Ralph Bowles of the First Baptist Church on 31 December 1856 to Julia Jennette Palmer. Neither were previously married or divorced. They had the following children (living in 1901): Fannie Augusta, born on 21 July 1859[906]; Lucy Jeanette, born on 14 February 1861; Joseph, born on 21 July 1864; and William, born on 21 March 1867. Since his discharge he lived at Branford. He was a member of the Mason Rogers Post No. 7 of Branford.

Paul Schenck died at Branford on 22 January 1913 and was buried there in Center Cemetery. A G.A.R. marker was on his gravesite in 1934 and 2011. He was born at Rosenberg, Kingdom of Wertenberg, Germany on 12 November 1836.

Jennette Schenck applied for widow's pension on 15 February 1913. She died at Branford on 7 November 1920 and was buried there in Center Cemetery. She was born at East Haven on 14 October 1840, daughter of Joel Palmer.[907]

SCRANTON, DAYTON H.
Co. H 2nd CVI & Co. F 12th CVI, enlisted 4 November 1861, wounded, died 18 December 1863, no pension

Dayton H. Scranton of North Branford enlisted at New Haven on 23 April 1861 and was mustered in on 7 May 1861 as a private in Co. H 2nd CVI, also known as Rifle Co. D. He was mustered out at New Haven on 7 August 1861 when his term expired. He reenlisted on 4 November 1861 as a sergeant in Co. F 12th CVI for a term of three years. Dayton Scranton was wounded at Port Hudson, Louisiana on 14 June 1863 and died on 18 December 1863 from his wounds. His name is inscribed on the North Branford Soldiers' Monument.

---

906   or born 20 July 1859, Branford Vital Records, 1852-1863, 19.

907   Her birth date and place were given by her in a letter to the pension board on 26 September 1916. Her death certificate at Branford gives her birth date as 14 October 1839 at North Branford.

He was born on 22 January 1840, son of Martin Scranton and Sarah Francis of North Branford.[908] He was one of four brothers who died in the war.

SCRANTON, FRANCIS S.
Co. H 2nd CVI & Co. I 14th CVI, corporal, enlisted 23 April 1861, wounded, died 13 December 1862, no pension

Francis S. Scranton of North Branford enlisted at New Haven on 23 April 1861 and was mustered in on 7 May 1861 as a private in Co. H 2nd CVI, also known as Rifle Co. D. He was mustered out at New Haven on 7 August 1861 when his term expired. He reenlisted, then of Guilford, on 15 August 1863 as a corporal of Co. I 14th CVI for a term of three years. Francis Scranton was severely wounded in the chest at the Battle of Fredericksburg, Virginia on 13 December 1862 and died the same day.

He was born on 6 December 1836, son of Martin Scranton and Sarah Francis of North Branford.[909] He was one of four brothers who died in the war.

SCRANTON, HENRY W.
Co. K 15th CVI, corporal, enlisted 11 August 1862, discharged 5 July 1865, no pension

Henry W. Scranton, age 26, of North Branford enlisted at New Haven on 11 August 1862 and was mustered in on 25 August 1862 as a private in Co. K 15th CVI for a term of three years. He saw action at the Battle of Fredericksburg on 13 December 1862 and at the Siege of Suffolk, Virginia in April 1863. From May through October 1863 he was detailed to the Pioneer Corps in the Peninsula Campaign and promoted to corporal on 1 June 1863. He was left sick at Balfour Hospital in Portsmouth, Virginia on 21 January 1864 and transferred to Knight Hospital, New Haven. He returned to duty on 23 July 1864. On 1 September 1864 his rank was reduced because of continued absence from the regiment. In November and December 1864 he was detached to Fort Hood, New York harbor in Company A Permanent Party until his discharge. Henry Scranton was discharged at New York City on 5 July 1865.

At the time of his enlistment he was described as five feet nine inches tall, fair complexion, blue eyes, sandy hair, occupation farmer. He was born at North Madison on 1 October 1835, son of John William Scranton and Lois Ann Hart of North Branford.[910] He was married to Rosanna Mack and was living at North Branford in 1870 and Huntington, Fairfield Co. in 1880. He did not apply for a pension. His name appears on the Northford Veterans' Monument.

SCRANTON, JAMES H.
Co. F 12th CVI, private, reenlisted, wounded, prisoner, died 27 January 1865, no pension

James H. Scranton, age 18, of North Branford enlisted at New Haven on 30 October 1861 and was mustered in on 19 November 1861 as a private in Co. F 12th CVI for a term of three years. In October 1863 he was sick in the hospital at New Orleans and reenlisted at New Orleans as a veteran in Co. F on 1 January 1864. He was wounded at the Battle of Winchester, Virginia on 19 September 1864. He was captured

908 Talcott, *Families of Guilford*, 1054.
909 Talcott, *Families of Guilford*, 1054.
910 Taloctt, *Families of Guilford*, 1051.

at Cedar Creek, Virginia on 19 October 1864, taken from Lynchburg to Richmond on 23 October 1864 and sent to Salisbury Prison on 4 November 1864. He was admitted to the hospital at Salisbury, North Carolina where he died on 27 January 1865 and was buried in a mass grave at Salisbury. At the time of his enlistment he was described as tan complexion, blue eyes, sandy hair, occupation farmer.

James H. Scranton was born on 23 February 1842 at North Branford, son of Martin Scranton and Sarah Francis.[911] He was one of four brothers who died in the war. His name is inscribed on the North Branford Soldiers' Monument.

SCRANTON, THOMAS MARVIN
Co. I 14th CVI, private, enlisted 15 August 1862, prisoner, died 3 January 1863, pension #86932 for his widow Mary

Thomas Marvin Scranton of Guilford enlisted at Hartford on 15 August 1862 and was mustered in on 23 August 1862 as a private in Co. I 14th CVI for a term of three years. He was captured at the Battle of Antietam, Maryland on 17 September 1862 and held prisoner. He was paroled on 16 November 1862 and was subsequently sick in camp. He was transferred to Lincoln General Hospital, Washington, D.C. on 26 December 1862 and died there on 3 January 1863 of encephalitis. Before the battle he was "an able and efficient soldier." Thomas M. Scranton was born at Guilford on 15 August 1824, son of Martin Scranton and Sarah Francis of Guilford and North Branford.[912] He was one of four brothers who died in the Civil War.

Mary Scranton of Branford applied for a widow's pension on 1 April 1865 and retained Henry Rogers of Branford as her attorney. She was living at Branford in 1870, age 53, a housekeeper with a child T. Mary Scranton, age 9. The 1880 census for Branford states she was divorced, age 63, living in the household of William D. Smith. She appears as a pensioner at Branford in 1883. She was married first at Branford by Rev. Timothy P. Gillette of the First Congregational Church on 20 August 1833 to John Gordon.[913] It appears they were divorced and he died in 1883.[914] She was married second as Mary Gordon at East Haven by Rev. William E. Vibbert on 17 April 1853 to Thomas Marvin Scranton.

Mary Scranton died at Branford on 22 February 1893[915] and was buried there in Center Cemetery.[916] She was born at Branford on 12 April 1817, daughter of James Beers and Mary Hopson.[917]

911   Talcott, *Families of Guilford*, 1054.
912   Talcott, *Families of Guilford*, 1054.
913   Branford Vital Records, 1786-1840, 361; Talcott calls her Mary Beers Gordon.
914   John Gordon died at Branford on 31 May 1883 and was buried there in Center Cemetery. He and Mary had four children.
915   Branford Vital Records, deaths, 1893, called "nee Mary Beers."
916   Trinity Episcopal Church Record, 176/7; no stone is listed in the Hale Collection.
917   Branford Vital Records, 1786-1840, 406.

SHANLEY, PATRICK
12th CVI, drafted 25 November 1864, failed to report, no pension

Patrick Shanley of Branford was drafted on 25 November 1864 and was unassigned in the 12th CVI. He was transferred to the regiment on 26 December 1864 but failed to report. There was no further record.

SHEPARD, CHARLES B.
Co. E 5th CVI & Co. A 10th CVI, enlisted 22 June 1861, wounded, discharged 15 June 1865, pension #600963 for the soldier and later for his widow Harriet

Charles B. Shepard, age 18, of Branford enlisted and was mustered in at Hartford on 22 June 1861 as a private in Co. E 5th CVI for a term of four years. From 25 December 1861 until 28 April 1862 he was sick and later served as a nurse. He was discharged for disability from Douglas Hospital, Washington, D.C. on 26 August 1862. He was the brother of Harvey G., John F., and Samuel S. Shepard.

He reenlisted at New Haven on 30 August 1862 as a private in Co. A 10th CVI for a term of three years. He was wounded at Kinston, North Carolina on 14 December 1862 in the right hand with the loss of one finger and a severe fracture of another. He was in Knight Hospital, New Haven or on furlough from 19 January 1863 until October 1863 and returned to duty. He was wounded again while on picket duty at Deep Bottom, Virginia on 1 August 1864. He was treated in General Hospital at Fort Monroe until October and at Knight Hospital, New Haven until February 1865. Charles Shepard was mustered out at Richmond, Virginia on 15 June 1865.

He applied for an invalid pension on 16 May 1892 under the act of 27 June 1890 for age related illnesses. At the time of enlistment he was described as five feet eight inches tall, dark complexion, blue eyes, brown hair, occupation farmer. He was married at Hartford by Rev. A. M. Smith on 13 July 1861 to Harriet Plaskett. Neither were previously married or divorced. They had the following children (living in 1899): Frederick Hudson, born on 8 July 1863; Curtiss Day, born on 27 September 1865; Harry Liston, born on 25 July 1867; C. Franklyn, born on 15 March 1872; Emma Gertrude, born on 7 August 1874; and Grace Rebecca, born on 21 August 1884. Since his discharge he lived at Branford in 1865, New Haven 1866 until about 1880, to Claremont, Virginia; and returned to New Haven in 1883 or 1884.

Charles Benjamin Shepard died at New Haven on 4 March 1905 and was buried there in Evergreen Cemetery. He was born at Branford on 3 September 1843, son of Benjamin Tyler Shepard and Hannah Stent.

Harriet Shepard of New Haven applied for a widow's pension on 11 May 1905. She was born at London, England on 3 October 1843, daughter of James Plaskett and Rebecca Rexworthy.[918] She died at West Haven on 29 May 1927 and was buried in Evergreen Cemetery, New Haven.[919]

---

918 Shepard, Gerald Faulkner, *The Shepard Families of New England* (New Haven: New Haven Colony Historical Society, 1971), I:445.
919 The Hale Collection, New Haven, 691.

SHEPARD, HARVEY G.
Co. B 13th CVI, private, enlisted 11 January 1862, discharged disability 15 June 1862, Co. B 27th CVI, private, reenlisted 10 September 1862, discharged 26 January 1863, pension #725287 for the soldier and later for his widow Mary

Harvey G. Shepard of Branford first enlisted at New Haven on 11 January 1862 and was mustered in on 22 January 1862 as a private in Co. B 13th CVI for a term of three years. He was discharged on 15 June 1862 for disability. While in the 13th he received a thigh injury from a shell or shot during battle. "He was discharged from the 13th while lying at New Orleans in July." He reenlisted on 10 September 1862 and was mustered in on 3 October 1862 as a private in Co. B 27th CVI for a term of nine months. In January 1863 he was sick in the hospital and was discharged on 26 January 1863 by General Couch from camp at Falmouth, Va. for disability. He was the brother of Charles B., John F., and Samuel S. Shepard.

He applied for an invalid pension on 4 January 1908. At the time of his enlistment he was described as six feet tall, light complexion, grey eyes, brown hair, occupation mechanic. "The cause of his disability was unavoidable from exposure at camp producing Rheumatism which renders him unfit for duty. He was injured in the war which caused him to limp." Since his discharge he lived at Branford, New Haven, Bridgeport, and spent summers at Short Beach, Branford. He was a member of the Admiral Foote Post No. 17 G.A.R. of New Haven.

He was married at North Madison by Rev. Phineas Blakeman of the 2nd Congregational Church on 17 January 1855 to Mary Caroline Johnson. He was age 20, born at Branford; she was age 16, born at Madison. They had the following children (living in 1908): Webster G., born on 5 September 1862; Mrs. Clara A. Thayer, born on 21 March 1859; John F., born on 10 January 1865; Arthur L., born on 25 October 1866; Mrs. Elsie L. Conger, born on 27 February 1872; and Homer H., born on 22 October 1877.

Harvey Gerald Shepard died at Shepard's Point, Branford on 22 April 1911 and was buried there in Center Cemetery. His company and regiment are engraved on his stone and a G.A.R. marker was on his gravesite in 1934. He was born at Branford on 25 July 1834, son of Benjamin Tyler Shepard and Hannah Stent, both born at Branford. He was a member of the Mason Rogers Post No. 7 G.A.R. of Branford.

Mary C. Shepard applied for a widow's pension on 6 May 1911. She was blind for over thirty years and lived at 27 Woolsey Street, New Haven with her daughter. In the file is a statement from her sister Clarissa A. Lane, age 70; and from her brother Leander F. Johnson. There is also a statement from Mary's sister-in-law Amelia W. Dorman, age 73, whose first husband was Samuel S. Shepard.

Mary C. Shepard died at New Haven on 11 April 1914 and was buried in Center Cemetery, Branford. She was born at North Madison on 18 March 1838, daughter of Luman Johnson and Eliza Crampton.

SHEPARD, JOHN F.

Co. A 10th CVI, private, enlisted 27 September 1861, wounded, prisoner, died 23 October 1864, pension #64991 for his mother Hannah Shepard

John Ford Shepard of Branford enlisted and was mustered in at Hartford on 27 September 1861 as a private in Co. A 10th CVI for a term of three years. With the rest of the regiment he fought at the Battle of Roanoke Island, North Carolina on 8 February 1862 and was wounded at Kinston, North Carolina on 14 December 1862. He was captured in a skirmish at St. Augustine, Florida on 30 December 1863 and died in Andersonville Prison at Millen, Georgia on 23 October 1864. There is a gravestone for him in Center Cemetery, Branford which reads "died in prison pens of Andersonville and Millen." He was born at Branford on 31 March 1841, son of Benjamin Tyler Shepard and Hannah Stent.[920] He was the brother of Charles B., Harvey G., and Samuel S. Shepard all of whom fought in the Civil War. His father Benjamin T. Shepard died at Branford on 27 October 1844.

His mother Hannah Shepard applied for a pension on 24 February 1865. She was dependent on her son for support and for five years before his enlistment he furnished provisions and necessaries for the family. While in the service he regularly sent his mother money.

Hannah Stent Shepard died at New Haven on 3 April 1898 and was buried there in Evergreen Cemetery.[921] Her gravestone reads "she gave her four sons to the Union Army."[922]

SHEPARD, LEWIS F.

see Daniel Sherman

SHEPARD, SAMUEL S.

Co. A 10th CVI, private, enlisted 8 September 1862, wounded, discharged 15 June 1865, pension #251403 for the soldier, his widow Amelia and daughter Lizzie L. Shepard

Samuel S. Shepard of Branford enlisted and was mustered in at New Haven on 8 September 1862 as a private in Co. A 10th CVI for a term of three years. With the regiment he fought at the Battle of Roanoke Island, North Carolina on 8 February 1862. He was severely wounded in the right arm at Kinston, North Carolina on 14 December 1862. He was admitted to Stanley Hospital at New Bern and was sent to Knight Hospital, New Haven on 19 January 1863 where he stayed nearly two years or was on furlough. He returned to the regiment in December 1864 but never returned to active duty, working in the hospitals. He was discharged at Richmond, Virginia on 15 June 1865 and after his discharge he was sick in Knight Hospital. He was the brother of Charles B., John F., and Harvey G. Shepard.

He applied for an invalid pension on 5 October 1865. At the time of his enlistment he was described as five feet eleven inches tall, light complexion, blue eyes, dark hair, occupation blacksmith. After his dis-

920   Branford Vital Records, Town Meeting Book A, 231.
921   *The Branford Opinion*, 9 April 1898.
922   Gerald Shepard, *The Shepard Families*, I:441.

charge and release from Knight Hospital he stayed with his brother Harvey G. Shepard at Bridgeport, also with his brother Charles B. Shepard at Fair Haven, and then returned to Branford.

Samuel Stent Shepard died at Branford on 14 June 1869 as a result of typhoid fever contracted while in the service and was buried there in Center Cemetery. His company and regiment are engraved on his stone and there was a G.A.R. marker was on his gravesite in 1934 and 2011. He was born at Branford on 3 January 1838, son of Benjamin Tyler Shepard and Hannah Stent.[923] The pension file is large with many affidavits regarding the cause of his death and whether it was contracted during his military service.

Amelia Shepard received a widow's pension on 15 June 1869. She was married to the soldier under the name of Amelia W. Matthews at Bristol by Rev. J. H. Gilbert on 28 April 1860. Neither were previously married or divorced. Lizzie Levina Shepard, their only child and a minor, received a pension on 25 October 1871 until the age of sixteen. She was born at Bridgeport on 11 February 1865. Lizzie was married at New Haven by Rev. D. McMullen of the Methodist Church on 17 December 1885 to William W. Cadwell.

Amelia Shepard of New Haven was married second at Whitneyville, Hamden by Rev. Austin Putnam on 25 October 1871 to Levi Dorman. Her pension claim ended upon her remarriage. Amelia W. Dorman, age 70, of New Haven reapplied for a pension on 7 November 1908. Her second husband, Levi Dorman died at New Haven on 12 February 1907.

Amelia Shepard Dorman died at New Haven on 29 March 1917 and was buried in Center Cemetery, Branford. She was born at Bristol on 1 January 1838, daughter of George William Matthews and Hannah Sheldon.

SHERMAN, DANIEL
Co. K 7th CVI, private, substitute, mustered in 30 November 1864, deserted

Daniel Sherman served as a substitute for Lewis F. Shepard of Branford. He was mustered in at New Haven on 30 November 1864 as a private in Co. K 7th CVI and deserted on 25 February 1865. He does not appear in the 1860 census at Branford.

---

923   Branford Vital Records, Town Meeting Book A, 231.

SLINEY, DAVID

Co. G 27th CVI, private, enlisted 3 September 1862, prisoner, mustered out 27 July 1863, pension #533538 for the soldier

David Sliney[924] of Branford enlisted on 3 September 1862 and was mustered in on 3 October 1862 as a private in Co. G 27th CVI for a term of nine months. "Dave Sliney is a regular customer at the Surgeons tent."[925] He was captured at the Battle of Fredericksburg, Virginia on 13 December 1862, marched that night to Acquia Creek, and paroled after four days. "Dave Sliney Stayed back in the city when we evacuated and was taken prisoner & parolled."[926] Sliney was mustered out with the rest of his regiment at New Haven on 27 July 1863.

He applied for an invalid pension on 24 September 1880 due to a hernia received during service. He claimed that after his capture at Fredericksburg and on the march to Acquia Creek, he fell causing the hernia. He was treated at Camp Parole, Annapolis, Maryland for about six weeks, sent to Knight Hospital, New Haven and never returned to his regiment. He was also treated at Knight Hospital after his discharge. The application was denied because he failed to prove the disability was contracted during his service. He was described as five feet five inches tall, dark complexion, black hair, blue eyes. He reapplied and received a pension under the act of 27 June 1890 due to age related illnesses. Since his discharge he lived at Branford. He was married to Elizabeth Dickson who died at Branford on 25 January 1893.[927] No children are listed in his pension file.[928] He was a member of the Mason Rogers Post No. 7 G.A.R. of Branford.

David Sliney died at Branford on 11 November 1896 and was buried there in St. Agnes Cemetery.[929]

SLOWMAN, JAMES or SLOMAN, SLOEMAN

Co. B 27th CVI, private, enlisted 28 August 1862, mustered out 27 July 1863, pension #502499 for the soldier

James Slowman, age 38, of Wallingford enlisted on 28 August 1862 and was mustered in on 3 October 1862 as a private in Co. B 27th CVI for a term of nine months. He fought at the Battle of Fredericksburg on 13 December 1862 with the rest of the company. He became sick right after the Regiment's return to camp and was in the camp hospital at Falmouth, Virginia from 15 December 1862 until his transfer to Stanton General Hospital, Washington, D.C. on 26 April 1863. On 1 June 1863 he was transferred to McDougall General Hospital, Fort Schuyler, New York Harbor. Slowman was mustered out with the rest of his regiment at New Haven on 27 July 1863.

---

924   For his biography see Beers, *Biographical Record of New Haven County*, 860; he should not be confused with another
       David Sliney of New Haven who died on 29 September 1864.
925   Letter, Samuel Beach to home, 18 November 1862.
926   Letter, Samuel Beach to home, 22 December 1863.
927   Branford Vital Records, 1863-1895, 249.
928   He did have grown children.
929   He was originally buried in St. Mary's Cemetery but disinterred and reburied at St. Agnes in 1945.

He applied for an invalid pension on 19 January 1887. He contracted chronic diarrhea, rheumatism, and heart disease by reason of exposure and fatigue while in the army and has been very much disabled and a great sufferer ever since. He was unfit for duty from about 15 December 1862 until his discharge when his term expired. Statements from neighbors attest to his disability and inability to work. In 1887 he was described as five feet four inches tall, light complexion, light hair, brown eyes, born in England. Since his discharge he lived at Wallingford. His wife Fanny died on 15 October 1859 age 26 and their two young children are all buried in Center Street Cemetery, Wallingford. It does not appear he remarried.

James Slowman died on 18 January 1895 age 71 and was buried in Center Street Cemetery, Wallingford.[930] There was a Civil War marker at his gravesite in 1934.

SMITH, A. JUDSON
Co. H 127th New York Infantry, corporal, enlisted 21 August 1862, mustered out 30 June 1865, pension #847535 for the soldier and later for his widow Augusta

A. Judson Smith[931] enlisted at Greenport, Long Island, New York on 21 August 1862 and was mustered in on 8 September 1862 as a private in Co. H 127th New York Infantry for a term of three years and was promoted to corporal. The regiment served in the defense of Washington, D.C. and in South Carolina for most of the war. Judson Smith was discharged with the rest of his regiment at Charlestown, South Carolina on 30 June 1865.

He applied for an invalid pension on 23 February 1892 under the act of 27 June 1890 for several age related illnesses. He had a gunshot wound to the left hand before the war. At the time of his enlistment he was described as five feet eight inches tall, light complexion, brown eyes, black hair, occupation tinsmith. He was married first to Ophelia Vesta Pyott[932] who died at Branford on 10 August 1877 age 27. He was married second at Patchogue, Long Island, New York by Rev. George Harding on 19 March 1878 to Mary Sophia Hand who died at North Branford on 5 November 1899 age 39. He had seven children (living in 1898): Nettie E., born on 14 June 1868; Etta M., born on 7 May 1870; Albert W., born on 24 December 1876; Mary E., born on 19 December 1880; Ruth E., born on 10 September 1884; Betsey C., born on 23 February 1886; and Margaret L., born on 3 October 1891. After his discharge he lived about twenty-five years at Branford, twelve years at North Branford, and moved to New Haven about 1904. He was a charter member of the Mason Rogers Post No. 7 G.A.R. of Branford.

He was married third at the First Swedish Church of Manhattan, New York by Rev. Emil Friborg on 23 June 1905 to Augusta Blomberg. It was his third marriage, he was age 60, living at New Haven; she was age 57, her first marriage, born in Sweden, daughter of John Blomberg and Mary Hirfeldt. She was not eligible for a pension.

---

930 The Hale Collection, Wallingford, 110.
931 For his biography see Rockey, *History of New Haven County*, II:105; and Beers, *Biographical Record of New Haven County*, 860.
932 Her name as provided by him on his application. Her name varies in the records - Vessie P., Jessie P., Ophelia V., Aphelia Fenti Pyatt, or Orphelia Testa Pyott.

A. Judson Smith died at New Haven on 22 February 1915 and was buried in Center Cemetery, Branford. A Civil War marker was on his gravesite in 1934 and 2011. He was born at Whitestown, Oneida Co., New York on 25 August 1841, son of Henry Smith and Emily Watson.

SMITH, DAVID L.
Co. A 10th CVI, private, enlisted 21 September 1861, discharged disability 13 April 1862, pension #133960 for his mother Ruth

David L. Smith, age 24, of Branford enlisted at Hartford on 21 September 1861 and was mustered in on 22 October 1861 as a private in Co. A 10th CVI for a term of three years. He was healthy before the war and contracted a severe cold while standing guard near camp at Annapolis, Maryland in a heavy rain about 1 January 1862. He was discharged for disability on 13 April 1862 at New Bern, North Carolina for phthisis pulmonalis.

David L. Smith died at East Haven on 30 May 1862 of consumption and was buried in East Haven Cemetery. At the time of his enlistment he was described as five feet nine inches tall, light complexion, hazel eyes, brown hair, occupation farmer, born at North Haven.

His mother Ruth Smith of New Haven applied for a pension on 26 February 1866. She was married at Hartford by Rev. Bisbee on 26 March 1827 to William Smith. William Smith died at East Haven on 13 July 1858 age 53. The soldier was unmarried and contributed toward her support.

Ruth Smith died on 26 March 1880. Henry C. Smith of New Haven wrote a letter to the pension board to receive compensation for her burial expenses.

SMITH, EDWARD L.
Co. A & Co. C 10th CVI, lieutenant, enlisted 18 September 1861, reenlisted, wounded, mustered out 25 August 1865, pension #148939 for the soldier, his widow Carrie and minor child

Edward L. Smith, age 18, of Branford enlisted at Hartford on 18 September 1861 and was mustered in on 21 September 1861 as a private in Co. A 10th CVI for a term of three years. With the regiment he fought at the Battle of Roanoke Island, North Carolina. He reenlisted at St. Augustine, Florida on 1 January 1864 as a veteran in Co. A and was promoted to corporal on 1 September 1864. He was wounded at Richmond, Virginia on 13 October 1864. He was promoted to sergeant on 1 November 1864 and to 1st sergeant on 1 January 1865 at Chapins Farm, Virginia. He was promoted to 2nd lieutenant of Co. C 10th CVI on 27 January 1865. He was wounded in action near Petersburg, Virginia at the charge of Fort Gregg on 2 April 1865 receiving three wounds; one in the head, and two in the left arm[933] and was admitted to General Hospital at Point of Rocks. Edward Smith was mustered out at Richmond, Virginia with the rest of his regiment on 25 August 1865 and discharged at Hartford on 5 September 1865. He served under Capt. James H. Linsley of North Branford.

He applied for an invalid pension on 27 September 1865 and was two thirds disabled from a gunshot wound to his head damaging his right eye and ear, loosing most of his sight and hearing. His condition was always poor after his discharge.

---

933   Crofut & Morris, *Military & Civil History of Connecticut*, 788.

Edward L. Smith died on 3 July 1868 age 26 and was buried in Old Cemetery, East Haven. There was a Civil War marker on his gravesite in 1934. He was born at Tobaccostick, Maryland. He was on the 1863 draft list for Branford but claimed by East Haven.

Carrie Smith applied for a widow's pension on 16 October 1868. She was married to the soldier under the name of Carrie B. Bradley at East Haven on 23 November 1866. He was age 26, born in Maryland, living at East Haven; she was age 18, born and living at East Haven. Henry J. Bradley, age 54, of East Haven is named in the file and was probably her father. They had one daughter Carrie E., born at East Haven on 5 April 1868 who received a pension until the age of sixteen.

Carrie Bradley Smith was married second at Branford by Rev. Warren Mason of the First Baptist Church on 13 February 1871 to Edward P. Bates of Jersey City, New Jersey. In 1874 she was living at Syracuse, Onondago Co., New York and was the guardian of her daughter Carrie Smith.

SMITH, ELBERT J.
Co. B 27th CVI, private, enlisted 1 September 1862, discharged 19 January 1863, no pension

Elbert J. Smith, age 18, of North Haven enlisted on 1 September 1862 and was mustered in on 3 October 1862 as a private in Co. B 27th CVI for a term of nine months. From November 1862 to January 1863 he was sick at Stuart's Mansion General Hospital at Baltimore, Maryland and discharged from there on 19 January 1863 for disability. There is a copy of his discharge paper in his file. He was described as five feet five inches tall, light complexion, hazel eyes, black hair, occupation mechanic. He was discharged for a variety of illnesses, totally unfit for duty.

Elbert J. Smith died on 2 February 1869 age 25 and was buried in Center Cemetery, North Haven.[934] He was probably the son of Julius Smith and Rebecca Eaton of North Haven. His name appears on the North Haven Civil War Honor Roll.

SMITH, FREDERICK alias ABRAM ARROWSMITH
28th Massachusetts Infantry, 100 & 116 Companies 2nd Battalion VRC, pension #372555 for his widow Alice E. Smith

Frederick Smith served under the name of Abram Arrowsmith and enlisted on 30 March 1864 as a private in the 28th Massachusetts Infantry, unassigned. He was transferred to the 116th Co. 2nd Battalion VRC on 9 January 1865. He was discharged from the 100th Co. 2nd Battalion VRC on 5 August 1865. He assumed the name of Frederick Smith after his discharge and moved to Branford.

Frederick Smith died at Branford on 28 May 1887 age 46 and was buried there in Center Cemetery. A Civil War marker was on his gravesite in 1934. He was born at London, England. Affidavits in his file claim he suffered from rheumatism since his return from the army.

---

934 The Hale Collection, North Haven, 21.

His widow states "My Husband was taken sick with Inflammatory Rheumatism [and was] in the Hospital in New York immediately after his Discharge, the Drs. saying it was due to exposure while in the Army."[935]

Alice E. Smith of Branford applied for a widow's pension on 14 December 1891 under the act of 27 June 1890. She was married to the soldier under the name of Alice E. Albee at Branford by Rev. Elijah C. Baldwin of the First Congregational Church on 8 October 1867. Neither were previously married or divorced. They had one daughter who lived to adulthood: Pauline L., born on 8 March 1872. Alice was the daughter of soldier Calvin Albee.

Alice E. Smith died at Branford on 15 May 1939 and was buried there in Center Cemetery. She was born at Durham on 9 May 1849, daughter of Calvin Goddard Albee and Hannah Maria Scranton.[936]

SMITH, HENRY C.
Co. A 10th CVI, corporal, enlisted 18 September 1861, reenlisted, wounded, discharged disability 31 July 1865, pension #53574 for the soldier

Henry C. Smith of Branford enlisted at New Haven on 18 September 1861 and was mustered in at Hartford on 21 September 1861 as a private in Co. A 10th CVI for a term of three years. With the rest of the regiment he fought at the Battle of Roanoke Island, North Carolina on 8 February 1862. He reenlisted at St. Augustine, Florida as a veteran in Co. A on 1 January 1864 and was promoted to corporal on 19 November 1864. He was wounded in action at Fort Gregg, Virginia on 2 April 1865 and treated at General Hospital at Hampton. Henry Smith was discharged for disability on 31 July 1865.

He applied for an invalid pension on 7 August 1865. At the time of his discharge he was described as age 24, five feet ten inches tall, light complexion, grey eyes, brown hair, born at North Haven, occupation farmer. He received a severe gunshot wound at the Battle of Petersburg, Virginia at a skirmish in front of Fort Gregg on 2 April 1865 resulting in an amputation above the left knee about four hours later. He received an artificial limb from the National Leg & Arm Company. He was married at Simsbury by Rev. George Curtis to Nancie E. Case (no date given). They had no children. After the war he lived at East Haven where they both appear in the 1880 census. There are no death dates in the pension file.

SMITH, IRA B.
Co. D 2nd CVI & Co. C 7th CVI, captain, enlisted 23 April 1861, reenlisted, prisoner, mustered out 20 July 1865, pension #C2576177 for the soldier

Ira B. Smith[937] of Derby enlisted at New Haven on 23 April 1861 and was mustered in on 7 May 1861 as a private in Co. D 2nd CVI for a term of three months. He fought at the first Battle of Bull Run and was mustered out at New Haven on 7 August 1861 when his term expired. He reenlisted on 23 August 1861 as a corporal in Co. C 7th CVI, then living at Meriden. He was promoted to sergeant on 1 September 1862. He reenlisted in Co. C on 22 December 1863 and was promoted to 1st sergeant on 16 April 1864. He fought at the Battles of St. John's Bluff, Florida; Pocotaligo, South Carolina; and Drury's Bluff, Virginia. He was captured at the Battle of Bermuda Hundred, Virginia on 2 June 1864 and spent three months in Andersonville Prison.

---

935   Affidavit, Alice E. Smith, 27 July 1893, in the pension file of Frederick Smith.
936   Branford Vital Records, deaths, 1939.
937   For his biography see *Commemorative Biographical Record of Hartford County, Connecticut* (Chicago: J. H. Beers & Co., 1901), 422.

He was transferred to a jail in Charleston then Florence, South Carolina. He was paroled on 11 December 1864, sent to Charleston harbor and transported home for a three month furlough. He rejoined his regiment at Wilmington, North Carolina and was promoted to captain of Co. C 7th CVI on 28 April 1865. Ira Smith was mustered out with the rest of his regiment at Goldsboro, North Carolina on 20 July 1865.

He applied for an invalid pension on 25 April 1886. After his discharge he lived at Gallain, Ohio, Meriden and moved to Short Beach, Branford in 1909. "He was employed in Derby and was the first man from that town to enlist when the war broke out. He was slightly wounded and a prisoner in Andersonville Prison for many months and was known as Cappy."[938] He was married at Meriden on 5 February 1864 to Susan K. Maynes, daughter of Alexander G. Maynes. She died in August 1937 age 96 and was buried In Memoriam Cemetery, Wallingford. She never applied for a widow's pension.

Ira Benham Smith died at Branford on 12 August 1934 and was buried In Memoriam Cemetery, Wallingford. He was born at Meriden on 16 August 1840, son of Lucius Benham Smith and Caroline Griswold.[939] At the time of his death he was one of two surviving Civil War veterans in Branford and the oldest member of the G.A.R. in the state for sixty-eight years. He was the last surviving member of the Gilbert W. Thompson Post No. 13 G.A.R. of Bristol   .

Ira B. Smith served in the 2nd CVI and was promoted to captain of Co. C 7th CVI in 1865. He moved to Branford in 1909 and was known as Cappy Smith. (Branford Historical Society photograph collection)

SMITH, JACOB A.
Co. K 15th CVI, private, enlisted 9 August 1862, died 3 October 1864, pension #53316 for his widow Marion

Jacob Augustus Smith, age 23, of North Branford enlisted on 9 August 1862 and was mustered in on 25 August 1862 as a private in Co. K 15th CVI for a term of three years. He saw action at the Battle of Fredericksburg, Virginia on 13 December 1862, during the Siege of Suffolk, Virginia in April 1863, and in the Peninsula Campaign of July 1863. In January and February 1864 he was detailed as a post teamster. He died at Foster General Hospital in New Bern, North Carolina on 3 October 1864 of yellow fever. There is a gravestone for him in Northford Cemetery, his company and regiment are engraved on his stone. His name appears on the Northford Veterans' Monument. At the time of his enlistment he was described as five feet seven inches tall, fair complexion, brown eyes, black hair, occupation farmer. Jacob A. Smith was born at North Branford, son of Nathaniel Stacy Smith and Eliza Frisbie.

938   Obituary, *The Branford Review*, 16 August 1934, 1; see also *The Branford Review*, 16 August 1932, 1.
939   Obituary, *The Branford Review*, 16 August 1934, 1; Branford Vital Records, deaths, 1934.

Marion W. Smith, age 20, of East Haven applied for a widow's pension on 10 November 1864. She was married to the soldier under the name of Marion W. Smith at East Haven by Rev. D. William Havens on 13 April 1864. They had no children. No further record for Marion was obtained.

SMITH, JOSIAH A.
Co. C 10th CVI, enlisted 15 October 1861, sergeant, reenlisted, wounded, mustered out 15 August 1865, pension #764177 for the soldier and later for his widow Jane

Josiah A. Smith of North Branford enlisted at Hartford on 15 October 1861 and was mustered in on 22 October 1861 as a private in Co. C 10th CVI for a term of three years. He was sick aboard a hospital ship at Hatteras Inlet in January and February 1862. He was discharged at St. Augustine, Florida on 31 December 1863, promoted to corporal the next day and reenlisted on 6 January 1864 as a veteran in Co. C. He was wounded at Darbytown Road, Virginia on 13 October 1864 and promoted to sergeant on 13 June 1865. Josiah Smith was mustered out with the rest of his regiment at Richmond, Virginia on 25 August 1865 and discharged at Hartford on 5 September 1865. He served under Capt. James H. Linsley of North Branford.

He applied for an invalid pension on 29 July 1890 under the act of 27 June 1890. At the time of his enlistment he was described as five feet one inch tall, light complexion, blue eyes, light hair, occupation tinner. After his discharge he lived at New London; Westfield, Massachusetts; and North Branford. In 1912 he was living at the Fitch's Soldier Home in Noroton, his conservator was Carrie M. Hodgetts (Mrs. H. W.) of Springfield, Massachusetts.

Josiah A. Smith died at the Norwich State Hospital in Preston on 9 March 1913 age 68 and was buried in New Northford Cemetery, North Branford. His rank, company and regiment are engraved on his stone and his name appears on the Northford Veterans' Monument. He was born at New London on 24 November 1844.[940]

Jane or Jennie Smith of Springfield, Massachusetts applied for a widow's pension on 5 April 1913. She was married to the soldier under the name of Jane Betsey Smith at Meriden by Rev. J. J. Wooley on 8 September 1866. He was age 23, born at New London, living at Meriden; she was age 19, born and living at Northford. Neither were previously married or divorced. They had one child Carrie M., born on 11 March 1867, 1913 living at Springfield, Massachusetts; married with one child.

Jane B. Smith died at New London on 23 March 1918 and was buried in New Northford Cemetery. She was born at Northford on 18 February 1847, daughter of Stephen Smith.

---

940   He gives both 1844 and 1845 as his birth year.

SMITH, STEPHEN
11th CVI unassigned, enlisted or drafted 28 March 1864, failed to report

Stephen Smith of Branford enlisted or was drafted on 28 March 1864. He was transferred to the regiment on 6 May 1864 but failed to report. There was no further record. He does not appear in the 1860 census at Branford.

SMITH, THOMAS
Co. I 29th CVI, corporal, enlisted 2 January 1864, mustered out 24 October 1865, no pension

Thomas Smith of Branford enlisted at New Haven on 2 January 1864 and was mustered in on 8 March 1864 as a private in Co. I 29th CVI for a term of three years. His service was credited to Branford. He was on detached duty to guard an ammunition train (no date given) and was promoted to corporal on 1 May 1864. He was sick at Corps d'Afrique U.S. General Hospital, New Orleans September 1865 and returned to his regiment on 11 November. Thomas Smith was mustered out with the rest of his regiment at Brownsville, Texas on 24 October 1865. His name appears on the Wall of Honor at Washington, D.C.

SNOW, LUTHER H.
Co. D 1st HA, enlisted 14 December 1863, private, mustered out 25 September 1865, pension #C2398651 for the soldier and later an application for his widow

Luther H. Snow of North Branford enlisted and was mustered in on 14 December 1863 as a private in Co. D 1st HA for a term of three years. He participated in the Siege of Petersburg and Richmond, Virginia with the rest of the regiment. Snow was mustered out with the rest of his regiment at Washington, D.C. on 25 September 1865 and discharged at Hartford on 1 October 1865.

He enlisted on 16 November 1865 at New York City and was commissioned as a sergeant in the 17th and 35th U.S. Army Infantry. He was discharged at San Antonio, Texas on 6 November 1868 when his term expired. At the time of this enlistment he was described as age 21, born at Providence, Rhode Island, five three inches tall, blue eyes, brown hair, fair complexion, occupation soldier.[941]

Luther H. Snow was living at Cincinnati, Ohio in 1912 and applied for and was granted an invalid pension on 10 December 1923. Mariah J. Snow of Ohio, perhaps an ex-wife, applied for a pension on 17 January 1890. He died at Cincinnati, Ohio on 6 May 1928. He may be the Luther H. Snow born at Little Compton, Rhode Island on 13 February 1844, son of George Taylor Snow and Alice Beal Andrews and appears with them at Providence in the 1850 and 1860 census.[942]

Carrie Snow, called the contested widow, applied for a pension on 12 June 1928. It does not appear either widow received a pension. His pension is at the Veterans Administration.

---

941   U.S. Army Record of Enlistments 1798-1914, www.ancestry.com.
942   Snow family tree, www.ancestry.com.

SQUIRE, LYMAN F.
Co. F 6th CVI, musician, enlisted 26 August 1861, reenlisted, mustered out 21 August 1865, pension #245302 for the soldier and later for his widow Lydia

Lyman F. Squire of New Haven enlisted at New Haven on 26 August 1861 and was mustered in on 7 September 1861 as a musician in Co. F 6th CVI for a term of three years. He reenlisted as a veteran in Co. F on 7 March 1864. Squire was mustered out at Petersburg, Virginia on 21 July 1865 and discharged at New Haven on 21 August 1865.

He applied for an invalid pension on 24 December 1885. He was described as five feet five inches tall, light complexion, auburn hair, gray eyes, occupation carriage maker. He claimed he contracted spotted fever resulting in consumption and disability in March 1863 while on board the transport "Cosmopolitan" during an expedition to Fernandina, Florida. He was treated on the ship by the regimental surgeon and later in quarters. Since his discharge he lived at New Haven and Hartford.

Lyman Frisbie Squire died at Hartford on 18 April 1888 and was buried in Center Cemetery, Branford.[943] A G.A.R. marker was on his gravesite in 1934 and 2011. He was born at Branford on 22 December 1842, son of Lyman Luzerne Squire and Elizabeth Lydia Palmer.

Lydia S. Squire of Hartford applied for a widow's pension on 27 April 1888. She was married to the soldier under the name of Lydia S. Stannard at Hartford by Rev. Edwin P. Parker on 15 September 1864. He was age 23, living at Branford; she was age 22, born and living at West Haven. Neither were previously married or divorced.

STANNARD, JOHN S.
Co. G 14th CVI, corporal, wounded, discharged disability 9 June 1865, pension #933588 for the soldier

John S. Stannard of Guilford enlisted at Hartford on 31 July 1862 and was mustered in on 23 August 1862 as a private in Co. G 14th CVI for a term of three years. With his regiment he fought at the Battle of Antietam, Maryland on 17 September 1862 and was promoted to corporal on 9 February 1863. He was wounded at the Battle of Gettysburg on 3 July 1863 resulting in a concussion and his rank was reduced due to sickness on 1 September 1863. He was wounded again at the Battle of the Wilderness, Virginia on 6 May 1864 by a gunshot to the foot. He was sent to Regimental Hospital then to Knight's Hospital, New Haven where he was discharged for disability on 9 June 1865 due to heart disease.

He applied for an invalid pension on 3 February 1892 under the act of 27 June 1890 due to worsening of his heart condition. At the time of his enlistment he was described as five feet six inches tall, florid complexion, blue eyes, light brown hair, occupation oyster man. He had a tattoo on his right arm with the Goddess of Liberty with his initials underneath. He was married at Guilford by Rev. DeLancy G. Rice on 9 July 1861 to Julia Cook Benton. She died on 25 August 1919. They had one adopted daughter Katie E.,

---

943   The Hale Collection, Branford, 61 & 62.

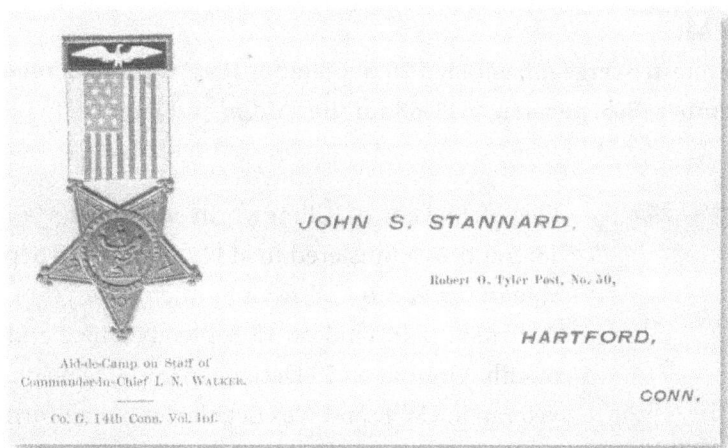

*John S. Stannard was a member of the Robert O. Tyler Post No. 50 of Hartford and
active in the local and state G.A.R. (Blackstone Library archives)*

born on 18 January 1886 who died on 29 December 1905. Since his discharge he lived at North Guilford in 1865, Fair Haven 1866, Branford 1868, Middletown 1871, Branford 1873, Hartford 1875, and Branford again since 1919. He was a member of the Robert O. Tyler Post No. 50 of Hartford and active in the local and state G.A.R. encampments.[944]

John Sefton Stannard died at Branford on 27 May 1923 and was buried in Center Street Cemetery, Wallingford. He was born at Westbrook on 8 August 1837, son of William H. Stannard and Catherine Stannard later of Branford.[945]

STERNBERG, JOHN
Co. K 11th CVI, private, enlisted 12 March 1864, deserted 14 May 1864, no pension

John Sternberg of Branford enlisted on 12 March 1864 as a private in Co. K 11th CVI and deserted on 14 May 1864. He does not appear in the 1860 census at Branford.

STEVENS, CHARLES C. or STEPHENS
Co. H 6th New York HA, private, enlisted 20 August 1862, discharged 28 June 1865, pension #136346 for the soldier

Charles C. Stevens enlisted at Morrisania, New York on 20 August 1862 and was mustered in on 2 September 1862 at Yonkers, New York as a private in Co. H 6th New York Heavy Artillery for a term of three years. He was wounded at Cedar Creek, Virginia on 19 October 1864. Charles Stevens was mustered out with the rest of his regiment at Petersburg, Virginia on 28 June 1865.

He applied for an invalid pension on 25 November 1874 for a gunshot wound to the right thigh. He first appears at Northford in 1880, unmarried, and appears there as a pensioner in 1883. He was still living at Northford in 1889 age 44.

---

944 His G.A.R. and encampment ribbons are in the Blackstone Library Archives, RG 5, box 3.
945 Branford Vital Records, deaths, 1923; his mother was also nee Stannard.

STEVENS, ELLIS M.

Co. K 8th CVI, quartermaster-sergeant, enlisted 20 September 1861, wounded, reenlisted,,
mustered out 12 December 1865, pension #545688 for the soldier and later for his minor child
Willie E. Stevens

Ellis M. Stevens of Killingworth enlisted at Meriden on 20 September 1861 and was mustered in at Hartford on 25 September 1861 as a private in Co. K 8th CVI for a term of three years. He was wounded at Antietam, Maryland on 17 September 1862 and discharged at Portsmouth, Virginia on 23 December 1863. He reenlisted the next day as a veteran in Co. K and was detailed as a mail carrier. He was promoted to quartermaster-sergeant of the 8th CVI on 1 July 1865. Ellis Stevens was mustered out at City Point, Virginia on 12 December 1865. He was probably the brother of Emmerson Stevens of the same company.

He applied for an invalid pension on 30 June 1880. At the time of his enlistment he was described as five feet six inches tall, fair complexion, light brown hair, blue eyes, occupation farmer. He was wounded in the knee at Antietam, Maryland on 17 September 1862 by a ten pound cannon ball rendering him unfit for active duty. The cannon ball killed five soldiers and wounded three others. Before his promotion to quartermaster he was detailed to headquarters as a clerk in Harland's Brigade. Just before applying for his pension he fractured his right leg and his wounded knee was worse. After his discharge he lived at Guilford and North Branford.

He was married to Sarah M. Burr. She remarried four years after his death and did not apply for a widow's pension. At the time of his death he had three children all under the age of sixteen: Elbert W., born on 27 October 1866; Flora B., born on 12 March 1869; and William E., born on 29 March 1880. Sarah M. Clark of Durham, post office box Middletown, wrote a letter to the pension board (no date) inquiring about a pension for her children who were minors when their father died. There is no application or evidence of a pension granted to Sarah in the file. His widow Sarah died at South Glastonbury on 26 February 1903.

Ellis M. Stevens died at North Branford on 22 April 1882 and was buried there in Bare Plain Cemetery. His rank and regiment are engraved on his stone. There was a G.A.R. marker on his gravesite in 1934 and 2011. He was probably the son of Daniel and Mercy Stevens of Killingworth.

Rebecca S. Clark, guardian, applied for a pension on 26 February 1892 on behalf of Willie E. Stevens, minor child of the soldier. The relationship of Rebecca to the child is not stated. In 1928 the soldier's daughter Mrs. Flora B. Fowler of Middletown, a widow, wrote to the pension board to try and obtain part of her father's pension.

STEVENS, EMMERSON R. or EMERSON

Co. K 8th CVI, private, enlisted 1 October 1861, discharged 10 October 1864, pension #774437 for the soldier

Emmerson R. Stevens, age 18, of Killingworth enlisted and was mustered in at Hartford on 1 October 1861 as a private in Co. K 8th CVI for a term of three years. He was discharged at Bermuda Hundred, Virginia on 10 October 1864 when his term expired. He was probably the brother of Ellis M. Stevens of the same company.

He applied for an invalid pension on 20 June 1891 under the act of 27 June 1890. At the time of his enlistment he was described as five feet four inches tall, light complexion, blue eyes, light hair, occupation mechanic. After his discharge he lived at Killingworth for one year, Chester for two years, East River about four years, Guilford for four years, Essex for three years, back to Guilford then to Branford. He was a member of the Mason Rogers Post No. 7 G.A.R. of Branford.

He was married at Prospect by W. W. Atwater right after the war to Mary E. Loper. She ran off with another man about 1879 while they were living at Essex and remarried without ever obtaining a divorce from Stevens and without his knowledge. They had the following children (living in 1898): Frederick E., born on 27 August 1866; William M., born on 12 February 1867; George M., born on 2 January 1871; and Ada May, born on 29 January 1872. In 1915 Mary E. Loper Stevens now Mary E. Reed was living at Wallingford and was alive in 1928 living with her daughter Mrs. Arthur James (Ada Stevens) at Kensington. The soldier lived with his son Frederick E. Stevens at Branford.

Emmerson R. Stevens died at Branford on 26 November 1928 and was buried there in Center Cemetery. A Civil War marker was on his gravesite in 1934. He was born at Killingworth on 23 February 1844.[946]

STEVENS, GEORGE

1st LA, private, enlisted 23 July 1862, transferred to the Navy, discharged 26 October 1865, pension #14226 for the soldier and later for his widow Pamelia

George Stevens, age 29, of Guilford enlisted and was mustered in on 21 July 1862 as a private in the 1st LA for a term of three years. He served with his regiment in South Carolina during 1863. He was discharged on 28 April 1864 and transferred to the Navy. He was a seaman on the U.S.S. *General Putnam, Malvern, Miami,* and *Constellation.* He may have also served on the U.S.S. *Minnesota.* George Stevens was discharged from the Navy at Fortress Monroe, Virginia on 26 October 1865. "He was a sailor and made voyages whaling. He enlisted in the Battery and obtained what he had long sought for, a transfer into the navy. He was a good soldier and held in esteem by all his comrades."[947]

He applied for an invalid pension on 10 December 1890 under the act of 27 June 1890.

---

946 Branford Vital Records, deaths, 1928; his death record states his parents were Emmerson and Mary Stevens which may be in error naming himself and his wife as his parents. He was probably the son of Daniel & Mercy Stevens of Killingworth.

947 Obituary, *The Short Line Times*, 25 January 1900.

At the time of his enlistment he was described as five feet ten inches tall, florid complexion, grey eyes, brown hair. "I was transferred to the Navy as coxswain on the U.S.S. General Putnam under Captain Savage. I was put on the recovery ship Minnesota and went from her to the Deep water Shoal Light on the James River until my discharge."[948] Since his discharge he lived at Guilford about fifteen years and since then at Branford. He was a member of the Mason Rogers Post No. 7 G.A.R. of Branford.

George Stevens died at Branford on 22 January 1900 and was buried in East Haven Cemetery. He was born at North Guilford on 28 July 1832, son of Anson Stevens.

Pamelia Stevens, age 62, of Branford applied for a widow's pension on 4 April 1900. She was married to the soldier under the name of Pamelia Cook at Guilford by Rev. Henry Robinson on 15 August 1858. He was age 26, born and living at Guilford; she was age 21, born and living at Portsmouth, New Hampshire. They had two children: Almira, born on 20 May 1859; and Albert P., born on 30 March 1867. She died at Branford on 8 January 1905 and was buried in East Haven Cemetery. She was born at Portsmouth, New Hampshire, daughter of John Cook.[949]

STEWART, JAMES or STUART

James Stewart, age 34, served as substitute for Benjamin Page, Jr. of North Branford. He was mustered in at New Haven on 19 August 1864 as a private for a term of three years. He was described as five feet seven inches tall, brown eyes, sandy hair, light complexion, unmarried, born in Scotland, occupation seaman.[950]

STONE, ELIZUR C.
Co. B 27th CVI, private, enlisted 20 August 1862, mustered out on 27 July 1863, pension #683888 for the soldier and later for his widow Sarah

Elizur C. Stone, age 35, of North Branford enlisted on 20 August 1862 and was mustered in on 3 October 1862 as a private in Co. B 27th CVI for a term of nine months. He was present at roll call in December 1862 and probably fought at the Battle of Fredericksburg on 13 December 1862. He was sick at the Regimental Hospital at Falmouth and Lincoln General Hospital, Washington, D.C. in March and April 1863. In May and June 1863 he was at Mower General Hospital, Chestnut Hill, Philadelphia, Pennsylvania. "I was taken sick and taken to the Hospital and never rejoined the Regiment until we were on our way home."[951] Elizur Stone was mustered out with the rest of his regiment at New Haven on 27 July 1863.

He applied for an invalid pension on 14 June 1880. Since his discharge he lived at North Branford. At the time of his enlistment he was described as five feet five inches tall, dark complexion, brown hair, hazel eyes. While on duty at camp near Falmouth, Virginia about

948   Affidavit, George Stevens, 23 January 1892, in his own pension file.
949   Branford Vital Records, deaths, 1905.
950   Muster & Descriptive Rolls of Substitutes, RG 13, box 97, 2nd Congressional District, Connecticut State Library; his service was not found in the *Record of Service of Connecticut Men*.
951   Deposition, Elizur C. Stone of North Branford, 13 March 1885, in the file of Nathan A. Harrison.

February 1863, he was attacked with rheumatism and chronic diarrhea. Statements from neighbors and family attest to his disability and inability to work since the war.

He was married at Durham in the house of Rev. David Smith on 3 January 1853 to Sarah Elizabeth Stevens. Neither were previously married or divorced. The following children were living (in 1897): Hattie M., born on 7 December 1855; Charles R., born on 12 July 1858; Edith J., born on 10 January 1863; George E., born on 4 October 1865; and Frank W., born on 20 August 1871.

Elizur C. Stone died at North Branford on 18 May 1909 and was buried there in Bare Plain Cemetery. His company and regiment are engraved on his stone. He was born at North Branford on 26 July 1826, son of Chauncey Stone and Lois Palmer, born at North Guilford and North Branford.

Sarah E. Stone applied for a widow's pension on 16 June 1909. She was born at Haddam on 19 February 1831. The pension board was informed of her death on 30 January 1923 by her son Frank W. Stone of North Branford. She was buried in Bare Plain Cemetery, North Branford.

STONE, HORATIO (THE YOUNGER)
Co. F 12th CVI, private, enlisted 15 October 1861, discharged disability 18 August 1862, pension application #1036001 for the soldier

Horatio Stone, age 26, of North Branford enlisted at New Haven on 15 October 1861 and was mustered in on 19 November 1861 as a private in Co. F 12th CVI for a term of three years. He was absent without leave on 31 January 1862. On 18 October 1862 while stationed at Camp Parapet, Louisiana he suffered from blood poisoning in his right hand and rheumatism.[952] Horatio Stone was discharged at Camp Parapet, Louisiana for disability on 14 August 1862 and mustered out at Hartford on 18 August 1862. He was the brother of Walter A. Stone.

He applied for an invalid pension on 30 June 1891 under the act of 27 June 1890. At the time of his enlistment he was described as five feet six inches tall, dark complexion, black hair, brown eyes. As early as 1867 he tried to obtain his discharge papers. His pension was rejected on the grounds of desertion and a dishonorable discharge. He tried unsuccessfully to have the charges removed claiming he was ill in the hospital when the alleged desertion took place. His application dated 16 March 1909 was also denied and he never received a pension. He was admitted to the Fitch's Soldier Home[953] at Noroton Heights on 14 February 1907. At the time of his death his possessions included his service certificate, a pocket knife, necktie, and scarf pin.

Horatio Stone died at the Fitch's Soldier Home in Noroton Heights on 6 January 1908, unmarried, and was buried in the North Branford Episcopal Cemetery.[954] His company and regiment are engraved on his stone. He was born at North Branford on 18 October 1835, son of Bennett Stone and Ruth Butler.

952 Bradley, *Our Soldiers*, 18.
953 Fitch's Home for Soldiers, Deceased Veterans Discharge Files 1882-1932, box 11, file 2640.
954 The Hale Collection, North Branford, 17; *The Branford Opinion*, 3 January 1908.

Photograph by Janet Gregan, 1985,
Totoket Historical Society

STONE, HORATIO (THE ELDER)
Co. K 13th CVI, private, enlisted 22 October 1861, discharged disability 19 June 1863, no pension

Horatio Stone, age 45, of North Branford enlisted at New Haven on 22 October 1861 and was mustered in on 27 November 1861 as a private in Co. K 13th CVI for a term of three years. In January and February 1863 he was sick at New Orleans. He was discharged for disability at Baton Rouge, Louisiana on 19 June 1863 for diarrhea and dysentery being unfit for duty for four months. Also, since landing on Ships Island in April 1863 he had been failing with cough and dyspnea and was "a broken down man."

At the time of his enlistment he was described as five feet nine inches tall, fair complexion, grey eyes, brown hair, occupation painter, born at North Branford, unmarried.

Horatio Stone died at Branford on 29 September 1873[955] and was buried in the North Branford Congregational Cemetery.

Photograph by Janet Gregan, 1985,
Totoket Historical Society

STONE, WALTER A.
Co. F 1st HA, private, enlisted 23 May 1861, prisoner, discharged disability 1 October 1862, pension #347901 for his mother Ruth Stone

Walter A. Stone, age 20, of North Branford enlisted and was mustered in at Hartford on 23 May 1861 as a private in Co. F 4th CVI which became the 1st HA. He was sick in the hospital at Savage Station, Cold Harbor, Virginia and captured while a patient there on 27 June 1862 when the Union abandoned the hospital to the enemy leaving behind the patients. He was confined at Libby Prison, Richmond on 13 July 1862 and paroled at Haxall's Landing, Virginia on 25 July 1862. Walter Stone was discharged for disability from Camden Street General Hospital, Baltimore on 1 October 1862. He was the brother of Horatio Stone (the younger). At the time of his discharge he was described as five feet seven inches tall, light complexion, gray eyes, brown hair, occupation joiner.

Walter A. Stone died at North Branford on 31 October 1862, unmarried, as a result of consumption contracted in the service. He was buried in North Branford Congregational Cemetery and his name is inscribed on the North Branford Soldiers' Monument. He was born at North Branford, son of Bennett Stone and Ruth Butler.

---

955   Branford Vital Records, 1863-1895, 215.

His mother Ruth Stone of North Branford applied for a pension on 10 April 1863 claiming her son helped support her and that her husband failed to support the family for a number of years. The application was denied due to failure to prove the support. She was married under the name of Ruth Butler at North Branford by Jesse Linsley, JP on 30 March 1836 to Bennett Stone. He died at North Branford on 12 March 1880 age 71. She reapplied for a pension on 10 June 1891 under the act of 27 June 1890 and received a pension. She died on 19 July 1894. She was the daughter of Jarius Butler and Sally Hale of North Branford.

STONE, WATSON W.
Co. L 2nd HA, private, enlisted 1 February 1864, discharged 2 April 1864, no pension

Watson W. Stone of Clinton enlisted on 1 February 1864 as a private in Co. L 2nd HA and was discharged by Special Order at Fort Ellsworth, Virginia on 2 April 1864. He was the brother-in-law of Edward J. Buell.

He was married first to Ellen Miller who died on 2 October 1877 age 33[956] and was buried in Indian River Cemetery, Clinton. After the war he lived at Clinton and first appears at Branford in 1880. He was mustered in on 8 November 1883 as a member of the Mason Rogers Post No. 7 G.A.R. and was living at Short Beach, Branford in 1910. In 1920 he was living at Seffner, Hillsborough Co., Florida. He was not eligible for a pension due to total time served.

Watson Wilbur Stone died on 24 May 1924 and was buried in Indian River Cemetery, Clinton.[957] He was born at Madison on 10 September 1843, son of Heman Stone and Mabel Field.[958]

His second wife Anna Amelia Stone died at Hartford on 18 April 1943 and was buried in Indian River Cemetery, Clinton. She was born at Clinton on 9 April 1867, daughter of George Buck and Ellen Tripp.[959]

STRICKLAND, ASA
Co. D 7th CVI, private, enlisted 24 August 1861, reenlisted, prisoner, discharged 14 June 1865, pension #598594 for the soldier and later for his widow Jane

Asa Strickland of North Branford enlisted at on 24 August 1861 and was mustered in on 5 September 1861 as a private in Co. D 7th CVI for a term of three years. He reenlisted as a veteran of Co. D on 22 December 1863. He was captured at Drewry's Bluff, Virginia on 16 May 1864, confined at Richmond and sent to Andersonville Prison, Georgia on 23 May 1864 where he was confined for eleven months. He was admitted to the hospital while in prison on 13 January 1865. He was released at Vicksburg, Mississippi on 17 April 1865 and paroled on 21 April 1865. He was in the hospital after his parole and discharged at Hartford on 14 June 1865.

He applied for an invalid pension on 14 September 1887. While confined at Andersonville Prison he contracted rheumatism and frozen feet. He was married at Middlefield by Rev. Samuel H. Smith on 3 July 1853 to Jane Derby. Neither were previously married or divorced. They had seven children (all living in 1899): Hattie A. Hollow [Harlow] age 45, born on 12 October 1853; Emily M. Miller age 42, born on 20 May 1855; Lizzie J. Culver age 39, born on 23 April 1858; Mary F. Peck age 32, born on 17 July 1865; Asa E., born on 13 August 1861; Horace E. age 28, born on 12 May 1869; and Bertha W. Knowlton age 26 years, born on 11 October 1872.

---

956   The Notebook of Elias Stevens of Killingworth 1809-1895, 85 at the Connecticut State Library.
957   The Hale Collection, Clinton, 26; his death is not in the Branford Vital Records.
958   Talcott, *Families of Guilford*, 1163
959   *The Branford Review*, 21 April 1943.

Asa Strickland died at West Granby on 24 March 1903 while visiting his sister Emily Griffing and was buried in West Granby Cemetery. He was the son of Lester Strickland and Emily Shepard.

Jane Strickland of Branford applied for a widow's pension on 21 June 1904. She died at Branford on 12 December 1906 and was buried there in Center Cemetery.

SULLIVAN, CHARLES
Co. B 12th CVI, private, enlisted 15 October 1861, died 2 October 1862, no pension

Charles Sullivan of Branford enlisted on 15 October 1861 and was mustered in on 20 November 1861 as a private in Co. B 12th CVI for a term of three years. He died on 2 October 1862. He appears at Branford in the 1860 census, age 24, born in New York, a farm laborer in the household of Harvey Towner.[960]

SULLIVAN, MATTHEW
Co. E 1st & Co. B 10th New Hampshire Infantry, sergeant, Co. I 4th VRC, pension #841695 for the soldier and later for his widow Catherine

Matthew Sullivan enlisted on 26 April 1861 at Concord, New Hampshire as a private in Co. E 1st New Hampshire Infantry and was discharged on 9 August 1861. He reenlisted at Nashua, New Hampshire on 7 August 1862 as a sergeant in Co. B 10th New Hampshire Infantry and was transferred to Co. I 4th Veteran's Reserve Corps on 25 January 1865. Matthew Sullivan was discharged at Springfield, Illinois on 20 July 1865. Before coming to the United States he served in the British Army.

He applied for an invalid pension on 4 October 1866. While in the service he developed severe varicose veins and rheumatism from which he never fully recovered. He was admitted to Grove General Hospital at Newport, Rhode Island on 26 May 1864 from Belfour Hospital, Virginia. At the time of his enlistment he was described as five feet five inches tall, light complexion, blue eyes, sandy hair, occupation carder.[961] After his discharge he lived at Nashua, New Hampshire and Branford since 1870. He was a member of the Mason Rogers Post No. 7 G.A.R. of Branford. In 1906 he was living at the Soldiers' Home in Togus, Maine and in 1908 at the National Soldiers' Home in Kennebec, Maine.

He was married at St. Patrick's Church, New Haven by Rev. Fitzpatrick on 6 October 1878 to Catherine McKeon. Neither were previously married or divorced. They had three children (living in 1915): John Joseph, born on 23 June 1879; Matthew Patrick, born on 4 November 1880; and Peter Paul, born on 30 June 1883; Bernard, born on 13 May 1887 died before 1898.[962]

---

960   U.S. census 1860, Branford, New Haven County, Connecticut, population schedule, M653-85, dwelling 943, family 1050, page 907, www.heritagequest.com.

961   His discharge papers differ, another says five feet three inches tall, light complexion, grey eyes, light hair, occupation laborer.

962   The soldier gives different dates for some of the children on different pension applications; from the Branford Vital Records - John was born on 22 June 1879 and Peter on 22 December 1883.

Matthew Sullivan died at Branford on 1 February 1917 and was buried there in St. Mary's Cemetery. He was born at Kenmare, County Kerry, Ireland on 20 April 1836, son of Matthew Sullivan and Ellen Downy.[963]

Catherine Sullivan of Branford applied for a widow's pension on 3 April 1917. She died at Branford on 12 October 1919 and was buried there in St. Mary's Cemetery. She was born at Liverpool, England on 3 April 1846, daughter of Peter McKeon.

SULLIVAN, PHILIP

Philip Sullivan, age 28, served as a substitute for H. Lynde Harrison of Branford. He was mustered in at New Haven on 13 September 1864 as a private in the 7th CVI for a term of three years. He was described as five feet ten inches tall, blue eyes, black hair, black complexion, unmarried, born Jamaica, occupation seaman.[964]

SUNDELOUS, PETER
Co. C 10th CVI, private, substitute 28 October 1864, wounded, discharged disability 15 March 1866, pension #559083 for the soldier, his widow Hulda and minor child

Henry Rogers of Branford received a certificate of exemption,[965] dated 28 October 1864, having furnished a substitute named Peter Sundeblas, age 25. Peter Sundelous[966] of Branford enlisted and was mustered in at New Haven on 28 October 1864 as a private in Co. C 10th CVI. He was wounded in the abdomen at Ft. Gregg, Virginia on 2 April 1865 and discharged for disability on 15 March 1866.

He applied for an invalid pension on 25 June 1866. He was described as six feet tall, ruddy complexion, grey eyes, brown hair, born in Sweden, occupation student.[967] Peter Sundelous died at Chicago, Illinois on 18 February 1896. Hulda D. Sunderlius of Illinois applied for a widow's pension on 28 February 1896. As Hulda D. Crawford of Illinois, guardian, she applied for a pension on 13 June 1923.

TALMADGE, GEORGE W.
Co. K 15th CVI, corporal, enlisted 11 August 1862, mustered out 27 June 1865, pension #436366 for the soldier and later for his widow Lois

George W. Talmadge of North Branford enlisted at New Haven on 11 August 1862 and was mustered in on 25 August 1862 as a private in Co. K 15th CVI for a term of three years. He was promoted to corporal on 1 June 1863. He saw action at the Battle of Fredericksburg, Virginia on 13 December 1862, during the Siege of Suffolk, Virginia in April 1863, and in the Peninsula Campaign of July 1863. He was on picket duty during the Battle of Kinston, North Carolina. George Talmadge was mustered out with the rest of his regiment at New Bern, North

---

963 A copy of his birth record in Ireland is in the pension file.
964 Muster & Descriptive Rolls of Substitutes, RG 13, box 98, 2nd Congressional District, Connecticut State Library.
965 Certificate of exemption, Henry Rogers, Branford Historical Society archives, RG 1, box 23, folder 26.
966 Various spellings - Sundelous, Sunderlous, Sundeblas, Sandelous, Sundelins.
967 Certificate of exemption, Henry Rogers, Branford Historical archives, RG 1, box 23, folder 26.

Carolina on 27 June 1865 and discharged at New Haven on 12 July 1865. His "Soldierly conduct was good." He served under Capt. Medad D. Munson of Wallingford.

He applied for an invalid pension on 18 July 1881. At the time of his enlistment he was described as five feet seven inches tall, dark complexion, brown hair, blue eyes, occupation farmer. He claimed he contracted chills, fever, and rheumatism from malaria in October 1864. "He was sent with [rebel] prisoners from New Berne, N.C. to Fortress Monroe, Va. on board the vessel 'Thorne' and upon arriving there was kept in quarantine ten days where he contracted chills and fever."[968] His claim was denied on the grounds there was no ongoing disability and an appeal was also rejected. He again applied on 10 January 1891 and received a pension under the act of 27 June 1890. His pension file is large containing many affidavits concerning his disability. He wrote many affidavits for other soldiers.

He was married first on 23 May 1866 to Maria A. Smith of Hartford who died at North Haven on 6 August 1876 age 32. She was the daughter of Julius Smith and Mary Frost. Since his discharge he lived at Northford, North Haven, New Haven, and returned to Northford.

George Washington Talmadge died at North Branford on 3 April 1896 and was buried there in Northford Cemetery. A Civil War marker was on his gravesite in 1934 and his name appears on the Northford Veterans' Monument. He was born at North Branford on 24 March 1842, son of Levi Talmadge and Marietta Foote.

Lois E. Talmadge of Northford applied for a widow's pension on 9 July 1896. She was married to the soldier as his second wife under the name of Lois Elizabeth Hull at North Haven by Rev. John Coleman on 26 September 1877. She was not previously married or divorced. The soldier had following children (living in 1896): Arthur Howard, born on 28 October 1871; Alice Elizabeth, born September 1879; and George Raymond, born at North Branford on 25 May 1892. About 1900 she moved to Branford.

Lois Elizabeth Talmadge died at Branford on 10 January 1924 and was buried in Northford Cemetery. She was born at North Haven on 4 November 1853, daughter of William Hull and Louise Delight Stevens.[969]

TALMADGE, WILLIAM
Co. E 15th CVI, private, enlisted 13 August 1862, prisoner, mustered out 27 June 1865, no pension

William Talmadge, age 32, of North Branford enlisted at New Haven on 13 August 1862 and was mustered in on 24 August 1862 as a private in Co. E 15th CVI for a term of three years. He saw action at Fredericksburg, Virginia on 13 December 1862, during the Siege of Suffolk, Virginia in the spring of 1863, and in the Peninsula Campaign of July 1863. He was captured with much of his regiment at the Battle of Kinston, North Carolina on 8 March 1865, confined at Libby Prison, Richmond on 23 March, and paroled at Boulware's & Cox's wharf on 26 March 1865. He reported to Camp Parole, Maryland on 30 March 1865, received a thirty day furlough and afterwards reported to Camp Convalescent, Virginia. William Talmadge was mustered out with the rest of his regiment at New Bern, North Carolina on 27 June 1865 and discharged at New Haven on 12 July 1865.

At the time of his enlistment he was described as five feet nine inches tall, dark complexion, blue eyes, brown hair, occupation farmer, born at Madison. He was married at Branford by Rev. Timothy P. Gillett of the First Congregational Church on 12 May 1852 to Harriet Louisa Johnson of Branford.[970]

968   Summary of pension application from the Dept. of the Interior, 30 April 1887, in the pension file of George W. Talmadge.
969   Branford Vital Records, deaths, 1924.
970   Branford Vital Records, Town Meeting Book A, 171.

William K. Talmadge died at Branford on 31 March 1872, a widower.[971] He was the son of Samuel Talmadge and Lucretia Salome Scranton.

TARBOX, AUGUSTUS G.
Co. D 1st HA, private, enlisted 2 January 1864, mustered out 25 September 1865, no pension

Augustus G. Tarbox of Branford enlisted and was mustered in on 2 January 1864 as a private in Co. D 1st HA. He participated in the Siege of Petersburg and Richmond, Virginia with his regiment. Tarbox was mustered out with the rest of his regiment at Washington, D.C. on 25 September 1865 and discharged at Hartford on 1 October 1865. He does not appear in the 1860 census at Branford.

TAYLOR, HENRY
Co. A 1st Cavalry, private, enlisted 19 December 1864, mustered out 2 August 1865, no pension

Henry Taylor of Branford enlisted and was mustered in on 19 December 1864 as a private in Co. A 1st Connecticut Cavalry. He was mustered out with the rest of his regiment at Washington, D.C. on 2 August 1865 and discharged at New Haven on 18 August 1865. He does not appear in the 1860 census at Branford.

TAYLOR, MICHAEL
Co. B 27th CVI, private, enlisted 9 September 1862, prisoner, mustered out 27 July 1863, pension #314530 for his widow Ann

Michael Taylor, age 25, of Wallingford enlisted on 9 September 1862 and was mustered in on 3 October 1862 as a private in Co. B 27th CVI for a term of nine months. He was wounded at the Battle of Fredericksburg on 13 December 1862 on the head and hand from the bursting of a shell. He was captured at the Battle of Chancellorsville, Virginia on 3 May 1863, held prisoner at Richmond, and was paroled at City Point, Virginia on 14 May 1863. He reported to Camp Parole, Maryland on 16 May 1863, was sent to Washington, D.C. on 20 May 1863 and spent the remainder of his service at Camp Convalescent, Virginia. With the rest of the Chancellorsville paroled prisoners, he rejoined the Regiment at Baltimore on 20 July 1863. Michael Taylor was mustered out with the rest of his regiment at New Haven on 27 July 1863.

Michael Taylor died on 16 January 1873 and was buried in Holy Trinity Cemetery, Wallingford.[972] His widow claimed that the wound to his head at the Battle of Fredericksburg disturbed his mental capacity and he had periods of insanity. He died by stepping onto the railroad track in front of a moving train at Wallingford.

> *"The 3:15 p. m. express train from New York ran over a man named Michael Taylor at Wallingford Tuesday and cut him in pieces. It is supposed that he was lying on the track asleep. A jury of inquest brought in a verdict to that effect, and exonerated the road from all blame."*[973]

Ann Taylor of Hartford applied for a widow's pension on 12 August 1890 under the act of 27 June 1890. She was married to the soldier under the name of Ann Pinkham at New Haven by Rev. E. J. O'Brien of St.

---

971 Branford Vital Records, 1863-1895, 212.
972 The Hale Collection, Wallingford, 149.
973 *The Daily Constitution*, 16 January 1873, www.genealogybank.com.

Mary's Church on 2 August 1852. Neither were previously married or divorced and she did not remarry after his death. At the time of the soldier's death she had the following children under the age of sixteen: Michael, born on 8 February 1862, died on 15 December 1884; and Joseph, born on 7 January 1864. She died on 12 May 1900 age 73.

TAYLOR, WILLIAM L.
Co. G 20th CVI, private, enlisted 19 August 1862, discharged 19 June 1865, pension #382429 for the soldier and later for his widow Louisa

William L. Taylor of North Branford enlisted on 19 August 1862 and was mustered in on 8 September 1862 as a private in Co. G 20th CVI for a term of three years and was discharged on 19 June 1865. He does not appear in the 1860 census at North Branford but is on the 1863 draft list for that town; age 31, born in Connecticut, married, occupation miller. He lived at Clinton in 1880 and applied for an invalid pension on 30 April 1886.

William L. Taylor died on 7 April 1893 age 70 and was buried in Clinton Cemetery. His company and regiment are engraved on his stone and there was a Civil War marker on his gravestone in 1934. Louisa Taylor applied for a widow's pension after his death.

Nicholas Terhune served in Co. E 2nd Maryland East Shore Regiment with Frederick Linsley. He came to Branford by 1870 and was a charter member of the Mason Rogers Post No. 7 G.A.R. (Bundy & Williams Studio, New Haven; courtesy of Virginia Page)

TERHUNE, NICHOLAS R.
Co. E 2nd Maryland Regiment, 1st sergeant, enlisted 26 December 1861, discharged 27 December 1864, pension #661742 for the soldier and later for his widow Lucy

Nicholas R. Terhune, age 19, of New Haven enlisted at Chestertown, Kent Co., Maryland on 25 December 1861 as a private in Co. E 2nd East Shore Maryland Volunteers for a term of three years and was promoted to 1st sergeant in 1863. The regiment served in Maryland and Virginia along the Potomac. On 31 December 1863 at Harper's Ferry, Virginia he was detailed to the quartermaster's department and was discharged from there on 27 December 1864 when his term expired.

He applied for an invalid pension on 15 April 1900 for age related illness. At the time of his enlistment he was described as five feet ten inches tall, gray eyes, dark hair, medium complexion, occupation wood carver.[974] He was married at Branford by Rev. Elijah C. Baldwin of the First Congregational Church on 28 December 1870 to Lucy DeEtte Averill. He was age 28, living at Winsted; she was age 21, living at Branford. Neither were previously married or divorced. They had the following children (living in 1903): Charles A., born on 9 September 1873; Walter, born on 3 July 1878; Lucy Edna, born on 18 March 1880; Clara S., born on 9 March 1885; and Olive, born on 23 July 1886. He was a charter member and commander of the Mason Rogers Post No. 7 G.A.R. of Branford.

---

974   His discharge papers differ, one states he was five eight inches tall, dark complexion, black eyes, black hair, occupation laborer, born at Hartford.

Terhune served in the Quartermaster Department at Harper's Ferry, Virginia. (Photographic History of the Civil War, 2:323)

Nicholas R. Terhune died at Branford on 24 August 1908 and was buried there in Center Cemetery. His company and regiment are engraved on his stone and a G.A.R. marker was on his gravesite in 1934 and 2011. He was born at Winsted on 17 January 1842, son of Nicholas A. Terhune and Sophia Wartendyke.[975]

Lucy A. Terhune of Branford applied for a widow's pension on 1 September 1908. There are affidavits from the soldier's brothers George D. Terhune age 63 and Stephen H. Terhune age 62 both of Branford stating they knew the soldier and Lucy before they were married.[976]

Lucy Averill Terhune died at Branford on 24 September 1920 and was buried there in Center Cemetery. She was born at Branford on 14 May1849, daughter of James Averill and Amanda Bassett.[977]

THAYER, ELWYN M.
U.S. Navy, enlisted 9 April 1864, discharged 22 August 1865, pension #C2581389 for the sailor

Elwyn M. Thayer of Branford enlisted in the Navy at the Brooklyn, New York Navy Yard on 9 April 1864 and was a landsman on the U.S.S. *Tritinia* on 30 April 1864, the *Fort Morgan* and the *Vermont* on 22 August 1865. He also served on the *North Carolina*. He was discharged on 22 August 1865.[978] After his discharge he returned to Branford. He was a charter member and commander of the Mason Rogers Post No. 7 G.A.R. of Branford and a charter member of the Branford Battery A. His pension is at the Veterans Administration. He was the brother-in-law of Daniel Averill, 2nd.

He was married first to Mary Geer and divorced. He was married second at Branford by Rev. Pascal G. Wightman of the First Baptist Church on 3 December 1896 to Mary Elizabeth Palmer.[979]

---

975   Branford Vital Records, deaths, 1908; also spelled Wortendyke.
976   Affidavit, George D. and Stephen H. Terhune of Branford, 5 September 1908, in the pension file of Nicholas Terhune.
977   Branford Vital Records, deaths, 1920.
978   *Index to Rendezvous Reports*, National Archives, T-1099, page 224, par 1; his name is spelled in various records Elwyn, Elwin, Edwin.
979   Branford Vital Records, marriages, 1896.

Elwyn M. Thayer, known as Cappie Thayer, served in the U.S. Navy and was the last surviving Branford Civil War veteran. He is buried in Center Cemetery. (Branford Historical Society photograph collection)

Elwyn Matton Thayer "Cappie" died at Branford on 20 May 1936 and was buried there in Center Cemetery. There was a G.A.R. marker at his gravesite in 2011. He was born at Shelbourne Falls, Massachusetts on 28 February 1849, son of Alvin S. Thayer and Myria G. Gilbert.[980] He was the last surviving Civil War soldier and G.A.R. member living at Branford.

His widow Mary E. Thayer died at Branford on 14 March 1943 and was buried there in Center Cemetery. She was born at Branford on 16 November 1864, daughter of James Bradley Palmer and Margaret Ann Smith.[981]

THOMAS, ELBRIDGE
Co. I 1st HA, private, enlisted 23 December 1863, mustered out 25 September 1865, no pension

Elbridge Thomas of North Branford enlisted and was mustered in on 23 December 1863 as a private in Co. I 1st HA for a term of three years. He participated in the Siege of Petersburg and Richmond, Virginia with the rest of his regiment. He was mustered out with the rest of his regiment at Washington, D.C. on 26 September 1865 and discharged at Hartford on 1 October 1865. He does not appear at North Branford in the 1860 census.

Elbridge E. Thomas died on 9 November 1880 and was buried in Woodlawn Cemetery, Everett, Massachusetts.[982]

980   Branford Vital Records, deaths, 1936.
981   Branford Vital Records, deaths, 1943.
982   Headstones for Deceased Union Civil War Veterans c1879-1903, National Archives M1845, www.ancestry.com.

THOMPSON, RICHARD E.

Co. B 24th CVI, private, enlisted 5 September 1862, wounded, mustered out 30 September 1863, pension #662434 for the soldier and later for his widow Mabel

Richard E. Thompson of Madison enlisted at Middletown on 5 September 1862 and was mustered in on 18 November 1862 as a private in Co. B 24th CVI for a term of ten months. He fought with his regiment at Irish Bend, Louisiana on 14 April 1863 and was wounded at Port Hudson, Louisiana on 14 June 1863. Thompson was mustered out with the rest of his regiment at Middletown on 30 September 1863.

He applied for and received an invalid pension on 25 August 1890 under the act of 27 June 1890 for rheumatism suffered during his service and for the loss of a finger on his left hand. He injured his hand after the war about 1865 while chopping wood at North Madison. There are very few documents in the file.

(Photograph by Tracy Thompson Tomaselli, with permission)

Richard Egbert Thompson died at North Branford on 7 March 1904 and was buried there in Bare Plain Cemetery. A Civil War marker was at his gravesite in 1934. He was born at Madison, son of Alvin Thompson and Abbie Watrous, born at Madison and Chester.[983]

Mabel K. Thompson of North Branford filed for a widow's pension on 30 July 1904. She was married to the soldier under the name of Mabel Kelsey Hopson at New Haven by Rev. H. M. Gallaher of the Calvary Baptist Church on 29 May 1878. She was age 32 and he age 35, both born and living at Madison. Neither were previously married or divorced and she did not remarry after his death. They had no children..

Her claim was sent for special examination due to questions concerning the value of her property. The examiner stated that she was "of good reputation and impressed me as an honest, plain spoken woman."[984] She owned a house and thirty-four acres in North Branford, twenty-five acres at Madison, a five acre salt meadow at Guilford, and a bank account. There are a number of depositions in the file including one from her brother John H. Hopson of North Branford. Her claim was rejected on 18 April 1905 on the grounds her annual income exceeded $250.00. As she got older, the income from her farm decreased and she reapplied and received a pension on 16 May 1908.

Mabel Hopson Thompson died at New Haven Hospital on 3 March 1925 and was buried in Bare Plain Cemetery, North Branford. She was born at North Madison on 31 January 1846, daughter of John Hopson and Roxana Kelsey.[985]

---

983   Copies of vital record information from Tracy Thompson Tomaselli of Guilford, 16 December 2010.
984   R. S. Coleman of New Haven, special examiner, 25 February 1905; in the pension file of Richard E. Thompson.
985   New Haven Vital Records, deaths, 1925.

TODD, ANDREW B.

Co. A 10th CVI, private, enlisted 14 September 1861, wounded, discharged disability 22 February 1863, pension #1159707 for the soldier and later an application for his widow Lucy J. Todd

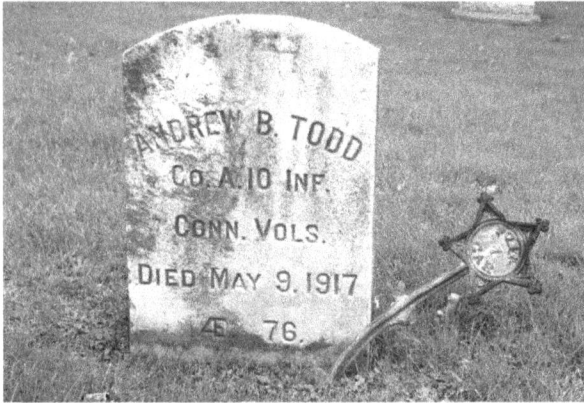

Andrew B. Todd of Hamden enlisted at Hartford on 14 September 1861 and was mustered in on 21 September 1861 as a private in Co. A 10th CVI for a term of three years. He was wounded at the Battle of Roanoke Island, North Carolina on 8 February 1862. He was discharged for disability at New Bern, North Carolina on 22 February 1863 due to a gunshot wound to his right hand.

He applied for and received an invalid pension on 4 May 1863 as a result of the wound to his right hand, the amputation of one finger, and loss of use of the hand. He eventually lost some use of his arm and shoulder. He received numerous payment increases through the years. After receiving a pension for forty-nine years, the pension board suddenly claimed in 1912 that the wound did not prevent him from performing manual labor. He was by then seventy-one years old. Though there were numerous affidavits in the file, he had to provide another physician's affidavit to continue receiving a disability pension. At the time of his enlistment he was described as five feet ten inches tall, fair complexion, blue eyes, brown hair, occupation farmer.

He was married first at Meriden on 24 June 1863 by Rev. Jacob Eaton to Eliza L. Thorp. Neither were previously married or divorced. She died at Short Beach, Branford on 15 January 1911 and was buried in East Lawn Cemetery, East Haven. She was born at Meriden on 21 January 1847, daughter of Gideon Thorp and Abagail Bowe. He was married second at Meriden by Rev. Charles K. Woodson on 3 January 1912 to Lucy J. Crowell. She was age 43, born at Middletown, living at Meriden, not previously married, daughter of Frank Crowell. He had three daughters by his first wife (living in 1915): Angie, born on 24 May 1866; Ada, born on 7 February 1869; and Bertha, born on 24 June 1871. Since his discharge he lived at Meriden, Southington, and Short Beach, Branford. He was mustered in on 21 September 1911 as a member of the Mason Rogers Post No. 7 G.A.R. of Branford.

Andrew B. Todd died at Short Beach on 9 May 1917 and was buried in Green Lawn Cemetery, East Haven. He was born at Ray, Macomb Co., Michigan on 6 May 1841, son of Jasper E. Todd and Mary Perkins.

Lucy J. Todd of Short Beach applied for a widow's pension on 11 June 1917 and again on 1 June 1920. Both claims were rejected because she had not been married to the soldier before 27 June 1905 as required by the pension acts. She was living at Meriden in 1920.

TODD, BERI M.

Co. B 27th CVI, private, enlisted 30 August 1862, mustered out 27 July 1863, no pension

Beri M. Todd, age 44, of New Haven enlisted at New Haven on 30 August 1862 and was mustered in on 3 October 1862 as a private in Co. B 27th CVI for a term of nine months. Throughout the war he was attached as a driver for the ambulance service. Beri Todd was mustered out with the rest of his regiment at New Haven on 27 July 1863.

Beri M. Todd of Co. B 27th Connecticut Volunteer Regiment was detached to the ambulance service during his enlistment. This photograph shows the New York Zouave ambulance crew. (Library of Congress, Prints & Photographs Division, LC-DIG-cwpb-03950)

Beri Moraldus Todd died on 5 September 1876 and was buried in Evergreen Cemetery, New Haven.[986] He was born on 7 April 1807[987] or 4 April 1808,[988] son of Melicu Todd and Polly Ray. He was married at North Haven by Rev. William J. Boardman on 12 November 1828 to Caroline S. Barnes, daughter of Joshua Barnes.[989] They lived at North Haven and his name appears on the North Haven Civil War Honor Roll.

TODD, HENRY D.

Co. B 27th CVI, private, enlisted 1 September 1862, mustered out 27 July 1863, pension #658531 for the soldier

Henry D. Todd, age 29, of North Haven enlisted on 1 September 1862 and was mustered in on 3 October 1862 as a private in Co. B 27th CVI for a term of nine months. He was present at roll call in November 1862. From 1 December 1862 through June 1863 he was sick at Satterlee General Hospital, West Philadelphia, Pennsylvania and returned to duty on 4 July 1863. Henry Todd was mustered out with the rest of his regiment at New Haven on 27 July 1863.

---

986   The Hale Collection, New Haven, 716.

987   Lorraine Cook White, editor, *The Barbour Collection of Connecticut Town Vital Records, North Haven 1786-1854* (Baltimore, Genealogical Publishing Co., Inc., 2000), 280, referring to North Haven Vital Records 2:14.

988   John Edward Todd, *The Todd Family in America or the Descendants of Christopher Todd 1637-1919* (Northampton, Mass., Press of Gazette Printing Co., 1920), 104 & 186.

989   John E. Todd, *The Todd Family*, 186.

He applied for an invalid pension on 9 May 1890. At the time of his enlistment he was described as five feet nine inches tall, light complexion, hazel eyes, brown hair, occupation farmer. He always resided at North Haven. He states he contracted rheumatism while at Camp Tuttle, Virginia on 15 November 1862 from exposure laying on the wet ground in the snow and rain. He contracted varicose veins on their march in the night from Long Bridge to Camp Tuttle. "We left him behind when the Regiment started for Aquia Creek and he was sent to the hospital in Washington, D.C."[990] Statements from neighbors attest to his disability, especially problems with his back.

He was married at North Haven by Rev. William T. Reynolds on 25 February 1868 to Grace Ann Hartley. Neither were previously married or divorced. They had no children. She died on 8 July 1914 and was buried in Center Cemetery, North Haven.[991] She was born on 5 March 1833.

Henry Dennis Todd died at North Haven on 10 December 1919 and was buried there in Center Cemetery. There was a Civil War marker on his gravesite in 1934 and his name appears on the North Haven Civil War Honor Roll. He was born at North Haven on 2 September 1832, son of Orrin Todd and Aurelia Clinton. There was no record of his birth since the North Haven records burned in 1864.

TODD, KIRTLAND
Co. B 27th CVI, private, enlisted 9 September 1862, prisoner, mustered out 27 July 1863, pension #358320 for his widow Ellen

Kirtland Todd, age 25, of North Haven enlisted on 9 September 1862 and was mustered in on 3 October 1862 as a private in Co. B 27th CVI for a term of nine months. He fought at the Battle of Fredericksburg on 13 December 1862 with the rest of the company. He was captured at the Battle of Chancellorsville, Virginia on 3 May 1863, held prisoner at Richmond, and was paroled at City Point, Virginia on 14 May 1863. He reported to Camp Parole, Maryland on 16 May 1863, was sent to Washington, D.C. on 20 May 1863 and spent the remainder of his service at Camp Convalescent, Virginia. With the rest of the Chancellorsville paroled prisoners, he rejoined the Regiment at Baltimore on 20 July 1863. Kirtland Todd was mustered out with the rest of his regiment at New Haven on 27 July 1863.

Kirtland Todd died at Wallingford on 13 March 1880 and was buried there in Center Street Cemetery. He died of pneumonia as a result of a severe cough contracted while in the service. He never applied for a pension. His name appears on the North Haven Civil War Honor Roll.

Ellen J. Todd, age 43, of Wallingford applied for a widow's pension on 11 May 1883. They were married under the names of Franklin Lathrop and Janett Judson at Orange by Rev. Raymond on 19 July 1861. They used false names because they had run away to marry. Her maiden name was Ellen J. Dervey. They had the following children born at Wallingford: William E., born on 13 September 1864; Martin B., born on 27 May 1867; Robert B., born on 18 July 1870; Clifford K., born on 30 September 1872; Whitney A., born on 21 August 1874; Fanny A., born on 6 August 1876; Nellie J., born on 6 December 1878; and Alison Dewd (son), born on 18 June 1880. She was admitted to the Wallingford Congregational Church from the Plainville Congregational Church on 6 May 1888.[992] Ellen Todd does not appear in the 1900 U.S. census.

---

990   Affidavit, Thomas O'Brien of New Haven, 31 March 1890, in the pension file of Henry D. Todd.
991   The Hale Collection, North Haven, 2.
992   Wallingford Congregational Church Records, 3:155.

TOWNSEND, SIDNEY
Co. D 1st HA, private, enlisted 2 January 1864, died 4 August 1864, pension #123921 for his widow Mary and minor children

Sidney Townsend, age 35, of Branford enlisted and was mustered in at New Haven on 25 January 1864 as a private in Co. D 1st HA. He died at Regimental Hospital, Broadway Landing, Virginia on 4 August 1864 of fever. He lived in Susquehanna Co., Pennsylvania and went with his friend Jedadiah Safford to Connecticut to enlist. At the time of his enlistment he was described as five feet seven inches tall, blue eyes, brown hair, ruddy complexion, occupation farmer. He was born in Wyoming Co., Pennsylvania. Mentioned in the file are Maria Townsend, wife of H. Finn of Susquehanna, Pennsylvania and Dillavan Townsend, both probably related to the soldier.

Mary E. Townsend applied for a widow's pension on 23 March 1865. She was married to the soldier under the name of Mary E. Hawk at Kingston Township, Luzerne Co., Pennsylvania by Rev. Charles Perkins on 8 December 1852. They had three children: Alvah, born on 10 August 1854; Fermin, born on 11 February 1858; and Francis M., born on 20 January 1860. In 1866 she was living at Lathrop, Susquehanna Co., Pennsylvania and the children were attending the Soldiers' Orphan School at Harford, Pennsylvania. There is no further information in the file.

TUBBS, JOHN E.
Co. A 13th CVI, private, enlisted 24 October 1861, mustered out 6 January 1865, no pension

John E. Tubbs of New Britain enlisted at New Haven on 24 October 1861 and was mustered in on 22 December 1861 as a private in Co. A 13th CVI for a term of three years. With his regiment he served in the New Orleans area and in Virginia. He was transferred to Co. A 13th Battalion C. V. on 29 December 1864 and was mustered out on 6 January 1865.

After the war he returned to New Britain. He was married at Bristol by Rev. Henry Fitch on 11 January 1852 to Clarissa Parmelee, both of New Britain.[993] She died on 25 January 1876 age 44 and was buried in New Britain. He was admitted to the Branford First Congregational Church on 7 March 1879 and was living at Branford in 1880 with his son-in-law and daughter Clifford & Annie Bartholomew. He was mustered in on 28 April 1882 as a member of the Mason Rogers Post G.A.R. No. 7 of Branford, transferred from the Stanley Post No. 11 of New Britain. He was age 51, born at Farmington, occupation engineer, a widower. He was transferred back to the New Britain post on 19 October 1885. He did not apply for a pension.

John E. Tubbs died on 11 January 1890 age 63 and was buried in Fairview Cemetery, New Britain.[994] His company and regiment are engraved on his stone and there was a Civil War marker on his gravesite in 1934.

---

993   The Barbour Collection, Bristol, 3:58.
994   The Hale Collection, New Britain, 157.

TUCKER, ALLEN
Co. D 3rd Rifle Co. & Co. F 10th CVI, sergeant, enlisted 23 April 1861, reenlisted, mustered out 25 August 1865, Congressional Medal of Honor, pension #911394 for the soldier and later for his widow Lucy

Allen Tucker[995] of Franklin enlisted at Sprague on 23 April 1861 and was mustered in at Hartford on 14 May 1861 as a private in Co. D 3rd Rifle Co. for a term of three months and fought at the first Battle of Bull Run. He was mustered out at Hartford on 12 August 1861. He reenlisted on 3 September 1861, then of Sprague, as sergeant of Co. F 10th CVI and his rank was reduced to corporal on 1 January 1862. He was sick in the hospital in May 1862. He reenlisted at St. Augustine, Florida on 1 January 1864 as a private in Co. F 10th CVI and was promoted to sergeant (no date given). He received the Congressional Medal of Honor at Petersburg, Virginia on 2 April 1865 for "Gallantry as color bearer in the assault on Fort Gregg, capturing the enemy's flag."[996] Allen Tucker was mustered out with the rest of his regiment at Richmond, Virginia on 25 August 1865 and discharged at Hartford on 5 September 1865.

He applied for an invalid pension on 15 March 1887. During the spring of 1862 he had malarial fever at New Bern, North Carolina and was treated at New Bern Hospital for four months and at Beaufort Hospital for two months. He developed a severe case of eczema on 27 July 1864 at Strawberry Planes [sic], Virginia from which he never fully recovered. In 1896 he broke his leg. At the time of his discharge he was described as five feet eight inches tall, light complexion, dark hair, blue eyes, occupation farm hand. After the war he lived at East Haven and worked as a farm hand for the Trowbridge family. He was mustered in on 15 February 1889 as a member of the Mason Rogers Post No. 7 G.A.R. of Branford.

He was married first at Sprague by Rev. Simon B. Bailey on 22 March 1864 to Amelia J. Bradley. She died at New Haven on 21 November 1897 age 51 years, 2 months & 8 days. She was born at New Haven, daughter of William and Susan Bradley, both born at Madison. He had three children living (in 1898): Carrie A., born on 27 July 1866; George A., born on 10 September 1896; and Leland T., born on 2 March 1877.

Allen Tucker died at the Springside Home, New Haven[997] on 22 February 1903 age 65 and was buried there in Evergreen Cemetery. His company and regiment are engraved on his stone and there was a Civil War marker on his gravesite in 1934. He was born at Old Lyme, son of Giles Tucker and Lucy Havens.

Lucy A. Tucker applied for a widow's pension on 14 April 1913 but abandoned her claim because she married the soldier after 1890. She began receiving a pension on 5 August 1918 when the date of marriage eligibility was increased to 1905. She was married first under the name of Lucy A. Deming at East Haven by Rev. Horace C. Hovey on 1 February 1880 to George William Stevens. He was born at Cheshire, son of William and Mary Stevens and died at Woodbridge on 16 April 1896 age 45 years and 4 months. He did not serve in the military. She stated that she had no children living (in 1919) but had two grandsons who served in the Navy during the World War but has had no contact; they were raised by a foster mother. She was married to the soldier at her sister's home in Hamden by Rev. Howard Mudie on 11 September 1898. He was living at New Haven and she at Seymour. She had no children with the soldier. A deposition from her brother William W. Deming of Bethany said he knew Tucker for

---

995   For information see Manzella, Nancy, Profiles of Connecticut Civil War Soldiers, *Connecticut Genealogy News*, Spring 2011, Vol. 4 No. 3, 11.

996   Congressional Medal of Honor Society at www.history.army.mil/moh; *The New York Times*, 22 June 1865, www.nytimes.com.

997   Springside Home on Springside Avenue is listed in the 1903 New Haven City Directory as a boarding house (Almshouse).

thirty-eight years before the marriage to his sister and that his first wife had died.[998] There are many statements in the file concerning her marriages.

She lived at Derby until 1909, Niantic until 1912 and since 1912 lived with her sister Mary E. Warner (Mrs. Charles A.) at Hamden.

Lucy A. Tucker died at Mt. Carmel, Hamden on 6 October 1922 age 69. She was born at New Haven, daughter of Calvin Deming and Lucy Ann Powers.

TUCKER, LEWIS M.
Co. B 27th CVI, private, enlisted 25 August 1862, died 10 October 1862, pension #85480 for his mother Betsey Tucker

Lewis Montgomery Tucker, age 25, of Branford enlisted on 25 August 1862 and was mustered in on 3 October 1862 as a private in Co. B 27th CVI for a term of nine months. "Said soldier contracted Typhoid Fever while doing Guard duty with his Co. in Camp Terry at New Haven and obtained a furlough authorized by his Captain and died while on said furlough."[999] He died at his home in Stony Creek, Branford on 10 October 1862 of typhoid fever, unmarried, and was buried in Damascus Cemetery. Lewis M. Tucker was born at Branford on 19 January 1834, son of Nelson Nathan Tucker and Betsey Griswold.[1000] His name appears on the Stony Creek Veterans' Monument. He was the brother-in-law of John Hotchkiss.

His mother Betsey Tucker applied for a pension on 22 January 1866 under the act of 14 July 1862. She was married at Branford on 30 November 1832 to Nelson Nathan Tucker. Tucker was stricken with paralysis in 1857 and was unable to support his family. The soldier contributed to his parents' support out of his own earnings as a butcher and bought them a small house and lot in Stony Creek. Nelson Tucker died at Branford on 16 August 1875 and was buried there in Damascus Cemetery.[1001]

Betsey Tucker died at Branford on 26 June 1892 and was buried in Stony Creek Cemetery.[1002]

TYLER, OBED L.
Co. B 27th CVI, private, enlisted 22 August 1862, prisoner, mustered out 27 July 1863, pension #892780 for the soldier

Obed L. Tyler, age 21, of Branford enlisted on 22 August 1862 and was mustered in on 3 October 1862 as a private in Co. B 27th CVI for a term of nine months. He fought at the Battle of Fredericksburg on 13 December 1862 with the rest of the company. He was captured at the Battle of Chancellorsville, Virginia on 3 May 1863, held prisoner at Richmond, and was paroled at City Point, Virginia on 14 May 1863. He reported

---

998   Deposition, William W. Deming, age 87, of Bethany, 10 December 1920, in the pension file of Allen Tucker.
999   Statement, Calvin L. Ely of Branford, 16 October 1866, in the pension file of Lewis M. Tucker.
1000   Branford Vital Records, Town Meeting Book A, 231.
1001   Branford Vital Records, 1863-1895, 217.
1002   Branford Vital Records, 1863-1895, 247.

to Camp Parole, Maryland on 16 May 1863, was sent to Washington, D.C. on 20 May 1863 and spent the remainder of his service at Camp Convalescent, Virginia. With the rest of the Chancellorsville paroled prisoners, he rejoined the Regiment at Baltimore on 20 July 1863. Obed Tyler was mustered out with the rest of his regiment at New Haven on 27 July 1863. He was the son-in-law of Benjamin F. Chaipel.

He applied for an invalid pension on 31 March 1898 under the act of 27 June 1890. He had difficulty receiving a pension. There are numerous letters of request and depositions in the file. At the time of his enlistment he was described as five feet eleven inches tall, dark complexion, brown hair, brown eyes, occupation iron moulder. Since his discharge he lived at Branford about 23 years, to Bridgeport in 1885, and was admitted to Fitch's Home for Soldiers, Noroton Heights in 1914. "I was born in Branford and lived there until 30 or 34 years ago when I went to Bridgeport and remained there till I came to this Home. I worked at the Branford Lock Shop."[1003]

At various times in the winter of 1863 he was treated for rheumatism. "He complained of rheumatism and loss of sight in his right eye when he returned from the war."[1004] "That while near Falmouth in the winter of 1862 and 1863 he was sick and had a bandage over his eye for a number of days before the Doctor sent him to the Hospital."[1005] "The first time I felt rheumatism was at Camp Ethan Allen near Washington, D.C. after I had been in the service about three months, I suppose by being wet and exposure while on picket duty. I was excused from duty at that time about three weeks by Dr. Hills the regimental surgeon. He treated me in quarters. I had another spell right after the battle of Fredericksburg and was treated for about three months in the Regimental hospital near Falmouth, Va. On the march to the Battle of Chancellorsville I was suffering from rheumatism. I was taken prisoner there. I was hardly able to walk when we were taken to Richmond. Sometime in the spring of 1863 near Falmouth I had trouble with my right eye. I was on picket duty and a strong wind was blowing, a stone and other pieces flew into my eye."[1006]

He was married first at Branford on 19 April 1864 to Mary J. Chappell [Chaipel]. She died at Branford on 21 September 1884 and was buried there in Center Cemetery. He was married second at Bridgeport by Rev. O'Brien on 16 August 1892 to Ann Barney, a widow, whose maiden name was Carroll. He was living with his second wife in 1915. His death certificate lists him as a widower, but names only his first wife. He had the following children by his first wife (living in 1898): Nettie, born on 2 April 1865; Martha, born on 29 November 1866; Mary, born on 21 February 1868; Willie, born on 27 December 1870; Arthur, born on 15 July 1875; and Lizzie, born on 29 April 1877. He was a charter member of the Mason Rogers Post No. 7 G.A.R. of Branford.

Obed L. Tyler died at the Fitch's Soldier Home on 6 June 1936 age 94 and was buried there in Spring Grove Cemetery. He was born at Branford on 14 December 1841, son of Benjamin Tyler and Hannah Spinks, both born at Branford.

TYLER, WILLIAM A.
Co. B 27th CVI, private, enlisted 10 September 1862, mustered out 27 July 1863, pension #462785 for the soldier

William A. Tyler, age 23, of Branford enlisted on 10 September 1862 and was mustered in on 3 October 1862 as a private in Co. B 27th CVI for a term of nine months. "I want to tell you that Will Tyler is detailed as guard of

1003 Deposition, Obed L. Tyler of Noroton, 23 May 1920 in the pension file of Michael O'Neil.
1004 Affidavit, Harriet Palmer of Branford, 10 August 1897, in the pension file of Obed L. Tyler.
1005 Affidavit, Daniel Averill of Branford, 19 March 1898, in the pension file of Obed L. Tyler.
1006 Deposition, Obed L. Tyler of Bridgeport, 12 November 1903, in his own pension file.

the ambulance train and got to sleep on his post and is under arrest at Hancocks head quarters. has just been to the camp and got his rations with a guard, wants to have the boys keep still and not write home about it."[1007] "I fought at the Battles of Fredericksburg, Chancellorsville, and Gettysburg." There are no medical records in his CMSR. William Tyler was mustered out with the rest of his regiment at New Haven on 27 July 1863. He was the first cousin of Daniel and David Averill.

He applied for an invalid pension on 26 March 1889. He was living at Mattituck, Suffolk Co., New York. "He contracted rheumatism and heart disease at Fredericksburg on 12 December 1862 and it has continued and grown worse. He fell down on the march to Gettysburg."[1008] "While in the line of duty at Fredericksburg, Va. about Dec. 12th 1862 he contracted Rheumatism from a severe cold while in Camp near Falmouth, Va."[1009] "He was an able bodied man when he entered the army and was a physical wreck when he returned."[1010] "When I got home my parents did not know me." In 1889 he was described as five feet eight inches tall, dark complexion, black hair, dark eyes, occupation carpenter and farmer.

William A. Tyler was one of many young men from Branford who served as privates in Co. B 27th CVI. After the war he lived at Branford and Mattituck, Long Island. (courtesy of John E. Tyler, Jr.)

In 1911 there is a series of letters from Tyler to the pension board commissioner asking for an increase in his pension rate and it appears the pension board accused him of fraud. "I wish for you to send me a good honest check now from $1.00 to $5.00 to which I am entitled or I will starve to death. I know what I write is the truth. The old Soldiers that fought the great Battles get the kicks [out] of the Gov. Pension dept. You are dealing with an honest Old soldier, 72 years old. I was always called an honest man until the Pension Dept. accused me. I fought in the 3 Greatest Battle in the whole War. I went from 165 lbs to 118 lbs in 2 months after the Battle of Chancellorsville. The Board tells a pack of lies for they never as much as asked me a question nor barely looked at me. I never even got into their office in New London, was just met at the door. That was Copperheads Treatment to an Honest old Soldier that was at the front. The Bullets were flying thick and one hit my hat at Gettysburg."[1011] "You gave me $2 a month that all my Neighbors call an insult to my disability. I was on my back for 18 months when I got home from the war and was under Dr. care. My father Payed the Dr. Bills."[1012] It is not clear whether he ever received his increase. He was a member of the Mason Rogers Post No. 7 G.A.R. of Branford.

He was married at New Haven to Sarah J. Farren who died at Branford on 4 July 1886 and was buried there in Mill Plain Cemetery.[1013] He remained a widower. They had three children, all living in 1898: Addie L., born on 7 September 1871; George L., born on 23 May, 1874; and Samuel G., born on 3 July 1879. His son Samuel G. Tyler was living at Mattituck, New York in 1913.

1007 Letter, Samuel Beach to home, 4 January 1863.
1008 Deposition, physician not named, 26 April 1893, in the pension file of William A. Tyler.
1009 Affidavit, Calvin L. Ely of Branford, June 1889, in the pension file of William A. Tyler.
1010 Affidavit, Joseph W. Pond of Branford, June 1889, in the pension file of William A. Tyler.
1011 Letter, William A. Tyler to Mr. Comm. Davenport [commissioner], 12 June and 25 July 1911, written from New London.
1012 Letter, William A. Tyler to Mr. Comm. [commissioner], 18 March 1912, written from New London.
1013 Branford Sexton Records, 1884-1932, 5; no stone.

William Averill Tyler died on 1 June 1913 and was buried in New Bethany Cemetery, Mattituck, New York. He was born at Branford on 13 April 1839, son of John Tyler and Eunice Averill.[1014]

UNDERWOOD, WILLIAM J.
Co. G 7th CVI, private, enlisted 27 August 1861, discharged disability 3 January 1862, pension #1054022 for the soldier

William J. Underwood of Branford enlisted at New Haven on 27 August 1861 and was mustered in on 7 September 1861 as a private in Co. G 7th CVI for a term of three years. He was discharged for disability on 3 January 1862. He was previously a member of Co. C & D 9th Rhode Island Light Artillery. He applied for an invalid pension on 25 January 1892 under the act of 27 June 1890. He does not appear in the 1860 census at Branford.

VALLELEY, FRANK or FRANCIS VALALY
Co. A 10th CVI & 2nd Battalion VRC, enlisted 29 August 1861, discharged 20 September 1864, pension #215856 for the soldier and later for his widow Ellen

Francis Valleley of Clinton enlisted at Hartford on 29 August 1861 and was mustered in on 21 September 1861 as a private in Co. A 10th CVI for a term of three years. With the rest of the regiment he fought at the Battle of Roanoke Island, North Carolina on 8 February 1862. On 11 July 1862 he suffered from sun stroke. He was reported as absent without leave but was sick in Knight Hospital, New Haven from 19 July 1862 until April 1864. He was transferred to the 159th Co. 2nd Battalion VRC on 7 May 1864 by reason of chronic rheumatism and was discharged on 20 September 1864.

He applied for an invalid pension on 30 June 1881. He was married at Branford by Rev. Campbell on 19 August 1870 to Ellen Collins, both were born in Ireland and living at Clinton.[1015] They do not appear in any Branford census.

Francis Valleley died on 31 January 1885 age 50 and was buried in St. Mary's Cemetery, Branford.[1016] Helen Valleley applied for a widow's pension on 15 February 1885 and appears at Clinton in the 1900 census. She died at Clinton on 27 September 1904 age 76 and was buried in St. Mary's Cemetery, Branford.[1017]

VANBENTHUYSEN, ISAAC E.
Co. F 71st New York Infantry, private, enlisted 25 April 1861, discharged disability 6 October 1862, pension #381318 for the soldier and later for his widow Josephine

Isaac E. VanBenthuysen, age 38, of New York enlisted on 25 April 1861 as a private in Co. F 71st New York Infantry for a term of three years. He was in the hospital from August 1862 until his discharge. He was discharged for disability at Alexandria, Virginia on 6 October 1862.

He applied for an invalid pension on 2 January 1877. At the time of his enlistment he was described as five feet eight inches tall, dark complexion, brown eyes, black hair, occupation blacksmith. "On the 2nd day of July 1862 between Malvern Hill & Harrison Landing Va. while on the retreat from Malvern Hill I accidentally fell over a stump & the but [sic] of my gun caught in the lower part of my stomach and caused

---

1014 Branford Vital Records, Town Meeting Book A, 243.
1015 Branford Vital Records, 1863-1895, 141; sometimes couples from other towns were married or buried here because Branford had a catholic church.
1016 Hale Collection, Branford, 104; the stone was not found.
1017 *The Branford Opinion*, 30 September 1904.

a rupture or hernia from which I have never recovered. I lay in camp & was treated at Harrisons Landing until about the first of August 1862 when I entered the Newark hospital & remained about 3 weeks & was then sent to Fort Hamilton & remained about 3 weeks & was then sent to Convalescent Camp Alexandria Va. where I remained until discharge."[1018] Since his discharge he resided at New York until 1870, then at Branford. He was a charter member of the Mason Rogers Post No. 7 G.A.R. and was transferred to the Douglas Fowler Post No. 48 of South Norwalk on 29 March 1892.

Issac Everett VanBenthuysen died at Branford on 10 March 1893 and was buried there in Center Cemetery. There is no stone but a Civil War marker was on his gravesite in 1934. He was born at New York City, son of John and Sarah VanBenthuysen.[1019] At the time of his death he had one son under the age of sixteen; Isaac Brown VanBenthuysen, born at Branford on 31 May 1879.

Josephine A. VanBenthuysen of Branford applied for a widow's pension on 6 April 1893. She was married to the soldier under the name of Josephine A. Cargill at New York City by Rev. Isaac Maguire of the Church of the Epiphany on 31 March 1872. He had been married first to Hannah who died at Branford on 20 January 1872 and was buried there in Center Cemetery. Josephine was married first to Oscar H. Cargill who died on 14 April 1867.

Josephine A. VanBenthuysen died at New Haven on 1 October 1902 and was buried in Center Cemetery, Branford. [1020]

VIBBERT, NELSON J.
Co. B 27th CVI, private, enlisted 10 September 1862, prisoner, mustered out 27 July 1863, Co. I 7th Vermont Infantry, private, enlisted 28 March 1865, discharged 12 May 1865, pension #450176 for his widow Laura

Nelson J. Vibbert, age 44, of Wallingford enlisted on 10 September 1862 and was mustered in on 3 October 1862 as a private in Co. B 27th CVI for a term of nine months. He fought at the Battle of Fredericksburg on 13 December 1862 with the rest of the company. He was captured at the Battle of Chancellorsville, Virginia on 3 May 1863, held prisoner at Richmond, and was paroled at City Point, Virginia on 14 May 1863. He reported to Camp Parole, Maryland on 16 May 1863 and spent the remainder of his service at Camp Convalescent, Virginia. With the rest of the Chancellorsville paroled prisoners, he rejoined the Regiment at Baltimore on 20 July 1863. Vibbert was mustered out with the rest of his regiment at New Haven on 27 July 1863. He was in Co. B 27th CVI Pioneer Corps.[1021] He reenlisted on 28 March 1865 in Co. I 7th Vermont Regiment and was honorably discharged on 12 May 1865.

He was married first at Hartford by Rev. J. S. Eaton on 14 August 1842 to Lucy A. Hosmer. She died at North Haven on 1 January 1882 age 62 and was buried in Center Street Cemetery, Wallingford. She was born at Hartland. Vibbert had two sons and one daughter.

He applied for a pension on 29 September 1890 under the act of 27 June 1890 but died before the pension was granted.

Nelson J. Vibbert died at Wallingford on 9 August 1892 age 69 and was buried there in Center Street Cemetery. He was born at East Hartford, son of John Vibbert, his mother's name was not given on his death certificate.

1018 Original pension application, 13 December 1876, in the pension file of Isaac E. VanBenthuysen.
1019 Branford Vital Records, deaths, 1893.
1020 *The Branford Opinion*, 4 October 1902; her death was not found in the Branford or New Haven Vital Records.
1021 Sheldon, *History of Twenty-seventh*, 122.

Laura Ann Vibbert applied for a widow's pension on 28 November 1892. Her application was rejected and was resubmitted on 30 June 1896. She was married first under the name of Laura A. Mix at Wallingford by Rev. Edward M. Gushee? of St. Paul's Church on 22 May 1864 to Calvin Wooding. Wooding died at Wallingford on 20 August 1880 age 82. He was born at Bethany, occupation farmer.

She was married second to Nelson Vibbert at Wallingford by Rev. H. P. Smith of the Baptist Church on 4 July 1882. Laura had life use of a house at Wallingford from her first husband. In 1897 she was living at Wallingford, a widow. There are affidavits in the file from Levi S. Vibbert, age 83, of Wallingford, brother of the late Nelson Vibbert and from Lucinda Vibbert, age 71, of Wallingford. In 1895 there was an affidavit from Albert N. Vibbert and from Lyman John Mix, age 43, the relationship of the latter three was not given.

WALLACE, WILLIAM J.
Co. B 27th CVI, private, enlisted 6 September 1862, mustered out 27 July 1863, pension #XC2664849 for his widow Augusta

William J. Wallace, age 18, of Wallingford enlisted on 6 September 1862 and was mustered in on 3 October 1862 as a private in Co. B 27th CVI for a term of nine months. He fought at the Battle of Fredericksburg on 13 December 1862 with the rest of the company. He was sick in Regimental Hospital January and February 1863. He was reported absent on leave in March 1863 and was given a furlough from 29 May 1863 until 6 April 1863. It was reported on 7 April 1863 at Falmouth, Virginia that he had deserted and on 17 May 1863 still had not reported back to camp. On 4 June 1891 it was determined that the charge of desertion was erroneous, that he was sick from 6 April 1863 until 27 July 1863 when the company was discharged. His honorable discharge certificate was furnished to the pension board. After his discharge he returned to Wallingford.

William J. Wallace died on 17 September 1878 age 31 and was buried In Memoriam Cemetery, Wallingford.[1022] He was the son of John and Harriett Wallace.

Augusta Wallace applied for a widow's pension on 13 March 1891 under the act of 27 June 1890. His pension is at the Veterans Administration.

WALLACK, GEORGE
Co. K 14th CVI & 2nd Battalion VRC, private, drafted 25 July 1863, wounded, discharged 23 September 1865, no pension

George Wallack of Branford served as a substitute or was drafted on 25 July 1863 as a private in Co. K 14th CVI. He was wounded at Morton's Ford, Virginia on 6 February 1864 and wounded again at Laurel Hill, West Virginia on 10 May 1864. He was transferred to 72nd Co. 2nd Battalion VRC on 20 October 1864 and discharged on 23 September 1865. He does not appear at Branford in the 1860 census.

WALTER, FRANK
Co. K 11th CVI, private, enlisted 10 February 1864, deserted, no pension

Frank Walter of Branford enlisted on 10 February 1864 as a private in Co. K 11th CVI and deserted to the enemy on 29 August 1864. He does not appear at Branford in the 1860 census.

1022 The Hale Collection, Wallingford, 202.

WEED, OSCAR

Co. F 17th CVI, private, enlisted 9 August 1862, prisoner, discharged 10 July 1865, pension #1085328 for the soldier and an application for his widow Helen

Oscar Weed of South Norwalk enlisted at Norwalk on 9 August 1862 and was mustered in on 28 August 1862 as a private in Co. F 17th CVI for a term of three years. He was captured at Dunn's Lake, Florida on 5 February 1865, held prisoner at Andersonville, and paroled on 21 April 1865. He was discharged at New York City on 10 July 1865 by General Gilmore as a paroled prisoner of war.

He applied for an invalid pension on 10 June 1892 under the act of 27 June 1890. At the time of his enlistment he was described as five feet four inches tall, light eyes, dark hair, light complexion, occupation farmer. He contracted rheumatism while imprisoned at Andersonville Prison. He was married first to Nettie Dolph who died at Branford on 12 January 1883. He was married second at New Haven by Rev. Elijah C. Baldwin on 19 October 1887 to Nellie M. Lee who died at Branford on 15 September 1905. He had no children living in 1915. Since his discharge he lived at South Norwalk until 1866, Branford until 1876, South Norwalk until about 1880, Branford until 1894; Canon City, Colorado until 1897, and finally back at Branford. He was a member and commander of the Mason Rogers Post No. 7 G.A.R. of Branford.

Oscar Weed died at Branford on 31 January 1919 and was buried there in Center Cemetery. His company and regiment are engraved on his stone and a G.A.R. marker was on his gravesite in 1934. He was born at New York City on 30 January 1846, son of Thomas Weed and Mary Simmons.[1023]

Helen Weed of New Haven applied for a widow's pension on 24 March 1919. She was married to the soldier under the name of Helen J. Scott at Farmington by Rev. Quincy Blakely on 27 May 1914 as his third wife. She was not previously married or divorced. She was not eligible for a pension since she married the soldier after 1905.

WHEATON, MERWIN or CHARLES WHEATON

Co. B 27th CVI, private, enlisted 10 August 1862, prisoner, mustered out 27 July 1863, pension #1106373 for the soldier

Merwin Wheaton, age 19, of North Branford enlisted on 10 August 1862 and was mustered in on 3 October 1862 as a private in Co. B 27th CVI for a term of nine months. He fought at the Battle of Fredericksburg on 13 December 1862 with the rest of the company. He was captured at the Battle of Chancellorsville, Virginia on 3 May 1863, held prisoner at Richmond, and was paroled at City Point, Virginia on 14 May 1863. He reported to Camp Parole, Maryland on 16 May 1863, was sent to Washington, D.C. on 20 May 1863 and spent the remainder of his service at Camp Convalescent, Virginia. With the rest of the Chancellorsville paroled prisoners, he rejoined the Regiment at Baltimore on 20 July 1863. Merwin Wheaton was mustered out with the rest of his regiment at New Haven on 27 July 1863. He was the brother-in-law of Josiah Johnson of the same company and regiment and first cousin of Albert F. Wheaton.

1023 Branford Vital Records, deaths, 1919.

He applied for an invalid pension on 3 December 1904. He was living at Paw Paw, Van Buren Co., Michigan. At the time of his enlistment was described as five feet seven inches tall, light complexion, hazel eyes, brown hair, occupation farmer. Since his discharge he lived at North Branford, Paw Paw 1868 to 1880; Cadillac, Michigan about 5 years; Chicago, Illinois; and returned to Paw Paw about 1903.

Merwin C. Wheaton was born at North Branford on 9 June 1844 but there was no public record of his birth. He states his birth was recorded by his father in the family bible but he does not know where the bible is. He was married at North Branford by Rev. William B. Curtis to Carrie J. Johnson (Caroline). She died at Paw Paw, Michigan on 22 January 1913, daughter of Chauncey & Julia Ann (Murray) Johnson. They had eight children (living in 1904): Walter J., born on 22 May 1866; Julia Ethelyn or Ethel, born on 30 August 1867; Earle M., born on 17 February 1869; Rolfe A., born on 30 August 1874; Mark L., born on 21 May 1876; Mabel C., born on 26 November 1884; M. C., Jr., born on 27 January 1886; and Harold L., born on 15 October 1891.

Merwin Charles Wheaton died at Paw Paw, Michigan on 31 December 1923 and was buried there in Prospect Hill Cemetery. He was the son of Albert Bishop Whedon and Martha Ann Harrison of North Branford.

> **Falmouth, Va. Jan. 9, 1863**
> *Dear Father*
>
> *...we went towards Fredericksburg and stopped just this side of the river. Such a cannonading as was heard has probably never been heard before on this continent. In the morning we crossed the river and Josiah and myself went around the city. It was completely riddled with shot and shell the houses were all blown to bits...About noon we were told we must go forward and take some batteries [Confederate] on the hill that were throwing their shells into the city. As we filled the streets the rebels shelled us terribly, four of the men in the next company were killed. We lay down on our faces the shells bursting so thick we could not stand up. I then began to realize the horrors of a battle field the groans of the wounded and the thunder of the shells all mixed together...We were soon ordered to charge and up we went the rebels poured shot into us and I felt rifle balls go past my ears. I did not go off the field untill about ten o'clock in the evening for I was looking for Josiah and some of the rest of our wounded boys...*
>
> *Give my love to mother, Emily and grandma besides all the rest of the friends. Write soon.*
>
> *Your Son*
> *Merrwin Wheaton[1024]*

WHEELER, GEORGE H.
Co. B 12th CVI, corporal, enlisted 1 November 1861, discharged disability 12 September 1862, pension #733854 for the soldier and later for his widow Lucy

George H. Wheeler of Branford enlisted at Hartford on 1 November 1861 and was mustered in on 20 November 1861 as a corporal in Co. B 12th CVI for a term of three years. He was discharged for disability at Camp Parapet, Louisiana on 12 September 1862.

1024 Letter, Merwin Wheaton, in the pension file of Josiah Johnson.

He applied for an invalid pension on 17 April 1900. At the time of his enlistment he was described as five feet eleven inches tall, fair complexion, blue eyes, sandy hair, occupation lock maker. He was married at Hotchkissville, now Riverside, Connecticut by Rev. L. W. Scofield on 28 March 1848 to Lucy Precilla Patridge. Neither were previously married or divorced. They had three children (living in 1900): Hubert F., born on 7 June 1852; George L., born on 7 August 1856; and Lillian M., born on 18 November 1861. In 1900 Lillian was the widow of George Babcock. Since his discharge he lived at Branford, then Barkhamsted, Litchfield Co. about 1885.

George H. Wheeler died at Barkhamsted on 4 November 1911 and was buried there in Riverview Cemetery. He was born at Granville, Massachusetts on 10 May 1828. Lucy P. Wheeler, age 81, of Barkhamsted applied for a widow's pension on 13 November 1911.

WHITE, ALBERT D.
Co. K 29th CVI, sergeant, enlisted 2 January 1864, mustered out 24 October 1865, no pension

Albert D. White of Branford enlisted at New Haven on 2 January 1864 as a corporal in Co. K 29th CVI for a term of three years. His service was credited to Branford. He was sent to Knight Hospital on 19 February 1864 from conscript camp and was sick again at Bermuda Hundred, Virginia beginning on 13 August 1864. He was promoted to sergeant on 1 November 1864. From 12 December 1864 until his discharge he was on detached duty in the ambulance corps. Albert White was mustered out with the rest of his regiment at Brownsville, Texas on 24 October 1865. His name appears on the Wall of Honor at Washington, D.C.

WHITE, JAMES alias JAMES LESTRANGER
Co. C 1st HA, private, enlisted 9 December 1864, mustered out 25 September 1865, pension #818234 for the soldier

James White of Branford, alias James Lestranger, enlisted and was mustered in on 9 December 1864 as a private in Co. C 1st HA. He participated in the Siege of Petersburg and Richmond, Virginia with the rest of his regiment. James White was mustered out with the rest of his regiment at Washington, D.C. He also served in the 20th Battery New York LA and Co. E 37th New York Infantry. He is probably the James White, age 26, born in Ireland, a farm laborer, living at Branford in 1860 in the household of Edward O'Brien.[1025] He applied for an invalid pension on 29 August 1891 under the act of 27 June 1890.

WHITE, WILLIAM H. alias JOHN B. KING
Battery C Rhode Island Infantry, bugler, enlisted 2 April 1862, U.S. Navy, seaman, enlisted 16 October 1863, discharged 16 October 1864, pension #58838 for the sailor

William H. White was perhaps a bugler in Battery C, Rhode Island Infantry[1026] but there is no mention in his pension file about serving in Rhode Island. He was living at Sag Harbor, New York when he reenlisted in the Navy at the Norfolk Naval Station, Virginia on 16 October 1863 and served as a seaman on the steamer U.S.S. *Florida* until 11 July 1864 and from 12 July until 16 August 1864 as coxswain. He was a seaman and

---

1025 U.S. census 1860, Branford, New Haven County, Connecticut, population schedule, M653-85, dwelling 1042, family 1157, page 921, www.heritagequest.com.
1026 Mason Rogers Post No. 7, transfer card.

quartermaster on the steamer *Quaker City* from 17 August until 14 October 1864. He was discharged from the sloop *Savannah* at the Brooklyn Navy Yard on 16 October 1864. While serving in the Navy he used the name John B. King.

He applied for an invalid pension on 6 August 1890 under the act of 27 June 1890 for injuries received while shooting the guns aboard the U.S.S. *Florida* in the spring of 1864, he was thrown on his left side. At the time of his Navy enlistment he was described as age 23, five feet nine inches tall, florid complexion, brown hair, blue eyes. After his discharge he was a seaman aboard various boats until 1869; he then lived at Lyme and Guilford. It does not appear he lived at Branford. He was mustered into the Mason Rogers Post No. 7 G.A.R. at Branford on 1 November 1906, transferred from the Admiral Foote Post No. 17 G.A.R. of New Haven.

He was married at Old Lyme by Rev. William Dixon on 8 March 1869 to Mary Jane Hall. She died at Guilford on 6 March 1918 and was buried there in Alderbrook Cemetery. She was born at Lyme on 14 February 1851, daughter of Jesse Hall and Abbie Champion. [1027] They had the following children: Stephen H., born on 8 August 1870, alive in 1910; Frank M., born on 5 July 1875, 1920 living at Guilford; Carrie P., born on 17 December 1880, 1920 living at Guilford; and Charles E., born on 17 June 1886, alive in 1910.

William H. White died at Madison on 1 August 1920 and was buried in Alderbrook Cemetery, Guilford. There was a Civil War marker on his gravesite in 1934. He was born at Southampton, Suffolk Co., New York on 17 February 1838, son of Stephen H. White.[1028]

WHITNEY, HENRY M.
Co. C 52nd Massachusetts Infantry, sergeant major, enlisted 9 September 1862, discharged 4 August 1863, pension #722848 for the soldier and later for his widow Frances

Henry M. Whitney[1029] of Northampton, Massachusetts enlisted on 9 September 1862 as a private in Co. C 52nd Massachusetts Infantry for a term of nine months. He was promoted to sergeant major on 14 October 1862. With his regiment he served at Baton Rouge and Port Hudson, Louisiana. He was discharged at Greenfield, Massachusetts on 4 August 1863. He joined the United States Christian Commission and was assigned to Virginia serving until 1865.

He applied for a pension for the first time on 8 March 1907. At the time of his enlistment he was described as five feet seven inches tall, light complexion, light brown hair, blue eyes. Henry M. Whitney was a graduate of Yale College in 1864, an ordained minister, and a professor of English at Beloit College in Wisconsin from 1871 until 1899. After attending Yale he lived at Princeton, New Jersey; Andover, Massachusetts from 1865-1868; Geneva, Illinois 1868-1871; Beloit, Wisconsin 1871-1899 and came to Branford in 1899 as the head librarian at the James Blackstone Memorial Library. He was the coauthor of the

Dr. Henry M. Whitney was sergeant-major of Co. C 52nd Massachusetts Infantry. He came to Branford in 1899 as head librarian of the James Blackstone Memorial Library and was a member of the Mason Rogers Post No. 7 G.A.R. (Branford Historical Society photograph collection)

1027 Guilford Vital Records, 1918-1920.
1028 Guilford Vital Records, 1918-1920.
1029 For his biography see John Howard Brown, *The Cyclopedia of American Biography* (Boston, Federal Book Co.:1903), 580. There are numerous biographical accounts of Dr. Whitney in various biographical encyclopedias. Some of his Civil War letters can be found in the "Henry Mitchell Whitney Papers" at the Massachusetts Historical Society.

History of the Fifty-second Massachusetts Volunteer Infantry. He was a member of the Mason Rogers Post No. 7 G.A.R. of Branford.

He was married at Geneva, Kane Co., Illinois by Rev. Edward M. Williams on 3 August 1869 to Frances Wurts. The minister performing the ceremony was Rev. Edward Williams, pastor of the Congregational Church in Austin, Minnesota. He was a schoolmate of Frances Wurts in Chicago and also a Yale classmate of Henry Whitney. The Whitneys had the following children (living in 1907): Albert Wurts, born on 20 June 1870; Elizabeth Barnes, born on 21 November 1876, married to Louis R. Moore, by 1926 she was Elizabeth Files of River Edge, New Jersey; Josiah Dwight, born on 11 November 1878; and James Lyman, born on 21 April 1881.

Dr. Henry Mitchell Whitney, clergyman, scholar, author, and librarian died at New Haven on 26 March 1911 and was buried in Center Cemetery, Branford. A Civil War marker was on his gravesite in 1934 and 2011. He was born at Northampton, Massachusetts on 16 January 1843, son of Josiah Dwight Whitney and Clarissa James, born at Westfield and Goshen, Massachusetts.

Frances Whitney applied for a widow's pension on 28 April 1911. She died at White Plains, New York on 20 August 1926 and was buried in Center Cemetery, Branford. She was the daughter of Alfred Wurts and Sarah Elizabeth Smith.

WILDER, JOHN K.

Co. B 27th CVI, private, enlisted 29 September 1862, prisoner, mustered out 27 July 1863, pension #661292 for the soldier and later for his widow Carrie

John K. Wilder, age 23, of Wallingford enlisted on 29 September 1862 and was mustered in on 3 October 1862 as a private in Co. B 27th CVI for a term of nine months. He fought at the Battle of Fredericksburg on 13 December 1862 with the rest of the company. He was captured at the Battle of Chancellorsville, Virginia on 3 May 1863, held prisoner at Richmond, and was paroled at City Point, Virginia on 14 May 1863. He reported to Camp Parole, Maryland on 16 May 1863, was sent to Washington, D.C. on 20 May 1863 and spent the remainder of his service at Camp Convalescent, Virginia. With the rest of the Chancellorsville paroled prisoners, he rejoined the Regiment at Baltimore on 20 July 1863. Wilder was mustered out with the rest of his regiment at New Haven on 27 July 1863.

He applied for an invalid pension on 29 March 1900 under the act of 27 June 1890. He was living at 766 Elm Street, Monroe City, Monroe Co., Michigan. He was married at Marietta, Ohio by Rev. Thomas Wicks on 26 May 1864 to Carrie P. Griggs. Neither were previously married or divorced. They moved to Monroe, Michigan in the winter of 1881. They had three sons (living in 1900): Edward S. age 33, John G. age 30 of Monroe, Michigan; and Frank A. age 27 of Damimes?, Iowa; all of whom were married.

John K. Wilder died at Monroe, Michigan on 27 December 1904 and was buried there in Woodlawn Cemetery. He was the son of Alonzo Wilder.

Carrie G. Wilder of Monroe, Michigan applied for a widow's pension on 1 May 1908. William Westgate, age 68, of Marietta, Washington Co., Ohio stated "I am a cousin of Carrie G. Wilder and have known her since infancy. Our parents lived opposite each other on the same street in Marietta when we were children. I

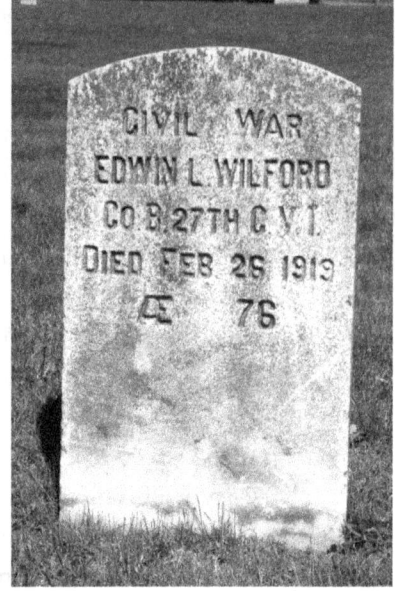

Edwin L. Wilford of Branford was a private in Co. B 27th CVI and was wounded in the leg at the Battle of Fredericksburg on 13 December 1862. (Photograph by W. Hunt, New Haven; Branford Historical Society collection)

was present at her marriage to John K. Wilder. Rev. Thomas Wickes was the officiating minister at Marietta. Her maiden name was Carrie P. Griggs and she was not previously married."[1030]

Rev. Henry B. Dye of Grundy Center, Iowa stated "I knew Carrie Griggs when she was a little girl in Marietta, Ohio. Her father moved before the war to Minnesota where he resided for a time at St. Anthony's Falls; then moved to Anoka, Minnesota. I married an elder sister of the claimant. Carrie Griggs lived between my home and a friends in Marietta before her marriage. I also knew John K. Wilder, his parents, and brothers who were neighbors. He and his parents were members of the church where I was pastor."[1031] In 1908 Charles Wilder, age 58, younger brother of the late John K. Wilder was living at Livermore, Almeda Co., California. Jason Wilder, 71 years, older brother of John K. Wilder was also living at Livermore, California.

Caroline Griggs Wilder died on 25 November 1911 and was buried in Woodlawn Cemetery, Monroe, Michigan. She was born on 28 August 1839.

WILFORD, EDWIN L.
Co. B 27th CVI, private, enlisted 22 August 1862, wounded, discharged 30 July 1863, pension #1138083 for the soldier

Edwin L. Wilford[1032] of Branford enlisted on 22 August 1862 and was mustered in on 3 October 1862 as a private in Co. B 27th CVI for a term of nine months. He was wounded at the Battle of Fredericksburg on 13 December 1862 and sent to Georgetown Hospital. "Ed Wilford was wounded in the leg but not so but that he walks on it."[1033] He was sent to Knight General Hospital, New Haven on 29 December 1862 where

---

1030 Deposition, William Westgate of Marietta, Ohio, 27 June 1908, in the pension file of John K. Wilder.
1031 Deposition, Rev. Henry B. Dye of Grundy Center, Iowa, 25 June, 1908, in the pension file of John K. Wilder.
1032 For his biography see Beers, *Biographical Record of New Haven County*, 1131.
1033 Letter, [George C. Baldwin] to home, 15 December 1862.

he remained until he was discharged on 30 July 1863. He was the first cousin of George G. Wilford of the same company.

He applied for an invalid pension on 18 September 1890 under the act of 27 June 1890. At the time of his enlistment he was described as five feet five inches tall, dark complexion, brown eyes, black hair, occupation farmer. Since his discharge he lived at Branford. He had a scar on the inside of his right leg caused by a rifle bullet wound at the Battle of Fredericksburg. He was a charter member of the Mason Rogers Post No. 7 G.A.R. of Branford and a delegate at state and national encampments.

Edwin Luzerne Wilford died at New Haven on 26 February 1919, unmarried, and was buried in Center Cemetery, Branford. His company and regiment are engraved on his stone and a G.A.R. marker was on his gravesite in 1934 and 2011. A second Wilford monument bears an engraving of a G.A.R. metal. He was born at Branford on 13 March 1842, son of Samuel Wilford and Susan Cook.[1034]

WILFORD, GEORGE G.
Co. B 27th, corporal, enlisted 21 August 1862, died 8 January 1863 from wounds, no pension

George G. Wilford, age 23, of Branford enlisted on 21 August 1862 and was mustered in on 3 October 1862 as a corporal in Co. B 27th CVI for a term of nine months. He was wounded at the Battle of Fredericksburg on 13 December 1862. "Geo Wilford when we went into the fight was my right hand man. he had Six balls hit him, one went through his hand, one through the leg, two in his back & two just grazed him."[1035] "Geo. Wilford was carried across [the river] on a stretcher."[1036] He was brought to the hospital, and died on 8 January 1863 from his wounds. "this morning we hear that Geo Wilford has died from his wounds. we are very sorry to hear such news a great loss to his family if Geo & his mother be both dead."[1037] His CMSR gives the date of death as 25 December 1862 at Campbell Hospital, Georgetown, Washington, D.C., but other documents in his file and his gravestone state he died on 8 January 1863. The cause of death was pyaemia from a gunshot wound, fracture of the left leg and all metacarpal bones in the right hand. There is a detailed physician's report. His possessions included clothing, a silver watch and $5.10 which were received by John Covert [of Branford]. His body was sent home for burial. "Sunday, January 18, 1863 To Church, George Willford was buried, he died from wounds received at the battle of Fredericksburg."[1038] He was the first cousin of Edwin L. Wilford of the same company.

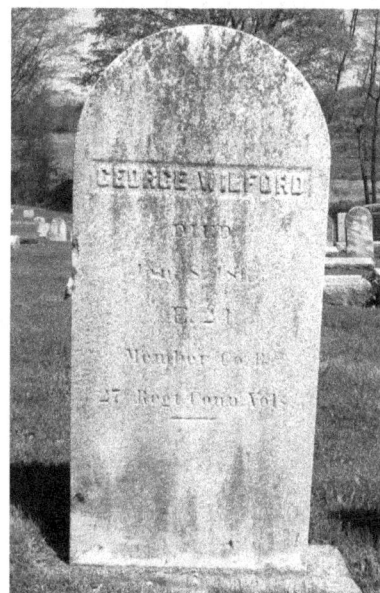

George G. Wilford was buried in Center Cemetery, Branford. His company and regiment are engraved on his stone and a Civil War marker was on his gravesite in 1934. He was born at Branford on 23 January 1839, son of John Wilford and Lucretia Goodenough.[1039]

1034 Branford Vital Records, deaths, 1919.
1035 Letter, Henry D. Boardman to his sister, 17 December 1862; see the chapter on Boardman.
1036 Letter, [George C. Baldwin] to home, 15 December 1862.
1037 Letter, Samuel Beach to home, 1 January 1863. Lucretia Wilford died 1 December 1862.
1038 Diary of Orrin H. Hoadley of Branford, courtesy of Ann Hitchcock, 2011.
1039 Branford Vital Records, Town Meeting Book A, 236.

George G. Wilford of Branford died at Campbell Hospital in Washington D.C. from wounds received at the Battle of Fredericksburg. (Photographic History of the Civil War, 7:15)

WILLIAMS, CHARLES M.
Co. I 15th CVI, private, enlisted 14 August 1862, Navy, discharged 24 May 1865, pension #822785 for the soldier

Charles M. Williams of New Haven enlisted on 14 August 1862 and was mustered in on 25 August 1862 as a private in Co. I 15th CVI for a term of three years. He claimed that while in the 15th he broke his right leg with resulting gangrene and had fractured ribs sustained at Port Tobacco while on the march to first Battle of Fredericksburg, Virginia. He was treated by Dr. H.V.C. Holcombe in his quarters. He deserted from camp opposite Fredericksburg on 28 February 1863 and returned on 26 April 1863. He was transferred to the U.S. Navy on 17 May 1864 while at Hampton Roads, Virginia. He was an ordinary seaman in the Navy and served on the U.S.S. *Minnesota* for a few days, then on the *Mercedita* from 21 May 1864 until 18 November 1864. He may have also served on the *Florida*, was on the *Atlanta* only a few days and discharged from the *Princeton* on 24 May 1865. At the time of his enlistment he was described as five feet six inches tall, dark complexion, black hair, black eyes. Since his discharge he lived at Branford. Before the war he was a blacksmith and afterwards a farmer.

He applied for an invalid pension on 5 September 1890 under the act of 27 June 1890 having reached the age of 70. He was married at New Haven in the fall of 1836 to Mary Elizabeth Newry. "She left me many years ago but we were never divorced." He had no children. Charles M. Williams died at Branford on 19 June 1895 age 78 and was buried there in Center Cemetery. He was born at Branford on 19 August 1817, son of Samuel N. Williams and Amy Moulthrop.[1040]

1040 Branford Vital Records 1786-1840, 418.

WILLIS, JOSEPH T.

Joseph T. Willis, age 20, served as a substitute for Franklin D. Linsley of Branford. He was mustered in at New Haven on 26 August 1864 as a private for a term of three years. He was described as five feet eight inches tall, brown eyes, brown hair, fair complexion, unmarried, born in Germany, occupation clerk.[1041]

WILLIS, L. MORTIMER or MORTIMER L.

Co. B 27th CVI, private, enlisted 1 September 1862, prisoner, mustered out 27 July 1863, pension #259361 for the soldier

L. Mortimer Willis, age 33, of Branford enlisted on 1 September 1862 and was mustered in on 3 October 1862 as a private in Co. B 27th CVI for a term of nine months. On 13 December 1862 at the Battle of Fredericksburg he received a buck shot wound to the index finger of his right hand. He states he was treated by Surgeon McDonald but was never treated in the hospital. On 31 December 1862 he returned to his company and worked as a nurse at a hospital.[1042] He was captured at the Battle of Chancellorsville, Virginia on 3 May 1863, held prisoner at Richmond, and was paroled at City Point, Virginia on 14 May 1863. He reported to Camp Parole, Maryland on 16 May 1863, was sent to Washington, D.C. on 20 May 1863 and spent the remainder of his service at Camp Convalescent, Virginia. With the rest of the Chancellorsville paroled prisoners, he rejoined the Regiment at Baltimore on 20 July 1863. Mortimer Willis was mustered out with the rest of his register at New Haven on 27 July 1863.

He applied for an invalid pension on 17 August 1878, living at Hutchinson, Reno Co., Kansas. "I was a tent mate of the claimant. I well remember the violent snow storm which we were exposed to when on picket duty in front of Fredericksburg, Va. at which time the claimant took a violent cold and was for some time sick in camp near Falmouth, Va."[1043] "He was disabled after exposure to a snow and sleet storm and was detailed for light camp duty. He was in action at Chancellorsville and taken prisoner. On his way to Richmond he was exposed in a severe rain storm without shelter and was again sick and was unable to continue the march to Richmond. He was taken on a special detail and met us at Richmond a few days later. He was sick until his discharge and was a physical wreck."[1044] At the time of his enlistment he was described as five feet five inches tall, light complexion, brown hair, black eyes, occupation farmer. There is no record of illness in his CMSR or any further information.

He was married at Branford by Rev. Henry Olmstead of Trinity Episcopal Church on 19 September 1858 to Mariette Squire. He is on the 1863 draft list for Branford; age 34, born New York, married, occupation turner. They had four children (living in 1897): Wilbur W., born on 13 October 1867; Florence E., born on 25 July 1869; May B., born on 8 May 1865; and Vinnie R., born on 2 December 1870. Marietta Willis died at Bartow, Polk Co., Florida on 26 May 1898.[1045]

Lord Mortimer Willis died at Bartow, Florida on 4 August 1905. He was born in New York on 25 February 1830.[1046]

1041 Muster & Descriptive Rolls of Substitutes, RG 13, box 98, 2nd Congressional District, Connecticut State Library; his service is not found in *Record of Service of Connecticut Men.*
1042 Probably at the Regimental hospital at camp near Falmouth, Virginia.
1043 Affidavit, Edward D. Sheldon of Branford, 9 May 1891, in the pension file of L. Mortimer Willis.
1044 Letter, Dr. Robert B. Goodyear of North Haven to Wm. Lochren of Washington, D.C., 13 October [no year] in the pension file of L. Mortimer Willis.
1045 *Shore Line Times*, 10 June 1898.
1046 Florida Deaths 1877-1939, www.familysearch.com.

WILSON, JOHN

Co. B 11th CVI, private, enlisted 11 March 1864, to U.S. Navy, deserted 15 December 186, no pension

John Wilson of Branford enlisted on 11 March 1864 as a private in Co. B 11th CVI. He was transferred to the U.S. Navy, served on the U.S.S. *Wyalusing* and deserted on 15 December 1864. He does not appear at Branford in the 1860 census.

WILSON, THOMAS

Co. H 15th CVI, private, enlisted 14 August 1862, died 28 September 1864, pension #54472 for his widow Eliza and minor children

Thomas Wilson of Branford enlisted at New Haven on 14 August 1862 and was mustered in on 25 August 1862 as a private in Co. H 15th CVI for a term of three years. "Tom Wilson is sick, has lung disease."[1047] He died at Regimental Hospital in New Bern, North Carolina on 28 September 1864 of yellow fever. He is the Thomas Willson at Branford in the 1860 census with a wife and child.[1048] He is on the 1863 draft list for Branford; Class 3, age 26, born in Scotland, married, occupation blacksmith.

His widow Eliza Wilson of Branford received a pension on 23 August 1865 for herself and her minor children. She was married to the soldier under the name of Elizabeth Wilson at New Haven by Fred Croswell, Esq. on 19 May 1858. He was age 21, she age 23, both born in Scotland and living at Branford. They had three children: Rebecca Jane, born on 13 November 1858 at Branford, living in 1870; Robert P., born on 12 October 1860, died on 18 March 1866; and Thomas, Jr., born on 13 April 1862 at Branford, living at New Haven in 1898.

Eliza Wilson did not remarry and lived at Branford until at least 1888. She died at New Haven on 27 January 1898 and was buried in Center Cemetery, Branford. [1049]

WINSHIP, HOYT F.

Co. E 11th CVI, private, enlisted 11 February 1864, discharged disability 8 June 1865, pension application #914969 for the soldier

Hoyt F. Winship of North Branford enlisted and was mustered in on 11 February 1864 as a private in Co. E 11th CVI. He was discharged for disability at Petersburg, Virginia on 8 June 1865.

He applied for an invalid pension on 12 September 1890 under the act of 27 June 1890. At Petersburg, Virginia in July 1864 he received a gunshot wound from a fragment of a shell when a mine exploded striking his forehead and fracturing his collar bone. He was treated at Point Rock Hospital near Bermuda Hundred, Virginia where he was discharged. After the war he lived mostly in the New Orleans area. His application was rejected for failure to prove his disability prevented him from performing manual labor. He applied for a pension several more times, all of which were rejected after review. The soldier gave conflicting information: that after the war he lost two fingers at New Orleans in a railroad accident, he later said at a saw mill; he also said it was at a cotton mill; he also claimed the loss of the fingers was from the gunshot wound during his service. In addition, he claimed that after the war he contracted rheumatism working in the cold at a packing house in Chicago. His file is large with many documents and he never received a pension.

1047 Towner letter, 13 November 1863.
1048 U.S. census 1860, Branford, New Haven County, Connecticut, population schedule, M653-85, dwelling 727, family 816, page 881, www.heritagequest.com.
1049 New Haven Vital Records, deaths, 1898; *The Branford Opinion*, 29 January 1898.

He was married at Cheshire by the rector of St. Peter's Church on 16 September 1865 to Laura Francis Checkeni? He had two children (living in 1897): Carrie F., born on 16 October 1866; and Frank A., born on 20 June 1871. There is no further information about his wife or children in the file.

In 1897 he was living at New Orleans, Louisiana, age 50, and in 1899 his mail laid unclaimed. His application was abandoned by the pension board.

WOERNLEY, PAUL
Co. D 1st HA, private, enlisted 4 January 1864, mustered out 25 September 1865, no pension

Paul Woernley of Branford enlisted on 4 January 1864 as a private in Co. D 1st HA. He participated in the Siege of Petersburg and Richmond, Virginia with his regiment. Woernley was mustered out with the rest of his regiment at Washington, D.C. on 25 September 1865 and discharged at Hartford on 1 October 1865. He does not appear in the 1860 census at Branford.

WOODRUFF, REV. CURTISS T.
Chaplain 6th CVI, enlisted 2 September 1861, discharged 18 April 1864, pension #348844 for his widow Julia

Rev. Curtiss T. Woodruff[1050] of Naugatuck enlisted on 2 September 1861 and was mustered in at New Haven on 13 September 1861 as chaplain of the 6th CVI for a term of three years. He resigned on 13 November 1862 and rejoined on 22 August 1863. He was discharged on 18 April 1864 when his term expired. He never applied for a pension.

He was born at Washington, Litchfield Co. on 8 September 1816, son of Curtiss Woodruff and Sarah Maria Trowbridge. He was a graduate of Yale College in 1849 and had under his charge parishes at Woodbury, Naugatuck, Ridgefield, and Norwalk. In 1866 he was an original trustee of the Connecticut Hospital for the Insane. From 1871 until the time of his death he was the superintendent of the New York City Missionary Society of the Episcopal Church.

Rev. Curtiss Trowbridge Woodruff died suddenly in his office at New York City on 1 February 1887 and was buried in Center Cemetery, Branford.[1051] A G.A.R. marker was on his gravesite in 1934 and 2011.

Julia L. M. Woodruff of Branford applied for a widow's pension on 27 August 1890 under the act of 27 June 1890. She was married to the soldier under the name of Julia L. M. Curtiss at New York City by Rev. Richard Cox of the Zion Episcopal Church on 10 February 1849. They had no children. She was an author and poet writing under the name of W.M.L. Jay. Julia Louisa Matilda Curtiss Woodruff[1052] was buried on 22 April 1909 in Center Cemetery, Branford.[1053] She was born at Newtown on 29 April 1832, daughter of Edwin Alfred Curtiss and Matilda Rogers.

1050 For his biography see Frank Bowditch Dexter, *Obituary Record of Graduates of Yale University* (New Haven: Yale University Press, 1913), 295.
1051 There is no record of the Woodruff family in Branford vital, church, city directories, or census records.
1052 For her biography see Leonard and Marquis, *Who's Who in America*, 1899, vol. I: 812.
1053 Branford Sexton Records, 1884-1932, 58; her death is not in the Branford Vital Records.

WOODWORTH, ALBERT P.

Co. B 10th CVI, sergeant, enlisted 30 September 1861, discharged 29 September 1864, pension #554787 for the soldier

Albert P. Woodworth of Coventry enlisted at Manchester on 20 September 1861 and was mustered in at Hartford on 30 September 1861 as a corporal in Co. B 10th CVI for a term of three years. With the rest of the regiment he fought at the Battle of Roanoke Island, North Carolina on 8 February 1862 and was promoted to sergeant on 18 October 1862. He was in General Hospital, Philadelphia, Pennsylvania and transferred to Knight Hospital, New Haven in April and May 1864. He was discharged at Hartford on 29 September 1864 when his term expired.

He applied for an invalid pension on 30 July 1890 under the act of 27 June 1890. After the Battle of Kinston, North Carolina in December 1862 on the march to New Bern, he was taken sick with rheumatism. He was sick at Seabrook and Morris Islands in the summer of 1863 and spent the winter in Florida for his health, returning to duty. At the time of his enlistment he was described as five feet eight inches tall, dark complexion, black eyes, dark hair, occupation carpenter. After his discharge he lived at South Coventry from 1864 until 1874, Mansfield from 1875 until 1879, South Coventry again from 1880 until 1906; Branford from 1906 until 1909; and back to South Coventry in 1909. While living in Branford he was mustered in as a member of the Mason Rogers Post No. 7 on 19 December 1907.

He was married at South Coventry by Rev. John Case of the Methodist Church on 20 November 1856 to Ellen Amanda Austin. Neither were previously married or divorced. She died in 1926 and was buried in Nathan Hale Cemetery, Coventry. They had the following children: Ida May, born on 1 November 1857, died on 1 March 1862; Albert Wesley, born at South Coventry on 12 December (year not given), died February 1865; Theron Palmer, born at Mansfield on 11 June 1858, died on 28 July 1860; Olin B., born at Mansfield on 19 May (year not given); Arthur Linus or Lucius, born at South Coventry on 18 February 1874, living in 1898; and Archie Everett, born at South Willington (Mansfield) on 22 January 1878, died there on 14 May 1878.

Albert Payne Woodworth died on 19 July 1926 and was buried in Nathan Hale Cemetery, Coventry. His company and regiment are engraved on his stone. He was born at South Coventry on 6 August 1836, son of Harry Woodworth and Roxanna Robinson.[1054]

1054 Behan, Jeanette Woodworth, *The Woodworth Family of America, Descendants of Walter Woodworth of 1630 Through Six Generations* (Newtown, Connecticut; 1988), 289.

WRIGHT, ELLIS C.

Co. G 28th Pennsylvania Volunteer Infantry, mustered in 28 June 1861, pension #12553 for the soldier

Ellis C. Wright of Sewickley, Alleghany Co., Pennsylvania was mustered in at Philadelphia on 28 June 1861 as a private in Co. G 28th Pennsylvania Volunteer Infantry also known as the Goldstream Regiment. He applied for a disability pension on 12 February 1863. In 1870 and 1880 he was living at Alleghany, Alleghany Co., Pennsylvania with a wife Mary and two daughters. He first appears at North Branford in 1880, a widower, with his daughter Florence A. Haight and her children.[1055]

Ellis W. C. Wright died at New Haven on 13 June 1927 age 84 and was buried in Bare Plain Cemetery, North Branford. His company and regiment are engraved on his stone and a G.A.R. marker was on the gravesite in 1934 and 2011. He was born June 1843 in Pennsylvania, son of Stephen and Margaret Wright.

YALE, SOLOMON

Co. B 27th CVI, private, enlisted 25 August 1862, discharged 27 July 1863, no pension

Solomon Yale, age 43, of Branford enlisted at New Haven on 25 August 1862 and was mustered in on 3 October 1862 as a private in Co. B 27th CVI for a term of nine months. He was wounded at the Battle of Fredericksburg, Virginia on 13 December 1862 and was sick in the hospital December 1862 and January 1863. He deserted about 31 January 1863 and was charged on 2 February 1863. On 10 April 1863 he was placed under arrest at division headquarters and held prisoner. On 24 April 1863 there is a note from the doctor stating that while he was charged with desertion, the soldier was under his care for sickness. On 2 June 1863 he was charged with derelict of duty while on the picket line by allowing Private Chas. Murray of Battery A 1st R. I. Vols to pass the line without authority and swim across the Rappahannock and after having arrived on the opposite shore to hold communication with the enemy. Yale was mustered out with the rest of his regiment at New Haven on 27 July 1863.

He never applied for a pension. He is probably Solomon Braddam Yale, born on 6 December 1812, son of Joel Yale and Polly Hill. Solomon B. Yale appears at Berlin in 1840 and Meriden in 1850. He was married on 11 June 1833 to Roxanna Goff. By 1860 only his wife Roxy A. [Roxanne] and two children appear at Berlin[1056] and she was living at Wallingford in 1870.[1057] There is no record of burial in the Hale Collection for the soldier.

1055 U.S. census 1900, North Branford, New Haven County, Connecticut, population schedule, T623-146, dwelling 122, family 128, page 276, www.heritagequest.com.

1056 H. Y. Andrews, *A Genealogy of the Descendants of Daniel Yale of Meriden, Conn.* (New Haven: Stafford Printing, 1872), 177; U.S. census 1860, Berlin, New Haven County, population schedule M653-79, dwelling 860, family 952, Timothy Root household, page 40, www.heritagequest.com.

1057 U.S. census, Wallingford 1860, New Haven County, population schedule M593-112, dwelling 68, family 78, page 673B, with son George W. age 17, www.heritagequest.com.

YOUNG, CHARLES A.

Co. B 27th CVI, corporal, enlisted 20 August 1862, prisoner, mustered out 27 July 1863, pension #1115537 for the soldier

Charles A. Young, age 25, of Branford enlisted on 20 August 1862 and was mustered in on 3 October 1862 as a corporal in Co. B 27th CVI for a term of nine months. He fought at the Battle of Fredericksburg on 13 December 1862 with the rest of the company. He was captured at the Battle of Chancellorsville, Virginia on 3 May 1863, held prisoner at Richmond, and was paroled at City Point, Virginia on 14 May 1863. He reported to Camp Parole, Maryland on 16 May 1863, was sent to Washington, D.C. on 20 May 1863 and spent the remainder of his service at Camp Convalescent, Virginia. With the rest of the Chancellorsville paroled prisoners, he rejoined the Regiment at Baltimore on 20 July 1863. Charles Young was mustered out with the rest of his regiment at New Haven on 27 July 1863. He was the brother-in-law of Edward D. Sheldon of the same company and regiment.

He applied for an invalid pension on 6 May 1905 under the act of 27 June 1890. At the time of his enlistment he was described as five feet six inches tall, light complexion, blue eyes, brown hair, occupation seaman. He was married at Branford by Rev. Jacob Miller of the First Congregational Church on 1 October 1860 to Sarah Cornelia Sheldon. She died on 25 February 1914 and was buried in Center Cemetery, Branford.[1058] They had two children: Anna Cornelia, born on 7 February 1862, died on 7 April 1864; and Franklyn Luther, born on 3 April 1864, died on 19 April 1864. Since his discharge he lived at Branford; New York City; Rahway, New Jersey until May 1879; Ashbury Park, New Jersey until 1905; Branford 1905; Daytona, Florida in 1915; and Springfield, Massachusetts in 1917.

Charles A. Young died at Springfield, Massachusetts on 8 July 1919 and was buried in Center Cemetery, Branford. A Civil War marker was on his gravesite in 1934. He was born at New York City on 15 December 1836.

YOUNG, WILLIAM E.

Co. G 7th Rhode Island Infantry, drummer, enlisted 11 December 1864, discharged 17 July 1865, no pension

William E. Young enlisted or was drafted on 11 December 1864 as a drummer in Co. G 7th Rhode Island Infantry. He was discharged on 17 July 1865.

He was born at Providence, Rhode Island. He was transferred from the R. R. Clarke Post No. 167 of Whitinsville, Massachusetts in 1902 to the Mason Rogers Post No. 7 G.A.R. of Branford. He does not appear in the 1900 or 1910 census at Branford.

1058 Her death is not in the Branford Vital Records.

ZINK, WALTER H. alias WALTER PATTON

Co. A & Co. G 95th New York Infantry, private, enlisted 26 August 1863, wounded, discharged disability 19 April 1864, pension #571644 for the soldier and later for his widow Caroline and minor child

Walter Patton, age 26, of New York City alias Dr. Walter H. Zink[1059] enlisted on 26 August 1863 as a private in Co. A 95th New York Infantry for a term of three years and was transferred to Co. G in March 1864. He was injured while marching through a thicket at night and fell, losing his right eye. He was discharged for disability at Culpepper Court House, Virginia on 19 April 1864.

His biographies and obituary state "he began his practice in New York City where he remained until the war of the rebellion broke out, when he went to the front as a surgeon."[1060] "He was given the post of surgeon and attached to the 5th Army Corps, he continued to discharge his duties in that capability for some two years."[1061] "During one of the fierce fights, while caring for a wounded soldier, a spent bullet struck him in the eye, depriving him of the sight for the rest of his life. The Doctor was very popular with the soldiers."[1062] There is no record in his pension file of his service during the war as a surgeon, only as a private. One of his biographies states he was surgeon of the 13th New York Regiment National Guard after the war. He did injure his eye during the war but not as stated in the biographies.

He applied for an invalid pension on 13 August 1866, a resident of New York City. He wrote on his application that he was injured while marching through a thicket at night and fell, losing his right eye. The vision in his left eye was also impaired. At the time of his enlistment he was described as five feet five inches tall, light complexion, blue eyes, sandy hair, occupation cook.

He had graduated from Wurzburg Medical School, Bavaria, Germany in 1862 and came to the United States in 1863. He began taking courses at Columbia Medical School in New York City and soon after enlisted in the New York Infantry. After his discharge he lived at New York City; then Newtown, Long Island and practiced in New York City for thirteen years. He moved to Branford in 1878 from Trenton, New Jersey taking over the practice of Dr. Newton B. Hall. He was a member, surgeon, and commander of the Mason Rogers Post No. 7 G.A.R. of Branford and surgeon for the state G.A.R. for twelve years.

Dr. Walter Henry Zink died at Branford on 26 August 1900 and was buried there in Center Cemetery. A G.A.R. medal is engraved on his stone and a G.A.R. marker was on his gravesite in 1934. He was born at Nuremberg, Germany on 21 March 1841, son of Charles Zink and Anna Maria Ernst. "Dr. Zink was a man of brusque exterior, but kind at heart and very sympathetic. Nearly all the stores in the business center were

Walter H. Zink served in the 95th New York Infantry and after the war was a practicing physician. He came to Branford in 1878 and was active in the Mason Rogers Post No. 7 G.A.R. He died in 1900 and was buried in Center Cemetery. (Branford Historical Society photograph collection)

1059 For his biography see Beers, *Biographical Record of New Haven County*, 902; Cutter, *Family History of Connecticut*, II:920; and *Proceedings of the Connecticut Medical Society, Annual Convention Held at New Haven* (Bridgeport: Farmer Publishing Co., 1902), 425.

1060 Obituary, *New Haven Register*, 27 August 1900.

1061 His pension file indicates he was in the service for only seven months.

1062 Beers, *Biographical Record of New Haven County*, 903; the biography in the book was provided by his family after his death. His biography in Cutter states "he became surgeon of the 13th Regiment New York National Guard."

closed for his service."[1063] "His full name was Walter Henry Patten Zink, his family name was Zink, his godfather's name was Patten. He enlisted under the name of Patten because he didn't want his mother to know of his enlistment. His mother lived in Germany but he enlisted with two of his friends from Germany, both were killed in battle. My husband had no relatives in this country. I think he had a step brother Charles Zink in Bavaria."[1064]

Caroline A. Zink of Branford filed for a widow's pension on 13 April 1901. She was married to the soldier under the name of Caroline Augusta Milling at Brooklyn, New York by Rev. Samuel Baker of the First Baptist Church at the home of William Weidmann on 26 September 1864. Neither were previously married or divorced. They had five children, three of whom were living in 1898: Louise Augusta, born on 7 June 1870, Charles Edward, born on 7 December 1874; and Walter Raymond, born on 5 July 1888. Her claim was sent for special examination due to the variations in the soldier's name and for an inventory of her assets.

Caroline A. Zink died at Branford on 10 June 1903 and was buried there in Center Cemetery. She was born in England on 9 March 1850, daughter of Phillip Milling and Catherine Minke, both born at Hesse-Cassel, Germany.[1065] "I was born in England in 1849 and came to this country with my parents when very small. I have no relatives living in this country besides my children except my brother's daughter Mrs. Baldwin[1066] of this town. I brought her up from the time she was 8 years old."[1067]

After Caroline's death, a pension claim was filed on 7 January 1904 for Walter Raymond Zink by guardian Charles F. Bradley of Branford (no relation). The claim was filed for retroactive payment until Walter R. Zink turned sixteen.

1063 Obituary, *New Haven Register*, 27 August 1900.
1064 Affidavit, Caroline A. Zink, 22 October 1902, in the pension file of Walter H. Zink.
1065 Branford Vital Records, deaths, 1903.
1066 Carolyn A. Milling later wife of Edwin E. Baldwin.
1067 Affidavit, Caroline A. Zink, 22 October 1902, in the pension file of Walter H. Zink.

APPENDICES

APPENDIX I: CIVIL WAR DRAFT RECORDS

The first Union draft, called The Enrollment Act, was enacted March 3, 1863 by the 37th Congress and signed by President Lincoln to enlarge the depleted Union army. The provost marshal of each state was in charge of canvassing every town to record eligible males between the ages of 20 and 45. The lists were compiled in ledger books, one for each class, and can be found in RG 110, U.S. Civil War Draft Registration Records, 1863-1865. These records were only available at the National Archives until recently.[1] The consolidated lists are organized by state, Congressional District within the state, alphabetical by surname, and by town within the surname list. For example, Branford is in the Connecticut 2nd Congressional District and entries for the town can be found by scanning each group of surnames in each ledger book. Some men were exempt: those mentally or physically impaired, the only son of a widow, the son of infirmed parents, or a widower with dependent children. Aliens who had declared their intention to become a citizen sixty days before the act could be drafted. Eligible males were divided into three classes:

Class I - all eligible men ages 20 to 35 and unmarried men above age 35 and under 45.

Class II - married men above age 35 and under 45

Class III - those who had previously or were currently serving

Recorded in the ledger were the resident's name, age on July 1, 1863, marital status, place of birth, occupation, and for Class III the military unit and rank in which they served or were serving. The data was collected between May and July 1863 and for Class III in August 1863. Some of the men volunteered before being drafted in order to collect a bounty.

For the town of Branford, 152 men were listed in Class I. Only five men enlisted and seventeen found substitutes. The low percentage of enlistments or draftees from the enrollment lists for Branford confirms other statistics that few men were drafted.

---

1   The records were digitized and made available at www.ancestry.com in April 2011.

Last Name	First Name	Town	Class	Age	Occupation	Marital	Birthplace	Military Service	Comment
Adams	John	North Branford	3	27	farmer	single	Ireland	27th Reg't Co. F	private
Albinger	John C.	Branford	3	33	farmer	single	Germany	15th Reg't Co. C	private
Allen	Henry L.	North Branford	2	36	blacksmith	[married]	Conn.	none	
Andrews	George H.	Branford	1	31	farmer	married	Conn.	none	
Appel	John	North Branford	2	44	farmer	[married]	Conn.	none	
Asher	Alford	North Branford	2	40	farmer	[married]	Conn.	none	colored
Augur	Daniel P.	North Branford	2	36	blacksmith	[married]	Conn.	none	
Averill	Daniel, 2nd	Branford	3	24	farmer	single	Conn.	27th Reg't Co. B	1st serg't
Averill	David	Branford	3	33	blacksmith	married	Conn.	1st Cav Co. B	private
Averill	Delbert	Branford	1	20	seaman	single	Conn.	none	
Averill	Edmund M.	Branford	2	41	sailor	[married]	Conn.	none	
Averill	George M.	Branford	1	24	seaman	single	Conn.	none	
Averill	Jarvis	Branford	2	37	sailor	[married]	Conn.	none	
Averill	Roland G.	Branford	1	20	sailor	single	Conn.	none	
Averill	Samuel	Branford	2	39	sailor	[married]	Conn.	none	
Babcock	Marcus M.	Branford	1	22	sailor	single	Conn.	none	
Baldwin	Charles E.	Branford	1	21	farmer	single	Conn.	none	
Baldwin	Elizur E.	Branford	1	23	sailor	married	Conn.	none	
Baldwin	Geo. W.	Branford	3	29	farmer	single	New York	27th Reg't Co. B	private
Baldwin	George	Branford	1	33	boatman	single	Conn.	none	
Baldwin	Giles H.	Branford	1	22	carpenter	married	Conn.	none	
Baldwin	Jerome	Branford	3	27	farmer	[single]	Conn.	7th Reg't Co. G	private
Baldwin	John U.	Guilford	1	27	butcher	single	New York	none	
Barker	Ami B.	Branford	3	19	mechanic	single	Conn.	15th Reg't Co. B	private
Barker	Harvey	Branford	1						[no other data given]
Barker	Harvey R.	Branford	II	36	farmer	[married]	Conn.	none	
Barker	John R.	Branford	1	29	farmer	married	Conn.	none	
Barker	Joseph	Branford	3	27	farmer	single	Conn.	6th Reg't Co. K	private
Barker	Moses H.	Branford	1	24	farmer	single	Conn.	none	
Barker	Samuel P.	Guilford	1						[no other data given]

Last Name	First Name	Town	Class	Age	Occupation	Marital	Birthplace	Military Service	Comment
Barnes	Charles	Branford	1	33	farmer	married	Conn.	none	
Barnes	Geo. H.	North Branford	3	25	farmer	single	Conn.	15th Reg't Co. K	private
Bartholomew	F. C.	Northford	2	42	manufacturer	[married]	Conn.	none	
Bartholomew	Isaac	Northford	2	39	machinist	[married]	Conn.	none	
Bartholomew	Isaac C.	Branford	1	33	boatman	married	Conn.	8th CV, discharged	
Bartholomew	John A.	Branford	3	25	mechanic	married	Conn.	13th Reg't Co. G	serg't
Bartholomew	Newton J.	Branford	1	24	locksmith	married	Conn.	18th CV, discharged	
Bartholomew	Rodolphus	Branford	3	44	farmer	married	Conn.	27th Reg't Co. B	wagoner
Beach	Harvey	Branford	3	28	miller	married	Conn.	27th Reg't Co. B	private
Beach	John B.	Branford	1	31	stage-driver	married	Conn.	none	"Don't live with wife"
Beach	John C.	Branford	1	36	farmer	single	Conn.	none	
Beach	Samuel	Branford	3	36	farmer	married	Conn.	27th Reg't Co. B	corp'l
Beach	William	Branford	1	26	farmer	married	Conn.	none	
Beach	Wm. H.	Branford	3	37	farmer	married	Conn.	27th Reg't Co. B	private
Beardslee	Edward	Branford	1						[no other data given]
Bears	William H.	Branford	1	32	shoemaker	single	Conn.	none	[Beers]
Beecher	Charles L.	Branford	1	22	locksmith	single	Conn.	none	
Beecher	Miles R.	Branford	1	22	sailor	single	Conn.	none	
Benton	Delos O.	North Branford	1	41	farmer	single	Conn.	none	
Benton	William J.	Branford	2	43	attorney	[married]	Conn.	none	
Bigelow	Joel	Branford	2	36	farmer	[married]	Conn.	none	
Bishop	George W.	Branford	1	25	sailor	single	Conn.	none	
Bishop	Martin C.	Branford	2	40	farmer	[married]	Conn.	3 years state service	
Bishop	Nathaniel H.	Branford	1	30	tinner	married	Conn.	none	
Bishop	Oliver H.	Branford	1	23	sailor	single	Conn.	none	
Blackstone	E. C.	Branford	1	23	farmer	single	Conn.	none	
Blackstone	James L.	Branford	1	30	farmer	married	Conn.	none	
Blackstone	John A.	Branford	1	33	farmer	married	Conn.	none	
Boardman	Henry D.	North Branford	3	20	sailor	single	New York	27th Reg't Co. B	private
Boardman	W. D.	Northford	1	24	painter	married	Conn.	none	

Last Name	First Name	Town	Class	Age	Occupation	Marital	Birthplace	Military Service	Comment
Booth	John H.	Branford	3	20	mechanic		Conn.	7th Reg't Co. G	private
Boylan	Luke	Branford	3	26	laborer	married	Ireland	15th Reg't Co. I	private
Bradley	Charles S.	Northford	2	40	hotel keeper	[married]	Conn.	none	
Bradley	Ebenezer T.	Branford	1	21	farmer	single	Conn.	none	
Bradley	Geo. G.	Branford	3	31	machinist	married	Conn.	10th Reg't Co. C	private
Bradley	Henry M.	Branford	1	28	boatman	married	Conn.	none	
Bradley	James A.	Branford	1	30	boatman	single	Conn.	none	
Bradley	Stephen	Branford	1	32	carriage maker	married	Conn.	none	
Bradley	Timothy	Branford	3	21	farmer	single	Conn.	10th Reg't Co. C	private
Brennan	Fred W.	Northford	1	30	tinsmith	married	Germany	none	
Brigs	George H.	Branford	1	33	machinist	married	Rhode Island	none	
Brocket	Atwater E.	Branford	1	29	merchant	married	Conn.	none	
Brockett	Benajah	North Branford	3	20	farmer			7th Reg't Co. F	private, claimed by East Haven
Brockett	Edgar	North Branford	3	20	farmer			7th Reg't Co. F	private, claimed by East Haven
Brockett	Edward	North Branford	3	20			Conn.	7th Reg't Co. F	private, claimed by East Haven
Buell	Edwin A.	North Branford	3	29	mechanic	single	Conn.	15th Reg't Co. K	private
Bunnel	Benjamin B.	Branford	1	32	moulder	married	Conn.	none	
Bunnell	Edward R.	Branford	1						[no other data given]
Bunnell	Henry	Northford	2	43	farmer	[married]	Conn.	none	
Bunnell	Luzerne	Branford	1	35	farmer	single	Conn.	none	
Bunnell	William	Branford	3	19	farmer	single	Conn.	27th Reg't Co. B	private
Bush	Timothy G.	Branford	3	22	carriage maker		Conn.	7th Reg't Co. G	private
Byington	Charles B.	Guilford	1	34	joiner	married	Conn.	15th CV, discharged	
Byington	Edwin M.	North Branford	3	19	carpenter	single	Conn.	15th Reg't Co. I	private
Byington	D.H.	Northford	2	44	joiner	[married]	Conn.	none	
Calkins	George W.	Branford	1	30	pedler	married	Conn.	none	
Carey	Thomas C.	North Branford	3	25	farmer	single	England	15th Reg't Co. E	private

483

Last Name	First Name	Town	Class	Age	Occupation	Marital	Birthplace	Military Service	Comment
Carter	Chas. E.	Branford	3	24	farmer	married	Conn.	20th Reg't Co. G	private
Cary	David	Branford	1	33	moulder	married	Ireland	none	
Cavitt	William	Branford	1	34	farmer	married	Conn.	none	
Chaipel	Benj. F.	Branford	3	44	farmer	married		12th Reg't Co. B	corp'l
Chaipel	Wm. H.	Branford	3	22	farmer	single		12th Reg't Co. B	private
Chidsey	Lambert R.	Branford	1	22	farmer	single	Conn.	none	
Chidsey	Leverett	North Branford	1	23	farmer	single	Conn.	none	
Chidsey	Merritt P.	North Branford	1	20	farmer	single	Conn.	none	
Clancy	James	Branford	2	38	moulder	[married]	Ireland	none	
Clark	Vincent C.	North Branford	1	30	farmer	single	Conn.	none	
Cline	Louis	Branford	1	34	carriage maker	married	Germany	none	
Coan	Jerome	Branford	3	29	clerk	single	Conn.	15th Reg't Co. E	private
Coe	Elbert H.	Branford	2	44	farmer	[married]	Conn.	none	
Colman	Josiah A.	Branford	1	29	farmer	married	Conn.	13th Reg., discharged	
Conley	Thomas	Branford	1	30	farmer	married	Ireland	none	
Connell	Patrick	Branford	1	30	farmer	married	Ireland	none	
Cook	Aaron J.	Branford	2	38	carpenter	[married]	Conn.	none	
Cook	Samuel S.	Branford	3	37	shoemaker	married	Conn.	27th Reg't Co. B	serg't
Cook	Samuel S.	Branford	1	34	boatman	single	Conn.	none	
Cook	William E.	Branford	1	21	farmer	single	Conn.	none	
Covit	John P.	Branford	2	35	merchant	[married]	Conn.	none	[Covert]
Cusher	Joseph	Branford	3	22	farmer	single	New York	27th Reg't Co. B	private
Daly	Jerry	Branford	1	26	engineer	married	Ireland	none	
Daly	John	Branford	2	38	farmer	[married]	Ireland	none	
Davis	Eckford	Branford	1	27	farmer	married	Conn.	none	
Davis	Harlow A.	North Branford	1	33	farmer	married	Conn.	none	
Davis	John	Branford	3	27	shoemaker	[married]	New York	7th Reg't Co. D	private
Davis	William F.	Branford	1	32	boatman	married	New York	none	
Dayton	Ambrose L.	Wallingford	3	20	mechanic	single	Conn.	15th Reg't Co. E	private, to VRC May 19, 1863

Last Name	First Name	Town	Class	Age	Occupation	Marital	Birthplace	Military Service	Comment
Desmond	John	Branford	2	43	farmer	[married]	Ireland	none	
Dibble	Elizur B.	Branford	3	21	farmer	[single]		27th Reg't Co. B	private
Dibble	Richard	Branford	2	44	farmer	[married]	Conn.	none	
Dolf	James	Branford	2	44	farmer	[married]	Conn.	none	[Dolph]
Dolph	Charles	Branford	3	30	farmer	[single]	Conn.	7th Reg't Co. D	private
Dougherty	Robert	Branford	3	23	farmer	[single]		9th Reg't Co. A	private
Douglas	James P.	Branford	1	29	depot agent	single	Conn.	none	[Joseph]
Dunn	Bernard	Branford	2	36	moulder	[married]	Ireland	none	
Dunn	Peter	Branford	1	33	moulder	married	Ireland	none	claims to be 36 yrs old
Eagan	George	Branford	3	22	soldier	single		1st Cav Co. B	private
Eaton	Harvey T.	Northford	2	44	mechanic	[married]	Conn.	none	
Eddy	Clayton	Branford	1	25	clergyman	married	Conn.	none	
Ely	Calvin	Branford	3	35	dentist	married	Conn.	27th Reg't Co. B	captain
Ennis	Edward	Branford	1	21	clerk	single	Conn.	none	
Evans	James B.	Branford	1	26	farmer	married	Conn.	none	
Evarts	Hamilton O.	Branford	1	29	locksmith	single	Conn.	7th CV, discharged	
Everts	Joel A.	Branford	2	35	farmer	[married]	Conn.	none	[Evarts]
Everts	Worthington C.	North Branford	1	30	farmer	single	Conn.	none	[Evarts]
Fahae	Luke	Branford	1	39	farmer	single	Ireland	none	
Farnham	James M.	Branford	1	34	locksmith	married	Conn.	none	
Field	Chancellor H.	Branford	1						[no other data given]
Field	George C.	Branford	1	27	farmer	single	Conn.	none	
Fields	Daniel F.	Wallingford	3	29	carpenter	married	Conn.	none	
Fitzgerald	John	Branford	2	38	blacksmith	[married]	Ireland	27th Reg't Co. B	1st lt, resigned
Fitzpatrick	Hugh	Northford	2	41	gentleman	[married]	Ireland	20th CV, discharged	
Foot	Elizur H.	North Branford	1	32	carpenter	married	Conn.	none	
Foot	Noah	Branford	2	38	farmer	[married]	Conn.	none	
Foot	Samuel	North Branford	1	20	farmer	married	Conn.	none	
Foot	Samuel A.	Branford	1	22	sailor	single	Conn.	none	
Foot	Samuel H.	Branford	2	44	farmer	[married]	Conn.	none	

Last Name	First Name	Town	Class	Age	Occupation	Marital	Birthplace	Military Service	Comment
Foote	E. D.	Northford	2	35	iron worker	[married]	Conn.	none	
Foote	Jerome W.	Northford	1	34	farmer	married	Conn.	none	
Foote	John M.	Northford	2	44	farmer	[married]	Conn.	none	
Foote	Lines H.	Northford	1	26	farmer	single	Conn.	none	[Lynde]
Foote	Russell	Guilford	1	29	farmer	married	Conn.	none	
Foote	William	Northford	1	20	mechanic	married	Conn.	none	
Forbes	Benjamin F.	Branford	1	34	farmer	married	Conn.	none	
Forbes	Edgar L.	Branford	3	20		[single]		1st Artillery Co. E	private
Forbes	Joseph	Branford	1	41	locksmith	single	Conn.	none	
Forbes	Levi	Branford	3	42	farmer	married		12th Reg't Co. B	serg't
Forbes	Levi S.	Branford	2	41	farmer	[married]	Conn.	12th CV, discharged	
Ford	George L.	North Branford	1	24	farmer	single	Conn.	none	
Ford	John B.	Northford	2	39	laborer	[married]	Conn.	none	
Ford	William D.	North Branford	1	29	farmer	single	Conn.	none	
Fowler	Degras, Jr.	Northford	1	23	machinist	married	Conn.	6 mons in 5th CV, resigned	
Fowler	Henry H.	Branford	1	36	farmer	single	Conn.	none	
Fowler	Herbert E.	Northford	1	20	mechanic	single	Conn.	none	
Fowler	Joseph S.	Branford	1	36	farmer	single	Conn.	none	
Fowler	Maltby	Northford	1	20	machinist	married	Conn.	none	
Fowler	Saml O.	Branford	3	41	farmer	single	Conn.	15th Reg't Co. I	private
Fowler	Thadeus	Northford	2	40	pin maker	[married]	Conn.	none	
Fowler	William S.	Branford	1	36	farmer	single	Conn.	none	
Francisco	Clifford A.	Branford	3	23	farmer	single	New Jersey	15th Reg't Co. I	private
Frisbie	Alonzo P.	Wallingford	3	41	tailor	married	Mass.	15th Reg't Co. K	private
Frisbie	Chas. H.	Branford	3	26	joiner	married	Conn.	15th Reg't Co. E	private
Frisbie	Harvey J.	Branford	1	21	sailor	single	Conn.	none	
Frisbie	Henry E.	Branford	1	32	farmer	married	Conn.	none	
Frisbie	James R.	Guilford	1	33	farmer	married	New York	none	
Frisbie	Louis	Branford	1	29	potter	married	Conn.	none	
Frisbie	Russell L.	Wallingford	3	19	clerk	single	Conn.	15th Reg't Co. K	private

Last Name	First Name	Town	Class	Age	Occupation	Marital	Birthplace	Military Service	Comment
Frisbie	Samuel E.	Branford	1	23	sailor	single	Conn.	none	
Frost	John C.	Northford	2	38	iron worker	[married]	Mass.	none	
Galpin	Joseph A.	Branford	3	40	manufacturer	widow	Conn.	15th Reg't Co. C	private
Gardner	Albert C.	Branford	2	38	machinist	[married]	Conn.	none	
Gates	Andrew M.	North Branford	1	31	farmer	married	Conn.	none	
Gates	John	North Branford	1	30	farmer	married	Conn.	none	
Gates	John H.	North Branford	1	32	farmer	married	Conn.	none	
Geland	James	Branford	1	25	sailor	single	Conn.	none	
Gilson	Bernard	Branford	2	40	moulder	[married]	Ireland	none	
Gilson	John M.	Branford	2	35	farmer	[married]	Conn.	none	
Giterslof	Christian	Branford	3	40	farmer	widow	Germany	15th Reg't Co. B	private, deserted Aug, 6, 1862
Glover	George H.	North Branford	2	43	farmer	[married]	Conn.	none	
Goodrich	Elizur B.	Branford	1	33	farmer	single	Conn.	none	
Goodrich	Horace A.	Branford	3	20	carriage trimmer	single	Conn.	20th Reg't Co. G	private
Graham	Richard	Branford	2	36	moulder	[married]	New York	none	
Graham	Wm. E.	Branford	2	44	carriage maker	[married]	Conn.	none	
Grannis	Albert	Branford	1	22	farmer	single	Conn.	none	
Grannis	James H.	Branford	1	38	farmer	single	Conn.	none	
Grave	Erastus	Branford	1	30	carpenter	single	Conn.	none	
Griswold	Joel	Branford	1	40	saloon keeper	single	Conn.	none	
Hadley	Benj. H.	Branford	2	42	machinist	[married]	Rhode Island	none	
Hadley	Henry H.	Branford	1	39	farmer	single	Conn.	none	[Hoadley]
Hadley	Orin H.	Branford	2	36	carpenter	[married]	Conn.	none	[Hoadley]
Hale	Samuel	North Branford	1	33	farmer	married	Conn.	none	
Hall	Eli	Branford	2	37	farmer	[married]	Conn.	none	
Hall	Newton B.	Branford	2	36	physician	[married]	Conn.	none	
Hall	Oliver B.	Branford	1	33	farmer	single	Conn.	none	
Hall	Roger	Branford	3	32	boatman	married	Conn.	27th Reg't Co. B	private
Hall	William	Northford	2	42	farmer	[married]	Conn.	none	
Hally	John	Branford	2	35	moulder	[married]	Ireland	none	

Last Name	First Name	Town	Class	Age	Occupation	Marital	Birthplace	Military Service	Comment
Hally	Michael	Branford	1	25	moulder	married	Ireland	none	
Harrington	Loring G.	North Branford	1	30	farmer	single	Conn.	22nd CV, discharged	
Harrison	Albert	North Branford	3	21	clerk	single	Conn.	27th Reg't Co. B	corp'l
Harrison	Elizur H.	North Branford	3	19	farmer	married	Conn.	1st Artillery Co. F	private
Harrison	Franklin	Branford	1	22	farmer	single	Conn.	15th CV, discharged	
Harrison	H. Lynde	Branford	1	24	attorney	single	Conn.	27 CV, 4 mons	
Harrison	Henry G.	North Branford	1	32	farmer	single	Conn.	none	
Harrison	Henry, Jr.	North Branford	1	33	farmer	single	Conn.	none	
Harrison	James C.	Branford	1	32	farmer	married	Conn.	none	
Harrison	John H.	Branford	2	39	farmer	[married]	Conn.	none	
Harrison	Jonathan L.	North Branford	1	24	farmer	single	Conn.	none	
Harrison	Lorenzo E.	North Branford	3	43	farmer	married	Conn.	15th Reg't Co. K	private
Harrison	Luther	North Branford	1	31	farmer	married	Conn.	none	
Harrison	Marcus	Branford	1	42	farmer	single	Conn.	none	
Harrison	Nathan	Branford	3	27	farmer	married	Conn.	27th Reg't Co. B	private
Harrison	Reuben	Northford	2	41	farmer	[married]	Conn.	none	
Harrison	Rufus	North Branford	1	42	farmer	single	Conn.	none	
Harrison	Russell	Branford	2	41	farmer	[married]	Conn.	none	
Harrison	Samuel	North Branford	1	43	farmer	single	Conn.	none	
Hart	Henry F.	Branford	3	22	farmer	single	Conn.	27th Reg't Co. B	private
Hart	Patrick	Branford	1	26	moulder	single	Ireland	none	
Hart	Timothy	Branford	2	37	boatman	[married]	Conn.	none	
Hawshel	Frederick	North Branford	1	30	carriage worker	married	Germany	none	
Hemingway	Amos A.	Branford	1	34	farmer	married	Conn.	none	
Hendrick	Wm. D.	Branford	2	39	shoemaker	[married]	Conn.	7 years Gov's Foot Guard	
Higgins	John	Branford	1	30	moulder	single	Ireland	none	
Hill	Allen C.	North Branford	1	30	farmer	single	Conn.	none	[Alden]
Hoadley	Henry M.	Branford	1	29	farmer	married	Conn.	none	
Hoadley	Miles A.	Branford	1	22	farmer	single	Conn.	none	
Holcomb	Geo. F.	Branford	1	27	carriage maker	married	Conn.	none	

Last Name	First Name	Town	Class	Age	Occupation	Marital	Birthplace	Military Service	Comment
Holcomb	H.V.C.	Branford	3	36	surgeon	married	Mass.	15th Reg't Co. F & I?	surgeon
Holcomb	John	Branford	1	32	farmer	married	Conn.	none	
Hopkins	Albert	Branford	3	20	farmer	single	Conn.	13th Reg't Co. G	private
Hopson	Charles R.	Branford	2	42	farmer	[married]	Conn.	none	
Hopson	Philander	Branford	2	36	carpenter	[married]	Conn.	none	
Hosley	Benj. A.	Branford	2	40	farmer	[married]	Conn.	none	
Hosley	Samuel B.	Branford	1	34	farmer	married	Conn.	none	
Howd	George W.	Wallingford	3	25	mechanic	single	Conn.	15th Reg't Co. K	private
Howd	Richard A.	Branford	1	30	farmer	married	Conn.	none	
Howd	William T.	Branford	3	21	farmer	single	Ireland	6th Reg't Co. K, private	enlisted U.S.A. Nov 3, 1862
Hubbard	Henry W.	Branford	3	30	blacksmith	married	Conn.	27th Reg't Co. B	private
Hubbell	Alonzo T.	Branford	3	24	carriage maker	single	Conn.	27th Reg't Co. B	serg't
Hubbell	Orgin A.	Branford	1	22	butcher	single	Conn.	none	
Hull	Eli	Branford	3	36	farmer	married	Conn.	20th Reg't Co. F	private
Hull	Morris	Branford	1	30	boatman	married	Conn.	none	
Ives	Wm. B.	Branford	3	33	farmer	married		1st Light Battery	private
Jefrey	William	Branford	2	39	locksmith	[married]	Conn.	none	[Jeffrey]
Johnson	Davis S.	Branford	3	20	farmer	single	Conn.	10th Reg't Co. A	private, claimed by East Haven
Johnson	Elizur C.	Branford	3	26	farmer	married	Conn.	10th Reg't Co. A	private
Johnson	Henry	Branford	3	29	farmer	married	Conn.	12th Reg't Co. B	private
Johnson	Henry H.	Branford	2	38	farmer	[married]	Conn.	none	
Johnson	Homer R.	Wallingford	3	26	farmer	single	Conn.	27th Reg't Co. B	private
Jones	Hubert	Branford	2	35	mason	[married]	England	none	
Jones	William S.	Branford	1	23	farmer	married	Conn.	14th CV, discharged	
Jones	Willis G.	Northford	1	30	farmer	married	Conn.	none	
Jordan	Frederick	Branford	2	44	farmer	[married]	Germany	none	[born Switzerland]
Kelsey	Hobart	Branford	1	28	farmer	married	Conn.	none	
Kennedy	James	Wallingford	3	37	burnister	single	Ireland	27th Reg't Co. B	private

Last Name	First Name	Town	Class	Age	Occupation	Marital	Birthplace	Military Service	Comment
Kennedy	Patrick	Branford	2	40	machinist	[married]	New York	none	
Kerr	John	Branford	3	37	wagoner	married		12th Reg't Co. B	wagoner
Kerringer	Matthias	Branford	3	44	tailor	married	New York	27th Reg't Co. B	private [Kneringer]
Kineen	James	Branford	3	29	farmer	married		12th Reg't Co. B	private
Kineen	Michael	Branford	3	20				1st Artillery Co. K	private
Lahe	Richard	Northford	1	28	farmer	married	Ireland	none	
Lane	Chauncey	Branford	1	25	sailor	single	Conn.	none	
Lanfare	Aaron S.	Branford	3	39	sea captain	married		1st Cav Co. B	corp'l
Lanfare	Franklin	Branford	1	20	farmer	single	Conn.	none	
Lanfare	Henry B.	Branford	1	28	sailor	single	Conn.	none	
Lanfare	John H.	Branford	1	28	farmer	married	Conn.	none	
Lann	Joel J.	Branford	1	30	farmer	married	Conn.	none	[Lund]
Latimer	John E.	Branford	1	32	carriage maker	single	Conn.	1 year in state service	
Leete	Isaac P.	Branford	2	43	physician	[married]	Conn.	none	
Linsley	Atwood	Branford	3	20				5th Reg't Co. E	private
Linsley	Charles M.	Branford	1	24	farmer	single	Conn.	none	
Linsley	Chas. F.	Branford	3	20	clerk	single	Conn.	15th Reg't Co. F	private
Linsley	Edgar	Branford	1	23	carriage trimmer	single	Conn.	none	
Linsley	Franklin	Branford	1	34	merchant	married	Conn.	none	
Linsley	George	Branford	1	34	carpenter	married	Conn.	2 years in state service	
Linsley	George C.	North Branford	1	21	farmer	single	Conn.	none	
Linsley	Gilbert H.	Branford	1	32	farmer	married	Conn.	none	
Linsley	Henry	Branford	2	38	carpenter	[married]	Conn.	none	
Linsley	Henry	Northford	1	20	farmer	single	Conn.	none	
Linsley	Henry B.	Branford	1	21	farmer	married	Conn.	none	
Linsley	Henry D.	Branford	1	20	farmer	single	Conn.	none	
Linsley	John W.?	Branford	1	26	sailor	married	Conn.	none	
Linsley	Obid	Branford	2	41	carriage maker	[married]	Germany	none	[Obed, born Conn.]
Linsley	Seth H.	North Branford	1	38	farmer	single	Conn.	none	
Linsley	Solomon	Northford	2	43	farmer	[married]	Conn.	none	

Last Name	First Name	Town	Class	Age	Occupation	Marital	Birthplace	Military Service	Comment
Linsley	William	Branford	2	40	farmer	[married]	Conn.	none	
Linsley	Wm. H.	Branford	3	20	mechanic	single	Conn.	15th Reg't Co. B	private
Lounsbury	John H.	Branford	1	20	machinist	single	Conn.	none	
Lyon	Joseph	Branford	2	38	farmer	[married]	Conn.	none	
Madison	Treat C.	Branford	1	30	farmer	single	Conn.	none	colored
Maguire	Thomas	Branford	3	20	teamster	single	Mass.	9th Reg't Co. E	private
Mahan	Jerry	Branford	2	41	moulder	[married]	Ireland	none	
Maltby	Charles	Northford	2	40	pin maker	[married]	Conn.	none	
Maltby	Charles D.	Northford	2	40	mechanic	[married]	Conn.	none	
Maltby	E. C.	Northford	1	33	farmer	married	Conn.	none	[Epaphras]
Maltby	Henry, Jr.	Northford	2	35	farmer	[married]	Conn.	none	
Maltby	William	Northford	2	38	farmer	[married]	Conn.	none	
MaNamara	Thomas	Branford	2	36	moulder	[married]	Ireland	none	
Markham	Francis	Branford	1	27	stone cutter	married	[not given]	none	
Marson	James R.	Branford	1	26	book keeper	single	Conn.	none	
Mason	Charles M.	Branford	1	29	farmer	married	Conn.	none	colored
McCenna	Thomas	Branford	2	36	melter	[married]	Ireland	none	[McKenna]
McDermott	John	Branford	1	25	moulder	single	Ireland	none	
McGovern	Patrick	Branford	1	30	moulder	single	New Jersey	none	
McQueny	Andrew	Branford	2	36	melter	[married]	Ireland	none	[McQueeny]
Merriam	Henry D.	Branford	1	26	carriage maker	married	Conn.	none	
Merriam	Lucien A.	Branford	1	23	butcher	single	Conn.	none	
Merrick	William	North Branford	1	32	druggist	married	Conn.		belong to Gov's Horse Guard
Miller	Harvey H.	Branford	1	32	sailor	married	Conn.	none	
Miller	Jacob G.	Branford	2	41	minister	[married]	Conn.	none	
Miller	Samuel	Branford	2	35	sailor	[married]	Conn.	none	
Monroe	Almon	Branford	1	34	moulder	married	Conn.	none	[Alvin]
Monroe	Josiah T.	Branford	1	34	farmer	married	Conn.	none	
Monroe	Merritt F.	Branford	1	32	sailor	married	Conn.	none	

Last Name	First Name	Town	Class	Age	Occupation	Marital	Birthplace	Military Service	Comment
Monroe	William T.	Branford	2	36	sailor	[married]	Conn.	none	
Mooney	Michael	Branford	3	43	farmer	married	England	20th Reg't Co. G	private, discharged Apr 14, 1863
Moran	John	Branford	3	22	farmer	single		1st Cav Co. B	private
More	Robert E.	Branford	2	44	farmer	[married]	Conn.	none	[Moore]
Morris	Lewis F.	Branford	1	22	student	single	Conn.	none	
Moulthrop	Joseph C.	Branford	2	41	carpenter	[married]	Conn.	none	
Munger	Charles E.	Branford	1	22	electroplater	single	Conn.	3 years in state service	
Munger	Wallace E.	Branford	1	29	pattern maker	married	Conn.	none	
Munson	William	Branford	3	19	farmer	single	Penn.	27th Reg't Co. E	private
O'Brien	Edward	Branford	2	37	farmer	[married]	Ireland	none	
O'Brien	John	Branford	3	21	farmer	single	Ireland	27th Reg't Co. B	private
O'Brien	Patrick	Branford	1	28	moulder	single	Ireland	none	
O'Conner	Charles J.	Branford	1	24	moulder	single	New Jersey	none	
O'Neil	Michael	Branford	3	21	farmer	single	Ireland	27th Reg't Co. B	private
Page	Albert L.	Branford	1	23	clerk	single	Conn.	none	
Page	Benjamin, Jr.	North Branford	1	22	farmer	single	Conn.	none	
Page	Charles	Branford	1	26	farmer	married	Conn.	none	
Page	Charles, Jr.	North Branford	1	22	farmer	single	Conn.	none	
Page	Darwin	Branford	2	41	farmer	[married]	Conn.	none	
Page	Dennis	Branford	1	30	butcher	single	Conn.	none	
Page	Edgar G.	Branford	2	36	farmer	[married]	Conn.	none	
Page	Elizur E.	Branford	3	33	farmer	married	Conn.	27th Reg't Co. F	private
Page	George H.	Branford	1	26	farmer	single	Conn.	none	
Page	James B.	Guilford	3	27	manufacturer	married	Conn.	27th Reg't Co. B	private
Page	Joel C.	Guilford	3	23	farmer	single	Conn.	15th Reg't Co. E	private
Page	John	Branford	1	25	sailor	married	Conn.	none	
Page	John N.?	Branford	1			[married]			[no other data given]
Palmer	Timothy	Branford	1	26	farmer	single	Conn.	none	
Palmer	Charles W.	Branford	1	23	farmer	single	Conn.	none	

Last Name	First Name	Town	Class	Age	Occupation	Marital	Birthplace	Military Service	Comment
Palmer	Edmond	Branford	2	43	farmer	[married]	Conn.	none	
Palmer	Henry	Branford	2	43	sailor	[married]	Conn.	none	
Palmer	James B.	Branford	1	26	carpenter	single	Conn.	none	
Palmer	James G.	Branford	1	22	farmer	single	Conn.	none	
Palmer	Wm. B.	Branford	3	22	farmer	single	Conn.	27th Reg't Co. B	private
Pane	Robert	Branford	1	20	farmer	single	Conn.	none	
Pardee	Henry N.	North Branford	3	39	mechanic	married	Conn.	15th Reg't Co. K	private
Parson	Edwin H.	Branford	3	44	bill agent	married	Mass.	27th Reg't Co. B	private
Patton	William H.	Branford	2	43	moulder	[married]	New Jersey	none	
Peck	Levi S.	Branford	1	24	butcher	married	Conn.	none	
Pelton	James B.	Branford	2	41	farmer	[married]	Conn.	none	
Plant	George W.	Branford	1	29	farmer	married	Conn.	none	
Pond	Joseph W.	Branford	2	42	sailor	[married]	Conn.	none	
Pond	Samuel	Branford	2	43	sailor	[married]	Conn.	none	
Prince	William	North Branford	1	22	farmer	single	Conn.	none	
Prior	Edward M.	Branford	2	39	farmer	[married]	Conn.	none	
Prout	Geo. M.	Branford	3	38	farmer	married	Conn.	27th Reg't Co. B	corp'l
Regan	William	Branford	1	26	locksmith	married	Ireland	none	
Regles	Charles H.	Branford	1	28	merchant	married	Conn.	none	
Rice	Edward	Branford	1	30	locksmith	married	Ireland	none	
Rily	Patrick	Branford	2	36	moulder	[married]	Ireland	none	[Riley]
Robinson	Edward	North Branford	1	23	farmer	single	Conn.	none	
Robinson	Elsworth	North Branford	1	34	farmer	married	Conn.	none	
Robinson	Euriah	North Branford	2	41	miller	[married]	Conn.	none	[Uriah]
Robinson	Henry P.	Branford	3	23	farmer	single	Conn.	15th Reg't Co. D	private, to Inv Corps July 1863
Robinson	James A.	Branford	3	20	student	single	Mass.	21st Reg't Co. K	private
Robinson	John S.	North Branford	3	26	fisherman	single	Conn.	27th Reg't Co. F	private
Robinson	William S.	North Branford	1	27	farmer	single	Conn.	none	
Rogers	Asa L.	Branford	2	36	blacksmith	[married]	Conn.	none	

Last Name	First Name	Town	Class	Age	Occupation	Marital	Birthplace	Military Service	Comment
Rogers	Frederick	Branford	1	36	farmer	single	Conn.	none	
Rogers	Geo. S.	Branford	3	21	farmer	single	New York	27th Reg't Co. B	private
Rogers	Henry	Branford	2	42	farmer	[married]	Conn.	none	
Rogers	Henry	North Branford	1	24	student	single	Conn.	none	
Rogers	John	Branford	2	40	farmer	[married]	Conn.	none	
Rogers	Munson	Northford	2	39	farmer	[married]	Conn.	none	
Rogers	Walter	Branford	3	27	tinner	single		1st Cav Co. B	private, enlisted U.S.A. Nov 1862
Rogers	William F.	Branford	2	37	farmer	[married]	Conn.	none	
Rose	Daniel M.	North Branford	2	36	farmer	[married]	Conn.	none	
Rose	Herbert M.	North Branford	1	21	carpenter	single	Conn.	none	
Rose	Russell M.	North Branford	1	23	farmer	single	Conn.	none	
Rose	Stephen H.	North Branford	2	41	farmer	[married]	Conn.	none	
Rose	Virgil H.	North Branford	1	31	farmer	married	Conn.	none	
Rowland	Geo. H.	Branford	3	24				1st Artillery Co. F	private
Rowland	Lynd	Branford	2	36	carriage maker	[married]	Conn.	none	[Lynde]
Rowley	Augustus R.	Branford	2	35	blacksmith	[married]	Conn.	none	
Russell	Jay E.	Branford	1	27	attorney	single	Conn.	none	
Russell	John B.	Branford	1	27	farmer	single	Conn.	2 years in state service	
Russell	Merrick M.	North Branford	1	21	farmer	single	Conn.	none	
Schenck	Paul	Branford	3	27	blacksmith	married		27th Reg't Co. K	private
Scranton	Dayton R.	North Branford	3	23	farmer	single		12th Reg't Co. F	serg't
Scranton	Henry W.	North Branford	3	27	farmer	married	Conn.	15th Reg't Co. K	private
Scranton	James H.	North Branford	3	20	coal business	single		12th Reg't Co. F	private
Sheldon	Edward D.	Branford	3	21	farmer	single	Conn.	27th Reg't Co. B	private
Shepard	Charles B.	Branford	3	20				5th Reg't Co. E	private
Shepard	Chas. B.	Branford	3	20	farmer		Conn.	10th Reg't Co. A	private
Shepard	Harvey	Branford	3	29	carriage maker	married	Conn.	13th Reg't Co. B	private
Shepard	Henry	Branford	2	43	boatman	[married]	Conn.	none	
Shepard	John F.	Branford	3	22	farmer	single	Conn.	10th Reg't Co. A	private

Last Name	First Name	Town	Class	Age	Occupation	Marital	Birthplace	Military Service	Comment
Shepard	Sam'l S.	Branford	3	25	blacksmith	[single]	Conn.	10th Reg't Co. A	private
Sheppard	Lewis F.	Branford	1	23	sailor	single	Conn.	none	
Sliney	David	Branford	3	39	farmer	married	Ireland	27th Reg't Co. G	private
Slyskie	William F. L.	Branford	2	35	carriage maker	[married]	Germany	2 years in state service	
Smith	Clinton	Branford	2	36	stone cutter	[married]	Conn.	none	
Smith	Edward L.	Branford	3	21	farmer	single	Maryland	10th Reg't Co. A	private, claimed by E. Haven
Smith	Elizur G.	Branford	3	19	clerk	single	Conn.	20th Reg't Co. A	musician
Smith	Henry	Branford	3	24	farmer	single	New York	18th? Reg't Co. C	private, claimed by East Haven
Smith	Henry C.	Branford	3	24	farmer	single	Conn.	10th Reg't Co. A	private
Smith	Jacob A.	North Branford	3	24	farmer	married	Conn.	15th Reg't Co. K	private
Smith	Riley O.	Branford	2	43	locksmith	[married]	Conn.	none	
Spencer	John	Branford	2	36	sailor	[married]	Conn.	none	
Spink	Shubil T.	Branford	2	36	carpenter	[married]	Conn.	none	[Shubael]
Stedman	Henry H.	Branford	1	23	farmer	single	Conn.	none	
Stone	Elizur C.	North Branford	3	36	farmer	married	Conn.	27th Reg't Co. B	private
Strickland	Azil	North Branford	3	37	teamster			7th Reg't Co. D	private, [Asa]
Sullivan	James	Branford	1	26	locksmith	married	Ireland	none	
Sullivan	Patrick	Branford	2	36	polisher	[married]	Ireland	none	
Tallmage	George W.	North Branford	3	21	farmer	single	Conn.	15th Reg't Co. K	private
Tallmage	William	North Branford	3	33	farmer	married	Conn.	15th Reg't Co. E	private
Taylor	Wm. L.	North Branford	3	31	miller	married	Conn.	20th Reg't Co. G	private
Thute	Patrick	Branford	1	30	locksmith	married	Ireland	none	
Toben	Michael	Branford	2	36	farmer	[married]	Ireland	none	[Tobin]
Todd	Albert	North Branford	1	28	farmer	married	Conn.	none	
Towner	Henry E.	Branford	2	36	farmer	[married]	Conn.	none	
Tucker	James T.	Branford	1	22	farmer	single	Conn.	none	
Tucker	Steven O.	Branford	1	20	farmer	single	Conn.	none	
Turner	Guy C.	Branford	2	36	stone cutter	[married]	Conn.	none	
Tyler	Almon	Branford	1	33	farmer	single	Conn.	none	

Last Name	First Name	Town	Class	Age	Occupation	Marital	Birthplace	Military Service	Comment
Tyler	John R.	Branford	1	27	farmer	married	Conn.	none	
Tyler	Obel L.	Branford	3	22	farmer	single	Conn.	27th Reg't Co. B	private
Tyler	Samuel	Branford	1	26	farmer	single	Conn.	none	
Tyler	Wm. A.	Branford	3	24	farmer	single	Conn.	27th Reg't Co. B	private
Vanwie	Ellick	Branford	1	30	locksmith	married	Conn.	none	[Alex]
Vogel	Louis	Branford	3	20	mechanic	single	Germany	6th Reg't Co. H	private
Waldin	Charles E.	Branford	1	30	sailor	single	Conn.	none	
Wallace	James	Northford	1	29	farmer	married	Conn.	none	
Wardell	Samuel B.	Branford	2	38	engineer	[married]	Conn.	none	
Way	James R.	Branford	2	38	farmer	[married]	Conn.	none	
Webb	Julius S.	Branford	1	30	carpenter	single	Conn.	none	[Junius]
Wells	Charles S.	Branford	1	30	farmer	single	Conn.	none	
Whaland	John	Branford	2	37	farmer	[married]	Ireland	none	[Whalen]
Wheaton	Merwin	North Branford	3	20	farmer	single	Conn.	27th Reg't Co. B	private
Wheeler	Geo. H.	Branford	3	34	locksmith	married		12th Reg't Co. B	corp'l, discharged
Wheeler	George H.	Branford	2	35	carpenter	[married]	Conn.	12th CV, discharged	
Wilcox	Lewis	Northford	2	35	tinner	[married]	Conn.	none	
Wilford	Charles H.	Branford	1	21	sailor	single	Conn.	none	
Wilford	Edwin L.	Branford	3	21	farmer	single	Conn.	27th Reg't Co. B	private
Wilford	Francis E.	Branford	1	23	moulder	single	Conn.	3 years in state militia	
Williams	Douglass	Northford	1	32	farmer	married	Conn.	none	
Williams	Henry A.	Branford	1	27	gunsmith	single	Conn.	none	
Williams	Philo	Northford	2	41	farmer	[married]	Conn.	none	
Willis	L. Mortimer	Branford	3	34	turner	married	New York	27th Reg't Co. B	private
Wilson	Thomas	Branford	3	26	blacksmith	married	Scotland	15th Reg't Co. H	private
Wise	Joseph	Branford	1	30	machinist	married	Conn.	none	
Wood	John	Northford	1	27	blacksmith	married	Conn.	none	
Yale	Solomon	Branford	3	44	carpenter	married	Conn.	27th Reg't Co. B	private, deserted Feb. 22, 1863
Young	Charles A.	Branford	3	26	sailor	married	New York	27th Reg't Co. B	corp'l

APPENDIX II: ARMY DIVISIONS AND RANK

Company: about 100 men, commanded by a captain and two lieutenants

Battalion: sometimes four companies banded together

Regiment: ten or twelve infantry, artillery or cavalry companies; commanded by a colonel

Brigade: four to six regiments; commanded by a colonel or brigadier general

Division: two or more brigades

Corps: two or more divisions

Army: one or more corps

Order of rank of enlisted men:

Private

Corporal

Sergeant

1st Sergeant

Order of rank of officers:

2nd Lieutenant

1st Lieutenant

Captain

Major

Lieutenant Colonel

Colonel

Brigadier General

Major General

APPENDIX III: MAJOR BATTLES AND TIMELINE
In which Branford and North Branford soldiers participated.

Abraham Lincoln (Library of Congress Prints & Photographs Division, LC-ppmsca-19469)

1861

February 9 - Confederate States of America (CSA) formed

March 4 - Lincoln sworn into office

April 12 - Fort Sumter captured by Confederate forces, the first engagement of the war

April 15 - President Lincoln calls for state militias

April 17 - Virginia secedes from the Union

April 19 - Lincoln begins the blockade of southern ports

Fort Sumter- (Library of Congress Prints & Photographs Division, LC-cwpb-03073)

1860

November 6 - Abraham Lincoln elected president

December 20 - South Carolina secedes from the Union, others soon follow

Port Royal (Library of Congress Prints & Photographs Division, LC-cwpb-01811)

May 3 - President Lincoln calls for volunteers

July 21 - Battle of the First Bull Run near Manassas, Virginia

November 7 - Capture of Port Royal, South Carolina

1862

February 8 - Battle of Roanoke Island, North Carolina

March through July 1862 - The Peninsula Campaign ends in the Seven Days Battles

May 31 - Seven Pines

June 8 - Cross Keys

Chickahominy (Harper's Weekly, 9 August 1862, 5)

June 9 - Port Republic

June 25 - Chickahominy

July 1 - Malvern Hill

March 20 through April 11 - Siege of Fort Pulaski, Georgia

April 6 & 7 - Shiloh, Tennessee

April - Siege of Fort Macon, North Carolina

April 24 - Union takes New Orleans

May 8 - McDowell, Virginia

May 25 - Winchester, Virginia

August 5 - Engagement at Baton Rouge, Louisiana

August 9 - Cedar Mountain, Virginia

August 29 & 30 - Second Bull Run

September 11 - Chantilly, Virginia

Antietam (by Alfred R. Waud, Harper's Weekly 11 October 1862)

September 17 - Antietam, Maryland
The Battle of Antietam near Sharpsburg, Maryland was the first major battle on Northern soil and the bloodiest single day battle in U.S. history. It was an inconclusive Union victory and General Lee's army withdrew back to Virginia without pursuit. The 8th, 11th, and 14th Connecticut Volunteers fought in the battle.

December 11 - Fredericksburg, Virginia
The Battle of Fredericksburg was the largest engagement for Branford and North Branford soldiers with six regiments in action. The Union forces under Major-General Ambrose E. Burnside suffered heavy losses particular at Marye's Heights. Burnside was replaced as commander after the battle.

Fighting in the streets of Fredericksburg (by Alfred R. Waud, Harper's Weekly, 3 January 1863)

1863

January 1 - The Emancipation Proclamation was signed by President Lincoln

March 3 - First Union draft

April 14 - Battle of Irish Bend, Louisiana

April 27 - Battle of Chancellorsville, Virginia
The Battle of Chancellorsville was a decisive victory for General Robert E. Lee against the Union forces under Major-General Joseph Hooker. Branford men in

A view of Gettysburg, Pennsylvania showing Cemetery Ridge in the center, Culp's Hill on the lower right, and the hill on the upper right is Round Top. (Photographic History of the Civil War, 2:211)

four regiments saw action during the battle sustaining heavy losses. Branford's Co. B of the 27th Connecticut Volunteer Infantry were captured and held at prisons in Richmond.

May 25 through June 9 - Siege of Port Hudson, Louisiana

July 3-5 - Battle of Gettysburg, Pennsylvania
The Battle of Gettysburg was a turning point for the Union army and had the largest number of casualties of any battle during the war. Many soldiers from Connecticut saw action at Gettysburg and the remnants of the 27th fought at the Wheatfield.

July 4 - Vicksburg, Mississippi surrenders

July 11 - Fort Wagner, South Carolina

July 18 - Second assault on Fort Wagner

July 28 through October 25 - Siege of Charleston, South Carolina

Vicksburg (by Kurz & Allison, Library of Congress Prints & Photographs Division, LC-USZC4-1754)

1864

February 6 - Morton's Ford, Virginia

May 4 through June - Advance toward Richmond, Virginia

    May 5-7 Battle of the Wilderness

    May 8-12 Battle of Spotsylvania Court House

    June 10 - Cold Harbor

May 9 through September - Sherman's march to

The Wilderness (by Edwin Forbes, Library of Congress Prints & Photographs Division, LC-ppmsca-20683)

Atlanta, Georgia
May 8-21 Battle of Spotsylvania, Virginia
May 14 & 15 - Resaca, Georgia
May 11 - Yellow Tavern, Virginia
May 16 - Drewry's Bluff, Virginia
Several regiments with Branford men fought at Drewry's Bluff and a series of battles called Bermuda Hundred as part of General Grant's march towards Richmond.

May 17 through June 27 - Bermuda Hundred, Virginia
June 3 & 6 - Cold Harbor, Virginia
June 15 - Siege of Petersburg, Virginia begins
June 26 - Strawberry Plains, Virginia
July 20 - Peach Tree Creek, Georgia
August 14, 15 & 27 - Deep Bottom, Virginia

Cold Harbor (engraving by Alfred R. Waud, Harper's Weekly, 25 June 1864, 404)

August 25 - Ream's Station, Virginia
August 25 through September 25 - Final Siege of Petersburg, Virginia and Atlanta, Georgia
September 2 - Atlanta, Georgia captured
September 19 - Third Battle of Winchester, Virginia
Several regiments associated with Branford fought at the Third Battle of Winchester, Fisher's Hill, and Cedar Creek in September and October 1864 as part of the Valley Campaigns under Major-General Philip H. Sheridan.

Winchester (by Kurz & Allen, Library of Congress Prints & Photographs Division, LC-pga-01855)

September 22 - Fisher's Hill, Virginia
September 29 - Chaffin's Farm, Virginia
October 13 - Darbytown Road, Virginia
October 19 - Cedar Creek, Virginia
October 1864 through April 1865 - Siege of Richmond, Virginia
November 15 through December 21 - Sherman's march to the sea
December 10 through 21 - Siege of Savannah, Georgia

Fort Fisher (Photographic History of the Civil War, 3:325)

1865

January 14 & 15 - Bombardment of Fort Fisher, North Carolina
February 5 - Hatcher's Run, Virginia

March 8-10 - Battle of Kinston, Virginia
The Battle of Kinston, Virginia was a significant battle for Branford soldiers where much of the 15th Connecticut Volunteer Regiment was captured.

March 16 - Averysborough, North Carolina
March 19 - Bentonville, North Carolina
March 25 - Petersburg, Virginia
March 29 - Appomattox campaign begins
April 1 - Five Forks, Virginia
April 2 - Capture of Petersburg, Virginia

April 6 - Sayler's Creek, Virginia last major engagement of the war
Aaron Lanfare of Branford received the Congressional Medal of Honor at Sayler's or Sailor's Creek for capturing the flag of the 11th Florida Confederate Infantry.

Lincoln's funeral procession through Washington, D.C. (Photographic History of the Civil War, 3:349)

Grand Review (Photographic History of the Civil War, 9:259)

April 9 - Surrender at Appomattox Court House, Virginia

A number of Branford soldiers from the 1st Connecticut Cavalry and 10th Connecticut Volunteer Infantry were at the surrender at Appomattox Court House.

April 14 - President Lincoln shot at Ford's Theatre and dies the next day

May 5 - Connecticut ratifies the Thirteenth amendment

May 23 - Grand Review at Washington, D.C.

Branford men from the 12th, 14th, and 20th Connecticut Volunteer Infantry units participated in the Grand Review at Washington, D.C. at the close of the war.

APPENDIX IV: LIST OF SOLDIERS BY REGIMENT
* has a pension or pension application

First Connecticut Cavalry
Averill, David Co. B
Callihan, Stephen Co. C (deserted)
Colwell, George W. Co. A
Connelly, James Co. C (deserted)
Dietrich, Joseph
Egan, George M.* Co. B (previously Co. C 3rd)
Gray, Samuel N.* Co. H
Hyde, James R. Co. F
Jones, Peter Co. E
Lanfare, Aaron S.* Co. B & K (Congressional
    Medal of Honor)
Martin, John Co. M
Moran, John Co. B
Nelson, William Co. M (deserted)
Riley, Thomas Co. I (deserted)
Rogers, Walter* Co. B (later Co. C & F 4th U.S.
    Infantry)
Taylor, Henry Co. A

First Heavy Artillery
originally the 4th Volunteer Infantry
Beach, George W.* Co. M
Boardman, Henry D.* Co. F (later Co. B 27th CVI)
Brown, Henry C.* Co. E
Bub, William Co. I (deserted)
Bush, Malachi C.* Co. E (died in prison)
Davis, James Co. B (died)
Foote, Lozelle* Co. F

Forbes, Edgar L.* Co. E (to Co. K 6th U.S.
    Veteran Corps)
Harris, Theodore* Co. E
Harrison, Elizur H. Co. F
Henry, James H. Co. G (deserted)
Hilline, Edward Co. F (deserted)
Hoyt, George E.* Co. E
Jergenson, Emanual Co. E
Kinneen, Michael* Co. K
Merring, Levi Co. G (deserted)
Phelan, Thomas* Co. M (later Co. G 24th V.R.C.)
Reynolds, Peter F.* Co. L (previously Co. G 9th
    CVI)
Robertson, Alexander
Rowland, George H.* Co. F
Snow, Luther H.* Co. D (later 17th & 35th U.S.
    Infantry)
Stone, Walter A.* Co. F (died)
Tarbox, Augustus G. Co. D
Thomas, Elbridge Co. I
Townsend, Sidney* Co. D (died)
White, James* Co. C (later 20th & 37th NY
    Infantry)
Woernley, Paul Co. D

First Light Battery
Behrens, Gustave
Clark, Thomas* (also U.S. Infantry)
Doolittle, Horace A.*

Ford, George
Ives, William B.*
Norton, Elias O.*
Stevens, George* (later Navy)

Second Connecticut Volunteer Infantry
Nettleton, Joseph F.* Co. D
Packard, Charles F.* Co. I (later Co. A 10th CVI)
Scranton, Dayton H. Co. H (later Co. F 12th CVI)
Scranton, Francis S. Co. H (later Co. I 14th CVI)
Scranton, James H. Co. H (later Co. F 12th CVI)
Smith, Ira B.* Co. D (later Co. C 7th CVI)

Second Heavy Artillery
Broom, James A. Co. M (deserted)
Cusher, Joseph (previously Co. B 27th CVI)
Demuth, Jacob Co. D (killed)
Fisher, Albert Co. L (deserted)
Hargent, John Co. M (deserted)
Harlow, Stephen P.* Co. K (later Co. K 22nd VRC)
Hipwell, John H. R. Co. K (killed)
Myer, William Co. L (deserted)
Russell, Charles Co. L (deserted)
Stone, Watson W. Co. L

Third Connecticut Regiment
Egan, George M.* Co. C 1st LA (later Co. B 1st
    Cavalry)
Galloway, William S.* 3rd LA
Tucker, Allen* Co. D 3rd Rifle Co. (later Co. F 10th
    CVI)

Fifth Connecticut Volunteer Infantry
Ackerman, John* Co. K
Barker, Ammi* (later Co. B 15th CVI)
Colwell, Thomas* Co. C (previously Co. B 9th,
    transferred to Co. F 20th)
Donovan, Jeremiah Co. C (failed to report)
Fowler, DeGrasse Co. E (died 1868)
Fuchs, Henry Co. K
Halling, William Co. D (deserted)
Jones, Elijah B.* Co. E (killed)
Linsley, J. Atwood* Co. E
Myers, George W. Co. C (deserted)
Palmer, Luzerne A.* Co. C & I
Reynolds, Stephen Co. C
Schaffer, Henry L.* Co. D
Shepard, Charles B.* Co. E (later Co. A 10th CVI)

Sixth Connecticut Volunteer Infantry
Barker, Joseph Co. K (killed)
Bradley, Leonard* Co. G
Butler, Jesse Co. F (killed)
Cobleigh, William C.* Co. G
Gilbert, Wells* Co. K (died)
Hanson, Peter Co. K
Howd, William T.* Co. K
Linsley, Solomon F.* Co. G
Paine, Richard J.* Co. K
Robinson, Lorenzo* Co. D & F
Squire, Lyman F.* Co. F
Woodruff, Rev. Curtiss T.*

Seventh Connecticut Infantry
Baldwin, Jerome A.* Co. G
Barry, Charles Co. E (deserted)
Beach, William H.* Co. K (previously Co. B 27th
    CVI & Co. H 15th CVI)
Blakeslee, Kirtland* Co. F
Booth, John H.* Co. G
Brockett, Benajah* Co. F
Brockett, Edgar L. * Co. F
Brockett, Edward * Co. F
Bush, Timothy G.* Co. G
Butler, Charles* Co. D (previously Co. D 15th)
Dargan, Pierce* Co. F (previously 11th CVI)
Davis, John* Co. D (died in prison)
DeBacque, Alfred Co. G (wounded, deserted)
Dolph, Charles C.* Co. D (later Co. I 19th)
Gilde, James* Co. D
Harrison, William H.* Co. A (died)
Johnson, Campbell
Martin, John Co. E (previously Co. E 15th)
Morse, James Co. E (previously Co. E 15th)
Page, Henry* Co. G
Sherman, Daniel Co. K (deserted)
Smith, Ira B.* Co. C (previously Co. D 2nd CVI)
Sullivan, Philip
Strickland, Asa* Co. D
Underwood, William J.* Co. G

Eighth Connecticut Volunteer Infantry
Bartholomew, Isaac C.* Co. K
Evans, Leverett E. Co. A (died of wounds)
Holcombe, Dr. H.V.C.* Co. F 8th (later Co. C 15th)
Stevens, Ellis M.* Co. K
Stevens, Emmerson R.* Co. K

Ninth Connecticut Volunteer Infantry

Colwell, Thomas* Co. B (later Co. C 5th and Co. F 20th)

Donohue, John Co. A (died)

Doherty, Robert* Co. A

McGuire, Thomas Co. A & E

McKeon, Francis* Co. E

Pratt, Eugene H.*

Reynolds, Peter F.* Co. C

Sanford, Daniel Co. C & F

Tenth Connecticut Volunteer Infantry

Adams, John Co. I (deserted)

Ames, Charles Co. H (deserted)

Bradley, George G.* Co. C (killed)

Bradley, Timothy* Co. C

Clanning, William Henry (also Navy)

Forrester, Julius Co. C

Harrison, Sylvanus* Co. C

Jennings, Barney* Co. G

Jepson, Benjamin* Co. A & K

Johnson, Charles Co. I

Johnson, Davis S.* Co. A

Johnson, Elizur C.* Co. A

Johnson, George Co. I

Lee, Frederick W.* Co. K (later Co. G 20th CVI)

Linsley, Benjamin M. (killed)

Linsley, James H.* Co. C

Linsley, John S., Jr.* (later 14th Regiment U.S. Infantry)

Packard, Charles H.* Co. A (previously Co. F 2nd CVI)

Palmer, John Henry* Co. K (killed)

Shepard, Charles B.* Co. A (previously Co. E 5th CVI)

Shepard, John F.* Co. A (died in prison)

Shepard, Samuel S.* Co. A (died shortly after the war)

Smith, David L.* Co. A (died of disease)

Smith, Edward L.* Co. A & C (died of wounds)

Smith, Henry C.* Co. A

Smith, Josiah A.* Co. C

Sundelous, Peter* Co. C

Todd, Andrew B.* Co. A

Tucker, Allen* Co. F (Congressional Medal of Honor, previously Co. D 3rd CVI)

Valleley, Francis* Co. A

Wheaton, Albert F.* Co. A (killed)

Woodworth, Albert P.* Co. B

Eleven Connecticut Volunteer Infantry

Albinos, John Co. H

Bamberg, Casper* Co. C

Bamberg, Martin* Co. C

Brown, Lawrence Co. D (deserted)

Dargan, Pierce* (to Co. F 7th CVI)

DeCourcey, Charles Co. B (later Navy)

Edge, Reuben D. Co. G (died)

Flynn, John Co. D (deserted)

Fuchs, Charles Co. H (died)

Hall, James Co. A (later Navy)

Harlow, Henry P.* Co. K

Lester, Thomas* Co. F (died soon after war)

Lynhan, James Co. I (deserted)

McGinley, James Co. K (deserted)

Murphy, John (later Navy, deserted)

O'Callahan, Philip Co. E

Reif, Christian* Co. C

Reif, Lorenz* Co. C

Smith, Stephen (failed to report)

Sternburg, John Co. K (deserted)

Walter, Frank Co. K (deserted)

Wilson, John Co. B (later Navy)

Winship, Hoyt F.* Co. E

Twelve Connecticut Volunteer Infantry

Chaipel, Benjamin F.* Co. B

Chaipel, William H. Co. B (deserted)

Curtiss, Joseph* Co. B

Forbes, Levi* Co. B (died from wounds 1866)

Johnson, Henry* Co. B

Johnson, Henry E.* Co. B

Kerr, John* Co. B & D

Kinneen, James* Co. B

Logan, Michael* Co. G

Lull, Oscar S. Co. E

Powell, John Co. B (died in prison)

Rich, James S.* Co. C

Scranton, Dayton H. Co. F (died, previously Co. H 2nd CVI)

Scranton, James H. Co. F (died, previously Co. H 2nd CVI)

Shanley, Patrick (failed to report)

Stone, Horatio* Co. F
Sullivan, Charles Co. B (died)
Wheeler, George H.* Co. B
Wilson, Thomas* Co. H (died)

Thirteenth Connecticut Volunteer Infantry
Bailey, Herman W.* Co. H
Bartholomew, John N.* Co. G
Frazier, John Co. A
Hopkins, Albert F. Co. G
Huntley, William* Co. H
Knight, Winthrop (died)
Morton, John Henry Co. A
Palmer, Theodore* Co. G
Robinson, Henry P.* Co. A (previously Co. D 15th
   CVI)
Russell, Alfred* Co. H
Shepard, Harvey G.* Co. B (later Co. B 27th CVI)
Stone, Horatio Co. K
Tubbs, John E.* Co. A

Fourteenth Connecticut Volunteer Infantry
Bartholomew, John L.* Co. F (died in prison)
Brennan, Michael Co. I (died in prison)
Brown, William* Co. I
Clifton, Robert Co. I (deserted)
Donohue, William* Co. G
Duffy, Thomas* Co. I
Green, John Co. K (deserted)
Jones, William S.* Co. G
Page, Henry B.* Co. G (died)
Palmer, Nathan A.* Co. I (previously Co. B 27th)
Scranton, Francis S. Co. I (killed, previously
   Co. H 2nd CVI)
Scranton, Thomas M.* Co. I (died)
Stannard, John S.* Co. G
Wallack, George Co. K

Fifteenth Connecticut Infantry
Albee, Calvin* Co. I (killed)
Albinger, John J.* Co. C
Barker, Ammi B.* Co. B (previously Co. C 5th
   CVI)
Barnes, George H.* Co. K
Beach, William Co. H (previously Co. B 27th CVI,
   later Co. K 7th CVI)

Bishop, Austin* Co. I (died)
Blakeslee, Charles P.* Co. E
Boylan, Luke* Co. I (died)
Brockett, William E.* Co. K
Brockett, William T.* Co. B
Buell, Edwin A.* Co. K
Butler, Charles* Co. D (later Co. D 7th)
Byington, Edwin M.* Co. I
Carey, Thomas J.* Co. E
Clark, Joseph Co. C (failed to report)
Coan, Jerome* Co. E
Crosby, Richard* Co. A
Dayton, Ambrose L.* Co. K
Donnelly, Edward Co. F
Dowd, Benjamin R.* Co. K (died)
Foote, Delizon B.* Co. A (later 2nd Battery)
Foote, Isaac* Co. K
Foote, Philo B. Co. K (died)
Fowler, Samuel O.* Co. I
Francisco, Clifford A. Co. I (died)
Frisbie, Alonzo P.* Co. K
Frisbie, Charles H.* Co. E
Frisbie, Russell L.* Co. K
Frost, Alva* Co. B
Galpin, Joseph A.* Co. C
Gutersloh, Christian Co. B (deserted)
Harrison, Franklin M.* Co. A (later Co. H 3rd
   VRC)
Harrison, Lorenzo E.* Co. K
Holcombe, Dr. H.V.C.* Co. C (previously Co. F
   8th)
Howd, George* Co. K
Hull, James C.* Co. H (died)
Jacobs, Egbert* Co. B
Linsley, Charles F. Co. F
Linsley, Jacob F. Co. K (died)
Linsley, Marcus M. Co. A & E (later Navy)
Linsley, Samuel M. Co. K (died)
Linsley, William H.* Co. B
Lynch, Daniel Co. A
Maher, John Co. G
Maltby, Charles D.* Co. K
Martin, James Co. E
McDermott, James* Co. G
Mix, Stephen* Co. K
Morse, James Co. E * (later Co. E 7th)
Munson, Medad D.* Co. K

Page, Joel C.* Co. E
Palmer, Ammi B.* Co. B
Palmer, Luzerne A.* Co. C & I
Pardee, Henry N.* Co. K
Plant, Albert E.* Co. B
Rath, Gottfried* Co. C
Robinson, Henry P.* Co. D (later Co. A 13thVRC)
Rogers, Mason Co. B (died)
Scranton, Henry W. Co. K
Smith, Jacob A.* Co. K (died)
Talmadge, George W.* Co. K
Talmadge, William Co. E
Towner, J. Edwin* Co. C
Williams, Charles M.* Co. I (later Navy)
Wilson, Thomas* Co. H (died)

Seventeenth Connecticut Volunteer Infantry
Allen, Henry* Co. F
Gilbert, Frederick A.* Co. G
Weed, Oscar* Co. F

Eighteenth Connecticut Volunteer Infantry
Clark, Francis L.* Co. A

Ninteenth Connecticut Volunteer Infantry
Dolph, Charles C.* Co. I (previously Co. D 7th)

Twentieth Connecticut Volunteer Infantry
Bliss, Howard* Co. H (died)
Carter, Charles* Co. G
Colwell, Thomas* Co. F (previously Co. B 9th and Co. C 5th)
Goodrich, Horace W.* Co. G
Hull, Eli* Co. F
Kelsey, Gilbert T.* Co. G 20th (died)
Lee, Frederick M.* Co. G (previously Co. K 10th CVI)
McGuinnis, John Co. B (failed to report)
Mooney, Michael* Co. G
Platts, Albert U.* Co. C
Smith, Elizur G.* Co. A
Taylor, William L.* Co. G

Twenty-first Connecticut Volunteer Infantry
Freeman, Wilbur* Co. I

Twenty-third Connecticut Volunteer Infantry
Blake, Halsey H.* Co. G & I
Ferguson, Charles M.* Co. F

Twenty-fourth Connecticut Volunteer Infantry
Thompson, Richard E.* Co. B

Twenty-fifth Connecticut Volunteer Infantry
Buell, Burton E.* Co. H
Hartson, Isaac Y.* Co. K
Hitchcock, Oliver A.* Co. I

Twenty-seventh Connecticut Volunteer Infantry
Adams, John* Co. F
Barnes, William H.* Co. A
Bradley, Franklin* Co. A
Calkins, Wilbur F.* Co. K (later Marine Corps)
Day, Thomas* Co. E
Munson, William W.* Co. E
Page, Elizur E.* Co. F
Robinson, John S.* Co. F (died)
Schenck, Paul* Co. K
Sliney, David* Co. G

Co. B Twenty-seventh Connecticut Volunteer Infantry
Averill, Daniel 2nd*
Backes, Michael*
Baldwin, George C. (died)
Baldwin, George W.
Bartholomew, Rodolphus*
Beach, Harvey W.*
Beach, Samuel*
Beach, William H.* (later Co. H 15th & Co. K 7th CVI)
Beaumont, Harvey*
Bennett, Joseph* (killed)
Boardman, Henry D.* (previously Co. F 4th CVI)
Bradshaw, William
Bunnell, William R.*
Callahan, Timothy*
Camp, Henry A.*
Camp, Joel

MUSTER-IN ROLL

OF

CAPT. CALVIN L. ELY'S (B) COMPANY, IN THE TWENTY-SEVENTH REGIMENT,

CONNECTICUT VOLUNTEERS, COMMANDED BY COL. RICHARD BOSTWICK.

CALLED INTO THE SERVICE OF THE UNITED STATES BY THE PRESIDENT OF THE UNITED STATES, FROM THE THIRD DAY OF OCTOBER, 1862, FOR THE TERM OF NINE MONTHS.

No. of each trade.	NAME.	RANK.	AGE.	JOINED FOR DUTY. WHEN.	JOINED FOR DUTY. WHERE.	No. of each trade.	NAME.	RANK.	AGE.	JOINED FOR DUTY. WHEN.	JOINED FOR DUTY. WHERE.
	CALVIN L. ELY,	Captain,	34	Aug. 19,	Branford,	21	DOUGLASS FAIRCHILD,	Private.	35	Sept. 10,	Wallingford,
						22	WILLIAM J. GALLAGHER,	"	29	Sept. 10,	Wallingford,
1	DANIEL W. FIELDS,	1st Lieut.	28	Aug. 25,	Wallingford,	23	HENRY W. HUBBARD,	"	29	Aug. 22,	Branford,
1	GEORGE W. ELTON,	2d Lieut.	32	Sept. 10,	Wallingford,	24	JOHN HOTCHKISS,	"	44	Aug. 25,	Branford,
						25	HENRY T. HART,	"	21	Aug. 19,	Branford,
1	DANIEL AVERILL, 2d,	Sergeant,	23	Aug. 21,	Branford,	26	ISRAEL HIGGS,	"	27	Sept. 8,	New Haven,
2	ROBERT B. GOODYEAR,	"	26	Sept. 1,	North Haven,	27	ROGER HALL,	"	37	Sept. 8,	Branford,
3	SAMUEL S. COOK,	"	36	Aug. 19,	Branford,	28	NATHAN HARRISON,	"	26	Sept. 9,	North Branford,
4	ALONZO F. HUBBELL,	"	23	Aug. 25,	Branford,	29	WILLIAM W. HOLMES,	"	24	Sept. 10,	Wallingford,
5	BILLIOUS C. HALL,	"	28	Sept. 10,	Wallingford,	30	JOSIAH JOHNSON,	"	21	Sept. 9,	North Branford,
						31	HOMER R. JOHNSON,	"	25	Sept. 10,	Wallingford,
1	GEORGE M. PROUT,	Corporal,	37	Sept. 10,	Branford,	32	RICHARD KELSEY,	"	21	Aug. 21,	Guilford,
2	ALBERT HARRISON,	"	20	Aug. 20,	North Branford,	33	MATTHIAS KNERINGER,	"	43	Aug. 22,	Branford,
3	SAMUEL BEACH,	"	35	Aug. 25,	Branford,	34	JAMES KENNEDY,	"	36	Sept. 10,	Wallingford,
4	HENRY D. BOARDMAN,	"	19	Aug. 29,	North Branford,	35	ADAM LAMM,	"	35	Sept. 1,	North Haven,
5	CHARLES A. YOUNG,	"	25	Aug. 20,	Branford,	36	JAMES McGOWAN,	"	18	Sept. 1,	Wallingford,
6	GEORGE S. ROGERS,	"	20	Aug. 25,	Branford,	37	MICHAEL O'NEIL,	"	20	Sept. 1,	Branford,
7	GEORGE G. WILFORD,	"	23	Aug. 21,	Branford,	38	THOMAS O'BRIEN,	"	31	Sept. 5,	North Haven,
8	ISAAC K. HALL,	"	27	Sept. 10,	Wallingford,	39	EDWARD O'BRIEN,	"	26	Sept. 10,	Wallingford,
						40	JOHN O'BRIEN,	"	21	Sept. 8,	Branford,
1	BRYAN HILL,	Musician,	21	Aug. 28,	Wallingford,	41	WILLIAM B. PALMER,	"	21	Aug. 21,	Branford,
1	HENRY Z. NICHOLS,	"	35	Sept. 10,	Branford,	42	EDWARD W. PARSONS,	"	44	Sept. 9,	Branford,
						43	NATHAN A. PALMER,	"	18	Sept. 10,	North Haven,
1	RODOLPHUS BARTHOLOMEW,	Waggoner	43	Aug. 22,	Branford,	44	CHARLES PADEN,	"	28	Sept. 10,	Wallingford,
						45	JAMES PAGE,	"	26	Sept. 10,	Guilford,
1	GEORGE C. BALDWIN,	Private.	19	Aug. 21,	Branford,	46	EDWARD D. SHELDON,	"	20	Aug. 20,	Branford,
2	WILLIAM H. BEACH,	"	36	Aug. 21,	Branford,	47	ELIZUR C. STONE,	"	35	Aug. 20,	North Branford,
3	JOSEPH BENNETT,	"	23	Aug. 25,	Branford,	48	ELBERT J. SMITH,	"	18	Sept. 1,	North Haven,
4	HARVEY BEACH,	"	27	Aug. 25,	Branford,	49	JAMES SLOMAN,	"	38	Aug. 28,	Wallingford,
5	WILLIAM BRADSHAW,	"	44	Sept. 1,	Wallingford,	50	HARVEY G. SHEPARD,	"	29	Sept. 10,	Branford,
6	HARVEY BEAUMONT,	"	25	Sept. 9,	Wallingford,	51	OBED TYLER,	"	21	Aug. 22,	Branford,
7	MICHAEL BACKUS,	"	32	Sept. 10,	Wallingford,	52	MICHAEL TAYLOR,	"	25	Sept. 9,	Wallingford,
8	GEORGE W. BALDWIN,	"	28	Aug. 21,	Branford,	53	KIRTLAND TODD,	"	25	Sept. 9,	North Haven,
9	WILLIAM BUNNELL,	"	18	Aug. 25,	Branford,	54	BERI M. TODD,	"	44	Aug. 30,	New Haven,
10	HENRY A. CAMP,	"	18	Sept. 2,	Wallingford,	55	HENRY D. TODD,	"	29	Sept. 1,	North Haven,
11	JOEL CAMP,	"	40	Sept. 10,	Wallingford,	56	LEWIS M. TUCKER,	"	25	Aug. 25,	Branford,
12	PATRICK CONDON,	"	18	Sept. 10,	Wallingford,	57	WILLIAM A. TYLER,	"	23	Sept. 10,	Branford,
13	JOHN CONDON,	"	30	Sept. 10,	Wallingford,	58	NELSON VIBBERT,	"	44	Sept. 10,	Wallingford,
14	TIMOTHY CALLAHAN,	"	30	Sept. 10,	Branford,	59	EDWIN L. WILFORD,	"	20	Aug. 22,	Branford,
15	JOSEPH CUSHER,	"	21	Sept. 10,	Branford,	60	MERWIN WHEATON,	"	19	Aug. 20,	North Branford,
16	ELIZUR DIBBLE,	"	20	Sept. 8,	Branford,	61	L. MORTIMER WILLIS,	"	33	Sept. 1,	Branford,
17	EDWARD B. DOLPH,	"	22	Sept. 9,	Wallingford,	62	WILLIAM WALLACE,	"	18	Sept. 6,	Wallingford,
18	JAMES ENNIS,	"	20	Sept. 17,	Wallingford,	63	JOHN K. WILDER,	"	23	Sept. 29,	Wallingford,
19	THOMAS H. EVANS,	"	44	Sept. 30,	Wallingford,	64	SOLOMON YALE,	"	43	Aug. 25,	Branford,
20	WALTER E. FOWLER,	"	22	Sept. 9,	Guilford,	65	ANDREW FOSTER,	"	28	Oct. 16,	New Haven.

Tuttle, Morehouse & Taylor, Printers, New Haven.

(Branford Historical Society archives)

Condon, John *
Condon, Patrick (killed)
Cook, Samuel S.*
Cross, Edmund B. (died)
Cusher, Joseph (later Co. A 2nd HA)
Dibble, Elizur B.*
Dolph, Edward B. (died)
Elton, George W.*
Ely, Calvin L.*
Ennis, James*
Evans, Thomas H.*
Fairchild, Douglas*
Field, Daniel W.*
Foster, Andrew * (previously Co. G 82nd NY)
Fowler, Walter E.*
Galligan, William J.*
Goodyear, Robert B.*
Hall, Billious C.*
Hall, Isaac K.*
Hall, Roger*
Harrison, C. Albert*
Harrison, Hart Lind
Harrison, Nathan A.*
Hart, Henry T.*
Higgs, Israel*
Hill, Bryon*
Holmes, William W.*
Hotchkiss, John* (died)
Hubbard, Henry W.*
Hubbell, Alonzo F.*
Johnson, Homer R.*
Johnson, Josiah* (died of wounds)
Kelsey, Richard T.*
Kennedy, James*
Kneringer, Matthias*
Lamm, Adam
McGowan, James* (later Navy)
Nichols, Henry Z.*
O'Brien, Edward*
O'Brien, John
O'Brien, Thomas*
O'Neil, Michael*
Paden, Charles*
Page, James B.*
Palmer, Nathan A.* (later Co. I 14th CVI)
Palmer, W. Bradley*
Parsons, Edwin W.*

Prout, George M.*
Rogers, George S.* (later Navy)
Sheldon, Edward D.*
Shepard, Harvey G.* (previously Co. B 13th CVI)
Slowman, James*
Smith, Elbert J. (died shortly after the war)
Stone, Elizur C.*
Taylor, Michael*
Todd, Beri M.
Todd, Henry D.*
Todd, Kirtland*
Tucker, Lewis M.* (died)
Tyler, Obed L.*
Tyler, William A.*
Vibbert, Nelson J.* (later Co. I 7th Vermont)
Wallace, William J.*
Wheaton, Merwin*
Wilder, John K.*
Wilford, Edwin L.*
Wilford, George G. (killed)
Willis, L. Mortimer*
Yale, Solomon
Young, Charles A.*

Twenty-eighth Connecticut Volunteer Infantry
Garlick, Seymour* Co. D

Twenty-ninth Connecticut Volunteer Infantry
Brown, Charles* Co. C
Butler, Samuel C. Co. G
Danby, William Co. I
Fowler, William N.* Co. G (died)
Green, Charles H.* Co. G (died)
Griffin, Alexander Co. I
Grimes, John R.* Co. H (died)
Mason, Charles Co. H
Morris, William H. Co. I
Parker, William H. Co. K
Smith, Thomas Co. I
White, Albert D. Co. K

Thirty-first U.S. Colored Infantry
Daniels, Josiah Co. C (died)

Navy
Averill, Adelbert C.*
Averill, Roland G.* (Marine Corp)

Babcock, Marcus O.*
Baisley, John W.* of New York
Calkins, Wilbur F.* (previously Co. K 27th)
Clanning, William Henry
Decourcey, Charles (previously Co. B 11th)
Graham, William F.*
Hall, James (deserted, previously Co. A 11th)
Hickman, John T.* (later Maryland Cavalry)
Hutchinson, John
Linsley, Charles E.*
Linsley, Jared, Jr.
Linsley, Marcus M. (previously Co. A & E 15th)
McGowan, James* (previously Co. B 27th)
Murphy, John deserted (previously Co. A 11th)
Rogers, George S.* (previously Co. B 27th)
Stevens, George* (previously 1st LA)
Thayer, Elwyn M.*
White, William*
Williams, Charles M.* (previously Co. I 15th)
Wilson, John (previously Co. B 11th)

Other states
Ashman, Robert A.* New York
Baisley, John W.* New York
Bird, Edward J.* New York
Bliss, George* Massachusetts
Buell, Edward J.* Ohio
Butler, Rufus A.* Ohio (died)
Carter, Edwin H.* Illinois (killed)
Colburn, Elisha H.* Delaware
Cooke, Samuel G.* Illinois
Daniel, Joseph* Vermont
Dory, George W.* Massachusetts
Downey, Timothy* New York

Foote, Frederick Illinois
Foster, Andrew* New York (later Co. B 27th CVI)
Frisbie, John R.* Illinois (died)
Hall, John G. (died)
Harrison, Dr. Benjamin F. New York
Hickman, John* Maryland
Hosley, Loring D.* Massachusetts
Hosley, William B.* Massachusetts (died)
Houghtling, William W. Massachusetts (killed)
Jost, Jacob* New York
Lay, James W.* Illinois
Lee, Joseph* Massachusetts
Linsley, Frederick A.* Maryland
Linsley, Joseph F.* Wisconsin (killed)
Neale, Daniel* Massachusetts
Rapp, William* career Army
Roberts, Amos, Jr.* Maine
Rogers, Albert T. Virginia
Smith, A. Judson* New York
Smith, Frederick* Massachusetts
Stevens, Charles C.* New York
Sullivan, Matthew* New Hampshire
Terhune, Nicholas R.* Maryland
VanBenthuysen, Isaac E.* New York
Vibbert, Nelson J. * Vermont (previously Co. B 27th CVI)
White, James* New York (previously Co. C 1st HA)
White, William* Rhode Island
Whitney, Henry M.* Massachusetts
Wright, Ellis C.* Pennsylvania
Young, William E. Rhode Island
Zink, Dr. Walter H.* New York

APPENDIX V: DEATHS DUE TO CIVIL WAR SERVICE

Albee, Calvin - killed at Kinston, North Carolina
Baldwin, George C. - of disease
Barker, Joseph - killed at Drewry's Bluff, Virginia
Bartholomew, John L. - in Salisbury Prison
Bennett, Joseph - from wounds at Fredericksburg, Virginia
Bishop, Austin - of disease
Bliss, Howard - of disease
Boylan, Luke - of disease
Bradley, George G. - killed at Darbytown Road, Virginia
Brennan, Michael - at Andersonville Prison
Bush, Malachi - in prison
Butler, Jesse - killed at Bermuda Hundred, Virginia
Butler, Rufus A. - of disease
Carter, Edwin H. - killed at Fort Donelson, Tennessee
Condon, Patrick - killed at Fredericksburg, Virginia
Cross, Edmund B. - of disease
Daniels, Josiah
Davis, James
Davis, John - in Andersonville Prison
Demuth, Jacob - killed at Petersburg, Virginia
Dolph, Edward B. - of disease
Donahue, John
Dowd, Benjamin R. - of disease
Edge, Reuben D.
Evans, Leverett E. - from wounds at Antietam, Maryland
Foote, Philo B. - of disease
Forbes, Levi - from wounds at Georgia Landing, Louisiana
Fowler, DeGrasse - died shortly after the war of disease
Fowler, William N. - of disease
Francisco, Clifford A. - of disease
Frisbie, John R. - from wounds at Missionary Ridge, Tennessee
Fuchs, Charles
Galligan, William - died shortly after the war of disease

Gilbert, Wells - of disease
Green, Charles H. - of disease
Grimes, John R. - of disease
Hall, John G. - of disease
Harrison, William H. - of disease
Hipwell, John H. R. - killed at Cedar Creek, Virginia
Hosley, William B. - of disease
Hotchkiss, John - of disease
Houghtling, William - killed at Petersburg, Virginia
Hull, James C. - of disease
Johnson, Josiah - from wounds at Fredericksburg, Virginia
Jones, Elijah B. - killed Cedar Mountain, Virginia
Kelsey, Gilbert I. - of disease
Knight, Winthrop - of disease
Lester, Thomas - of disease
Linsley, Benjamin M. - killed at the Wilderness, Virginia
Linsley, Jacob F. - of disease
Linsley, Joseph F. - killed at Perry's Ferry, Mississippi
Linsley, Samuel M. - of disease
Page, Henry B. - of disease
Palmer, John Henry - from wounds at Petersburgh, Virginia
Powell, John - in Salisbury Prison
Robinson, John S. - of disease
Rogers, Mason - of disease
Scranton, Dayton H. - from wounds at Port Hudson, Louisiana
Scranton, Francis S. - killed at Fredericksburg, Virginia
Scranton, James H. - from wounds at the Battle of the Wilderness, Virginia
Scranton, Thomas M. - of disease
Shepard, John F. - in Andersonville Prison
Shepard, Samuel S. - of disease contracted during the war
Smith, David L. - of disease
Smith, Edward L. - from wounds at Fort Gregg, Virginia
Smith, Elbert J. - of disease contracted during the war
Smith, Jacob A. - of disease
Stone, Walter A. - of disease
Sullivan, Charles
Townsend, Sidney - of disease
Tucker, Lewis M. - of disease
Wheaton, Albert F. - killed at Kinston, North Carolina
Wilford, George G. - from wounds at Fredericksburg, Virginia
Wilson, Thomas - of disease

APPENDIX VI: SUBSTITUTES

Ames, Charles for John B. Russell of Branford
Arlington, Willoughby for George M. Prout of Branford
Barry, Charles for Edwin A. Ennis of Branford
Brown, Lawrence for Virgil H. Rose of North Branford
Bub, William for William Bryan, Jr. of Branford
Clark, Thomas for Lyman H. Foote of North Branford
DeBacque, Alfred for Augustus R. Rowley of Branford
Dietrich, Joseph for John H. Harrison of Branford
Donnelly, Edward for Elias E. Potter of North Branford
Forrester, Julius F. for Ralph Blackstone of Branford
Fuchs, Charles for Orrin H. Hoadley of Branford
Flynn, John for Henry B. Lanphier of Branford
Hilliner, John for John Higgins of Branford
Hogan, Michael for George H. Page of Branford
Jennings, Barney for George C. Field of Branford
Johnson, Campbell for John Spencer of Branford
Johnson, Charles for Joseph P. Douglass of Branford
Johnson, George for Henry Palmer of Branford
Jones, Peter for John H. Gates of North Branford
Lamb, John for William D. Ford of North Branford
Lynch, Daniel for Reuben N. Augur of North Branford
Martin, James for Merrick M. Russell of North Branford
McGinnis, James for Jarvis Averill of Branford
Morse, James for John C. Harrison of North Branford
O'Callahan, Philip for Martin Bishop of North Branford
O'Neal, John for Edmund M. Averill of Branford
Robertson, Alexander for Leverett Chidsey of North Branford
Sherman, Daniel for Lewis F. Shepard of Branford
Stewart, James for Benjamin Page, Jr. of North Branford
Sullivan, Philip for Lynde Harrison of Branford
Sundelas, Peter for Henry Rogers of Branford
Willis, Joseph T. for Franklin D. Linsley of Branford

APPENDIX VII: FURTHER RESEARCH

Opportunity for further research on Branford and North Branford soldiers is available, particularly in state and federal records. The Connecticut State Library has a variety of government generated records in their archives, most of which are sorted but not indexed. Federal records of interest include court marshals, more compiled service records, national soldiers' homes, pension payment vouchers, and pensions not retrieved by this researcher. More research could be done on individual sailors and their experience in both published and archived records relating to the Navy.

Multi-volume published records referenced in the bibliography provide extensive detail to military activities, battles, officers, and correspondence. Those interested in Connecticut regiments should also consult regimental histories, local newspapers, Records of Events, and Compiled Military Service Records. Further research on individual soldiers might uncover additional genealogical information or primary material such as letters and photographs. The political climate in the state and nation provides the backdrop for the war and the state's communities. Events planned throughout the country acknowledging the 150th anniversary of the Civil War will generate new ideas and scholarship.

Unidentified image but based on provenance is probably Elizur B. Dibble with his wife Ann G. Meigs, perhaps for their wedding in 1864. On her lap is his Civil War kepi with the symbols depicting his service—a bugle (for Infantry), 27 (for Regiment) and a B (for Company) (Branford Historical Society photograph collection)

APPENDIX VIII: GROUP PHOTO IDENTIFICATION

A. Atwood Linsley
B. Dr. Walter Zink
C. Henry Hubbard
D. Bradley Palmer

E. Nicholas Terhune
F. Samuel O. Fowler
G. John Huchinson
H. Samuel S. Cook

I. Elizur Johnson
J. Edward Bird
K. Edward Sheldon
L. Rodolphus Bartholomew

M. James W. Lay
N. Elwyn Thayer
O. Samuel G. Cooke
P. James Rich

Q. Ammi Barker
R. Dr. Calvin Ely
S. Michael Kinney
T. Albert Plant

U. Joseph Lee
V. Eddie Wilford
W. Said to be the daughters
   of Elwyn Thayer (N)

GLOSSARY

Adjutant - a staff officer who serves as an assistant to a commanding officer

Adjutant general - an officer who is the chief administrative assistant to the commanding general of a corps

Army of the Potomac - principal Union force in the eastern theater

Artillery company - a branch of the army carrying cannon or other large caliber firearms, sometimes called a battery, could be light or heavy. Most artillery

Battery at Petersburg (Photographic History of the Civil War, 3:381)

companies belonged to a regiment, a few were independent and scattered in different assignments

Aquaduct Bridge - bridge connecting Washington, D.C. with Virginia, now the Key Bridge

Battery - an artillery company or unit with more than six cannon

Bivouac - a temporary encampment that could be easily disassembled, provided no shelter for the soldiers

Breastwork - an entrenchment of earth and wood to protect defenders, often fronted by a ditch

Brigade - a division of the army made up of four to six regiments, usually led by a colonel or brigadier general, had a number designation

Camp Seward - named for Secretary of State William H. Seward

Camp Tuttle - named for General James M. Tuttle

Campaign - a series of military operations

Captain - the commander of a company, had administrative duties and led the company in battle

Carte deviste (CDV) - a 2 ¼ X 3 ¾ inch photograph mounted on card stock, the soldier often had his photo taken shortly before or after enlisting or while away from home to send to loved ones

Cavalry - a branch of the army mounted on horseback, were sometimes called a troop, usually carried sabers, pistols or short rifles but often fought on foot. Some horseback units were called mounted infantry

Breastwork at Petersburg (Library of Congress Prints & Photographs Division, LC-cwpb-02604)

Chevron - a V-shaped bar or bars worn on the sleeve of a military uniform showing rank. For enlisted officers, sergeants wore three strips and corporals two

Commutation - paying a fee to avoid the draft

Company - a group of 75-100 soldiers led by a captain, given letter descriptors A-M except J; ten or twelve companies made up a regiment

Conscript - a draftee

Copperhead - phrase used by Republicans for anti-war Democrats, or a Northerner opposed to the war

Corps - made up of two or three divisions of approximately 36,000 men led by a general

Diphtheria - a bacterial infection of the tonsils and pharynx, it spread quickly among the soldiers in camp

Discharge - to release a soldier from duty; often used interchangeably with muster out

Division - contained three to five brigades of approximately 4,000 men, was commanded by a major general

Dysentery - a disease manifested by abdominal pain, increasing intestinal disease and weakness, was the leading cause of death by disease among soldiers in the Civil War

Enlist - to register or enroll for service in a branch of the armed forces

Engagement - a high level of combat below a battle but sometimes used interchangeably

Finding Aid - instructional material for using archival records

Flank - either end of a battle line or line of troops

Garrison - military personnel assigned to a fort or fortress

Haversack - small bag issued to and carried by the soldier

Infantry - branch of the army in which soldiers are on foot

Kepi - a French style military cap used during the Civil War with a flat circular top and a visor

Lieutenant - an officer second in command of a company or battery, assisted the captain

Long Bridge - connects Washington, D.C. to Virginia, now called the 14th Avenue Bridge

Malaria - a parasite infection transmitted by mosquitoes causing fever, chills, was contracted by soldiers serving in warmer climates

Militia - a local or state military group

Minie bullet - standard rifle bullet used during the war, sometimes spelled minnie

Musician - each company had a fifer and drummer who were trained by a lead musician, most had some ability before they enlisted, others were sent to school in New York for instruction

Long Bridge (Library of Congress Prints & Photographs Division, LC-cwpb-04247)

Pontoon bridge over the James River
(Library of Congress Prints & Photographs
Division, LC-cwpb-01896)

Muster - to assemble troops for roll call, inspection, or service, or to formally enroll. Muster out was often used interchangeably in the pension records with discharge

Orderly sergeant - the first sergeant of the company, conveys the orders

Parapet - a wall or bank used to screen troops from frontal enemy fire, sometimes placed along the top of a rampart, made of logs and packed behind by dirt

Parole - release of prisoners upon taking an oath that the prisoner will not fight for a specific amount of time. General Grant discontinued prisoner parole and exchanges later in the war

Phthisis - tuberculosis

Picket - guard duty along the front lines

Pioneer - enlisted men detailed for building roads, temporary bridges, general construction, and carpentry

Pontoon - a temporary bridge supported by flat bottomed boats

Provost duty - police duty in an occupied territory

Provost marshal - head of the policing force, used to enforce the draft and make arrests for desertion or other military crimes. They also managed the troops used to guard captured cities

Quartermaster - officer in charge of clothing and supplies for the soldiers

Quinine - medicine used for the treatment of malaria

Rampart - an earthen embankment for defense against an enemy, also called a bulwark

Recruit - to strengthen the army by enlisting more personnel

Regiment - unit of the Army of about 1,000 men or ten to twelve companies, usually commanded by a colonel. Had a numerical designation i.e. 15th Connecticut. Sometimes was known by the name of the commander such as the Lyon Regiment

Secesh - someone in favor of the attempt of the Southern states to withdraw from the union, short for secession

Sergeant - could have specific administrative duties, such as ordinance or quartermaster sergeant

Siege - the military blockading of supply and travel routes to a city forcing its army to surrender

Provost marshal (Photographic History of the Civil War, 7:187)

Surgeon (Harper's Weekly, 12 July 1862, 436)

Surgeon - held the rank and pay of a major, an assistant surgeon held rank equal to captain

Sutler - a private business man who sold goods to soldiers

Theater - a large area of military campaigns

Typhoid fever - a systemic bacterial infection with a slow onset of sustained fever and profound weakness, the bacteria was found in contaminated food

VC or VRC - Veteran Reserve Corps or Invalid Corps was authorized by the War Department on April 28, 1863, allowed retention of disabled soldiers to perform hospital or other light duty

Yellow fever - an acute viral disease transmitted by mosquitoes causing fever, headaches, jaundice, and gastrointestinal hemorrhage. It was rampant among some troops

A Sutler's Tent (Library of Congress Prints & Photographs Division, LC-stereo-1s02746)

BIBLIOGRAPHY

CONNECTICUT IN THE CIVIL WAR
See text footnotes for histories of individual regiments.

Bradley, Marion Doody, *Our Soldiers*, North Branford: The Totoket Historical Society, 1995.

Catalogue 6th, 7th, 8th, 9th, 10th and 11th Regiments of Infantry, First Light Battery and First Battalion of Cavalry, Connecticut Volunteers 1861, Hartford: Case, Lockwood & Co.

Connecticut History, The Association for the Study of Connecticut History, "Connecticut Commemorates the Civil War 1861-2011," volume 50, number 1, Spring 2011.

"Connecticut at Gettysburg, *The New Haven Register*, 26 June 1938.

Connecticut Explored, Spring 2011, volume 9, number 2; "Connecticut in the Civil War."

Connecticut Grand Army of the Republic, Hartford: Case, Lockwood & Brainard Co., annual encampment booklets (Connecticut State Library)

Crofut, W. A. and Morris, John M. *The Military and Civil History of Connecticut During The War of 1861-65*, New York: Ledyard Bill, 1868.

Dedication of the Monument at Andersonville, Georgia October 23 1907, In Memory of the Men of Connecticut who suffered in Southern Military Prisons 1861-1865, Hartford: State of Conn., 1908.

Fitch's Home for Soldiers, Deceased Veterans Discharge Files 1882-1932, RG 73, Connecticut State Library.

Hamblen, Charles P., edited by Walter L. Powell. *Connecticut Yankees At Gettysburg*, Kent, Ohio: Kent State University Press, 1965.

Hines, Blaikie. *Civil War, Volunteer Sons of Connecticut*. Thomaston, Maine: American Patriot Press, 2002.

History of Battle Flag Day, September 17, 1879, Hartford, Connecticut: Lockwood & Merritt, 1879. (Has a brief history of each regiment).

LaLancette, Thomas & Donna, *A Guide to Civil War Monuments, Memorials and Markers of Connecticut*, 1997.

Lane, Jarlath R., *A Political History of Connecticut during the Civil War*, Washington, D.C., Catholic University Press, 1941.

Lee, Will, *Post-Civil War Soldiers' Monuments in New Haven County, Connecticut*, Journal of the New Haven Colony Historical Society, Fall 1989, vol. 36, No. 1, 25-51.

Muster and Payroll, List of Substitutes, RG 13, Boxes 98-100, Connecticut State Library.

Niven, John, *Connecticut For The Union, The Role of the State in the Civil War*. New Haven: Yale University Press, 1965.

Noble Pension Records, Record Group 13, Connecticut State Library. (Case numbers are ascending, alphabetical by last name, and arranged in boxes by the case number, files of William H. Noble).

Pelland, Dave, *Civil War Monuments of Connecticut*, published by the author, 2011, see also www.CTMonuments.net.

Program of Exercises at the Dedication of a Soldiers Monument at the Broadway Park, New Haven, June 16, 1905 Erected by The First Connecticut Light Battery, The Sixth, Seventh and Tenth Connecticut Volunteers Monument Association Upon the Forty-First Anniversary of the Battle of Bermuda hundred and Petersburg Turnpike, Virginia; New Haven: The Price, Lee & Adkins Co., 1905.

Ranson, David F., *Connecticut's Monumental Epoch: A Survey of Civil War Memorials*, Hartford: Connecticut Historical Society Bulletins, 1997, volume 58 towns A-L & volume 59 towns M-W.

Ray, Ben C., *Old Battle Flags, Veteran Soldiers Souvenir*, 1879. (Has a brief history of each Connecticut regiment and their engagements)

Record of Service of Connecticut Men in the Army and Navy of the United States during the War of the Rebellion, Hartford, Connecticut: Case, Lockwood & Brainard, 1889.

Robert, J., *A Political History of Connecticut During the Civil War*, A Dissertation, Washington, D.C.: The Catholic University of America Press, 1941.

Selectman's returns of volunteers and men drafted 1862-1864, RG 13, Box 111 & 112, Connecticut State Library. (The collection is somewhat by county but largely unsorted. Contains list of men, returns, claims, releases, and petitions).

Smith, Sharon B., *Connecticut's Civil War, A Guide for Travelers*, Milford: Featherfield Publishing, 2010.

The Connecticut Civil War Centennial, Connecticut Civil War Commission 1961-1965; a series of pamphlets.

The Connecticut War Record, New Haven, J. M. Morris editor, Peck, White & Peck Publishing, August 1863-July 1865. (on microfilm at the Connecticut State Library).

Walsh, Mark C., *The Story of Connecticut's Organized Militia from 1636*, Hartford: Connecticut National Guard, 1991.

Warshauer, Matthew, *Connecticut in the American Civil War, Slavery, Sacrifice, and Survival*, Middletown: Wesleyan University Press, 2011.

TWENTY-SEVENTH CONNECTICUT VOLUNTEER INFANTRY

DeCusati, Andrew. "Connecticut Men Answer Lincoln's Call." essay, c. 1995.

Dedication of the Monument at Gettysburg, October 22nd, 1885. An Account of the Excursion From New Haven to Gettysburg and Return. New Haven, Connecticut: Price, Lee & Co., 1885.

Leinster, David R., *The Twenty-Seventh Connecticut Volunteer Infantry 1862-1863*, typescript, 1961 (copy at the James Blackstone Memorial Library)

Order Book, 27th Connecticut Volunteer Infantry, RG 13, box 169, item 240, Connecticut State Library (orders from headquarters for the 27th and the entire brigade)

Sheldon, Winthrop D. *"Twenty-Seventh" A Regimental History*. New Haven, Connecticut: Morris & Benham, 1866.

Sloat, Frank D. "History of the Twenty-Seventh Regiment C. V. Infantry", *Record of Service of Connecticut Men During the War of the Rebellion*, 1889, 825.

The Connecticut War Record. A series of articles written by "Winthrop" about the history of the 27th began in the November 1864 issue. The articles by Winthrop Sheldon became the basis of the published history of the 27th cited above.

MILITARY SERVICE RECORDS

Amann, William F. *Personnel of the Civil War*. New York: Thomas Y. Yoseloff, 1961, 2 volumes.

"Civil War Soldiers and Sailors System," National Park Service, Civil War. www.nps.gov.

Glasson, William H. *Federal Military Pensions in the United States*, New York: Oxford University Press, 1918.

Hamersly, Thomas H. S. *Complete Regular Army Register of the United States: For One Hundred Years 1779-1879*. Washington, DC. 1881.

Heitman, Francis B. *Historical Register and Dictionary of the United States Army, From Its Organization, September 29, 1789, to March 2, 1903*, 2 volumes. (list of officers, battles, and actions)

Hewett, Janet B. *Supplement to the Official Records of the Union and Confederate Armies*, Wilmington, N.C.: Boardfoot Publishing Co., 1994-1999, 95 volumes. For Connecticut regiments, see Part II - Record of Events, volume 4, Serial No. 16.

Powell, William H. *Officers of the Army and Navy (Regular) Who Served in the Civil War*. Philadelphia: L. R. Hamersly & Co., 1892.

Roll of Honor: Names of Soldiers Who Died in Defense of the American Union. Quartermaster General's Office, Washington, D.C.: 1865-1871, 27 volumes.

The Roster of Union Soldiers, 1861-1865. Wilmington, N.C.: Broadfoot Publishing Co., 1996-2001, 33 volumes.

The War of the Rebellion: A compilation of the official Records of the Union and Confederate Armies. Washington, D.C.: U.S. War Department, 1880-1900, 128 volumes.

RECORDS AT THE NATIONAL ARCHIVES
RECORDS ADMINISTRATION (NARA)
For other records, see www.nara.gov.

Adjutant General Records, R694.

Card Records of Headstones for Deceased Union Civil War Veterans c1879-1903 (M1845). There are other cemetery records - RG 292, entry 628 & 592 1909-1924 (gravestones in private cemeteries) and entry 2110C 1925-1963.

Complied Military Service Records, RG 94.

Compiled Records Showing Service of Military Units in Volunteer Union Organizations (National Archives Microfilm Publication M594), called the Records of Events.

General Index to Pension File, 1861-1934 (National Archives Microfilm Publication T288).

Index to Pension Application Files of Remarried Widows Based on Volunteer Service in the Civil War and Later Wars and in the Regular Army After the Civil War (National Archives Microfilm Publication M1785)

Index to Rendezvous Reports, Civil War 1861-1865, T-1099 (Navy).

Medical Information, Regular Army, 1821-1885. RG 94, entry 529.

Muster Rolls of Regular Army Organization, 1784-1912. RG 94, entry 53.

Numerical Index to Pension Records, 1860-1934 (National Archives Microfilm Publication A1158).

Organizational Index to Pension Files of Veterans Who Served Between 1861 and 1900 (National Archives Microfilm Publication T289).

Plante, Trevor K. *Military Service Records at the National Archives*, Paper 109. Washington, D.C.: National Archives and Records Administration, 2009.

Records of Movements and Activities of Volunteer Union Organizations (National Archives Microfilm Publication RG 94 and 407), Connecticut regiments are on rolls 5-8.

Register of Enlistments in the U.S. Army, 1798-1914 (M233), Civil War rolls 27-37.

Registers for National Homes for Disabled Volunteer Soldiers, 1866-1938. R15 (M1749).

Registers of the Records of the Proceedings of the U S. Army General Courts-Martial, 1809-1890.

Regular Army Enlistment Papers, 1798-1912. RG 94, entry 91.

GENERAL BIBLIOGRAPHY

Abbott, John S. C., *The History of the Civil War In America*, Springfield, Mass:Gurdon Bill, 1866, 2 volumes.

Bradford, Ned, *Battles and Leaders of the Civil War*, New York: Meridian Press, 1986.

Cannan, John, *Great Campaigns, The Antietam Campaign, August – September 1862*, Pennsylvania, Combined Books, 1994.

Commemorative Biographical Record of New Haven Country, Connecticut, Chicago: J. H. Beers & Co., 1902.

Dyer, Frederick, *A Compendium of the War of the Rebellion*, Cedar Rapids, Iowa: Torch Books, 1908.

Forbes, Edwin, *Thirty Years After, An Artist's Story of the Great War*, New York: Fords, Howard & Hulbert, 1890.

Furgurson, Ernest B., *Chancellorsville 1863, The Souls of the Brave*, New York: Alfred A. Knopf, 1992.

Geary, James W., *We Need Men, The Union Draft in the Civil War*, Northern Illinois University Press, 1991.

Griess, Thomas, *The West Point Military History Series, Atlas for the American Civil War*, Wayne, New Jersey: Avery Publishing Group, Inc., 1986.

Horn, John, *The Petersburg Campaign June 1864 – April 1865*, Pennsylvania: Combined Books, 1993.

Johnson, Robert Underwood; Buel, Clarence Clough editors; *Battles and Leaders of the Civil War*, New York, Thomas Yoseloff, Inc., 1956, 4 volumes. Originally published as "The Century War Series" in *The Century Magazine* November 1885, vol. 29 through November 1887, vol. 35.

Kennedy, Frances H., *The Civil War Battlefield Guide*, Boston: Houghton Mifflin Co., 1990.

Long, E. B., *The Civil War Day By Day, An Almanac 1861-1865*, New York: Da Capo Press, Inc., 1971. The book includes a number of summaries about the Civil War such as casualties, immigrants, slavery, prisons, etc.

Lowenfels, Walter, *Walt Whitman's Civil War*, New York, Da Capo Press, Inc., 1960.

McPherson, James M., *Battle Cry of Freedom: the Civil War Era*, Oxford University Press, 2003.

Miller, Francis Trevelyan, *The Photographic History of the Civil War*, New York: The Review of Review Co., 1911, 10 volumes.

Official Records of the Union and Confederate Navies in the War of the Rebellion, Washington, D.C.: Government Printing Office, 1895, 30 volumes.

O'Reilly, Francis Augustín, *The Fredericksburg Campaign, Winter War on the Rappahannock*, Baton Rouge: Louisiana State University Press, 2008.

Robertson, William Glenn, *Back Door to Richmond, The Bermuda Hundred Campaign April-June 1864*, Newark: University of Delaware Press, 1987.

Roll of Honor, Names of Soldiers Who Died in Defense of American Union Interred in National and Other Cemeteries, Washington, D.C.: Government Printing Office, 1865-1871, 27 vols.

Sears, Stephen W., *Chancellorsville*, Boston: Houghton Mifflin Company, 1996.

Sears, Stephen W., *Land-Scape Turned Red, The Battle of Antietam*, New York: Ticknor & Fields, 1983.

Sutherland, Daniel E., *Fredericksburg & Chancellorsville, The Dare Mark Campaign*, Lincoln, Nebraska: University of Nebraska Press, 1998.

Swinton, William, *Decisive Battles of the Civil War*, New York: Promontory Press, 1992.

The Medical and Surgical History of the War of the Rebellion, Washington, D.C.: Government Printing Office, 1870, 3 volumes.

The Official Military Atlas of the Civil War, New York: The Fairfax Press, 1983; originally published from 1891-1895 as *Atlas to Accompany the Official Records of the Union and Confederate Armies* by the Government Printing Office.

The War of the Rebellion: a Compilation of the Official Records of the Union and Confederate Armies, 128 volumes (known as the Officials Records or OR).

INDEXES

NAME INDEX

ABBOT
Sophie T. 418
ABELL
Lucy Ann 364
Virginia Victoria 322
ABERCOMBIE
General John J. 18
ACKERMAN
Cora DeWolf 198
Harriet M. (Beckwith) 198
John B. 84, **197-198**, 504
Lulu Hopper 198
ADAMS
James 198
John **198**, 480, 505, 507
Rev. J. L. 170
Rev. R. J. 290, 304, 333, 354
ADDIS
Austin 217
Clarissa Ann 217
Lucy Ann (Phillips) 217
AHERN
John 164
Mary 164, 165
Mary (Dusee) 164
ALBEE
Alice E. 430
Benjamin 199
Calvin Goddard **199**, 430, 506, 511
Ellen J. 199
Harriet Maria (Scranton) 199, 430
Lydia (Otis) 199
ALBINGER
Anne 200
Bridget (Curtin) 200
John 200
John Francis 200
John Joseph **199-200**, 480, 506
Josephine 200
Loretta 200
ALBINOS
John **201**, 505
ALFORD
Nancy E. 135
ALGER
Mary 335
ALGIER
James 359
ALLARD
Mary E. 170
ALLEN
Colonel 341
Dora E. (Kelsey) 305
Dora M. 305
Frances Almena (Remington) 202
Henry **201-202**, 480, 507
Margaret 336
Maria F. 391
Rev. 142
Rose M. 305
Sophia 202

William 202
William J. 305
Willie C. 305
AMES
Charles **202**, 505, 513
ANDREW
George W. 309
ANDREWS
Alice Beal 433
Delia (Harrison) 329
George H. 480
George W. 404
Julia L. 278
Lucretia 227
Lucy Ann 404
Lucy Ann (Andrews) 404
Rebecca 278
Rhoda 223, 341
ANDRUS
Silas 393
ANGEL
Rev. 212
APPEL
John 480
APPLEBY
Alice Gibson 221
Almira 173
Charles 222
Jane (Gibson) 222
ARLINGTON
Willoughby **202**, 405, 513
ARNOLD
Bethia 259
ARROWSMITH
Abram **429**
ASHER
Alford 480
ASHLEY
Sylvester 279
ASHMAN
Charlotte (McElroy) 203
David Steel 203
Frederick William 203n304
Maria (Rhutten) 203
Mary Alice (Hotchkiss) 203
Mollie (Caruth) 203
Robert Adolphus **202-203**, 510
Winston 203n304
ATWATER
Rev. Lucius 120
W. W. 437
AUGUR
Daniel P. 480
Rebecca Amelia 245
Reuben N. 203, 375, 513
Tryphena 383
AUSTIN
Ellen Amanda 472
Sophronia 299
AVERILL
Adelbert Charles **203-204**, 480, 509

Almira (Hemingway) 207
Amanda (Bassett) 205, 447
Carrie M. [Carolyn] 207
Charles Adelbert 79, 84, **203**, 206
Daniel **204**, 457
Daniel, 2nd **204-205**, 206, 447, 480, 507
David 84, 104, 203, 205, **206**, 457, 480, 503
Edmund M. 206, 389, 480
Elizabeth Charlotte (Foote) 206
Estella Nancy (Shepard) 204
Eunice 458
Fannie M. (Palmer) 207
George 262
George M. 480
Harry R. 207
James 205, 447
Jane (Bradley) 204
Jarvis 206, 378, 480, 513
John 207
Lucy DeEtte 446, 447
Lucy Elizabeth (Pond) 205
Polly (Morris) 206
Roland Gelston 79, 84, 203, **206-207**, 480, 509
Roy Victor 204
Samuel 480
AYERS
Marguerite 411
BABCOCK
Anna (Beach) 110
Anson Tyler 208
Austin 110
George 463
Lauretta Hobart 208
Lillian M. (Wheeler) 463
Marcus O. 79, 84, **207-208**, 480, 510
Rebecca Hobart (Robinson) 208
Russell William 208
Wealthy Ann (Emmons) 208
William Robinson 208
BABSON
Lydia E. 413
BACKES
Catherine 208
Catherine (Helmstalder) 208
Elizabeth 208
Grace 208
John 208
Michael **208**, 507
Rebecca 208
BADGER
Iminild T. 263
BAILEY
Anna A. (Scranton) 209
Caroline 304
Carrie Louise 215
Cora Josephine (Burchard) 209
Damaris 209
Eleazer 209
Elmer James 209

JACOBS
Celia (Brockett) 348n720
DeForest 348
Egbert **347-348**, 506
JAMES
Ada May (Stevens) 437
Arthur 437
Clarissa 465
JARVIS
Dr. 272
JAY
W.M.L. 471
JEFFREY
William 488
JENETT
John 305
JENNINGS
Barney **348**, 505, 513
Lena (Drybread) 348
JEPSON
Arthur Wiswell 350
Benjamin **349-350**, 505
Clara Louise 350
Emelia (Bromhead) 350
Harry Benjamin 350
John 350
Mary Louise (Wiswell) 350
JERGENSON
Emanual **350**, 503
JERROLDS
Ida Augusta (Hubbard) 341
JEWETS, JEWITT
Major P. A. 260
Dr. 178
JOHNSON
Abigail Anna (Hosley) 351-352
Adella A. 354
Bertha M. 352
Betsey 405
Campbell **350**, 504, 513
Carrie J. [Caroline] 355, 462
Charles **350**, 353, 505, 513
Charles E. 354
Chauncey 355, 462
Clarissa 353
Clarissa A. 423
Cornelia Augusta 335
Daisy May 354
Davis S. 81, 86, **351**, 488, 505
Edna 352
Eleanor Bonney (Linsley) 146
Eliza (Crampton) 423
Elizabeth H. 352
Elizur C. 86, 87, **351-352**, 488, 505, 515
Emily C. 356
Frank S. 352
Franklin 354
Frederick W. 335
George **352**, 505, 513
George William 351, 352
Harriet Louisa 444
Henrietta (Page) 353
Henrietta Amelia 218
Henry 86, **352-353**, 488, 505
Henry E. 295, **353**, 505
Henry H. 488

Homer R. **353-354**, 488, 509
Ida F. 352
Jane Elizabeth (Hotchkiss) 353
Jennie Elizabeth 293
Jerome 331
John Benjamin 218
Josiah 23, 28, 94, **354-355**, 461, 462, 509, 512
Julia 331
Julia Ann (Murray) 355, 462
Leander F. 423
Lillie A. 352
Lottie H. 352
Luman 423
Margaret (McNulty) (Hobbs) 351
Maria (Cook) 351, 352
Maria (Moulthrop) 218
Mary Caroline 423
Mary E. (Bradley) 354
Nanch (Linsley) 335
Samuel 353
Sarah J. (Mallory) 353
Sarah Jane (Shepard) 293
Sidney H. 293
JOHNSTON
Mary Josephine (O'Connor) 164
Thomas 164
JONES
Caroline C. 329
Edward F. 90
Edwin L. 356
Elijah B. **355**, 504, 512
Elijah Bradley 355
Emily C. (Johnson) 356
Hubert 488
Julia Amelia 403
Mary E. (Gray) 355
Nellie Cornelia (Russell) 356
Peter **356**, 503, 513
Rev. Elisha C. 297, 303, 404
William S. **356**, 488, 506
Willis G. 488
JORDAN
Frederick 488
JOSEPH
Amelia A. 301
JOST
Jacob 86, **357**, 510
JUDD
Elizabeth 227
Henry Green 261
Mary Francis 261
Sarah Rebecca (Raymond) 261
JUDSON
Janett 452
KANE
Ann 271
John 271
Winnifred 271
KATELL
Rev. G. F. 289
KELLEHER
Catherine 164
KELLEY, KELLY
Father 377
Ellen 280
Joseph Case 307

Laura Melinda (Service) 307
Mary Frances 307
KELSEY
Agnes Fayette 358
Albert 357
Alvah 358
Ann J. (Post) 357
Dora E. 305
Eliza Ann (Hurd) 357
Ernest Russell 358
Gilbert Isaiah **357**, 507, 512
Gustave Baldwin 358
Hobart 488
M. Antoinette (Baldwin) 358
Martha 113
Mary Almira (Higgins) 358
Polly 243
Richard Percy 358
Richard Taylor **357-358**, 509
Roxanna 449
KENDAL
William F. 236
KENNEDY
James **358-359**, 488, 509
Margaret (Hayes) 359
Mary 359
Mary (Shanahan) 359
Patrick 489
KERR
John 86, **359**, 403, 489, 505
Mary (Barr) 359
Rebecca (Haydock) 359
KEUCHMAN
Antoinette 407
KIDDER
Alice L. 339
KIMBALL
Charlotte 346
KING
Alexa 245
KINNEEN, KINNEY
James **360**, 489, 505
James Henry 360
Joseph 360
Mary (McQueeney) 360
Mary Ann 360
Michael 82, 86, 87, **361**, 489, 503, 515
William 360
Catherine (McGowan) 361
Francis J. 361
Hannah (Greeley) 361
John 361
John F. 361
Mary Jane 361
KIRBY
Rev. 217
KIRKPATRICK
Captain 413
KIRTLAND
Delight 318
KISSINGER
Elizabeth 235
KNERINGER
Adele 362
Hannah E. (Mitchell) 362
Harry 362

STONE, con't.
Mary A. 239
Mrs. David M. 318
Ruth (Butler) 439-441
Sarah Elizabeth (Stevens) 439
Walter A. 60, 94, 439, **440-441**, 503, 512
Watson Wilbur 86, 242, 295, **441**, 405
STOWE
Amelia (Boardman) 115
STRICKLAND
Anna Louise 328
Asa **441**, 494, 504
Asa E. 441
Bertha W. 441
Emily 442
Emily (Shepard) 442
Emily M. 441
Hattie A. 441
Horace E. 441
Jane (Derby) 441, 442
Lester 442
Lizzie J. 441
Mary F. 441
Mary Louise (Hayden) 329
Royal Nelson 329
STRONG
Rev. Edward A. 371
SULLIVAN
Bernard 442
Catherine (McKeon) 442, 443
Charles **442**, 506, 512
Ellen (Downy) 442
James 494
John Joseph 442
Matthew 86, **442-443**, 510
Matthew Patrick 442
Nellie 265
Patrick 494
Peter Paul 442
Philip **443**, 504, 513
SUMNER
General Edwin V. 21
SUNDELOUS
Hulda D. 443
Peter **443**, 505, 513
SWAIN
Rev. Charles W. 292
Rev. W. 304
SWAN
Rev. Jabez S. 198
SWEIZER/SCHITZER
Captain 105, 115
SYKES
General George G. 29
TALMADGE
Alice Elizabeth 444
Arthur Howard 444
George Raymond 444
George Washington **443-444**, 494, 507
Harriet Louisa (Johnson) 444
Levi 444
Lois Elizabeth (Hull) 444
Lucretia Salome (Scranton) 445

Maria A. (Smith) 444
Marietta (Foote) 444
Martha M. 233
Samuel 445
William **444-445**, 494, 507
TARBOX
Augustus G. **445**, 503
TAYLER, TAYLOR
Jane E. 268
Adison 130
Ann (Pinkham) 445, 446
George Lansing 249
Henry **445**, 503
Joseph 446
Louisa 446
Michael **445-446**, 509
Rev. George Lansing 399
William L. **446**, 494, 507
TERHUNE
Charles A. 446
Clara S. 446
Dora E. (Kelsey) (Allen) (Frisbie) 305
George D. 447
Lucy DeEtte (Averill) 446, 447
Lucy Edna 446
Margaret 224
Nicholas A. 447
Nicholas R. 86, 87, 205, 369, **446-447**, 510, 515
Oliver 446
Sophia (Wartendyke) 447
Stephen H. 447
Walter A. 446
TERRY
Dr. 178
General Alfred H. 18, 67-69, 76, 119
THAYER
Alvin S. 448
Clara A. (Shepard) 423
Elwyn Matton 81, 84, 86, 87, **447-448**, 510, 515
Mary (Geer) 447
Mary Elizabeth (Palmer) 447
Myria G. (Gilbert) 448
THOMAS
Elbridge E. **448**, 503
THOMPSON
Abbie (Watrous) 449
Alvin S. 449
Gilbert W. 431
Mabel Kelsey (Hopson) 449
Richard Egbert **449**, 507
THORP
Abagail (Bowe) 450
Eliza L. 450
Gideon 450
THUTE
Patrick 494
TOBIN
Michael 494
TODD
Ada 450
Albert 494
Alison Dewd 452

Andrew B. 86, **450**, 505
Angie 450
Antoinette 327
Aurelia (Clinton) 452
Beri Moraldus **450-451**, 509
Bertha 450
Caroline S. (Barnes) 451
Clifford K. 452
Eliza L. (Thorp) 450
Ellen J. (Dervey) 452
Fanny A. 452
Grace Ann (Hartley) 452
Henry Dennis 40, **451-452**, 509
Jasper E. 450
Kirtland **452**, 509
Lucy J. (Crowell) 450
Martin B. 452
Mary (Perkins) 450
Melicu 451
Nellie J. 452
Orrin 452
Polly (Ray) 451
Polly Eliza 273, 299
Robert B. 452
Whitney A. 452
William E. 452
TOMLINSON
Emma 366
TONEY
Harry 307
Mary Frances (Kelly) (Frisbie) 307
TOPLIFF
Rev. Calvin H. 135
TORREY
Susan 324
TOWNER
Anna Pearl 183
Davis 319
Emily S. 185
Harriet 188
Henry E. 494
John 183
John Edwin 49, 53, 86, 87, 137, **182-192**, 507
Laura Emily 183
Martha (Tyler) 183
Merle Eugene 183
Nancy 413
Susan Driver (Hoadley) 183
TOWNSEND
Alvah 453
Dillavan 453
Fermin 453
Francis M. 453
Maria 453
Mary E. (Hawk) 453
Sidney 60, **453**, 503, 512
TRACY
Almira (Nichols) 374
Lucy A. 374
Solomon F. 374
TREADWAY
Dr. 288
TRIPP
Ellen 441

PLACE & SUBJECT INDEX

www.ingramcontent.com/pod-product-compliance
Lightning Source LLC
Chambersburg PA
CBHW062019090426

42811CB00005B/902